The Shell Guide to

BRITAIN

TIMES OF OPENING
AND
CHARGES FOR ADMISSION

Details giving the latest information may be obtained from any of the sources mentioned below:

The owner, curator, agent, or occupier of the place itself.

"Historic Houses, Castles, and Gardens in Great Britain and Ireland" (available at most booksellers'), issued yearly at 5s. by the British Travel Association, Tourist Information Centre, 64 St. James's Street, London S.W.1; *tel.*, 01-629 9191.

The British Travel Association direct, by letter or telephone.

The National Trust, 42 Queen Anne's Gate, London S.W.1; *tel.*, 01-930 0211.

(For Ancient Monuments) The Ministry of Public Building and Works, C.I.O. Branch, Lambeth Bridge House, London S.E.1; *tel.*, 01-735 7611.

The Scottish Tourist Board, 2 Rutland Place, West End, Edinburgh 1; *tel.*, FOUntainbridge 1561.

The National Trust of Scotland, 5 Charlotte Square, Edinburgh 2; *tel.*, CALedonian 2184.

Use of Gazetteers and Maps

THE GAZETTEERS. Each place mentioned is followed by its map reference and (with the exception of towns and villages of under 2,000 population) by its early closing day (EC) and approximate population figure. All places in the Gazetteers are of interest for the reasons given, but a single * indicates a place of particular interest, and a double ** a place of exceptional interest and worth a special journey. The abbreviation NT indicates property or land controlled by the National Trust; AM indicates an Ancient Monument or Historic Building in the care of the Ministry of Works. MAP REFERENCES in the text indicate the squares in which the places concerned are to be found. Map squares correspond with the 10,000-metre squares of the National Grid, except in the London map.

THE SHELL GUIDE TO
BRITAIN

Edited by
GEOFFREY BOUMPHREY

EBURY PRESS
in association with George Rainbird
London 1969

This book was designed and produced by George Rainbird Ltd,
Marble Arch House, 44 Edgware Road, London W2,
and was printed and bound by Jarrold & Sons Ltd, Norwich

First published 1964
Second edition 1969
Reprinted 1970

© Shell-Mex and B.P. Limited, 1964 and 1969

7181 4029 X

EDITORIAL BOARD: Geoffrey Boumphrey
Edward Young
Yorke Crompton

Gazetteer: Douglas Garman
F. G. Stokes
Mrs Hazel Thurston

Cartography: J. B. P. Angwin, FRICS
John R. Flower

CONTENTS

GENERAL INTRODUCTION

The forty-eight sections that follow describe the counties of Britain; this Introduction sketches in the background. First, in ROCK AND LANDSCAPE, we make a brief tour of the country's geology, noticing its effect on the scenery. Next, SOIL AND PLANT (p. xv) shows how the character of the vegetation can reveal the nature of the soil on which it grows. Climate, too, is shown to have its effect on plant life. Further on, PREHISTORY IN BRITAIN (p. xxii) and ARCHITECTURAL STYLES IN BRITAIN (p. xxiv) provide quick references to the principal archaeological and architectural periods. Finally, in HOLIDAY WEATHER (p. xxviii), with its six sunshine maps, we are concerned with the effect of climate on ourselves.

Rock and Landscape

BY TERENCE MILLER

To the geologist, the word 'rock' conveys anything from the hardest granite to the softest sand. He excludes only soils from his consideration. It happens that Britain has an astonishing variety of rock types, almost every major kind being found. In a single day's journey the observant traveller, with a little knowledge, may recognize many different varieties without even leaving the roads. He can see, too, how the rock, even when it is largely hidden, controls not only the shape of the land, but often the location of industry, town and even hamlet.

Rocks are classified as *igneous* (originating in a molten state) or *sedimentary* (accumulations of various kinds, such as seashells, sand, mud or rock-fragments). Rocks of either group when severely changed by heat and/or pressure are called *metamorphic*. As all these processes are continuous, rocks may be termed old, or middle-aged, or young. In Britain it happens that the older rocks are harder and more resistant than the younger, so that where they occur, in the west and north-west, they tend to stand out as moorlands and mountains. The eastern and southern parts are younger and correspondingly gentler and lower. The oldest rocks of the kingdom, in north-west Scotland, are some 2,700 million years old; the chalk of south and south-east England is about 100 million, and the sands and clays of East Anglia less than one million years old.

South-east England

Chalk is, of course, a sedimentary rock, composed chiefly of the fossilized remains of minute sea-creatures. As these are only loosely stuck together, the resulting soft, porous limestone lets rainwater soak straight in, so that few surface streams are seen, and no sharp or jagged shapes remain in the landscape. Between the rolling chalk country of the North and South Downs (pp. 131, 133) lies the Weald, a region of lower, sandy, hills and stretches of heavy, badly drained clay. These sandstones and clays are *older* than the chalk; but near Salisbury (p. 80) the chalk surface slants gently southwards under another set of sands, clays and gravels, *younger* than the chalk, which are the bedrock of the New Forest. Under the Solent the chalk flattens out and then slants upwards much more steeply, to reappear, now standing almost vertical, in the Needles, at the western tip of the Isle of Wight, with the younger rocks still there, but now to the north of the chalk 'rib'.

The chalk of the North Downs dips gently northwards beneath London and the Thames valley, to come up again as the Chilterns (p. 179). So London is built on soft clays, sands and gravels like those of Hampshire. The sands and gravels which lie on the chalk of East Anglia and east Lincolnshire are younger still. These are the comparatively recent deposits left by the last Ice Age. Good examples of glacial debris are the ridge of gravelly sand that runs along the north Norfolk coast behind Cromer, and the similar sheet under the heathland around Brandon.

The Geological Midlands

West and north-west from London, after a slow climb up, the chalk 'rim of the saucer' ends with a drop to lower ground – as just before Cambridge, Aylesbury, Thame, Swindon, Devizes, or Shaftesbury. Beyond lie the geological 'midlands' of England, where the rocks are 'middle-aged'. This region extends to the edges of Exmoor and Dartmoor, the Bristol Channel and the Severn; north-westwards to Herefordshire and Shropshire, and eventually to the sea in Liverpool Bay; northwards, to the east side of the Pennines, to the Cleveland Hills, and finally to the coast between Scarborough and South Shields.

The ups and downs in this rather subdued landscape are related to alternate sheets of clay, sandstone and limestone, rarely visible except when artificially exposed. In the extreme south-west are the great Portland stone quarries (p. 51), and those for other building-stones around Bath and Cheltenham. In the Banbury and Kettering districts huge mechanical excavators work the ironstone; and ironstone occurs again at Scunthorpe and in the Cleveland Hills. Near Bedford and Peterborough, rows of slim, tall chimneys tell of claypits for brickmaking.

By this time, the traveller is well on into the midlands, and he will have noticed the predominantly red colour of the rocks, whether he is on the borders of Devon, or in Warwickshire or Leicestershire. These rather elderly midland rocks, known as the New Red Sandstone, were once part of a desert plain which covered most of England. Through them stick isolated patches of a more ancient rock – as in and about Charnwood Forest in Leicestershire, and, more extensively, in the Malvern Hills (p. 241). In both cases, hard, splintery dark-green and purple rocks make a striking contrast with the surrounding sandy and marly red – and much softer – varieties.

South-west England

On the south coast a strip of the red midlands runs down to the sea at Torquay, just as it does in the Cheshire Wirral, and, on the other side of England, at the mouth of the Tees; but beyond Exeter we come to something quite different. The granite of Dartmoor (p. 27) is part of a vast underground wedge pushed up, about 300 million years ago, into the dark-grey mudstones and sandstones of Cornwall (p. 3) and Devon. With it, hot 'gassy' fluids deposited veins of copper, tin, zinc and even a little uranium. In places they attacked the granite itself, converting it into crude china-clay. Today one sees the ruined remains

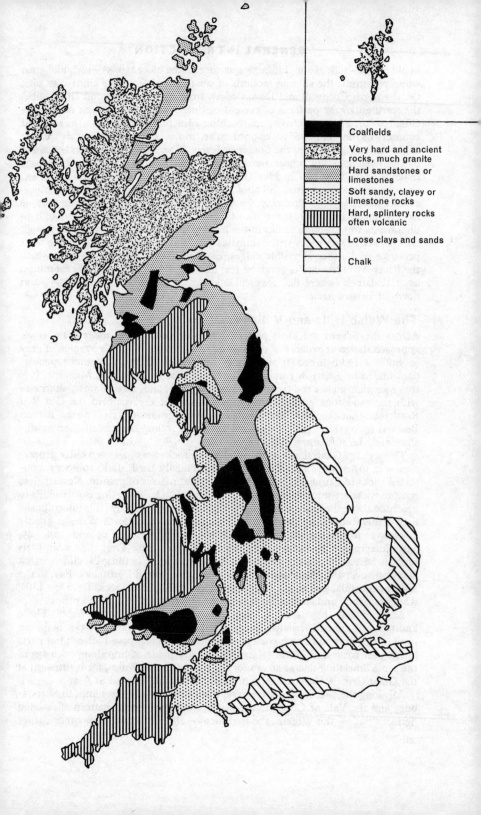

████	Coalfields
░░░░	Very hard and ancient rocks, much granite
═══	Hard sandstones or limestones
∴∴∴	Soft sandy, clayey or limestone rocks
‖‖‖	Hard, splintery rocks often volcanic
⫽⫽⫽	Loose clays and sands
	Chalk

of old mines – tall, gaunt chimneys standing on the moors (p. 5) – and, like great white pyramids, the shining mounds of waste gravel from the china-clay pits. On the north Cornwall and Devon coast, from St Ives to beyond Ilfracombe, the tortured zigzag patterns of the old, splintery rocks can be seen in the sea-cliffs (p. 19). Then, suddenly, approaching Minehead, we are into the soft, red contours of the 'midland' rocks once more, and soon even into a small brother of the East Anglian fens, the Somerset levels. These are bounded on the north by the Mendip Hills, whose smooth, bare tops remind us of other limestone uplands. The famous Cheddar Gorge (p. 43) was probably once a narrow, sinuous cave, whose roof collapsed long ago. Branching off it are other, smaller caves (p. 35). Probably the whole range, like other limestone hills, is honeycombed by caves, the work of rainwater, which is just acid enough to dissolve its way through cracks in the limestone. North of the Mendips, though the blanket of red rocks still dominates the landscape, older rocks make their presence felt, either as visible ridges, like the limestone ridge through which the River Avon has cut its gorge, or less directly, as the head-gear of coal mines, as at Radstock (where fine fossil plants can be found on the tip-heads), and north of Bristol itself.

The Welsh Hills and Valleys

Across the Severn the same pattern continues but on a grander scale as we approach the great expanse of the South Wales coalfield. This is a region of grey or buff or reddish-brown sandstone, sometimes shaley, sometimes pebbly, surrounded by a narrow rim of the limestone that we saw in the Mendips. It is this rock that makes the coast of Gower (p. 209), and, farther west, alternates with the sandstone around Tenby. North-east of the coalfield the Old Red Sandstone (not the New Red Sandstone of the midlands) rises as the Brecon Beacons (p. 231), and falls away into the lower rolling country of Monmouth-shire and Herefordshire.

Throughout Central and North Wales, the rocks are of an even older genera-tion – in many ways like the younger but equally hard, dark, splintery, con-torted rocks of Cornwall, but without the great masses of granite. Nevertheless igneous rocks are important, though on a smaller scale, in causing isolated hills to protrude above the enveloping sedimentaries – as the Prescelly Hills interrupt the flattish Pembrokeshire countryside. Much of mid- and north Wales is greatly given over to sheep grazing. The landscape is one of rolling uplands (pp. 225, 239), interrupted by sudden, irregular crags and peaks. Thus the Cader Idris range is based on sheets of granitic rock, clearly visible in the great cliff face that looks out over the Mawddach estuary. Similarly, round Portmadoc Bay, in the Lleyn peninsula, and throughout Snowdonia, the igneous rocks form the hills, while the sandy and slaty rocks occupy the hollows or form upland plateaux.

Anglesey can show some of the oldest rocks of England or Wales. These knotted and gnarled, twisted, grey, green and purple-spotted types make up most of the west and north coasts – they are less well exposed inland; but parts of the east coast and Puffin Island beyond are made of limestone once again, the same limestone that seems to form a rim all round Wales, for it turns up at the Great Orme's Head, near Llandudno, and inland around St Asaph.

All along the Welsh border country, from Chepstow in the south, to Shrews-bury and the Vale of Clwyd in the north, the same general pattern of isolated 'igneous' hills – the Wrekin, the Breiddens – alternating with smoother shapes based on mudstones, shales and sandstones, with occasional patches of pale grey limestone – persists. But beyond the rich Cheshire Plain, with its thick beds of rock-salt below, supporting a flourishing chemical industry above, beyond the Mersey flats and the Lancashire coalfield, we approach the main ridge of the Pennines.

The Pennines

The Pennines rise up out of the flanking 'red midlands' as a spine running up the middle of England from Staffordshire and Derbyshire to the Scottish border. The main English coalfields 'lean' on this spine from either side. In most of the southern part the dominant rock is a coarse, pebbly sandstone called Millstone Grit. Long crags of this rock form the 'edges' of the Peak District. Further north the sandstone is replaced by alternating beds of limestone, sandstone and shale. This 'layered cake' arrangement accounts for the terraced shape of many of the valley sides in Wharfedale, Wensleydale (p. 592) and Swaledale, and of such flat-topped hills as Ingleborough and Pen-y-Ghent, the sandstone layers, and often the limestones as well, tending to stick out, while the shales form gentle grassy slopes between. Of the occasional igneous rocks found in this area, chief is a great sheet of basaltic rock, known as the Whin Sill. This is responsible for High Force, in Teesdale, for crags along the east side of the Vale of Eden, and for Bamburgh Castle's rocky seat (p. 598).

The Lake District and South Scotland

It is in the Lake District that igneous rocks return in force. Geologically the Lake District is very like North Wales. The same dark grey slaty contorted rocks appear in road cuttings, in dry stone walls, and in the hill crags themselves. But in the Lakes the jagged outlines of the igneous rocks (here mainly volcanic), which in Wales are more or less at random, are concentrated in a strip of country centred on Scafell and Borrowdale (p. 617). The hills on either side, though quite high perhaps, have gentler shapes, being carved out of softer, more homogeneous rocks. But there remain patches, often of granite, in Eskdale and Ennerdale – and most obviously in the huge quarry near the summit of Shap.

Beyond Shap, the road to Penrith runs back into red rocks of 'midland' type (notice also the familiar limestone around Shap itself), and these persist right through the Vale of Eden and over the Border to Annan and Dumfries. But most of the country beyond the Solway and the Border – Galloway – Ettrick Forest (p. 648) and across to Berwickshire – is a third repetition of Wales and the Lakes, with the same dark, hard, crumpled rocks, and the same patches of granite – the Mull of Galloway, Criffel, Loch Doon, and others. Near Thornhill and Sanquhar the observant motorist might think himself back in the English Midlands, for buff-coloured sandstones appear, and the pithead gear of coal mines. These are just patches of the middle-aged rocks left lying on the older 'floor'. But a little farther on, past Dalmellington, Biggar, or Peebles, the midland rocks reappear in force, the old 'floor' rocks having dived down below the great central Scottish industrial belt which, as in the English midlands, is based on coal seams, ironstone, limestone, and oil-shale. Unlike England, however, here quite large masses of igneous rock appear, as in the hills about the lower Clyde or such relatively small isolated hills as those of Edinburgh and Stirling Castles (pp. 675, 671), Ailsa Craig (p. 635) and the Bass Rock (p. 676).

The Highlands

North-west of a line drawn across Scotland from Helensburgh to Stonehaven – not quite, but very nearly, the 'Highland Line' – we run into the most extensive area of very ancient rocks in Britain, and therefore into an area with a special flavour of its own. The important feature of these old rocks is that nearly all of them belong to the class of 'changed' (metamorphic) rocks, i.e. they have had a peculiarly long and tortured history – in this resembling the country whose foundation they are – stretching back over many hundreds and even thousands of millions of years. They are therefore harder, more splintery, more twisted and distorted even than the rocks of Wales, the Lake District, or South Scotland. They contain a variety of sparkling new minerals, such as shining mica flakes or little dark red garnets, and they often contain veins, sheets, and lumps of granite or its like. Almost the whole country, from Kintyre to Cape Wrath, and across to Aberdeen, is made of these rocks (pp. 739, 748).

As variants, along the north-west coast, in Western Ross, Coigach and up to Cape Wrath, one sees flat thick sheets of the dark reddish-brown pebbly 'Torridon Sandstones', often forming isolated steep-sided peaks – Stack Polly, Quinag, Suilven, Cul Mhor – which seem to be standing guard along the coast. In the closely connected narrow strip running up from Loch Carron through Ullapool to Durness are crags of limestone, and near the village of Durness on the north coast the usual limestone cave, at Smoo. Again, in the north-east, sandstones lie almost flat on top of the old floor – but these are far younger than the Torridon rocks: in fact, they are of the same general age as the rocks of south-east Wales, of Cornwall and of parts of Devon. These Caithness 'flag-stones' – so called because they were once quarried on a big scale for paving stones – form the bleak and savage coast southwards from Duncansby Head to the Dornoch and Moray Firths, and all the country round Dingwall and the Black Isle. They also form nearly all the Orkney Isles, whereas most of Shetland is formed of the typical central Scottish metamorphic rocks, with, as usual, a good deal of granite.

The Islands

The outer isles of the west (p. 752) are also entirely of the ancient floor, in fact, the main rock of the region takes its name – Lewisian – from the island of Lewis. The inner isles, particularly Skye, Mull, Rhum, and Arran, are all in part of volcanic origin – though nothing today bears any relation to an actual *volcano*, however much some of the hills may suggest volcanic cones. But the red and black Cuillin (pp. 737, 741, 751) of Skye, the central parts of Mull and Rhum, and the north and centre of Arran – together with the westernmost tip of the Ardnamurchan peninsula – are all relics of the roots, as it were, of groups of volcanoes. In fact, the western parts of both Skye and Mull consist almost entirely of the lava sheets which flooded out from the volcanoes, just as lava flows out from modern volcanoes in southern Italy, Iceland or Hawaii today.

Books for further reading

L. DUDLEY STAMP *Britain's Structure and Scenery* 1946
A. E. TRUEMAN *Geology and Scenery* 1949
W. G. FEARNSIDES and O. M. B. BULMAN *Geology in the Service of Man* 1944

Soil and Plant

BY GEOFFREY BOUMPHREY

If it is to the rock beneath that we owe the shape of the landscape, its colour and texture are in the main due to the trees, shrubs and other plants that cover its surface. And the link between rock and plant is the soil. The rock, one might say, is the skeleton, vegetation the skin, hair and complexion – but soil the flesh through which flow the vital fluids. Several writers in this guide draw attention to the remarkable diversity of British scenery; and as most changes of scene are marked by changes in vegetation, it is not surprising to read in A. G. Tansley's *Britain's Green Mantle* (a book for anyone wanting to learn more about the subject of this article): 'There are few if any countries which contain within so small a space a greater variety of soils than England possesses' – the variation is rather less marked in Scotland and Wales.

The Nature of Soil

All soils except peat are mainly composed of various kinds of rock which have been broken down into powder by the combined action of weather, water and, later, of plants and micro-organisms. In their first crude state they are relatively infertile; but as algae and lichen, followed by mosses, ferns and other forms of plant life establish themselves, fertility is increased by the accumulation of 'humus', the decaying remains of the various plants. Humus is particularly valuable for two reasons. Firstly, it contains in handy form just those foods which a plant needs and must otherwise extract from the soil-minerals as and when it can find them. Secondly, its presence improves the physical quality of the soil, lightening and aerating a heavy clay, or filling in the gaps between the much larger grains of a sandy soil and so helping it to retain water. Peat soils are almost wholly humus. They are formed by the accumulation of successive layers of plants growing under conditions where lack of oxygen prevents the lower, dead layers from rotting away completely. When there is enough alkaline water (usually containing lime) to neutralize the acids caused by this partial decomposition, the result is fen peat, such as occurs in East Anglia. When this is drained, the 'black soil', often many feet deep, is exceptionally fertile, growing wonderful crops. Not so bog peat, such as we find on Dartmoor, on the badly drained slopes of the Pennines, in Wales and in Scotland. Here the absence of lime or any other alkali results in a peat soil so acid that it can be tolerated by only a few plants, such as bogmoss (sphagnum), heather, bog-asphodel, cotton-grass and dwarf willow.

Of the mainly mineral soils, sand is the least fertile. It is formed from rocks consisting largely of quartz (silica) which breaks down into grains so large that water drains quickly through it, carrying away the dissolved minerals and humus which all plants need for survival. The soil with the smallest particles is clay. In this the grain may be so fine that water can hardly penetrate, and there is little space for air, which is needed by the decay-causing bacteria and also to improve the insulating properties of the soil. Pure clay, then, although it may be extremely rich in minerals, is a cold, 'late' soil, hard as concrete in dry weather, sticky as glue in wet. Clearly the best is something between the two, a mixture of coarse and fine grains that will hold a certain amount of water and yet drain freely. Such a soil, provided it is also well supplied with humus and contains enough lime and other necessary minerals, is called a loam.

Lime-haters and Lime-tolerators

Whether the soils are acid or alkaline in reaction has a great bearing on what trees, shrubs and plants we see as we travel about the country. Everyone who gardens on limy soil knows that it is no good hoping to grow such plants as azaleas, rhododendrons or most heathers. On the other hand he will expect to beat his acid-soil rivals with, let us say, yews, dogwoods, clematis or rock-roses. The first group will not grow on alkaline soil; the latter at least tolerate it. If on a map of Britain you draw a straight line from the mouth of the Tees to the boundary of Dorset and Devon on the English Channel, it is roughly true to say that to the south and east of it the hills are made of chalk or limestone, while to the north and west of it the older, more rugged hills and mountains are made of acid rocks. This by no means implies a neat division into alkaline soil one side and acid the other: it merely marks a probability. There are plenty of exceptions – for instance, between the chalk and limestone districts of midland and southern England lie great stretches of clay, usually acid and highly fertile, or of sand, again usually acid but of low fertility; while in the mainly acid north and west, limestone crops up here and there, even in Scotland.

But it is not only the nature of the underlying rock which determines whether a soil is acid or alkaline: climate may play a part too. Britain has almost as wide a range of climates (sub-climates to the botanist) as of scenery. Where the air is usually moist and the rainfall high, as in the west, more water is likely to reach the soil by precipitation (rain, mist, etc.) than is normally lost by evaporation and transpiration from trees and plants. Here, then, the movement of water through the soil is likely to be downwards, so that there is a steady 'leaching' away of valuable minerals, such as lime, and of humus, while if the nature or lie of the underlying rock prevents the water flowing away, peat bogs or moors are likely to form. For all these reasons the soils of the west are in general less fertile than those of the east, though there are many exceptions. In the east the least fertile regions are those where great beds of sand have been laid by the flow of water in ages long past. Dry, poor in useful minerals and usually acid, these are today the heathlands of East Anglia (Breckland), Berkshire, Sussex (Ashdown Forest), Dorset and the New Forest, or the commons of Surrey, growing little but gorse, heather, bracken, birches and pines or other conifers. Fortunately for the landscape lover the picturesqueness of a countryside does not depend on its fertility: almost any type of soil with its characteristic vegetation has its own beauty.

Chalk Country

The chalklands of England stretch from the white cliffs of Dover to Yorkshire's Flamborough Head, though by no means uninterruptedly. They include the North and South Downs, Salisbury Plain, the Downs of Dorset, Hampshire and Berkshire, the Marlborough Downs, the Chilterns and the Wolds of Lincolnshire and Yorkshire. The soil is shallow, over-well drained, and of course alkaline – since chalk is a form of limestone. The characteristic tree is the beech. However, this should be thought of less as a lime-lover than as a tree that will tolerate lime. What makes it the predominant tree on chalk is that its shallow roots, lacking the deep tap-root of the oak, can accommodate themselves to the thin soil layer. But like most trees the beech really does best on a deep, rich loam – provided it is well drained. The real chalk-loving trees and shrubs include yew, box, juniper, wayfaring-tree, blackthorn, dogwood, guelder-rose and buckthorn. Any of these may be found either alone or growing round the edges of beechwoods – the spreading, shallow roots of beech and the deep shade it casts discourage competition actually inside the woods. In the south, the plant which signals the presence of chalk soil most clearly is traveller's joy (or old man's beard). There is, too, a whole series of 'flowers of the chalk', of which the most striking, perhaps, are the curiously chequered snake's-head fritillary and the beautiful mauve pasque-flower (*anemone pulsatilla*). When oaks or hornbeam are found in chalk country, as in Savernake Forest, their presence implies a layer of some other soil, probably clay, on the chalk.

Clay-loam Country

There is an obvious connexion between the facts that the oak is the commonest tree in Britain and that clay or some variant of it, such as loam, or marl (a limy clay), is by far the most widely distributed type of soil. It would hardly be an exaggeration to say that wherever chalk, mountain limestone, 'Cotswold-type' limestone or the older acid rocks do not stick up through it, the soil is basically of the clay-loam type. The exceptions would be chiefly sands, gravels or peat. Between the North and South Downs of Kent and Sussex lies the clay of the Weald; the London Basin, much of the Hampshire Basin of East Anglia and most of the Midland Plain are clay; so, too, the Vales of Severn and Evesham; the soil of the Cheshire Plain is marl, becoming clay in south Lancashire. North of the Border, too, most of the soil of the Lowlands has been deposited there in past ages by the melting of ice or the flowing of water, and is usually clay or loam. If we leave mutton and fish off our menu, we can truthfully say that we are fed off clay; because it is clay – or what centuries of good farming have made of it – that grows our crops and fattens our livestock. In its raw state it may be intractable enough, and often too acid. But break it up, weather it, lime or marl it whenever necessary, add coarser material or muck to it if need be – and it will release the mineral riches it holds. The range of trees and plants that will flourish on it is limited more by such considerations as climate, drainage, or light and shade than by anything else. To the traveller, the oak is the tree above all others which hints at the presence of clay (the common oak, not the 'durmast', which is more usually found on the acid hill-soils of the west). Luckily the oak is a generous host and, unlike the beech, allows light and space to accommodate a rich variety of flowering plants, from bluebell to primrose and from woodsorrel to lesser celandine beneath its widespread boughs, while as companions it may have wych elm, hornbeam, sweet chestnut or a dozen other kinds of tree. On limy clays, such as are found round South Cambridgeshire, for instance, the place of oak may be taken by ash, accompanied by other lime-tolerating plants.

Mountain Limestone Country

If beech is the commonest tree on chalk, our other alkaline soil, that found on limestone, undoubtedly favours the ash. Mountain limestone is the beautiful grey rock so prominent in the Cheddar Gorge, the Mendips in Somerset, in the

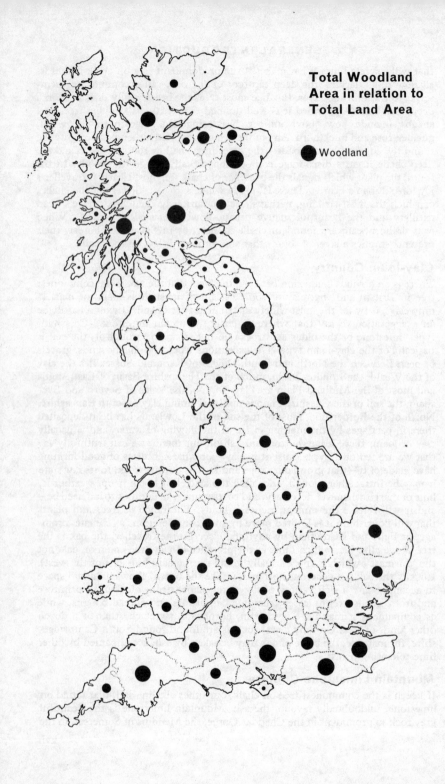

Total Woodland Area in relation to Total Land Area

● Woodland

Classification of High Forest as mainly Coniferous or mainly Broadleaved

Mainly Coniferous   Mainly Broadleaved

Derbyshire Dales and in the West Riding of Yorkshire. It occurs also in North Wales, in north Lancashire, and here and there in central Scotland. The fact that all these places have a higher, often a much higher rainfall than the chalk districts, explains the predominance of ash over beech: the latter needs a well-drained soil; the ash will grow with its roots actually in water, though it prefers better conditions. On the younger, softer limestones of Dorset, Somerset and the Cotswolds, with richer soil and milder climate, both trees are found, with many others. Like the oak, the ash is a generous host, allowing plenty of light to reach other lime-lovers, great and small. As well as those already mentioned, ashwoods often include such trees and shrubs as whitebeam, aspen, bird cherry, hazel, hawthorn and elder, while on the ground lily-of-the-valley, dog's mercury, hairy St John's wort and ground ivy, among many others, often find conditions to their liking.

The Acid-rock Soils

This heading must serve for all those widely scattered areas, mostly in the north and west of Britain, where nearly all forms of plant life find the going difficult – and most do not even make the attempt. They include Dartmoor and much of Cornwall, the hills and mountains of Wales, the Peak District and the Pennines, the Lake District and the Highlands of Scotland. Dr Johnson said of such places: 'An eye accustomed to flowery pastures and waving harvests is astonished and repelled by this wide extent of hopeless sterility. . . . It will readily occur that this uniformity of barrenness can afford very little amusement to the traveller: that it is easy to sit at home and conceive rocks and heath and water-falls; and that these journeys are useless labours which neither impregnate the imagination nor enlarge the understanding.' Today our point of view is different, and we find in such country some of the most beautiful and all the grandest scenery in Britain. Subject to a heavy rainfall, swept by high winds and often at a high altitude, the soil in such regions is shallow, poor and (like the very old, often igneous rocks beneath) acid. The principal vegetation is heather, with perhaps bilberry and, in damp places, cotton grass. Where trees can grow, they will be birch, pine or rowan (mountain ash), though in valleys, glens or on lower slopes, the durmast oak may join them. Of these, birch and pine will grow at heights of 1500 feet or so, and the rowan, common in North Wales and one of the commonest trees in the Highlands, even higher. One other class of plant must be mentioned, if only for the unexpectedness of such miniature beauty in surroundings of such grandeur. Far above the tree-line in the mountains of North Wales, the Lake District and the Scottish Highlands, at heights of 3,000 feet and more, where the snow may lie for ten months of the year, gay little flowering plants can be found making the best of the few weeks of intermittent sunshine. Alpine azalea, saxifrages white, yellow or purple, stemless campion, mountain woodrush and others, they are called Arctic Alpines – and they are believed to be relics of the last Ice Age, which ended ten thousand years ago.

Man-made Landscape

It is not always realized how large a part man has played in shaping the British landscape. If we except mountains, moors and loose sands, almost the whole British scene is very unlike what Nature alone would have made of it. When the Romans came, almost all the low-lying parts of the Midlands and East Anglia were covered either by swamp or forest or both. It was the Romans who started the centuries-long work of draining the Fens. The Anglo-Saxons were great clearers of forests, preferring valleys to live in rather than the uplands largely favoured by the pre-Roman Britons. Their ploughs, too, were able to cultivate the heavy clay soils as these became available. Throughout the succeeding centuries, the forests were slowly driven back, except where they were preserved for the chase – as the New Forest or Sherwood Forest (though by no means all Royal Forests were tree-covered). By the sixteenth and seventeenth centuries there was a serious shortage of timber. Landowners began to plant trees, at first as an elegant hobby but later in earnest. In Scotland one laird alone planted fifty million trees in his lifetime, from 1716 on. In that country the Scots pine (our only native conifer, except for yew and juniper) was the favourite; but in England, coinciding as it did with the great interest in beauty and good taste which reached its peak in the eighteenth century, tree-planting was practised largely as a means of creating beautiful landscapes, under the direction of such artists as Capability Brown. Fifty years ago probably saw the results of their work at its best. Even now, though much of the best has gone or is going, throughout the country in general we can recognize much for which we should bless our tree-planting forebears. The late eighteenth and early nineteenth centuries saw the end of another process which has left its happy mark on the country we see today – the Enclosures, by which the 'wastes' and 'open fields', used and cultivated in common for centuries by the villagers, were taken away from them and enclosed. However hard and unjust this may have been on the villagers, it did replace what must have been a dreary landscape with our familiar checkerboard of fields separated by hedgerows of quickthorn interspersed with oaks, elms and other decorative trees and shrubs. Such fences were by no means the cheapest: they were planted for their beauty as well as for the shelter they gave – and we can be as thankful for that as for the pleasure we get from the birds that frequent them. But hedges are having to give way before the needs of mechanized farming, as fields and trees to new housing. All in all, we shall do well to seek out and gaze at the beauty of our country – with some understanding – before even more has been whittled away.

Acknowledgment

The publishers are very grateful to the county librarians for their assistance in preparing the revisions for this edition.

All the maps in four and two colours are based on the Ordnance Survey Map with the sanction of the Controller of H.M. Stationery Office (Crown Copyright reserved).

For permission to reproduce the forestry maps on pages xviii and xix from the *Census of Woodlands 1947–9*, acknowledgment is due to the Forestry Commission.

The six sunshine maps on pages xxx–xxxii are reproduced by permission of the Meteorological Office.

Prehistory in Britain

BY GEOFFREY BOUMPHREY

Approximate Dates B.C.	General Conditions	Site Survivals	Other Finds
500,000 to 10,000	**Old Stone Age** (Paleolithic). Recurrent Arctic conditions, bringing glaciers over most of Britain, alternating with much warmer periods. All through Old and Middle Stone Ages man lived by hunting and food-gathering.	Caves and other habitation sites.	*Early Paleolithic.* 'Eoliths' – crudely shaped (?) pear-like flints. Bones of mammoth, elephant, hippo, bear, bison, reindeer, etc. Swanscombe skull (c. 200,000), earliest known ancestor (?) of modern Briton. Flint tools improving slowly. *Late Paleolithic.* Human fragments. Evidence of fire-making. Cutting tools of flint. Spear-throwers (first mechanical device). Carved and decorated bones; but no cave-paintings in Britain.
10,000 to 2,300 6,000	**Middle Stone Age** (Mesolithic). Last Ice Age ending. Climate gradually becoming much warmer and drier than today. Land surface sinking. Forests encroach on plains. At about this time Britain became an island. Climate still warm, but now wetter.	Caves and camping places. Traces of crude huts.	No art; but much better and lighter tools in flint and bone. (Bows and) arrows. Axes and other tools with handles. Dug-out canoes. Dogs domesticated. Cold-climate animals replaced by red deer, wild pig, etc.
2,300 to 1,900	**New Stone Age** (Neolithic). Settlers of long-headed Mediterranean type introduce farming (cattle, sheep, pigs and wheat-cultivation) and pottery.	Ditched camps with causeways. Sunk hut circles. Stonehouses. Flint-mines. Long barrows. Stone-axe factories. Megalithic (great stone) tombs. Megalithic circles and timber sanctuaries.	Shapely, thin-walled pottery. Polished stone tools, including hoes. Beautifully made flint tools in wide variety. Crude oil-lamps. Carved fertility figures. Primitive carpentry. Crouched burials in communal tombs.

Date	Period	Sites and structures	Objects
1,900 to 450	**Bronze Age.** Climate became drier again. Grasslands spread. Round-headed, warlike invaders bringing copper and bronze implements and weaving. Mainly nomadic herdsmen, tending to neglect tillage – though they introduced oats. Commerce at home and abroad developed.	Sunk hut sites. Stone hut circles. Round barrows and cairns. Avebury and, in its final form, Stonehenge. Embanked sanctuaries. Stone circles. Urn cemeteries. Dwellings on piles in Thames estuary. Stone houses.	Flint daggers. Polished flint knives. Copper and bronze axes, daggers, spears, swords, halberds. Stone axe-club-hammers, pierced for handles. Turned shale cups. Ornaments of gold, bronze, amber and jet. Linen and woollen fabrics. Pottery. Individual crouched burials with objects for use in next world. Occasional dug-out, boat-like coffins. Cremations and cinerary urns.
800	First invasions by Celtic peoples, bringing two-ox plough. Great increase in population and in prosperity.	Squarish Celtic fields. Embanked cattle enclosures. Flatter round barrows.	Pots with handles. Great development in bronze working. Wooden and bronze shields. Carpenters' tools. Cauldrons and buckets of sheet bronze.
450 to A.D. 43	**Iron Age.** Climate became wetter and much cooler – i.e. as today. Increasing invasions by Celts, who brought with them iron weapons and implements.	Hill-top camps. Stone-walled ring forts. Lake villages. Stone villages. Sites of round, timbered houses. Storage pits.	Thin-walled, decorated pottery. Wine vessels. Polished bronze mirrors. Many examples of superb Celtic decorative art. Chariots and carts. Dice. Ingots of tin.
75 B.C.	First invasions of Belgae.	Small round barrows. In Scotland, brochs or 'Pictish towers' and vitrified forts.	Clay bullets and pebbles for slings. Rotary querns for grinding. Iron currency bars. Expensive funerary objects.
A.D. 43 to early 5th century	**Roman Britain.** Claudius began the conquest of Britain in A.D. 43. The last Roman troops were recalled in about A.D. 410.		

Note. The dates given are approximations only: the more nearly they approach historic times, the more accurate they become.

For further reading: JACQUETTA & CHRISTOPHER HAWKES, *Prehistoric Britain* 1958. This also contains an annotated bibliography.

Architectural Styles in Britain

BY GEOFFREY BOUMPHREY

Since all periods were to some extent 'transitional', the dates given are approximate and, indeed, arbitrary. Only ecclesiastical buildings are considered under the first five headings.

Anglo-Saxon (500–1066)

Crude and heavy, based on Roman architecture (itself not famed for lightness). Windows deep-set and semi-circular (occasionally triangular) at the top. Doorways also round-headed. Tendency to use stone as though it were timber – i.e. pilaster strips and long-and-short corner stones, as on tower of Earls Barton church, Northants (p. 405). The rare surviving vaults (arched roofs) are, like the Roman, semi-circular (p. 479).

Norman (1066–1189)

Also heavy, but dignified and reposeful. Round-topped arches, doorways and windows, ornamented with vigorous mouldings, the 'chevron' being particularly characteristic (pp. 15, 139, 252). Massive cylindrical piers (columns) and flat buttresses. Vaults still circular, but groins (where cross-vaults meet) gradually replaced by ribs which support panels of stone. This innovation led to the pointed arch. Later Norman work is often termed TRANSITIONAL.

Early English (1189–1307)

Higher and more graceful, owing to the use of rib-and-panel vaulting and the introduction of the pointed arch. Windows are tall and lancet-shaped to match, while externally buttresses, pinnacles, steep roofs and spires (in place of the square Norman tower) increase the effect of soaring lightness. So, too, the groups of slender pillars encircling the much-reduced piers, to which they are joined by stone bands (pp. 38, 69). Delicate carvings of leaves decorate the capitals and the 'dog-tooth' is a favourite ornament.

Decorated (1307–1377)

Most marked by its windows. Whereas the Early English lancets could at best only be grouped in threes, the central one being taller, it now became possible to pierce the walls with much larger openings and to frame the windows in these with light and flowing stone tracery (p. 28). The piers are now so deeply fluted as to resemble sheaves of slim, equal-sized columns. Vaulting ribs become more numerous, forming patterns of great complexity and beauty. Leaf carvings are more naturalistic.

Perpendicular (1377–1485)

The name indicates the main feature of this exclusively English style. The desire of the builders to extend all vertical lines to the limit resulted in the development of a much-flattened arch and to roofs much less steep. Windows become enormous and so tall that the stone verticals are stayed by horizontal members (pp. 205, 386, s.59). Vaulting is even more complex, reaching its culmination in 'fan-vaulting' (p. 387). Battlements, like almost all non-structural stonework, are pierced, and much is made of the flying buttress.

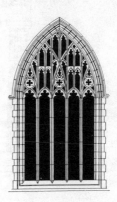

Tudor and Early Renaissance (1485–1603)

Ecclesiastical buildings continued in the previous style; but for the first time since Roman-Britain, domestic architecture began to claim serious attention. The house was planned, not for defence, but for living in (p. 442). Square-headed mullioned windows were often of enormous size, following a great reduction in the price of glass (p. 97); bays and oriels proliferated. Tall chimneys, elaborately decorated, were grouped as 'features'. Under Renaissance influence, the random if picturesque grouping of the medieval mansion was replaced by the classical symmetry and proportion of such masterpieces as Longleat (p. 75) and Montacute.

Renaissance - Jacobean, Queen Anne, Georgian and Regency (1630–1830)

In these two centuries British architecture reached the peak of refinement. So far as the medium or small house in town or country is considered, its achievements

Doric

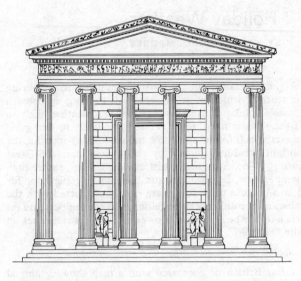

Ionic

cannot be paralleled. Two figures dominate the first 120 years: Inigo Jones,
working between 1615 and 1652, mastered
the Palladian (Italian) idiom, and Wren,
between 1663–1723, was much influenced
by the French Renaissance. They were
followed by other great names, such as
Gibbs, Nash, Kent, the Woods (of Bath),
the Adam brothers and Soane. Between
them they transformed classical architecture, originally evolved for very different conditions, into something essentially
British (pp. 47, 56, 104, 312). Today the
words 'Georgian' or 'Queen Anne' are
almost synonymous with good taste –
taste which spread downwards even to
the small local builder. Many examples of
such work will be found in these pages;
here one can do no more than depict
the three Greek 'Orders of Architecture'
which began it all.

Corinthian

The Corinthian façade does not in general
differ from the Ionic. The distinction
of the third classical order lies in its
developed capital.

Holiday Weather

BY GEOFFREY BOUMPHREY

The purpose of this section is to offer the reader some guidance in answering two questions, one or other of which must present itself to many of us each year. (i) If the *time* of one's holiday is fixed, *where* is the best weather likely to be found? And (ii) If the *place* is fixed, *when* is one most likely to find good weather there? The charts which follow show, for the six holiday months, the average amounts of bright sunshine enjoyed by the various parts of Great Britain during the years 1931–60. Sunshine statistics were chosen, rather than those for rainfall or temperature, because it is sun that most people hope for when on holiday and also because the last two are closely connected with the first: if the sun is shining, rain is unlikely to be falling, and the temperature (at least out of the wind) is likely to be agreeable. However, a few general notes on all three factors may be helpful.

Rainfall

If a contour map of Great Britain be compared with a map showing annual rainfall, the similarity of the two is most striking – high ground, high rainfall; low ground, low rainfall. In fact, the wettest parts of the country are Snowdonia, the Lake District and the north-west Highlands, followed by Cornwall and west Devon, most of the rest of Wales, the high ground of Lancashire and the Pennines, the south-west Lowlands and the remaining high areas of Scotland. One sometimes hears it said that 'Mountains attract rain' and certainly in our country they appear to do so. What really happens is rather different. Most of the weather affecting Britain comes to us across the Atlantic; and so the prevailing westerly winds tend to be heavily laden with water vapour. When this damp air strikes rising ground, it is forced upwards, often to considerable heights. By rising it is cooled. But since cool air cannot hold so much water vapour as warm, any surplus moisture has to condense as cloud or, if the excess is still greater, as rain. This process is by no means the only one leading to the formation of cloud or rain; but it does provide the main reason for the facts noted above. It explains too, the maddening way in which Snowdon, Ben Nevis and other of our great peaks so often veil their summits. And to some extent it justifies such rhymes as:

> 'When Bredon Hill puts on its cap,
> Men of the vale, beware of that.'

– the appearance of cloud-cap signifying an increase in humidity, which makes rain more probable. When we are considering holiday weather, however, total annual rainfall is of less importance than the records of the various holiday months. Here, I am afraid, August, to which so many are compelled, does not show up very well. If the year's rain were to be distributed equally between the twelve months, each would have a percentage of 100 ÷ 12 – i.e. 8·3%. In fact the figures for Great Britain are May, 6·4%, June 5·8%, July, 7·4%, August, 9·4% and September 7·6%. So far as August is concerned, only the south and

xxviii

south-east coasts show relatively good figures; in Snowdonia and the Lake District it is the wettest month of the year except for September and October.

Temperature

If low rainfall were the only consideration in deciding where to go for a holiday, most of us would unhesitatingly make for the eastern half of our island. Draw a curved line from north to south down the centre of Great Britain and you will find that the rainfall to the east of it is little more than half that of the west. But apart from scenic and other personal questions, there is one other main factor to be considered – temperature. It is widely believed that we enjoy a temperate climate, rather than the far colder conditions to which our latitude would otherwise condemn us, thanks to what is popularly miscalled the Gulf Stream, a slow drift of water across the North Atlantic from Florida. We should rather thank the prevailing westerly winds which have been long in contact over the Atlantic with the relatively warm water. In proof, think how inevitably cold weather grips us in winter if the normal flow of Atlantic depressions is deflected by anything, such as a shift of the Polar front or the spread of an anticyclone from across the North Sea. On the east coast, however, even in summer the sea is considerably colder than on the west. Consequently, when the sun warms up the land, the air above is heated and rises, drawing in colder air from the sea. Hence a chilly east wind which, though you may call it 'bracing', contrasts sharply with the balmy sea-breezes of the west coast. The sea everywhere takes much longer than the land to warm up, and so does not reach its highest temperature until about six weeks later – the end of August or the beginning of September. For this reason the three autumn months, September, October and November, are warmer than the spring months of May, April and March respectively. Once it is warm, the sea is correspondingly slow to cool, and in cooling it releases an enormous amount of heat. In fact, the relatively warm Atlantic with its associated westerly winds affects Great Britain much in the manner of a gigantic fan-heater. So much is this so that in winter – despite popular belief – lower temperatures are found not as one goes farther north, but as one moves east. The January temperature of the extreme north-west of Scotland is no lower than that of east Kent.

Sunshine

Here the charts which follow speak for themselves; but a few general notes may be added. The sunniest places in Great Britain are on the Channel coast: but why does not north Scotland, with two and a half hours of more daylight at midsummer, record more hours of bright sunshine? The answer lies mainly in the last two words. The official instrument used records only *bright* sunshine. In the long early morning and evening hours which so much lengthen northern daylight, the sun is rarely bright enough to make its mark. There is, too, a greater probability of haze or cloud in those damper latitudes. In discussing sea breezes in the last paragraph, I described how air, heated over the land, may rise. Clearly, this action may result in the formation of cloud, just as it may when the air has been deflected upwards by a hillside. Here, then, is the explanation of the sunny coastal strips so evident on the charts and so much appreciated by seaside holidaymakers who see the clouds piling up just inland.

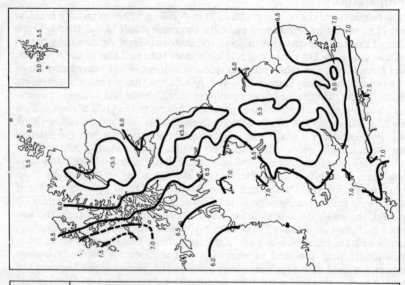

May

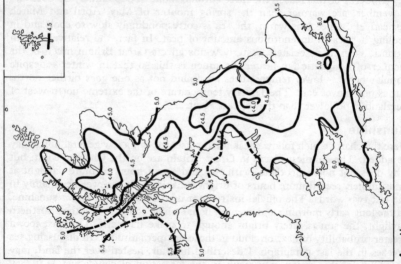

April

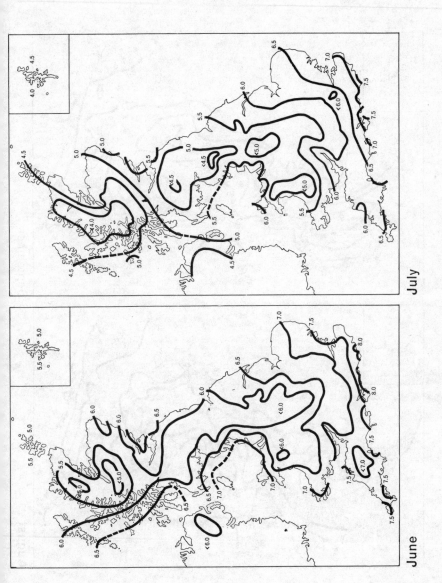

July

June

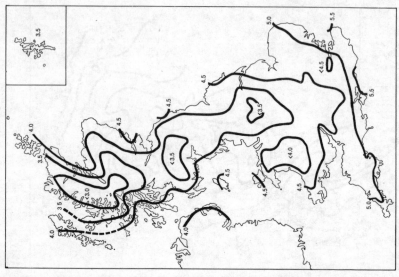

August

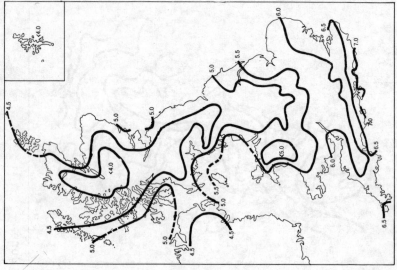

September

Gurnard's Head *J. Allan Cash*

CORNWALL
and the Isles of Scilly

AN INTRODUCTION BY GEOFFREY GRIGSON

Until the railway came to the far west and crossed the Tamar into Cornwall by
Brunel's tall Saltash bridge of 1859 (which now has the modern road bridge as
neighbour), Cornwall was a most isolated county. For centuries the Tamar,
twisting in a narrow valley, then widening into a tidal estuary, had kept Cornwall
and Devonshire, Cornwall and the rest of England, considerably apart. There
was not a bridge below the narrow medieval New Bridge at Gunnislake miles
up from the sea. So Cornwall retained its antiquities, its small, rather secretive
fishing ports, its little Tudor and Jacobean manor houses, its holy wells and
wayside or churchyard crosses, its Celtic sentiments and its dialect – English
indeed, but peppered with words surviving from the old Cornish language.

Cornwall, whatever a very patriotic Cornishman may allege, is not at all

Opposite: Detail from the original painting by Richard Eurich.
This imaginary landscape epitomizes the character of the county: the sea cutting deeply into wooded
hills; the church with its square, buttressed 15th-century tower; the wheel-headed wayside cross, a relic
of medieval Cornwall.

purely Cornish. The English fought their way over the Tamar more than eleven centuries ago. When the visitor crosses out of Devonshire into Cornwall (a name which began on English lips as a term for the Cornish people, meaning the Welshmen of the land of Kernow), the signpost names which greet him will be fairly divided at first between the English and the Cornish languages. If he enters, not by the 20th-century bridge at Saltash, but by the 14th-century bridge I have mentioned at Gunnislake, the steep climb from the Tamar, past the chimney-stacks of abandoned mines, will set him under the heather-heights of Hingston Down, which was where King Egbert defeated the Cornish, with Viking allies, as long ago as 838, and so opened their country to English settlers. It is over a thousand years now since Cornish was regularly spoken in the east of the county. Still, the Anglo-Cornish on the Cornish side of the Tamar did not have so much to do with the English people on the Devonshire and Dartmoor side; and as you drive west you quickly see more Cornish place-names written up, beginning with *pen*–(head or end), *tre*–(farm), *lan*–(church), etc. The first town of some size on the road from Gunnislake is Liskeard, as Cornish as could be, meaning the *lis*, the court or capital, of a Cornish king, a petty one but still Cornish, whose name was Cerruyt. The road continues along the moorland spine of Cornwall, it comes to Bodmin, Cornish for the 'House of the Monks', it makes for Cornish-named town after town – Truro, Redruth, Camborne, Penzance (which means 'Holy Headland') – passing signposts with the names of unfamiliar saints, such as St Mabyn, St Breock, St Wenn, St Columb, St Enoder, St Piran, St Erth, St Ives, and so on, all holy men or women of the British Christianity of 1,300 and 1,400 years ago, which continued, in Wales, in Cornwall and across the water in Brittany, when the newly arrived English were still pagans, their worship centring around such fierce deities as Woden.

Cornwall is astonishingly full of entertaining and rewarding things to see, and for the holiday-maker this favourite of all the holiday counties of England divides into four, Cornwall of the seaside, Cornwall of the granite moors, the ferny luxuriant Cornwall tucked out of the wind along tidal creeks and wooded combes, and the Cornwall of small villages and small fields and deep lanes and isolated lichen-rough churches, which often seem to grow out of hill flanks in the most intimate and natural way.

The Coast

Cornwall of the seaside is exceedingly various. The long peninsula of the county has a rougher side and a gentler side, and it slopes from one to the other. Down the coast on the northern rougher side, from the Devon border to Land's End, you have the Atlantic, the considerable intermittent savagery of abrupt headlands and high cliffs, and small difficult harbours. Make an Atlantic northern journey from Morwenstow to Boscastle and Tintagel, and on, till you reach St Agnes and the Reskajeage cliffs and Cape Cornwall and Land's End, if you like the sight and sound of long rollers and the sentiment of land and rock resisting the sea (and if you like surf-bathing – but watch out, for the undertow can be dangerous in places). Make a southern journey along the milder, less aggressively resistant Channel coast – Looe, Talland, Polperro, Fowey and its river or estuary, Mevagissey, the many tide-inlets which constitute the green-watered, oak-banked complex of the Fal, and so round the Lizard to the sub-tropical shelter of Mounts Bay and Penzance – if you like

2

colour, fertility, mildness of air, coves of sand, bland little grey harbours, un-ruffled inland tide-waters, and a sense (which the weather does not always maintain) of comfort and enclosure, spiced with the recurrent wilderness of rock, and wind-rounded gorse and blackthorn.

Opposites in combination are one of the marks of this county. If it is rough and rocky, with rocks which vary from the bluntness of granite to red and purple slates, it has also its extraordinary exuberance of vegetation and flower-colour (bluebells, primroses, foxgloves especially) out of the wind, and under the shelter of the rock. If it seems – and is – remote, as well as rough and primitive, it is a county also where the valleys and hills crowd together, and where you may have half a dozen or more parish churches within a few square miles. If hills break out, they emerge from an unusually close pattern or embroidery of small earth- and stone-hedged fields, medieval or still older in origin, irregular in outline and fitted closely to the swell and curve of the land.

Cornish Buildings

Neither churches nor mansions nor towns are architecturally of great merit. Cornwall is no treasure-county of the arts; and as far as buildings go, the great pleasure afforded by Cornwall is that house or church or village or small town – or railway viaduct – seldom does violence to its landscape.

This is even true of the relics of Cornwall's industrial period of the late 18th and early 19th centuries. The engine-houses of the abandoned mines of West Cornwall, on the moors, along the cliffs, or in the valleys, are stony outgrowths of Cornwall no less than its churches or low white cottages, or the small ruined lime-kilns often to be found on the creeks and above the beaches. Yet internally

Engine-house of deserted mine near Redruth　　　　*Reece Winstone*

vagissey harbour　　*Aerofilms*

many of the rather low almost cave-like parish churches – for instance Lanteglos-by-Fowey, Talland, Lanreath, Blisland, Morwenstow – are very full of the flavour of a late medieval, Tudor and Jacobean past which liked colour and image and symbol, and provided them liberally in its own provincial way.

Several of the small Cornish houses or small mansions on show are eloquent of the wakeful, grasping, alert time in Cornwall after the Reformation, when the Cornish gentry were building up estates, and were busy, in this Atlantic county, with maritime speculation and the chancy profits of a New World. No one should miss two of the National Trust houses, Cotehele, on the Tamar, which has the strongest early Tudor feeling, furniture, tapestries and all, of a Cornwall just leaving the Middle Ages, and Lanhydrock, built a hundred years later by a Puritan who was one of the wealthiest merchants of Cornwall, and one of its principal Cromwellians. Both are rather squat granitic houses. Near Cotehele, the little 15th-century building of Dupath Well, with water running through it, gives one a feeling of a Cornwall as old as its saints, and older still.

The Towns

The best of the Cornish towns, for different reasons, I believe to be Launceston in the far east, Truro in the west, and Penzance in the far west. Those who come into Cornwall by A30 from Okehampton too often rush uphill and by-pass Launceston, which is a town of many eras, compact, encircled with green views, and satisfying for church, Norman castle ruins, Georgian houses, and an uncommon look of having missed – so far, and for lack of funds – the nastiness of 20th-century town commerce. Truro, the cathedral town of the county, is made satisfying by its clean Georgian look, its surrounding hills, its runnels of fresh water along the edge of the streets, and its luck in having a small, almost entirely delightful museum and art gallery. Penzance speaks still of the discovery of the pleasures of the seaside early in the last century, a town of terraces, villas and gardens with bedding-out and tender shrubs on one side, and of an overcrowded main street on the other – a town, too, with an antiquarian bookshop specializing in books on Cornwall and the Isles of Scilly. Both Penzance and Truro are in debt to the fortunes made out of tin and copper in the era of Cornish shaft mining. The geological museum at Penzance and the geological collections in the museum at Truro are full of strange crystals brought up from the dark galleries of the mines.

Across Mounts Bay from Penzance, St Michael's Mount (an island at high

St Michael's Mount

Reece Winstone

The Longships Lighthouse off Land's End *J. Allan Cash*

water) is the noblest and most exciting of the National Trust properties in Cornwall. Capped now with a mansion and a chapel, which survive from a medieval priory, there is not much doubt that this was the 'certain island lying off the coast of Britain called Ictis', where the merchants of the Mediterranean bought ingots of tin from the Cornish, some 2,000 years ago.

The Moors

Cornwall of the granite moors is not quite as attractive as it is supposed to be – at any rate in the eastern Cornwall of Bodmin Moor, of which the best part is the extreme western edge, Sharp Tor, Twelve Mens Moor, and Hawkstor Downs: these give, from their great height, a huge hollow view of the valleys of the Lynher and the Tamar and the myriad, many-coloured, tiny fields of every farm between Bodmin Moor and Devonshire's Dartmoor. But then Penwith, the Land's End district, once the end of the known world, is also granite moorland, and in right conditions one of the most emotive stretches of Britain, brilliant in sea-light, and spattered with neolithic tombs and with the forts and villages of prehistoric tinners, and ruined 19th-century mines – including the engine-houses of Botallack mine, like cliff castles one after another down to the crumping volume of the Atlantic, which swells roundly forward and swells roundly back from the rock with a dull weight.

Scillonia

The Isles of Scilly (never to be called the Scilly Isles, by the way) are Cornwall extended, across more than twenty miles of ocean. But that is only true of the stuff they are made of: they are knobbly, low, hard little islands of granite, softened between the rock by an abundance of blown sand. But in spirit and in look they are different altogether from Cornwall or anywhere else in or round the British Isles. The light of the islands is more brilliant, the surface pattern of small bulb plots protected by the tallest grey-green pittosporum hedges makes a landscape of its own. But this is the pattern only of a fold or a flat here and there between wastes of green or ochre or dark red fern and slabby uplifts of granite, under a vast concave of surrounding sky, inside a blue, white-edged surround of limitless ocean.

St Mary's is the metropolitan island, longest, most 'developed', with the conveniences of its small town, but the least attractive scenery. Of the other inhabited islands, each – Bryher, Tresco, St Agnes and St Martin's – has an individuality, and independence. Each is a pocket of freedom from the pressures and limited views of mainland living; Tresco (with its sub-tropical abbey gardens) the most urbane, Bryher the most ragged and broken, St Agnes the most oceanic, St Martin's offering the greatest variety of beach and scenery. The necessary warning is that these are islands for the extrovert visitor who enjoys walking, air, light, colour, slightly chilly oceanic bathing, natural history, history, and archaeology – any or all of these. Others often condemn these islands as deserts with nothing to do.

7

Some houses and gardens open to the public

Antony House 2m NW of Torpoint *Map CE 05. Splendid, unspoilt Queen Anne house, with panelled rooms and contemporary furniture and portraits.* NT.

Cotehele House *Map CE 06. A romantic 15th-cent. mansion high on the wooded banks of the River Tamar. Within are the furniture, tapestries and armour of the Earls of Mount Edgcumbe. Pools and rills add to the interest of a garden on different levels (see also p. 9).* NT.

Godolphin House 5m NW of Helston *Map BG 02. Tudor with later additions inc. granite colonnaded front.* S. E. Schofield, Esq.

Lanhydrock House *Map CA 06. 17th-cent. mansion with formal gardens (see also p. 11).* NT.

Pendennis Castle Falmouth *Map BJ 03. Henry VIII castle on headland.* Ministry of Public Building and Works.

Penfound Manor nr Poundstock *Map CC 09. Oldest inhabited manor in Britain, part Saxon with later additions.* Mrs Kenneth Tucker.

St Michael's Mount nr Marazion *Map BF 03. See pp. 6 & 14.* NT.

Trelissick Gardens 4m S of Truro *Map BJ 04. Rhododendrons, camellias and sub-tropical shrubs.* NT.

Trerice nr Newlyn East *Map BJ 05. Manor house rebuilt 1571.* NT.

Tresco Abbey Gardens Tresco *Map AJ 01. Terraced gardens with finest collection of sub-tropical plants in Europe. Museum of shipwreck figureheads.* Lt-Cdr T. M. Dorrien-Smith.

Books for further reading

Cornwall in general

W. G. V. BALCHIN *Cornwall: an illustrated essay on the history of the landscape* 1955
JOHN BETJEMAN *Cornwall* (Shell County Guides series) (in preparation)
W. H. HUDSON *The Land's End* 1908
ROBERT HUNT (ed.) *Popular Romances of the West of England* 1865
A. K. JENKIN *The Cornish Miner* 1927
HENRY JENNER *A Handbook of the Cornish Language* 1904
NIKOLAUS PEVSNER *Cornwall* (Buildings of England series) 1951

Cornwall in history

MARY COATE *Cornwall in the Great Civil War and Interregnum, 1642–1660* 1933

LEONARD ELLIOTT-BINNS *Medieval Cornwall* 1955
F. E. HALLIDAY *History of Cornwall* 1959
H. O'NEILL HENCKEN *The Archaeology of Cornwall and Scilly* 1932
JOHN ROWE *Cornwall in the Age of the Industrial Revolution* 1953
A. L. ROWSE *Tudor Cornwall* 1941
NICHOLAS THOMAS *Guide to Prehistoric England* 1960

The Isles of Scilly

CLIVE MUMFORD *Portrait of the Isles of Scilly* 1967
B. H. ST J. O'NEILL *Ancient Monuments of the isles of Scilly* 1958

Gazetteer

CORNWALL
and the Isles of Scilly

Altarnun (CC 08). Fine moorland church, Norman font, rood-screen, carved bench-ends. Pack-horse bridge.

Bodmin Moor (CB 07). A hundred square miles of moorland averaging some 800 ft. above sea level. Highest points, with rewarding views, are Brown Willy (1,375 ft.) and Rough Tor (1,312 ft.), both N of main road. Source of the Camel and the Fowey. Earlier inhabitants left numerous stone monuments. Bolventor (CB 07) is good starting-point for walks to Brown Willy, etc., and to Dozmary Pool.

Boscastle (CB 09). A narrow cleft winding between high wild cliffs, almost blocked by stone pier. Impressive even on a calm day, terrific in a gale. This little harbour was built for the export of slate from the huge Delabole quarries.

Botallack Mine. 19th-cent. tin mine on the Atlantic cliffs of St Just-in-Penwith (BD 03), which extended far under the sea. The engine-houses descend the cliff almost to the water's edge.

Bude (CC 10) EC Thurs (3,583). Originally a small seaport town which has now grown into a thriving seaside resort. Renowned for its long sandy beaches and excellent surfing.

The Cheesewring (CC 07). One of Nature's jokes. A pinnacle of granite weathered into the shape of the stones forming an old-time 'wringcheese' or cheese press. A gold cup found in 1818

in a Bronze Age barrow on the moors near here, and now in the British Museum, was used by George V as a shaving mug.

Chysauster* (BE 03). Excavated remains of an Iron Age village of tin-smelters, c. 200 BC–100 AD (AM), with huts, a street, and a panoramic view of Mount's Bay. Roger's Tower, a romantic 'folly' of the early 19th cent., stands on higher ground of an Iron Age hill camp.

Cotehele House* (CE 06). A very remarkable early Tudor manor house, above the Tamar. Worth a special visit for its enclosed courtyard, hall, chapel, furniture, delft, tapestries, etc. Beautiful gardens on many levels (NT).

Duloe (CC 05). Hill-crest village inland from Looe, notable for its church, its holy well (St Cuby), and its stone circle (c. 1600–1000 BC) of very large stones which are cooped up in a very small field.

Dupath Well (CE 06) not far from **Cotehele** (*above*). Medieval holy well enclosed in a pinnacled 15th-cent. building, the water flowing across the floor into a basin. Probably visited by sufferers from skin diseases (AM).

Falmouth (BJ 03) EC Wed (17,500). Happy blend of seaside resort and seaport. Excellent buildings of early 19th cent., especially the Customs House, and late 18th cent. On the lofty headland projecting into the broad estuary of the River Fal, Henry VIII built Pendennis Castle (AM), with another opposite at St Mawes to complete the defences of this magnificent natural harbour. The wooded rivers and ramifying creeks of the Fal estuary are best appreciated from a boat, but they are tidal and the

The Helford River   *Aerofilms*

upper reaches are apt to dry out with disconcerting suddenness.

Fowey* (CB 05) EC Wed (2,340). Pronounced 'Foy'. A maze of narrow streets on the steep west bank of the estuary. Quays upstream busy with the export of china clay (used for making not only pottery but also paper, paint, chemicals, lipstick, stomach powders, etc.); elsewhere pleasure-boats of all kinds. A ferry (cars carried) crosses to Bodinnick, saving the long detour via Lostwithiel. Exquisite creek and river scenery (by tide to Pont, Lerryn, Lostwithiel).

Harlyn Bay (BJ 07). An Iron Age cemetery under drifted sand. Skeletons on view in stone chests, enclosed in cucumber frames. Small museum.

Helford River (BH 02). Popular centre for yachting, fishing and creek-

exploring. The Duchy of Cornwall Oyster Farm, hereditary property of the Prince of Wales, is one of the best in Britain, millions of oysters being laid in the river every year.

Helston (BG 02) EC Wed (7,100). Attractive old town with good Georgian buildings. Celebrated for the Furry (or Floral) Dance which takes place annually on May 8.

Lamorna Cove (BE 02). Celebrated picturesque cove 'discovered' by 19th-cent. artists. A small brook winds by the road down a wooded valley to the strip of turf above the boulder-strewn beach. There is a bathing beach round the corner.

Land's End* (BD 02). Some 290 miles by road from London, about 870 from John o' Groats. Fine granite-piled cliffs. For centuries the point of mystery, the end of the known and threshold of the unknown for the English and the Cornish.

Lanhydrock House* (CA 06). Secluded 17th-cent. mansion of Lord Robartes, Cornish parliamentarian leader in the Civil War, approached by a noble sycamore avenue (a Cornish speciality). Long gallery, ceiled with Creation scenes in plaster, contains Puritan library and family portraits by Cornelius Johnson of high quality. Granite church alongside unites with the house in a charming hillside group (NT).

Lanreath (CB 05). 15th-cent. church, with rood-screen, carved bench-ends, and monuments, facing a pretty green, flanked on one side by inn and cottages, on the other by early 17th-cent. manor-house.

Lanyon Quoit* (BE 03). Chamber of a New Stone Age long barrow: a granite slab 18 in. thick, 8 ft. 9 in. wide and over 17 ft. long, balanced on three upright slabs, *c.* 2000–1600 BC (NT).

Bench-end, Launcells Church
Reece Winstone

Launcells (CC 10). Church with wonderful collection of sixty carved bench-ends, and medieval tiles. Holy well.

Launceston (CD 08) EC Thurs (4,500). One of the least spoilt towns of England, built on a steep hill with

Lanyon Quoit, near Penzance
Reece Winstone

fine views of the surrounding country. Up and down streets, early Tudor church crusted with granite carvings, early medieval remains of a castle with a Norman mound; pretty 18th-cent. houses.

Linkinhorne (CD 07). 15th-cent. St Melor's Well. Fine granite church. The three Bronze Age circles of the Hurlers are in this moorland parish.

The Lizard★ (BG 01). Most southerly point on England's mainland, a breezy moorland peninsula some 300 ft. above sea level, dropping down to

Mullion Cove   Reece Winstone

many-hued rocks, golden sands, flowers and coves: Poldhu, Mullion, Kynance, etc. In 1901 Marconi received the first trans-atlantic wireless signals at Poldhu, and in 1962 the first television pictures from America via Telstar satellite were received on Goonhilly Downs.

Looe, East and West (CC 05) EC Thurs (3,900). Two valleys unite in a narrow estuary dividing the twin fishing towns. East Looe has a pier and a

sandy shore; a bridge connects the two towns. Good centre for deep-sea fishing and for exploring East Cornwall. The tide journey up the West Looe River to Watergate is one of Looe's time-honoured pleasures.

Lostwithiel (CB 05) EC Wed (2,160). Here, 5 m. above its mouth, is the first bridge, built in the 15th cent., across the R. Fowey. Restormel★, 1 m. north, a round moated castle, mainly 13th cent., belonged to the Earls of Cornwall; exquisite in shape and site (AM).

Mevagissey (CA 04) EC Thurs (2,200). Steep narrow streets, pier-sheltered harbour; one of the most delightful of small Cornish fishing towns.

Morvah★ (BD 03). Here is the remarkable Chun Castle, a ring-fort with granite walls dating from about 250 BC and occupied till about AD 500. Probably a fort of tin-miners and smelters.

Morwenstow (CC 11). Lonely cliff-top church with Norman pillars and carvings, and vicarage built by the poet R. S. Hawker (1803–75).

Mount Edgcumbe (CE 05), facing Plymouth Sound. Sea-girt grounds open to public; mansion burnt out in Second World War and now rebuilt after the same style. Magnificent views of the Sound.

Mousehole (BE 02). Charmingly apt name for this pleasant fishing village crowded round its near-circular harbour.

Mylor (BJ 03). Beautifully situated partly Norman church with rood-screen and very tall Cornish wheel-headed cross of the Middle Ages. A tombstone in the churchyard tells its story with exemplary brevity:

'His foot it slip And he did fall, Help help he cries and that was all.'

Newquay (BJ 06) EC Wed (11,850). A town built on cliffs. Its sandy bays, 'pirate' caves and surf-bathing have made it the most popular resort in N Cornwall, far removed from its days as a fishing village when, from the Huer's House on the headland, the lookout watched for shoals of pilchard. About 3 m. W is Holywell Bay with its holy well and a magnificent stretch of sands and caves.

Padstow (BK 07) EC Wed (2,850). Charming small Cornish harbour town. (*See also* **Harlyn Bay** *above*.)

Penzance (BE 02) EC Fri (20,600). Terminus of the old Great Western Railway; busy shopping, marketing and holiday centre of the Land's End peninsula, sheltered and sunny, with pretty terraces and villas. Penzance developed as a Regency wateringplace and winter resort. Dracaena trees and other sub-tropical plants abound. Antiquarian bookshop specializing in Cornish books. Geological Museum. The boat for the Isles of Scilly leaves from Penzance.

Polperro (CC 05). Chapel Rock on the W side of the harbour provides a good gull's-eye view of this diminutive, picturesque fishing-port crammed into a rocky gulf. Within easy reach are some interesting Cornish churches: Lansallos, Lanteglos-by-Fowey, Talland, Pelynt.

Rame Head* (CE 04). The most easterly headland of Cornwall, with panoramic views of Plymouth Sound and the coastline from Cornwall's Lizard Point to Devon's Bolt Head, anciently capped by a chapel of St Michael, the saint of high places. Do not be deceived by the long crescent of Whitesand Bay immediately to the W: it is a death-trap for bathers.

Roche Rock   *Reece Winstone*

Reskajeage Cliffs, between Navax Pt and Portreath (BG 04). Stretch of Atlantic cliffs in W Cornwall forming an extraordinary series of sharp, grim triangles.

Roche Rock, about 4 m. N of St Austell (CA 05). Granite outcrop in the china-clay district capped with the hermit's cell and chapel of St Michael, built 1409.

St Agnes (BH 05). A holiday village with a good beach and surf bathing, surrounded with old tin mines, some on the cliff edge. Rugged, most remarkable cliff scenery.

St Austell (CA 05) EC Thurs (23,650). About a million tons of china-clay are dug out of the surrounding country every year; the white pyramids of waste are visible for miles, like Mountains of the Moon. Old pits form deep pools of celadonblue water.

13

St Buryan★ (BE 02). Fine 15th-cent. church with notable rood-screen. Not far away are three Bronze Age monuments (*c.* 1600–1000 BC), the stone circles of Boscawen-Un and the Merry Maidens, and the standing stones called The Pipers.

St Cleer★ (CC 06). Church with noble granite tower. St Cleer's holy well, under a little granite building of the 15th cent., close by. In this parish is Trevethy Quoit, very fine chamber of a Neolithic tomb (*c.* 2000–1600 BC).

St Clether, 2½ m. N of Altarnun (CC 08). 15th-cent. holy well and baptistery, beautifully set in the valley of the Inney.

St Germans (CD 05). A priory church with a deep-set Norman porch between two massive towers. Port Eliot mansion, designed by Sir John Soane, adjoins, on the site of the priory buildings.

St Ives (BF 04) EC Thurs (9,050). The art centre of W Cornwall. Exhibitions are held during the summer. A harbour crowded with boats, an 'old town' riddled with courts and alleys. Cliffs, sandy bays, and a sparkling brilliance of light and colour.

St Juliot, just E of Boscastle (CB 09). When Thomas Hardy came here in 1870 to restore the church, the rectory door was opened by his future wife, and his best poems – all of them love poems – were written about the 'shagged and shaly Atlantic' scenery of the parish.

St Mawes (BJ 03). Boating, fishing, idling village resort on the E side of the Fal estuary opposite Falmouth. Henry VIII's castle (AM) looks across to Pendennis Castle on the other side. (*See* **Falmouth** *above.*)

St Michael's Mount★ (BF 03). Almost certainly the 'island of Ictis' from which Mediterranean merchants obtained tin during the first century BC. A priory on the Mount belonged to the Breton abbey of Mont St Michel. The priory buildings were transformed into the mansion of the St Aubyn family, which with the rest of the Mount now belongs to the NT. The castle dates from the 14th cent. Access by boat or, at low tide, by causeway.

St Neot★ (CB 06). In a wooded valley on a tributary of the Fowey, a church justly celebrated for its fifteen stained-glass windows of the 15th and 16th cent. St Neot's holy well is just outside the village.

St Piran's Oratory, 1½ m. N of Perranporth (BH 05). A minute Celtic church of the 6th or 7th cent., encased in a concrete shelter, among ragwort-yellow sandhills which overwhelmed it in the 11th cent. Found again in 1800. The Normans built a new church, abandoned because of sand in 1804 and excavated in 1919. This was a pilgrimage centre where they preserved the head, body, bell and staff of St Piran, patron saint of the tin trade.

Saltash (CE 05) EC Wed (7,400). Here are two notable bridges spanning the Tamar estuary: one built for the railway by Brunel, opened in 1859 and still going strong; the other, the new suspension bridge opened in 1962 to provide a much-needed additional road link between Devon and Cornwall. Cornishmen are reputed (by Devonshire men) to leave their tails in the cloakroom of Saltash station when they cross to Devon. The 13th- and 14th-cent. Trematon Castle, 2 m. W, is well worth a visit.

The Norman porch of St Germans Church

Reece Winstone

Scilly, Isles of ** (AK 01). An Atlantic archipelago of granite rocks, sandy islets and islands, which form the most delectable of all the holiday areas of Cornwall. Five islands are inhabited. The boat from Penzance (40 m., often a rough passage) docks at Hugh Town, the small capital and chief settlement of the largest island, St Mary's. The 'Off Islands', reached by launch, are St Martin's (the most beautiful), Tresco (notable for the sub-tropical gardens of Tresco Abbey, and the 17th-cent. Cromwell's Castle), Bryher, St Agnes (lighthouse of 1680). The Elizabethan fort of Star Castle (1593–4) above Hugh Town is the most remarkable building in the Islands. Remains of little Celtic monastery on St Helen's. The small daffodil fields are cleared of their crops between early winter and early spring. BEA helicopters (several flights a day) cross from Penzance to St Mary's in about 20 minutes.

Sennen. The westernmost village in England, on Whitesand Bay just NE of Land's End (BD 02).

Tintagel* (CA 08) has more to offer than legends of King Arthur, Merlin, King Mark, Tristan and Iseult. The 12th–14th-cent. remains of the castle (AM) are magnificently perched on black shaly cliffs and a projecting spur of rock. Excavations have shown that the castle was preceded by a Celtic monastery (c. 500–800).

Trecarrel, 4 m. S of Launceston (CD 08). The early 16th-cent. hall and chapel of Sir Henry Trecarrel, builder of Launceston parish church.

Trevelgue Head, 1 m. NE of Newquay (BJ 06). Sea-cut promontory massively defended by ditches and banks, forming a tin-traders' cliff-fort of the 3rd cent. BC to post-Roman era.

Truro (BJ 04) EC Thurs (12,860). Administrative centre of Cornwall. Has dignity, charm, good Georgian buildings. The cathedral (1880, incorporating part of 16th-cent. church) with its three spires, splendidly dominates the town. The Royal Institution of Cornwall (in River Street) has a collection of pictures and drawings that is full of pleasant surprises. The river trip down to Falmouth is well worth doing.

Newquay

Reece Winstone

Beer: bay, cliffs and Beer Head

DEVON

AN INTRODUCTION BY W. G. HOSKINS

The special quality of Devon is apparent immediately we cross the county border from the east, indeed a few miles before we get to the actual boundary. Coming from Bristol and the Midlands, we cross the River Parrett at Bridgwater in western Somerset and the landscape changes at once. Gone are the compact villages, clustered about their stately perpendicular churches: in their place we see white farmsteads scattered about the hillsides, and in the combes off the main road an occasional whitewashed cob-built hamlet of three or four farms. Its rather plain 15th-century church, buried among tall trees, stands either on its own or beside 'the barton' – the west-country name for the principal farm of the parish. These bartons are invariably of great antiquity. They were the 'home farms' of the Norman lords when Domesday Book was compiled, and they can be traced back without a break to Anglo-Saxon times. On most of them the farming has gone on continuously for well over a thousand years. In certain richer parts it is likely that there has been no break for two thousand years or more, from the Iron Age times onwards.

Coming down from London on A303 or A30, or on the A35 from Bournemouth and Dorchester, we see ahead the massive dark wall of the Blackdown

Hills, the geographical frontier of the South-west, the former Celtic kingdom of Dumnonia. Together, the Blackdowns and the River Parrett marked off this ancient British kingdom, and they still bring a sudden change in the landscape, in human settlement, in dialect, even in the colour of the cows. We enter the lush pastoral west by steep climbs followed by sudden drops into green combes.

But Devon is by no means all lush green pastures and red cliffs or soil: the New Red Sandstones, so beloved of railway advertisements, underlie about one-seventh of the county, mostly in the east and round Exeter. For the rest, the geographical range is vast, from the crumbling chalk at Beer Head to the granite of Dartmoor and – that most ancient of all rocks – the Pre-Cambrian of the extreme south, round Bolt Head and Prawle Point. Slate formations of various ages cover a good deal of the South Hams and the northern parts of Devon, giving dramatic tormented coasts both north and south. The cliffs of North Devon, from Hartland Point southwards, are considered by some to offer the most magnificent coastal scenery in the whole of England and Wales. The ancient rocks of Bolt and Prawle give hardly less dramatic cliff scenery.

Between the uplands of Dartmoor and Exmoor stretches a broad expanse of Devon which hardly sees a tourist. Though its yellow clay has always given a poorer living than the rich soils of much of the county, the area has a scenic quality and a charm of its own. Here are small forgotten hamlets on the upper reaches of rivers like the Taw and the Torridge which are better known in their estuaries. Their small parish churches, built in the local brown dunstone, are redolent of the past life of yeoman farmers and backwood squires whose modest memorials, from the 16th to the 19th centuries, hang on the plain walls or grace the floors in beautifully engraved floor-slabs. You can meander quietly round these places day after day, on winding roads between high hedges, meeting hardly another car for hours on end.

Hills and valleys

Both the geography and the topography of Devon are broken up and rather complicated. The core of the county is the granite mass of Dartmoor, a plateau with an average elevation of some one thousand two hundred feet, rising in two places (High Willhays and Yes Tor) to just over two thousand feet above sea level. Some hundred or more jagged tors break the skyline, the rocks which form their summits denuded of soil by centuries of wind and rain. Heather covers their upper slopes, giving way lower down to rough grazing, crossed here and there by stone walls or little streams, and lower still to fields of pasture or the more treacherous green of bogs. Exmoor is a gentler moor altogether, rising to one thousand seven hundred and five feet at Dunkery Beacon (which is in Somerset). Outside the two moors, many hills rise to eight or nine hundred feet and command magnificent views, the finest perhaps from Haldon, the range just to the west of Exeter, and from the hill-forts of Woodbury, Cadbury or Posbury – but it is idle to choose between so many that are equally fine. Of the valleys, the Exe is the least known, despite its pastoral beauty throughout its entire length; while the river trip up the Dart, from Dartmouth to Totnes, is a memorable experience. Most of the river valleys are well wooded: all are beautiful.

Industries

The largest industry in Devon today is the holiday trade, larger even than farming. There used to be an important woollen industry; but few of the large

mills now remain in operation. Mining (tin and copper, with some silver and gold) dated from at least the 12th century, but now it is finished – though it has left behind some spectacular landscapes, of which Blanchdown near Tavistock is well worth exploring. The only other industries today are small and local: brewing, agricultural machinery, and so forth, with some shipbuilding.

Architecture

Everything is on a small scale in Devon. There are really no great country houses. Most typical are the little medieval manor houses that can be found all over the county. There are, indeed, important houses like Powderham Castle and Castle Hill, but it is houses like Wear Giffard, Little Hempston and Higher Hareston (which take some finding even on a large-scale map) that are the true Devon at this social level. Many of these manor houses are now farmhouses, generally well cared for as far as a working life permits.

Of the churches, Exeter cathedral is supreme. On the site of a Saxon abbey, founded in 670, it is not very impressive externally, except for its Norman towers; but internally it is perhaps the most harmonious of all the English cathedrals. Monastic ruins are few and disappointing in Devon, though the rebuilt abbey at Buckfast (completed in 1938), also on a Saxon site, is worth a pilgrimage. Of castles, Totnes is the best, small but perfect. Exeter possesses a fine Norman gatehouse but little else; otherwise there is little to compare with castles elsewhere.

Though I have suggested that the parish churches of Devon are generally small and often plain, their great glory is in their woodwork. Probably no other county can show such glorious rood-screens and such a wealth of late medieval bench-ends. The former cloth towns, such as Totnes, Crediton, Ottery St. Mary, Cullompton and Tiverton, have, of course, more splendid churches, worthy to stand beside parish churches anywhere; but it is the smaller churches that are possibly more appealing, more profoundly characteristic of old Devon: churches above all which because of poverty escaped the Victorian 'restoration' two or three generations ago, and survived to be rescued more gently. Such are Honeychurch (as appealing as its name), Molland, Ashton, Torbryan (a delightful building all through), Hittisleigh and a score of others. As most of the Devon churches were rebuilt in the great days of the cloth trade and the tin-mining in the 15th and early 16th centuries, one gets perhaps a little tired of Perpendicular Gothic; but their charm lies in less obvious features – in their medieval woodwork, the engraved floor-slabs commemorating local families, or simply in their churchyard settings among quiet green landscapes.

Apart from the many Elizabethan farmhouses, there are few buildings of a later date worth travelling far to see – though one may always meet with the odd surprise. Devon can show very little good Georgian architecture. As for the 20th century, the new Plymouth will stimulate some as much as it depresses others. To me, the rebuilt Exeter is dull – suburban of the 1930s – but not all would agree with me. It is, perhaps, too soon to judge these new streets and buildings.

Archaeology

Archaeologically, the granite upland of Dartmoor is one of the richest regions in Britain. It was used as a vast summer pasturage during the New Stone Age; but from the Bronze Age (c. 1900 B.C.) until the end of the Iron Age (c. A.D. 250),

21

when the climate deteriorated, mixed farming took the place of the earlier nomadic, pastoral life. Dating from this period we have several hundred hut-circles (i.e. the foundations of prehistoric farmsteads), stone avenues, stone circles, cattle pounds and burial chambers. Exmoor has fewer monuments, and the best of them are on the Somerset side of the border.

From the 12th century onwards, with the discovery of the richest deposits of tin in Europe, Dartmoor was reoccupied. There survive many monuments of this period also, such as the 'blowing houses' where the tin ore was smelted on the spot. Farmers followed the tin-workers, building their houses of granite as their Bronze Age ancestors had done some three thousand years earlier. The remains of these medieval peasant houses may be seen in various parts of the Moor, notably at Challacombe, near the prehistoric village of Grimspound. Recently a complete deserted medieval village was found near Hound Tor. This is being excavated, and seems to consist of a number of houses abandoned at the time of the Black Death. Among other medieval monuments on the Moor are the famous Clapper Bridge at Postbridge, once thought to be prehistoric but now believed to be early medieval, and the numerous wayside crosses, like Bennett's Cross and Marchant's Cross, which marked the way across the Moor in the 13th century.

Of the Roman period, when Dartmoor was a silent wilderness, the most important survival is the City of Exeter. First settled some two or three hundred years before the Romans came, it became the tribal capital of the Dumnonii, and is still the mother-city of the South-West. It was walled round by the Romans about A.D. 200, and some of the original Roman walls may still be seen. In the countryside there are numerous hill-forts of the period immediately before the coming of the Romans. The grandest of these is Hembury, which was first occupied in the New Stone Age and was finally abandoned when the Romans took over Exeter. Cadbury and Woodbury are other notable Iron Age hill-forts near Exeter.

Kent's Cavern in Torquay is unique. In this cave was found the earliest evidence of man in Britain, dating back perhaps twenty-five thousand years – long before our own species *homo sapiens* had appeared on the earth. It is now open to the public.

Flora and fauna

The flower most characteristic of Devon is the primrose. Begin looking for them in late February in the deeper lanes, but remember that the removal of wild primrose roots is an offence against the county by-laws. Cowslips are rare; but in a few secluded places wild daffodils grow by the million. The other notable plant is the whortleberry, which fruits on the rougher hills and moors in late summer. Flowers bloom all the year round – I have picked over twenty different kinds of wild flower in the Tamar valley on Boxing Day. Blackberries are common on rougher ground, though with the improvement of farming standards they are rarer than they were thirty or forty years ago.

Of the fauna, the most distinctive are the wild red deer of Exmoor, where they have lived for centuries and are still hunted, and the Dartmoor ponies. These attractive little animals are no longer entirely wild: they all belong to someone and are periodically rounded up and sold – no longer as pit ponies, but now mainly as pets for children. Devon is a great county for riding of this harmless and pleasant kind. The Dartmoor ponies are the lineal descendants of the 'wild horses' referred to in Saxon times as roaming these moorlands. They were themselves the descendants of the small horses domesticated by the Iron Age people more than two thousand years ago. They are easily tamed today, and are therefore not true wild horses.

In the world of birds, the noble buzzard is a common sight anywhere in the rougher parts of Devon away from traffic – above all, in wooded combes. Peregrine falcons are common on the north coast of Devon, and the estuaries in winter are full of migrant birds that are rare elsewhere – especially, perhaps, the Exe estuary with its ample mudflats and sandbanks. The movements of the rarer birds are periodically reported in the *Western Morning News*.

Specialities for the gourmet

Devonshire cream is a delicacy which has been made for many centuries. The best cream should have a thick yellow crust and be firm enough to hold a spoon upright. Probably because of an ancient addiction to clotted cream, Devon, unlike its neighbours Dorset and Somerset, has no special cheeses – a curious deficiency in a county that makes so much excellent butter. Half a dozen rivers produce fine salmon, usually served on local menus under the river names – Torridge salmon, Exe salmon and so on. On a lower level, fresh mackerel, caught off the south Devon coast and cooked the same day, is a much underrated dish, at its best about midsummer. Devon spring lamb is such a delicacy that it is flown to expensive restaurants in Paris at Easter and few locally can afford to buy it. In the realm of drink, there used to be much beautiful cider made (and much 'rough' stuff too); but with the spread of bottled brands it is becoming rare. With luck you will find village inns that are still supplied from neighbouring farms. Quality varies, but the best is a genuine '*vin du pays*'. This genuine cider seems a harmless enough drink, but it goes to the knees very quickly. Cider on a close Devonshire afternoon in some deep combe must be one of the most powerful sleeping draughts known to science. As a restorative, Brixham crab or lobster may be recommended for supper, or scallops freshly caught at Budleigh Salterton. Euphoria, a sense of well-being, is common in Devonshire – and this perhaps accounts for the outstanding kindliness with which the Devonians greet and treat strangers fortunate enough to cross their borders.

The estuary of the River Dart, below Dartmouth J. Allan Cash

Some houses and gardens open to the public

A La Ronde 1½m N of Exmouth *Map* DA 08. *Circular house modelled on San Vitale in Ravenna; shell gallery, 18th-cent. pictures, furniture etc.* Miss M. L. Tudor.

Arlington Court nr Kentisbury *Map* CG 14. *Early 19th-cent house with model ships, pewter, sea-shells; spacious grounds.* NT.

Bicton Gardens East Budleigh *Map* DA 08. *Magnificent landscaped and ornamental gardens, countryside museum, narrow gauge railway.*

Bradley Manor Newton Abbott *Map* CJ 07. *Roughcast 15th-cent. manor house.* NT.

Buckland Abbey nr Yelverton *Map* CE 06. *13th-cent. monastery now museum (see p. 26).* NT.

Cadhay Ottery St Mary *Map* DB 09. *Unspoilt, 'lived-in' Tudor manor house in lovely setting.* Lady William-Powlett, DSC, RN, JP.

Compton Castle 3m NW of Paignton *Map* CJ 06. *Fortified manor house built 1320–1520.* NT.

Killerton Gardens nr Broad Clyst *Map* CK 09. *Fifteen acres hillside pleasure grounds containing unique collection of rare trees and shrubs.*

Kirkham House Paignton *Map* CJ 06. *Restored Tudor house with good timbers.* Ministry of Public Building and Works.

Knightshayes Court 2m N of Tiverton *Map* CK 11. *Magnificent gardens: rhododendrons, azaleas, alpines etc.* Sir John Amory, Bt. *Gdns only open.*

Oldway Mansion Paignton. *Map* CJ 06. *'The Little Versailles', Palladian Mansion with Marble Hall, Staircase, Painted Ceiling, Hall of Mirrors, Ballroom and Italian and water gardens, as well as the more usual varieties, also tennis, putting, bowls, café.*

Powderham Castle *Map* CK 08. *The present Earl of Devon, who lives in the castle, is direct descendant of Sir Philip Courtenay who built it c. 1400. Fine furniture, portraits, park stocked with deer.* Inf. from Secretary: Starcross 243.

Saltram House 2m W of Plympton *Map* CF 05. *A George II mansion embodying the remains of a Tudor and late Stuart house, situated in a landscaped park. Magnificent interior plasterwork and decoration. Two important rooms designed by Robert Adam. Fine period furniture and pictures including many portraits by Sir Joshua Reynolds. Also a unique 18th/19th-century kitchen. Enquiries for parties:* Administrator, Saltram House (Tel. Plymouth 36546). NT.

Wortham Manor 1½m N of Lifton *Map* CD 08. *11th-cent. manor house of granite & local stone.* Capt. P. W. Burgess.

Books for further reading

Devon surveyed

R. DUNCAN *Devon and Cornwall* 1966
W. G. HOSKINS *Devon* 1954
D. ST. L. GORDON *Devonshire* 1950 (County Books, Hale)
A. MEE *Devon* 1965
B. WATSON *Devon* 2nd edn 1955 (Shell Guide)
N. PEVSNER *Buildings of England—Devon* 2 vols 1952

Geology and natural history

A. W. CLAYDEN *History of Devonshire scenery* 1906
W. S. M. D'URBAN and REV. M. A. MATHEW *Birds of Devon* 1892
DEVONSHIRE ASSOCIATION *Flora of Devon* 1939

Traditions, legends, folklore

S. B. GOULD *Devonshire characters and strange events* 1908
J. R. W. COXHEAD *Devon traditions and fairy tales* 1959
S. HEWITT *Nummits and crummits* 1900

R. ST. L. GORDON *Witchcraft and Folklore of Dartmoor* 1965

Some areas of special interest

H. HARRIS *Industrial Archaeology of Dartmoor* 1968
L. A. HARVEY and D. ST. L. GORDON *Dartmoor.* 2nd edn 1962 (New Naturalist)
L. MEYNELL *Exmoor* 1953
W. E. MINCHINGTON *Industrial Archaeology in Devon* 1968
P. T. ETHERTON *Lundy, tempestuous isle* rev. edn 1960
P. RUSSELL *A history of Torquay and the famous anchorage of Torbay* 1960
W. G. HOSKINS *2,000 years in Exeter* 1960
R. A. J. WATLING *Story of Plymouth* 1950
M. WILLY *The South Hams* 1955

Fireside reading

The Dartmoor Novels of EDEN PHILLPOTTS (esp. *Secret Woman*) and JOHN TREVENA; HENRY WILLIAMSON'S 'Village' books and incomparable nature stories; the prose of RONALD DUNCAN

Gazetteer

DEVON

Appledore *Jarrold*

Appledore (CE 13). On the corner where the Torridge and Taw rivers unite. Pleasant fishing village with cobbled streets, Georgian cottages, a quay, a stony beach, boating and boat-building, and fishing.

Ashburton (CH 06) E C Wed (3,050). An important town in the heyday of tin-mining. The church has an extremely fine tower. Robert Herrick was the vicar of near-by Dean Prior in the 17th cent., but there is no gravestone to mark his burial-place in the churchyard there.

Axminster (DD 09) E C Wed (2,700). Famous for the carpets that originated and are still made here. Handsome Georgian and other houses.

Bampton (CK 12). A little market town among wooded hills on a tributary of the Exe. A great sight here is the annual Fair for Exmoor ponies held on the last Thursday in October.

Barnstaple* (CF 13) E C Wed (16,340). The bridge (built late 13th cent., well restored and widened) spans the Taw at the head of its estuary. Engaging little town with a long history reflected in some of its buildings. Note the colonnaded house crowned with a statue of Queen Anne: this was the exchange of the Barnstaple Merchant Venturers. Note also the twisted spire of St Peter's Church. The Pannier Market (Fridays) should be seen, and the Great Fair if you are there in September.

Beer (DC 08). No longer a simple fishing village in an opening of the cliffs, but still a friendly place for boating, fishing and bathing from its shingle beach. The Beer quarries have provided the stone for many famous buildings.

Berry Pomeroy* (CJ 06). 1½ miles E of **Totnes**. Ruins of a 13th-cent. castle partly converted in the 16th cent. into what would have been a handsome mansion if it had been completed. Note the screen in the church.

Bideford* (CE 12) E C Wed (10,850). A prosperous port in the days of sail, when it carried on a considerable trade with America. Charles Kingsley wrote part of *Westward Ho!* in a room in the Royal Hotel, and such adventurers as Sir Richard Grenville bestrode its quay. An ancient 24-arch bridge spans the Torridge, linking Bideford proper with 'East-the-Water', and the town is beautified with many good houses built by the shipowners of old.

Bovey Tracey (CJ 07) E C Wed (3,650). Pleasant town set beside the little Bovey river, though the scene is somewhat spoilt by the china-clay workings. In the church note the

Buckfast Abbey, Buckfastleigh

Aerofilms

coloured 15th-cent. screen and pulpit. A member of the Tracey family was concerned in Becket's murder, but there is no evidence that he built Bovey church in expiation.

Branscombe (DB 08). Village of stone and cob cottages among broken cliff-top hills, with paths leading down to the beach. Beautiful church with an unusual three-decker pulpit, box pews and an imposing tower.

Braunton (CE 13) EC Wed (3,800). At the edge of the sandy tract known as Braunton Burrows. Formerly a well-known haunt of nature-lovers, its peace has been threatened by Service amphibious training.

Brixham (CK 05) EC Wed (10,700). Active fishing port looking out across Tor Bay and well protected from SW gales. Besides the inner harbour with its fish quay is a large outer harbour protected by a stone mole. A statue of William of Orange on the quay commemorates his landing here in 1688. The Rev. H. F. Lyte composed the words of *Abide With Me* at Berry Head House. Part of the new Borough of Torbay since April 1968.

Buckfastleigh (CH 06) EC Wed (2,530). The main attraction of this old town is Buckfast Abbey★ just to the north of it. This is a modern rebuilding on the site of a pre-Conquest abbey. It was the almost unaided work of the Benedictine monks, who also produce honey from their famous apiaries for sale to visitors.

Buckland Abbey★ (CE 06). 13th-cent. monastery granted by Henry VIII to Sir Richard Grenville, grandfather of the hero of *The Revenge*, who also lived here. Sir Francis Drake bought it on his return from his circumnavigation of the world. Now a naval and Devon folk museum, with Grenville and Drake relics.

Budleigh Salterton (DA 08) EC Thurs (3,830). Seaside town of fairly recent growth, but with some attractive Georgian houses from the time when it was a 'fashionable' resort. Near by, East Budleigh is a typical pretty Devon village; its church has interesting bench-ends. A farmhouse at Hayes Barton was the birthplace of Sir Walter Raleigh, and in the church is the Raleigh pew. The gardens at Bicton Park are magnificent.

Clovelly* (CD 12). Perhaps the most picturesque village in all Devon. The street descends 400 ft. in a few hundred yards, and vehicles are not admitted. On either side are flower-decked cottages; at the foot, a stone 16th-cent. jetty guards the pebbled beach.

Crediton (CJ 10) EC Wed (4,880). Busy market town whose church is large enough for a cathedral. Indeed the See of Devon and Cornwall was here from 909 to 1050, when it was moved to Exeter.

Dartington Hall (CH 06). The centre of a successful scheme for utilizing the resources of a large old estate. The Hall is partly 14th cent., partly Elizabethan. Around it are scientifically run farms, sawmills, workshops and building yards, and here too is the well-known co-educational school.

Dartmoor* (CF 08). A great elevated mass of granite, 200 square miles in extent, which fills most of the western part of S Devon. Much heathery moorland, a walker's paradise, interspersed with valleys and streams, with rocky outcrops known as Tors. Highest point: High Willhays, 2,038 ft. The boggy northern part is the source of most of Devon's rivers. Stone monuments (mainly Bronze Age) abound. Botanists and ornithologists will not be idle here.

Dartmouth* (CJ 05) EC Wed (7,190). Its long and honourable history is mostly concerned with

Saddle Tor, Dartmoor

J. Allan Cash

voyages and exploration, and Dartmouth ships and men have taken part in nearly every naval battle for centuries. Stroll in the piazza-like Butterwalk; and for one of the finest painted rood screens in Devon visit St Saviour's Church. N of the town is the famous Royal Naval College. S is Dartmouth Castle (AM), the outcome of an offer by Edward IV to pay the Dartmouth burgesses £30 a year 'for ever' if they would build a defensive new 'towre with a cheyne sufficient in lengthe and strengthe to stretch a travers the mouth of the haven'.

Dawlish (CK 07) E C Thurs (7,830). Seaside resort two miles south of the long sandy tract at the mouth of the Exe. A stream ripples quietly through the town. Sandy beach, good bathing, picturesque red cliffs.

Devonport (CE 05). Part of the County Borough of **Plymouth** (*see below*). The Royal Naval Dockyard, parts of which may be visited, faces the part of the Tamar estuary known as the Hamoaze. Good views of the waterway from Mount Wise, where there is a monument to Captain Scott, born here in 1868.

Doone Valley (CH 14). For many, Lorna Doone is as much a reality here as King Arthur is at Tintagel. An interesting exercise is to try to follow the topography of R. D. Blackmore in his novel.

Exeter* (CK 09) E C Wed and Sat (92,550). Ancient city with a wonderful variety of buildings – medieval, Regency and modern – the last-named due to heavy bombing raids in 1942 (many churches and nearly 2,000 other buildings were damaged or destroyed). The choir screen in the cathedral can hardly be missed, but note also the bishop's throne, the little minstrels' gallery in the N wall of

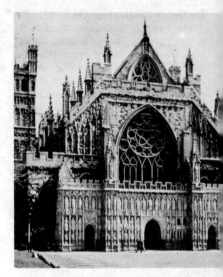

Exeter Cathedral, the West Door

Jarrold

the nave, and the various chapels. See the 15th-cent. Guildhall (the oldest municipal building in England), the Tuckers' Hall, and the remains of Rougemont Castle (Norman). Visit also the city's medieval passages which run underneath the main streets. The Museum and Art Gallery shows pictures by Devon artists. Exeter University is in its own estate of 250 acres on the N side of the city.

Exmouth (DA 08) E C Wed and Sat (22,420). Exeter's seaside resort. Good sands, with rocks at low tide, and a little harbour for small-boat sailing. Ferries across the Exe to Starcross.

Hartland (CC 12). Hartland 'Town' was an important borough with a portreeve, a town hall and a charter dated 1285. Today it is a pleasant village 2 miles inland from Hartland Point. Here, however, is none of the softness usually associated with Devon scenery, but harsh black cliffs rising 300 ft. above the waves, which in storms whip spray over the top. On a plateau below the cliffs, but still 120 ft. above the sea, is the lighthouse.

Honiton (DB 10) EC Thurs (5,260). It is good to be able to record that lace is still made here, though not on the scale which made Honiton famous a century ago.

Ilfracombe (CF 14) EC Thurs (8,240). The oldest and most unusual of the N Devon holiday resorts, built in and among small hills, its beaches reached by tunnels in the rocks. Steamer and other trips from the ancient harbour; cliff walks, concerts and all modern amenities.

Kingsbridge (CH 04) EC Thurs (3,320). Busy market town at the head of the tidal estuary extending up from Salcombe. The centre of the prosperous farming area known as the South Hams. Local 'sons': William Cookworthy, porcelain manufacturer, and Dr John Wolcot, satirist ('Peter Pindar'). Note the 16th-cent. arcade known as 'The Shambles'.

Lundy Island (CB 14). Some 11 miles NW of Hartland Point, it has, so far, sustained its claims to be extra-territorial and therefore exempt from income and other taxation. The island is a huge mass of granite 3½ miles long, about ½ mile wide and bounded by cliffs rising almost sheer for 400–500 ft. Lobsters are caught, seals breed on the rocks, and the island itself is a naturalists' paradise. Bird life is strictly preserved. Boats from Ilfracombe, Barnstaple and Bideford.

Lydford Gorge (CF 08). Where the River Lyd emerges from the 2 miles of deep-cleft gorge is a fine waterfall.

Lynton and Lynmouth (CH 14) EC Thurs (1,900). Motorists approaching Lynmouth from the E should take the warning notices seriously. Lynton is on the cliff top some 400 ft. above the point where the East and West Lyn rivers join to flow into the sea by Lynmouth harbour. Much of Lynmouth is new, following

Kingsbridge   *Jarrold*

Lynmouth, the Rhenish Tower and harbour *Jarrold*

the flood disaster of 1952 (the River Lyn takes its name, significantly, from the Old English word *Llynn*, a torrent), but Lynton retains something of a Victorian air. The river and coastal scenery is some of Britain's finest. Watersmeet, where the East Lyn and one of its tributaries unite, is extremely popular (NT).

Ottery St Mary* (DB 09) EC Wed (5,100). Small market town with a great church dating partly from the 14th cent. and bearing a striking resemblance to Exeter Cathedral. The most interesting piece of ecclesiastical architecture in Devon. The bells are a notable feature; so too are the unusual medieval clock and the minstrels' gallery. S. T. Coleridge, author of *Kubla Khan* and *The Ancient Mariner*, was born in the vicarage.

Plymouth* (CE 05) EC Wed (247,400). The site might have been designed by nature for a seaport – a broad tongue of land, its coast fretted by creeks and coves, looking out on to the estuary of five rivers. It is old, but reconstruction after war damage has been on such a scale that the City Centre, for example, has a completely new look. However, one can still enjoy the Hoe, where Drake played out his game of bowls; the aquaria of the Royal Marine Biological Laboratory in the cliffs below; and Sutton Pool, departure-point of the *Mayflower*. On the Hoe, too, is Smeaton's Tower, upper part of the previous Eddystone Lighthouse, removed in 1878 to make way for the present lighthouse, visible (in clear weather) 14 miles to seaward.

Princetown (CF 07). Nearly 1,400 ft. above the sea, it is one of the highest towns in England. The grim prison was built in the early 1800's to house French and American P.O.W.s.

Salcombe (CH 03) EC Thurs (2,420). The little town clings to the steep hillside overlooking the winding estuary which enters the sea between

Bolt Head and Prawle Point. Sheltered yacht haven, sandy beach, good bathing, sub-tropical vegetation.

Sheeps Tor (CF 06). The view from the Tor (1,010 ft.) ranges over the village and Burrator reservoir, whence Plymouth draws water. Sir James Brooke ('Rajah Brooke of Sarawak') lived for some years in the village and is buried in the churchyard.

Sidmouth (DB 08) EC Thurs (11,750). Fashionable in the early 19th cent., it lies where the River Sid cuts through the high cliffs to the sea. A sheltered spot, with eucalyptus trees and other sub-tropical vegetation.

Sticklepath (CG 09). Motorists hurrying past on the A30 miss the anachronistic sight of an engineering works powered by water-wheels, a form of power used here successfully for 100 years and more. Open to public.

Stoke Gabriel (CJ 05). Quiet creeks of the River Dart, spreading trees, an old watermill, and a Regency mansion by Nash which was the home of John Davis, the navigator. A fascinating blend of history and beauty.

Tavistock (CE 07) EC Wed (6,600). Built around an abbey (demolished after the Dissolution), and once the centre of tin-mining and woollen industries, Tavistock has many signs of former prosperity. The church has a window designed by William Morris, an organ played by Samuel Wesley, and two huge thigh-bones alleged to be those of Ordulf, founder of the abbey.

Teignmouth (CK 07) EC Thurs (12,130). Built on the broad spit of land where the River Teign joins the sea, Teignmouth has the advantage of a river aspect as well as a sea front, the town extending some way up the valley. The bridge across the river to Shaldon is said to be one of the largest of its kind in the country.

Tiverton (CK 11) EC Thurs (14,370). Prosperity founded first on wool and then on lace has endowed Tiverton with an unusual number of good buildings. The church has a fine

Tiverton Church   *Jarrold*

tower and S porch; the organ by 'Father' Smith is in a case attributed to Grinling Gibbons; see too the well-carved Greenway chapel. Blundell's school (founded 1604) occupies new buildings at Horsdon, a mile out of town; the altar in the chapel was designed by Eric Gill.

Torbay (CK 06) EC Wed (98,000). New County Borough created April 1968, comprising the three towns of Torquay, Paignton and Brixham. Sands, harbours, parks. Except for the remains of 14th-cent. Torre Abbey, hardly a building pre-dates the Napoleonic Wars, when houses were built for officers and their families awaiting orders. The design and siting of these so-called 'villas' is one of the engaging features of the older part of the town, which has now spread far inland. The climate has aided the growth of many trees not seen elsewhere in England. Contrasting with the more modern town is the old-world suburb of Cockington, with its well-known forge.

Kent's Cavern*, Ilsham Road, consists of two parallel caves with stalactites and flood-lighting. It is of outstanding archaeological interest owing to the discovery there in the 19th cent. of remains of people who may have been among the very earliest inhabitants of Britain. Some of the remains are now in the Torbay Museum.

Totnes* (CJ 06) EC Thurs (5,630). Ancient town at the head of the Dart estuary, with gated, winding streets, narrow and steep, the ruins of a Norman castle (AM), a 17th-cent. Guildhall with a colonnaded front and a church with the finest stone screen in Devon. It was an important wool town and is still a busy market and shopping centre for the South Hams. (*See also* **Berry Pomeroy**.)

Westward Ho! (CE 12). Named after Kingsley's novel. An open-air resort overlooking Bideford Bay, with golf, bathing and a pebble ridge some 2 miles long and 20 ft. high. Beyond the ridge are remains of a submerged forest.

Widecombe-in-the-Moor (CH 07). A pretty stone-and-thatch Dartmoor village which has suffered from the popularity of the well-known song. But it has a fine church with a magnificent granite tower and a Church House of *c*.1500 (NT).

Totnes Castle

J. Allan Cash

Opposite: Detail from the original painting by Thomas Swimmer.

Devon is warm, fertile, damp, velvety – and rough. The rich pastures of fields and valleys are the home of the Red Devon cattle (whose milk yields Devonshire cream), and in the same soil cider-apple orchards and foxgloves flourish. Inlets on the south coast are reminders of Devon's long naval importance. Of her famous men, here are two: Sir Walter Raleigh and Samuel Taylor Coleridge.

AN
ESSAY
CONCERNING
HUMAN
UNDERSTANDING

JOHN
LOCKE

LONDON

Ponies on Exmoor

SOMERSET

AN INTRODUCTION BY W. G. HOSKINS

Somerset has everything to offer the visitor except a decent coastline. Towards the extreme west, it is true, from Minehead to Porlock, the great hog-backed cliffs fall from the moorland a thousand feet above into a wrinkled, crawling sea far below; for the rest, there are but few oases (like Brean Down) between the long spoilt stretches.

Inland, Somerset has a serene natural beauty – a beauty enhanced by man's activities during the past two thousand years. I call to mind those wonderful Perpendicular church towers in and around the Vale of Taunton, a group that would be outstanding in any country; the massive stone barns almost everywhere, which speak of centuries of rich farming; the miles of willow-lined Levels under rain-washed skies in the middle of the county; the little stone-built towns like Somerton and Shepton Mallet, and lively, brick-built Taunton itself, the county town, with above all the Georgian city of Bath. And from another world, the grey fragments of the ancient abbey of Glastonbury, the earliest site of the Christian faith in England, even if one does not accept the legend of Joseph of Arimathea having come here just after the Crucifixion to construct 'with twisted twigs' the very first Christian church in Britain. Whatever one thinks of this story, first written down in the 12th century, Glastonbury is holy ground where saints have trod.

Opposite: Detail from the original painting by David Gentleman.

A county of flats and hills, and of baskets made from Sedgemoor withies. Superb churches tower above the orchards. A relic of older beliefs is the Romano-British carving of the goddess Sul, deity of the hot springs at Bath. One of Somerset's famous men is John Locke, the philosopher. On Sedgemoor in 1685 the Duke of Monmouth lost his bid for the throne; Judge Jeffreys's 'Bloody Assize' wreaked vengeance on the rebels.

Geology and Scenery

To understand even a little geology is to appreciate vastly more the colour and
the shape of the man-made landscape in Somerset: for example, the little
lilac-coloured town of Somerton, the many golden country houses, the little
towns built of the local Blue Lias stone, and the great houses of Ham Hill stone
from near Montacute. And the natural landscape takes on meaning, too – especially the hills of Somerset: Mendip, Quantock, Exmoor, Brendon, and Polden,
and the strange isolated hummocks like Brent Knoll and Glastonbury Tor that
rise suddenly from the Levels to a height of four hundred feet or so.

The Levels themselves, so much more attractive than this dull word would
suggest, were once under the sea, which laid down sands and silts and slowly
raised the land above the waters. Silt and peat now overlie the old sea-bed.
Man came into this landscape later, from the 7th century onwards (though he
was living on the hills round the margins thousands of years before) and completed the process of drainage. Indeed, it was the monasteries which created this
landscape. So we have the miles of ditches, some broad and straight and some
narrow and winding (these are the oldest), known locally as *rhines*, with willow-
lined roads running along the top of ancient causeways or along medieval
embankments, giving those sharp bends for no apparent reason today, a few
brick houses here and there (often showing signs of subsidence as the peat
shrinks), and occasional stone-built villages clustered on the summits of old
islands that rose some twenty or thirty feet above the Levels. The higher hills
are outliers of Lias limestones and shales that often give terraces on the hillsides. The lower gentler islands, so easily missed in a car, are much more important from the human standpoint, for they were better suited for the siting
of early villages than the abrupt Lias hills. Sedgemoor's villages, for example,
stand on islands of the so-called Burtle Beds, rising only thirty to fifty feet above
the winter floods.

Across the middle of the Levels run the Polden Hills, a long backbone of the
Lias again, rarely more than 300 feet above sea-level, but giving wonderful
views in all directions. Along the northern edge of the Levels runs the long flat-
topped upland of the Mendips (averaging about 800 feet but rising to 1,068 feet
at Blackdown), formed of the grey Carboniferous Limestone. This plateau,
rather dull country on the top (though here were the Roman and medieval lead
mines), is most striking along its broken edges, where ancient streams cut into
the rock and then disappeared underground, leaving us with the magnificent dry
gorge of Cheddar in the south, and Burrington Combe in the north. Cheddar is
painfully overcrowded during the summer, when the northern edge is perhaps
better worth visiting.

Coming back to the Levels again, the western horizon is bounded by the
rolling, almost down-like profile of the Quantocks (1,260 feet at their highest
point). This is broken into by deep, wooded combes, especially on the eastern
side, rising to miles of heather-covered upland from which can be seen the
distant Welsh mountains on a good day. Beyond the Quantocks, to the west, lie
the long smooth curves of Exmoor (1,705 feet at Dunkery Beacon), a quiet land
of ravens, curlew, wild red deer, and (in late summer) whortleberries. This is
the country of *Lorna Doone*. Southwestwards the greensand escarpment of the
Blackdown Hills closes the horizon, the old frontier of the Celtic kingdom of
Dumnonia. South and eastwards from the Levels lies a very tumbled kind of
country, small hills and hidden valleys – the oolitic limestone country that gives

Cave in the Mendip Hills near Pri

some of the best building stones, such as the famous Ham Hill, quarried in Roman times and since.

Industries

Somerset has a large and growing tourist industry – today, perhaps, even more important than farming in terms of money turnover. Apart from this and farming, Somerset has no large-scale industries. There is only one coalfield left in the Midsomer Norton/Radstock area, and this is likely to close in the near future. Brick and tile-making in and around Bridgwater used to be important but is now declining. However, many modern industries are appearing, and Bridgwater has a flourishing cellophane works. Of the large centuries-old woollen industry little remains except old mills at Frome, Wellington and Wiveliscombe. Printing, clothing and footwear have tended to take over here. The glove trade is important in and around Yeovil, and the Mendip quarries make Somerset the fourth largest producer of limestone in England. On the Somerset Levels, the ancient industry of peat-cutting has been taken over in a big way, especially at Ashcott and Meare, for garden use rather than as fuel. Basket-making on Sedgemoor is locally very important, and the withy-beds are very beautiful in winter. Keynsham, near Bristol, has a very large chocolate factory, and sheep-skin goods and shoes are made at Glastonbury and Street, respectively.

Flora and Fauna

With its many soils, Somerset has a wide range of wild-life – best brought out, perhaps, by looking at the various Nature Reserves. That on Bridgwater Bay (6,076 acres) is notable for its population of wildfowl and waders. The Stert Island area here, to which access is prohibited, is now visited by such rare birds as the avocet and the spoonbill. On Steep Holm, an island in the Bristol Channel, is a reserve mainly for the study of the large herring-gull colonies. The Nature Reserve at Rodney Stoke (eighty-six acres), on the south escarpment of the Mendips, is the best surviving example of a characteristic Mendip ashwood. Shapwick Heath (484 acres) in the Levels was made into a Nature Reserve in 1961. It contains some of the last remnants of the raised bogs which once covered most of central Somerset. Not only has it a wide range of distinctive fauna and flora (e.g. the rare Royal Fern), but the peat diggings have produced evidence of human occupation from the Neolithic, the Bronze and Iron Ages, and the Romano-British period, including clear traces of timber causeways built in the late Bronze Age between the Polden Hills and the islands in the Levels as the climate grew wetter. Neolithic trackways have also been found in the peat. The peat deposits, where they remain uncut, give a wonderful opportunity for studying changes in vegetation, climate and human activity from about 4000 B.C.

Of the larger fauna, the red deer and the semi-wild ponies of Exmoor are the most noticeable. The ponies are the descendants of wild horses first domesticated by the Celtic population before the Romans came. The red deer, which are hunted, are probably of the same ancient origin. Exmoor was recently made a National Park, administered by both Devon and Somerset. It is gentler by far than Dartmoor, but archaeologically less rewarding.

37

moor, viewed from Dunkery Beacon   *J. Allan Cash*

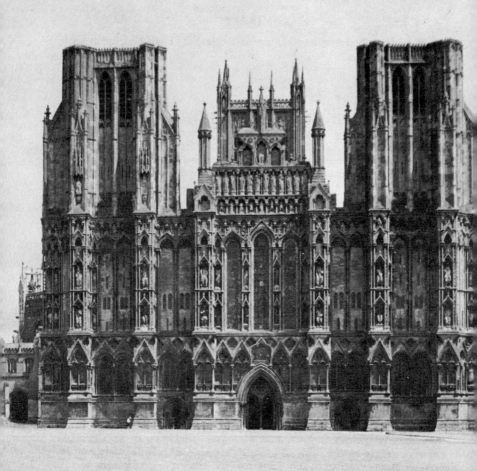

Wells Cathedral, West Front

Archaeology

From this standpoint, Somerset is one of the most fascinating regions of Britain. In the Old Stone Age, in the late Iron Age, and in Roman times, it was one of the great cultural centres of Britain, as indeed it continued to be during historic times in such places as Glastonbury (Dark Age and Medieval) and Bath (Georgian). In the Old Stone Age (Palaeolithic) the Mendips with their deep dry caves were the homes of the Magdalenian hunters. So the caves at Cheddar and Wookey, though much commercialized, should be visited. Many other caves along the north and west sides of the Mendips were important during this period. In the succeeding Bronze Age we leave the caves for the high dry uplands like Exmoor, the Quantocks, the Brendons, and the Mendip top, where numerous barrows and occasional stone circles tell of this period. In the Iron Age that followed, the lake villages of Glastonbury and Meare show a high level of culture again – Glastonbury in particular was 'a great Celtic emporium' at this time. Of this, little trace now remains; but the massive hill-forts of the period are well seen at Cadbury and Hamdon. Cadbury Castle is becoming an increasingly important site for the Arthurian controversy, and is now considered to be possibly the legendary Camelot. The most outstanding survival of Roman times is the city of Bath (*Aquae Sulis*), rightly called 'one of the leading therapeutic establishments in the Western Empire'. Sufferers from rheumatism and the like came here from all over Britain and Gaul, and the baths remain perhaps the grandest monument of the Roman Age in Britain. Somerset was favoured by the upper class in Romano-British times and is particularly rich in villas or country houses. The succeeding Dark Ages have left the great earthwork of Wansdyke as their most impressive monument. Running from near Bristol across Wiltshire and into Hampshire, it is between fifty and eighty miles long, the longest earthwork of its kind in Britain. It is Roman and post-Roman in date, possibly finished in the late 5th century, and undoubtedly a massive defence by a southern people (British) against attackers from the north (the Anglo-Saxons); but much still remains to be found out about it.

Architecture

Somerset was rich in monasteries. Glastonbury, the richest and oldest of them all, is perhaps the most evocative; but more substantial remains are to be found at Cleeve Abbey (near Watchet) and at Muchelney in the Levels, both well worth a long visit. Bath Abbey, a completely Perpendicular building, begun in 1499 and finished in the early 17th century, is not strictly an abbey church at all. Somerset is poor in castles, but rich in country houses, probably for the same reasons that led the Romano-British to build so many villas in this serene countryside. The Elizabethan period was, of course, the great age for building country houses, though Barrington Court is earlier (begun *c.* 1514) and Lytes Cary (a highly attractive house) has considerable medieval remains. Montacute is the best of the country houses (built *c.* 1588–1600), large but not ostentatious (most Elizabethan country houses were vulgar, the typical expression of the New Rich). This was the great age also for the rebuilding of the ordinary houses in towns and countryside. Somerset contains an extraordinary number of beautiful stone-built villages with farmhouses and cottages dating from the 16th to the 18th century. Most of the parish churches were rebuilt during the 15th century and early 16th, and are rather monotonously Perpendicular in style. But they are usually far statelier and richer than their Devonshire counterparts, their great glory being their towers – spires are rare. In the towns the outstanding things are perhaps the medieval Vicars Close at Wells (1348), Wells Cathedral itself (a superb example of English 13th-century Gothic), Shepton Mallet for its early 18th-century merchants' houses, and Taunton for many things, including the excellent County Cricket Ground – that historic ground where Jack Hobbs equalled and then surpassed W. G. Grace's record number of centuries in 1926.

I have left till the last, the best: Bath. This beautiful city, as rebuilt from 1725 onwards, and so largely unspoilt today, has no rival in Britain, and few peers the world over. It would be presumptuous to try to describe its loveliness in the short space remaining: let it be my close.

Some houses and gardens open to the public

Barrington Court *Map* DE 11. *Fine Tudor house, externally little altered, with Gothic windows and twisted pinnacles.* NT.

Claverton Manor 3¾m SE of Bath *Map* DH 16, via A36. *The house, built 1820 by Sir Jeffry Wyatville, contains a museum of furniture and paintings illustrating American domestic life from late 17th cent. to mid 19th cent. American teas with home-made cookies.* The American Museum in Britain.

Clevedon Court Clevedon *Map* DE 17. *A once-fortified manor house, 12th cent. and later, with 14th-cent. chapel & 18th-cent. terraced garden.* NT.

Coleridge Cottage Nether Stowey *Map* DB 13. *S. T. Coleridge lived here from 1797–1800 and wrote 'The Ancient Mariner'.* NT.

Dunster Castle Dunster *Map* CK 14. *Part 11th cent., part 13th cent., this historic castle dominates the town. Owned by the Luttrell family for nearly 600 years.* Mrs G. F. Luttrell.

Lytes Cary 2½m NE of Ilchester *Map* DF 12. *Typical Somerset manor house, with 14th-cent. chapel & 15th-cent. great hall. Home of the Lyte family for 500 years.* NT.

Montacute House 4m W of Yeovil *Map* DF 11. *One of the most important houses in the West Country, built 1588–1600. Tapestries, English portraits and furniture, heraldic glass, plasterwork and panelling. Early Jacobean garden.* NT.

Prior Park Combe Down nr Bath *Map* DH 16. *Splendid Palladian mansion standing in beautiful grounds with lakes and magnificent views.* The Order of Christian Brothers.

Tintinhull House 1½m N of Montacute *Map* DF 11. *A fine small house rebuilt c. 1700. Beautiful formal garden.* NT.

Books for further reading

Topography – general

M. FRASER *Companions into Somerset* 2nd edn 1951
M. HUTCHINGS *Inside Somerset* 1963
E. HUTTON *Highways and Byways in Somerset* 6th edn 1955
M. L. TURNER *Somerset* (County Books series) 1949
G. W. and J. H. WADE *Somerset* (Methuen Little Guide) 10th edn 1949
A. WALLER (ed.) *Smiling Somerset* 1968
WARD LOCK'S 'RED GUIDES'

Buildings

N. PEVSNER *South and West Somerset* 1958 *North Somerset and Bristol* 1958 (Buildings of England series)
A. K. WICKHAM *Churches of Somerset* 1965

Special localities

G. ASHE *King Arthur's Avalon* 1957
S. H. BURTON *Exmoor* 1952
A. W. COYSH and others *The Mendips* 1954

D. HAWKINS *Sedgemoor and Avalon* 1954
B. LITTLE *Bath Portrait* 1961
V. WAITE *The Quantocks* 1964

Scenery, geology, natural history

H. E. BALCH *The Mendip Caves* 1947–48
A. BULLEID *The Lake Villages of Somerset* 1938
G. FARR *Somerset Harbours*
W. H. P. GRESWELL *The Forests and Deer Parks of the County of Somerset* 1905
R. P. MURRAY *Flora of Somerset* 1896. Supplement by E. S. Marshall 1914
E. M. PALMER and D. K. BALLANCE *Birds of Somerset* 1968

Novels

R. D. BLACKMORE *Lorna Doone* (Exmoor)
A. D. CRAKE *Last Abbot of Glastonbury*
A. CONAN DOYLE *Micah Clarke*
A. DUGGAN *King of Athelney* 1961
G. HEYER *Black Sheep* 1966
W. M. JONES *The "Jarge Balsh" Books* 1967
J. C. POWYS *A Glastonbury Romance*

Gazetteer

SOMERSET

Athelney (DD 12). The legend of King Alfred and the cakes is better remembered than the great battle he was planning while taking refuge here in 878 – the battle in which (at Ethandune in Wiltshire) he put an end to the domination of the Danes. Nothing remains of the abbey he built at Athelney to celebrate the victory, but there is a monument on the little hill called the Mump.

Bath** (DH 16) EC Thurs and Sat (80,850). Its medicinal waters have been used at least since it was the Roman city of *Aquae Sulis*. In the 18th cent. a tremendous planning scheme was carried out by the architect John Wood – so successfully that Bath became the most fashionable place in Britain (though perhaps more of its visitors went there to bask in the glory of Beau Nash than to be cured of gout or rheumatism). Smollet, Fielding, Jane Austen and Dickens (Pickwick said the waters tasted 'like warm flat-irons') have all given us pictures of Bath at various periods. In spite of modern reconstruction Bath retains its Regency air: the new chain stores look out on scenes hardly changed since Wood's days. See the Baths (including the Pump Room), the Abbey, the Holbourne of Menstrie Museum, etc. The Festival of Music and Drama takes place in May.

Bridgwater (DC 13) EC Thurs (25,600). Important, sprawling town in which the A38, A39 and A372 meet for the crossing of the River Parrett. Admiral Blake was born here in 1599; his house is now a museum.

Bath, colonnade in Bath Street
Reece Winstone

Bristol* (DF 17) EC Wed (436,450). Partly in Gloucestershire, partly in Somerset, but since 1373 a county in its own right, with a long history of maritime adventure and commerce. The boat basin by the city centre marks the position of the harbour around which Bristol grew up. As ships became larger, deeper docks were built at the mouth of the Avon. As an importer of tobacco leaf Bristol naturally made (and still makes) cigars and cigarettes – so with numerous other imports. To understand Bristol fully, go to the docks. Then see the soaring St Mary Redcliffe Church; the restored but ancient Cathedral; the museum and art gallery, adjoining the towered University building and facing the Cabot tower which celebrates Cabot's discovery of North America in 1497. In front of the Exchange are four short pillars called *nails*, on which merchants conducted cash transactions: hence 'paying on the nail'. Notable is the 18th-cent. Theatre Royal. At Clifton, NW of the city, the Avon gorge is spanned by Brunel's spectacular suspension bridge.

Bruton (DG 13). Pleasant little town on the river Brue. Note the old packhorse bridge and, half a mile S, the remains of a little 16th-cent. dovecot (NT) which belonged to a 12th-cent. abbey now in ruins.

Burnham-on-Sea (DD 14) EC Wed (9,850). Many towns have lighthouses, but Burnham has two: the queer wooden affair on the sands and the more solid one which pops up among the trees and houses inland. They serve as leading lights for vessels making for Bridgwater. 7 miles of sands.

Burrington Combe* (DE 15). One of the major gorges of the Mendips. Sheltering from a storm, Augustus Toplady here wrote the hymn *Rock of Ages*.

Cadbury Castle* (DG 12). Splendid Iron Age hill fort – the finest in Somerset.

Castle Cary (DG 13). 'Capital' of Caryland – an old yellow-stone town, the home of good cheddar cheese. Note the little 'pepper-box' lock-up and the remains of the Norman castle.

Chard (DD 10) EC Wed (5,800). Rain falling in the main street may eventually swell either the Bristol Channel or the English Channel, according to which side of the main street it falls on. John Stringfellow, first to make (and fly) a power-driven aeroplane (1848, now in Science Museum, London), was born here, as was Margaret Bondfield, the first British woman Cabinet minister.

Cheddar* (DE 15) EC Wed (2,600). A little cheese is still made here, but the place is best known for its caves, though any romantic leanings are soon dispelled by the sight and sound of the booths and shops around the entrances

at the foot of the gorge. Flood-lighting and other effects cannot entirely disguise the beauty of stalactite and stalagmite. How much of the Mendip limestone is riddled with similar, still silent, caverns, excavated by underground rivers? Do not omit to explore the gorge, hardly appreciated by those who go no further than the caves.

Cleeve Abbey (DA 14). *See* **Watchet**.

Clevedon (DE 17) EC Wed (10,650). Relatively quiet little town built around a small rocky bay with trees coming down to the water's edge. Memories of Coleridge (who spent his honeymoon here) and of Arthur Hallam (for whom Tennyson wrote *In Memoriam*). Thackeray did some of his writing at Clevedon Court (NT).

Crewkerne (DE 10) EC Thurs (4,200). Attractively planned around a central market-place, with good stone buildings. Since Nelson's day Crewkerne has made sails; today it makes parachute harness as well. In the SE corner of the church is a chamber once thought to have been an anchorite's cell – more probably a shrine.

Culbone Church   *Reece Winstone*

Culbone* (CJ 14). Near Porlock. One of England's smallest churches (35 ft. by 12 ft.) lies hidden in a wooded combe. Cars cannot come

near. All is quiet. The Bristol Channel lies below. At the farmhouse above the church Coleridge wrote *Kubla Khan*.

Downside Abbey (DG 14). The abbey was founded by English Benedictine monks expelled from Douai in 1793. The Gothic church was consecrated in 1935. Here is the well-known Roman Catholic boys' school.

Dunster* (CK 14). Notable are the wide main street, the picturesque 17th-cent. yarn market, and the ancient, restored, still inhabited castle rising impressively in the background (*see p.* 40). In the church note the 14-bay rood-screen, 11 ft. high and beautifully carved.

Exmoor (CH 14). Over 250 square miles of wild moorland scored with deep valleys: highest point Dunkery Beacon (1,705 ft.). Most of it is in Somerset, but a small portion is in Devon. Though its official title is Exmoor Forest, it is mainly open

heather and grass country, with red deer and small shaggy ponies roaming at large, numerous sheep, and a great variety of birds, rare plants and flowers. The National Trust has done much to protect the wild life.

Frome (DH 14) EC Thurs (11,450). Once one of the busiest wool towns in the West Country, Frome (pronounced 'Froom') is now busy with printing and other industries. *See* Cheap Street – narrow and with a runnel of water down the middle.

Glastonbury** (DF 13) EC Wed (5,800). Before exploring the town it is well to clear one's mind of the legends concerning Joseph of Arimathea, King Arthur and Guinevere. The Abbey ruins are sufficiently rewarding. They are all that is left of a famous shrine of the Middle Ages, 'an house meet for the King's Majesty and no one else'. Founded in Celtic times; suppressed by Henry VIII in 1539; bought by the Church of England in 1908 and vested in trustees, under whom intelligent

Dunster Castle

Reece Winstone

Glastonbury, Abbey ruins

Reece Winstone

excavations have revealed many interesting features. A landmark from afar is Glastonbury Tor (525 ft.) crowned by a 14th-cent. tower marking the site of a chapel destroyed by a landslide in 1271. Note the stone-fronted George Hotel, formerly a hostel for pilgrims, and the near-by museum with models and relics illustrating ancient lake villages.

Hinton St George (DE 11). The church is notable for the many monuments (showing appropriate contemporary costumes) of the Paulett family – notables of Tudor and medieval times.

Ilminster (DD11) EC Thurs (2,800). Stone-built town: conspicuous church with the tombs of Nicholas and Dorothy Wadham, founders of Wadham College, Oxford.

Kilve (DB 14). At the foot of the Quantocks. One of the best points to observe the beds of oil-bearing shale which extend for more than 10 miles. As one looks up the Severn Estuary from here, the atomic power station at Hinkley Point can be seen, towering above the natural scenery.

Lytes Cary (DF 12). 2½ m. NE of Ilchester, visit the manor house with 14th-cent. chapel and 15th-cent. Great Hall (NT).

Mendip Hills (DF 15). A typical limestone range which subterranean rivers have over the centuries riddled with caves, potholes, gorges (besides Cheddar visit also Ebbor Gorge, S of Priddy); they extend some 30 miles NW from the valley of the Frome almost to the Bristol Channel. Average height over 600 ft., highest point Blackdown (1,068 ft.). Wide views over Sedgemoor to the Quantocks from the steep western escarpment. Everywhere are evidences of Roman (and later) lead mines. (*See also* **Cheddar** and **Priddy**.)

Minehead (CK 14) EC Wed (7,675). Most westerly of Somerset resorts, lying at the foot of the wooded hill culminating in Selworthy Beacon (1,104 ft.). Splendid walking country around. Sands and sheltered gardens; steamers connect with Bristol Channel ports.

Hinton Charterhouse Priory (now in ruins). At the foot of the church tower is the tomb of two ladies described by Pepys as having 'two bodies upwards and one stomach'.

Nunney (DH 14). Impressive ruins of a moated rectangular castle built in 1373 (AM).

Porlock (CJ 14). Modern cars make less of the notorious hill on the Lynmouth road than did their forerunners;

Minehead

Montacute* (DF 11). Tudor domestic architecture at its best produced this immense mansion with its formal Early Jacobean gardens (NT). In the village see the old-world square of Ham Hill stone houses called The Borough.

Norton St Philip (DH 15). The 15th-cent. George Inn – stone-built ground floor and two storeys of timber and plaster – was once a guest house for

but it is still a long pull up, and many people prefer the toll road, which is incidentally prettier. The Ship Inn in Porlock village has associations with the poets Coleridge and Southey. Porlock Weir, $1\frac{1}{4}$ miles NW, is a small natural harbour with wooded cliffs overlooking Porlock Bay.

Priddy (DF 15). Scattered village on the Mendips with entrances to mysterious caves and channels known only to pot-holers. Hurdles stacked on the wide village green are held to carry the right to hold the 600-year-old Sheep Fair.

Quantock Hills* (DB 13). A dozen miles of superb wooded undulating upland extending to the sea from between Taunton and Bridgwater. Fringed by pretty villages. Nether Stowey and Alfoxton have associations with the Wordsworths; at Stowey the National Trust care for the cottage where Coleridge lived from 1797–1800 and wrote *The Ancient Mariner*.

Sedgemoor. Extending SW from the Mendips to Taunton and Ilminster, this great low-lying area with its dykes and pumping stations is more like the Lincolnshire Fens than the popular conception of Somerset. Great crops of withies are cut, cured and made into basket-ware. Here is the site of the Battle of Sedgemoor (DD 13), where the rebellious Duke of Monmouth and his followers were routed in a terrible hand-to-hand struggle, the last battle to be fought on English soil. (*See also* **Athelney,** *above*.)

Shepton Mallet (DG 14) EC Wed (5,500). Ancient sheep-market town on a hill, once famous for cloth and stockings. Note the excellent hexagonal market cross, *c.* 1500. This small town has become famous in recent years for its output of champagne-perry.

Tarr Steps. About 4 m. NW of Dulverton (CK 12). Ancient, probably prehistoric bridge across the River Barle, formed by huge stone slabs. Some of them weigh nearly 5 tons, yet such was the force of the water during the great storm in 1952 that they were washed away and the bridge had to be rebuilt.

Taunton (DC 12) EC Thurs (35,200). The county town of Somerset and the bustling, prosperous centre of a

Tarr Steps, Exmoor   Reece Winstone

thriving agricultural centre (markets Tues and Sat) with other industries ranging from the printing of Admiralty charts to wickerwork and the making of church organs. Note the fine tower of St Mary's Church. Good museum in the remains of the ancient castle, in the Great Hall of which Judge Jeffries held his 'Bloody Assizes' over the survivors of the Battle of **Sedgemoor** (*see above*).

Trull (DC 12). In the church the pulpit, rood-screen and bench ends are excellently carved – though not all by 'Simon Warman, maker of thys worke Ano Dni 1560', who did the linen panelling in the N aisle.

Watchet (DA 14) EC Wed (2,600). An old little town with large paper mills, a harbour and cliffs containing vari-coloured strata of gypseous alabaster. The harbour, although relatively dormant for many years, has been given a new lease of life, and trade is gradually increasing. 3 miles SW at Old Cleeve are the well-preserved ruins of 12th-cent. **Cleeve Abbey*** with its fine refectory (AM).

Wellington (DB 12) EC Thurs (7,500). The conspicuous monument on the highest point of the Blackdown Hills to the S (NT) commemorates the great Duke of Wellington who took his title from the town. Cloth has been made here since the time of Elizabeth I.

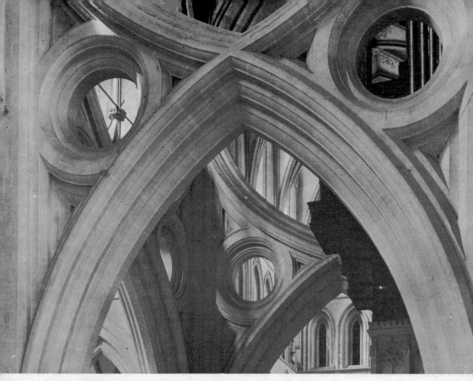

Wells Cathedral, the great arches

Wells** (DF 14) EC Wed and Sat (6,700). A city within a city, for inside the municipal boundary is the ecclesiastical city, enclosed by walls and containing the Cathedral, Chapter House, Bishop's Palace, and Deanery. The Cathedral west front is famous for its array of carved figures; notable inside are the inverted arches (installed in 1337 when the tower foundations began to give way), the Chapter House and the humorously carved pillar capitals in the S transept. The swans at the Bishop's Palace ring the bell when they are ready for lunch.

Weston-super-Mare (DD 16) EC Thurs (44,000). Weston is to Bristol what Margate is to London – a grand place for a lively holiday or a good day out. Splendid sands, piers and all modern amenities. Boat trips to the twin islands of Steep Holm and Flat Holm, 5 miles off shore. Flat Holm is identifiable by its lighthouse.

Wookey* (DF 14). Here the River Axe issues from the Mendips by way of Wookey Hole, into which the general public can penetrate for some way. The museum displays objects found in the caves proving that they were occupied in prehistoric times. Less spectacular than Cheddar, the Glen is quieter and prettier than the Gorge. The handmade-paper mills are commendably unobtrusive.

Yeovil (DF 11) EC Thurs (24,550). The glove-making industry here is at least 350 years old. More recent are the Westland aircraft works (occupying in part the site of a Roman settlement inhabited as late as 367). Interesting things are to be seen in the museum in the municipal buildings.

Lulworth Cove and the coastline towards Weymouth   *Aerofilms*

DORSET

AN INTRODUCTION BY GEOFFREY BOUMPHREY

It is often claimed that the British Isles hold a wider variety of scenery for their size than can be found anywhere else in the world. Whether this be true or not, there can be little doubt that no county of Britain offers a richer diversity than Dorset. High uplands rising in places to eight or nine hundred feet, bare for many miles save for the earthworks of prehistoric man, or, in contrast, richly wooded; lush vales of arable and pasture land threaded with quiet streams; sombre heaths where the sandy soil is hidden (or not) by heather and bracken, scrub oak or silver birch; and a long coastline that in itself offers a variety from sandy beaches or shingle banks to high golden cliffs or cliffs of grey limestone scalloped out into caves and arches or delicious coves – could more be asked of an area measuring some fifty miles from east to west and averaging about half that distance from north to south?

49

The rock beneath

As with the British Isles in general, it is the great variety of geological formations occurring close together that gives Dorset so wide a range of scene. Truly, it is the rock beneath that paints the landscape. Four main types are responsible, though with many subdivisions and interpenetrations which make the coastline in particular a geologist's paradise.

First the chalk. Originating in the uplands of Salisbury Plain and the Marlborough Downs, a dominating ridge crosses the county diagonally from the north-east, near Shaftesbury, to the south-west, near Bridport. From this point another narrower ridge doubles back due east and reaches the coastline between Swanage and Poole Harbour.

In the triangle which lies between the two ridges of chalk, its points at Studland, Dorchester and Cranborne, lie the sands, occupying about one quarter of the county, to the chalk's one half.

Third are the limestones. These lie along the coast between the chalk and the sea, forming the 'Isle of Purbeck' (Purbeck stone), the Isle of Portland off Weymouth (Portland stone of building fame) and a wonderfully spectacular line of cliffs. At the western end of the county they form the southern extremity of the great belt of building stone that runs north-eastwards across England, through Bath, the Cotswolds, Northamptonshire (as ironstone) and so to Lincolnshire.

Finally come the clays, one quarter of the county in extent, lying chiefly in the west, north-west and north. It is these – as in the Vales of Marshwood and Blackmoor – which constitute the richest farmlands in the county, growing first-class wheat and barley (and immense oak trees) and no doubt justifying the claim that 'Dorset butter is the best in the world'.

Local industry

Happily, from the point of view of the visitor or tourist, large-scale industry has made little mark on Dorset. Quarrying for stone is primarily carried out on the Isle of Portland, which has its own strange beauty, as the work of certain modern artists testifies. Purbeck marble, stuffed as full of fossils as a plum cake of raisins, is in short supply nowadays; but many churches, in Dorset and far beyond, can show highly polished evidence of an earlier vogue. The fine clays found near Poole and Wareham provide the raw material for local potteries and for other industries elsewhere.

The quays of the old port of Poole are furnished with the usual gear of such places, some pleasant to see and others less so. Weymouth today is not so much a naval base as a holiday resort, with many charming architectural reminders of the day when it found favour with George III. Incidentally, it was Weymouth which saw the birth of the bathing-machine, that strange but passing witness to the English love of the sea. It was invented in 1763 by one Ralph Allen, who also was the first to use it 'to bathe his body in the open sea – a treatment so extreme and so strange that it savoured of madness'. His example can be happily and safely followed today along much of the lovely Dorset coast – though not, presumably, from a bathing-machine.

Another place that has changed its character is the picturesque and precipitous little town of Lyme Regis. Once a thriving port, it retains atmosphere enough of the past to have quite unusual charm. Quaint old houses cling to its steep streets – almost the only level ground in the older part is its unsophisticated Parade and the sand left behind by the falling tide. The Pretender,

50

Monmouth, landed here in 1685 on his way to defeat at Sedgemoor – but visitors are on the whole more interested to recall that the Cobb, as the four-teenth-century breakwater is called, was the scene of Louisa's famous fall in Jane Austen's *Persuasion*.

Rope-making has left a not unwelcome mark on Bridport in the great width of the main streets which allowed each or any house to have its own rope-walk. But today net-making (or 'braiding') survives as the little town's main activity. The only recent incursion of industry into the county is that of the Atomic Energy Establishment at Winfrith Heath, half-way between Wareham and Dorchester. Set low down in country which, as its name suggests, is on the relatively barren sands, its presence is unobtrusive enough.

Thomas Hardy's 'Wessex'

And so today Dorset still looks much as it must have looked two or three centuries ago, or as Thomas Hardy describes it so incomparably well in his novels. There are many ways to approach it, and none better, perhaps, than through his writing. *Under the Greenwood Tree* or *Far from the Madding Crowd* will make a good enough introduction, if you don't already know him; but, if you want something weightier, read *Tess of the D'Urbervilles*, one of the few novels in any language comparable with the Greek tragedies. No one, after reading these books, can fail to see Dorset with clearer vision, to perceive a greater depth in its beauties. The faint disguises of his place-names are easily pierced: his 'Shaston' is Shaftesbury, Dorchester becomes 'Casterbridge', and for 'Egdon' see Puddletown Heath.

If pilgrimages appeal to you, Hardy's birthplace, his school, his home, and old Stinsford Church where his heart is buried, all lie within a radius of a very few miles. The Hardy Monument, by the way, a tall column prominent for many miles on a hill-top near Portesham, commemorates not the novelist and poet but the Admiral who was present at the death of Nelson. Thomas Hardy's memorial statue by Eric Kennington stands (or rather sits) in the county capital, Dorchester.

The archaeological record

Should your tastes extend further into the past, there is a far older Dorset than Hardy's to be explored. In no other county are the traces of Roman and pre-Roman habitation more abundantly evident, and in no other county, I think, do they lie in such lovely settings.

When the Romans came, they found a country uninhabited for the most part in the low-lying districts where we live today. It was on the downs and uplands where the light shallow soil was easily tilled, that the Ancient Britons preferred to live. The Romans, and still more the Saxons who followed them, were the first to tackle the heavier soil and tougher trees and undergrowth of the valleys. As civilization moved downhill, it left almost untouched the evidence of earlier days; and it is these which we can still see and wonder at today. Ignorance of at least a glimmering of their significance robs the traveller of half the interest and joy in his journeyings and keeps him from some of the loveliest parts of Dorset.

If you drive down on the A354, the main road from London after Salisbury, you cross the county boundary about ten miles beyond Sarum. At this point you are on the old Roman road that ran almost straight (as Roman roads did) from Old Sarum to Dorchester. On your left is to be seen a high embankment with a broad ditch on the near side. This is the Bokerly Dyke. It runs for miles; and excavation has proved that it was dug and raised right across (and thus must be later than) the Roman road. So it was probably dug as a defence against raiders from the east, culminating in the Saxons, who eventually drove the Britons westwards as far as Cornwall and Wales after the fall of the Roman power. A mile and a half further on, the modern road bends slightly to the right; but if you look you will see clearly the line of the old road running dead straight ahead over the downs to the distant skyline. Next, on the left of your road, in the angle between the new and the old, you will come to the finest group of round barrows or tumuli in the country. These circular mounds of earth, often with a ditch round them, are the graves and monuments of important Britons. They are anything up to four thousand years old or older. It may be wondered whether later stone monuments – even cathedrals – will last so long.

A mile south-west of Dorchester lies Maiden Castle, the largest hill-top camp in Britain. Three and sometimes four lines of ramparts up to sixty feet high surround the great oval of nine hundred by four hundred yards – and all this dug with red deers' antlers for picks and their shoulder-blades for shovels. The site was originally inhabited as far back as the New Stone Age, say ten thousand years ago; but the last great fortifications were raised against the impending Roman invasion. When the Romans did take it by storm in A.D. 45 or thereabouts, little wonder that they decided to rehouse the surviving tribesmen on a less easily defended site at Durnovaria, the modern Dorchester. Here again, a visit to the County Museum will add to the interest of 'the Maiden' itself.

Rocks and plants

To go yet further back in time: even the amateur geologist is likely to know what Dorset has to offer him in his chosen field. Nowhere else in Britain can be seen such examples of various and contorted strata. Fault, syncline, anticline and many such other can be seen in the cliffs as plain as in textbook, and with these for good measure are thrown in such fossils as petrified tree-trunks, dinosaurs' footprints, bones of plesiosaurus, prehistoric elephant and crocodile and, of course, innumerable shellfish. If he cannot hope to collect all these, he can at least take his hammer along and hope for the best. At worst he will be allowed to visit the family quarries at Purbeck and may well be shown any fossils that have recently come to light.

For the botanist, many rare plants – in particular ferns and orchids – are to be found. The neighbourhood of Swanage and Studland is perhaps the likeliest area. In the same part, the butterfly collector may hope to capture the rare and unique Lulworth Skipper – though we may hope not too often.

Special to Dorset

The gourmet will like to know that many of the villages and towns along the coast make something of a speciality of lobsters. Afterwards, he may eat Dorset's own cheese, Blue Vinny, a close rival to Stilton. Nothing goes better with it, of course, than Dorset butter spread generously on Dorset knobs. These are like very miniature cottage loaves, but crisp right through. Other specialities of the county include the indigenous Dorset Horn Sheep – horn-rimmed spectacles indeed, and on both sexes! And where is the equal of the Swannery at Abbotsbury? There you will see over five hundred birds living on the placid waters of

The stratified cliffs of the Stair Hole at Lulworth Cove *Jarrold*

the Fleet, the narrow eight-mile-long lagoon that lies between the Chesil Bank and the mainland.

Castle and minster and ancient church – these are listed in the Gazetteer which follows. What cannot be given is the beauty of the countryside itself, of the thatched roofs (and thatched walls), of the stone in the houses and cottages, grey-white to the east, sun-drenched gold in the west of the county: for this, and much else, only Dorset can bestow.

Some houses and gardens open to the public

Athelhampton nr Puddletown *Map* D H 09. *Medieval battlemented house. Formal and landscape gardens.* Robert V. Cooke, Esq., MP.

Chettle House nr Tarrant Hinton *Map* D K 11. *Early 18th-cent. Baroque.* Mrs E. M. Bourke.

Compton Acres nr Poole *Map* D K 08 *Famous gardens.* Mr & Mrs J. R. Brady.

Creech Grange nr Wareham *Map* D K 08. *Tudor and William & Mary house. Furniture and paintings. Gardens.* Lt-Col Ashley R. Bond.

Forde Abbey 5m S of Chard, 6m. w of Crewkerne *Map* D E 10. *Fine 12th-cent. Cistercian monastery, set in 15 acres of gardens and lakes on the banks of the river Axe. Martlake tapestries.* G. D. Roper, Esq.

Hardy's Cottage 3m NE of Dorchester *Map* D G 09. *Birthplace of Thomas Hardy.* NT.

Minterne nr Cerne Abbas *Map* D G 10. *Important rhododendron garden.* The Lord Digby.

Parnham House nr Beaminster *Map* DE 10. *Tudor. Panelling, plasterwork and carvings. Gardens.* National Assn. for Mental Health.

Purse Caundle Manor nr Sherborne *Map* D G 11. *Medieval. 15th-cent. Great Hall and Great Chamber.* R. E. Winckelmann. *Open May–Sep Wed Thurs & Bk Hols 2–6. 2/6.*

St Giles's House Wimborne St Giles *Map* EA 11. *Jacobean. Furnishings and tapestries. See also p. 64.* The Earls of Shaftesbury.

Smedmore nr Kimmeridge *Map* D K 07. *17th–18th-cent. manor house. Paintings, china, antique dolls. Walled garden.* Major J. C. Mansel.

Yaffle Hill Broadstone 3m N of Poole *Map* EA 09. *Six acres of gardens, trees, shrubs, azaleas, etc.* Cyril Carter, Esq. *Gardens only open.*

Books for further reading

The 'feel' of Dorset

WILLIAM BARNES *Poems Grave and Gay* sel. Giles Dugdale 1949; *Selected Poems* ed. Geoffrey Grigson 1950; *The poems of William Barnes* ed. Bernard Jones 1962

THOMAS HARDY 'Wessex' novels; particularly *Tess of the D'Urbervilles*: *The Mayor of Casterbridge*; *The Trumpet Major*; *Under the Greenwood Tree*

F. S. HINCHY *North-East Dorset Towns and Downs* 1957; *Dorset Days* 1963; *Dorset Today and Yesterday* 1965

MARGARET GOLDSWORTHY (ed.) *Dorset Bedside Anthology* 1951

J. S. UDAL *Dorsetshire Folklore* 1922

LLEWELYN POWYS *Dorset Essays* 1935

RALPH WIGHTMAN *Abiding Things* 1962; *Portrait of Dorset* 1965

Scenery, geology, natural history

LLEWELYN PRIDHAM *The Dorset Coastline*; from a personal and photographic point of view 1954

G. M. DAVIES *The Dorset Coast* 2nd edn 1956

RONALD GOOD *Geographical handbook of the Dorset Flora* 195–; *The Old Roads of Dorset* 1966

F. L. BLAYTHWAYT *A revised list of the birds of Dorset* 1946

ERIC BENFIELD *The Town of Maiden Castle* 1947

MONICA HUTCHINGS *Dorset River* 1956; *Hardy's River* 1967

Topography – general

ERIC BENFIELD *Dorset* (County Books series) 1950

F. R. HEATH *Dorset* (Little Guides series) 10th edn by E. T. Long 1949

WARD LOCK'S 'RED GUIDES' *Dorset Coast* 1966

ARTHUR MEE *Dorset* 1967

ARTHUR OSWALD *Country Houses of Dorset* 2nd edn 1959

MICHAEL PITT-RIVERS *Dorset: A Shell Guide* 1966

Gazetteer

DORSET

Abbotsbury swans   Reece Winstone

Abbotsbury (DF 08). Famous for its Swannery, this village of stone and thatch lies near the western end of the Fleet, the narrow lagoon that runs for some 8 m. between the **Chesil Bank** and the mainland. There are the ruins of a Benedictine Abbey (AM) and a noble 15th-cent. tithe barn 276 ft. long. On a hill-top between village and sea stands the chapel of St Catherine (patron saint of spinsters) of the same date. It has a remarkable stone roof. Garden-lovers should not miss the Sub-tropical Gardens*, approached from the Bridport road, especially in magnolia and camellia time (earlier here than usual).

Affpuddle (DJ 09). In the valley of the River Puddle – also called the Piddle or Trent. The church, close to the mill, has a 13th-cent. chancel, a Norman font, and rare Early Renaissance carved pulpit and bench-ends.

Badbury Rings* (DK 10). One of the most impressive Iron Age camps. Tree-crowned and sombre, it stands beside the disused Roman road from Old Sarum to Dorchester, which here makes a bend. Legend associates it with King Arthur, who is said to have won his last great victory over the Saxons nearby, in the battle of Mons Badonicus, where he also received his death-wound.

Batcombe, 3 m. NW of Cerne Abbas (DG 10). The rebuilt church retains its 15th-cent. tower and stone screen. The font is 12th cent. On Batcombe Down, worth the climb for the view

alone, stands the carved Cross-in-Hand pillar, which will be remembered by readers of Hardy's *Tess*.

Beaminster (DE 10) EC Wed. As a result of wars and fires, this ancient market town looks younger than it is. The church has a fine Tudor tower, with carvings of the Virgin, the Crucifixion, the Resurrection and the Ascension. Two notable Tudor manor houses in the neighbourhood are Mapperton and Parnham.

Bere Regis (DJ 09). Its name shows that this ancient place held a royal residence in Saxon times. The church is of particular interest, with a splendidly carved and painted roof. It contains the tombs of the Turbervilles, a name associated with Hardy's *Tess*. Cloud's Hill (NT), T. E. Lawrence's cottage, is 3½ m. SW.

Blandford Forum (DJ 10) EC Wed (3,650). Handsome market town on the Stour. Apart from the Almshouses and the Old House, there are few antiquities, since fire almost wiped out the old town in 1731; but many fine 18th-cent. houses prove the quality of two local architects, the Bastard brothers. Their stately church contains a canopied mayor's chair and other contemporary fittings. Bryanston House, now a public school, is a mile NW of the town. Among numerous pre-Roman earthworks in the neighbourhood, Pimperne Barrow, dating from the New Stone Age, has been rated the finest earthern long barrow in the country.

Bradford Abbas (DF 11). A village on the River Yeo with one of the great churches of Dorset. Wyke Farm, to the east, is a moated house with a splendid medieval tithe barn.

Bridport (DE 09) EC Thur (6,500). Pleasant old rope-making town, with a wide street of fine red-brick houses; produced cables for the Royal Navy from time immemorial until recent years, and net-making is still carried on. It lies nearly 2 m. from the port of West Bay, in magnificent country.

Broadwindsor (DE 10). Two landmarks look down on this village: Lewesdon Hill (894 ft., NT) and Pilsdon Pen (908 ft.). The latter, the highest point in the country, is a fine viewpoint. The church (Norm. and Perp.) has a 12th-cent. font and a Jacobean pulpit. Five m. to the W, near Chard, stands Forde Abbey, founded by the Cistercians in 1138. Among later additions it has a Tudor entrance-tower and work by Inigo Jones.

Cerne Abbas★★ (DG 10). The 180-ft. figure of the celebrated Cerne Giant (NT), Britain's most uninhibited monument, is cut in the chalk of the hill-side above this charming village. Among the ruins of the Abbey are a

The Cerne Giant   *Aerofilms*

fine gatehouse, a guest house, and a tithe barn. Opposite the church (mainly Perp.) is a most lovely row of overhung Tudor cottages and a Georgian house with a shell porch. Two m. N, at Minterne, is a wild shrub garden specializing in rhododendrons.

Charminster (DG 09), 2 m. N of Dorchester, has a church of 12th-cent. origin, re-fashioned in the 18th. Its fine tower, of Ham Hill stone, dates from the latter century. Wolfeton House, a Tudor manor, is open to the public on occasion, but only by appointment.

Charmouth (DD 09). Attractive little resort with Regency houses, little altered since Jane Austen wrote of it in *Persuasion*, describing the 'sweet retired bay'.

58

Chesil Bank is a remarkable pebble ridge extending about 10 m., from Portland to Abbotsbury, and in a lesser form for another 7 m. to a point near Bridport. Unique in its formation, the bank is composed of graduated pebbles. It is one of the most dangerous beaches in Europe.

Corfe Castle* (DK 08). The gaunt ruins of the Norman castle (AM) stand splendidly above the town, with its old stone houses and inns. The church suffered badly in the Civil War, but its fine 15th-cent. tower survives. The Town Hall Museum is open daily. The Purbeck Hills run E to Swanage and W to Worbarrow Bay, above which rise the earthworks of Flower Barrow Camp, an Iron Age hill-top fortress that is worthy of its magnificent natural setting. Two m. NW of Corfe is the famous Blue Pool, the largest of many small lakes that fill the old clay pits on Wareham Heath. Five m. SW is Smedmore, an 18th-cent. manor house with a collection of antique dolls.

Cranborne (EA 11). Small village with a great church built in the 13th cent., near the borders of Wiltshire and the disafforested Royal forest of Cranborne Chase. The fine Jacobean manor house has Renaissance loggias and a brick gatehouse. It was often visited by James I and Charles I when they hunted in the Chase. In Saxon times the Hundred Court used to assemble on Castle Hill, a large fortified mound 1 m. S of the town.

Dorchester* (DG 09) EC Thur (13,570). Founded by the Romans, the city is surrounded by traces of far earlier habitation, notably the forts of Poundbury and Maumbury Rings (*see also* **Maiden Castle** *below*). The County Museum contains many Roman and pre-Roman finds and much else of Dorset interest, including a Hardy Memorial Room. There is also the Dorset Regiment Military Museum (open daily). 'Max Gate', which Hardy built and where he spent the last years of his life, lies off the Wareham road, about 1 m. out. The

Badbury Rings

Reece Winstone

Hardy's birthplace   *Reece Winstone*

cottage where he was born (NT) is at Higher Bockhampton, 3 m. NE. The lodgings of the notorious Judge Jeffreys, the old Grammar School, and the Old Crown Court, where the Tolpuddle Martyrs were sentenced in 1834, are all of interest.

Eggardon Hill (DF 09). Has a magnificent example of an Iron Age promontory camp, and breath-taking views.

Lulworth Cove★ (DJ 07). An almost land-locked bay, is as beautiful as it is interesting geologically even to those who are not geologists. Along the cliffs westward lie the 40-foot rock arch of Durdle Door and the chasm of Stair Hole. Eastwards, the Fossil Forest of petrified tree-stumps slopes down to the sea; beyond that are the stratified rocks of Worbarrow Bay. Inland, the village of East Lulworth has thatched cottages and the shell of a 16th-cent. castle, gutted by fire in 1929. Roads are sometimes closed when the military firing range is in use (times advertised in *Dorset Daily Echo* and *Bournemouth Echo*), but there is always access to both East and West Lulworth.

Lyme Regis (DD 09) EC Thur (3,300). Seaside town of charm and

distinction with a quay 600 ft. long known as the Cobb, where the Duke of Monmouth made a landing in 1685 and Louisa Musgrove (in Jane Austen's *Persuasion*) jumped and fell. There are almshouses dated 1549 and handsome Georgian houses. The cliffs are of great geological interest.

Maiden Castle★ (DG 08). Two m. SW of Dorchester rise the 60-foot ramparts of the greatest of our prehistoric forts. The vast scale of its quadruple walls and the intricacy of the two entrances make this site as impressive as any medieval fortification (AM).

Milton Abbas★ (DJ 10). An 18th-cent. model village (now rated as the prettiest in England) of thatched cottages on a wide street, built by the first Earl of Dorchester to replace older dwellings which marred the privacy of his own newly built home. Milton Abbey, with its ancient Abbot's Hall, is now a school. In the beautiful Abbey Church, which dates from the 14th cent., should be noted in particular the vaulting of the tower, the sacrament house, the altar screen and a unique Gothic pyx. On a hill east of the Abbey stands the small St Catherine's Chapel. Four miles to the south-west is Bingham's Melcombe, a great Tudor house with ancient bowling-green and yew hedge. Bulbarrow Hill, 4 miles NNW, gives one of the most extensive views in the county.

Poole (DK 08) EC Wed (97,500). The largest town in Dorset, a port and a resort, with much character and much history. The old town is 14th cent.: almshouses, an old postern gate, and some admirable 18th-cent. buildings including the Guildhall and the Custom House. The almost land-locked harbour is ideal for sailing; its shores, with many beautiful creeks and inlets, measure nearly 100 miles. Near

Maiden Castle, near Dorchester

Aerofilms

the entrance lies Brownsea Island (NT), a wild-life sanctuary. Compton Acres Gardens, on the Canford Cliffs road, contain remarkable statuary in marble and bronze. At Yaffle Hill, Broadstone, are 6 acres of gardens with many rare trees and shrubs (*see p. 56*).

Portland (DH 07) EC Wed (12,010). A high rocky peninsula, with the naval harbour and breakwater to the N, **Chesil Bank** to the W, and Portland Bill with its lighthouse (site of fine bird observatory) and Pulpit Rock on the southern point. Both coast and interior of the 'Isle' are full of interest. Portland Castle was built by Henry VIII, on the site of a Saxon castle. Since the 18th cent. the fine oolitic stone has been extensively quarried for building purposes; Wren used it for St Paul's Cathedral. Interesting also is Avice's Cottage, given to Portland by Dr Marie Stopes; now home of the Portland Museum.

Puddletown (DH 09). To E and W of the village are splendid manor houses: Athelhampton Hall is 15th cent; Waterston Manor is Jacobean. There is a great church (mainly Perp.) with a splendid nave roof, a Jacobean gallery, and a tumbler-shaped early Norman font.

Pulpit Rock, Portland   *Reece Winstone*

61

Gold Hill, Shaftesbury

Shaftesbury* (DJ 12) EC Wed (3,430). Busy market town with a great past, splendidly placed above the Blackmoor Vale. The Abbey was founded by King Alfred, who made his daughter the first Abbess. There are a few remains of the Abbey, a few old houses, and the picturesque cobbled Gold Hill. St Peter's Church has a remarkable crypt and a finely vaulted porch. The Historical Society's Museum is at the top of Gold Hill. Two miles SE, Zigzag Hill climbs the downs with wide views over Cranborne Chase.

Sherborne (DG 11) EC Wed (7,730). Historic town on the northern border, once the capital of Wessex, with houses that date from the 15th cent. and a magnificent Abbey Church (Norm. to

15th cent.) notable for its fan vaulting, choir and chapels. In its tower hangs 'Great Tom', the tenor bell, gift of Cardinal Wolsey. The adjacent school occupies part of the former Abbey buildings: it was founded in the 8th cent. The beautiful 14th-cent. Abbey Conduit stands at the foot of Cheap Street. The Sherborne Castle of today was built in part by Sir Walter Raleigh, to whom Queen Elizabeth gave the estate. But there are still remains of the original Norman castle to be seen in a park at the E of the town.

Stinsford, 2 m. E of Dorchester (DG 09). This village is the 'Mellstock' of Thomas Hardy's novels, and in the ancient church there is a Hardy memorial window. His heart is buried in the churchyard, beside the grave of his first wife and near many of his ancestors. His ashes are in Westminster Abbey. Kingston Maurward, a fine Elizabethan manor house, stands in the grounds of a later mansion.

Studland (EA 08). Seaside village of great charm, as yet almost unspoilt. It has a sandy beach and good bathing. Its church is 'a singularly perfect and unaltered specimen of Norman style'. There is a fine walk to Swanage over Ballard Down. In the opposite direction, on the way to Poole Haven are two massive upright stones, the Agglestone and the Puckstone, and the lake called Little Sea—a very lovely landscape.

Sturminster Newton (DH 11) EC Wed (1,800). An old market town of stone buildings, standing on a great loop of the River Stour. A fine bridge of six arches unites Sturminster with Newton, and carries one of the county's 'transportation tablets'. The birthplace of the Dorset poet William Barnes.

Swanage (EA 07) EC Thur (7,800). A pleasant resort in a beautiful position, with sandy beach, rugged cliffs, and good anchorage for yachts. The town is for the most part modern, but there are some old stone houses, notably near the mill pond, overlooked by the 13th-cent. tower of the church.

Tarrant Hinton (DK 11). The beautifully placed 13th-cent. church has a Norman font and piscina and a remarkable 16th-cent. Easter sepulchre. Two m. to the N are the ruins of Eastbury House, designed by Vanbrugh. Two m. to the NE stands Chettle House, a good example of 18th-cent. Baroque work. Tarrant Rushton, to the S has a very unusual church, shaped like an equal-armed cross, dating from the 12th cent.

Toller Fratrum and **Toller Porcorum** (DF 09). Two villages 1 m. apart in the valley of the River Hooke, at the foot of the fortified **Eggardon Hill**. The 'Brethren' of the first name are the Knights Hospitallers of St John, who had granaries here; the fine manor house, with twisted chimneys and heraldic beasts, stands on the site of their ancient home. The church, dedicated to Basil the Great, has an early Norman font. The second village, 'Toller of the Pigs' (which were once bred here), has an interesting church with a 13th-cent. chancel arch and a Roman capital as pedestal of the font.

Tolpuddle (DH 09). Hamlet that became famous when, in 1834, six agricultural labourers were condemned to transportation for the crime of asking for a wage increase. The 'Tolpuddle Martyrs' are commemorated by the 'Martyrs' Tree' (NT).

Wareham (DK 08) EC Wed (3,500). A delightful old town near the mouth of the River Frome, almost surrounded by pre-Roman earthworks. The small restored Saxon church of St Martin has a figure of T. E. Lawrence in Arab dress sculptured by Eric Kennington. St Mary's Church contains a unique six-sided lead font, and the marble coffin of Edward the Martyr. Three m. S stands Creech Grange, a Tudor Manor in wooded gardens. Morden Bog to the N and Arne Heath to the E are nature reserves of great beauty.

Weymouth (DG 07) EC Wed (42,160). Finely placed on Weymouth Bay, the modern resort, grown up round the old seaport and the 18th-cent. watering-place, still retains memories of its past. There are some charming Georgian houses, and fine portraits in the Guildhall. No. 3,

Trinity Street, composed of converted Tudor cottages, is completely furnished with objects of the 17th cent. George III lived at Gloucester House (now an hotel); his likeness on horseback is cut in the turf of the downs behind the town, and his statue presides on the sea front. There are good sands and bathing, fishing and sailing. The ruins of Sandsfoot Castle, a blockhouse built by Henry VIII, stand on the cliff overlooking Portland Harbour.

Wimborne Minster★ (EA 09) EC Wed (4,160). This venerable town in the valley of the River Stour is dominated by its great Minster. The lantern formed by the partly Norman central tower is of particular interest; so are the chained library, the 14th-cent. Astronomical Clock, and many fine monuments and tombs. Two m. NW stands Kingston Lacy, home of the Bankes family for 300 years.

Wimborne St Giles (EA 11). The church, restored and enlarged in 1908, is still an excellent example of Georgian architecture. St Giles's House, the home of the Earls of Shaftesbury, is mainly 17th cent., incorporating late 16th-cent. work. There is an 18th-cent. Shell Grotto in the grounds; and in the kitchen garden, it is claimed, was grown the first cabbage to be raised in this country.

Wool (DJ 08) EC Thur (4,300). Beside the handsome 15th-cent. bridge over the Frome stands Woolbridge— the 'Wellbridge House' of Hardy's *Tess* and one of Dorset's most perfect manor houses. The ruins of the 12th-cent. Bindon Abbey lie to the E. Six m. to the W is Woodsford Castle, now a farm, with ancient tower and a fine thatched roof. The large military camp of Bovington has a museum of armoured fighting vehicles, open daily.

Worth Matravers (DK 07). Quarrying and lobster fishing occupy the inhabitants of this village on the Purbeck Downs, the site of the first radar station. There is much fine Norman work in the church, particularly the chancel arch. Two m. of rough road lead SW to St Alban's (or Aldhelm's) Head, with a Norman chapel and a magnificent view.

Lyme Regis, the Cobb

Reece Winstone

Opposite: Detail from the original painting by John Nash.

Dorset ends, or begins, with the strangest coast of any county. Here the view is eastward; the long sea-piled wall of pebbles known as the Chesil Bank curves towards the peninsula of Portland, home of Portland stone. In the foreground a lobster sprawls near ancient fossils from the Dorset cliffs and a portion of Blue Vinney cheese.

"WHEN I SET OUT FOR LYONNESSE"

Stourhead Gardens

WILTSHIRE

AN INTRODUCTION BY GEOFFREY GRIGSON

Wiltshire is one of the lonelier counties, its towns rather few and small, except for industrial Swindon in the north and cathedral Salisbury in the south, its villages, or most of them, widely scattered. It is not much of a railway county, or for that matter much of a road county, although a portion of the M4 will eventually go through the northern part of the county. In spite of Swindon with its railway factory (and its Railway Museum) the railways slip across in a hurry to get elsewhere, and the Great West Road has long been the county's one famous and considerable highway, also in a hurry to link London to Bath in next-door Somerset, indifferent to most of the Wiltshire towns, and giving no more than the quickest glimpse, along downland stretches west of Marlborough, of the county's very ancient past.

The prime things in Wiltshire are few, yet remarkable and famous. They are Stonehenge, Avebury, Salisbury Cathedral, Wilton House and Stourhead Gardens, all of which have a special relation to the heart of Wiltshire loneliness, in other words to Salisbury Plain.

Opposite: Detail from the original painting by Keith Grant.
Corn is harvested alongside the burial mounds of ancient people. Thatched chalk walls reveal Wiltshire's dependence on chalk, flint, and crop. Apt symbols of the county are the White Horses, of which seven were cut on the chalk slopes between 1741 and 1937.

Stonehenge

In the Middle Ages (which did not bother to take any notice of Avebury with its rampart, its great ditch, and its stones) Stonehenge was already listed among the Wonders of Britain. All by itself in the wide sheep-walks and cornfields of Salisbury Plain, yet mysterious and suggestive, small in such immensity, yet made up of gigantic stones, Stonehenge has been for England the chief symbol of remotest and most enigmatic antiquity. Poets, novelists, painters, and romantic mystifiers have been to Stonehenge, and have drawn after them the archaeologists and the preservers. Even more than at present, when there are fences around Stonehenge, when it has a ticket office and a car park, and when one can see on the horizon one of those great military establishments which occupy too much of the loneliness of Wiltshire, the reputation of the monument has always been a solemn one. People imagined it – as we still imagine it – to have been a 'temple' of some kind (though it is as likely to have been the stockaded 'palace' or HQ or seat of government of a New Stone Age and then Bronze Age kingdom). The poet William Wordsworth, when he was young, in 1793, watched the fleet off Portsmouth, preparing for the French·Wars. Very soon after, depressed by the thought of a war which would be long and full of misery, he spent two days travelling on foot over Salisbury Plain, where the sight of the tall trilithons and the fallen stones of grey Stonehenge and of the prehistoric barrows or burial mounds of the dead round about, made him think all the more of past and present and the disasters of war – caused him to write a poem, which contains, incidentally, one of the best of all descriptions of the Plain, where roads (but nowadays they are tarred) 'their bare white lines extend'. The forlorn wanderer of Wordsworth's stanzas came to Stonehenge in the night (which is a good time for a visit, by the way, if there happens to be a moon). He had crossed the Plain as the light failed, looking back first to the thin spire of Salisbury Cathedral. He found no house, or hut, or human being –

> *could only hear*
> *Winds rustling over plots of unripe grain,*
> *Or whistling thro' thin grass along the unfurrowed plain.*

It rained, it grew dark, and the Wanderer at last found shelter in Stonehenge, which Wordsworth in the poem called an 'inmate of lonesome Nature's endless year' – which it certainly is.

Stonehenge, then, is the necessary thing above all things which must be visited in this county. It should be at the head of the tourist's programme – and when he reaches it, he can meditate upon one fact established firmly by modern archaeological research, that the grey Stonehenge is some 3,800 years old.

Avebury

Item Two in the explorer's programme will probably be – since they are so close to Stonehenge – either Salisbury itself, or Old Sarum, which is the fortified site of the first cathedral, on what is now the suburban fringe of the city. But out of order, let us have a first look at Avebury (which is hardly less wonderful and no less enigmatic than Stonehenge), even though it lies north of the Plain, across the Vale of Pewsey in the Swindon sector of the county. Avebury was perhaps an earlier chalkland capital which was deserted for Stonehenge. Its neighbourhood is rich with an extraordinary medley of objects. Here you have a

Stonehenge

Aerofilms

museum, a manor house, an ancient church, an ancient village half in, half out of the huge circle of rampart, ditch and massive squat stones. Here, as well, you have a winding avenue of stones, and the unexplained enormous mound of Silbury, as well as the camp or corral on Windmill Hill, which was the home, some 5,000 years ago, of some of the first herding and corn-growing people of Britain. Here too is the West Kennet Long Barrow, a damp Neolithic family tomb recently excavated, and restored, some of the stones of which are smooth with the polishing of stone axes. Sarsens (the Avebury circles and most of Stonehenge are made of sarsens) lie on the Marlborough Downs above Avebury; and the A4 (by which you approach Avebury from London) is in part, hereabouts, that ancient highway of the Romans which began in London with the straight line of Oxford Street. Between Avebury and Devizes the main road cuts across a striding, strongly defined length of Wansdyke (i.e. Woden's Dyke), which the West Saxons probably built, more than a thousand years ago, to check the Mercians who pushed hard against them from the north. Also between Avebury and Calne, one of the finest of Wiltshire's stud of White Horses is cut clear into the chalky hillside. A few miles the other way another White Horse

67

extends on the chalk and harebell slope of Hackpen Hill. All in all, Avebury is the best centre in Wiltshire – and one of the best centres in any county of Great Britain – for a combination of walks, distances, huge skies, and a superabundant quantity of ancient monuments. Its genuine rurality is unimpaired.

Salisbury

Salisbury is Wiltshire of the valleys – a meadow city where three chalk streams, the Nadder, the upper part of the Avon, and the Bourne, join into one, after draining the chalk country of Salisbury Plain. The city is below the Plain and yet its product – 13th-century successor to the original Old Salisbury or Old Sarum (Sarum is the medieval Latin – and conveniently shorter – form of Salisbury), which was built within the multiple ramparts of an Iron Age hill fort on the border of the Plain, in a position the 13th-century ecclesiastics of the first cathedral found too windy and waterless. So Salisbury is the natural capital of the ancient sheep wealth, wool wealth and corn wealth of the great open lands extending to the north, north-east, west and south-west. As Wiltshire's county town (though not its administrative capital, which is Trowbridge, a town without much to offer to the visitor), Salisbury is also successor to Wilton, once the aboriginal capital of the Wiltshire English, three miles upstream on the little River Wylye, which joins the Nadder. 'Wilton' means the farm settlement on the Wylye; Wylye in turn means the tricky or twisty river, and Wiltshire means the Shire of Wilton; and Wiltshire people, more than a thousand years ago, were the *Wilsaetan*, or the Wylye dwellers.

Salisbury contradicts the common idea that medieval cities were jumbles without plan. It was planned, alongside the new cathedral, on a grid system of intersecting streets, roughly parallel. Traffic still follows the old grid in part, but a new inner ring road, parts of which are already in use, is beginning to relieve traffic congestion. The cathedral still stands by itself in the middle in its own river-meadow precinct or close, where the foundation stones were laid on an April day in 1220. Most cathedrals are a mixture of the different medieval styles and centuries. Nearly all of Salisbury Cathedral was built between 1220 and 1280. In the early decades of the next century they added the great spire which can be seen from so many points of Salisbury Plain.

This small city flourishes, and looks a credit to the civilization of England, with good shops (including a good secondhand bookshop near the principal gate into the Close), good buildings, a good museum, and good markets. It is a town of entry, not only to the Plain, but to the serene intricate system of chalk valleys with their valley villages along the banks of chalk-streams, which are clear, and white in the early summer with the crowded flowers of water-crowfoot.

Wilton and Stourhead

Wilton House, upstream at Wilton, bedded between two shoulders or flanks of Salisbury Plain, I have mentioned as another of the prime things of the county. As mansions go, Wilton House is not overlarge or super-grand. But, for its 17th-century architecture (Inigo Jones), its extraordinary pictures (Van Dyck, Rembrandt, Lucas van Leyden, etc.), its grounds, and its associations with many of the greater Elizabethan and Jacobean writers, Wilton is as much a national shrine and a European treasure-house as unique Stonehenge is a national and European antiquity, or Salisbury Cathedral a national and European master-work of medieval art and piety. Westward beyond the source of the

68

Wilton House

Wylye, on the border of Wiltshire, there is yet another beautiful and peculiar attraction of European and national importance, in the shape of the 18th-century landscape gardens, with temples, grotto, and lakes, attached to the mansion of Stourhead (National Trust). Not only on the edge of the county, but on the extreme edge of Wiltshire chalkland, which is visible from the portico, Stourhead is the last of a westward-extending line of mansions all of which are rooted in the ancient wealth of Salisbury Plain.

Towns and Villages

So much for the greater things of Wiltshire, which few other counties can rival. The best of the small towns and the prettiest villages of the county, with few exceptions, are to be found west and south-west of the Plain, bordering Somerset and Gloucestershire. Here the building influence of Bath, in the next county, extended into Wiltshire. Here, instead of soft chalk, good building-stone was available for wall and roof, and in the westward valleys of Wiltshire streams run fast enough to turn the cloth mills which earned very considerable wealth.

Bradford-on-Avon, which has a concentration of seemly houses of the 17th and 18th centuries (as well as its Saxon church), was such a clothier's town. Malmesbury, which, with Devizes, I prefer to all the smaller Wiltshire towns, had the benefit of water, clothiers and building stone, and carried over a tradition of well-being or self-importance from the great abbey of Benedictine monks, part of whose church survives, with its involved and elongated Romanesque carvings, in the porch, of angels and apostles. Clothiers, too, gave its stony character to the small town of Corsham, where one of them in the church has a memorial blandly remarking:

> *The labouring poor he never did contemn,*
> *And God enriched him by the means of them.*

Castle Combe, which has been voted England's prettiest village (it is pretty, but not that pretty, by any means), lies by a mill-swift stream in a deep stony valley, a cloth-centre once of a smaller kind. Other stony villages of note are Sherston, Biddestone, Lacock (with its nunnery), and Steeple Ashton, marked by a clothier's church, factory and manor house.

Contrariwise it is the chalk, the chalk escarpments and the valley views they afford, which give Wiltshire much of its more select scenery, away from its better villages. For example, not much in the south or west of England surpasses the downland chalk near Baydon, in the north-east of Wiltshire, or the views of the Pewsey Vale from the chalk spurs of Martinsell Hill, which is an outlier of the Marlborough Downs, or the lofty and lonely country around Haydown Hill on the border of Hampshire, north-west of Hampshire's Andover.

Corsham: The Flemish Buildings *Reece Winstone*

Some houses and gardens open to the public

Avebury Manor Avebury *Map* EB 17, *16th-cent. manor with famous topiary gardens.* Sir Francis Knowles, Bt.

Burderop Park 1½m W of Chiseldon *Map* EB 17. *Part-Elizabethan house, altered later. Original ceiling. Attractive garden.* Miss Calley.

Corsham Court Corsham *Map* DJ 16. *Elizabethan manor, with later alterations. Georgian State Rooms, old masters and furniture. Park laid out by Capability Brown.* The Lord Methuen, RA, FSA.

Great Chalfield Manor 2½m NE of Bradford-on-Avon *Map* DJ 16. *Moated house built c. 1480, skilfully restored.* NT.

Lacock Abbey *Map* DK 16. *See p. 75.* NT.

Littlecote Froxfield *Map* EC 16. *Large Tudor manor of c. 1500. Plasterwork, panelling, paintings, furniture, glass, Cromwellian relics.* Mr. D. S. Wills.

Longford Castle 3½m S of Salisbury on A338 *Map* EB 12. *Elizabethan with later additions. Pictures & furniture.* The Earl of Radnor.

Longleat *Map* DJ 14. *One of the finest Elizabethan houses in Britain. See p. 75.* The Marquess of Bath.

Lydiard Mansion Lydiard Tregoze *Map* EB 18. *Medieval house reconstructed in 18th cent. For church see p. 76.* Corporation of Swindon.

Philipps House Dinton *Map* EA 13. *Former seat of Wyndham family, completed 1816.* NT.

Stourhead Stourton *Map* DH 13. *Mansion & landscape gardens of outstanding interest. See p. 79.* NT. *House, built in 1722 by Colen Campbell, contains furniture designed by Thomas Chippendale the younger and fine paintings. Lake in 18th-cent. garden is surrounded by temples, grottos and rare trees. Sculpture by Rysbrack.*

Wilton House Wilton *Map* EA 13. *Important mansion of great historical and architectural interest. See p. 80.* The Earl of Pembroke.

Books for further reading

Wiltshire life and customs

W. H. HUDSON *A Shepherd's Life* 1961
A. R. STEDMAN *Marlborough and the Upper Kennett Country* 1960

Archaeology and natural history

R. J. C. ATKINSON *Stonehenge* 1956
D. CRAMPTON *Stonehenge of the Kings* 1967
P. J. FOWLER *Regional Archaeologies – Wessex* 1967
G. S. HAWKINS *Stonehenge Decoded* 1966

NICHOLAS THOMAS *Guide to Prehistoric England* 1960

Topography

GEOFFREY GRIGSON *The Wiltshire Book* 1957
NIKOLAUS PEVSNER *Wiltshire* (Buildings of England series) in preparation
H. W. TIMPERLEY *The Vale of Pewsey* (Regional Books series) 1954
RALPH WHITLOCK *Salisbury Plain* (Regional Books series) 1955

Gazetteer

WILTSHIRE

Adam's Grave. Neolithic long barrow overlooking the Pewsey Vale, above the village of Alton Priors (EB 16). Area of lofty, breezy downland, crossed by **Wansdyke** (*see below*).

Avebury** (EB 17). The village is built in and out of the great companion-piece to Stonehenge. The Avebury monument (AM) is a complex of circular rampart and ditch, stone circle and small interior circles, carefully (though not completely) excavated and restored. The stones are lumpier and dumpier than those of Stonehenge; and Avebury presumably had a similar function, religious or secular or the two combined, at a somewhat earlier date in the New Stone Age (late 3rd millennium to early 2nd millennium BC). Avebury is a good centre for the Marlborough Downs; and among other things to see are the museum, the manor, the church (partly Saxon); the huge artificial prehistoric mound of Silbury (AM); the West Kennet chamber-tomb (recently opened and restored) alongside Silbury, an underground aisle of huge sarsens (AM); the early Neolithic camp of Windmill Hill (AM), which has given its name to the earliest culture of Neolithic settlers, *c.* 3000 BC.

Bemerton (EB 12). The great poet George Herbert (1593–1633) lies buried near the altar under a stone marked with his initials in Bemerton Old Church. The ugly church of 1860 is the Church of England's memorial to Herbert.

Bridge chapel, Bradford-on-Avon *J. Allan Cash*

Biddestone (DJ 17). One of the prettiest stone-built villages of NW Wiltshire.

Bowood*, 2 m. W of Calne (DK 17). 18th-cent. mansion of the Marquises of Lansdowne, designed by the Adams, in a magnificent park, with lake by Capability Brown. The house is closed to the public, but visitors without dogs or cars may walk along the main drives.

Bradford-on-Avon* (DJ 16) EC Wed (7,310). Ancient, sunny, stone-built town mostly on a steep slope. Notable things: Saxon church with carved angels (10th cent.); medieval church house for church feasts, etc.; medieval hermitage; stone bridge (14th–17th cent.) with bridge chapel, later used as lock-up; tithe barn (14th cent.) (AM); John Hall's almshouses (1700). This decorous grey-gold town owes much to its neighbour Bath, across the Somerset border.

Bremhill (DK 17). Hill-top village. Wick Hill in this parish is joined to Chippenham by Maud Heath's Causeway, endowed in 15th cent. to provide a dry passage to market. Remarkable early 19th-cent. statue to Maud Heath crowns the hill.

Bromham (DK 16). Church with noble late medieval Baynton chapel, and churchyard cross over the grave of the Irish poet Tom Moore.

Castle Combe (DJ 17). Village in a deep valley with a 15th-cent. market cross, stone houses and cottages beside a placid trout stream, small bridges, and a church surmounted by a good tower. The former peace of this clothiers' village was shattered in 1962 when it was proclaimed the Prettiest Village in England and became even more a target of excursions, and again in 1966 when Hollywood invaded the village to film parts of 'Dr. Doolittle'.

Castle Eaton, 3 m. NE of Cricklade (EB 19). Lonely and charming small church on grassy bank of the Thames.

Cley Hill (DJ 14). Lofty isolated chalk hill. Notable landscape feature (NT).

Corsham (DJ 16) EC Wed (3,490). Handsome little 17th–18th-cent. clothiers' town in Bath stone (extensive subterranean quarries). Good church, and alongside it Corsham Court, a fine 16th–18th-cent. house.

Cranborne Chase (DK 11). In the SW corner of Wiltshire, a medieval hunting-ground extending into Dorset, notable for downland scenery and prehistoric antiquities – barrows, earthworks, etc. Visit the fascinating Pitt-Rivers Museum just across the county border at Farnham in Dorset.

Devizes (EA 16) EC Wed (9,000). This small town has seemly 18th-cent.

houses, a wide market place, churches (St Mary's, St John's) notable for light-enclosing 15th-cent. architecture; the admirable museum of the Wiltshire Archaeological Society; and a series of locks by which the disused Kennet and Avon Canal climbs into the Pewsey Vale. The Bear Inn contains mementoes of Sir Thomas Lawrence, whose father was landlord ('Gentlemen, here's my son. Will you have him recite from the poets or take your portraits?'). Roundway Down above Devizes is the remarkable downland site of the Civil War battle of 1643, near the Iron Age camp (c. 250 BC) of Oliver's Castle.

Dinton★ (EA 13) has an unusual conglomeration of NT houses, largest of which is Philipps House.

Edington (DK 15). Large, light-filled 14th-cent. church surviving from a priory of the brethren known as the Bonshommes, or Boni Homines. It is well placed under the chalky flank of Salisbury Plain. Good monuments.

Everleigh (EB 15). Salisbury Plain village with an isolated Gothic revival church of 1813 of considerable beauty. Note 17th-cent. brass and poem tenderly commemorating a former incumbent's wife.

Fonthill★ (DK 13). William Beckford, writer, dilettante and millionaire, demolished his father's mansion and built the great 'Gothic' fantasy of Fonthill Abbey (1796–1800), of which only a cloister fragment remains at Fonthill Gifford. From Fonthill Bishop the public road passes under the huge classical gate which led to the old mansion, then along the ornamental lake over romantic artificial caverns opening into a grove of yews.

Great Yews and Grims Ditch★ near Homington, 2½ m. SSW of Salisbury

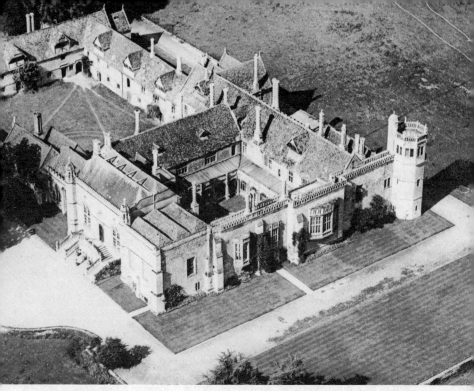

Lacock Abbey

Aerofilms

(E B 12). Remarkable, eerie yew wood of some 8o acres, in a downland neighbourhood of Neolithic and Bronze Age barrows. The double rampart of Grims Ditch (which forms the northern boundary of Great Yews) is part of the fence of a prehistoric ranch or tribal area, built *c*. 8oo BC.

Haydown Hill (E D 15). On the Hampshire border, near Tidcombe, encircled by a great bend of Roman road running N W from Winchester, and crowned (833 ft. above sea-level) by the Iron-Age Fosbury Camp. Hereabouts is some of the best Wiltshire scenery of chalk combe and down.

Heddington, 3 m. S of Calne (D K 17). A village in itself of little note, below shapely downland escarpment of exceptional attraction: Kings Play Hill, Beacon Hill, with disused section of old Bath Road, and the Roundway battle site of 1643 (*see also* **Devizes**).

Inglesham (E C 19). Lonely Thames-side church, with box pews; minute, simple and beautiful. William Morris helped to preserve it.

Lacock★ (D K 16). Village and abbey both belong to the N T. Much of the village is late medieval. The abbey housed a community of Augustinian canonesses from 1232 to 1538. Cloister, sacristy, chapter-house, warming-house, lavatory, kitchen, etc, remain.

Longleat★ (D J 14). The mansion of the Marquises of Bath, an architecturally important Elizabethan building (1559–78), beautifully set in grounds landscaped by Capability Brown in the 18th cent. The contents are somewhat grandiose. Note memorial stones to dead pets.

Lydiard Tregoze (EB 18) 3 m. W of Swindon. Isolated church (with numerous coloured monuments) and 18th-cent. mansion of the Bolingbrokes, approached by a tree tunnel. The mansion is open to the public.

Malmesbury (DK 18) EC Thurs (2,680). Little hill-top town between two streams, which grew up around the precincts of a major Benedictine Abbey. The mainly 12th-cent. part of the abbey church remains. The Romanesque carvings of the Twelve Apostles, etc, in the porch, are one of the major works of early medieval art surviving in Great Britain. 'Athelstan Cinema' is named after King Athelstan, buried in the earlier abbey church, 941. Churchyard stone with verses to victims of a circus tiger. Late medieval market-cross.

Marlborough (EB 16) EC Wed (5,910). Small town on the Bath road, 'capital' of a downland area. Remarkable 16th- to early 19th-cent. main street, partly arcaded; good bookshop, antique shops, autumn fair. The famous public school has many features of historical importance.

Marlborough Downs (EB 17). Continuation on N side of the Pewsey Vale of the chalk downland of Salisbury Plain. Areas on either side of A4 have sarsen stones still *in situ*. Good walking, mushrooms, etc. *See* **Marlborough, Avebury, Adam's Grave, Martinsell.**

Martinsell Hill, 4 m. SW of Marlborough (EB 16), above the village of Oare and the Pewsey Vale. Remarkable scenic perch, 964 ft. above sea-level, capped by an Iron Age camp. A smooth spur projects entrancingly into the Vale.

Mere (DJ 13) EC Wed (1,920). Grey, stony little town on the county border, under Salisbury Plain, and directly below the mound of a (long-destroyed) castle. Roomy, rewarding church. Otherwise the best building is the Ship Inn, a 17th-cent. mansion with an earlier-timbered dining-room and

Malmesbury Abbey: medieval carving

Reece Winstone

Old Sarum *Aerofilms*

elaborate 18th-cent. curling iron work upholding the inn sign.

Old Sarum* (EB 13). The original site of Salisbury (New Sarum) on a hill between Salisbury and Salisbury Plain, two miles from the city centre. Fortified in the Iron Age, later the site of a Norman Castle and of a cathedral built by St Osmund, nephew of William the Conqueror. Lack of water, the windy exposed position and the insolence of the castle soldiery led to the decision to build a new cathedral and city down by the river (AM).

The Ridgeway (EB 17). Ancient 'green road' keeping for the most part to high, dry chalkland, crossing the county NE into Berkshire; a trackway for earlier inhabitants, Neolithic, Bronze Age, etc, making for the northern chalklands of the Yorkshire Wolds. A good stretch will be found left and right of the Marlborough-Wootton Bassett road, on Hackpen Hill, its course marked here by beech clumps.

Salisbury** (EB 12) EC Wed (35,990). Wiltshire's most pleasant and civilised town, laid out on a grid plan by Bishop Poore in the 13th cent., alongside his great cathedral, most of which was built 1220–80. The spire (404 ft.) was added in the 14th cent., on foundations insufficient for so great a tonnage – both the worry and pride of the cathedral authorities ever since (note weight-buckled columns

77

Salisbury Cathedral: the cloisters

at the crossing). The 13th-cent. cloisters added after 1260 are a masterpiece of serenity. See in the cathedral library Anglo-Saxon manuscripts and Sir Christopher Wren's report on the spire. Pleasures of the city include the clear waters of the Avon, the 15th-cent. painting of the Last Judgement in St Thomas's Church, 15th-cent. hall of John Hall (cinema foyer), the Salisbury Museum (huge processional figure of St Christopher), an excellent antiquarian bookshop, the Saturday market with junk stalls, etc.

Salisbury Plain A great undulating area of chalk extending westward from Amesbury (E B 14) for some 20 m. at an average height of 400–500 ft.; highest point 755 ft. just above Westbury (D J 15). Much of it is now under cultivation – and much more in possession of the War Department for training purposes – but the scarcity of streams and villages, coupled with the numerous earthworks and barrows, distinguish it from any other part of England. But it cannot be appreciated from the busy main roads. (*See also* **Stonehenge**.)

Savernake Forest (E C 16). Remnant of a royal deer forest. The part bordering the Bath Road (A4) conveys only a hint of the magnificence of the older trees and glades, especially oak and beech. Celebrated for woodland fungi.

Silbury. *See* **Avebury.**

Steeple Ashton (D K 15). Cloth trade village of stone houses. Noble late 15th-cent. church, 17th-cent. market cross, and stone round-house or lock-up for those who broke the peace.

Stonehenge** (E B 14). Remote in Salisbury Plain, the major prehistoric monument – and mystery – of Great Britain (AM). It began as a bank and ditch without stones, *c.* 1850 BC. Later in Neolithic times stones were transported from Wales and incorporated in a complex of standing sarsen stones from Wiltshire. About 1600–1500 BC, in the Bronze Age, Stonehenge was grandly remodelled with taller uprights and cross-stones, regularly fashioned and combined. The function of Stonehenge (*see also* **Avebury**) was probably religious, though it may also have formed a royal 'palace', the power-centre of the farming and herding communities of the surrounding chalkland. Bronze Age barrows are particularly numerous and impressive in the Stonehenge neighbourhood.

Stourhead** (DH 13) in Stourton. The mansion and landscape gardens of Stourhead are interesting NT properties of exceptional importance, created by a member of the Hoare family (of Hoare's Bank). The 18th-cent. mansion is notable for furniture, pictures, library and position, facing the last slopes of the Wiltshire chalk country. In a valley below, the gardens are an exquisite pictorial composition embracing village, parish church, medieval cross from Bristol, artificial lakes, classical temples, a grotto and splendid banks of foliage. Brought into being 1730–80, and the finest surviving example of the English landscape garden. Best seen in autumn. Do not miss King Alfred's Tower (1766) above the gardens, a prospect tower

raised as a memorial to King Alfred and a tribute (from a banker) to constitutional monarchy.

Swindon (EB 18) EC Wed (97,920). Industrial and railway workshop town, rapidly changing and increasing. Good Railway Museum, opened in 1962, with locomotives, drawings, relics of Brunel, etc., alongside the original model village set up for the craftsmen of the railway workshops.

Vale of Pewsey (EA 16). Sheltered, ultra-fertile greensand vale, between Salisbury Plain and Marlborough Downs, traversed by the railway and the Kennet and Avon Canal from Bath.

Wansdyke (EB 16). An intermittent 60-mile bank and ditch, once reaching from the Bristol Channel near Portishead to the E of Savernake Forest. Now considered to be a West Saxon defensive work against the Mercians. A good section crosses the downs and the main road (A361) between Beckhampton and Devizes. The name

Stonehenge

means 'Woden's Dyke', as if only the great god Woden could build himself so vast a work.

Wardour Castle, SW of Tisbury (DK 12). Wardour Old Castle, once seat of the great Arundell family, was split by mines when besieged in the Civil War. Cedar trees and a romantic grotto (AM). The new 'castle' near by is a classic mansion (now a girls' school) by James Paine (1768).

West Dean (EC 12). Neglected fragment of a church, replete with an unusual, colourful collection of memorials to members of the Evelyn and Pierrepoint families.

White Horses. Wiltshire 'white horses' cut into chalk scarps will be found at Bratton, 2½ m. NE of Westbury (DJ 15), ancient but remodelled 1741; Cherhill, 1780 (EA 17); Marlborough, 1804 (EB 16); Milk Hill, N of Alton Priors, 1812 (EB 16); Hackpen Hill near Broad Hinton, 1838 (EB 17); Broad Town, just NW of Broad Hinton (EB 17), now faint, 1864; Pewsey, 1937 (EB 15); and on

SW of Marlborough-Broad Hinton road (EB 17), 18th or 19th cent., only visible after ploughing.

Wilton House** (EA 13). Seat of the Earls of Pembroke; has the national importance of Stonehenge, Avebury, Stourhead and Salisbury Cathedral among the treasures of the county. Many of the greatest Elizabethan poets were entertained here by the Countess of Pembroke, sister of Sir Philip Sidney. A considerable portion of the house is among the few surviving works which Inigo Jones (1573–1652) designed. He was responsible for the Double Cube Room, for which Van Dyck painted the huge portraits. The visitor sees other fine paintings, e.g. by Rembrandt, Lucas van Leyden and Honthorst (Prince Rupert). The contents of this not very large mansion reach a level of taste which few other aristocratic families attained in the decoration of their homes. The riverside park (good trees, mossy statues) is peaceful and in keeping.

Visitors are welcomed in the celebrated carpet factory in the small town of Wilton outside the walls.

The Cherhill White Horse   Reece Winstone

The yachtsman's Hampshire: Solent creeks and rivers   *J. Allan Cash*

HAMPSHIRE
and the Isle of Wight

AN INTRODUCTION BY CHARLES COLES

There are four distinct Hampshires. Much of the county consists of chalk uplands, typified by sheep and skylarks, moving cloud-shadows and tiny flowers, Celtic barrows and seas of barley. This is my favourite country. I lived in a chalk village for ten years, and when I moved a mere five miles across the river to the New Forest, friends came to wish me a very final good-bye. They assured me that I was moving to quite another world with different people. This was true. There is a very different feeling about the Forest. Physically the deeply wooded, silent parts are very beautiful, with their historic oases of very old oak and beech, interlaced by peaty brown streams. There are also wildernesses of holly and honeysuckle, silvery beams and dark yews.

Different again are the tranquil green watermeadows, where the last of the drowners and eelpot men still work, and where the finest dryfly fishing and some of the best coarse angling in the country are to be found. This is also the sketch-book Hampshire of thatched cottages, prize dahlias and Norman churches – intimate and welcoming but not peculiarly Hampshire. Incidentally, the county was always noted for anglers: Izaak Walton retired to the 'silver streams' of the Meon, and Charles Kingsley used to fish the Itchen.

Lastly there are the 'vilainous heaths' of Cobbett (where I spent part of my boyhood) – the sandy wastelands of the north-east, with their counterpart in the form of the lonely acid moors and bogs of the south-west. On a bleak overcast day, when the horizon is bare except for a group of Scots pines and a row of telegraph poles, and when the over-all colour of the vegetation is brownish, the sandy tracks grey and the cotton-grass a dirty white, the landscape has a melancholy about it. But this same heath country has another face, and also produces miles and miles of vivid mauves and purples and heady golden gorse. It's a question of timing!

Beneath the Surface

Hampshire is a splendid county for 'bones and stones'. Geologically, the most obvious feature is the chalk. The South Downs cross the border near Butser Hill and range north-west to the far side of Winchester. Another limb of chalk extends northwards towards Alton and her hop-gardens, eventually linking up with the North Downs and the Hog's Back. North-west from Alton the Hampshire Downs curve towards Sidown Hill (*c.* 900 feet) near the Berkshire border. The north-east corner of Hampshire, from, say, Aldershot to the Hartfordbridge flats, is mostly heathland on London Clay and Bagshot Sands. In the south-west the New Forest consists largely of Bagshot and Bracklesham Beds, with small areas of London Clay. Deep down below the Forest, fossils of cinnamon and fig-leaves have been discovered, relics of the warmer climate of past ages.

On the Isle of Wight there is an east–west backbone of chalk downs, with further chalk roughly from St Catherine's to Shanklin. Much of the southern half of the island shows the Lower Greensand, upon which rests the 'blue slipper' Gault clay – so named because it causes landslips. Some of the landslips along the Undercliff near Ventnor, and further west near Niton, are of great antiquity, and though the scars are softened by vegetation they are still spectacular. The limestone at Binstead and Bembridge, which provided the material for several famous buildings (such as Winchester Cathedral) is important; the multi-coloured cliffs at Alum Bay are not – but in a thousand attics there must be a host of forgotten jam-jars full of those coloured sands, collected by holiday children of the past.

People and Places

After Vespasian's capture of the Isle of Wight in A.D. 43, Hampshire quickly became romanized. Many villas were built – one at Rockbourne having been discovered under a cornfield, where the rabbits were seen scuffing out oyster-shells which were recognized as being like those cultivated by the Romans at Poole! Of Silchester, the 'lost city of Calleva' – much is to be seen in Reading Museum. Apart from its walls, the once-great city has now returned to its grave under the green grass.

It was after the Romans that Hampshire really came into its own, with Winchester as King Alfred's Wessex capital. There is still a good deal of Saxon

Reece Winstone **The River Itchen near Winch**

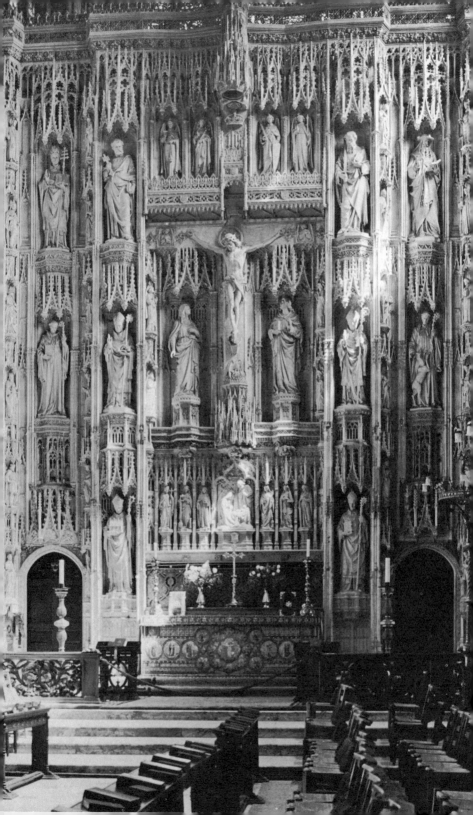

work to be seen in some of the village churches today, and the many -worthies, -bournes and -hams in Hampshire speak of Saxon settlements. Of Norman times we have many solid reminders, castles at Southampton, Odiham and Winchester – where there is also beautiful Norman work in the cathedral and in Henry de Blois' Hospital of St Cross (*c.* 1133).

The old capital city still retains a dignity and a beauty: the suburbs do not intrude. View it first from St Giles Hill – the site of that famous, boisterous Fair of the Middle Ages – and look over the Cathedral and the many other centuries-old buildings, with the great chalk downs away to the east. Then enter by the medieval gate to the town itself for a closer look at (dare I say it?) the town where English history started. And English schooling, too, for there you will find the illustrious College, founded in 1387 by William of Wykeham, of 'manners makyth man' fame. It might almost be claimed as the birthplace of English weather too, for St Swithun was a Bishop of Winchester in Saxon times. At his own request his body had been buried outside the Cathedral, 'where the rain of heaven might fall upon him'; but (according to the popular legend) Authority decided that the grave should be transferred to a more appropriate place near the altar. The moment they tried to move the body it started to rain, and operations were delayed for forty days while the rains continued. Authority was slow to take the hint!

Romsey Abbey probably provides one of the best examples in the county of a great Norman church, and the countryside around in almost any direction is beautiful and typical of this part of the county: Christchurch and Portchester Priories are also fine specimens of the period.

The New Forest scene deserves leisurely exploration, though it is traversed by roads of tempting excellence. The story that William the Conqueror ruined scores of villages and churches to enlarge his hunting preserve is incorrect: research has shown that they just weren't there to destroy! And there is now a theory that Rufus the Red was more likely done away with by ritual murder than accidentally killed by Walter Tyrell's arrow. Anyway, you can see the Rufus stone, marking the supposed spot in the Forest near Cadnam. Beaulieu Abbey, completed in 1246, destroyed in the Dissolution, belongs to Forest history, as does the little village of Buckler's Hard just down the river. It was here that some of the Trafalgar men-of-war were built of New Forest oak – many of the sails being woven at the Fordingbridge mill. Perkin Warbeck, Monmouth, and Lady Alice Lisle, who was condemned to death by the notorious Judge Jeffreys, are other notables in Forest history. Other great Hampshire names are the Duke of Wellington (of Stratfield Saye) and Nelson, whom one always associates with Portsmouth. To see the surgeon's cabin on *Victory's* orlop deck – painted red to disguise the bloodstains – is a macabre reminder of conditions at sea a hundred-and-fifty years ago. The whole ship is very much alive, and yet full of ghosts: not just a place to visit on a wet afternoon. A gentler ghost may be felt to haunt Jane Austen's home at Chawton, now partly a museum.

After Winchester, Southampton has probably played the greatest part in the county's history. It claims to be the 'Gateway of England': it was certainly once the gateway to the New World, for it was from this port that the Pilgrim Fathers set sail for America. It is now a queer but not always unattractive mixture of new houses, factories and shopping areas (replacing the blitzed

chester Cathedral: the Great Screen in the Choir   *Reece Winstone*

ones), medieval battlements and odd, tucked-away places like Norman wine-vaults, and the funnels of the Cunarder 'Queens' all mixed up with old chimney-pots. From here (as from Lymington or Portsmouth) you can cross with your car to the Isle of Wight, or from Southsea you can sometimes skim across to Ryde in a spray-shrouded hovercraft.

The Isle of Wight

The Garden Island is small, only twenty-two miles from one side to the other and thirteen miles from north to south. I know it almost better from seaward than inland – the loom of the great St Catherine's light on the dark horizon having many times welcomed me home after a wet night in the Channel. Indeed the island looks almost at its best from seaward: the coastal scenery, the deep chines, the trees down to the water's edge – and at the right time of the year the wild fuchsias, hydrangeas and rhododendrons are surely at their loveliest when seen across the water. The little towns and villages too: Ventnor terraced up the steep hillside almost Italian fashion; Sandown and Shanklin looking cosy behind their bright sands.

In some obscure way the island is unlike Hampshire, possibly because the inhabitants regard us 'overners' from the mainland as not belonging. In places one still meets a staid and prosperous Victorian atmosphere which is most delightful.

Cowes Week takes place during the first week in August. If you are prepared to walk you can still be alone or nearly so even in holiday time, and you will get some spectacular views – St Boniface Down, or the cliffs above the Needles. This is the place from which to watch the round-the-island race, often with over a hundred yachts taking part. With a fleet of striped spinnakers bellying out over a sparkling sea this race is as picturesque as any in the world.

A great deal of history has been buried or built on the island since the Romans first invaded it. The villa at Brading is one of the best preserved in the whole country. In Carisbrooke Castle, built as a Norman fortress, the betrayed King Charles was imprisoned before his execution. There are also several fine old manor houses. Osborne House, the seaside home of Queen Victoria, is where she died. To this day there *is* something final about it, as though it marks the end of an era of island remoteness and the start of a new period of fashion and popularity.

Hampshire Occupations

Though light industry increases all the time, Hampshire is still predominantly an agricultural county, and I hope you will admire the work of our skilled thatchers and hurdlemakers. There were always a number of old iron-works, and some remain. The silk mills have vanished; but one historic business, started in 1727 by the Portal family at Laverstoke, is thriving today, making the paper for Bank of England notes. Along the coast, oil refineries, aircraft works and the Royal Navy provide the main interest – with the Army much in evidence at Aldershot and test pilots at Farnborough.

Hampshire claims Hambledon as the birthplace of modern 'crickett'. This famous club was started in the mid-18th century, and so skilled were the players that they used to play and often beat the All-England XI. In 1778 they played them for 1,000 guineas, and in 1783 for 'eleven pairs of white corded dimity breeches and eleven handsome pink striped waistcoats'. Mr Thomas Lord, the proprietor of the original Lord's cricket ground in London, which was opened in 1797, is buried not far away at West Meon.

Natural History

In the home county of that famous naturalist, Gilbert White of Selborne, there is a rich variety of wild life. Most species of deer, including Sika, are to be found in the New Forest: if you get up early enough you will probably see them, and at rutting time you will smell them and hear them. If you are not an early riser, you may see them in the headlights of your car; but beware of the good straight Forest roads – the deer and the ponies cause hundreds of accidents every year. The unauthorized feeding of these animals can lead to a fine of £5. For the specialist there are slow-worms and crested newts. Biting horseflies are the only creatures to be wary of, except adders and, perhaps, the leeches in some of the Forest pools. The lampreys may look equally revolting but they are good eating. For red squirrels you will have to go to the Isle of Wight. The Forest is still a good centre for the bug-hunter – White Admirals, and some of the less common fritillaries and hairstreaks are to be seen. If a pinpoint of greenish light stares at you from near the ground, it will be a glow-worm.

The little fly-catching sundews of the bogland are common, and beds of wild lilies-of-the-valley are by no means rare. The nightingale is a truly Hampshire bird, and in the Forest you may see a nuthatch or a Dartford Warbler, a Montagu's Harrier or a hobby.

Food and Drink

The day of the once famous 'Hampshire Hog' – when pork and pudding was the farm worker's staple diet – is virtually over, though the commoners' pigs are still turned out to free-range in the Forest during the pannage months, the season of beech-nuts and acorns. And though the county boasts no truly regional dishes or local cheeses, her watercress farms, the early strawberries sold by the roadside, and the Christchurch salmon caught in salt water, are widely known. Crayfish, abundant in many streams, have a better chance of survival nowadays than when catering was more difficult. Eels, too, locally termed 'the pork of the river', are neglected: properly crumbed and grilled they are as good as Dover sole. Local roe and fallow venison is delicious, but it must come from young beasts. The Romans, who first brought the vine to Hampshire, would have been amused to know that grapes are still grown near Hambledon and wine made regularly.

New Forest ponies at Cadnam   *Reece Winstone*

Some houses and gardens open to the public

Arreton Manor I.O.W. *Map* EF 08. *Early 17th-cent. manor retaining original panelling and carving. Furniture, toy & doll & folk museums.* L. H. Slade, Esq.

Avington Park *Map* EF 13. *16th–17th-cent. house. Painted Hall and Red Drawing Room, Orangery, library and notable ballroom ceiling.* Major J. B. Hickson.

Beaulieu Abbey and **Palace House** Beaulieu *Map* ED 10. *Ruins of Cistercian Abbey built 1204. See p. 80. Also home of the celebrated Montagu Motor Museum.* The Lord Montagu of Beaulieu.

Breamore House Breamore *Map* EB 11. *Elizabethan manor house. Paintings, tapestries, porcelain, furniture. Gardens.* Sir Westrow Hulse, Bt.

Carisbrooke Castle I.O.W. *Map* EE 08. *History-ridden medieval castle. See p. 90.* Ministry of Public Building and Works.

Coles Privett *Map* EG 12. *Gardens in woodland setting. Shrubs, borders, rose garden, water garden.* Brigadier O. W. Nicholson.

Exbury Gardens *Map* EE 09. *Large woodland gardens, rhododendrons, azaleas, camellias, etc.* Edmund de Rothschild, Esq. *Gardens only open.*

Mottisfont Abbey *Map* ED 12. *Former 12th-cent. Augustinian Priory converted to mansion. Painted drawing-room by Rex Whistler.* NT.

Osborne House I.O.W. *Map* EF 09. *Former home of Queen Victoria. See also p. 92.* Ministry of Public Building and Works.

The Vyne nr Sherborne St John *Map* EG 15. *Beautiful Tudor mansion of diaper brick, with later alterations. Oak gallery & chapel date from c. 1510. Palladian Portico from 1650; 'Treatric' staircase 1764. Charles II, Queen Anne, & Chippendale furniture.* NT.

West Green House nr Hartley Wintney *Map* EH 15. *Very charming early 18th-cent. house.* NT.

Books for further reading

Topography

C. P. CHATWIN *The Hampshire Basin* (British Regional Geology) 3rd edn 1960

L. COLLISON-MORLEY *Companion into Hampshire* 4th edn 1950

J. C. COX *Hampshire* (Little Guides) rev. Jowitt 7th edn 1949

JUANITA BERLIN and others *The New Forest* 1960

BRIAN VESEY-FITZGERALD *Hampshire and the Isle of Wight* (County Books) 1949

S. E. WINBOLT *Hampshire and the Isle of Wight* (Penguin Guides) 1949

In the past

WILLIAM COBBETT *Rural Rides* 1830

ELEANOR DUCKETT *Alfred the Great and his England* 1957

L. V. GRINSELL *The Archaeology of Wessex* 1958

HUGH ROSS WILLIAMSON *The Ancient Capital* 1953

DOUGLAS WOODRUFF *The Tichborne Claimant: a Victorian mystery* 1957

Out of doors

H. S. ALTHAM and others *Hampshire County cricket* 1957

K. ADLARD COLES *Creeks and Harbours of the Solent* 6th edn 1959

W. H. HUDSON *Hampshire Days* 1903

S. L. RITCHIE *Hampshire Coast Ways* 1958

GILBERT WHITE *The Natural History and Antiquities of Selborne* 1789

The Isle of Wight

AUBREY DE SELINCOURT *The Isle of Wight* 1948

MONICA M. HUTCHINGS *The Isle of Wight* 1953

R. L. P. and D. M. JOWITT *The Isle of Wight* 1951

J. P. HUGHES *The Isle of Wight* 1967

N. PEVSNER, ed. *Hampshire and the Isle of Wight* 1967

L. WILSON *Portrait of the Isle of Wight* 1965

Some writers with Hampshire associations

Jane Austen
Charles Dickens
John Keble

Charles Kingsley
Mary Russell Mitford
Charlotte M. Yonge

Gazetteer

HAMPSHIRE
and the Isle of Wight

Brading Church   Reece Winstone

Alresford (EF 13) EC Wed (2,420). Pleasant small 18th-cent. town. Mary Mitford, author of *Our Village*, was born here, and Admiral Rodney was buried in the church at Old Alresford.

Alton (EH 13) EC Wed (9,150). Busy little town on the route of the Pilgrims' Way. Good Georgian buildings, a handsome church (note S door with marks of bullets fired by Parliamentary troops in 1643) and the Curtis Agricultural Museum. Hopfields all around, and a brewery. 4 m. N is Lasham, where gliders ride serenely in the air. At Froyle near by is a splendid wooden waterwheel plant.

Alum Bay, I.O.W. (ED 08). Notable for its cliffs of many-hued sands, its view of the line of chalk rocks called 'The Needles' and the lighthouse on the end.

Avington (EF 13). Both the little brick church (built *c.* 1770), with its original pews, gallery and pulpit, and the neighbouring mansion of Avington Park have associations with Shelley.

Basing, 2 m. E of Basingstoke (EG 15) EC Wed (2,000). Under the 5th Marquess of Winchester, Basing House (now a ruin) withstood a long siege before yielding finally to Cromwell himself (1645). Note the 16th-cent. dovecote.

Beaulieu* (ED 10). Beautifully set beside the river are the remains of the Cistercian abbey founded by King John in 1204. The Great Gatehouse forms part of Palace House, which is now the residence of Lord Montagu of Beaulieu; the Refectory is the parish church (note reader's pulpit). Amid these ancient buildings is a museum of veteran and vintage cars and motor-cycles.

Bembridge, I.O.W. (EG 08). A yachting centre at the mouth of Brading Haven, home of the famous 'Redwings'. There is a windmill (NT) open to visitors, and at Bembridge School an important collection of Ruskin's manuscripts and drawings.

Bonchurch, I.O.W. (*See* **Ventnor**)

Bournemouth (EA 09) EC Wed/Sat (154,000). One of the largest and most prosperous resorts on the S coast, with good sandy beaches, pines and rhododendrons.

Brading, I.O.W. (EG 08). Once a seaport, now a quiet inland town, with a good church containing monuments of the Oglander family. See stocks under old town hall and the bull ring at near-by crossroads. To the S is a Roman villa with well-preserved pavements and hypocausts (underfloor heating) and a small museum.

Breamore (EB 11). On the downs above the village is the Miz-Maze, a

89

medieval labyrinth cut in the turf. Above the door of the Saxon church is a Saxon rood. Breamore House is notable.

Buckler's Hard* (EE 09). Where New Forest oak was turned into 'wooden walls of old England'. Three of Nelson's ships at Trafalgar were built on the slipway here. The present-day charm of the place rests in the brick-built cottages where the shipwrights used to live, and the delightful setting beside the Beaulieu River. The tiny church can accommodate a congregation of perhaps 30 people at a squeeze.

Burghclere (EE 15). The Sandham Memorial Chapel (just N of Highclere station) was built in 1927 in memory of a soldier who died in the First World War (NT). It is filled with wall paintings of wartime scenes by Stanley Spencer.

Carisbrooke, I.O.W. (EE 08) EC Thurs (3,330). The Castle** is the most interesting building in the Isle of Wight, its keep one of the most perfect of Norman shells. Fine machicolated gatehouse with inner doors dating from 1470. Charles I was imprisoned here 1647–8 shortly before his execution; there is a museum of island history, including objects associated with Charles I. In the Well House is a donkey-wheel for drawing water (AM).

Chawton (EH 13). The house in which Jane Austen spent her last eight years, and wrote *Emma* and *Persuasion*, is now a museum. She died in Winchester, and is buried in the Cathedral there.

Christchurch (EB 09) EC Wed (26,500). A world apart from the busy main street is the grand Priory Church* with its massive Norman nave, 16th-cent. Salisbury chantry, rood screen and carvings. S of the church is a busy quay whence boats make their way to Hengistbury Head and Mudeford quay.

Corhampton (EG 11). Set in the quiet Meon valley is this 11th-cent. Saxon church with wall paintings and its original stone altar.

Cowes, I.O.W. (EE 09) EC Wed (17,820). The main part of the town is on the W side of the Medina river. Here are Cowes Castle (headquarters of the Royal Yacht Squadron) and the principal boatyards and moorings. Cowes Week in August is one of the great events of the yachting world. Regular steamer and hovercraft connection with Southampton. Trips round the Island, etc.

Freshwater, I.O.W. (ED 08) EC Thurs (3,400). The little river Yar rises so close to the S coast that it almost turns this corner of the Isle of Wight into another island. Hills rise steeply on either side of the valley. Tennyson's Down, to the W, is crowned by a tall monument commemorating the poet; Tennyson spent many years at Farringford House, which he bought out of the proceeds of *Maud*. Splendid walk westward from the cross to the point looking down on the Needles. To the N is **Alum Bay** (*see above*).

Hamble, popular yachting centre near the mouth of the River Hamble (EE 10).

Hambledon (EG 11). The cradle of cricket. The Hambledon Club was founded in 1760; see the memorial on Broadhalfpenny Down opposite the *Bat and Ball* inn.

Hengistbury Head (EB 09). From this airy point survey the whole sweep of the coast from Purbeck to the Solent and across to the Isle of Wight. By boat from Christchurch harbour

or by road to Double Dykes, pre-historic defence works at the foot of the headland; the site was populated from early Neolithic times to the 4th cent. A.D.

Laverstoke (EE 14) lies pleasantly beside the River Test, with cottages and a church that has an impressive reredos. Laverstoke House (18th-cent.) was built by Joseph Bonomi.

Lymington (ED 09) EC Wed (28,650). An ancient borough enjoying a new lease of life with the modern popularity of sailing. Substantial ferry boats carry cars and passengers past the yacht moorings and down the winding fairway, across to Yarmouth in the Isle of Wight.

Lyndhurst (ED 10) EC Wed (2,620). The 'capital' of the **New Forest** (*see below*). A village with no definite boundaries, where wild ponies roam the streets and there are plenty of stables for trained ones. The church has a wall painting by Lord Leighton and glass by Burne-Jones and Rossetti.

Mattingley, 2 miles N of Hook (EH 15). Here is an unusual and de-lightful little 15th-cent. half-timbered church.

Netley (EE 10) EC Wed (2,300). Among trees and unalluring more recent buildings are the remains of a Cistercian Abbey* (1239) of con-siderable beauty (AM).

New Forest* (EC 10). To the SW of Southampton, well over 100 square miles in extent and containing some of the finest oaks and beeches in Eng-land. In addition to woodlands there are considerable areas of open heath-land rising in places to 400 ft. with views extending to the Isle of Wight. Numerous ponies roam the Forest,

and motorists should remember that they frequently walk or lie on the roads (where they have priority). Camping by permit only – weekdays, from the Queen's House, **Lyndhurst;** weekends or public holidays, from the keepers' cottages.

Newport, I.O.W. (EF 08) EC Thurs (19,690). The capital of the Isle of Wight, at the head of the navigable part of the Medina river. Meeting-place of most of the island's main roads and a busy market town. The church has a good Marochetti monu-ment to Charles I's daughter (who died in captivity at Carisbrooke) and a medallion of the Prince Consort. Small Roman villa in Avondale Road.

Odiham (EH 15). A pleasant town with Georgian houses and other interesting old buildings. Note the old pest-house in the churchyard of the 14th-cent. church. About a mile to the W are the Norman remains of Odiham Castle.

Osborne House, I.O.W. (EF 09). Long the home of Queen Victoria, who died here in 1901. A building in the Palladian style, designed by Thomas Cubitt and the Prince Con-sort. Part of it was used as a Naval College in World War I (King George VI was trained there); it is now a convalescent home for officers and civil servants, but visitors can see the State Apartments – a notable excur-sion into 'Victoriana', which is con-tinued in Whippingham Church, also of the Prince Consort's designing. Osborne House is in the care of the Ministry of Public Building and Works.

Portchester Castle* (EG 10). A castle within a castle; Henry II built his inside the walls of one built by the Romans to protect the Saxon shore. Also within the Roman walls is the

Osborne House

church, built in 1133. A historic spot, for here Henry V assembled his Agincourt expedition. (AM)

Portsmouth (EG 09) EC Wed (215,000 inc. Southsea). 'Pompey' to the Royal Navy, and for long England's chief naval base, it is still an important naval port. Every corner is redolent of the sea. The great sight is Nelson's *Victory**, in dry dock near the entrance to the Royal Dockyard. St Thomas's Church is now Portsmouth Cathedral. E of the town is Southsea, a place with many holiday attractions, but few to match the view of the constant coming and going of ships of all kinds through the swiftly flowing harbour mouth – including submarines from the base in Fort Blockhouse on the Gosport side.

Ringwood (EB 10) EC Thurs (6,340). Market town at W edge of the New Forest. Fishing in the River Avon.

Rockbourne, 3½ m. NW of Fordingbridge (EB 11). Here the remains of a Roman villa were discovered under a cornfield (*see p. 82*).

Romsey (ED 12) EC Wed (6,230). An old-fashioned market town notable for its Abbey Church*, founded in the 10th cent., but mainly a Norman building with typically massive piers and many remarkable details. Note the Saxon crucifix in the S choir aisle – a relic of the nunnery of which the church was a part.

Ryde, I.O.W. (EF 09) (21,200). The largest of the Island's holiday resorts and the main port of entry with ferry and hovercraft services to the mainland. The pier is nearly half a mile long with sections for foot-passengers and cars, trains and trams. Quarr Abbey is nearby.

Sandown, I.O.W. (EF 08). A holiday resort with a zoo housed in the old fort. There is a geological museum at the public library. Behind the town lie the Island's main airport and principal golf-course (18 holes).

Selborne (EH 13). Quiet, unspoilt village made famous by Gilbert White (1720–93), the naturalist and writer who spent most of his life here. In the churchyard where he lies is a magnificent yew. 'The Wakes', the house in which he lived, is now a museum, and the NT owns some 240 acres on Selborne Hill, where he observed and recorded much of the material for *The Natural History of Selborne*.

Shalfleet, I.O.W. (EE 08). The squat rectangular tower of the church is so wide as to be almost a cube. The walls are 5 ft. thick, and it may have originated as a place of refuge. Note Norman carving over inner doorway.

Shanklin, I.O.W. (EF 08) EC Wed 14,250). The wooded Chine and the

93

Old Village with its thatched cottages distinguish this resort from others on the Island. Good sands and a cliff lift. South towards **Ventnor** (*see below*) the downs rise to nearly 800 ft.

Shorwell, I.O.W. (EE 08). Attractive village among the downs. Over N door of church is a good 15th-cent. wall painting of St Christopher. Note Elizabethan pulpit, brasses, and the chained Cranmer and Vinegar Bibles.

Silchester* (EG 16). The high Roman walls of the Roman town *Calleva Atrobatum* still stand – over a mile in circumference – but of the town they once enclosed there is now no sign. Its ruins were excavated, and the important finds removed for safe keeping in Reading Museum.

Southampton* (EE 11) EC Wed (204,700). An ancient town that is now Britain's chief terminal port for Transatlantic traffic and many other routes besides. The largest liners afloat can use the Ocean Terminal (for permits to go aboard apply at Dock Office); smaller vessels conduct sightseers round the harbour. Southampton is favoured by a double tide arising from its position opposite the Isle of Wight. Consequent on war damage there is much that is new; but stretches of the medieval wall remain, also the 14th-cent. Bar Gate, the Norman House, the Wool House and many other ancient buildings. From West Quay in 1620 the Pilgrim Fathers set sail for Plymouth in the *Mayflower*, on the first stage of their voyage to America.

Southampton Docks

Aerofilms

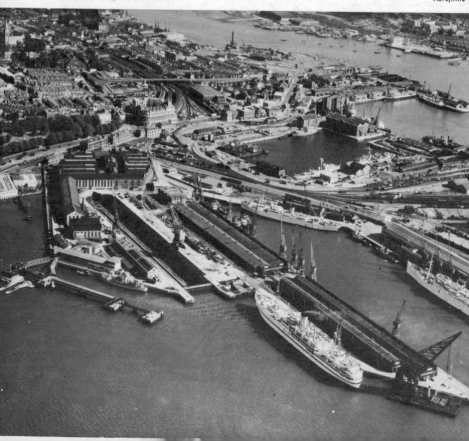

Steventon (EF 14). The village in which Jane Austen was born in 1775. Unfortunately nothing remains of the rectory in which she spent her first 26 years and where she wrote *Pride and Prejudice* and *Northanger Abbey*.

Stockbridge (ED 13). Noted for the trout fishing in the River Test.

Stratfield Saye (EG 16). The mansion and estate were given by the nation to the Duke of Wellington in gratitude for the victory at Waterloo. The lofty monument on Heckfield Heath at the entrance to the park is capped by a statue by Marochetti.

Tichborne, 2 m. S of New Alresford (EF 13). The ancient ceremony of the annual dole is still observed in early spring. The Tichborne Claimant trial was a famous law case in 1871.

Titchfield (EF 10) EC Wed (2,950). Taking materials from the 13th-cent. church of an abbey dispossessed at the Dissolution, the Earl of Southampton in the 16th cent. built the huge Tudor mansion called Place House. For a portrait of him see the monument in the church. The remains of Titchfield Abbey are in the care of the Ministry of Works.

Ventnor, I.O.W. (EF 07) EC Wed (6,250). A terraced resort with a Victorian and Edwardian flavour, built at the foot of the steep slopes of St Boniface Down*, which rises behind it to 785 ft., the highest point in the Isle of Wight. Good winter climate; pier, sands. Eastward is Bonchurch, where A. C. Swinburne (1837–1909) is buried; beyond is the Landslip, a tumbled mass of chalk and limestone through which the road makes a picturesque way.

The Norman church at Bonchurch near Ventnor   *Reece Winstone*

Winchester** (EE 12) EC Thurs (28,650). Parliaments have met here regularly, kings have been crowned and kings buried. For long the city was the kingdom's joint capital with London. Winchester has had a cathedral since the 7th cent.; curfew has rung nightly since the time of William the Conqueror. Recent excavations have produced new evidence of 2nd-cent. Roman Winchester and of the Saxon forerunners of the present inspired Cathedral built by the Normans. The remains of Canute are among those in the mortuary chests on the screens enclosing the choir of the cathedral. Among more modern graves are those of Izaak Walton and Jane Austen. Graceful ironwork abounds throughout this most beautiful of all English cathedrals. Note well the chantry of William of Wykeham to whom the splendid nave is due, as also Winchester College and New College, Oxford. Of Winchester's historic castle only the Great Hall remains; the so-called Round Table of King Arthur may date from the 13th cent. (it was already ancient in the time of Henry VIII, when it was repainted in the Tudor colours of green and white). The endowment of St Cross Hospital or almshouses (c. 1133) provides for a 'wayfarers'

dole' of bread and beer to all comers – so long as the daily ration lasts.

Yarmouth, I.O.W. (ED 08). Southern terminal of the car-carrying ferry from Lymington; its harbour a popular sailing centre. A busy little place with an air of the past. Remains of a Henry VIII castle (AM); a quaint little town hall rebuilt 1763 and a church with a curious statue whose body represents Louis XIV of France and the head Sir Robert Holmes (d. 1692), who captured New York from the Dutch.

Tombstone in the precincts of Winchester Cathedral   Reece Winstone

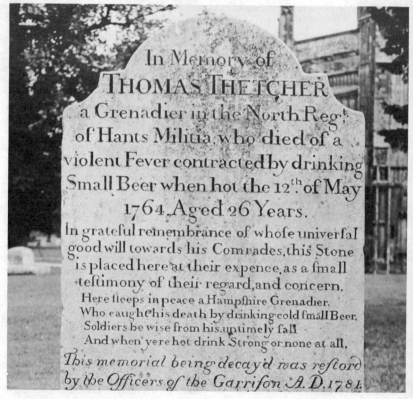

Opposite: Detail from the original painting by Keith Shackleton.
The tidal creeks of the Solent, with New Forest oak to hand, are ancient centres of shipbuilding. Inland Winchester was England's joint capital with London when, in Winchester Cathedral, William the Conqueror was crowned a second time. Not far away, the stone curlew haunts the chalk hills that give rise to some of the finest trout-streams in Britain.

Ockwells Manor, near Bray

Geoffrey Boumphrey

BERKSHIRE

AN INTRODUCTION BY GEOFFREY BOUMPHREY

The Royal County of Berkshire may be likened in shape to an old boot, with its toe at Windsor (hence the 'Royal') conveniently poised for kicking Middlesex and London well out into the North Sea. I see it as a football boot; for the toecap is heavily reinforced, rising up in a bulge as it follows the Thames upstream through Maidenhead and Henley before dipping southwards to Reading. There the laces start, and the river boundary curves gently northwards through Streatley, Wallingford and Abingdon to Oxford, where we may tie the laces. Round the ankle to Lechlade we still follow the river; and in the low ridge of hills running parallel to us in the south, from Boars Hill to Faringdon, is found the only building stone in Berkshire – a circumstance that has done much to determine the general appearance of the county. South of this ridge and parallel to it stretches the Vale of White Horse. Here the soil is good arable clay, with some gravels, the dead flat of the vale pleasantly relieved by lines of innumerable willows and whitebeams, with occasional church spires sticking up almost in Dutch fashion – country of a platinum sheen for three parts of the year, even though the mist broods over it at times in the fourth.

Now follow the back of the boot roughly southwards, rising to more than 700 feet above sea-level on the Downs, losing height to cross the Kennet Valley at

---

Opposite: Detail from the original painting by Barbara Jones.
The poet Matthew Arnold was inspired to write of Berkshire; its Thames-side meadows and rolling downs, overlooked by Windsor Castle, are now used as gallops for racehorses in training. Other notable persons are remembered in the effigies of Aldworth's downland church. Reading is noted for its biscuits.

Hungerford, and then climbing to almost a thousand feet at Inkpen Beacon and Walbury Camp, the highest chalk downs in England. Combe Gibbet still stands near by – what a marvellous view must have been his last for many a poor devil, doomed to dangle from the gibbet till he rotted away! But at this point our boot has oddly developed a stiletto heel: the county boundary turns north again to find the Kennet Valley south-west of Newbury, and then proceeds due east (with a break at the instep to pass north of the old Roman-British tribal town at Silchester) to Sandhurst. From here, on its way past Ascot and across Windsor Great Park to complete our circuit, it passes over the most infertile stretch of soil in Berkshire, poor sands or gravel, capable of growing little but silver birch and bracken.

In this part, man (rich man especially) has done much to improve upon Nature. Virginia Water was made for the Duke of Cumberland in the middle of the 18th century; and an artificial landscape of great beauty was created round the lake by the planting of carefully considered clumps of beeches, oaks and other trees. A little later George IV, while Prince of Wales, did much to improve Windsor Great Park, and had many thousands of conifers planted on the waste land near Sunninghill and Ascot. From the late 18th century onwards many grand mansions were built in the district, their gardens elaborately landscaped. With the coming of the railways more and more rich people built houses in the 'toe' of Berkshire, so near to London and the land of so little use for anything else, and therefore (at that time) so cheap. Mention the racecourse at Ascot laid out for Queen Anne in 1711, with later golf-courses and country clubs – and the description will serve well enough for the present day. A more recent addition is the creation of the Savill Gardens in Windsor Great Park, not far from Virginia Water, which draw keen gardeners like a magnet.

Let us now return to Sandhurst with its Royal Military Academy and retrace our attention due westwards along the sole of the boot. At Aldermaston the Kennet Valley from Reading joins us; with it the Bath road and the main line from Paddington to Taunton. The Bath road: what memories the words conjure up! – of nobility and gentry making their slow way by coach or carriage to the Bath of Beau Nash and Jane Austen – and of highwaymen on Maidenhead thicket. Nowadays the sprawl of factories and new housing beside it reaches almost to Newbury. To the south of the river, broad stretches of heather and bracken or extensive pinewoods tell of poor, acid soil. But by the side of the stream the water-meadows are lush, and rising from the north bank towards the Downs are clays which, if not ideal farming land, can be fertile enough, though even here tracts of bracken tell of the sand beneath. North-eastwards from Newbury the hills are covered with lovely dingled woods which persist until the land drops steeply down to Pangbourne and Streatley.

The River

We have taken a short cut across the instep of our boot and have come back to the Thames, which we left at Windsor, the toe. It is along this stretch between Streatley and Pangbourne that the Chiltern Hills of Oxfordshire most nearly approach their fellow chalk of the Berkshire Downs. The Goring Gap, as it is called, is a most beautiful stretch of river – quiet meadows with poplars and willows by the river, and the woods on the Berkshire side rising almost precipitously 600 feet to the Downs, balanced by their Oxfordshire fellows. But the river valley is almost uninterruptedly lovely all the way down to Windsor, if you

except an odd half mile or so past Reading. And so, for the most part, are the villages along it – Sonning, Wargrave, Hurley, Cookham (where the new Stanley Spencer Gallery is well worth a visit), Bray, and the rest. Riverside architecture of the turn of the century is in a taste which I, personally, have not acquired; but where the houses may not be thought beautiful, the settings almost always are. It was along these tree-hung reaches that fashionable Victorian and Edwardian society used to take its pleasure at summer weekends, the men in flannel blazers and straw boaters, the ladies in more elaborate creations. Today the river is still busy enough, though the screw-propeller has largely replaced the oar, the paddle and the punt pole.

In our quick tour I have left the best of Berkshire to the last. Streatley may be held to mark the end of the 'commuter's range': beyond this point a daily journey to London and back is too daunting for most people. North and west of the Goring Gap the county is, in general, peopled by those whose business and interests are local, and is spared the daily leeching which enfeebles all dormitory areas. The little riverside towns of Wallingford and Abingdon managed to keep clear of the Paddington-Oxford line when the railway followed the river and road through the Gap, and so they were spared most of the horrors of industrial development. They remain today friendly country towns full of beautiful buildings from bygone centuries – especially Abingdon, which suffered less from the ravages of old wars. I know of no lovelier town in Britain, though many of its beauties lie hidden at least five minutes away from the main streets.

The Downs

For me the peculiar charm of north Berkshire lies in the contrast between the lushness of the river valley and the austere beauty of the Downs. Along the northern crest of these runs a road as old as any in Britain, the Berkshire Ridgeway, making for Avebury and Stonehenge (though their ancient monuments had not been reared when early Britons first trod its turf). Thyme-scented, lark-haunted, it can still be followed, a hundred yards and more wide in places, right across the county from Streatley to Ashbury – a twenty-mile walk or ride that takes one as near to heaven as seems likely on this earth. For the motorist I would recommend as the most beautiful road in the county the one that runs north of and parallel to the Ridgeway, along the foot of the Downs – especially the section westwards from Wantage. The modelling of the little green valleys round which the road twists and turns in miniature alpine fashion is quite perfect. Northwards you look right across the breadth of the Vale of White Horse to the hills beyond, and, on the nearer side, to the thatched roofs of farms and villages half-hidden by trees. The climax of both scenery and interest is reached at the White Horse itself, believed to date from about 100 B.C. Here you can drive your car almost to the top; and it is imperative that you park it and climb to the summit of 856 feet. Below you is the huge ribbed bowl of the Manger, and the flat-topped Dragon Hill on which St George is said to have fought and killed the monster; as proof, you can still see that no grass grows where its blood once trickled down. The Horse itself is better seen from the Vale below (though if you care to walk across and stand on its eye, it should bring you luck); but while you are up here you must look southwards and get a just idea of the vastness and beauty of the Downs. To confirm this, on regaining the road follow it westwards for a couple of miles to Ashbury and then turn left for Lambourn. From this townlet, whose main business is racehorses (like many

White Horse, near Uffington   *Aerofilms*

villages on and around the Downs), follow the road beside the little River
Lambourn to Great Shefford, where you can either turn north for Wantage or,
forking right through Farnborough, the Ilsleys, Compton and Aldworth, make
your way back to Streatley. In either case, you will have tasted the full flavour
of the Berkshire Downs.

History

If history is mostly a tale of wars, as it seemed to be when I was at school, then
Berkshire has seen plenty of it. Passing over earlier evidence of warfare in the
shape of bronze spear-heads, shields and leaf-shaped swords dredged out of
the Thames or its gravel, we find a statue of Alfred the Great dominating the
market square of Wantage, his birthplace; it was on the Berkshire Downs that
he defeated the Danes at the famous battle of Assendun – one of the turning
points of our national history. It should be read about in Chesterton's *Ballad of
the White Horse*. After the battle of Hastings, William the Conqueror marched
as far as Wallingford in order to cross the Thames and descend on London.
He provided the county with castles at Windsor, Reading, Wallingford and
Newbury. In Henry I's reign others were built at Faringdon and Brightwell:
this last was obliterated by Stephen, who also largely destroyed that at Newbury.
Subsequent troubled times resulted in battles near Faringdon and on Maidenhead Bridge. Of the Civil War it is enough to say that Berkshire lay between
the Parliamentarians, based on London, and the Royalists who held Oxfordshire. Long before this the Reformation had put paid to the abbeys of Abingdon
and Reading. Their ruins today are not very impressive. All things considered,
need we wonder at Berkshire's lack of castles (only Windsor and a ruined
gateway at Newbury), of cathedrals (here St George's Chapel, Windsor, must
serve) and indeed of any great medieval buildings (one vast tithe-barn of stone
at Great Coxwell, a few large churches, such as Uffington, Lambourn and
Faringdon, and a dream of an Elizabethan manor-house, Ockwells, near
Bray).

Building Materials

One other factor I have already mentioned: the absence of building stone in
Berkshire, apart from the one narrow ridge across the extreme north of the county.
Faringdon is its only town built in stone, a warm grey limestone. Berkshire is
mainly a county of brick buildings. But to see what the 17th and 18th centuries
could do with brick you have only to note the warm and intimate beauty of little
towns like Hungerford and Newbury, Abingdon and Wallingford. In the villages,
farms and scattered cottages, other local materials are put to fitting and almost
always picturesque use: thatch in place of lichen-gilded tiles; chalk, either cob
or block, for walls, combined perhaps with a few sarsen stones brought from
the Downs where the Ice Age left them stranded; flints, dressed or not, with
mellow brick, maybe, round doors and windows; timber-framed buildings, their
panels filled in with almost any combination of these materials or with wattle-
and-daub. Imagine villages built of such homely materials, set low in the fold of
some valley by a willow-hung stream with watercress beds. Add a thatched wall
or two – its chalk laced, quite possibly, with the horns of oxen that once tilled
the fields around. This is the kind of scene you may come upon in almost any
part of Berkshire once you leave the main roads.

Farm and Factory

Eighty-five per cent of the county is still grass, farm or woodland, though industry has spread and is spreading. Reading makes biscuits, beer and boats, among other activities; Abingdon succeeds in concealing a large motor-car factory. There was a time in the Middle Ages when the Berkshire Downs and the Cotswolds supplied most of the wool on which England's wealth was founded; and the county grew fat on the various processes concerned with turning it into cloth. Today one sees more arable farming than sheep on the Downs. When the gold of the harvest has been erased by the plough, the fields are still no less beautiful, the soil shading in colour from coffee to cream as the chalk lies deeper or less deep. Harwell was famous for cherries long before atomic energy was thought of: a strip of greensand running along the northern foot of the Downs still supports many broad orchards, mainly of cherry or plum. In the Vale of the White Horse cheesemaking is added to general and dairy farming. Hop-fields are to be seen only at Kingston Bagpuize. The importance of pig-keeping to the county is proved by the fame of the snub-nosed, black Berkshire breed. Racehorses I have mentioned: their training is a major industry. All over the Downs you may come across their 'gallops', neatly marked out, and (if you and your car are not in a hurry) very beautiful a string of them can look on their way to or from exercise.

Wild Flowers

On the Downs, too, you may find the rare purple Pasque-flower (*anemone pulsatilla*) – almost half an acre of it in one place near Lowbury Camp. If there is truth in the local belief that it grows wild only 'where Danish blood was shed', perhaps this marks the true site of the battle of Assendun. Another wild flower in which Berkshire claims a priority interest is the tall snowdrop-like 'Loddon Lily', so called because it can be found in early summer beside the River Loddon. By this stream lies Swallowfield, on the Reading–Basingstoke road, where the authoress Mary Mitford is buried. If you would learn what life in the county was like a hundred and fifty years ago, read *Our Village*. Then browse through the first few chapters of *Tom Brown's Schooldays* – but, above all, read Thomas Hughes' other book, *The Scouring of the White Horse*. I should be very happy to think that my own picture of Berkshire today was half as vivid as theirs of yesterday.

Some houses and gardens open to the public

Ashdown House N of Lambourn *Map ED 17. 17th-cent. hunting-box, built of chalk blocks with stone quoins, roof crowned by cupola. Great staircase.* NT. *Open May–Sep Wed & 1st & 3rd Sat 2–6. 1/6.*

Buscot *Map EC 19. Adam-style late 18th-cent. house with later alterations. Paintings by Rembrandt, Murillo, Reynolds, etc., and furniture.* NT. *Open Apr–Sep 1st & 2nd Sat & following Sun 2–6. 2/6.*

Charney Manor *Map ED 19. Built about 1260, probably the earliest open-plan manor-house still extant. Walled garden with rare shrubs.* Managed by Society of Friends as a guest house, private guests, conferences, meals by arrangement.

Milton Manor House *Map EE 19. Early 17th-cent. manor-house, believed designed by Inigo Jones. Gothick library and chapel, also*

Georgian wing, added in 18th cent. Wooded park, walled garden. Surgeon Capt. E. J. Mockler. *Open May–Sep Sat Sun & Bk Hols 2.30–6. 2/6, 1/– child.*

The Savill Gardens Windsor Great Park *Map EK 17. Beautiful woodland gardens, with streams and ponds and fine collection of rhododendrons, azaleas, primulas, etc. Extensive herbaceous borders, rose garden and other features.* Crown Estate Commissioners. *Open Mar–Oct daily 10–6. 2/–, 1/– child.*

Windsor Castle *Map EK 17. Largest inhabited castle in the world. See p. 112.* Residence of H.M. The Queen. *Castle precincts open daily all year round 10–sunset. Admission free. State Apartments open* (exc. when Her Majesty is in residence) *Mon–Sat Apr May Oct 11–4, Jun–Sep 11–5, Nov–Mar 11–3; also Sun May–Sep 1.30–5, Oct 1–4. 1/6, 6d. child. State Apartments also include: Queen's Doll's House, 6d.; The Old Master Drawings, 6d.*

Books for further reading

Bygone Berkshire – fact and fiction

THOMAS HARDY *Jude the Obscure*
THOMAS HUGHES *The Scouring of the White Horse; Tom Brown's Schooldays*
E. A. G. LAMBOURN *History of Berkshire* 1909
MARY RUSSELL MITFORD *Our Village*
H. PEAKE *The Archaeology of Berkshire* 1931
VICTORIA *History of the County of Berkshire* 4 vols and index 1906–27
J. E. VINCENT *Highways and Byways in Berkshire* 1906

Towns and Buildings

T. E. HARWOOD *Windsor Old and New* 1929
J. K. HEDGES *The History of Wallingford* 2 vols 1881
M. HINTON *A History of the Town of Reading* 1954
MARY RUSSELL MITFORD *Belford Regis* (Reading) 1835 etc.
WALTER MONEY *The History of Newbury* 1887
SIR OWEN MORSHEAD *Windsor Castle* 1951
N. PEVSNER *Berkshire* (Buildings of England series) 1966
W. W. SKEAT *The Place-names of Berkshire* 1911
J. TOWNSEND *A History of Abingdon* 1910
J. W. WALKER *A History of Maidenhead* 1931

Depicting the Royal County

J. H. BAKER *Land of the Gap* 1937
R. P. BECKINSALE *Companion into Berkshire* 1950
JOHN BETJEMAN and JOHN PIPER *Berkshire: architectural guide* 1949
H. J. M. BOWEN *The Flora of Berkshire* 1968
F. G. BRABANT *Berkshire* (Little Guides) 1934
G. C. DRUCE *The Flora of Berkshire* 1897
J. R. A. HOCKIN *On Foot in Berkshire* 1934
ARTHUR MEE *Berkshire* (King's England series) 1964
N. H. PIZER *A Survey of the Soils of Berkshire* 1931
M. C. RADFORD *The Birds of Berkshire and Oxfordshire* 1966
F. S. THACKER *Kennet Country* 1932
IAN YARROW *Berkshire* (County Books) 1952

Sweet Thames

ROBERT GIBBINGS *Sweet Thames Run Softly* 1941; *Till I End My Song* 1957
ERIC DE MARE *Time on the Thames* 1952
L. R. MUNK *The Thames: An Eating, Drinking and Cruising Guide* 1967
J. H. B. PEEL *Portrait of the Thames from Teddington to the Source* 1967
R. PILKINGTON *Small Boat on the Thames* 1966
F. S. THACKER *The Thames Highway: . . . inland navigation* 1968, *. . . locks and weirs* 1968

Gazetteer

BERKSHIRE

Abingdon* (EE 19) EC Thurs (16,770). The perfect approach is on the A415 from Dorchester – just meadows, the old bridge with boathouses, and across the river the tall spire of St Helen's Church drawing the old town round it. Abingdon is so full of good things that they can only be listed: the superb Charles II County Hall; St Helen's and St Nicholas' Churches, with the beautiful close at the W end of the former, bounded by almshouses of 1446, 1707 and 1797; the Prior's House (c. 1250) and the Guest House (c. 1400), their interiors now accurately restored; the Tompkins almshouses (1733) in Ock Street, and many other medieval to Georgian buildings. Of the Abbey church (AD 573) only fragments remain, but several of its secular buildings can still be seen.

Aldermaston (EF 16). The proximity of Britain's 6th atomic energy station has not yet spoilt this village of peace and quiet in the Kennet valley, with its pleasant brick and tiled cottages and its church with medieval wall paintings. It was here that the William pear was first grown. Near by is Ufton Court, a good Tudor gabled mansion with priests' holes.

Aldworth*, 2 m. W of Streatley (EF 17). Elizabeth I turned aside to view the effigied tombs of the de la Beche family under elaborate crocketed canopies in the church. Note also the magnificent yew in the churchyard.

Appleton (EE 20). The moated manor house includes portions dating back to King John. In the church see the monument to Sir John Fettiplace (1593). Note too the handsome brick and timber barn.

Ascot (EK 16) EC Wed (5,140). The most fashionable racecourse in Britain. 'Ascot Week' (June) is famous all over the world.

Avington (ED 16). Ignored by the traffic of the Bath Road, this little cedared hamlet, set by a Kennet weir 2 m. E of Hungerford is worth visiting for its unspoiled Norman church.

Bisham Abbey (EJ 18). Among lawns beside the Thames is the Elizabethan mansion now occupied by the Central Council of Physical Recreation. It was built by Sir Philip Hoby, whose family are commemorated by fine monuments in the adjoining church. Note steps in the river bank for those attending service by boat.

Blewbury (EF 18). Lovely downland village with good 17th–18th-cent. houses, gardens and orchards with thatched chalk walls. Memories of the miserly Rev. Morgan-Jones who figures in *Our Mutual Friend* as 'Blackberry Jones'.

Blowing Stone*, Kingston Lisle (ED 18). A perforated sarsen that used to stand on the Ridgeway. A strong and sustained blast down one of the holes can produce a horn-like note. Legend says that Alfred the Great used to sound it as an alarm to gather his chiefs against the Danes. He must have had exceptional lungs.

Bracknell (EJ 16) EC Wed (30,000). One of the New Towns on the A329 between Wokingham and Ascot, covering the former villages of Bracknell and Easthampstead. Begun in 1952, its goal is a community of 60,000 welded into the combination expressed in the Development Corporation's motto "Home, Industry, Leisure". Here are the Meteorological Office and the Royal Air Force Staff College.

Ufton Court, near Aldermaston

Bradfield, 3 m. SW of Pangbourne (EG 17). The Public School, founded in 1850 with an 18th-cent. manor house as nucleus, is famous for its open-air Greek theatre.

Bray, 1 m. S of Maidenhead (EJ 18) (4,860). Remembered for Simon Alleyn who would always be vicar 'whatsoever king may reign' rather than give up his living. Looking round the pleasant Thames-side village, we do not wonder. One and a half m. W is the beautiful Elizabethan Ockwells Manor, with its original window-glass.

Buckland (ED 19). Former home of the Throckmortons, designed by Wood, junior, of Bath in the 18th cent.

Buscot (EC 19). Here is the second lock on the Thames and a good stone village. The church has glass by Burne-Jones and a painted pulpit, but Buscot is best known as a great centre of agricultural experiment in the 19th cent. The house and grounds of Buscot Park are under the NT.

Combe (ED 16). Of all the odd clauses in a lease, surely the oddest is that of the farm given the responsibility of maintaining in good order the gallows

on the hill between Inkpen and Walbury Hill. (*See also p.* 98.)

Cookham*, 3 m. N of Maidenhead (EJ 18) (5,500). The river scenery is not excelled anywhere else on the Thames; the lock gardens are as gay as any. Cookham has been the home of many artists from Fred Walker to Stanley Spencer (whose Gallery is here). At Cookham Dean (2 m. W) Kenneth Grahame wrote *The Wind in the Willows.*

Cumnor* (EE 20). Scott's version (in *Kenilworth*) of the death of Amy Robsart departs somewhat from the facts, and in any case Cumnor Hall is no more. Cumnor Church, however, is worth seeing, especially the very fine spiral wooden staircase in the tower.

Donnington, 1 m. N of Newbury (EE 16). Remains of a 14th-cent. castle (AM) which withstood two sieges during the Civil War.

East Hendred, 4 m. E of Wantage (EE 18). An unusually beautiful and well-kept village of 16th- and 17th-cent. cottages, timber-framed and brick or chalk. It has a disused 15th-cent. stone chapel or shrine, with the Priest's House of the same date near by. The church has one of the earliest clocks (1525) still in use. To compensate for the lack of face and hands, this strikes all the quarters and, on occasion, plays a hymn.

East Ilsley (EE 18). Famous for training racehorses, strings of which may be seen on the downs. Before horses Ilsley was deeply involved in sheep – it is said that as many as 80,000 were gathered in one day.

Faringdon (EC 19). EC Thurs (3,400). This remote little market-town has two claims to distinction. It is the only stone-built town in the county and it contains what is probably the last 'folly' to have been built in England – the stone tower built in 1936 among and overtopping the clump of firs on the hill known as Faringdon Folly. It is in the grounds of Faringdon House (1780) and is a landmark for many miles round.

Great Coxwell, 2 m. SW of Faring-don (EC 19). The cathedral-like tithe barn*, built by the monks of Beaulieu in the 14th cent., is considered by many the finest in England.

Harwell (EE 18). The A.E.R.E., Britain's first nuclear research station, is fortunately out of sight from this little village of cherry-orchards and picturesque old cottages. The church is noteworthy for a number of quaint and even comic 14th-cent. stone carvings.

Hungerford (ED 16) EC Thurs (3,400). Here the Kennet runs close beside the road. Hungerford treasures a horn alleged to have belonged to John of Gaunt; also some good Georgian buildings. The wide main street is fortunately well away from the busy Bath Road. A favourite centre for anglers. A picturesque ceremony is held every Hocktide (the first Tuesday after Easter) to elect the Constable in whom the government and manor of Hungerford are vested for the year. In this a bellman and two tutti-men (tithe-men) with decorated poles play a prominent part.

Great Coxwell: the tithe barn
Reece Winstone

Newbury: bridge over the River Kennet

Reece Winstone

Hurley (EJ 18). Here the Thames is divided by several islands and the backwaters are among the prettiest on the river. A picturesque 16th-cent. timbered inn, remains of a 13th-cent. monastery and a Norman or possibly pre-Conquest church (restored) are other attractions.

Lambourn (ED 17) EC Wed Thurs (2,700). Famous for its racehorse training stables. A little old town with a grand medieval church and some good buildings. At Seven Barrows, 2 m. N, are some twenty round barrows of various types and a chambered long barrow.

Long Wittenham, 2½ m. W of Dorchester (EF 19). An attractive village with an interesting church. The thatched Barley Mow inn by the river, at Clifton Hampden bridge, is associated with Jerome K. Jerome's *Three Men in a Boat*.

Maidenhead (EJ 18) EC Thurs (43,700). Busy residential town and popular boating centre, its 18th-cent. bridge now saved from through-traffic by the M4. Two miles upstream,

beyond Boulter's Lock, the famous house of Cliveden stands high above the river on the Buckinghamshire bank (NT).

Newbury (EE 16) EC Wed (21,980). A cheerful-looking old town with a narrow balustraded 18th-cent. bridge over the Kennet. Its importance as a cloth-making town was established in the 16th cent. by John Winchcombe (Jack O'Newbury), part of whose house still survives, as does his memorial brass in the tower of the church which he built. Newbury's prosperity has continued – as proved by the choice of charming 16th-, 17th- and 18th-cent. buildings still to be seen, including many almshouses. The ancient Cloth Hall, with overhanging upper storey, is now a museum. The racecourse is beautifully sited east of the town. Two m. S is Sandleford Priory (1781), built by James Wyatt for Mrs Elizabeth Montagu, the original 'blue-stocking'.

Padworth, 1 m. E of Aldermaston (EF 16). The little church here is almost pure Norman, the interior being 'overwhelmingly grand', despite its size.

Pangbourne (EG 17). A boating village where the Thames is joined by the Pang. Pangbourne College was founded in 1917 to train boys to become officers in the Merchant Service, but it is now a public school.

Radley, 2 m. NE of Abingdon (EE 19). The 18th-cent. mansion, Radley Hall, was the original nucleus of Radley College, the Public School founded in 1847. The little village church is sumptuously furnished with carved oak and contains wonderful heraldic glass of the 15th and 16th cent.

Reading (EH 17) EC Wed (126,380). At the junction of the Rivers Kennet and Thames. It is difficult to recognise in the bustling industrial town of today the Reading whose Abbey first echoed to the lovely sounds of 'sumer is icumen in', written by a monk in the 13th cent. and inscribed on a stone tablet in the Abbey chapter-house; the Abbey itself was so despoiled at the Dissolution that the few remains hardly help the imagination. Reading has played its part in history. Here Edward IV defied Warwick 'the Kingmaker' and announced his marriage to Elizabeth Woodville. It was the birthplace of Archbishop Laud (1593). Jane Austen went to school in the abbey gatehouse. Here the imprisoned Oscar Wilde wrote *De Profundis* and *The Ballad of Reading Gaol*. Nowadays Reading is known for its shops, its river interests, its biscuits and seeds and especially for its University, with considerable interest in agriculture. Life in Roman times is fascinatingly portrayed in Reading museum★ by the many objects found when Silchester (in near-by Hampshire) was excavated. Life in more recent days is admirably recorded in the Folk Museum in Whiteknights Park.

The Ridgeway. Men and cattle have walked this way along the top of the Berkshire Downs at least since the Bronze Age and it is still a glorious route, floored with resilient turf and with far-spreading views on each side. It crosses the county westwards from above the Goring Gap (EF 18), where

The Ridgeway, looking across the Goring Gap *Geoffrey Boumphrey*

tracks from three river-crossings unite, to near Ashbury (EC 18), from where, in Wiltshire, it turns southwards to Avebury, Stonehenge, and beyond. Every 9 or 10 m. (a convenient day's drive for cattle) are enclosures or camps: Lowbury Camp (Roman), Segsbury Camp and Uffington Castle (Iron Age), and others.

Sandhurst (EJ 16). In the Royal Military College here is to be found The National Army Museum.

Shottesbrooke, 3 m. SW of Maidenhead (EJ 18), has 'one of the most celebrated Decorated churches in the country'.

Sparsholt, 3 m. W of Wantage (ED 18). This little village is worth visiting for itself alone, as well as for the three 14th-cent. carved wooden effigies in the church.

Steventon (EE 19). A series of beautiful 17th-cent. houses (NT) of brick and plaster, all half-timbered, can be seen from the mile-long, roughly paved Causeway, as can the cooling towers and chimney of the new electricity generating station at Didcot.

Uffington (ED 18). A little village of chalk-and-thatch cottages, with a fine stately church dating from *c.* 1150. The village and district are well described in *Tom Brown's Schooldays.* *See* **White Horse** and **Wayland Smith's Cave.**

Wallingford (EG 18) EC Wed (5,870). A charming old riverside town, its best approach by the many-arched bridge from Oxfordshire. Its fine 17th-cent. Town Hall in the market square is raised on Tuscan pillars, and it has many beautiful Georgian buildings. But its history goes back still further (it has held a Charter for over eight centuries). Here, in 1066, William the Conqueror crossed the Thames to take London in the rear; here, to its castle, fled Queen Maud when she escaped from Oxford Castle one icy night in 1142. Wallingford, on the side of King Charles in the Civil War, was the last

Wayland Smith's Cave, near Uffington   Reece Winstone

town to surrender. Of these old times only ancient earthworks and a few fragments of the Castle remain today.

Wantage (ED 18) EC Thurs (7,660). The statue of King Alfred the Great in the market-place commemorates his birth here in 849.

Wayland Smith's Cave, nr Uffington (ED 18). Here if you leave your horse overnight, with a coin, legend tells that you will find it shod in the morning. The 'cave' is actually a cromlech, the exposed stones of a long barrow (recently restored). In Scandinavian mythology, Wayland the Smith has a white horse – and this barrow, most beautifully sited in a clump of beeches by the Ridgeway, is only 1 m. or so from the Uffington White Horse. But it is 1,000–2,000 years older (AM).

The White Horse* (ED 18). Probably the oldest and certainly the most famous of its kind, this gigantic figure (374 ft. from nose to tail) is carved out high up on the chalk flank of the downs near Uffington. Since at least the 12th cent. it has given its name to the broad vale it overlooks, and from time immemorial its periodic 'scouring' has been an occasion for local junketing, well described by Thomas Hughes in *The Scouring of the White Horse.* Its style – beaked muzzle and two legs completely detached – is far more impressive than any naturalistic representation could be, and the design is, in fact, very like one to be found on certain British coins of the late Iron Age. Possibly it represents the totem animal of a Celtic tribe living in Uffington Castle just above. The ribbed dry-valley just to the W is known as The Manger, and near-by stands the flat-topped Dragon Hill, on which St George is reputed to have slain the dragon (the Horse?). The White Horse and its surroundings are

Wytham   Reece Winstone

best seen when the sun is low in the sky (AM).

Wickham, 2 m. S of Great Shefford (ED 17). The late Saxons who built the tower of this flint church (largely for defence, it seems) would have been surprised to see that the roof of the N aisle is apparently supported by huge elephants' heads, coloured and gilded – an unusual feature in any English church. The whole interior is a perfect example of the early Victorian Gothic Revival.

Windsor (EK 17) EC Wed (29,920). Thames-side town dominated by the royal castle**, and with Eton close at hand on the other side of the bridge; in between, the river with its boats and swans. The town hall was completed by Wren, though he inserted the internal pillars (which do not in fact support the upper floor) against his will.

Kings and queens have lived in the

castle since the 11th cent. William the Conqueror founded it – but none of his original building survives, though the Round Tower crowns the original Norman mound. The present structure contains work of every age from medieval to the early 19th cent. St George's Chapel is a magnificent example of 15th-cent. work, ablaze with banners of the Knights of the Garter. Henry VI, Edward IV, Henry VIII, Charles I and all monarchs from George III to George VI are buried here. The State Apartments have valuable pictures, furniture and gifts and trophies presented to successive monarchs. In St George's Hall hang the banners and coats of arms of the Knights of the Garter since the Order was founded by Edward III in 1348. From the top of the Round Tower or Keep it is possible to see parts of 12 counties. The Home Park and the Great Park extend S as far as Virginia Water.

Old Windsor, about 1½ m. SE, was a seat of Saxon kings long before William the Conqueror appeared on the scene. Remains have been found of a building which may have been Edward the Confessor's palace.

Wokingham (EJ 16) EC Wed (17,980). Flourishing market-town on A329, 2 m. E of Reading. Attractive blending of old and new, with modern town centre surrounded by half-timbered cottages – and the curfew ringing at 8 o'clock in winter.

Wytham, 3 m. NW of Oxford (EE 20). A charming Oxfordshire-style stone village looking across river-meadows to Godstow Nunnery and sheltered from the W by rising woods. The E window in the church is said to have come from the chamber in Cumnor Place, now demolished, in which Amy Robsart spent her last night.

Dragon Hill, below the White Horse

Geoffrey Boumphrey

The Seven Sisters

SUSSEX

AN INTRODUCTION BY CLIFFORD MUSGRAVE

The fame of Sussex owes much to one distinctive kind of scenery: the South Downs with their whale-back shapes, grass-covered slopes and exhilarating air. Yet these Downs are but the backbone of a county that in a length of some seventy miles, with a width of twenty to thirty, possesses a variety of scenery that must satisfy every type of personality or mood. The county is no less rich and diverse in its wealth of historical associations, and in its splendid heritage of the works of man, as seen in its towns and buildings. Sussex offers not only the delights of numerous small ancient towns and villages, but also the glittering attractions of large modern resorts, culminating in the cosmopolitan sophistication of a town where a legendary monarch created a fabulous pleasure-palace.

The Structure of Sussex

As elsewhere in Britain, the rapid changes of geological formation that occur within a small distance give the county its delightful variety of scenery. Three principal formations, the chalk, the sands and the clay, create the distinctive character of Sussex. The great rampart of the Downs is but a remnant of the immense dome of chalk, 3,000 feet high, that was formed ages ago when primeval cataclysms thrust upwards the floor of the ocean. Cracks occurred in the chalk dome, and the broken surface was carved and washed away by glaciers and rain, until nothing remained but the broken edges of the dome, forming the

113

North and South Downs. Rivers cut their way from north to south through cracked furrows, dividing the Downs into six great blocks of land.

Between the sea and the Downs, where they enter the county westwards beyond Chichester, lies a triangular section of coastal plain forming rich horticultural land. As the line of the Downs approaches the sea closer and closer eastwards, this coastal plain narrows to a strip. From the beaches of Brighton onwards, the Downs break into tall cliffs that dip and rise until they reach their climax in the breath-taking height of 536 feet at Beachy Head. Beyond, the land falls into the broad sandy levels of Pevensey, out of which rise the little medieval towns of Rye and Winchelsea near the borders of Kent.

Across the north-eastern part of the county stretches the Forest Ridge, a range of the sandstone and gravel of the Wealden sand or Hastings Beds, so called because this formation reaches the sea at that place. Beginning near Horsham, it comprises the dense woods of St Leonards Forest and Ashdown Forest, and the bare uplands where the ridge reaches its maximum height at Crowborough Beacon (792 feet). A second wooded ridge runs across the county farther south through delightful old towns and villages such as Cuckfield, Lindfield, Fletching, and Heathfield, and through Burwash, the centre of the ancient iron industry of Sussex. Between the chalk downs and the sandstone ridges lies the Weald, the ancient inland forest of Sussex where once great oak trees grew so thickly that they were called 'the Sussex weed'. These broad expanses of rich clay pastureland are diversified by low hills of sandstone and gravel, outcrops of the Forest Ridge. Westwards beyond Petworth are other sandy hills covered with pine, fir and silver birch, and bracken-clothed heathland, rising to 918 feet at Blackdown, near the Surrey border, the highest point in Sussex.

Ancient Sussex

In prehistoric times the dense forests of the Weald left only the shores of Sussex and the open hilltops free for human habitation. On the principal summits of the Downs are still to be seen the remains of the hill camps that were built in a chain throughout the county by the Bronze Age farming people of the 'Windmill Hill' culture about 2,000 years BC. In the Iron Age they were fortified, and eventually became a final defence against the Romans.

The largest and finest of the hill camps is at Cissbury, near Worthing, which was a centre of the Neolithic flint industry supplied by the flint mines within the camp boundary. Other surviving works of ancient man in Sussex are the round barrows, long barrows and cultivation terraces, and the downland trackways that stretch from the coast westwards inland towards Stonehenge. One of the principal Roman roads of England, the Stane Street, runs through Sussex from *Regnum* (Chichester) to London over Bignor Hill, near which lies one of the finest Roman villas in the country, Bignor Villa, with its wonderful mosaic pavements of Medusa, Venus and the Four Seasons. The Roman Palace at Fishbourne, near Chichester, is a recent discovery worth visiting. Found accidentally in 1960, the site has been uncovered and purchased by the Sussex Archaeological Society and was opened to the public in the summer of 1968.

The Romans and Romanized Britons were the first to push back the Wealden forests from the foot of the Downs; but it was the Saxons who made great clearings in the woodlands and drained the land for cultivation. When the Normans came, they used the great natural divisions of the county as the basis

J. Allan Cash **Looking down on the Lighthouse from Beachy He**

for parcelling out Sussex into six areas of government, the six 'Rapes', each with its strip of coastland, a portion of downland for grazing flocks and herds, a river, a stretch of cleared and cultivated Wealden land, and on the north an area of wild forest for hunting and for the feeding of hogs. Each of the Rapes – Chichester, Arundel, Bramber, Lewes, Pevensey and Hastings – was dominated by its castle, not only for protection, but also to hold the country in subjection.

Pevensey Castle, first built by the Romans to protect Sussex against the Saxons, and later enlarged and strengthened by the Normans, still stands to remind us that after the departure of the Romans the last of the Britons perished there when the Saxons overran Sussex. Not far away, at Battle, the Saxon Kingdom itself under Harold was destroyed by William the Conqueror.

Arundel Castle, with its Norman gates, barbican and keep, second only to Windsor in the romanticism of its castellated skyline, is the greatest of Sussex castles. Bodiam, standing foursquare in its lily-covered moat, is of the 14th century. Herstmonceux was one of the first great castellated houses of brick. Lewes Castle commemorates Simon de Montfort's victory there that gave us the beginnings of Parliament.

In the 14th century some prosperity came to Sussex from the sheep-farming that flourished on the downland grass, and this is reflected in the richness of the improvements that were made to many of the Sussex churches at this time, endowing them with the elaborate tracery in the stone-carving of windows and towers of the Decorated period of Gothic. Because of this new wealth, also, several of the ancient Saxon manors were developed into great estates in Tudor times, as at Parham in the west and Firle in the east. Medieval piety brought European culture and fine ecclesiastical foundations to Sussex. Battle Abbey, with its beautiful 14th-century gatehouse, commemorates the Battle of Hastings; Michelham Priory, moated on an island in meadows near Hailsham, shows us with its ancient buildings and restored rooms the life of an Augustinian priory. Medieval wall-paintings in the churches of West Chiltington and Hardham still testify to the arts of painting that were disseminated with other learning and culture through Sussex from the great Cluniac priory at Lewes, which was founded by the Conqueror's sister Gundrada and destroyed by Henry VIII. Bayham Abbey and Boxgrove Priory have impressive remains of similar religious establishments; Wilmington Priory is on a smaller scale.

Hundreds of fascinating village churches and the austerely magnificent Chichester Cathedral, with its ancient Saxon stone-carvings, tell us of past religious life, and continue into our own day the Christian tradition that was brought to Sussex, not from Canterbury by St Augustine, but from the sea by the wandering Bishop Wilfrid, who taught the starving pagan South Saxons the art of fishing.

Industries Ancient and New

Museums at Brighton, Hastings, Worthing and Lewes preserve many remarkable treasures of past ages, together with relics of the bygone agricultural and social life of the county. They are rich in examples of the Sussex ironwork that was the chief industry of the county from Roman times until 1823. The first English cannon was cast at Buxted in 1543; but the most enduring traces of this vast industry are to be found in the names that commemorate the iron-workings – Iron Hill, Smoke Alley, Furnace Wood and Mine-Pit Copse.

Bodiam Castle Aerofilms

Although the shape of Sussex has been worked almost entirely by natural forces, the hand of man has played no little part in giving the landscape its character. The eastern part is far less densely wooded than the western, and this is to some extent due to the destruction of the woodlands of the forest ridge to feed the iron-smelting furnaces.

The contrast between the primitive and the sophisticated still persists in Sussex industries. Such ancient crafts as the making of wattle-fencing and trug-baskets, those long shallow baskets of bentwood, are still carried on in the villages. An old craft that has developed with the times is that of the blacksmith, whose work of shoeing horses has now almost completely vanished. Instead he has turned to the making of decorative ironwork for garden gates, sign-brackets, balcony and staircase railings, and even iron jewellery on a tiny, delicate scale. Around the principal towns, highly advanced modern electrical, electronic, engineering and other light industries have become established, while inland the new town of Crawley is a vast centre of modern industries, with a huge population of new residents flowing out into the neighbouring countryside and towns for recreation, shopping and entertainment.

Around the western harbour towns, boat-building reflects the world-wide boom in this industry. Shoreham harbour has been enormously improved in recent years and is visited every day by cargo boats from Holland, Scandinavia, Germany and Russia, chiefly carrying timber and vegetables. Newhaven remains an important cross-Channel port.

Sussex for the Naturalist

Strange as it may seem, the open Downs and the seashore offer a greater variety of plant-life than the Forest Ridges on the Weald. The extremely rare spiked rampion is possibly the only British plant belonging specially to Sussex, and it is found in parts of the forest land. Other rare plants of this region are the Cornish

117

money-wort, the slender cicendia and the wood forget-me-not. The Downs are chiefly remarkable for many species of the orchis family, including the great and lesser butterfly, the tway-blade, the bird's-nest, the bee, fly, spider, green-man, and the small white orchid. Perhaps the prettiest flower of the downland is the dark blue round-headed rampion, often called 'the Pride of Sussex'.

In the coastal regions grow sea-pinks, sea-poppies, and various different vetches, especially the yellow vetch and the starry-headed trefoil.

Sussex is a paradise for the bird-watcher, particularly because many lines of migration pass through the county. The merlin and the hobby are to be seen along the coast. The gulls include the common gull, black-headed, herring, and greater black-backed gull, and the cormorant is not unknown. The whimbrel, oyster-catcher, plovers and terns frequent the beaches. Occasionally the golden oriole is seen in the Weald, and herons are fairly common on the rivers. Among the butterflies the adonis blue, marbled white and clouded yellow are frequently seen in sheltered valleys of the downland. Seals have frequented the shore from early times and are still to be seen, and schools of porpoises disporting themselves off the beach are an entertaining sight.

Gourmet's Delight

The delicacy for which Sussex has been most widely renowned, Southdown mutton, has been little heard of since the Southdown sheep were taken away from the Downs at the beginning of the last war, when Sussex was threatened with invasion. Later these immemorial grazing grounds were ploughed for cultivation. The rich meadows of the Weald produce wonderful butter, an excellent but not widely known cheese, and honey. Sea foods are now the most distinctive regional fare. Lobsters are plentiful at many places along the coast, and fresh south-coast plaice rival the best Dover soles. Locally caught shrimps, whelks and cockles have for years been symbolic of the delights of the cockney day-tripper's excursions to the sea.

Sussex Houses

As in so many other respects, Sussex is rich in the variety and beauty of its houses, ranging from the small manor houses of the Middle Ages like Brede and Great Dixter, to fine Elizabethan houses like Glynde Place, Parham Park and Danny Park, and to the great houses of the years of William and Mary and the Georges: Uppark with its gloriously decorated rooms and furniture of

several successive periods of style; noble Petworth with its paintings by Turner and carved room by Grinling Gibbons; Firle Place near Lewes, a splendid gem of Georgian decoration, with fine pictures and furniture; and at Brighton a past royal residence, the exotic Royal Pavilion, built by the Prince Regent in oriental

The Royal Pavilion, Brighton
Reece Winstone

style as a monument to Britain's connections with the Far East, and with its original decorations and furniture restored. In these houses are to be found some of the most splendid rooms in this country, and many works of art.

The Arts

As befits a county that was given urban sophistication by the patronage of an art-loving monarch, King George IV, the arts have always held a high place in the life of Sussex. Brighton's Theatre Royal is famous for the large number of successful plays it puts on before London production, and Chichester's revolutionary new Festival Theatre, a 'theatre-in-the-round', brings fresh vitality into the world of drama. The superb productions of opera, especially of Mozart, performed each year in the opera-house near Lewes make the name of Glyndebourne as famous as Salzburg and Bayreuth. The Dome at Brighton is the centre of the Brighton Philharmonic Orchestra, which presents a season of symphony concerts and recitals every year by its own members and by famous orchestras from all over the world.

The Art Galleries and Museums of Sussex are treasure-houses of works of art: Brighton with its collection of Old Master paintings and modern paintings, silver, porcelain, miniatures, jewellery, and the astonishing Willett Collection of pottery; Worthing and Hastings with their local collections and lively programmes of art exhibitions; Eastbourne, specializing in the work of modern artists. Almost all the towns, and especially Lewes, Chichester, Shoreham, Newhaven, Steyning and Battle, and even villages such as Rottingdean, have their art centres for exhibitions, concerts and discussions. As in so many other respects, in Sussex the arts have immense vitality and offer a wide range of interests to the visitor on an intimate and informal level as well as on a grand scale. Simplicity and sophistication, grandeur and intimacy, these are the qualities that enhance the life of Sussex no less than its scenery, and which ensure the enjoyment of a world of delight for all who visit the county.

Some houses and gardens open to the public

Arundel Castle Arundel *Map* FA 10. *See p. 121.* His Grace the Duke of Norfolk.

Bodiam Castle Bodiam *Map* FH 12. *See p. 122.* NT.

Charleston Manor Westdean, Seaford *Map* FE 09. *Ancient manor house of Norman, Tudor & Georgian construction. Tithe barn. Large gardens of romantic beauty.* Lady Birley.

Danny Hurstpierpoint *Map* FC 11. *Late Elizabethan house with notable Great Hall.* Mutual Households Association Ltd. *Open May–Sep Wed Thurs 2–4. 2/6, 1/– child.*

Field Place 2m W of Horsham *Map* FB 13. *Shelley's birthplace. Built c. 1325, with 1680 additions. Attractive garden.* Miss D. Charrington. *Garden only open.*

Glynde Place 4m SE of Lewes *Map* FE 11. *Early Elizabethan house, panelled Long Gallery, bronzes, portraits, documents, pottery.* Mrs Humphrey Brand.

Goodwood House 3½m NE of Chichester *Map* EJ 10. *Fine example of Sussex flintwork, built late 18th cent. Rich collection of paintings. French furniture, porcelain, tapestries. See also p. 124.* Goodwood Estate Co. Ltd. Closed during 1969 for alterations.

Great Dixter Northiam *Map* FJ 12. *Finely restored 15th-cent. half-timbered manor house, formal & informal gardens with a wide variety of plants.* Mrs Nathaniel Lloyd.

Leonardslee Lower Beeding 4½m SE of Horsham *Map* FC 12. *Valley garden with lakes, rhododendrons, azaleas, camellias, magnolias, etc.* Sir Giles Loder, Bt. *House not open.*

Michelham Priory 4m W of Hailsham *Map FF 10. Augustinian Priory founded 1229, surrounded by large moat. Unique & imposing gatehouse c. 1400. Tudor buildings, fine furniture, tapestries, ironwork, picture gallery.* Sussex Archaeological Trust.

Newtimber Place 2m S of Hurstpierpoint *Map FC 11, nr junction of A22 & A281. 17th-cent. house surrounded by water-filled moat at foot of Downs.* Trustees of the late Earl Buxton.

Nymans Gardens Handcross 4½m S of Crawley *Map FC 12. 30 acres of rare conifers, shrubs, magnolias, camellias, etc. Also 570 acres of woodland & farmland.* NT.

Parham nr Pulborough *Map FA 11. Splendid Elizabethan mansion with notable paintings, furniture & needlework.* Mrs P. A. Tritton.

Petworth House Petworth *Map EK 12. Magnificent house, mainly late 17th cent., with 320-ft.-long W front, standing in park of 738 acres. 13th-cent. chapel. Fine pictures, including many Van Dycks and Turners, & carving by Grinling Gibbons. See also p. 126* NT.

Royal Pavilion Brighton *Map FD 10. Built for George IV when Prince Regent by Henry Holland, later completed by John Nash after the style of the Moghul palaces of India. State Apartments decorated in the Chinese manner.* County Borough of Brighton.

St Mary's Bramber *Map FB 11. Mid-15th-cent. timber-framed house of monastic origin, finest example of its kind in Sussex. Rare 17th-cent. painted room. Fine collection of handicrafts.* Miss D. H. Ellis.

Sheffield Park Gardens 1m NW of Fletching on E side of A275 *Map FE 12. Gardens, lakes, woods & parkland, with rare shrubs and trees. Five lakes on different levels.* NT.

Uppark S Harting *Map EH 11. Late 17th-cent. house with 18th-cent. wallpapers, curtains & other furnishings.* NT.

Wakehurst Place Ardingly, nr Horsted Keynes *Map FD 12. Satellite garden for Royal Botanic Gardens, Kew, with fine tree and shrub collection on 462 acres.* Royal Botanic Garden.

Books for further reading

Topography – general

A. A. EVANS *On Foot in Sussex* 1933

V. G. HOWE *Something of Sussex* 1959

R. F. JESSUP *Sussex* (Little Guides series) 1957

E. V. LUCAS *Highways and Byways in Sussex* 1935

S. P. B. MAIS *The Land of the Cinque Ports* 1949

A. MEE (ed.) *Sussex* (The King's England) 1950

E. MEYNELL *Sussex* (County Books series) 1949

C. MUSGRAVE *The Sussex Book* 1957

WARD LOCK'S 'RED GUIDES' *The West Sussex Coast* and *The East Sussex Coast* (also issued for individual towns)

IAN NAIRN and N. PEVSNER *The Buildings of Sussex* 1965

N. WYMER *Companion into Sussex* 1950

History

W. V. COOK *The Story of Sussex* 1920

W. E. P. DONE *Looking Back in Sussex* 1953

A. BARR-HAMILTON *In Saxon Sussex* 1953

T. W. HORSFIELD *The History, Antiquities and Topography of the County of Sussex* 2 vols 1835

Literature

M. GOLDSWORTHY *The Sussex Bedside Anthology* 1950

R. T. HOPKINS *Sheila Kaye-Smith and the Weald Country* 1925

R. T. HOPKINS *The Kipling Country* 1924

RUDYARD KIPLING *The Sea and Sussex* 1926 also his *Puck of Pook's Hill* and *Rewards and Fairies*

Gazetteer

SUSSEX

Lullington Church, near Alfriston
Reece Winstone

Alfriston (FF 10). Snugly placed in the valley of the Cuckmere, a village with smuggling traditions. The Star Inn is a good example of 16th-cent. half-timbered work (the ferocious lion on the corner was a ship's figurehead). The 14th-cent. Priest's House (NT) has a very fine roof. Alfriston Church is so large that it has been called 'the cathedral of the Downs'. Lullington, across the river, has a church reputed to be the smallest in England; it is, however, only part of a once larger building.

Amberley (FA 11). A village that apparently never knew a planning scheme: well-kept brick-and-flint and thatched cottages lining a handful of winding lanes leading to the Norman church and the lofty remains of a 14th-cent. castle (the garden is sometimes open). This looks out on to Amberley Wild Brooks – luscious pasture in summer, but often a lake in winter.

Arundel* (FA 10) EC Wed (2,600). Though originally built about 20 years after the Battle of Hastings, much of the Duke of Norfolk's castle is modern (he and his family now live in an even more modern house in the park), but from across the wide curve of the River Arun it still presents the vision of an authentic medieval stronghold. Adding to the richness of the scene is the Roman Catholic church of St Philip Neri, built in the 19th cent. in French Gothic style. Adjoining is Arundel parish church (14th cent.), with a dividing wall separating the E end (known as the Fitzalan chapel) from the nave and aisles which serve

for the parish church. Thus under one roof are held Roman Catholic and Anglican services. The castle park has magnificent beech trees and the picturesque Swanbourne Lake. Lovely walks along the river; rowing boats are available.

Ashburnham, 3 m. W of Battle (FG 11). The chancel and side chapels of the church were built after the Restoration by John Ashburnham, who attended Charles I in his flight from Oxford to Scotland, when Parliamentary forces closed in on the town, and at his execution. Garments worn by the King in his last hours are preserved at Ashburnham.

Ashdown Forest, W of Crowborough (FF 13) and N of Uckfield (FE 12). Splendid walking country on the Wealden ridges, thousands of acres of lofty undulating heath and woodland interspersed with lovely streams and ponds. Highest point, Crowborough Beacon (792 ft.). Despite the name, ash trees are in a minority; oaks, Scots pines, hazel and sweet chestnuts predominate.

Battle* (FH 11) EC Wed (4,300). Before the famous battle of 1066 (which was fought, not at Hastings, but just to the SW of the Abbey Gate here) William of Normandy vowed he would build an abbey should the day be his. Here, now part of a school, are the remains of the abbey he built on the historic slope, with the high altar over the actual place where King Harold fell. The grounds are open to the public every weekday.

Bexhill (FH 10) EC Wed (29,000). Notable in the annals of road transport as the site of the first public motor racecourse in Britain (half a mile long!), laid out by Earl de la Warr when he was developing Bexhill as a holiday resort.

Bignor Hill* (EK 11). Near here are the important remains of a Roman villa (*see p.* 114).

Bodiam Castle** (FH 12). A 14th-cent. stronghold, reflecting its imposing walls amongst the water-lilies in the surrounding moat. Perhaps the most romantic castle ruin in the whole of England (NT).

Bosham (EJ 10) EC Thurs (2,800). A popular centre for artists and yachtsmen near the head of a creek in Chichester harbour. The village is old enough for its Saxon church to figure in the Bayeux tapestry; remains dug up by the chancel arch in 1865 may well be those of Canute's little daughter.

Boxgrove, 4 m. W of Slindon (EK 10). The beautiful remains of an 11th-cent. Benedictine Priory.

Bramber (FB 11). Where the Adur cuts through the Downs, with remains of a well-placed Norman castle and a museum with glass cases of stuffed birds supposed to illustrate such rhymes as *Cock Robin*.

Brede (FJ 11). Peter Pan's Captain Hook lived here – or at least his real-life original. He was J. W. Mahler, who became rector after retiring from a life of piracy on the high seas. It was while staying at Brede that Barrie heard the story of Mahler and of his blackmailer Smith, who figured as 'Smee'. Brede Place is notable.

Brighton* (FD 10) EC Wed, Thurs and Sat (162,750). In 1724 Brighton was 'a poor fishing town'. But when Dr Russell taught the medicinal value

Tombstone in St Nicholas's Churchyard, Brighton   Reece Winstone

of sea-bathing and the Prince Regent brought the Court here to relax, the small town was set on the way to becoming the great popular resort we know. Fine Regency terraces still defy the encroachments of modern hotels and blocks of flats. The unique Pavilion, built for the Prince Regent in Chinese style, is now an indispensable ingredient of the Brighton 'flavour'.

On the downs near Falmer, NE of the town, is the new University of Sussex, and heading the list of very good schools is Roedean College for girls. Hove, closely adjoining Brighton, not only keeps its curiously sedate air but jealously retains its identity as a separate borough.

Brighton Front seen from the Pier

Camber Castle (FK 11). One of the best examples of Henry VIII's coastal defence castles built when French invasion threatened. The extent of the coastal changes hereabout can be gauged from the fact that originally the castle was close to the shore (*see also* **Winchelsea**). This is a favourite corner of Sussex for bird-watchers.

Chanctonbury Ring* (FB 11). This ring of beeches is a well-loved landmark from many distant spots – even from the outskirts of London. Conversely the view from the Ring is equally extensive. The trees were planted in 1760 around a small Iron Age camp. They are 779 ft. above the sea. Near by is a 19th-cent. 'dewpond'.

Chichester* (EJ 10). EC Thurs (20,000). The Romans founded it (calling it *Regnum*) at the intersection of two important roads, a point now

marked by the beautiful 16th-cent. Butter Cross. The site of the Roman amphitheatre is at the E end of the town. The Normans built the cathedral on the site of a Saxon church; two sculptures in the N choir aisle are almost certainly Saxon work. Note the striking picture by Graham Sutherland, the cope designed by John Piper and modern glass by Christopher Webb in the N aisle. In St Martin's Square is the almshouse known as St Mary's Hospital, a lovely 13th-cent. building which stands almost as built. The 15th-cent. church of St Andrew's contains the grave of the poet William Collins, who died here in madness in 1759; and in the medieval Guildhall William Blake, the great artist and poet, was tried for high treason in 1804 – and acquitted. A modern structure of more than usual interest is the theatre built in 1962 for the Festival. Chichester 'harbour' is an extensive inlet from the sea reaching from Chichester across to Hayling Island; a wonderful stretch of water for small-boat sailing, full of delightful creeks and protected from the sea swell by a narrow entrance with a shallow sand 'bar'.

Cissbury Ring* (FB 10). Remarkable example of a prehistoric hill fort, on the Downs above the village of Findon to the NE of Worthing. The shafts of Neolithic flint mines are still visible. The ramparts were built about 300 BC and the fort was occupied until 50 BC. Views to the Isle of Wight and Beachy Head.

Ditchling Beacon* (FD 11), at 813 ft., crowns the downs NNE of Brighton. The view is superb; worth choosing a clear day for the visit.

Eastbourne (FG 09) EC Wed (60,900). A former fishing village which became popular during the threatened Napoleonic invasion, when officers 'standing by' sent for their families. Later, the Duke of Devonshire took a hand; the western part of the town is a mark of his enlightened ideas about town planning – wide, tree-lined roads with houses set in good gardens. Between this and Eastbourne's parish church (12th cent.) is a wide gulf filled with buildings of every style. Eastbourne makes a feature of good music and beautifully kept gardens, and those who find the 3-mile promenade too short for their exercise may climb the hill to the dizzy summit of Beachy Head.

Glyndebourne (FE 11). In 1934 the late John Christie courageously established a summer festival of music at his lovely part-Tudor manor-house, adjoining which he built an opera house. The Glyndebourne opera season is now famous the world over.

Goodwood (EJ 10). In this lovely undulating stretch of parkland lies Goodwood House, the home of the Duke of Richmond and Gordon, with its splendid array of pictures (*see p.* 119). Here too is the racecourse which brings enormous crowds to the annual meeting in July. And in recent years Goodwood has become the scene of some of the most important events in the motor-racing calendar.

Hastings and St Leonards (FJ 10) EC Wed (66,350). Hastings was the first seaside borough to build an underground promenade and car park. At the E end of the long front are the tarred net-lofts and red-tiled cottages

Net-lofts in old Hastings   *Reece Winstone*

of the fishing village. Rising above them are the remains of the Norman castle, built to protect the ancient harbour by virtue of which Hastings became a Cinque port. St Clement's Caves, some 3 acres in extent, are entered from near the castle. The Hastings Museum and Art Gallery has a good collection of Sussex ironwork, prehistoric relics – and birds.

Herstmonceux Castle (FG 11). Brick built in the 15th cent. and set within a wide moat, this picturesque castle is now the home of the Royal Greenwich Observatory, moved to the clearer atmosphere from London smoke and haze.

Horsham (FB 13) EC Thurs (21,150). From the centre of this picturesque old town the quiet tree-lined Causeway leads to the museum (large collection of riding and driving bits for horses) and the church. Among monuments in the church is one commemorating P. B. Shelley, who was born at Field Place. Many of the older buildings in the town are roofed with slabs ('Horsham slabs') of stone quarried in the neighbourhood. Two m. SW is Christ's Hospital, the famous 'Bluecoat' boys' school.

Hove (FC 10) EC Wed (73,000). *See* **Brighton** *above.*

Lancing (FB 10) EC Wed (11,900). The cathedral-like chapel of the College, well seen from the coast road near Worthing, is a splendid example of modern Gothic architecture begun in 1868. The interior is equally fine, with canopied stalls from Eton, and paintings by Rubens, etc. The College is a public school for boys, founded in 1848. The chapel is open to visitors.

Lewes (FE 11) EC Wed (13,650). Built in a gap through the South Downs made by the River Ouse and with a Norman castle built to defend that gap. A town for leisurely wandering. South-eastward Mount Caburn rises steeply to 490 ft.; westward is Mount Harry (639 ft.) with the racecourse. In Barbican House, by the Castle Gateway, is the museum of the Sussex Archaeological Society. See Anne of Cleves' interesting house at Southover and the tomb of Gundrada, William the Conqueror's daughter, in

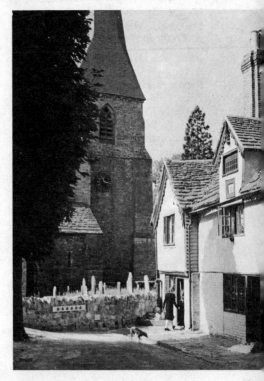

Horsham Church　　　*Reece Winstone*

the church across the way. In the old tilting ground attached to the castle is a rare (intentionally) undulating bowling green.

Lullington. *See* **Alfriston.**

Midhurst (EJ 12). The name is apt, for on every hand are lovely woods. Midhurst has few outstanding buildings but a number of very attractive 16th–17th-cent. houses. Note Elizabeth House, its half-timbering revealed by removal of plastering a few years ago. The road to Petworth undulates through the beautiful park of Cowdray. Near the famous polo grounds are the ruins of the splendid 15th-cent. mansion burnt down in the 18th cent. (some say because of a curse

125

on the Browne family to whom it belonged). The present Cowdray Hall was built in the 19th cent.

Petworth (E K 12) E C Wed (2,730). A compact little town at the gates of Petworth House*, the home of Lord Leconfield, who in 1947 conveyed it to the NT. Interesting in itself, it is a treasure house of pictures, furniture and ornaments. Turner stayed here and painted several of his well-known pictures. The park (included in the gift) is 14 m. round.

Pevensey (F G 10). Here, as at Portchester in Hampshire, the Normans built a castle inside a Roman one. Both were for the protection of a harbour (now silted up and built over by Pevensey village) which served as beach-head for the respective invading armies. Here was fought the savage battle in 961 when the Saxons attacked the castle 'and slew all that dwelt therein, nor was there a Briton left'. William the Conqueror landed at Pevensey in 1066 before advancing to attack King Harold at Senlac, some 9 m. to the N E and now the site of the present Abbey at **Battle** (*see above*).

Rye* (F K 12) E C Tues (4,430). In its original form the name meant 'island', and the town still rises impressively out of the surrounding flat lands which have more than once been submerged by the sea. Rye is certainly 'quaint' and 'picturesque' with its steep, cobbled streets, but it also has a solid background of good and historic building and its story goes back to medieval times. Before the sea receded it was an important Cinque Port. After seeing the church with its famous clock and

Ancient ammunition dump in Pevensey Castle   Reece Winstone

Mermaid Street, Rye

its many monuments, and Mermaid Street, and Lamb House where the writer Henry James lived, find the Gun Garden outside the Ypres Tower and enjoy the views of Rye Harbour and along the coast.

Selsey Bill (EJ 09) is not nearly so pointed as maps would suggest, but it is at the tip of a peninsula with good sandy beaches. Terns and other sea-birds nest in Pagham harbour on the E; on the W is Bracklesham with its beds of fossils.

Shoreham-by-Sea (FC 10) EC Wed (17,400). The silting-up of the mouth of the Adur has produced a canal-like waterway nearly 2 m. long, the water in which is now warmed by the effluent from the power-station recently built on the narrow bank which divides it from the sea. Great activity here, with boats of all kinds. Marlipins Museum has much of local interest and there is a fine Norman church. Here we are at *New* Shoreham; the original port and town were at *Old* Shoreham, upstream, until silting blocked the river to larger craft.

Steyning (FB 11) EC Thurs (2,500). Old-fashioned little town beside the Adur with a number of very attractive buildings including a Norman church and a market hall with an interesting clock tower.

Wilmington★ (FF 10). The 'Long Man', whose portrait is cut in the steep chalk side of Windover Hill above the village, is possibly a relative of the Cerne Abbas giant in Dorset, but he is larger (over 200 ft. tall). First recorded in 1764, he is of uncertain age and origin.

Winchelsea* (FK 11). 14th-cent. town-planning with some very nice flint-and-brick building and a splendid church. The old town down by the shore was engulfed by the sea in 1287, but three of the original gateways survived: one of them is the Strand Gate at the top of the hill leading up from the Rye road. Only the E end was completed of the huge church originally conceived, but even so it is large and impressive. Note the famous Alard tombs. The town never recovered from repeated French raids in the 14th cent. and except during the holiday season still justifies the description of 'a town in a trance'.

Worthing (FB 10) EC Wed (80,150). Holiday and residential borough where glasshouses produce vast quantities of tomatoes and grapes. Repertory theatre, concert hall, pier, good library and easy access to the Downs. In Broadwater cemetery are the graves of two great naturalists, Richard Jefferies and W. H. Hudson. (*See also* **Cissbury Ring** *above*.)

Georgian houses at Winchelsea   *Reece Winstone*

Opposite: Detail from the original painting by Rowland Hilder.
Chalk downs, gapped by rivers and crumbling at the sea's edge into splendid white cliffs, hide much of Sussex from the English Channel. Wild orchids are common, and the wheatear sings on the downland summits. Among those remembered in Sussex is George IV, who brought fame to Brighton.

On Leith Hill, south of Dorking   *J. Allan Cash*

SURREY

AN INTRODUCTION BY JOHN MONTGOMERY

Although one of the smallest counties in England, Surrey is eighth in the scale of population, and the number is increasing rapidly. Guildford alone has doubled its population since 1900. Croydon is larger, and Kingston is older; but the big towns are not typical of the county. For although large farming areas near the sprawling metropolis of London have fallen victim to suburban ribbon development, there still remain beyond the fringe of hastily built housing estates and semi-detached 'bypass Tudor' villas many wild, unspoiled acres of pine and heather, white chalk downs, fertile valleys and rich woodlands. The county owes much of its reputation to its wealth of trees, covering over 12 per cent of its soil, the remains of the great Forest of Windsor which was once a hundred miles in circumference.

The 'Cockney's back yard', Surrey has been called; but it is really a neat green back garden. Thomas Fuller compared it in the 17th century to 'a cynamon tree, whose bark is far better than the body thereof. For the skirts and

Opposite: Detail from the original painting by S. R. Badmin.
For all its neat homes and gardens and its dense population, much of Surrey is still an exquisite blend of sandy heath and green valley, of pine and silver birch, of dark yews and the trees of Box Hill.

borders bounding this shire are rich and fruitful, whilst the ground in the inward parts thereof is very hungry and barren, though, by reason of the clear air and clean waves, it is full of many gentile habitations.'

The county is about thirty-eight miles across at its greatest length, with a maximum breadth of twenty-five miles. In the north there is a low-lying belt of clay along the Thames valley; in the west there are the Bagshot Beds, a relaxing area of pine and fern; to the south lies the rich clay soil of the garden lands of the Weald. But perhaps the best-known feature is the long chalk ridge of the North Downs, crossing the middle of the county from east to west, and narrowing into the Hog's Back. The hills predominate: on their heights, particularly at Leith Hill, Box Hill, the Hog's Back, Newland's Corner and other vantage points, motorists picnic and survey the pleasant views of the wooded weald.

The rivers are small, nearly all flowing northwards into the Thames. The Blackwater, Hog's Mill River, Wandle, Beverley and Bourne brooks might almost escape notice. The larger Wey, formed from several branches rising in the Haslemere area, is navigable at Godalming and meanders sluggishly through Guildford. But the most attractive of the Surrey streams is the Mole, which starts in Sussex and curves and bends its way through rich meadows and lush waterfields to cut the North Downs between Dorking and Leatherhead before joining the Thames opposite Hampton Court Palace. At Burford Bridge near Dorking it appears to burrow underground. Perhaps no stream in England has been honoured by so many poets. Spenser wrote of it in his *Faerie Queene*:

> Mole, that like a nousling mole doth make
> His way still underground, till Thames he overtake.

Milton called it 'sullen Mole, that runneth underneath', and Pope, in his *Windsor Forest*, mentions the 'sullen Mole, that hides his diving flood'.

The Past

There are few early British or Roman relics, although some of the hills are crested with ancient camps. But everyone has heard of Stane Street (meaning Stone Street), the great Roman highway which ran from Chichester to London. It entered Surrey near Oakwood Hill, crossed Ockley Green, cut through the North Downs in the Mole gap, and went straight to Southwark. It may still be traced, and you can travel by car over parts of the original route where Roman chariots once passed. Crossing the county is another ancient highway, the Pilgrim's Way, popularly regarded as the path travelled on foot and horse by religious pilgrims from Winchester to Canterbury.

At Ockley, in 851, the Danes fought a fierce battle with the men of the south. The invaders had arrived off the coast of Kent in three-hundred-and-fifty ships. Having sacked Canterbury, they swept along the Thames and marched down Stane Street, intending to capture Winchester, the capital. But at Ockley Green they met and were defeated by the English Army. 'Blood stood ankle deep', says an account of the battle. Hardly a Dane escaped alive, so great was the slaughter.

The Saxons called this part of the country Sudrie or Suthrige, and they crowned their kings at Kingston-upon-Thames, where you can see the King's stone. In 873, after the sacking of Chertsey Abbey by the Danes, the little kingdom came under the rule of the West Saxon kings. Most of the land belonged to Earl Godwin; but after the Norman invasion William the Conqueror

gave thirty-eight manors to his supporter, Richard of Tonbridge, who built his castle at Bletchingley.

The people of Surrey have made several successful protests against the tyranny of their overlords. Magna Carta was signed at Runnymede, near Egham, in 1215; the rebellion led by Wat Tyler in 1381, although ending in Tyler's death and the capture of Guildford, helped to end the old feudal system of villeinage; and in the rising of 1450 the men of the county played an important part, led by Jack Cade, who was probably a Surrey man.

Things to see

From the motorists' point of view there is much to see. One can go to Kew to the famous Royal Botanic Gardens or to Wisley for the R.H.S. Gardens, to Richmond Park to picnic and see the deer, to Epsom Downs where the Derby is run, or further afield westwards to Blackdown, the highest point in the south after Leith Hill. Here, about two and a half miles south of Haslemere, is an extensive, unforgettable view across the Weald. On a fine day the South Downs are clearly visible, a long bare ridge extending to Mount Harry above Lewes, some thirty-five miles away, with the crown of trees on Chanctonbury Ring standing out clear against the sky, and 'green Sussex fading into blue, with one gray glimpse of sea' visible through the Arun Gap.

Haslemere itself is between five and six hundred feet above sea-level, as high as Newland's Corner. Although not so picturesque as Farnham, it has some attractive red 17th-century houses, with weather-tiled gables and tall chimneys. A window by Burne-Jones in the church is dedicated to the memory of Tennyson, who lived at Aldworth on Blackdown. And on nearby Hindhead you will be 895 feet above sea-level when you stand on Gibbett Hill, where three men were hanged in chains for the murder in 1786 of an unknown sailor on the old Portsmouth road.

Kingston, although an excellent shopping centre, has kept little of its past; Leatherhead has old buildings by the river; Ripley Village with its broad cricket green lies fresh and white in the sun, an excellent place to stop for beer or tea.

Travelling for pleasure around the county is best in April, May or October, when the hotels and inns are less full and the roads not so congested. At these times the countryside is at its richest, the lanes and banks and hedgerows are bedecked with wild flowers, the views from the hills are more clear, and the narrow side-roads, which the wise motorist will prefer, are less crowded. From Box Hill one looks across the Mole stream to the long lime avenue of Betchworth Park and the spire of Brockham Green, one of the most attractive of villages: Dorking town is to the right, with Leith Hill behind it, and a glimpse of blue heather shows us where Hindhead lies far to the west. Nearer, to the east, is the spire of Reigate church and the tree-crested summit of Priory Park. Far beyond, southwards, is green Ashdown Forest. One of the most popular views in the south of England, this noble prospect has changed little with the passing years.

The gardens at Polesden Lacey, near Dorking, are magnificent. In the grounds of Esher Place you will find the oldest tulip tree in the country, planted in 1685. At Albury, with the nearby silent pool, the gardens were made by John Evelyn, the diarist, the cedars planted from seeds brought from Lebanon; and at Pain's Hill, Cobham (where Matthew Arnold lived), there stands the largest cedar in England. But if you seek a fine expanse of water, where there is yachting, you

Frensham Great Pond

J. Allan Cash

should visit the great pond at Frensham, surrounded by woods and heather. And for tea in delightful surroundings you cannot do better than go to Shere, with its gabled cottages and a stream running through the village. On the way back to London is the pilgrims' chapel of St Martha on the hills above Guildford, with the Tillingbourne valley below, and the great new cathedral near by, begun in 1936.

Cobbett thought Guildford 'the prettiest, and taken altogether the most agreeable and most happy-looking town that I ever saw in my life'. Today it is a far busier place than in Cobbett's day; but its High Street, rising steeply from the river, is still picturesque with many historic buildings. At the top, the Abbot's Hospital, founded as an almshouse in 1619, confronts the old Grammar School of a century earlier; and in many of the surrounding streets quaint gabled houses survive to remind us of an older England.

In Godalming, a small town hall (now a museum), with graceful clock tower and copper cupola, sits squarely in the middle of the High Street. It slows down the traffic; but since 1814 all attempts to have it removed have failed. In the little church at Stoke d'Abernon, on the north bank of the Mole between Leatherhead and Cobham, are the oldest brasses in England. One commemorates the death of Sir John d'Abernon in 1277, and the other bears the name of his son, who died in 1327. If you have time, stay to admire the view from the churchyard across the stream, over a broad stretch of meadow grassland. And at Cobham you will again meet the Mole, and see a silent water-mill with swans floating on the stream by the roadside.

The county is rich in ancient buildings, all within easy reach of London by car. There are Norman walls at Guildford castle, overlooking the grey and red slates of the town; Farnham castle, although ruined by Cromwell, has a keep which dates partly from Henry III, and round it a deer park, lawns, and a cricket ground, with old cedars. Compton church contains the oldest piece of Norman woodwork in the land – but for the rest I must refer you to the Gazetteer.

Many great names have lived and stayed in Surrey: George Meredith at Box Hill, Tennyson and George Eliot and George Macdonald at Haslemere, Jonathan Swift at Moor Park near Farnham, Lewis Carroll at Guildford (where you can see the house in which he died), Cobbett at Farnham, Eadweard Muybridge, the pioneer of motion pictures, born and buried at Kingston, Sir Richard Burton, the Arabist, buried at Mortlake, Lord Howard of Effingham who lies at Reigate, and (it is believed) Sir Walter Raleigh who is buried, headless, at Beddington.

Industries, old and new

Today there are modern industries at Woking, Mitcham, Kingston, Weybridge and Guildford; there are extensive market gardens in the Thames Valley; gloves and hosiery are made at Godalming; there is a fine airport at Gatwick; and new factories are being built in the greater London area. But in Tudor times there were iron forges at Shere, Abinger Hammer, Cranleigh, Witley, Hasle-

Shere

Reece Winstone

Farnham

Reece Winstone

mere and Dunsfold. The sandstone provided the ore, while the fuel for the charcoal furnaces came from the dense woods. And glass was made by Normandy refugees at Chiddingfold in the 14th century for the windows of Westminster Abbey, St George's Chapel at Windsor, and many great mansions. Guildford, Godalming, Wonersh, Farnham and the surrounding villages were once famous for their cloth, which was woven by housewives and daughters in timbered cottages; beautiful tiles were made at Chertsey Abbey; delft-ware came from Lambeth; and gunpowder was made at Wotton and, from Elizabeth I's reign until recently, at Chilworth, where banknotes were also made (which greatly distressed the travelling historian, Cobbett).

There are many famous hostelries in the county, such as the Bush, which Thackeray described in *The Virginians* as having stood in Farnham town for three hundred years; or the Burford Bridge Hotel, near Dorking, where Nelson, Keats and Stevenson stayed. But perhaps more typical of the county are the small village inns, many unspoiled by the centuries; often near by you will find a village pond, a blacksmith's forge, a cricket-ground or a green, some timbered cottages with neat gardens, and perhaps an old post office and a cattle pound. Here is the true Surrey, unspoiled by the chain stores and multiple shops of the suburban towns and nearby London. England is constantly changing; but many of us hope that the backwaters of this beautiful county will remain unspoiled for future generations to enjoy.

135

Some houses and gardens open to the public

Clandon Park West Clandon 3m E of Guildford *Map* FA 14. *Palladian house built c. 1735. Fine plaster decoration.* NT.

Feathercombe 2½m SW of Godalming *Map* EK 14. *Gardens with flowering trees and shrubs, a heath garden and wide views.* Miss M. R. Parker.

Ham House Petersham nr Richmond *Map* FB 17. *Notable example of Stuart domestic architecture, with fine collection of late Stuart furniture.* NT.

Hatchlands East Clandon 4m E of Guildford *Map* FA 14. *18th-cent. house with Robert Adam interior.* NT.

Kew Gardens Kew *Map* FB 17. *Finest botanical collection in the world, with Palm House, Temperate House, Orangery, Herbarium etc. 300 acres. Satellite garden is found at Ardingly, Sussex (see p. 120).* Royal Botanic Gardens.

Kew Palace (The Dutch House) Kew *Map* FB 17. *Gabled brick house in Dutch style. Pictures, furniture and other mementoes of George III. 17th-cent. garden.* Ministry of Public Building and Works.

Loseley House 1½m N of Godalming *Map* EK 14. *Historic mansion built by Sir Wm More 1562. Panelling, furniture, large parkland.* J. R. More-Molyneux.

Polesden Lacey nr Dorking *Map* FB 15. *Regency & Edwardian house in beautiful wooded parkland. Greville collection of pictures, furniture, tapestries, etc.* NT.

White Lodge Richmond Park *Map* FB 17. *Early 18th-cent. Palladian house with later alterations.* Governors of the Royal Ballet School.

Willmer House Farnham *Map* EJ 14. *Built 1718, with richly moulded brickwork. Panelling, good doors and staircase, carved archways. Walled garden.* Farnham UDC.

Winkworth Arboretum 3m SE of Godalming *Map* EK 14. *Rare trees & shrubs on 95 acres of hillside. Two lakes and many wild birds.*

Wisley Gardens NE of Ripley *Map* FA 15. *The famous & extensive show gardens of the Royal Horticultural Society.*

Books for further reading

Architecture and landscape

GEOFFREY CLARK and W. HARDING THOMPSON *The Surrey Landscape* 1934
JACK HILLIER *Old Surrey Water-Mills* 1951
IAN NAIRN and NIKOLAUS PEVSNER *Surrey* (Buildings of England series) 1962
ERIC PARKER *Surrey Gardens* 1954

History

J. E. B. GOVER and others *The Place-Names of Surrey* 1934
F. J. C. HEARNSHAW *The Place of Surrey in the History of England* 1936
D. C. WHIMSTER *The Archaeology of Surrey* 1931
Victoria History of the County of Surrey 1902–14

Wild Life

JOHN A. BUCKNILL *The Birds of Surrey* 1900
ERIC PARKER *Surrey Naturalist* 1952
CHARLES E. SALMON *Flora of Surrey* 1931

Topography

FRANCIS RICHARD BANKS *Surrey* (Penguin Guides) 1956
JOHN CHARLES COX *Surrey* (Little Guides series) 7th edn rev. by E. F. Peeler 1952
R. W. GALLOIS and F. H. EDMUNDS *British Regional Geology: the Wealden District* 1965
RALPH LAWRENCE *Surrey* (Vision of England series) 1950
ARTHUR MEE (ed.) *Surrey* (The King's England series) 1966
L. COLLISON-MORLEY *Companion into Surrey* 2nd edn 1949
WILLIAM THOMAS PALMER *Odd Corners in Surrey* 1951 and *Wanderings in Surrey* 1949
ERIC PARKER *Highways and Byways in Surrey* 1935 and *Surrey* (The County Books series) 1947
W. A. POUCHER *The Surrey Hills* 1949

Gazetteer

SURREY

Population figures are based on the 1961 Census. Figures for large towns may include other places within the borough or urban administration.

Abinger Hammer (FB 14). The stream once worked the hammer-mill when the village was a centre of the iron industry – hence the name. The figure of a working blacksmith on the clock projecting over the road is a further reminder of Abinger's industrial past. A motte and pit-dwelling indicate early inhabitation. The watercress beds, for which the village is noted, are fed by underground springs.

Albury (FA 14). The mansion, remodelled by Pugin, contains a valuable collection of paintings, clocks and some notable chimney-pieces. Note the 63 chimneys, all different. The Yew Walk is very fine. Albury old church has Saxon and Norman work.

Betchworth, 3 m. W of Reigate (FC 14). One of the most attractive villages on the winding Mole, with a venerable barn and a church with a font carved by Eric Kennington.

Bisley (EK 15). The ranges of the National Rifle Association are the scene of important international shooting competitions. Prizes worth £10,000 are awarded during the annual meeting in July.

Bletchingley, 1½ m. W of Godstone (FD 15). Pleasant old houses border the wide street. The church has a sturdy Norman tower but is mostly 15th cent. In the wall of the south chapel note the 'Hermit's Hole' and then (by contrast) turn to the huge Clayton monument. There are some remains of Bletchingley Castle.

Abinger Hammer: blacksmith clock

Burford Bridge, 1 m. N of Dorking under Box Hill (FB 15). The Mole, the bridge and the trees make a background to memories of Keats (who completed *Endymion* here) and Nelson (here the night before he left for Trafalgar). Here is the most popular approach to Box Hill.

Burstow (FD 14). A little church with an unusual tower entirely of timber.

Camberley (EJ 15) EC Wed (30,350). The centre of an important military training area. Here is the Royal Staff College. The Royal Military College, Sandhurst, is half a mile N. See the very moving War Memorial chapel. The National Army Museum, opened in 1960, has a wonderful collection of pictures, models, weapons, uniforms, etc.

Chaldon (FD 15). The church has a well-preserved medieval painting of St Michael weighing souls in the

137

balance while a demon leans heavily on the scales and rampant devils pitchfork the bad souls into hell. In its day no doubt more effective than the most violent of sermons.

Charlwood (FC 14) EC Wed (2,750). The church has a very fine 15th-cent. screen, also traces of medieval wall paintings.

Cheam (FC 16) EC Wed (79,000). Nonsuch Park retains the name – but only the name – of an enormous palace built by Henry VIII which has completely vanished, although traces have been found in recent years. In 1670 Charles II gave it to Barbara Villiers who straightway pulled it down and sold the materials! It was here that the first lilacs in England were planted.

Chiddingfold (EK 13). Picturesque old houses border the green. The Crown Inn dates from the 14th cent. Chiddingfold was once a centre of glass-making: see examples in the church

Cobham* (FB 16) EC Wed (7,250). Church Cobham and Street Cobham stand beside the Mole with its old watermill. There are several good houses in the neighbourhood. Cedar House (15th cent.) (NT) may be seen on application: note the fine opentimbered roof of the Great Hall. Pain's Hill mansion stands in magnificent gardens laid out in the 18th cent. and noted for their fine cedars. On Chatley Heath is a five-storey tower, part of a chain of semaphore stations by which messages were sent from London to Portsmouth (in less than a minute) in pre-telegraph days.

Compton, 2 m. NW of Godalming (EK 14). Unique is the 12th-cent. chapel built over the vaulted sanctuary of the church*. The Norman screen is among the oldest woodwork in England. Limnerslease, a little to the N, was long the home of G. F. Watts, some of whose works are in the Watts Picture Gallery behind the Pottery which he and his wife established.

Crowhurst (FD 14). A yew tree beside the church is over 30 ft. in girth. It is still growing, although the trunk is so hollow that a dozen people are said to have gathered round a table inside it. Note the striking gatehouse of Crowhurst Place, a moated mansion dating from the 15th cent.

Dorking (FB 14) EC Wed (23,000). At the S end of the gap worn through the North Downs by the river Mole, with Box Hill rising to 590 ft. to the N and Leith Hill, 965 ft. high, to the S. Excellent centre for walking. George Meredith's grave is in the cemetery. At one time Dorking was noted for its edible snails. *See also* **Leith Hill.**

Egham (FA 17) EC Thurs (31,700). The church contains memorials of the barons who confronted King John with Magna Carta at **Runnymede** (*see below*).

Epsom (FC 15) EC Wed (72,400). Epsom salts are named after the same mineral spring which brought the town 18th-cent. fame as a spa. Nowadays it is the racecourse on Epsom Downs which brings the crowds, to see the Derby and the Oaks.

Esher (FB 16) EC Wed (63,000). The wide street retains a countryfied air and pleasant Georgian buildings. In the former parish church* note the handsome chamber pew with fireplaces and the high pews at the back for servants. Cardinal Wolsey once lived in the 15th-cent. gatehouse in the grounds of Esher Place.

Farnham (EJ 14) EC Wed (29,800). A busy little market town with many attractive Georgian buildings and

Reece Winstone **Compton C**

literary associations. William Cobbett is buried in the church (he was born in the house which is now the *Jolly Farmer* inn); Waverley Abbey, 2 m. E, provided Sir Walter Scott with a title for his novels; and at Moor Park Swift wrote *The Battle of the Books* and met Stella. The 12th-cent. Farnham Castle, for centuries the home of the Bishops of Winchester, is now the residence of the Bishop of Guildford; parts are open to the public (A M).

Frensham Ponds (EJ 14). Popular lakes for sailing and fishing. The larger of the two ponds covers over 100 acres. Under the tower in the church is a great cauldron, nearly 3 ft. across, probably used at wedding feasts.

Friday Street. *See* **Leith Hill.**

Godalming (EK 14) EC Wed (17,800). 'The most considerable town in the county' – that is how Godalming was described in 1749 when it was an important centre of the clothing industry. Many good old houses remain from those times. The old town hall, with its clock and cupola, was built in 1814 by public subscription; it is now a museum. Godalming's history goes back a long way – at least as far as King Alfred. Charterhouse School is 1 m. N, and 3 m. SE is the National Trust Winkworth Arboretum.

Guildford* (FA 14) EC Wed (55,500). Well placed in the valley of the River Wey, with a steep main street beautified by the half-timbered Guildhall with its projecting clock (note the nice ironwork and also the buttresses upholding the little balcony, carved like ships' figureheads). On the other side of the street are the remains of the Castle built by Henry II and for a time used as a gaol: the Keep crowns

a knoll probably raised by the Romans. Lewis Carroll died in the house called 'The Chestnuts' near the Castle in 1898 and is buried in Guildford cemetery (Guildford Museum has some relics). Chained books are in the library of the 16th-cent. Grammar School; there is much good woodwork in the adjoining Abbot's Hospital (1619). The first stage of the University of Surrey on Stag Hill was completed in 1968 and by the early 1970's there will be 5,000 students at this technological institution. The new Yvonne Arnaud theatre on the bank of the River Wey, was completed in 1965. The new Guildford Cathedral stands on Stag Hill, NW of the town. The foundation stone was laid in 1936, but owing to the war consecration did not take place until 1962; Sir Edward Maufe's design, a simplified treatment of Gothic, was accepted as long ago as 1932.

Haslemere (EK 13) EC Wed (13,500). Beautifully placed among wooded hills close to **Hindhead** (*see below*). Well known for the July Musical Festival founded by Arnold Dolmetsch in 1925 and featuring medieval music played on old-time instruments. There is a fascinating Educational Museum, founded in 1888 and since copied elsewhere. Aldworth, 2 m. E, was built by Tennyson; he died here in 1892.

Hindhead (EJ 13) EC Wed (2,750). 'The most villainous spot God ever made' – so wrote William Cobbett. But he must surely have been unlucky with his weather, for Hindhead (800 ft. up) is one of Southern England's finest viewpoints, surrounded by woods and heathlands, much of which is protected by the NT. A mile or so to the SW are the well-known ponds of Waggoners' Wells. The highest point in the area is Gibbet Hill*

Reece Winstone   **Guildford : Castle Gate, with the Museum on the ►**

The Palm House, Kew Gardens

(894 ft.) above the deep hollow of the Devil's Punch-bowl. Note the sombre inscription on the Sailor's Stone close at hand.

Kew (FB 17) EC Wed (4,250). It is not always appreciated that the beautiful and world-famous Botanical Gardens★★ (nearly 300 acres) have a severely practical purpose. But for Kew, which supplied the seeds, there might have been no rubber plantations in Malay and Ceylon, or quinine in India. Kew Palace is a pleasant house with relics of George III. Gainsborough and Zoffany are buried beside the church on Kew Green. Strand-on-the-Green, just below Kew bridge, is an unspoiled row of 18th-cent. Thames-side houses.

Kingston-upon-Thames (FB 16) EC Wed (36,500). The Coronation Stone on which Saxon kings were crowned is still preserved – in the open, hard by the Market Place. Lovekyn's Chapel and the parish church date from the 14th cent. But Kingston today is an extremely busy shopping and residential suburb with many boating interests. Across the River Thames, in former Middlesex, begins the greenery of Hampton Court Park.

Leith Hill★★ (FB 14). The highest (965 ft.) of a series of hills among some of the choicest scenery in Surrey and with wonderful views over the Weald. This is the highest point in SE England. From the top of the tower (1,029 ft. up) thirteen counties can be seen on a clear day. Large areas of this lovely countryside are now cared for by the NT. About 2 m. NNW is the hamlet of Friday Street, a row of detached brick-built cottages with ample gardens. The lane from the main road comes down through a miniature tree-shaded defile and continues through the trees to the panoramic view from the summit of Leith Hill.

Limpsfield (FE 15). A peaceful village almost lost among the modern residential areas. It looks out from the greens and hills to the North Downs above Titsey Hill and has a fine common with gorse and birch trees. In the churchyard are the graves of Frederick Delius, the composer, and J. Arthur Thomson, the scientist.

Mickleham (FB 15). A quiet village on the NW slopes of Box Hill, with high chalk hills on either side and lovely woods by the River Mole.

North Downs. This chalk range runs through the county from W to E, starting with the narrow ridge of the Hog's Back near Guildford and gradually widening and rising until at the Kentish border it nears the 900 ft. mark. Its steep southern escarpment is largely covered with yew, box, juniper and beech trees. Two rivers have breached this green wall: the Wey, which provided Guildford with its valley situation; and the Mole, responsible for the fine wooded scenery along the Leatherhead–Dorking dual carriageway (A 24).

Nutfield, 2 m. E of Redhill (FC 14) on A 25. Note the extensive workings of the 'Fuller's Earth' beds beside the road. Once mainly used in connection with cloth-making, 'Fuller's Earth' is now an important ingredient in the refining of oil.

Outwood (FD 14). Here is one of the best-preserved windmills in England. Built 1665, restored 1961–2. Its tall companion, once beautiful in its decay, sadly collapsed in 1960.

Pilgrims' Way. It is commonly supposed that pilgrims from Winchester to Canterbury used this ancient track. Possibly they did, but it was certainly not they who first trod it out. Note how it avoids steep gradients and keeps mostly to the sunny southern slopes of the Downs, well above the low ground which in former days was often soggy with marshland. Much of it is now clearly marked by NT signposts.

Reigate (FC 14) EC Wed (56,400). An ancient town which has become a popular residential and commuting area. Of the Norman castle there are only a few ruins and a subterranean excavation known as the Baron's Cave. St Mary Magdalene's Church has a valuable library of about 2,000 volumes and the tomb of Lord Howard of Effingham (1536–1624), 'Admyrall of Englande, Generall of Queen Elizabeth's Royale Navey at Sea against the Spanyards invinsable Navey'. From the Pilgrims' Way on Colley Hill panoramic views extend to the South Downs.

Richmond★★ (FB 17) EC Wed (41,000). New buildings and the conversion of old buildings have not destroyed the flavour of this Thames-side borough, which has been a Londoners' pleasure resort at least since the 18th cent. It stands between two good open spaces – Kew Gardens and the Old Deer Park to the N, and on the S the fine extent of Richmond Park, reached by Richmond Hill, with delightful views down to the Thames. The park is a magnificent extent (2,350 acres) of turf and trees and bracken, with ponds and streams high above the 18th-cent. bridge spanning the river. In the summer the river is gay with pleasure-boats. The gem of the town is Richmond Green, bordered by 17th–18th-cent. buildings. Near by are the remains of Richmond

143

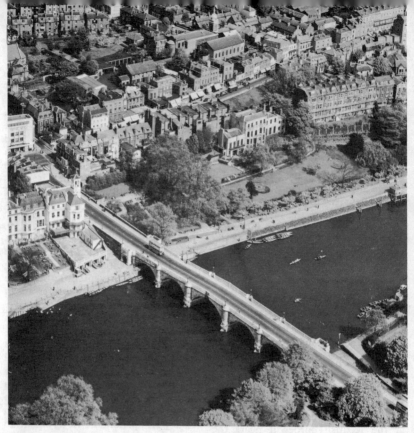

Richmond Bridge

Palace and 1½ m. S the splendid 17th-cent. Ham House. In the Old Deer Park is Kew Observatory (founded 1768).

Runnymede* near Egham (FA 17). The riverside meadows where King John affixed his seal to Magna Carta in 1215 were given to the NT in 1931. Memorial buildings and kiosks designed by Sir Edward Lutyens. Among the trees on Cooper's Hill to the S is the Air Forces Memorial, designed by Sir Edward Maufe and unveiled in 1953.

Shere (FA 14) EC Wed (3,800). Beautiful old village with a Norman church, among wooded hills and now mercifully preserved from the roar of traffic by a by-pass. Visit the Silent Pool, 1 m. W.

Stoke D'Abernon 3 m. NW of Leatherhead (FB 15) EC Wed (2,950). The church has Saxon and Norman work employing Roman materials and good medieval and Renaissance glass. The brass effigy of Sir John d'Abernon (1277) is the earliest in England.

Wotton (FB 14). At the foot of the long rise to Leith Hill, and now used as a Fire Service College, is Wotton House, where John Evelyn, the diarist, was born and died; the house is the old home of the Evelyn family, whose tombs are in the 13th-cent. church. Note wooden belfry on early Norman tower.

Apple orchard near Sutton Valence   *J. Allan Cash*

KENT

AN INTRODUCTION BY DEREK CHAPMAN

An unimaginable time ago Kent lay buried under the sea. For millions of years generations of microscopic shellfish lived and died, leaving their hard outer cases to form a charnel-house of lime superimposed on the sea-bed layers of sand and clay. With the shrinking of the earth's crust, giant pressures from north and south heaved the whole mass of rock into an arch; and when the sea went down, the topping of calcium shells was revealed as a vast whaleback of chalk rising to half a mile high at its loftiest point. From the exposed uplands rivers emerged; abetted by the weathering forces of frost and rain they began their long process of demolition. The chalk, now reduced at its highest to under a thousand feet, remains today as two east-west ridges of beautiful hills: on the one hand the South Downs of neighbouring Sussex; on the other the North Downs, which run westward across Surrey into a corner of Hampshire, and eastward from Westerham through the full length of Kent until, laid bare as the white cliffs of Dover, they tower impressively above the seaborne traveller from France.

The North Downs are broken at three points by north-bound rivers. Near Sevenoaks the Darent has quite worn through them on its way to Dartford; the Medway breaches them near Maidstone; further east, from Ashford to Canterbury, the Stour flows abrasively through the Wye gap. Although every year the ploughman ploughs yet higher up their flanks, the Downs remain largely

covered with thin, springy turf, sympathetic to walk on. From a hundred vantage points they provide some of the most breath-taking views of England: at the
eastern end the sea and the Channel traffic, coming close in here to avoid the
Goodwin Sands, and across the water, on a fine day, the town of Calais clearly
visible through binoculars; northward the age-old accretions of silt and saltings
which have made the low-lying fringes of the Thames estuary and the mouth of
the Medway; and southward – the Weald of Kent.

The Weald, which occupies most of Kent, was originally a vast forest, the
Andredsweald of the Anglo-Saxons. Though exploited for two thousand years
by piecemeal clearing for timber and farming, wealden scenery is still heavily
wooded. The locals distinguish between the High Weald and the Low, the
former being the sandstone hills that run high into Goudhurst and Cranbrook,
the latter the wealden clay lowland encircling them. The High Weald is a garden
where everything grows; the Low Weald is quieter, heavier, colder and sleepier
country.

Between the Weald and the sea, south of the Tenterden-Hythe road, lies the
flat, secretive country of the Romney Marsh, an area that was added to Kent,
almost as an afterthought, when the Romans first built its defending sea-wall.
It is a fascinating triangle of fertile flats, precariously kept from the sea by a
system of drains and embankments; the land seldom rises more than a dozen
feet above sea-level. The sunsets, when good, are incomparable. In spring and
summer the fields are dense with grazing sheep, but when the cold winter winds
sweep in from the sea and drive them to more sheltered pastures inland, the
Marsh settles down to brood over its smuggling past. The Marsh men are a
race on their own.

Local Industries and Activities

In Kent they mainly farm, producing everything from sugar-beet to the native
Kent (or Romney Marsh) long-woolled sheep – a hardy, adaptable breed that
has colonized most of the world's sheep farms. On the chalk Downs they grow
barley of fine malting quality, and rather boast about it, while some of the
pastures in the marshland fatten more beasts to the acre than any in Britain.
Sheep grazing in a flowered orchard, a group of cowled oast-houses set among
hop-fields – these are the familiar views of Kent. Orchards are everywhere: to
view them in their greatest profusion, start from Tonbridge or Maidstone.
Cherries, apples and plums are abundant. The hop gardens are concentrated
largely in three areas: around Maidstone; between Paddock Wood and Ashford;
and again between Faversham and Canterbury.

Manufacturing takes second place. Paper-making is a notable industry in the
north and north-west; engineering works occur by the Thames from Gravesend
to London; there is the huge new BP oil refinery on the Isle of Grain; Ashford
is associated with the making of railway carriages and farm machinery, and,
latterly, with the canning of peas and other foodstuffs.

Of the mineral resources the most improbable is coal, mined in the east of
the county. The lower greensand, such as prevails in the Maidstone district,
yields the attractive building stone called Kentish Rag, used in the construction
of churches in all periods. The chalk and mud vales of the lower Thames and
Medway are quarried for making cement; the gault clay is made into bricks.

In a few districts bordering Sussex you may come across relics of the days
when the Weald was noted for its ironworks. For centuries iron ore was dug

J. Allan Cash **Hop-pick**

from the Hastings beds and smelted over charcoal derived from the exploitation of the wealden forests. All that was altered when coke replaced charcoal: the industry packed up and left for the coal-mining districts of the Midlands and the north country. The last wealden furnace went out in 1828, and today you may see the hammer ponds, dead and stagnant, evidencing the site of a centuries-old foundry.

Archaeology and Early History

The high plateaux of the Downs in west Kent have yielded examples of man's oldest known handiwork, the roughly worked flints known as eoliths. Signs of Old Stone Age occupation are abundant in the river valleys, while mesolithic (6000 B.C.) dwelling pits have been excavated at Sevenoaks, Ightham, and East Malling. In the Medway gap are to be seen several New Stone Age tombs, the most famous being Kits Coty House, near Aylesford. These same tomb-builders – centuries before Chaucer – trod out the Pilgrim's Way, which runs along the foot of the Downs.

The Roman occupation of Britain began in Kent, and Kent still uses the earliest Roman road, Watling Street, linking Canterbury with London. At Richborough a fortified Roman township (still impressive) guarded what was then the coast, from the time of Claudius, in A.D. 43, until the legions departed.

The succeeding ages were to give Britain to the Angles and Saxons. It is said that the first Saxon invaders, Hengist and Horsa, landed at Ebbsfleet in 449 and founded the Kingdom of Kent, its extent roughly matching the present county boundaries. But Kent was largely inhabited by Jutes from the lower Rhine, who established themselves first in the north coastal zone, and presently spread out as far as the Medway. The distinction still made between the Kentish Men, born on the London side of that river, and the Men of Kent, born on the east and south side of it, may descend from the differences between Saxon and Jute.

The Jutes introduced customs and laws very different from those in the neighbouring kingdoms of Wessex and Mercia, the most striking being gavelkind, whereby on a man's death his property was divided equally among all his sons. Gavelkind made for more but smaller farms and for a large middle class of Kentish yeomen rather than a few rich and powerful landlords. Today you may note a prevalence of isolated farmsteads, the absence of large estates, and an indefinable yeomanness about the Kentish men.

Towns and Buildings

Canterbury, of course, is *the* tourist attraction in Kent, perhaps the most visited city outside London. It flourished in Roman times (below Butchery Lane you may see a display of mosaic tiles), and the prominent knoll known as Dane John is a first-century burial ground. The medieval city walls survive in parts; and the west gateway has hardly altered for 600 years. In the last war they bombed pretty sharply the city centre; the rebuilding is not undistinguished.

St Augustine, who is popularly believed to have brought Christianity to England through Kent, founded the cathedral in 597. After a fire, it was rebuilt in 1070, and for four centuries adders-on, improvers, and embellishers contributed to its amalgam of styles. Important as the city was to the churchmen of England, Canterbury achieved international fame with the murder of St Thomas Becket in 1170. Pilgrims came from all over Europe to pray at his shrine and contribute gifts. Chaucer's pilgrims, who set out from Southwark and spun

Canterbury Cathedral

J. Allan Cash

their Canterbury Tales to enliven the journey, arrived two hundred years later. The spot where the four knights struck Becket down, in the Chapel of the Martyrdom, is precisely known, and in the right mood the right guide will re-enact the murder with chilling realism. Christopher Marlowe, the great drama-tist who could have written Shakespeare but did not, was born in Canterbury in 1564 and, like Becket, stabbed to death, but in a tavern brawl in Deptford in 1593.

In contrast to the hushed Gothic air of Canterbury, Tunbridge Wells has an 18th-century sensibility. The discovery of health-giving springs persuaded the 'quality' to summer out of London and to cure all those ills the Restoration flesh was heir to. By 1750 a town had arisen; socially it rivalled Bath, from which spa it lured for a time the uncrowned king, Beau Nash, to advise upon fashions and modes of merrymaking. In the Pantiles, a raised walk with shops, trees and quiet, you may sample the waters if your taste runs that way – for black bile, alias melancholia, the traditional dose is twenty pints at a sitting.

Of the Cinque Ports that for centuries commanded the narrow seas and, in fact, maintained the navy, all but Hastings lie in Kent. The office of Lord

Warden of the Cinque Ports continues to survive as a gift of the crown bestowed upon distinguished men, and with it the right to reside in Walmer Castle.

Dover, the chief Cinque Port, is now the only one with a harbour. The great keep of its castle, which gives as fine a view of an approaching enemy as ever it did, goes back to 1180 and compares in size and strength with the Tower of London. Sandwich, today, is two miles from the seashore it once commanded. Some of its houses have a Flemish look, influenced by the refugees who fled from the Netherlands in Elizabethan times and brought with them their skill in weaving. New Romney, too, is now an inland town, the old port lying well within the Marsh. Its church is exceptionally fine, with an impressive pinnacled Norman tower. The main street presents an array of Tudor and Georgian fronts. Finally, Hythe: it remains on the sea, although the old town on the hill is farther from the beach than when it supplied eleven ships, as against neighbour Folkestone's four, to meet the Armada.

Folkestone owes its prosperity to the holidaymaker. As a seaside resort it retains pretensions to fashion, despite the excursions and incursions of non-passport trippers to France. The old town and the harbour have not yet lost all their fishing-village character. On the north coast, Margate and Ramsgate both speak for themselves, not wholly in measured tones. Herne Bay is rather less extrovert, Birchington residential. Broadstairs, the farthest east, radiates the same charm that attracted Charles Dickens. He frequently stayed there, and for a time settled in Bleak House overlooking the harbour. Even now, at the height of the season, you may encounter the ghost of an Edwardian nanny searching the beach for her vanished charges.

The Dover Road traveller, soon after shaking off London, finds himself in the curious complex of Medway towns, one leading into another. The most pause-worthy, Rochester, straddles the Medway. Augustine, in 604, founded a bishopric there. The cathedral, a Norman foundation, took the place of the early church. Although the cathedral and the castle are major attractions, Rochester is full of smaller but history-rich houses and inns, many of them associated with Dickens. On the north side of Rochester, Strood is manifestly industrial; to the east, Chatham and Gillingham speak, in the passing tense, of docks and shipbuilding.

Kent can show castles, or fortified houses, of every period and in every state of preservation, from the primarily Norman keep of Dover castle to the coastal Martello towers, part of a chain constructed during the Napoleonic Wars. Stately homes include Knole, Leeds Castle and Penshurst Place. Ightham Mote, which dates from about 1340, is a splendid example of a moated manor-house.

Most villages contain one or two timber-framed houses, particularly in the wooded wealden area. Brick with infillings of flint is more typical of the Downland country, where flints are found among the chalk. Elsewhere, indeed almost everywhere, the weather-boarded cottage, with its horizontally lapped white-washed clapboards, is very characteristic.

Flora and Fauna

Of Great Britain's fifty species of wild orchid, three-quarters can be found in Kent. A similar richness extends to wild flowers in general, especially in the valley of the Medway. Blean Woods, north of Canterbury, harbour endless varieties of birds, insects and fungi. The tree-lover should visit the Forestry Commission's national pinetum at Bedgebury near Goudhurst.

Many migratory birds and butterflies halt in Kent, if only to rest their wings. The Foreland is a favourite landing-place for bird visitors in spring. Butterfly immigrants mostly prefer the cliffs of Folkestone and Fairlight.

In Romney Marsh there is the marsh frog, a biggish creature with a stentorian croak. A few who were imported by a frog-lover in 1935 proceeded to breed out of hand, and in May they bring insomnia throughout the district. Unfortunately they are not edible – or their spread might be halted. The disappointed gourmet would be well advised to solace himself with Whitstable oysters instead.

Knole, near Sevenoaks   *Aerofilms*

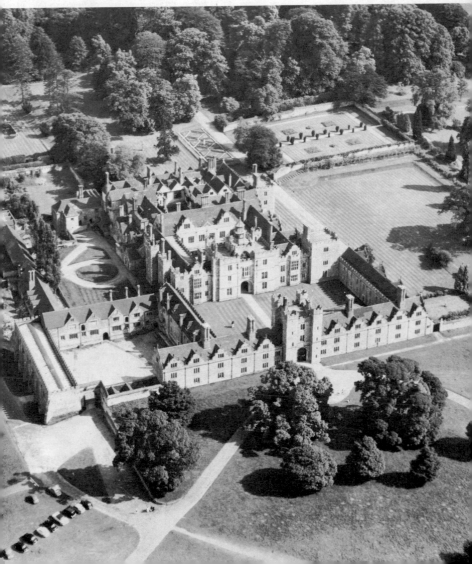

Some houses and gardens open to the public

Boughton Monchelsea Place *Map* FH 14. *Stone battlemented manor house in deer park. Dress collection, tapestries, furniture.* M. B. Winch, Esq.

Chiddingstone Castle *Map* FE 14. *Picturesquely situated castle mansion, with unusual collections of Ancient Egyptian and Japanese art, Buddhistic images, also royal Stuart and Jacobite collections.* Denys E. Bower, Esq.

Chilham Castle, Chilham *Map* GA 15. *Jacobean castle built by Inigo Jones in 1616, with Norman keep on Roman foundations. Beautiful gardens.* Viscount Massereene & Ferrard, DL.

Godington Park 2m W of Ashford *Map* GA 14. *Stuart mansion with fine Jacobean panelling and carving. Portraits, furniture, china.* Alan Wyndham Green, Esq.

Knole Sevenoaks *Map* FF 15. *Begun in 1456 by an Archbishop of Canterbury, granted by Elizabeth I to Thomas Sackville, who enlarged it into one of the most imposing private houses in England. Large collection of pictures, furniture, etc.* NT.

Lympne Castle Lympne Old Village, 3½m NW of Hythe. *A small Medieval castle, built 1360 on the foundation of an older building. Stone door-jambs, archways, fireplaces all of architectural interest and the King Post bedroom, almost untouched since the 14th cent.*

The Owl House Lamberhurst *Map* FG 13. *16th-cent. tile-hung half-timbered cottage with smuggling associations and woodland gardens.* The Marchioness of Dufferin and Ava.

Owletts Cobham *Map* FG 16. *Red-brick house of Charles II's reign. Carolean staircase, plasterwork.* NT.

Penshurst Place *Map* FF 14. *Mainly Elizabethan mansion, with Great Hall dating from 1340. Furniture, portraits, armour. See also p. 159.* The Rt Hon. Viscount De L'Isle, VC.

Quebec House Westerham *Map* FE 15. *Brick 17th-cent. house with mementoes of General Wolfe.* NT.

Sissinghurst Castle *Map* FH 13. *The late V. Sackville-West created the lovely gardens surrounding the Tudor house (Spring Garden Apr–May, Old Roses Jun–Jul).* NT. *Gardens only open.*

Sissinghurst Place Gardens *Map* FH 13. *Beautiful gardens in and around ruins of house burnt down in 1948. Specimen trees, flowering shrubs, walled garden, etc.* Mrs Lindsay Drummond.

Smallhythe Place 2m S of Tenterden *Map* FJ 13. *Half-timbered house c. 1480, from 1899–1928 home of Ellen Terry. Relics of famous actors and actresses.* NT.

Books for further reading

History

EDWARD HASTED *The History and Topographical Survey of the County of Kent* 2nd edn 12 vols 1797–1801

F. W. JESSUP *A History of Kent* (Darwin Finlayson, 1958); *Kent History Illustrated* 1966

Topography

RICHARD CHURCH *Kent* (The County Books Series) 1948; *A Portrait of Canterbury* 1968

J. C. COX *Kent* (Little Guides Series) 7th edn by R. F. Jessup 1950

MARCUS CROUCH *Kent* 1968

DOROTHY GARDINER *Companion into Kent* 2nd edn 1947

R. H. GOODSALL *The Ancient Road to Canterbury* 1960

R. H. GOODSALL *The Medway and its Tributaries* 1955

R. F. and F. W. JESSUP *The Cinque Ports* 1952

SHEILA KAYE-SMITH *The Weald of Kent and Sussex* 1953

W. J. S. MURRAY *Romney Marsh* 1953

Natural History

J. M. HARRISON *The Birds of Kent* 2 vols 1953

Two personal views

FRANK KENDON *The Small Years* 1930

C. HENRY WARREN *A Boy in Kent* 1937

Gazetteer

KENT

Population figures are based on the 1962 Census. Figures for large towns may include other places within the borough or urban administration.

Kentish oast-houses   *Jarrold*

Appledore (FK 12). As attractive as its name, a peaceful wide-streeted village of good cottages and houses looking out over Romney Marsh from its slight eminence above the Royal Military Canal. There is a good 14th-cent. church with fine stained glass and Flemish wood-carving; the church was partially burned in one of those 14th-cent. raids by French marauders.

Aylesford* (FH 15) EC Wed (4,450). Notwithstanding Aylesford's paper-making activities, the picturesque old village remains beside its restored 14th cent. bridge over the Medway – its peace, too, mercifully restored since the building of the Maidstone by-pass. Since 1949 Carmelite monks and sisters have returned to the Friary which their order inhabited as long ago as 1284. On the hills around are many ancient monuments, the best being Kit's Coty House*, 1½ m. NE, the earliest prehistoric monument in SE England (AM). A mile upstream, from Aylesford, beautiful by the river, stands the restored Norman castle of Allington*, now occupied by Carmelite nuns but open to the public in the afternoons in summer.

Barfreston*, app. 4 m. E of Barham (GC 15). The church is a rare and exquisite specimen of Norman architecture, rich with carving and moulding. Notice especially the S doorway, and the church bell in the yew tree.

Biddenden (FJ 13). Two sisters who were joined together at birth and lived to the age of 34 provide the village legend. More interesting are the many ancient weavers' cottages lining the street, the old Cloth Hall and the 14th–15th-cent. church with its unusual collection of portrait brasses.

Bigbury 2 m. W of Canterbury (GB 15). Iron-Age settlement on the brow of a hill overlooking Canterbury. Here, too, Britons tried unavailingly to defend themselves against the onslaught of Roman legions in 54 BC.

Biggin Hill (FE 15) EC Wed (3,675). Famous R.A.F. airfield in the Battle of Britain. Some of the aircraft are exhibited beside the road.

Broadstairs (GD 16) EC Wed (20,300). Smallest and most individual of the Thanet coast resorts. Sandy bay below gardened cliffs overlooked by Georgian houses and sheltered by the same old pier that pleased Dickens. Although he lived there, there is no evidence that the Bleak House on the cliff is the one of which he wrote (open in the afternoon in summer).

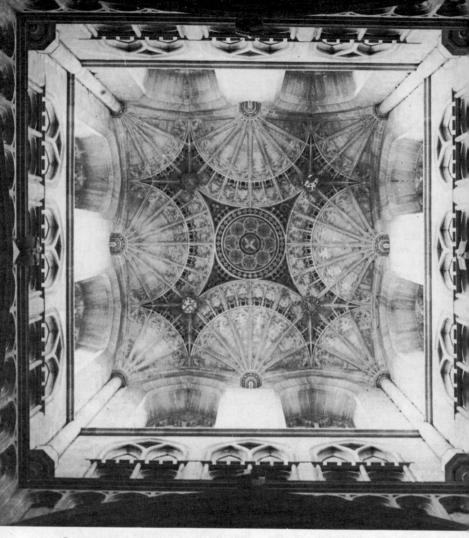

Canterbury Cathedral: looking up into the Bell Harry Tower   Reece·Winstone

Canterbury** (GB 15). EC Thurs (32,900). Busy centre of prosperous farming country, a town rich in history going back to pre-Roman days, but above all dominated by its famous and venerable cathedral. When St Augustine arrived here in 597 he found Christian worship already being conducted in St Martin's Church (which though restored is perhaps the oldest in England so used). King Ethelbert

followed his conversion by a gift of land, on which Augustine founded a monastery outside the city walls and the Cathedral within. The early bishops were buried at St Augustine's, which was then more important than the cathedral, but after the murder (1170) and subsequent enshrinement of Becket the pre-eminence of the cathedral became absolute. Parts of St Augustine's are used as a missionary college. Excavations have revealed the graves of the early bishops and of the little church of St Pancras, formerly a pagan place of worship.

The cathedral, basically 11th cent., was considerably altered in the 15th cent. One striking feature is the way in which the choir is raised above the nave and the altar above the choir. Do not miss the site of Becket's murder, the Black Prince's Tomb, the Norman crypt, the beautiful stained glass. The city's 14th-cent. West Gate has a good museum. Of its 11th-cent. castle only the keep remains. In a vault in St Dunstan's Church lies the severed head of Sir Thomas More. The earliest thing in Canterbury is the mound known as the Dane John, originally a burial mound, fortified later by the Normans and now the centre of a park.

Canterbury Cricket Festival, in early August, is famous.

Charing (FK 14). Good timbered houses and remains of a palace of the Archbishop of Canterbury where Henry VII and Henry VIII were entertained.

Chiddingstone (FE 14). Picturesque village with 16th–17th-cent. timber buildings (NT) and attractive groups of oast houses. The mansion known as Chiddingstone Castle has a collection of Stuart and other relics.

Chilham* (GA 15). Round the spacious square at the top of the village are gracious timbered houses, an old inn, a richly monumented 15th-cent. church, and the imposing gateway to the present castle built in 1616. Among the beech-trees in the park are the Keep of a Norman castle and the largest and oldest heronry in England.

The Cinque Ports. A defence system of fortified ports built up during the Middle Ages to protect SE England against raiders and invaders from the Continent. In return for certain customs and other privileges (often abused by smugglers), the ports provided men and ships when required by the King. The original Cinque Ports were Dover, Sandwich, Romney, Hythe, Hastings.

Cobham (FG 16). A name well known to readers of *Pickwick*: the Leather Bottle Inn has Dickens relics. Owletts, a 17th-cent. brick mansion, is open to the public (NT). The church has a celebrated collection of medieval brasses.

Cranbrook (FH 13) EC Wed (4,150). Former cloth-weaving town of painted weatherboard houses, with a splendid windmill said to be the largest working mill in England. In the 15th-cent. church is a baptistery for total immersion, and a room over the S porch was used as a prison during the Marian persecution.

Deal (GD 15). EC Thurs (26,800). For centuries a naval dockyard, Deal has no sheltered harbour; stores have always had to be carried off in small sailing or rowing boats. Deal therefore has a maritime tradition strengthened by the reputation of its pilots – and lifeboatmen (the treacherous Goodwin Sands lie only a few miles off shore here). Deal is a good place for fishing and golf. Deal and Walmer castles (open weekdays and Sunday afternoons) were built by Henry VIII to protect the shipping in the Downs: Walmer Castle is the official residence of the Lord Warden of the Cinque Ports.

Dover* (GD 14) EC Wed (36,000). Thousands of years ago the famous White Cliffs were part of a much higher ridge of chalk which continued across to the cliffs of Calais (clearly visible on a fine day). Ancient past and bustling present mingle in this busiest of cross-Channel ports, once chief of the medieval Cinque Ports. To guide their legionaries across the water the

Dover: the Roman pharos
Reece Winstone

Romans (who called the place Dubris) built a pharos, or lighthouse; much of it still stands in the Castle precincts. The great Norman castle* (AM, open weekdays and Sunday afternoons) is grimly impressive on its steep height overlooking town and sea, especially when floodlit at night. Near the eastern dock German shellfire from Calais during the last war laid waste an area now occupied by modern blocks of flats and a hotel. An ever-fascinating town.

Downe (FE 16). Charles Darwin lived at Down House for 40 years until he died there in 1882. Here he wrote *The Origin of Species* and made notable experiments with orchid cultivation. (House open daily, except Fridays.)

Dungeness (GA 11). A vast sheet of shingle, deposited by the swift Channel tides and still growing seaward. Once a place of melancholy solitude and a famous bird sanctuary, it is now dominated by the huge nuclear power station visible for miles along the coast. Another newcomer is the modern lighthouse of revolutionary design, tall and slender, with an automatic light and a fog signal booming from sixty loudspeakers. The old lighthouse still stands close by. The shore here descends very steeply, and bathing is *most dangerous*.

Ebbsfleet, Pegwell Bay (GD 16). A full-scale model of a Viking ship (sailed over from Norway in 1949) commemorates the landing of Hengist and Horsa in 449. Landing here a century and a half later St Augustine brought the first great Christian missionary effort to Kent and S Britain.

Faversham* (GB 16) EC Thurs (14,260). The attractive town centre lies north of the A2. Abbey Street, with an array of timber-framed houses, leads to the site of the abbey where King Stephen was buried. Arden's House still survives, once belonging to a town mayor whose murder in 1550 inspired the Elizabethan melodrama 'Arden of Faversham'. The church is notable for its crown spire (1797) and medieval aisled transepts, 100 feet long.

Folkestone (GC 13) EC Wed (43,880). The parish church, well placed on the cliffs, stands between the old town down by the harbour (whence steamers sail for Boulogne) and the more modern hotel and shopping area. The Leas is the finest seacoast promenade in England, with views extending to the French coast. E of the harbour the cliffs have fallen away to form the Warren, a great place for fossils and flowers.

Fordwich, 2 m. NE of Canterbury (GB 15). A picturesque cul-de-sac, once the port of Canterbury. On the N end of the timbered tiny Town Hall is the crane from which nagging wives were dipped in the River Stour.

Godmersham, 2 m. S of Chilham (GA 15). Jane Austen often stayed here when her brother owned the Georgian house known as Godmersham Park. A 12th-cent. bas relief of Thomas Becket in the church is the earliest known.

Goudhurst (FH 13) EC Wed (2,675). Attractive little hill-top town with a swan-graced pond and a wide view over undulating acres of orchards and hop gardens. In the 15th-cent. church are excellent monuments to the Culpepers, once a force in this land. Two m. S at Bedgebury is the beautifully laid-out Pinetum, planted when the one at Kew began to succumb to London smoke and fumes.

Gravesend (FG 17) EC Wed (54,900). Busy Thames-side town. The famous Red Indian princess Pocahontas lies buried in St George's Church.

Groombridge, 3½ m. SW of Tunbridge Wells (FF 13). Large triangular green rising to a long row of brick and tiled cottages; larger houses looking on. The whole delightful. Do not miss the moated manor house or the curious clock in the church.

Hever, 2 m. SE of Edenbridge (FE 14). Henry VIII met Anne Boleyn at the moated 14th–15th-cent. castle where she had spent much of her girlhood. Fine trees in the grounds, which are open to visitors on stated occasions.

Hythe (GB 13) EC Wed (11,100). Pleasant little shopping town set back from its shingle beach. Under the partly Norman church is a crypt stacked with bones and skulls. Hythe was one of the original Cinque Ports, but like Sandwich and Romney it has seen its harbour turn to dry land. Through the town runs the Royal Military Canal, a 'moat' built during the Napoleonic invasion scare and running all the way to Rye; it now provides boating and fishing. Hythe is the terminus of the world's smallest-gauge public railway (all stations to Dungeness). About ½ m. N is the fine restored Norman castle of Saltwood, whence on a winter's evening in 1170 rode four knights on their way to murder Thomas Becket in Canterbury Cathedral; it is now a private home, but the grounds are open at certain times.

Ightham* (FF 15). The 14th-cent. moated manor-house known as the Mote (open Friday afternoons) is one of the few extant specimens of its kind. Lovely gardens. On Oldbury Hill, to the SW of the village, is a large prehistoric hill-fort and the site of Stone-Age rock shelters (NT).

Kit's Coty House. *See* **Aylesford.**

Lamberhurst (FG 13). Village of timbered houses, once a centre of the iron industry. Two m. W are the remains of Bayham Abbey, and just to the SE the lake-side ruin of Scotney Castle (gardens open Wed & Sat in summer).

Leeds Castle* (FJ 15). Through the trees beside the A20 romantic glimpses may be had of the magnificent 12th–14th-cent. castle on its island in the lake. Still privately inhabited, it is open to the public only occasionally.

Lenham (FJ 15). The 13th–15th-cent. church is notable for its woodwork.

Lullingstone (FF 16). Excavated remains of a Roman villa★ with a fine mosaic floor. The Tudor mansion known as Lullingstone Castle (open Wednesday afternoons in summer) was long the centre of a silk-growing enterprise; the silk for the Queen's wedding dress was produced here, but the silk farm is now at Ayot St Lawrence in Hertfordshire.

Lydd (GA 12) EC Wed (4,170). The airport (Ferryfield) serves the air car-ferry to Le Touquet. The Anglo-French cable by which electric power is exchanged comes ashore at Dungeness and at Lydd is fed into the British grid system. Lydd gave its name to the explosive lyddite, first developed at the military research depot here. The spacious 14th-cent. church with its massive tower is justly called 'The Cathedral of the Marshes'.

Lyminge (GB 14). The chancel of the present church is part of an earlier church built about 975 which incorporated Roman materials. The massive tower was added in the 16th cent.

Lympne (GB 13). In Roman days, before the sea receded, this was a port. The fortress which guarded it fell into ruins after a landslip; its remains, known as Studfall Castle, are still to be seen at the foot of the hill. From Lympne the Roman 'Stone Street' ran (and most of it still runs) straight to Canterbury along a ridge of the Downs with long views of weald and sea. Lympne is now an airport for cross-Channel passenger traffic. The house known as Lympne Castle includes part of a 15th-cent. moated manor.

Maidstone (FH 15) EC Wed (65,790). Capital and chief market town of Kent, straddling the River Medway. Local industries: timber, paper, cement, beer. Alongside the 14th-cent. church is the Archbishop's Palace, once belonging to the Archbishops of Canterbury; it has a fine panelled banqueting hall. Opposite, in the old stable, is a museum of old carriages. Maidstone museum, in the former Chiddingstone Manor in St Faith's Street, has good art and archaeological collections.

New Romney (GA 12) EC Wed (2,600). One of the original Cinque Ports, it replaced Old Romney (still there, 2 m. farther inland, with its 13th-cent. timber-roofed church)

Maidstone: the Archbishop's Palace

Reece Winstone

when the sea receded. But a violent storm in 1287 altered the course of the River Rother and left even the new town without access to the sea (now a mile away at Littlestone). New Romney's church is largely Norman, with a fine tower and nave.

Penshurst (FF 14). In the gracious 14th-cent. mansion of Penshurst Place★ Sir Philip Sidney was born in 1554; it has been the home of the Sidney family for over 400 years.

Reculver (GC 16). The still visible remains of a Roman fort (AM) and the Western wall of an ancient

Reculver Towers   *Jarrold*

church. Early 19th-cent. prints show the twin towers still surmounted by tall spires; these went long ago, but the towers were so useful as a navigational guide to Thames shipping that they were taken over by Trinity House; they are now in the care of the Ministry of Works (AM).

Richborough★ (GD 16). Quietly impressive ruins of the huge fort built by the Romans to protect their harbour (since silted up by the River Stour) and the entry to what was then a wide navigable channel (also silted up) cutting behind the island of

Thanet to Reculver. Acres of ground are enclosed by stout walls still bonded by Roman mortar, and remains of the amphitheatre are visible (AM). Good museum.

Rochester (FH 16) EC Wed (55,100). Since Roman days Rochester has been a place of great strategic import. Here Watling Street crosses the Medway and here the Medway opens out to a wonderful natural harbour. In 604 Augustine founded the third English bishopric here. On the site of his church the Normans raised a cathedral; they also built a great castle. The remains of these two buildings are still the principal historic features of the town. Rochester has many Dickens associations; his home at Gad's Hill is on the NW outskirts of the town.

Romney Marsh. (*See p.* 146.)

Sandwich (GD 15) EC Wed (4,590). A town of ancient ghosts: ghosts of the days when it was an important Cinque Port and fishing and smuggling throve. Now the nearest sea is $1\frac{1}{2}$ m. away. Rebuilding and street-widening are changing the town's face, but the huge echoing churches still tell their vivid story.

Sevenoaks (FF 15) EC Wed (18,200). Pleasant dormitory town on greensand hills 400–500 ft. above sea-level. Beside Sevenoaks School (founded 1432) is an entrance to the great deer park of Knole★, one of England's largest and finest private mansions. Built 1456, enlarged in the early 17th cent., it still belongs to the Sackville family. Valuable collection of pictures, furniture, etc. (NT).

Tenterden (FJ 13) EC Wed (5,620). Attractive town with old buildings and an unusually wide green-verged main street. The church has a notable shingled tower from which it is said one can sometimes see the French

Tenterden *Jarrold*

coast. William Caxton, first English printer, was born here in 1422. Ellen Terry, the actress, spent her last years at Smallhythe, 2 m. S.

Tonbridge (FF 14) E C Wed (28,550). The bridge spans the Medway, a busy point guarded since Norman times by a castle of which the gatehouse is the best remnant. The well-known public school for boys dates from 1553. Tonbridge, a busy shopping and market town with many fine old buildings, has become a notorious bottleneck on the A21 London–Hastings road.

Tunbridge Wells (FF 13) E C Wed and Sat (43,490). This busy residential town has expanded enormously since it became a fashionable 18th-cent. spa centred round its chalybeate spring. Then, as now, the tree-shaded, colonnaded promenade known as the Pantiles★ (where the waters may still be taken) was the gem of the town.

Walmer (GD 15) E C Thurs (5,820). *See* **Deal** *above.*

Westerham (FE 15) E C Wed (4,080). General Wolfe, who spent his early years in the square brick house known as Quebec House (NT), is commemorated by a monument on the small village green. Not far to the S is Chartwell, home of the late Sir Winston Churchill.

Whitstable (GB 16) E C Wed (22,570). The world-famous oyster beds have been in continuous cultivation for at least 2,000 years. Old houses, harbour for small yachts, modern jetty for small cargo ships. The Canterbury–Whitstable railway, laid by George Stephenson, was the first passenger line to be opened (1830); the engine which pulled the first train, the Invicta, still stands by the S E gate of Canterbury's city wall.

Wrotham (FG 15). Splendid view of the Weald from the roadside at the top of the hill. The conspicuous mast is the BBC's VHF transmitter. The attractive village at the foot of the hill has an interesting 13th–15th-cent. church with a fine collection of portrait brasses.

Wye (GA 14). Quiet little town under the Downs. Fine old oak beams and good modern glass in the church; an attractive Georgian mill-house by the bridge. Wye is well known for its racecourse and for its Agricultural College (offshoot of London University).

Opposite: Detail from the original painting by Rowland Hilder, 'The Garden of England' well describes this county of hop-gardens, oast-houses, and orchards. Many of the Kentish Roman roads are still in use today. Samuel Palmer, painter of visionary landscapes, lived in Kent.

The Goring Gap

Geoffrey Boumphrey

OXFORDSHIRE

AN INTRODUCTION BY MARTYN SKINNER

Many people think of Oxfordshire only in connection with Oxford and the Thames, and picture its landscape as one of watermeadows, willows and a spire in the background. And although one of its chief characteristics is in fact variety, there is some justification for this restricted view, since the county is centred on the basin of the Thames; and the river, fed by four tributaries, the Evenlode, the Windrush, the Cherwell and the Thame, forms its southern boundary for 71 miles. Nor is the flat country confined to the neighbourhood of the Thames. The great Oxfordshire plain, formed largely of clay, spreads north towards Bicester and east to where the steep scarp of the Chilterns extends its striking horizon. To the west of this plain the Cotswolds rise less conspicuously (their steep side is in Gloucestershire) and blend in the north-west with the ironstone area round Banbury. It is these three ranges of hills – chalk, limestone and iron-stone – that bring to Oxfordshire such distinctive variety, and give Oxford its one undeniable advantage over Cambridge: a surrounding countryside of singular interest and character.

Opposite: Detail from the original painting by Walter Hoyle.
This county of dreaming rivers (Thames, Cherwell, Windrush, Evenlode), of willows and green meadows, is famous for its University city. Here we see towers and spires, a dinosaur and other objects from the University Museum, and (crossing Magdalen Bridge) a reminder of the near-by car industry.

The Thames Valley

Indeed, an undergraduate at Oxford who wished to spend a day exploring the country would have the choice – without leaving the county – of four regions, each quite different from the other, and each with a distinctive scenery and architecture of its own. Even if he kept to the river he would find contrast enough: the Thames at Henley, where a magnificent, wide, straight reach forms 'the finest regatta course in the world' (partly in Bucks), being very different from what Matthew Arnold called 'the stripling Thames at Bablock Hythe', winding through rather remote, flat country of willowed fields, grey humped bridges, and occasional pleasant pubs beside them. In this part are Kelmscott, where William Morris devised the Kelmscott Chaucer, and Bampton, where Morris dancing is still performed in the village street.

In some ways the Thames gives the county a kind of substitute coastline. Regatta Week at Henley and Eights Week at Oxford are great social as well as sporting events; and the increased popularity of boating, due to the development of the cabin cruiser, has given places like Goring and Henley the status of holiday resorts. It is in the Goring Gap, where the river cuts through the chalk, and the Chilterns and Berkshire Downs rise steeply on either side, that the scenery is most spectacular. Here, if anywhere, history and geography mingle. It is one of the great thoroughfares and crossroads in the south of England, the only railway-worthy gap between London and Bath, and the point where those ancient roads, the Icknield Way and the Ridgeway, join and intersect the Thames.

The Oxfordshire Chilterns

The Romans were not a people to neglect so strategic an area, and no doubt they made good use of the Icknield Way. Where it crosses a farm near Goring a field is still called the Vineyards, supposed relic of their attempt to grow grapes (it faces south-east as a vineyard should). A little farther north the Way intersects Grim's Dyke (or Ditch), 'the most mysterious and elusive earthwork of any of its kind in England', and skirts a hill named after St Birinus, the Apostle of Wessex, who converted its king, Cynegils, in 634, and founded the See of Dorchester.

The Chilterns are typical chalk country: valleys without streams, steep grassy banks sprinkled with juniper and spindle, beechwoods with flinty floors and the occasional yew, thin-soiled fields that gleam white in March. Estate records show that some of the beechwoods are centuries old, their management based on a system of selective felling and regeneration. In them until quite recently the chair-bodgers and the tentpeg-makers pitched their cabins (piled high with shavings on three sides) and worked their treadle lathes, a craft now extinct like many of the rare flora – coral root, golden saxifrage, *Daphne mezereum*, the great pig-nut, the man and military orchises – that used to be found on the hills, and in some cases perhaps still are. Where the hills are more open, the chalk is well suited to the growing of barley, and the area round Goring is noted for the quality of its malting samples.

The Oxfordshire Cotswolds

Barley is a staple of the Cotswolds too – but what a contrast they are in other respects, after the flint and brick buildings and white soil. (And how pleasant to be beside a stream again after the dry chalk.) Dry-stone walls instead of hedges,

grey limestone houses and barns with Stonesfield slates that attract moss and lichen – take away the villages and the farms and the unique quality of the Cotswold landscape would be lost. Sheep harmonize with the grey stone of the walls; and when wool was a national staple, the Cotswolds were prosperous: the size of the Cotswold sheep (a few years ago there was still one flock in existence), the largest of the native breeds, was evidence of the demand for large fleeces and family joints.

The Oxfordshire Ironstone

In the north-west corner of the county the presence of ironstone becomes apparent as the honey-coloured stone replaces the grey. The character of the countryside alters too, as the high, walled wolds become more wooded and broken. Round Wroxton Abbey, opencast iron mining has been in progress. After the ore has been extracted, the topsoil is replaced, and the land is fit to be cultivated, if not to be seen. Even the area round Great Tew was recently threatened; but local opposition was fortunately successful – fortunately because it is one of the finest parts of the county.

Great Tew, gold and thatched cottages steeply embowered in splendid trees; Burford, a single-streeted masterpiece of grey stone; Ewelme, incomparably grouped round its fine flint church; Dorchester, with its willowed abbey, and curving bridge and street that wind like the Thames beside it – each of these four contrasting villages seems to sum up its own region. A county that contains such diversity is rich indeed.

Country Houses, Towns and Churches

Like its villages, Oxfordshire's country houses are representative: Broughton of the north, Cotswold Chastleton unchanged for centuries, Chiltern Stonor and Mapledurham by the Thames. There are many others, notably Blenheim Palace, Oxford's Versailles, where Winston Churchill was born. Churchill's grave is in Bladon Churchyard, nearby. During the Civil Wars the county was the Royalist stronghold, and many of its mansions took knocks from Cromwell's artillery. Rycote, near Thame, was the scene of a battle. Its enormous house was burnt down in the 18th century, leaving only a tower, an exquisite chapel and a ghost behind.

The county's smaller towns are most of them famous for something: Witney for blankets, Banbury for its cross and its cakes (apart from marmalade, the only item for the gourmet the county offers), Woodstock for Blenheim, Henley for its Regatta, Thame for having the largest one-day show in England, and Watlington for being the smallest town.

Its churches are many of them noted for their spires – it has been suggested that this may be because Oxford Cathedral had one of the earliest spires in England – if not the earliest. Witney, Burford, Cassington, Bampton, Shipton and Broadwell are a few examples. In the north, the churches of Bloxham, Adderbury and King's Sutton (just over the border in Northants) are locally proverbial as typifying length, strength and beauty.

Off the Beaten Track

Oxfordshire has its remote places and minor curiosities. Otmoor, for instance, that strange inland marsh north of Oxford with no road across it – an obvious place for a bird sanctuary (it became a bombing range instead). Or Wychwood,

ord : Tom Tower, from the cloisters of Christ Church   *Reece Winstone*

once a medieval royal forest, equally atmospheric. Or what has been called the Flora Thompson country, the uplands near Brackley, where the hamlet of Juniper Hill is the *Lark Rise* of a book that has become a classic as a description of a cottage childhood in the Victorian countryside. Typical local curiosities are the Rollright Stones in the north of the county; the monument at Chalgrove to John Hampden, fatally wounded in the battle there; a Roman well with a Jacobean well-head in a farmyard at Headington; the Maharajah's Well at Stoke Row near Henley, presented to the village by the Maharajah of Benares to requite an obligation to the local squire; the ruins of Godstow Nunnery, associated with Fair Rosamund; or – in Oxford itself and hardly off the beaten track – the queer circle of classic heads at the base of the Sheldonian Theatre, faceless with weather, and once described as 'a collection of Bernard Shaws'.

Oxford – the University

It is a varied list, and brings us back to Oxford itself, as any consideration of the county must. Historically Oxford was of great importance in the 17th century, when Charles I made it an alternative capital and started it off as a home of lost causes. Few cities are so packed with ancient and notable buildings – its very railway station is unique as being on the site of an ancient abbey. And in spite of cars and Cowley it is still possible to get an idea of the city as it once was: either from the National Trust property on Boar's Hill, where the distant view resembles one of those engravings by Hoefnagle or Farington still to be found in its own print-shops; or from the top of the Sheldonian Theatre, an amazing roofscape of domes, spires, towers and pinnacles; or early on a Sunday or Bank Holiday morning, from the end of the High Street itself, a majestic curve of colleges, 'Europe's loveliest street'. Trees play a great part in the Oxford landscape: 'Towery city and branchy between towers' remains a true and vivid description. Another feature is the gardens – what other city (except possibly Cambridge) can rival these? Apart from the noted University buildings, like the Sheldonian Theatre or the Bodleian Library and Divinity School or the Radcliffe Camera, the finest architecture is to be found in the many colleges, of which University is the oldest, Christ Church the largest and Magdalen the loveliest. The last of these alone would be worth visiting England to see. Visitors, coming from all over the world, are themselves a characteristic sight: 'Oxford they see, and Oxford sees them too'.

Oxford: the City

Oxford is a well-known city in its own right, and has given its name to a motor-car, a marmalade and a religious movement. In the 19th century it narrowly escaped being Swindon, through a proposal to establish the railway works on meadows to the west of the city. In the 20th, owing to the accident of a Mr W. Morris setting up a bicycle shop in one of its suburbs, it developed into a large industrial centre. Although the industrial area is well away from the old city, the increase of population and traffic has affected the latter's character. It is difficult, as one waits to cross the traffic procession in the High Street, to imagine that not many decades ago grass grew in the cobbles where now the vibration of wheels threatens the fabric of the colleges.

As might be expected in so venerable a place, curious customs have survived. Every year the city's bounds are beaten; and each May-Day morning the college choir sings from Magdalen Tower, listened to by a crowd on the bridge beneath.

OXFORDSHIRE

For two days in September the wide street of St Giles is given over to an annual Fair, to the dislocation of local traffic – which was also once dislocated on another occasion when (according to local legend) some undergraduates discovered that an ancient charter gave them the right to practise archery in the High Street, which they proceeded to do until the prerogative was hastily repealed.

Oxfordshire has no Hardy (few counties have), though Oxford is mentioned as Christminster in his novels. Through Oxford it has been associated with many literary names: Johnson endured the University; Gibbon rejected it; it rejected Shelley. Perhaps the literary names most closely associated with Oxfordshire are those of Robert Bridges and Matthew Arnold; and on Oxford itself, Arnold has certainly the final word:

> *That sweet city with her dreaming spires,*
> *She needs not June for beauty's heightening,*
> *Lovely all times she lies, lovely tonight!*

Oxford: St John's College Library

Reece Winstone

Some houses and gardens open to the public

Blenheim Palace Woodstock *Map* EE 21. *Vanbrugh's impressive masterpiece. See p. 176.* His Grace the Duke of Marlborough.

Botanic Garden Oxford *Map* EF 20. Opposite Magdalen College. *Famous botanic gardens founded in 1621.* University of Oxford.

Broughton Castle nr Banbury *Map* EE 23. *Moat-surrounded castle built 1306, 'modernised' 1554. Civil War family relics. Chinese wallpaper. Pictures.* The Lord Saye and Sele.

Chastleton House *Map* EC 22. *Jacobean manor-house entirely unaltered. Fine panelling, plasterwork, tapestries. Original furnishings. 17th-cent. topiary garden.* Alan Clutton-Brock, Esq.

Ditchley Park 2m NE of Charlbury *Map* ED 21. *Important 18th-cent. mansion designed by Gibbs. Now Anglo-American Conference Centre.* Ditchley Foundations Ltd.

Greys Court 2½m W of Henley-on-Thames *Map* EH 18. *13th-cent. manor-house, fortified in 14th cent. by Lord Grey who fought at Crecy.* Sir Felix Brunner.

Rousham House 8m W of Bicester *Map* EE 22. *Built 1640, with 18th- & 19th-cent. alterations. Fine collection of pictures and bronzes. Only surviving William Kent landscape garden.* C. Cottrell-Dormer, Esq.

Books for further reading

City and University

DACRE BALSDON *Oxford Life* 1957

R. FASNACHT *History of the City of Oxford* 1954

W. GAUNT *Oxford* 1965

CHRISTOPHER HOBHOUSE *Oxford: as it was and as it is today* 5th edn rev. Marcus Dick 1952

J. MORRIS *Oxford* 1965

A. R. WOOLLEY *Oxford: University and City* 1951

Natural History

W. B. ALEXANDER *A revised list of the Birds of Oxfordshire* 1947

W. J. ARKELL *The Geology of Oxford* 1947

G. C. DRUCE *The Flora of Oxfordshire* 2nd edn 1927

R. PLOT *The Natural History of Oxfordshire* 1677, 1705

History, topography, general

F. G. BRABANT *Oxfordshire* (Little Guides series) 1933

JOANNA CANNAN *Oxfordshire* (County Books series) 1952

M. GELLING *The Place-Names of Oxfordshire* 1953–4

S. JENNETT (ed.) *Oxford and District* (The Travellers Guides) 1965

R. L. P. JOWITT *Berkshire and Oxfordshire* (Penguin Guides) 1950

R. M. MARSHALL *Oxfordshire Byways* 1949

A. F. MARTIN and R. W. STEEL (ed.) *The Oxford Region, a scientific and historical survey* 1954

A. MEE *Oxfordshire* 1965

JOHN PIPER *Oxfordshire* (Shell Guides) rev. edn 1953

FLORA THOMPSON *Lark Rise to Candleford, a trilogy* 1945

REGINALD TURNOR *Oxfordshire* (Vision of England series) 1949

E. C. WILLIAMS *Companion into Oxfordshire* 2nd edn 1943

Victoria County History

Vol. 1 ed. by L. F. SALZMAN 1939

Vol. 2 ed. by WILLIAM PAGE 1907

Vol. 3 ed. by H. E. SALTER and M. D. LOBEL 1954

Vol. 5 ed. by M. D. LOBEL 1957

Vol. 6 ed. by M. D. LOBEL 1959

Vol. 7 ed. by M. D. LOBEL 1962

Vol. 8 ed. by M. D. LOBEL 1965

Gazetteer

OXFORDSHIRE

Adderbury. On the hills above the Cherwell, 3 m. S of Banbury (EE 23), a village of thatched cottages and fine 17th-cent. houses. The early 15th-cent. church* is noted for its spire and its carved stonework; corbels, capitals and roof bosses are decorated with human figures, flowers and grotesques.

Bampton (ED 20). Quiet little town in the upper reaches of the Thames Valley. Noted centre of Morris Dancing. The Elizabethan manor house was formerly used by the deans of Exeter. The partly Norman church has a Saxon chancel arch.

Banbury (EE 24) EC Tues (21,000). The present Banbury Cross at the bottom of the hill on the A41 is a Victorian replacement of the original Cross of the nursery rhyme, which was destroyed by Puritans in 1602. A century later the church, too, was destroyed, to be replaced by the present 18th-cent. Palladian building. Genuine Banbury cakes are still being made. There is a busy and important cattle-market. Wroxton Abbey stands 3 m. NW. *See also* **Adderbury, Broughton.**

Bicester (EF 22) EC Thurs (5,500). Old-fashioned town with a market square. A well-known hunting centre. The church, neighboured by some good stone houses, has a typical small Saxon arch and some Norman work, but is mainly 14th cent. One and a half m. S is the site of the Roman town of Alchester.

Black Bourton, 1 m. N of Clanfield (EC 20). So called because it once belonged to the Black Canons of

Banbury Cross   Reece Winstone

Osney Abbey. A splendid series of 13th-cent. wall paintings* in the church has been revealed and restored.

Blenheim Palace*. *See* **Woodstock** *below.*

Bloxham* (EE 23). The 198-ft. church spire of this hill-top village makes a beautiful landmark for miles around. In the church note the painted screen, and the humorous carvings over the W door.

Broughton*, 2 m. SW of Banbury (EE 23). The moated castle, mainly 14th-cent., with 15th-cent. gatehouse, has been the seat of the Fiennes family (Lords Saye and Sele) for over 500 years. It was built by Thomas Broughton, whose coloured effigy is in the church he also built. In the chancel is a monument to William Fiennes, one of the founders of Connecticut in the 17th cent.

Burford* (EC 21). Numerous variations of the Cotswold building theme border the lovely street leading down to the bridge over the Windrush. The exterior of the fine 13th–15th cent.

Broughton Castle

Reece Winstone

church was defaced during the Civil War, when it was used as a temporary prison (*see inscription scratched on the font*). The interior with its chapels and monuments contains all the history of Burford. A busy little town, beautiful – and mercifully unspoilt.

Chalgrove (E G 19). Small village of thatched cottages, with an obelisk commemorating the battle (1643) at which John Hampden was fatally wounded.

Charlbury (E D 21). In the Evenlode Valley, looking over to the remaining parts of Wychwood Forest. A pleasant, stone-built little town: note 17th-cent. Lee Place and the splendid wistaria covering houses near the church. Two m. NE is Ditchley Park, an imposing 18th-cent. mansion.

Chastleton* (E C 22). Lovely secluded village with a great manor-house built c. 1610 by a Witney wool merchant. The manor was once owned by Robert Catesby, of Gunpowder Plot fame, and it has many Civil War associations. In its lovely grounds are a topiary garden, a box garden and a splendid old dovecote.

Chinnor (E H 20). On the Icknield Way at the foot of the Chilterns. The cement works repel but the village is pleasant enough with its elm trees and moated manor house. The church has pictures by Sir James Thornhill, 14th-cent. glass and brasses.

Chipping Norton (E D 22) E C Thurs (4,250). An old wool town, still making tweeds, overlooking a tributary of the Evenlode. Stone-built 18th-cent. houses and 17th-cent. almshouses.

Chislehampton (E F 19). Here is a Georgian church of a beautiful and rare simplicity with box pews, panelled pulpit and reader's desk. A narrow many-arched bridge crosses the Thames.

Burford

Churchill (E C 22). Warren Hastings was born here (1732). So was William Smith (1769), the pioneer geologist who produced the first geological map of England. The church tower is a deliberate copy of that of Magdalen College, Oxford.

Clifton Hampden (E F 19). The bridge over the Thames was designed by Gilbert Scott. The village of mellow red brick and thatch was the background to one of the uproarious incidents in *Three Men in a Boat*.

Cornwell (E C 22). Typical Cotswold stream-threaded village, thoroughly restored by Clough Williams-Ellis. The fine mansion with its formal gardens is well seen from the road.

Cropredy (E E 24). Rivers and streams were important features in the Civil War: here is another of the bridges where Royalists and Parliamentarians fought it out (1644). Suits of armour and some of the cannon balls are in the church.

Cuddesdon (E G 20). Well-situated village with a Theological College and a 17th-cent. house built as a palace for the Bishops of Oxford, later rebuilt by the celebrated, but unloved, Doctor Fell.

Deddington (E E 23). Village of honey-coloured stone with a remarkable number of large old houses. Only earthworks remain of the castle. The tower of the 14th-cent. church fell down in the 17th cent. and had to be rebuilt.

Dorchester* (E F 19). A cathedral city from 634–707, now a charming village on the Thames with a variety of good buildings and a huge Abbey church (12th–13th cent.). Do not miss the fine 'Jesse' window in the chancel. Wittenham Clumps are conspicuous across the river.

Elsfield (E F 20). Hill village with views over Oxford. Long the home of John Buchan, who is buried in the churchyard.

Enstone (E D 22). On one side of the sharp valley of the River Glyme is Neat Enstone; on the other, Church Enstone. Here is a fine tithe-barn built by the Abbot of Winchcombe (Glos.) in 1382. The church has chained books and coloured effigies.

Ewelme* (E G 19). One of the best villages in Oxfordshire. The 15th-cent. church has the tomb of Alice, Duchess of Suffolk, a granddaughter of Geoffrey Chaucer. The author, Jerome K. Jerome, is buried in the churchyard.

Great Milton, 4 m. W of Tetsworth (E G 20). The 14th-cent. church has a fine relief of Sir Ambrose Dormer encamped at Calais, a splendid four-poster Dormer monument and good brasses. Little Milton near by is a lovely village of thatched stone houses.

Great Tew (E D 22). A model village in the best sense; church, manor house and cottages being perfectly related to their surroundings. This was the work of John Claudius Loudoun, the landscape gardener, at the beginning of the 19th cent.

Henley-on-Thames* (E H 18) EC Wed (9,150). Beautifully situated among wooded hills, with a picturesque 18th-cent. bridge over a wide curve of the Thames, and many good-looking Georgian and older houses. The annual regatta, held in the first week of July, makes a gay and fashionable scene along the straight mile of river on the downstream side of the bridge. The church has monuments to many people notable in their day and still remembered: the tower is a prominent feature in distant views of the town.

Iffley*, 2 m. S of Oxford (E F 20). Here is one of the finest Norman churches in England; it has rich stone carving and an imposing W doorway.

Henley-on-Thames   *Jarrold*

Oxford: the medieval St Edmund Hall

Kelmscott (EC 19). From 1871 to 1896 the manor house was the home of William Morris, poet, printer, designer and social reformer. His printing press at Hammersmith was named after it. His tomb is in the churchyard here. The house is now owned by the Society of Antiquaries.

Mapledurham (EG 17). Between the Thames and the wooded hills, a village with a watermill, a church and a fine pink-brick Elizabethan manor house which played its part in the Civil War.

Minster Lovell* (ED 21). Attractive old village on the River Windrush with a fine central-towered 14th-cent. church and the ruins of a 15th-cent. manor house (AM).

North Leigh, 1 m. NE of Witney (ED 21). The village with its disused windmill is on the hill; the old church at the foot of the slope has a collection of beautifully wrought coffin plates. A short distance to the NE are the remains of a Roman villa (AM).

Oxford** (EF 20) EC Thurs (106,150). One of Europe's most important and ancient universities and, historically and architecturally, Britain's second most interesting city. A busy administrative, marketing and shopping centre, its streets almost invariably crowded and its traffic problems always acute.

The earliest colleges – University, Balliol, and Merton – were founded in the 13th cent.; Nuffield College is the most recent. The largest is Christ Church, which has for its chapel the ancient cathedral. Nearly every college has its lawned quadrangle, its chapel and its hall to which visitors are admitted at stated times, and most of them have valuable collections of pictures and books. Nearly every college is of considerable architectural importance, even down to the modern annexe to Magdalen College. The

173

Rollright Stones

catalogue of notable buildings goes on: the Bodleian Library (Duke Humphry's Room, 1480); the Radcliffe Camera (Gibbs, 1737); the Sheldonian Theatre (the University's ceremonial hall, designed by Wren; the Ashmolean Museum (the first public museum to be opened in Europe), the University Museum and the 17th-cent. Botanic Garden, the oldest of its kind in Britain. At Magdalen Bridge punts may be hired for the exploration of the tree-embowered Cherwell; below Folly Bridge college boats are usually at practice. And beyond this wonderland of beauty is the great hive at Cowley whence motor-cars, refrigerators, etc., pour in an unending stream.

Rollright Stones* (E D 23). Famous prehistoric stone circle, less impressive than the larger circles at Stonehenge and Avebury, but set high up on a ridge commanding wide views over Warwickshire (A M).

Rousham (E E 22). The large Jacobean mansion, well placed above the Cherwell, has delightful grounds laid out by William Kent.

Shipton-under-Wychwood (E C 21). Many good houses, built in the days when 'sheep towns' and wool markets meant prosperity. Note Shipton Court (1603) and the Shaven Crown inn with its Tudor archway.

South Newington (E E 23). Where the Swere stream runs out from the hills, a village church with wall-paintings long concealed (and preserved) under layers of whitewash.

Stanton Harcourt (E E 20). Delightful village among water meadows of the upper Thames Valley. The great house of the Harcourts was pulled down in 1780 but the tower, gatehouse and huge kitchen indicate the size of the place. In the tower Pope worked on his translation of the *Iliad*. In the churchyard is the grave of George Orwell, pen-name of Eric Blair.

Swinbrook Church: Fettiplace monum

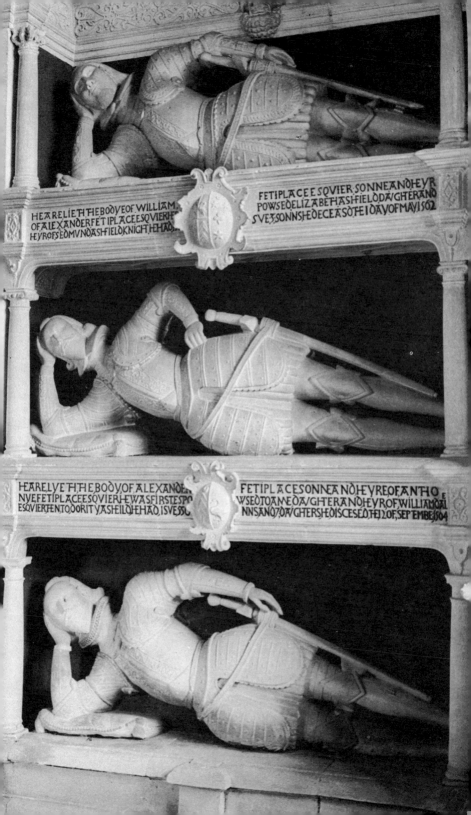

HEARE LIETH THE BODY OF WILLIAM
OF ALEXANDER FETIPLACE ESQVIER H
HEYR OF SE OMVNDASHFIELD KNIGHT HE HAD

FETIPLACE ESQVIER SONNE AND HEYR
POWSE DELIZABETH ASHFIELD DAVGHTER AND
SVE 3 SONNS HE DECEASD TE I DAY OF MAY 1562

HEARE LYETH THE BODY OF ALEXANDER
NVE FETIPLACE ESQVIER HE WAS FIRSTE SPO
ESQVIER FENTODORITY ASHEILD HE HAD IS VESSO

FETIPLACE SONNE AND HEYRE OF ANTHO
WSED TO A MEDAVGHTER AND HEYR OF WILLIAM DAL
NNSANO 7 DAVGHERS HE DISCESED TE 12 OF SEPTEMBER 1504

Swinbrook (EC 21). A church so small that effigies of the Fettiplace family, depicted reclining on their sides, are arranged bunk-fashion against the wall. Note the 'woolpack' gravestones in the churchyard, long rounded stones representing the wool-packs which once meant such prosperity to the Cotswolds. Lovely riverside views.

Taynton, 1½ m. NW of Burford (EC 21). Taynton stone has gone into many good buildings, including St Paul's Cathedral, the New Bodleian Library at Oxford, and Blenheim Palace, but no industry now disturbs the peace of this little village beside the Windrush.

Thame (EH 20) EC Wed (4,200). Very attractive market town with a wholly successful mixture of archi-tectural periods and an unusually wide street designed for markets and fairs. Beside the river is the imposing church. John Hampden was but one of many famous men educated at Thame School. The fine old Spread Eagle inn was made famous by John Fothergill's *Innkeeper's Diary.*

Watlington (EG 19). Charming small 17th–18th cent. town built around its market hall. A mile to the NE is Shir-burn Castle, originally 14th-cent., given a moat and drawbridge in the 19th; it is not open to the public.

Witney (ED 20) EC Tues (9,200). Blankets have been made here for centuries and they still provide the main industry. The best part of the town is above the many-gabled 17th-cent. Butter Cross and the Town Hall. Here good stone buildings stand back behind wide grass verges, the vista being closed by the very fine church. Note the old Blanket Hall and the 17th-cent. Grammar School. (*See also* **North Leigh** *above.*)

Woodstock (EE 21). Small town on the edge of the Cotswolds, long famous for gloves. Many good stone houses, some built when Woodstock still had a royal palace (demolished when neigh-bouring Blenheim was built). The Black Prince was born here.

On the very edge of the town lies the great park of **Blenheim Palace***, the imposing pile given to the Duke of Marlborough for his victories in the Low Countries, including Blenheim (1704). Vanbrugh designed it and the park owes much to Capability Brown, the whole job taking nearly 20 years and costing £300,000. Furniture, por-traits, and in the chapel the marble tomb of the Duke and Duchess (*see p.* 168).

Yarnton, 2 m. N of Oxford (EF 20) on the left of the Woodstock road. The splendid Tudor manor house was built about 1611 by Sir Thomas Spencer; was partly pulled down and after being used as a farmhouse was restored in 1897. Adjoining it is the parish church, with good Spencer monuments and some medieval glass.

Amersham High Street

BUCKINGHAMSHIRE

AN INTRODUCTION BY FRANK MORLEY

Topographically, Buckinghamshire is like a lettuce that has bolted. There is the compact, leafy region of South Bucks, rising gradually to the Chiltern Hills; towards the north the Chilterns present a steep escarpment, after which the county bolts away across the Vale of Aylesbury to Northamptonshire.

Each half of the county has its own characteristics, but they are rarely spectacular. Geological forces in this region were gentle: it was an area not given to convulsions. The traverse escarpment of the Chilterns as a physical feature is not so startling as the Cotswold Edge. The chalk barrier is rather to be compared with the downs of Berkshire or Sussex, but with a difference – other downs tend to be bald, but the Chilterns exhibit a splendid growth of beechwoods which becomes thin only as the hills draw north-east towards Dunstable. So thick are the beechwoods (and lovely at any time of the year), that even when crossing the escarpment there are not apt to be wide views; though here or there (as at Coombe Hill) one may see the flat vale to the north, spread out below like the chess-board country of *Alice Through the Looking Glass*.

North of the Chilterns, Bucks is a land of many little rivers, a low-lying clay plain riddled with small streams and marshes. South of the Chilterns the plateau, sloping down towards London, alters from chalk to clay with flints; what characterizes South Bucks is thus light, hungry soils scored by dry valleys, with a comparative absence of rivers. There are only five streams to be counted from west to east: Hamble, Wye, Misbourne, Chess and Colne. All these streams flow southwards to join the Thames, which forms, from Remenham near Henley to Egham near Staines, a southern boundary of the county.

The few river courses of South Bucks thus run from north to south, and they have scored deeply into the dry plateau, leaving sharp ridges between, so that in early days east–west traffic across South Bucks must have been difficult. Along the northern edge of the Chilterns there was the east–west Icknield Way, and to the south of the area there might be transport on the Thames, but the main routes were and are up and down the few river valleys. From London the northernmost of the early routes skirted South Bucks altogether: it entered the hills at Watford, passed Berkhamsted and Tring and then (this was the Roman Akeman Street) pushed straight to Aylesbury. This was the flattest way of getting through the Chilterns, and the first part of Akeman Street was therefore the course now followed – with a minimum of locks – by the Grand Junction Canal, the only water to pierce the Chiltern escarpment. The second of the main routes from London was past the Chalfonts and Amersham and up the pretty valley of the Misbourne (Little Missenden and Great Missenden retain their prettiness today) to cross the escarpment at Wendover. The third followed the valley of the Wye, striking across from Bradenham to Princes Risborough, between the bluff of Bledlow Ridge and the hills of Whiteleaf – Bledlow and Whiteleaf each bearing on the northward hill-face a white cross carved into the chalk, none knows by whom. Departing from this third route at West Wycombe, the present-day A40 goes slap over the escarpment at Stokenchurch and on to Oxford. Gradients which were troublesome for horse-traffic do not amount to much for modern cars and lorries, and in the north–south traffic which now streams across South Bucks many a driver, I suppose, scarcely notices the Chilterns.

The Past

The archaeological features of Buckinghamshire contain nothing so breath-taking as some of the monuments of the West Country: there is no Avebury, Stonehenge or Maiden Castle. A specialist may see a mound; to the layman, even when it is pointed out, it is only a mound. Nevertheless, the flints which are a curse to the gardener in South Bucks were to the prehistoric weapon-maker as valuable as diamonds. In the British Museum are treasures from South Bucks representative of all the early periods. In addition to prehistoric tools and pottery, urns (and a pigmy cup) and weapons, there are the exquisite blue-and-white marbled 1st-century glass bowl and other objects from the Radnage Roman burial. Here, too, are the princely trappings from the famous grave of an Anglo-Saxon chieftain at Taplow. In his book on *Early Man in South Buckinghamshire* Mr J. F. Head remarks: 'The Taplow burial must rank after Sutton Hoo as one of the most important and wealthy deposits of this period found in England.' In prehistoric times South Bucks, as Mr Head well says, was a back-water. It was so in Roman times: there is no relic of a Roman city, such as Silchester near Reading. As to Saxon times, when you leave the Thames there is scanty evidence. Mr Head is forced to end his account of this period with the mournful phrase of a 7th-century chaplain – *deserta Ciltine*, 'the deserts of Chiltern'.

J. Allan Cash **Ivinghoe Bea**

In later times what contrast there is! The wealth of Buckinghamshire may not reside in spectacular topography or spectacular ancient remains, but there is no county that can excel it for small beauties, if you have capacity to stand and stare. That is the essential 'feel' of the county – put away your telescope. Forget the past that is very far away, forget the long distances, and be prepared to look for little things: then you will find much in small compass to reward the sight and stir the memory. The Thames – Bucks cannot claim much of it, but what it claims is good. Bucks cannot claim Windsor Castle, but it can claim the best view of it, and it has Eton over the bridge. It can claim at least an equal share of Boveney and Bray (a famous reach for punting) and Boulter's Lock and Cliveden Reach. Marlow and Medmenham and the pleasant lazy meadows of Hambleden are on the Buckinghamshire bank. This whole stretch of the Thames is apt to be crowded nowadays in summer, but from a vantage-point on shore (Medmenham can be as good a point as any) the river in the sun can be blue, the ripples dancing, and the sail-boats and launches colourful to watch. Stop for a moment – you will find you have stayed for an hour.

At Cliveden one remembers George Villiers, the powerful, versatile, insolent Duke of Buckingham in the time of Charles II, who started the building of the original house, and who after his scandalous duel with Shrewsbury fled 'to Cliveden's proud alcove'. That was an episode which made Pepys angry: 'This will make the world think that the King has good councillors about him, when the Duke of Buckingham, the greatest man about him, is a fellow of no more sobriety than to fight about a whore.'

Medmenham, where the Hell-Fire Club met in the Abbey, is a reminder of Sir Francis Dashwood, and of the Mausoleum which he put up in 1762 at West Wycombe. It may be seen there today, with the urns in the niches which were to contain the hearts of full-fledged members of the Hell-Fire Club. But though a certain number of wealthy and wild eccentrics can be associated with this particular part, what was in general always more characteristic of the county was the life represented by such small villages as West Wycombe itself, or Turville and Fingest on the way between Medmenham, Hambleden and West Wycombe.

I have an early map of Buckinghamshire which shows how sparsely inhabited the country once was south of the line of the Chilterns; north of the Chilterns the map is simply speckled with churches. That does not mean there are no small churches in the southern half – Fingest, just mentioned, or Little Missenden (with February snowdrops), or Chalfont St Giles towards the east of the county (where Milton's cottage also attracts visitors). But it is impossible in a short space to treat adequately the variety of churches, villages and houses to be seen in North Bucks, which, bordering on Oxfordshire and Northamptonshire, is scenically part of the Midlands. I can only refer you to the Book List and Gazetteer which follow. If these do not draw you north through Aylesbury to Buckingham, to churches such as Dinton, to villages such as Olney ('Cowper's Olney'), I don't know what will.

Famous People

Mention of Cowper reminds me not to neglect all of the notables who have had particular associations with the county. I might have remarked, when mentioning Windsor, that it was at Datchet Mead that Falstaff was thrown from the basket into the Thames and cooled, glowing hot, in that surge, like a horse-shoe; where as his size had a kind of alacrity in sinking, he might have been drowned had not the shore been shelvy and shallow. At Stoke Poges 'visitors by the hundred', says Murray's *Guide*, 'attempt to catch the atmosphere in which Gray composed the Elegy, but it is dispersed by the neighbouring Slough Trading Estate'. I differ on two counts: the church at Stoke Poges retains atmosphere, and though it is fashionable to sneer at Slough because it is a centre for light industry, I can find interests there. Slough is handling its planning problems better than many towns I can think of elsewhere. Granted that Slough has little architectural beauty to offer, it does have open spaces and the parks are well designed; it has an unusually excellent public library; and many who sneer at other shoppers nevertheless go to Slough for their shopping. Windsor and Eton always cocked a snook at Slough: and at the beginning of the railway age, when the Great Western was refused access by rail to the noble places, a clause was forced into the Companys' Act forbidding the erection of a station even at lowly Slough. The clause was promptly evaded, and Great Western trains stopped at Slough as soon as the rails were laid. For what had been prohibited was the erection of a station; instead, a public house of old standing (on the site of the present station) willingly co-operated, tickets were sold and passengers refreshed comfortably enough. The evasion may have pleased Dickens, for it was at Elizabeth Cottage on the south side of the High Street (where a shop now stands, at Nos. 162 and 164) that he established himself with Ellen Ternan when he was evading Victorian convention. *Our Mutual Friend* records his feelings for the country between Slough and High Wycombe.

Evasion of authority would seem to have been typical of South Bucks from the beginning. As an islanded region it was a natural underground for rebels. All of Buckinghamshire was of course much fought over in the Civil Wars. John Hampden (a statue to him stands at Aylesbury) received his fatal wound from Rupert's cavalry in the Chilterns. In later religious struggles Quakers could find sanctuary at Pennington because that estate, although well within South Bucks, escaped local jurisdiction by pretending to be part of Hertfordshire. William Penn (buried not in the State of Pennsylvania but at the small Friends' Meeting House at Jordans) must have had trouble assisting some of his 'scrupulous' followers in this county of churches. What is now sometimes called the Penn country was also gypsy country: broom-handles and wood for the 'Windsor chairs' made at High Wycombe were traditionally scrounged by the gypsies though the sound of the 'bodger's' pole-lathe is no longer heard in the beech-woods. What I am saying is that South Bucks could harbour people of all kinds of contradictory habits. At Beaconsfield, Edmund Burke and his wife and son are commemorated by a simple oval monument in the church in the Old Town; Disraeli is commemorated by a pub in the New Town; G. K. Chesterton lived in the New Town and used the pub. Protestant, Jew, Catholic, Quaker, Gypsy are each recorded.

Literary Figures

It was from Beaconsfield that we first heard of *The Innocence of Father Brown*. It was at Marlow, at Albion House in West Street, that Mary Shelley, while expecting a child, worked away quietly at her story, *Frankenstein's Monster*. Shelley and Thomas Love Peacock ranged the surrounding country within a radius, they are meticulous to say, of sixteen miles. We read of dinners within that orbit. Peacock maintained that the infallible sign of a good inn was the state of its mustard-pot; nearing an inn he would stalk ahead, ask without explanation for a mustard-pot and, according to its condition, leave or stay.

There was not then, nor is there now, any cuisine peculiar to Bucks, except that Aylesbury duckling is always better the nearer you are to Aylesbury. At one time (but this was very long ago) some of the edible dormice introduced by the Romans escaped from Verulamium and settled in the area from Tring to Amersham, and when cooked and served with honey sauce they were a delicacy much esteemed. I have not seen them served up lately, though much good honest fare at roadside inns I have found.

Buckinghamshire is a county which has defended itself stubbornly, and on the whole very well, against the traffic which now rushes through it. High Wycombe is sometimes glared at by motorists for the congestion caused by the motorists themselves, but the town hall, market hall and church are all worth stopping for. The main street of Old Beaconsfield holds up well, and Amersham High Street is one of the best in the country. South Bucks has also defended itself against the London sprawl. Each time I leave Marylebone and cross the county line at Denham I am the better for it. Just after passing Denham East Signal Box there is an angle of the River Colne which always seems to smile at me. Then one is in farmland (very well farmed too) and into a county where, if they are looked for at the right time, there are snowdrops, daffodils, primroses, bluebells, blackthorn hedges and fruit blossom; a county not of great dimension but, when you know your way around, a county of great beauty.

West Wycombe Church and Mausoleum *Aerofilms*

Some houses and gardens open to the public

Ascott Wing *Map* E J 22. *Houses the important Anthony de Rothschild collection of French and Chippendale furniture, paintings by Rubens, Hogarth, Gainsborough, etc., and Oriental porcelain. Gardens have unusual trees, bulbs.* N T.

Claydon House 1½m E of Steeple Claydon *Map* E G 22. *Mid 18th-cent. house containing series of fine rococo staterooms. Florence Nightingale museum.* N T.

Cliveden *Map* E K 18. *Mansion built 1851 on site of two earlier houses. Tapestry and furniture. Beautiful wooded grounds overlooking Thames.* N T.

Hughenden Manor 1½m N of High Wycombe *Map* E J 19. *The home of Benjamin Disraeli from 1847 to 1881. See p. 189.* N T.

Nether Winchendon House 2m W of Dinton *Map* E H 21. *Tudor manor-house with late 18th-cent. Gothic additions. Specimen tree collection in garden.* J. G. C. Spencer Bernard, Esq.

Stowe *Map* E G 23. *One of the finest 18th-cent. mansions and landscape gardens with temples by Vanbrugh, Gibbs & Kent. See p. 191.* Governors of Stowe School.

Waddesdon Manor Waddesdon *Map* E H 21. *Built 1880–9 for Baron Ferdinand de Rothschild in the French Renaissance style. See p. 191.* N T.

West Wycombe Park 3m W of High Wycombe *Map* E J 19. *Rebuilt c. 1765 for Sir Francis Dashwood in Adam manner. Painted ceilings. Pictures, tapestries, furniture. Park with temples and artificial lake.* N T.

Books for further reading

The 'feel' of Buckinghamshire

H. HARMAN *Buckinghamshire Dialect* 1929
H. HARMAN *Three Traditional Folk Songs of Buckinghamshire*
H. EVELYN HOWARD *At the Sign of the Swan: a collection of fifty poems of Buckinghamshire* 1937

Scenery, geology, natural history

GEORGE CLARIDGE DRUCE *The Flora of Buckinghamshire* 1926
ERNEST HARTERT and FRANCIS C. R. JOURDAIN *The Birds of Buckinghamshire and the Tring Reservoirs* 1920
M. S. TEMPLE *A Survey of the Soils of Buckinghamshire* 1929

Topography – general

G. ELAND *Old Works and Past Days in Rural Buckinghamshire* 1921 2nd edn called 'In Bucks' 1923
MAXWELL FRASER *Companion into Buckinghamshire* 1950
DONALD MAXWELL *Unknown Buckinghamshire* 1935 (The County Books series)
J. H. B. PEEL *Buckinghamshire Footpaths* 1949
NIKOLAUS PEVSNER *Buckinghamshire* 1960
E. S. ROSCOE *Buckinghamshire* (Little Guides series)
ALISON UTTLEY *Buckinghamshire* 1950 (The County Books series)

Gazetteer

BUCKINGHAMSHIRE

Amersham (EK 19) EC Thurs (10,900). A charming old town in the Misbourne valley with a modern suburb on the hills northward. The spacious main street is bordered by a lovely sequence of 17th- and 18th-cent. buildings with a town hall on arches and attractive small almshouses. A monument on the hill commemorates Lollards and other martyrs burnt at the stake during the Marian persecutions.

Aylesbury (EJ 21) EC Thurs (27,900). The county town, with a busy market on Wednesdays and Saturdays. There are many old houses in the byways leading from the market-place. Ducks are no longer produced on a large scale; printing, engineering, and a creamery are now the main industries. The church tower has an unusual spirelet: inside note the Lady Chapel and the misericords in the choir stalls. The Bucks County Museum has interesting collections of antiques and bygones.

Beaconsfield (EK 18) EC Wed (10,000). Here the London–Oxford Road (A40) becomes a fine wide street between mellow Georgian red-brick buildings. The 17th-cent. church has a great pinnacled tower and memorials to Edmund Burke and Edmund Waller the poet. The half-timbered rectory dates from 1543.

Bradenham (EJ 19). NT village among the beech-clad hills NW of High Wycombe. The manor house (not open to the public) was the home of Isaac Disraeli, and here his son

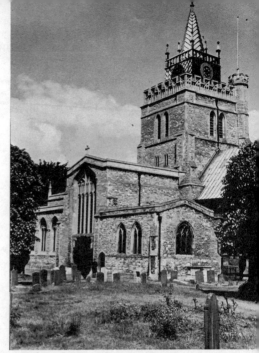

Aylesbury: St. Mary's Church
J. Allan Cash

Benjamin (*see* **Hughenden** *below*) spent his youth. The church has the oldest door (1100) in Buckinghamshire, and two bells made by Michael de Wymbis in 1300 which are among the oldest in England.

Brill (EG 21). Noted for its hill-top post-mill dating from the 17th cent. At one time the village had pretensions to being a spa; there are several good 15th–17th-cent. buildings. Two miles W is the conspicuous 14th-cent. Boarstall Tower (NT), the remnant gatehouse of a fortified and moated house long in possession of the Aubrey family.

Buckingham (EG 23) EC Thurs (4,370). The swan atop the clock tower of the town hall is the county emblem and a reminder that Buckingham was the county town until superseded by Aylesbury. In the wide market-place is a squat castle-shaped erection that was at one time used

185

as a gaol. Close by is a chantry (NT) built by the Normans, rebuilt and restored; in Henry VI's reign it became the Royal Latin School. A splendid beech avenue leads from the town to **Stowe** (*see below*).

Burnham Beeches, 3 miles E of Maidenhead (EJ 18). A large area of beautiful woodland and heath bought for the public by the City of London Corporation in 1879. To this was added the 215 acres of Dorney Wood, given to the National Trust during the last war, with house and contents, by Lord Courtauld-Thomson as a residence for a Secretary of State or Minister of the Crown.

Chalfont St Giles (EK 19) EC Thurs (4,380). Beyond the pond is the cottage to which Milton fled in 1665 to escape the plague ravaging London. Here he finished *Paradise Lost*, began *Paradise Regained*. There is a small museum. The fine 14th-cent. church has wall paintings and brasses.

Chenies (FA 19). Red-tiled timbered cottages around the green look down to the Chess Valley. Adjoining the red-brick manor house is the church, with a magnificent collection of tombs of the Dukes of Bedford.

Chequers (EJ 20). The owner of the original 13th-cent. house was Henry de Scaccario (i.e. of the Exchequer), hence the name. The present Tudor building and the surrounding estate were presented to the nation during the First World War by Lord Lee of Fareham as a country residence for successive Prime Ministers.

Cliveden* (EK 18). Beautifully wooded estate on the cliffs looking across the Thames to Maidenhead. With the mansion it was presented to the National Trust by Lord Astor in 1942. Another handsome gift to the National Trust is the Canadian Hospital in the grounds presented to the nation by the Canadian Red Cross in 1946.

Denham (FA 18) EC Wed (4,850). An unspoiled old-fashioned village, complete with pond, which has figured in many films made by the huge Denham studios. Denham Place stands at the end of the village.

Dinton (EH 21). The ruin beside the Aylesbury road is mock-ancient, having been built to display the splendid ammonites inset among the flints. Dinton, a pleasant village among farms, has stocks and a whipping-post on its green and a good Tudor manor house. Excellent Norman door to church.

Eton* (EK 17) EC Wed (3,900). The college founded by Henry VI in 1440 is the most famous school in England. Mellow red brick buildings and a splendid greystone chapel. The 4th of June is Eton's great day, with a procession of boats on the river, followed by fireworks.

Fawley, 3 m. N of Henley (EH 18). Beautifully set among beech- and yew-clad hills, with good 17th-cent. farms and cottages and a church with carving by Grinling Gibbons. Fawley Court, 2 m. S, was rebuilt by Wren; there is a large heronry on the estate.

Fingest* (EH 19). Tiny village in a hollow of the Chilterns. The unusual church tower is Norman, with a 13th-cent. double saddle-back roof. The church itself is 12th cent.

Haddenham (EH 20). Attractive village with several ponds, a large green, and a church with curious carvings and some 15th-cent. glass.

Hambleden (EH 18). About 1 m. N of the lovely combination of locks and weirs on the Thames between Marlow (EJ 18) and Henley. A typical Buckinghamshire village among the hills, with Georgian and Stuart red-brick houses. A curiosity in the church is a

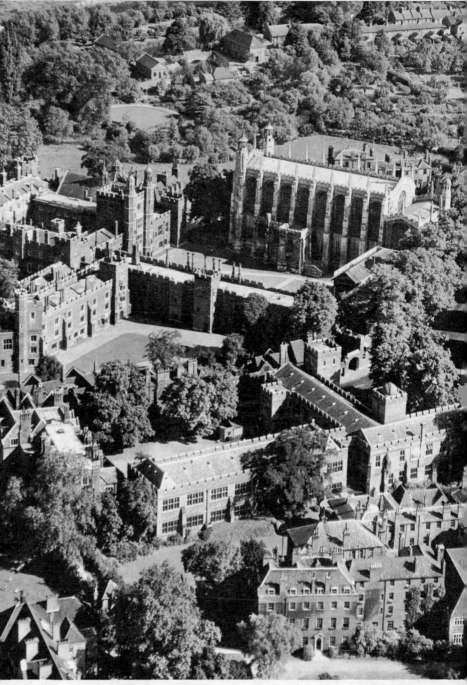

Eton College and Chapel

panel said to have been part of Cardinal Wolsey's bed. A Roman villa was excavated in 1912 and there is a nice little museum.

Hampden (EJ 20). John Hampden, who in 1636 refused to pay the tax known as Ship Money, is buried in the church at Great Hampden which adjoins the house (now a school) in which he lived. Across the valley is Little Hampden, with a tiny church with a half-timbered porch, a Saxon altar and faded wall paintings.

Hanslope (EJ 24). The tower and spire are the tallest in the county. They are seen from afar, but only on closer approach does one become aware of the church attached.

High Wycombe (EJ 19) EC Wed. (50,300). In proportion to its width this must be one of the longest towns in Britain, the A40 and the River Wye running side by side through the valley for over 2 m. Fortunately for the inhabitants and for the exasperated Oxford-bound motorist, this traffic bottleneck is to be relieved by a new by-pass on the S.

Note the octagonal market hall with its lantern, and the excellent Guildhall raised on arches and surmounted by a good cupola. Furniture-making founded on the local beechwoods still flourishes here, but Wycombe today is the home of many and various industries. (*See also* **Hughenden** *below*.)

Hughenden Manor* (EJ 19). The home of Benjamin Disraeli, who died here in 1881. The house (NT – *see p.* 184) contains much of his furniture, books, etc. His insignia as Knight of the Garter was brought from Windsor and placed over the chancel arch in Hughenden Church, and his grave is in the churchyard.

Ivinghoe (EK 21). The village from which Scott took the title for his novel *Ivanhoe*. The church has an interesting

roof and good carving on the pillars in the nave. The view from the Beacon (904 ft.) above the village includes a large NT acreage of the Chiltern Hills, the historic landmark of the ancient Ivinghoe Windmill, the lion carved in the chalk hill to the eastward which marks the site of Whipsnade Zoo, and the horizon reaching as far as Edge Hill in Warwickshire.

Jordans* (EK 19). The simple redbrick Quaker Meeting House (1688) among the beechwoods had early associations with William Penn, who returned after founding Pennsylvania and was buried here beside members of his family. The Mayflower Barn, at Old Jordan's Farm, is believed (on reasonable though unconfirmed evidence) to incorporate beams from the original *Mayflower* in which the Pilgrim Fathers sailed to America in 1620.

Latimer, 1 m. W of Chenies (FA 19). Picturesque hamlet in the best part of the Chess Valley with a pretty waterfall by a bridge. Paths round the fountain on the tiny village green are paved with Roman tiles, etc., found in the vicinity. Latimer House is now the home of the Joint Services Staff College.

Long Crendon (EG 20). A village of notable buildings, large and small. The 14th-cent. Courthouse now belongs to the NT. The manor house, built on the site of a Norman castle, has a fine hall, open from floor to roof.

Ludgershall, 3 m. N of Brill (EG 21). Note amusing carvings on the pier capitals in the church, the fine roof and the tomb of Anne Englische and her daughter and a child—all in Tudor costume.

Marlow (EJ 18) EC Wed (8,700). The wide, pleasant High Street leads to the suspension bridge over the Thames which provides a good view of the tumbling weir downstream and

Stowe

of Bisham Abbey upstream on the Berkshire bank. On the N side of West Street is the house in which P. B. Shelley lived. In the church is a monument to Sir Miles Hobart (1682) who courageously locked the King's Messengers out of the House of Commons and was subsequently killed in a carriage accident (depicted on the monument).

Medmenham* (EH 18). Thames-side village among trees below steep chalk hills. The church has a chancel 'arch' formed of kingpost tie-beams with curved braces. The village became notorious in the 18th cent. for the curious activities of the Hell-Fire Club which held its meetings in the ruined Abbey here (*see also* **West Wycombe** *below*).

Olney (EJ 25) EC Wed (2,340). The first of the annual Shrove Tuesday pancake races is said to have been run in 1445. In 1950 Olney was challenged by Liberal, Kansas, USA, and the transatlantic contest is now an annual event. The *Olney Hymns* were written here by the poet William Cowper (1731–1800) and John Newton, the former slave-trader who saw the error of his ways and became pastor of Olney. There is a Cowper museum in the village.

Stewkley (EJ 22). Village on a hill-crest some 500 ft. up, with the finest Norman church* in Buckinghamshire. Note especially the W doorway and the chancel arch with its intricate carving.

Stoke Poges (EK 18). The scene which inspired Thomas Gray (1716–71) to write his *Elegy Written in a Country Churchyard* would seem to have changed little since his day, despite the proximity of Slough. The NT now cares for Wyatt's statue of the poet, who is buried in the churchyard. In the church is the 'Bicycle Window', showing a man riding a form of hobby-horse.

Stowe* (EG 23). The public school for boys occupies the former seat of the Dukes of Buckingham, whose title became extinct in 1889. It is a magnificent mansion in Vanbrugh's best style, with details by Robert Adam and Grinling Gibbons. The exquisite parkland was laid out by William Kent, Capability Brown and others. The 13th-cent church in the grounds is the only vestige of the village left after it was removed when the park was made in 1713.

Waddesdon* (EH 21). The great manor house on the edge of the village was bequeathed to the NT in 1957 by James de Rothschild, together with its magnificent collection of French furniture, paintings, porcelain and books, second only to that in the Wallace Collection.

Wendover (EJ 20) EC Thurs (4,870). One and a half m. to the W of this attractive little town is one of the highest points in the Chilterns, Coombe Hill (NT), 852 ft. above sea-level, with wonderful views towards Aylesbury and Thame and over the woods surrounding Chequers.

Waddesdon Manor *Aerofilms*

West Wycombe*, 2 m. NW of High Wycombe (EJ 19). The whole village, threatened with demolition in 1929, is now owned by the NT. Good 17th- and 18th-cent. buildings border the main road. On the hill above is the curious mausoleum built in 1762 by the eccentric Sir Francis Dashwood of 'Hell-Fire Club' fame (*see* **Medmenham** *above*). The church was planned on the lines of a drawing-room. Caves in the hill are shown to the public. At the W end of the village is the Adam-style house of West Wycombe Park (NT).

Wing (EJ 22). The village church is largely Saxon and contains five monuments to the Dormer family. The important house of Ascott*(NT) contains the fine Anthony de Rothschild collection of French and Chippendale furniture, etc.

Winslow (EH 22). Neat village with thatched cottages and a church with an unusually large porch. Winslow Hall, with its imposing façade, contains tapestries and baroque wall paintings, and is believed to be the work of Wren.

Winslow .   Reece Winstone

Opposite: Detail from the original painting by Rowland Hilder.
A county of vale and clay, and, to the south of the Chilterns, smooth and sudden slopes and squirrel-haunted beechwoods. Stacked here in a clearing are beech logs destined for the chair factories at High Wycombe; and, just visible on the tree-stump alongside Gray's *Elegy* (written in the churchyard at Stoke Poges) and the bust of Milton (who finished *Paradise Lost* at Chalfont St Giles), is one of the edible dormice that have made the Chilterns their special home.

The River Coln at Bibury

GLOUCESTERSHIRE

AN INTRODUCTION BY JOHN MOORE

In the sense of landscape there are three Gloucestershires: Cotswold, Severn Vale and Forest of Dean. Each of these is as different from the others as chalk is from cheese. The whale-backed oolitic Cotswold Hills present an unspoilt skyline 50 miles long, from Chipping Campden in the north down to the extreme south of the county (and indeed to Bath in Somerset). The Severn Vale, whence you can look up at this heart-lifting sight, goes down from Tewkesbury – where the river is joined by Shakespeare's Avon – to the City of Gloucester. Beyond are the tidal reaches of the great river, with the Vale of Berkeley on the left bank and on the right the coal-bearing, oak-wooded Forest of Dean, bounded on its west side by the swift tumbling Wye.

The Cotswolds

The image of Gloucestershire which perhaps most readily comes to mind is one of 'galloping country' – stone walls dividing the great sweeping sheep-pastures of short-cropped fescue grass, trout-streams, and what Belloc called

> 'The hundred little towns of stone
> Forgotten in the Western Wold.'

Opposite: Detail from the original painting by David Gentleman.
A county divided by the wide gleam of the Severn – on one side the Forest of Dean, on the other the Cotswold uplands, the sheep, the dry walls, the stone-chambered neolithic long barrows, the country of mosaic-floored Roman villas, and tall churches founded by medieval wool merchants.

Bourton-on-the-Water, with the River Windrush

Reece Winstone

It was a sheep-country in Shakespeare's day also, and Shallow asked a Cotswold man's question when he said 'How a score of ewes, now, Cousin Silence?' meaning how much were they fetching at market. Indeed, long before then the Cotswolds were producing the fleeces which enriched the 15th-century wool-merchants, who spent part of their great wealth in building the handsome churches which tower over the little towns – such as Chipping Campden's, the lordly burial place of William Grevel, or Fairford's, paid for out of the fortune earned by Cotswold sheep for John Tame. As a lavish extra, he gave it some of the best stained-glass in England, including the famous West Window with its lively picture of the Eternal Pit, into which the host of the damned (all notice-ably women) are being pitchforked and prodded by cheerful imps with animal faces. Cirencester and Northleach have fine churches too, and the country towns of Stow-on-the-Wold ('where the Devil caught cold') and Moreton-in-the-Marsh, such villages as Bourton and Bibury, indeed almost all the hamlets and habitations in the heart of the Cotswolds, look as if they had grown naturally out of the ground, like the trees; and in a sense so they have, as the old over-grown stone-quarries bear witness.

The trout-streams, such as the Coln, the Evenlode, and the sweetly named Windrush, go briskly but never turbulently between the gently sloping hills. As well as trout, they contain a plentiful supply of crayfish. Myriads of mayflies dance over them in early June. The 'monkey-flower', *Mimulus*, grows freely along their banks. The meadows and pastures show some rarer flowers: butter-fly-orchids, even man-orchids, fritillaries, and the slaty-violet *Anemone pulsatilla* or Pasque-flower; lilies-of-the-valley, Herb Paris and Solomon's-seal are found in the woods. Buzzards have recently become common, quail are seen by the partridge-shooters now and then, and the Garganey teal has nested by these Cotswold streams. The very rare Large Blue Butterfly still survives, though precariously, in one or two colonies; but the localities are necessarily kept secret.

Reece Winstone **Gargoyle on Winchcombe C**

Cheltenham: the Promenade

J. Allan Cash

Close under the Cotswolds lie the towns of Cirencester and Cheltenham. Ciren, as the locals call it (*not* 'Cister') was the Roman town of Corinium, where the two great roads, the Icknield Way and Ermine Street, joined the Fosse Way. The Roman villa among the beechwoods at Chedworth, not far from Cirencester, was found by accident when a keeper was digging out his ferret that had killed a rabbit in a bury, and was 'lying up'. More than fifty of these luxurious villas, with tessellated floors and elaborate heating systems, are known to have existed in Gloucestershire, which is rich in Roman relics of all kinds.

Cheltenham possesses at least as much good Georgian building as Bath; but it is scattered all over the large town instead of being concentrated in one small area. The 'garden-town', with its tree-lined Promenade and beautiful parks, used to be famous for peppery retired colonels; they are no more, and light industry, which they would have deplored, keeps Cheltenham busy and prosperous. Its annual Cricket Week brings to mind memories of W. G. Grace and Gilbert Jessop, whose famous swipe once smashed the clock-face in Cheltenham College pavilion.

GLOUCESTERSHIRE

The Severn Vale

From the flat river-meadows around Tewkesbury you lift up your eyes unto the hills whichever way you turn: to Cotswold or to Malvern. A Gloucestershire poet, F. W. Harvey, wrote in the trenches during the First World War of his homesick longing

> 'To see above the Severn plain
> Unscabbarded against the sky
> The blue high blade of Cotswold lie,
> The giant clouds go royally
> By jagged Malvern with a train
> Of shadows . . .'

The vale itself is not beautiful; at best it is ordinary pastoral England, a green and pleasant land; but it offers you, at sunrise or at sunset, some heartening horizons.

The seven-mile drive from Cheltenham to Tewkesbury takes you back, architecturally, from Georgian to Tudor. The black-and-white half-timbered buildings in the High Street mostly date from the late fifteen-hundreds. In a jumble of back-streets and alleys (now mostly tidied up and modernized) the old and new join together to form a remarkable hotchpotch. Over all stands the tower of one of the finest churches in Britain, the tremendous Norman abbey. Here, among the tombs and the memorials of Despencers, Warwicks and De Clares, of a knight that fell at Agincourt and of a baron who witnessed the signing of Magna Carta, there lie in a dark, damp, and appropriately sinister vault the remains of that Duke of Clarence who is supposed to have been drowned in a butt of Malmsey wine. His bones, in a glass case, are confusedly mixed up with those of his lady. A stone's-throw away from him Edward Prince of Wales is buried, concerning whom Clarence had a dreadful nightmare (according to Shakespeare) while he languished in the Tower:

> 'Then came wandering by
> A shadow like an Angel, with bright hair
> Dabbled in blood; and he shriek'd out aloud,
> *Clarence is come, – false, fleeting, perjur'd Clarence –*
> *That stabb'd me in the field by Tewkesbury; –*
> *Seize on him, Furies, take him to your torments!'*

The field, still called the Bloody Meadow, is to be found near the junction of the Severn and the Swilgate Brook, on the south side of the town. Great slaughter was done here in 1471, when Queen Margaret and her Lancastrians were utterly routed, and the Wars of the Roses ended (for the time being) with the triumph of the White:

> 'Now is the winter of our discontent
> Made glorious summer by this sun of York.'

Tewkesbury, world-famous for its abbey and its battle, in Shakespeare's day had another claim to fame. 'His wit's as thick as Tewkesbury mustard,' said Falstaff of Poins. In Victorian days the town became associated with the novel *John Halifax, Gentleman*, by Dinah Maria Mulock, who subsequently married her publisher and became Mrs Craik. Various Tewkesbury landmarks – the Bell Hotel and the old Flour Mill, for instance – are recognizable in the book; but it is a tedious story, and its interest for us nowadays is mainly topographical.

The River Severn, roaring over Tewkesbury Weir, flows down through a quiet pastoral landscape to the city of Gloucester.

> 'The men that live in West England
> They see the Severn strong,
> A-rolling on rough waters brown
> Light aspen leaves along.'

These rough waters brown, upon the first floods of autumn, carry with them the silver-coated eels on the first stage of their journey to their breeding-place in the far-off Sargasso Sea; the fishermen string wicker traps called 'putcheons' across the river and count their catch sometimes in hundredweights. In the early spring another generation of eels, no thicker than bootlaces, the tiny, wriggling gelatinous fry that have drifted and swum 3,000 miles from that breeding-place, swarm upriver by the million million, and themselves are caught in nets of cheese-cloth stretched on frames of withy. They are locally regarded as a delicacy, fried in bacon fat or jellied into 'elver-cakes'. Double Gloster cheese would go well with them, to make a Gloucestershire mid-day meal. The Severn salmon provide another harvest for the fishermen; so in a very small way do the curious lamperns, from a surfeit of which Henry the First is said to have died. The city of Gloucester, by ancient custom, makes them into a pie for the monarch, on the occasion of a Coronation. King John, who never missed the chance of laying his hand on some cash, levied a fine upon the city of Gloucester of 40 marks because 'they did not pay him sufficient respect in the matter of his lamperns'. Porpoises and sturgeons (which are another royal prerogative) have been known to swim up the Severn upon its tides, which are very powerful and produce the inrush of waters known as the Bore. This noisy wave, which races through the winding narrows below Gloucester, is caused by a tide which may have risen as much as 18 feet in an hour and a half. When there is a big Bore the wave is 7 feet high, and it travels at 15 knots. Stonebench is a favourite place from which to watch it when there is a high spring tide.

The upper estuary would be difficult to navigate, because of its shifting sands; but a ship canal 17 miles long, from Gloucester to Sharpness, gives passage to vessels of up to 1,000 tons burden. Timber is the main cargo they carry up to Gloucester, which is no quiet Cathedral city, but a sizeable inland port and a buzzing hive of workshops and factories. Its matches are sold all over the world; the Gloster Gladiator during the late 1930's took its name into the sky.

The canal passes through a countryside somewhat reminiscent of Holland: flat grassland grazed mainly by black-and-white Friesian cattle, and veined with little watercourses which are frequently criss-crossed by narrow lanes having humpback bridges. This Berkeley Vale, some 50,000 acres of it, is very thinly populated, and in winter there are more geese than people there. The Severn Wildfowl Trust has its headquarters at Slimbridge; and in some seasons as many as 6,000 Whitefronts feed upon the foreshore area quaintly called the Dumbles.

Dr Jenner practised in Berkeley Vale; and here on the 14th May 1790 he inoculated a farm labourer's son, James Phipps, with lymph taken from a cow-pox pustule on the hand of a dairymaid, Susan Nelmes; six weeks later he inoculated the boy a second time, but with smallpox. James did not develop the disease; and so demonstrated for the first time the advantages of vaccination.

View from the Cotswold Hills across the Severn Valley   Reece Winstone

Jenner was also a pleasant minor poet, as well as a first-rate naturalist who anticipated some of Darwin's discoveries by a century.

The Forest

About twenty million trees, many of them fine oaks, grow in the Royal Forest of Dean, which Michael Drayton about 1600 called 'The Queen of Forests all'. Deep down under the roots of the trees is a coalfield of some 22,000 acres. The 'tips' rise up in the neighbourhood of the collieries, neat little man-made hills, and provide vantage points from which you can look down on some of the most magnificent woodland scenery in Britain. The older of these tips are pleasantly overgrown with birch-scrub and broom, and the whole area is unique in being the only coalfield which has been exploited and yet remains beautiful. Scattered among the oaks are ancient hollies, the largest in England, some of them 40 feet high. Groves of birches, daffodil-fields on the Forest fringe, plantations of conifers, here and there an open heath, tall bracken, and the abundant fox-gloves which are said to be at their best on St Swithin's Day, make a varied landscape in a forest which offers you about 2,000 miles of woodland path for your walking.

Not long ago, Purple Emperor butterflies glided down these rides between the oak-trees. Within living memory, they seem to have vanished. About half the forest is fenced; the other half is grazed by the foresters' sheep, an ancient privilege rather than a right of common. The 'ship-badgers', as these commoners call themselves – presumably because, as shepherds, they 'badger' the sheep – may own 200 sheep or only one cherished ewe. They also have the privilege of letting their pigs feed among the Queen's oaks at the season when the acorns fall – the 'right of pannage', as it is called, upon 'the open and unenclosed woods and woody lands of our Lady the Queen'.

These and other rights they guard jealously. Old customs and old trades are cherished in this ancient forest – where charcoal-burning and iron-mining have been practised since prehistoric times. The Foresters are very different both in speech and manners from the Gloucestershire people who live upon the hills; as different as their rough, tough hard-living sheep are from the fat deep-fleeced flocks on Cotswold. The Forest of Dean accent has a lilt in it which perhaps comes from Wales, across the river which forms the boundary of Gloucestershire on the western side, the turbulent, beautiful, half-Welsh River Wye.

199

Some houses and gardens open to the public

Badminton House Map D J 18. *Internationally famous for the Three Day Event Horse Trials, it has been the home of the Dukes of Beaufort since the 17th cent. A fine example of the Palladian style, it contains a very valuable collection of paintings of the Italian, Dutch and English schools, together with carving and furniture of great interest.*

Berkeley Castle Map D G 19. *One of England's most historic homes, and scene of murder of Edward II. See p.* 201. Capt. R. G. Berkeley, MFH.

Blaise Castle House 4m NW of Bristol *Map* D F 17. *Late 18th-cent. mansion now housing fascinating Folk Museum.* Bristol Corporation.

Daneway House Sapperton 5m W of Cirencester *Map* E A 20. *14th-cent. Cotswold house with 17th- & 18th-cent. additions. Period doll's house. Lovely small garden.* Mrs Titania Hill.

Dodington House 200 yds N of M4 roundabout on A46 Bath–Stroud *Map* D H 18. *Fine Regency house by James Wyatt. Grand staircase and halls. Landscaped park by Capability Brown.* Major Simon Codrington. Chipping Sodbury 8606 for information.

Dyrham Park Map D H 17. *Beautifully situated mansion built 1698. Contemporary panelling, tapestries, furniture, paintings.* N T.

Hidcote Manor Garden 4m N E of Chipping Camden *Map* E B 23. *A series of beautiful formal gardens, with rare trees, shrubs, bulbs, 'old' roses, large collection of herbaceous plants and superb hedges.*

Red Lodge Park Row Bristol *Map* D F 17. *Late 16th-cent. house with early 18th-cent. staircase. Furniture, plasterwork, panelling.* Bristol Corporation.

Snowshill Manor 3m S of Broadway *Map* E A 23. *Unspoilt Tudor house, with a 1700 front. Collections of musical instruments, clocks, toys, etc.* N T.

Sudeley Castle Winchcombe *Map* E A 22. *Historic castle of mellowed Cotswold stone, dating partly from 15th cent. Pictures, furniture, tapestries, glass, etc.* Mrs J. H. Dent-Brocklehurst.

Books for further reading

The 'feel' of Gloucestershire

HARRY BEDDINGTON *Forest of Dean Humour* 1961

FREDDIE GRISEWOOD *Our Bill: guide – counsellor – friend* rev. edn 1950

LAURIE LEE *Cider with Rosie* 1959

JOHN MOORE *Blue Field* 1948 with the companion volumes *Brenshaw Village* 1946, and *Portrait of Elmbury* 1945

JENNIFER TANN *Gloucestershire Woollen Mills* 1967

Scenery, archaeology, natural history

O. S. G. CRAWFORD *The Long Barrows of the Cotswolds* 1925

H. P. R. FINBERG *Gloucestershire: an illustrated essay on the making of landscape* 1955

EARNEST NEAL *The Badger* 1948

REV. H. J. RIDDELSDELL and others, eds *Flora of Gloucestershire* 1948

Topography – general

R. P. BECKINSALE *Companion into Gloucestershire* 5th edn 1948

ROBERT COOKE *West Country Houses* 1957

J. CHARLES COX *Gloucestershire* rev. edn 1949 (The Little Guides series)

ANTHONY WEST *Gloucestershire: a Shell Guide* rev. by David Verey 1959

Berkeley Vale and Severn Vale

BRIAN WATERS *Severn Tide* 1947, and its sequel *Severn Stream* 1949

LEWIS WILSHIRE *The Vale of Berkeley* 1954

Forest of Dean

F. W. BATY *The Forest of Dean* 1952 (Regional Books series)

Cotswolds

EDITH BRILL *Portrait of the Cotswolds* 1964

WILSON MACARTHUR *The River Windrush* 2nd edn 1948

CHARLES and ALICE HADFIELD *The Cotswolds* 1966

Gazetteer

GLOUCESTERSHIRE

Aust (DF 18). Eastern end of the great new suspension road bridge across the Severn. The brightly coloured strata of the cliffs are well worth a special note.

Badminton* (DJ 18). The Palladian mansion (*c.* 1680), seat of the Duke of Beaufort, was altered by Kent *c.* 1740 A noted hunting centre and scene of the annual Three Day Horse Trials. Beaufort monuments in church.

Belas Knap. *See* **Winchcombe** *below*.

Berkeley* (DG 19). The splendid castle is a 12th-cent. feudal stronghold on rising ground looking out over the Severn. Built of vari-coloured stones and set among lovely gardens; a place of winding stairways and arched door-ways. Within these walls Edward II was hideously murdered in 1327. The castle has been occupied by the Berkeley family continuously since the 12th cent. In the parish church (which has a detached tower) is the grave of Edward Jenner (1749–1823) who introduced vaccination. Near the river is a large nuclear-powered generating station.

Bibury* (EB 20). Stone cottages and the Swan hotel look out across the rippling Coln to the NT row of early 17th-cent. cottages known as Arling-ton Row, and a fairer scene would be hard to find. Lean on the bridge and watch the trout in the current below, or go a little way along the Quenington

Bibury: Arlington Row   Reece Winstone

road for the view of the attractive manor house against a background of wooded hills.

Bisley (DK 20). Village of excellent stone houses and a 14th-cent. church. The near-by house of Lypiatt Park had connections with the Gunpowder Plot.

Bourton - on - the - Hill* (EB 23). Picturesque village of bow-windowed stone cottages. The manor house has a fine tithe-barn. A mile or so S is the Indian-style mansion of Sezincote, which was the inspiration for the Brighton Pavilion.

Bourton-on-the-Water*(EB 22). The Windrush flows between lawns along-side the main street and is crossed by

201

Bristol: Avonmouth Docks

graceful stone bridges. All around are good Cotswold houses, and at one end is an old mill. Behind the New Inn is a model of the village constructed from local stone.

Bristol* (D F 17) E C Wed (436,450). Partly in Gloucestershire, partly in Somerset, but since 1373 a county in its own right, Bristol has a long history of maritime commerce. The boat basin by the city centre marks the position of the harbour around which the city grew up. As ships became larger, deeper docks were built at the mouth of the Avon. As an importer of tobacco leaf Bristol naturally made (and still makes) cigars and cigarettes – so with numerous other imports. To understand Bristol fully, go to the docks. Then see the soaring St Mary Redcliffe Church; the restored but ancient Cathedral; the museum and art gallery, adjoining the towered University building and facing the Cabot tower which celebrates Cabot's discovery of North America in 1497. In front of the Exchange are four short pillars called *nails*, on which merchants conducted cash transactions: hence 'paying on the nail'. Notable is the 18th-cent. Theatre Royal. At Clifton, N W of the city, the Avon gorge is spanned by Brunel's spectacular suspension bridge. The Clifton Zoo is well worth a visit.

Chedworth* (E A 21). On the N of Chedworth wood, just off the Fosse Way near Fosse Bridge, are the comprehensive remains of a large Roman villa (with mosaic pavements) dating from between AD 180 and 380 (N T). Lilies-of-the-valley abound in the woods.

Cheltenham* (D K 22) E C Wed and Sat. (72,000). Well cared for Regency buildings, wide streets, and a wealth of trees preserve the character of this beautiful town despite the pressure of modern commerce. No shopping street in England can compare with the Promenade for beauty. Cheltenham developed as a spa during the 18th cent. (the waters are still dispensed at the Town Hall), but it is as a residential and educational centre, with festivals of music, etc. that it is best known today. St Mary's Church has a fine rose window. Excellent centre for exploring the Cotswolds. The famous steeplechase race-course is at Prestbury Park to the N.

Chipping Campden* (E B 23) E C Thurs (2,600). Home of some of the wealthiest of the 14th-15th cent. Cotswold wool merchants. Many excellent buildings (note especially Wm. Grevel's house) and an arched market hall. Good brasses in the fine church, and near by a row of almshouses in typical Cotswold style.

Chipping Sodbury* (D H 18) E C Thurs (1,100). Georgian brick houses mingle with Cotswold stone cottages. The fine 14th-cent. church has a high tower with pinnacles; the pulpit is entered through a hole in an adjacent pier, and there is curious carving on the chancel arch.

At Little Sodbury, 1 m. N, is a Romano-British camp occupied by the Saxons before the battle of Dyrham in 577 and by Edward IV in 1471 when he was preparing for the battle of Tewkesbury.

Cirencester* (E A 20) E C Thurs (11,850). The feature of the town is the elaborate three-storied 16th-cent. porch in front of the parish church. The church has a good tower, and fan vaulting in St Catherine's Chapel.

Cirencester was the Roman *Corinium*, and excavations have revealed the lay-out of the entire town. See the excellent Corinium Museum. Earl Bathurst's 3,000-acre park has a notable 5-mile avenue of chestnuts (the house itself is not open to the public).

Dean, Forest of. Extends roughly N and E of Chepstow (D F 19). One of the few true forests remaining in England; an extensive hilly area of oak and birch between the Wye and the Severn, with excellent views from some of the high points. For centuries coal and iron have been worked, but the pits were mostly small and in recent years all have been closed. The Speech House Hotel, in the centre of the Forest, was once the Verderer's Court. (*See also p.* 199.)

Deerhurst (D J 22). Tiny village among the fields, worth visiting for its church*, one of the most complete Saxon buildings in England, though aisles and other features are Norman.

Dursley (D H 19) E C Wed (4,870). The 18th-cent. market house, raised on pillars, gives no hint of the industries tucked away down the hill. Good old houses are solid evidence of the town's former cloth-making prosperity, but they are now being crowded out by the rapid spread of new building.

Elkstone (D K 21). Cotswold village with an unusually good little Norman church.* Note the dovecot over the E end.

Elmore. *See* **Severn Bore** *below.*

Fairford (E B 20) E C Sat (2,440). Famous for the 28 windows of its church*, filled with late 15th-cent. glass illustrating Biblical themes. Popularly said to have been salvaged

Gloucester Cathedral: the West Front

from a wrecked ship, the glass was more probably made especially for these windows when the church (except the tower) was rebuilt by the rich wool-merchant John Tame.

Frocester, 5 m. WSW of Stroud (DJ 20). A small village under the Cotswolds, with a good Elizabethan manor house and a splendid 13th-cent. tithe barn 60 yds. long and 36 ft. high, reputed to be the largest in England. From Frocester Hill, 1 m. SW, magnificent views over the Severn valley.

Gloucester (DJ 21) EC Thurs (69,700). For centuries the city has guarded the lowest crossing of the Severn and the routes into Wales. It was the Roman fortified town of *Glevum,* the British *Caer Glowe*; the Normans walled it and built a castle (destroyed in the 17th cent.). The glory of the city is the Cathedral★★ built mainly in the 12th cent. as a monastic church but refounded by Henry VIII as a cathedral. The pillars of the nave have been standing there for nearly 900 years. Note especially 14th-cent. glass in E window, largest in England, and (15th-cent.) in the Lady Chapel. The cloisters display the earliest fan vaulting in England. In Northgate Street is the 15th-cent. 'New' Inn with its galleried courtyard. Modern Gloucester is a busy inland port and manufacturing centre.

Hailes Abbey (E A 22). 2 m. N E of Winchcombe. Little but ruins marking the ground plan remain. This once great 13th-cent. Cistercian foundation was the burial place of Richard Earl of Cornwall, King of the Romans (1209–72), and attracted pilgrims with a phial said to contain drops of the Holy Blood. A small museum preserves various relics of the abbey (N T and A M).

Lechlade (E C 19). Where the River Leach joins the Thames the counties of Gloucestershire, Berkshire and Wiltshire meet. A charming little place with quiet Georgian houses; it has clearly changed little over the years. The 15th-cent. church has an interesting priest's door.

Moreton-in-Marsh (E C 23). Not 'Marsh' but 'March' gives the true meaning of the name, march being used in the sense of 'boundary'. Moreton's old curfew bell is still in its tower overlooking the Fosse Way.

Nailsworth (D J 19) E C Thurs (3,600). Among wooded Cotswold hills and steep winding roads (the 'ladder' is a famous hill-climb test) leading to widespread commons with views in all directions.

Northleach (E B 21). Stone-built little town, once an important centre of the Cotswold wool trade. The church*, with its splendid carved S porch, is one of the finest of those built by the old wool merchants. Among the brasses are some which portray the kind of sheep which produced the Cotswold Golden Fleece.

Painswick (D J 20) E C Thurs (2,750). Hillside town with a remarkable number of good stone buildings dating from the heyday of the wool trade. The churchyard is famous for its collection of ninety-nine clipped yews.

Splendid views from Painswick Beacon, 2 m. N. Painswick House is open to the public on Sunday afternoons in summer.

Prinknash Abbey. About 3 m. S E of Gloucester (D J 21), in a hamlet called Paradise, Benedictine monks (who until 1924 lived on an island off the Welsh coast near Tenby) have started work on the building of an immense new abbey.

Pucklechurch (D H 17). About 2½ m. E of the village is the N T house of Dyrham Park, built c. 1700, in beautiful grounds.

St Briavels (D F 20). In a wooded valley with a small, restored, partly 12th-cent. castle, now a youth hostel. Views down the valley towards the **Forest of Dean.**

Severn Bore*. A phenomenon which occurs at certain high-water spring tides when the waters of the Bristol Channel surge up and roll back the waters of the Severn. The best views of it are in the neighbourhood of Elmore, some 3 m. downstream from Gloucester (D J 21).

Slimbridge, 4 m. E of Sharpness (D G 20). The Severn Wild Fowl Trust founded here by Peter Scott (and open to visitors) protects the largest and most varied collection of wild water fowl in the world. The nave in the church has 12th-cent. carved arcades.

Stanton* (E A 23). A single street of 16th–17th-cent. houses and barns, with a partly Norman church. One of Cotswold's loveliest villages, restored with skill and restraint.

Stow-on-the-Wold (E B 22). Small hill-top town at the conjunction of eight roads (the Fosse Way is one of them); it is not surprising that it was once an important market town.

Owlpen Manor, Uley

Reece Winstone

Hence the large market-place in which the great annual sheep fairs were held. Good village cross. In the church is a large painting of the Crucifixion by a pupil of Rubens.

Stroud (D J 20) E C Thurs (17,460). A famous manufacturing centre of the cloth trade, especially in the late 18th cent. It is now a bustling modern town.

Sudeley Castle. *See* **Winchcombe** *below.*

Tetbury (D J 19) E C Thurs (2,500). Quiet, dignified houses, an Elizabethan market hall mounted on pillars, and a church with an unusual arrangement of numbered box pews.

Tewkesbury★ (D J 23) E C Thurs (5,800). Old-fashioned town of timbered houses, venerable inns, and above all a splendid Norman abbey church★ to which a series of chantries and chapels were added in the 14th cent. Here the Rivers Severn and Avon unite, and Tewkesbury is a popular sailing and boating centre. Parts of the bridge over the River Avon are over 750 years old. (*See also p.* 197.)

Uley (D H 19). An old weaving village in a valley among steep wooded hills. The 14th-cent. Owlpen manor house (1 m. E) with its clipped yews is one of the most picturesque of all the smaller Cotswold manors. Above the village is the prehistoric long-barrow known as Hetty Pegler's Tump (AM), with splendid views across the Severn Valley into Wales.

Westonbirt, $2\frac{1}{2}$ m. S W of Tetbury (DJ 19). The well-known girls' school is in an Italian mansion built by Lewis Vulliamy for R. S. Holford. The arboretum is one of the best in England: a rarity is an avenue of tulip trees.

Winchcombe* (EA 22) E C Thurs (2,800). Attractive little grey-stone town in the Cotswolds. A Benedictine abbey, founded c. 800 by Kenulf of Mercia, was rebuilt, and then dissolved and razed by Henry VIII. Two stone coffins in the 15th-cent. church are said to be those of Kenulf and his son. One of the altar cloths was the work of Catherine of Aragon. Near-by **Sudeley Castle** provides the parallel to the Vicar of Bray, for rather than give up his castle the Lancastrian Lord Sudeley changed coats and became a Yorkist. Here came Sir Thomas Seymour, lately married to Catherine Parr, who died here and is buried in the chapel.

On a hilltop to the S of Winchcombe, and nearly 1,000 ft. above sea-level, is the famous long barrow of **Belas Knap***, a Stone-Age burial mound with a false portal, masked by dry walling at one end, with burial chambers opening in the sides (AM). *See also* **Hailes Abbey** *above*.

Woodchester (D J 20). The Roman villa covering 26 acres, one of the largest Roman villa sites in Britain, is generally kept covered with earth for preservation, but it is opened up from time to time as announced in the local press.

Wotton-under-Edge (D H 19) E C Wed (3,500). Old market and cloth town on the western escarpment of the Cotswolds with widespread views over the Severn. The church organ came from St Martin-in-the-Fields, London. Handel played on it.

Winchcombe *Jarrold*

The Mumbles, near Swansea *Aerofilms*

GLAMORGAN AND MONMOUTHSHIRE

AN INTRODUCTION BY C. J. O. EVANS

These two counties in the south-east corner of the Principality of Wales lie on the north shore of the Bristol Channel. Glamorgan is mountainous in the north with deep valleys and ravines through which rivers course their way to the sea; its south is a pleasant land, largely agricultural and extremely picturesque. Its westernmost part, the peninsula of Gower, open to the Atlantic Ocean and unsullied by industry, compares favourably with England's West Country. The north-west of Monmouthshire also has its lofty hills, which rise to 2,000 feet; but its easternmost part is pastoral, falling south to low-lying lands skirting the Severn estuary.

Among the hilly districts of both counties are the famous coal-mining areas of South Wales; but the fair region of the south and east, fertile and pleasant to the eye, is flecked with interesting towns and villages, numerous archaeological remains, ruined castles and woodlands. Along the coast of Glamorgan are popular seaside resorts with safe bathing, such as Penarth, Barry Island, Porthcawl, Aberavon and Swansea Bay, with many charming bays along the Gower coast.

Among the river valleys, those of the Wye and Usk are famed for their beauty; while at Kenfig Burrows, between Bridgend and Port Talbot, is an area very different in its appeal. Here the sands have buried an ancient borough and its castle (all but part of one tower), and now support a range of plants fascinating to the botanist. On the seventy-acre lake which they encircle, wildfowl are found in abundance. Nor far away is the village of Merthyr Mawr, quaint and unspoiled, with thatched cottages.

Physical Features

The physical appearance of the two counties is determined in a marked degree by the underlying rock formations – in the north-west the coal measures, and in the east the Old Red Sandstone. Limestone is quarried throughout the area, and is well exposed along the coast of Glamorgan and in the beautiful Wye valley. Near Penarth, bands of gypsum appear among the strata. This, known locally as 'Penarth Alabaster', has been worked and used in local buildings. The coast of Glamorgan is rocky and interesting between Cardiff and the mouth of the River Ogmore, and again along the southern reaches of the Gower peninsula. Monmouthshire's coastline is less interesting – the tracts of low levels are mainly composed of deposits of silt, terraces of gravel, and stretches of mud and alluvium.

Natural History

The wild cat and pine-marten ceased to exist within the last century; the polecat occasionally appears from adjoining counties where it is still common. Otter, now becoming rather rare owing to river pollution, is still hunted, and the fox is the quarry of several hunts. There are a few 'earths' of badger, happily not seriously worried; and the red squirrel more than holds its own. The grey squirrel is all too common. Schools of porpoise are often seen frolicking offshore in the summer.

The large birds of prey have mostly disappeared, and black grouse is very rare; but red grouse is preserved in the north, and pheasants and partridges breed well. Heronries are few, and pairs appear to be decreasing. Razorbills and guillemots breed in large numbers on the peninsula of Gower, and peregrines and raven are common. The ringed plover and oyster-catcher are seen along the coast.

In most rivers and streams fish were plentiful in early times; but industrial pollution caused severe loss. This is now being reduced and, in the main rivers, good fishing of trout and salmon, as well as of a migratory trout called sewin, is possible, Wye and Usk salmon and trout being famous beyond the county boundaries.

The flora is richer than one might expect. In the uplands coarse grass with its thin layer of earth on solid rock gives good pasturage for sheep, despite an abundance of gorse, heather and bracken. In the valleys are many varieties of fern and, occasionally, Cornish moneywort, the lesser bladderwort and green spleenwort. The lower ground is mainly rich agricultural land, arable pasture, with luxuriant hedgerows dividing field and meadow. Bluebells deck the woodlands, wild clematis and monkshood line the hedges, and on the sandy warrens and river estuaries are varieties of glasswort, sea-lavender, sea-aster, milkwort, wormwood, spurge and others. Several areas in the hills have been planted with fir, and there is a flourishing nursery of the Forestry Commission near Bonvilston.

Margam, Port Talbot

Aerofilms

Antiquities

Prehistory is well represented in the two counties. The Old Stone Age left evidence of its inhabitants in a cave at Paviland on the seashore of Gower, where a human skeleton was found near part of an elephant's skull and tusks, the molar teeth of a mammoth, and the bones of other animals such as bear, rhinoceros and wild horse. There are many remains of the Later Stone Age in Glamorgan – notably chambered tombs: one in particular at St Nicholas is well maintained. Many Bronze Age burials and 'beaker folk' interments have given us increasing knowledge of the period. The new culture which preceded the Christian era by a few hundred years, when iron supplanted bronze to a great extent, introduced a craftsmanship now known as Late Celtic Art. This reached a marvellous standard of design in decorative work, with flowing curves and scroll ornament. In the higher regions many hilltop camps of this period still survive, and several promontory camps are found on the coast. At Llyn Fawr, a pool in the north of Glamorgan, was found a surprising hoard of weapons and implements of both the Bronze and Iron Ages.

At the time of the Roman invasion Monmouthshire was part of a large area inhabited by the Silures, a tribe whose leader was Caradoc (Caractacus). The Romans completed their domination of South Wales by A.D. 90, by which time they had erected a fort, named *Isca*, on the side of the River Usk. This became the fortress of the Second Augustan Legion and is the most important Roman site in Wales. Today Caerleon, although mostly built over, is still an interesting place. It held a force of approximately 6,000 men, and outside its walls was erected a stone amphitheatre, which still remains to recall former gladiatorial combats. The Romans also established a township eight miles to the east at Caerwent, which they named *Venta Silurum*, market town of the Silures. Little but its walls remains today. Other military stations were at Abergavenny, Usk and Monmouth in Monmouthshire, and Cardiff, Neath and Loughor in Glamorgan. A Roman villa existed at Llantwit Major, but although its mosaic floor has twice been exposed, it is now turfed over.

The early Christian era bequeathed to us a large number of stone monuments. Only a few are in Monmouthshire; but Glamorgan has several with noteworthy inscriptions, such as those in the Lapidary Museum at Margam and in the church at Llantwit Major. In the National Museum of Wales at Cardiff are to be seen all the prehistoric finds of the area, as well as casts of inscribed stones. There is also a small Roman Museum at Caerleon.

Historical Outline

The only part of South Wales mentioned in the Domesday Survey extended to a small area west of the River Usk. The Normans came to the rest of Monmouthshire and Glamorgan some years later, driving the Welsh to the uplands, where they continued to be such a nuisance that the intruders had to build strongholds for defence. This accounts for the many castles in the lowlands. The powerful Norman magnates thus acquired extensive holdings which were held as 'marcher lordships' – petty kingdoms assuming extraordinary privileges. Within their boundaries knights and vassals owed service only to the lords of the marches – even the King's writ had no authority except for treason. Castles were erected at Chepstow, Usk, Monmouth, Abergavenny, Cardiff, Neath and Swansea – to mention but a few – and lesser knights erected castles in their respective fiefs.

213

y Christian symbol of the Holy Trinity, on a stone in Tintern Abbey   *Reece Winstone*

These autocratic marcher lordships (the envy, by the way, of the English barons) continued until the Act of Union in the reign of Henry VIII.

The Welsh remained restless throughout the medieval period and many insurrections occurred, the last being that of Owen Glyndwr, who in 1403 laid in utter waste the whole of South Wales in an abortive effort to regain independence. During the Civil War, local sympathies were divided, and many leading people changed sides during the conflict. A considerable engagement was fought at St Fagan's, Glamorgan, and the Castles of Chepstow and Raglan fell to the Cromwellian troops. The Chartist movement was particularly violent in Monmouthshire, the Mayor of Newport being shot and wounded in 1839 while attempting to read the Riot Act.

Architecture

Ecclesiastical buildings in Glamorgan are not very imposing. Llandaff Cathedral (the only cathedral in the country not built on the plan of a cross) has little Norman work. It was badly damaged by a land-mine in January 1941. In its rebuilding an unusual addition in the modern style was made to the nave: Epstein's fine figure of Christ in unpolished aluminium and 18 feet high. Ewenny Priory Church is the finest example of Norman ecclesiastical architecture in Wales. Margam Church, also late Norman, is (except for its ruined chapter house) all that is left of a Cistercian abbey. St John's Church at Cardiff has a beautifully designed tower. The church of Llantwit Major has many unusual points, including a number of inscribed Early Christian stones.

It has been said that while Glamorgan had the largest castle in the country, it had also some of the smallest. Cardiff Castle, with its keep and imposing curtain walls, is now in the hands of the Cardiff Corporation and is well worth a visit even though it has been modernized. St Donat's Castle, with its lovely terraced gardens dropping down to the sea, has been in continuous occupation since the 13th century. It was added to by its former owner, the late William Randolph Hearst of the U.S.A., and has now become the Outward Bound Atlantic College. Caerphilly Castle, second only to Windsor Castle in area, has a leaning tower that has been strengthened to stand even in its ruined state for years to come. Other castles in Glamorgan are in the safe hands of the Ministry of Works.

In Monmouthshire most of the churches are comparatively modern architecturally, though many show vestiges of early foundation. St Woolos, formerly the parish church of Newport but now the cathedral of the Diocese of Monmouthshire, is a small edifice in various styles of architecture beginning with the Late Norman entrance to its nave. There is also a fine east door of the same period at Chepstow Church. But the gem of this county's ecclesiastical architecture – and one of the most lovely sights in Britain – is the noble ruin of the Cistercian abbey at Tintern, so beautifully situated on the banks of the Wye. Another ruin worth a visit as much for its beauty as for its associations, is Llanthony Priory, set in a secluded valley of the Black Mountains, and once a monastery of Black Canons of the Order of St Augustine. In more recent times it was for some years the home of Walter Savage Landor, the poet and author.

Monmouthshire, too, had numerous strongpoints. Chepstow Castle, built on solid rock almost at the mouth of the Wye, is an inspiring sight as you cross into the county from Gloucestershire. Newport Castle is a mere shell, so is the one at Abergavenny; Caldicot is well preserved; Usk Castle stands on a commanding eminence. The 'Three Castles' (Grosmont, Skenfrith and White Castle), although not of absorbing interest, each have their features and are kept in good condition; and finally, Raglan Castle, besieged by Cromwellian forces during the Civil War, is picturesque. Monmouthshire is richer in good domestic architecture than Glamorgan. These often beautiful houses were, of course, built when the need for solid defence works became unnecessary. St Fagan's Castle in Glamorgan, a Tudor manor house, is now a Welsh Folk Museum, part of the National Museum of Wales.

Industries

Until the industrial revolution at the end of the 18th century, Glamorgan and Monmouthshire were mainly agricultural, with a few rural industries such as weaving, pottery-making and quarrying. Mining for metals had been explored by the Romans, and a little coal was dug from early days. The manufacture of iron became a profitable adventure in the 16th century; but two centuries later came the discovery that iron could be smelted with coal instead of charcoal. This utterly changed the face of the northern part of the area: it became the great iron-producing centre of the world. It was from Penydarren, Merthyr, in Glamorgan, that the first railway locomotive in history successfully hauled a train loaded with bar iron for nearly ten miles, thus settling a wager between two ironmasters. It had been built by the Cornish engineer Richard Trevithick in 1804 – ten years before Stephenson's 'Puffing Billy'.

With the introduction of the Bessemer process, about the middle of the 19th century, steel came into its own and became the principal product of the former flourishing ironworks. Today the Steel Company of Wales at Margam, Port Talbot, extending $4\frac{1}{2}$ miles along the coast of the Bristol Channel, is one of the largest and most modern steelworks in Europe. At Llanwern in Monmouthshire, just east of Newport, another large steelworks for Richard Thomas and Baldwins Ltd. has been in production since 1962.

A mile or so west of the giant works of the Steel Company of Wales is a new petroleum chemical plant, soon to be extended, at a cost of £60 million at Baglan Bay. Within the bay itself a great new harbour to take large ore-carrying ships is now being constructed.

Cement-making has long been established in South Glamorgan, and oil refining at Llandarcy is a flourishing innovation of the county. The docks at Newport, Cardiff, Port Talbot and Swansea continue to hold their own, though coal exports are not what they were. Today, the traditional industries of coal, iron and steel have been considerably augmented by a variety of light industries. At Mamhilad near Pontypool is a large factory producing nylon yarn. In 1936 a government-sponsored trading estate was established at Treforest to the north-west of Cardiff, and today the Industrial Estates Management Corporation for Wales is responsible for some 350 factories in Treforest, Bridgend, Swansea, Hirwaun, Wrexham and other parts. They cover industries of an exceedingly wide range, with products of light engineering, transformers, switchgear, electric motors, die-casting, plastics, chemicals, textiles, furniture, etc.

An industry which came and went during the first half of the century was the manufacture of Swansea and Nantgarw china by Joseph Billingsley, a talented potter and painter. It is still prized by collectors for its beauty.

For the Visitor

There are many first-class hotels in Glamorgan and Monmouthshire, and a few country clubs which welcome visitors. The Royal Porthcawl and Southerndown are only two of many which cater for the golfer. Glamorgan is the only Welsh county in the County Cricket Championship (which it won in 1948); but its native players come from all parts of Wales. The gourmet may be interested to know that scarcely any of the well-known Caerphilly cheese is made in the town of that name, although it is now being manufactured in one of the factories on the industrial estate on the outskirts of the town. Two products of the sea that should not be despised are the homely cockle, harvested on the north shore of the peninsula of Gower, and a native dish known as laver-bread, made from a special kind of seaweed; sprinkled with oatmeal and fried with bacon, it is delicious eaten at breakfast.

Some houses and gardens open to the public

Cardiff Castle *Map* DB 17. *Norman castle built on site of Roman fortification.* Cardiff City Council.

Castell Coch 5m NW of Cardiff *Map* DB 17. *Remarkably successful 19th-cent. reconstruction of 13th-cent. castle on its original foundations, built for the 3rd Marquess of Bute.* Ministry of Public Building and Works.

Cefntilla Court 3m NE of Usk *Map* DD 20. *Historic manor house built 1616, restored 1856. Pictures, porcelain, military relics. Painted*

heraldic frieze of 1510. Lord and Lady Raglan.

Llanvihangel Court 4½m N of Abergavenny *Map* DD 21. *Elizabethan manor house with 17th-cent. alterations.* Col and Mrs Somerset Hopkinson.

St Fagan's Castle 4m W of Cardiff *Map* DB 17. *The 16th-cent. house and its gardens are part of the Welsh Folk Museum, which includes several re-erected buildings (farmhouses, cottages, chapel, tannery, woollen mill, etc.) from different parts of Wales.*

Books for further reading

Glamorgan

H. L. EDLIN (ed.) *Glamorgan Forests* 1961
C. J. O. EVANS *Glamorgan: its History and Topography* 2nd edn 1953
C. HOULDER and W. H. MANNING *South Wales* 1966 (Regional Archaeological series)
MRS ABEL JONES *The Story of Glamorgan* 1955
H. J. RANDALL *The Vale of Glamorgan* 1961
S. WILLIAMS *The Garden of Wales* 1961; *Saints and Sailing Ships* 1962

Monmouthshire

W. T. BARBER *West of the Wye: with a camera in Gwent* 1966

H. DURANT *Raglan Castle* 1966
C. J. O. EVANS *Monmouthshire: its History and Topography* 1954
SIR CYRIL FOX and LORD RAGLAN *Monmouthshire Houses* 1954
F. J. HANDO *Here and there in Monmouthshire* 1964
F. J. HANDO *Monmouthshire Sketch Book* 1954
F. J. HANDO *Out and About in Monmouthshire* 1958
ARTHUR MEE (ed.) *Monmouthshire* (King's England series) 1951

Gazetteer

GLAMORGAN AND MONMOUTHSHIRE

Abergavenny, *Mon.* (DD 21) EC Thurs (9,620). 'The Gateway of Wales', so called from its position on the Usk between two prominent hills. Agricultural town with cattle-markets. Good centre for exploring the valleys running up into the Black Mountains. Ruins of 12th-cent. castle (AM). St Mary's Church has interesting altar tombs.

Barry, *Glam.* (DB 16) EC Wed (42,000). The docks were built to provide additional facilities for the export of coal. The town became a borough in 1939. Barry Island, Whitmore Bay and Porthkerry Bay are highly popular seaside resorts.

Bonvilston, *Glam.* (DA 17). Here the Forestry Commission raise seedlings for planting in the new forests (*see* **Neath**, for example). Near by is a Roman camp.

Bridgend, *Glam.* (CK 17) EC Wed (15,150). Market town on the Ogmore river, about midway between Cardiff and Swansea. Good fishing.

Caerleon*, *Mon.* (DD 19) EC Thurs (4,200). The parish church stands in the centre of the site of Roman *Isca*, a legionary fortress with room for 6,000 men. The chief feature today is the amphitheatre (AM). One of the many places associated by the romantically inclined with the Arthurian legends.

Caerphilly*, *Glam.* (DB 18) EC Wed (36,000). The ruins of the great

Caerphilly Castle   Aerofilms

13th–14th-cent. castle (AM) cover 30 acres, an area exceeded only by Windsor among the old castles of Britain.

Caerwent*, *Mon.* (DE 19). Small village on the site of an extensive Roman town, *Venta Silurum,* of which many parts have been excavated. Relics in the church and in Newport Museum. About a mile S is Caldicot castle, small, but notable for the excellence of its masonry work.

Cardiff, *Glam.* (DB 17) EC Wed (256,300). An intensely busy city with a large dock area and the first planned city centre in Britain. Here is the castle*, with a Norman keep on an artificial mound; the Central Library with priceless manuscripts and books; the City Hall and Law Courts; the National Museum of Wales, and the University College of South Wales and Monmouthshire. Cardiff Arms Park, well known to cricketers and Rugby footballers, is but one of a number of good open spaces. The

Empire Bathing Pool has competition facilities unsurpassed in Britain. Formerly engaged almost entirely in the shipping of coal and iron, Cardiff now handles the products of over a hundred other industries and is the principal distributing centre over a wide area of South Wales.

Chepstow, *Mon.* (DF 19) EC Wed (6,000). Here on a high rock at the lowest crossing of the Wye the Normans built an imposing castle (AM)★ which is well seen from the eastern bank of the river. SE of the town is the new Severn road bridge: with a central span of 3,246 ft. and two side spans of 1,000 ft. each, the bridge is one of the largest of its kind in Europe, with a clearance above high water of about 110 ft.

Coity, *Glam.* (CK 18). Here are the well-preserved remains of a medieval castle (AM). A few hundred yards N is a long-cairned chambered tomb probably dating from 2000 BC.

Ebbw Vale, *Mon.* (DB 20) EC Wed (28,650). The most notable feature of this important coal-mining town is the huge tinplate strip mill, one of the largest in Europe.

Ewenny★, *Glam.* (CK 17). The fine Norman church is the chief remnant of the fortified Priory built here in the 12th cent. Note the chancel roof and the stone screen in front of the choir.

Gower, *Glam.* (CE 18). Peninsula extending some 15 miles westward of Swansea and having an average width of 5 miles. The S and W coasts are cliff; bays and coves shelter many pleasant villages with sandy beaches that are popular holiday resorts. Rhossili Bay, at the western end, has nearly 3 miles of sand. The N coast is low-lying and marshy in places. The NE corner is involved in the industrial area around Llanelly. (*See also* **Paviland Caves** *below*.)

Grosmont, *Mon.* (DE 22). Old-world town on the River Monnow (good fishing) with remnants of a 13th-cent. castle (AM) which even in Elizabethan times was reported to be 'ruinous, time out of mind'. The Ministry of Works have done good work on what is left.

Kenfig, *Glam.* (CJ 18). Among the sandhills W of Porthcawl are a 60-acre freshwater lake and the remains of a borough and castle which were overwhelmed by a great sandstorm in the 16th cent.

Llandaff, *Glam.* (DB 17) EC Wed (19,850). Though now a part of Cardiff, Llandaff retains the air of a cathedral city, with its Bishop's Palace, Deanery and Canons' Residence. The Cathedral has Norman work, but misguided alterations in the 18th cent. necessitated a thorough restoration in the 19th cent. The most important feature of the interior is Epstein's huge figure of Christ.

Llanthony★, *Mon.* (DC 22). Far up the narrow Honddu valley in the Black Mountains are the beautiful remains of a 12th-cent. priory (AM), once the home of Walter Savage Landor. Four miles farther up the valley, at Capel-y-ffin, are the remains of a monastery begun in 1870 but never completed.

Llantwit Major, *Glam.* (CK 16) EC Wed (5,000). An unusual church, the eastern end being a late 13th-cent. addition to a former plain erection. It is traditionally claimed to be the earliest home of Christianity in Wales and was famous as a centre of learning in Celtic times. The western end of the church has many Early Christian inscribed stones.

Reece Winstone   **Llandaff Cathedral: Epstein's 'Christ in Maje**

Ogmore Castle

Merthyr Tydfil, *Glam.* (DA 20) EC Thurs (59,000). Once the Welsh metropolis of the iron and steel trades, where Richard Trevithick in 1804 demonstrated the world's first steam-driven locomotive. Now a busy and prosperous town of many industries. Art gallery and museum in Cyfarthfa Park.

Monmouth (DF 21) EC Thurs (5,500). Quiet little market town lying in the valley where the River Monnow meets the famous Wye (both fine fishing rivers). The 13th-cent. fortified gatehouse on the bridge, built somewhat earlier, over the Monnow at the SW end of the town is unique in Britain. Monmouth is celebrated as the birthplace of Henry V. In the centre of the town is a statue of the Hon. C. S. Rolls (the 'Rolls' of Rolls-Royce), who was the first man to fly from England to France and back again. The Nelson Museum has the largest sextant collection of its kind.

Mumbles, *Glam.* (CG 18) EC Wed (12,000). On the W side of the curving Swansea Bay, a popular seaside and residential suburb which includes the village of Oystermouth. Bells in All Saints' Church came from Santiago Cathedral when it was burned down. In the graveyard lies Thomas Bowdler, whose expurgating of Shakespeare in the early 19th cent. added the word 'bowdlerise' to the English language.

Nantgarw, *Glam.,* 3 m. SW of Caerphilly (DB 18). In the mouth of a deep green valley is a huge coke-oven and by-products plant. Once 'Nantgarw China' was manufactured here.

Neath, *Glam.* (CH 19) EC Thurs (30,875). Busy market and industrial town at the point where the River Neath emerges from its beautiful narrow valley. At Briton Ferry, now included in the borough, an eleven-span viaduct carries the South Wales road high above the docks. On the hills above Neath in 1922 the Forestry Commission planted Rheola Forest, which now supplies pit-props and sawmill timber. There are remains of a 12th-cent. Benedictine abbey (AM) and a Norman castle. Due W across the river is the great BP refinery at Llandarcy.

Newport, *Mon.* (DD 18) EC Thurs (108,000). Busy industrial town and seaport not far from the point where the Usk joins the Bristol Channel. The tidal range in this part of the Channel is among the highest in the world; this of course affects the Usk – hence the transporter bridge 177 ft. above the water. Very good museum of archaeology and natural history and a small art gallery. St Woolos's Church is now the cathedral of the diocese of Monmouth, created 1921.

Newton Nottage, *Glam.*, 1½ m. E of Porthcawl (CJ 17). Here is a curious freshwater spring which ebbs and flows with the rise and fall of the Bristol Channel tides.

Ogmore-by-Sea, *Glam.* (CJ 17). Near the Ogmore river are the remains of a Norman castle (AM).

Paviland Caves, *Glam.* (CE 18). When Buckland discovered these limestone caves in the Gower peninsula in 1823 he found what he called 'The Red Lady' – in fact the skeleton of a young man whose bones were stained red, perhaps by the action of oxide of iron percolating through the cave walls. Can be visited at low water.

Penarth, *Glam.* (DB 17) EC Wed. (20,900). Only 2 miles S of Cardiff, it is a very popular seaside resort extending south towards Lavernock. Turner House (National Museum of Wales) has paintings by Turner, Cox, Cotman, etc.

Pontneathvaughan, *Glam.*, 2 m. N of Glyn-Neath (CJ 20). Here two rivers meet in a region of wooded hills, deep gorges and waterfalls.

Pontypool, *Mon.* (DC 20) EC Thurs (39,900). A historic place in the development of South Wales industry.

Newport

Aerofilms

Raglan Castle

Reece Winstone

Here the first hammer-mill, worked by the River Llwyd, was opened in 1770, enabling the first tin-plate to be made. A large factory for the manufacture of nylon yarn, on the outskirts of the town, has been operating for the past 20 years.

Pontypridd, *Glam.* (DA 18) EC Thurs (35,550). Busy town among the hills at the junction of the Taff and Rhondda valleys, shopping and social centre for a wide area. When the bridge over the Taff was built in the 18th cent., the town's original name of Newbridge was retained in the great ironworks largely concerned with making naval anchors and chains.

Porthcawl, *Glam.* (CJ 17) EC Wed (11,100). On a rocky promontory at the end of the long line of sand dunes lining Swansea Bay. Popular seaside resort.

Port Talbot, *Glam.* (CH 18) EC Thurs (50,250). Busy coal and iron port S of Aberavon. SE are the great steel works of the Steel Company of Wales on Margam burrows.

Raglan, *Mon.* (DE 20). Even as a ruin the 14th–15th cent. castle (AM) is imposing with its gateway and machicolated towers. Note huge fireplace in kitchen.

Rhondda, *Glam.* (CK 19) EC Thurs (100,300). Once one of the 'problem' valleys of the South Wales coalfield, whence the population migrated owing to industrial depression. However, new industries have recently been introduced, and to some extent at least the densely populated area wears a brighter face.

St Donat's, *Glam.* (CK 16). One of the most perfect old baronial halls of Wales – 'a 14th-cent. castle with an Elizabethan courtyard' and other anachronisms. Randolph Hearst, the American newspaper magnate, who bought the castle, brought here part of Bradenstoke Priory in Wiltshire.

St Fagan's, *Glam.* (DB 17). A small village on the River Ely, some 4 miles W of Cardiff. The castle, a Tudor manor-house with nearly 100 acres of

St Donat's Castle

ground, was presented by the Earl of Plymouth to accommodate the Welsh National Folk Museum, well worth a visit. The church has windows with Welsh inscriptions.

St Lythan's, *Glam.* (DB 17). Here at Dyffryn House are gardens containing rare trees and plants, including many from China. St Lythan's Cromlech was a prehistoric burial chamber, though the earth which covered the long barrow is gone (AM).

St Nicholas, *Glam.* (DA 17). Near by is the remarkable neolithic tomb at Tinkinswood, with a roof capstone weighing about 40 tons (AM).

Skenfrith, *Mon.* (DE 22). Here are the remains of a Norman castle (AM and NT) built as a defence against the Welsh, with a fine interior courtyard. This is one of the 'Three Castles', the others being **Grosmont** (*see above*) and White Castle, 6 miles SW of Skenfrith.

St Fagan's Castle

Swansea, *Glam.* (CG 19) EC Thurs (166,750). Thriving port for oil, tin-plate, and much else. Town-planning has removed war damage. Parts of the 14th-cent. castle remain. The Guild-hall, the Glynn Vivian Art Gallery, and the Royal Institute of South Wales have collections of pictures and Swansea china.

Tintern Abbey**, *Mon.* (DF 20). One of the most beautiful Cistercian ruins in Britain, with the wooded hills of the Wye valley all around. Dating from the 12th cent. it is far more extensive than a glimpse from the road would suggest. The Ministry of Works have done good service in excavating the ground plan and repairing weak points.

Usk, *Mon.* (DD 20). Small town and popular fishing centre on the River Usk. Remains of a fine Norman castle and a Benedictine nunnery. Three miles to the NE is Cefntilla Court, built 1616.

Tintern Abbey

Edward Young

Opposite: Detail from the original painting by John Elwyn.
Ancient lands rich in relics of Celtic Christianity – notably the Great Cross of Conbeline – and of still earlier days. Crude urns from Bronze Age barrows, and red-ochred bones from a cave of the Gower coast, lie with pottery from Swansea.

View from the A44 road near Goginan, east of Aberystwyth   *Reece Winstone*

CARDIGANSHIRE AND BRECONSHIRE

AN INTRODUCTION BY F. V. EMERY

On a map showing the Welsh counties, Brecon and Cardigan together have the rough shape of an hour-glass. Cardigan, slightly the smaller of the two, lies uppermost and reaches to the sea in Cardigan Bay. The waist of the hour-glass, where the counties meet, is a bleak stretch of high moorland, 1,500 feet and more above the sea, acting as a kind of barrier between these two counties. Not a single main road passes directly from one into the other, only the old drovers' tracks along which thousands of young cattle, mostly small Welsh blacks, were driven to England in the days before the railway. (Now the railway lines in their turn are in danger of becoming as deserted as the drove-ways.) Breconshire spreads north to within a mile or two of Rhayader, whence its boundary follows

Opposite: Detail from the original painting by Keith Grant.
From Cardigan Bay the blue hills of Wales roll inland to Breconshire. Here is a land of rough uplands and deep valleys, where foxgloves and bindweed are plentiful. A solitary and mysterious monolith, the Corbelanus Stone, records the burial of an unknown Corbelanus of the Dark Ages.

the River Wye south-eastwards to Hay and runs between Hereford and Monmouth along the eastern Marches of Wales. Returning, it skirts the industrial congestion of the South Wales coalfield. Since the two counties face opposite ways, it is not surprising to find them differing one from the other in their scenery and way of life. Travelling along the A40 through Brecon, then by the A482 through a corner of Carmarthenshire before entering Cardiganshire at Lampeter, you pass from semi-English to thoroughly Welsh landscapes and communities. You make a cross-section, scenically and historically, of the whole of Wales: whereas the Welsh language is known by just one-third of the people in Breconshire, over three-quarters of the population in Cardiganshire are Welsh-speaking.

Mountains, Rivers and Lakes

If you are looking for dramatic mountain scenery, as climber, walker, or ponytrekker, Breconshire has more to offer. Pride of place goes to the Brecon Beacons, a massive rampart culminating in Pen-y-Fan (2,906 feet) and well worth their membership of the hierarchy of the loftiest Welsh peaks. The Beacons dominate the whole county as a north-facing scarp of great majesty. They are capped with very resistant bands of Devonian conglomerate or 'pudding stone', a rock so called because of the assorted pebbles bound together in it, like the fruit in a plum-pudding. Their scarp-face is scalloped by hollows like gigantic armchairs, known as *cirques* or *cwms*, and the seats of local glaciers during the Ice Age. Llyn Cwm-llwch is a small lake now ponded back within one of them. Although the range becomes more subdued as it passes westwards into Fforest Fawr, the entire Beacons National Park is splendidly wild country: it has broad sweeps of stubborn moorland grasses, patches of peat and cottongrass on boggy glacial clays, sudden sharp boulders, and thin streams cascading whitely through their pebbly gulleys. Waterfalls, wooded gorges, and underground caverns are worth exploring in the south-westernmost corner of Breconshire, where five head-streams cross a narrow belt of limestone before coming together as the River Neath. This is the only locality where the geology offers much to collectors of fossils. Elsewhere the rocks are ancient mudstones, giving deep red soils in the valleys, or tough grits like those underlying the Black Mountains (2,660 feet) or Mynydd Epynt (1,560 feet) between the Usk and Wye valleys.

These rivers, the Usk and Wye, with their many tributaries, are renowned far and wide for their beauty and for their riches in salmon and trout. Indeed, both Breconshire and Cardiganshire provide superlatively fine sport for the angler. Llangorse Lake, or, to give it its more melodious Welsh name, Llyn Safaddan, is also worth a visit. It has a reputation for its pike, perch, and very large eels. The ornithologist will find its shores and waters rewarding, as it is traditionally the breeding-place of uncommon birds like the coot and the bittern. The lake also has more than its fair share of legends. In the Middle Ages and even to quite recent times it was thought miraculous when its waters became 'tinged with red, as if blood flowed partially through certain veins'. How prosaic it seems now to know that the River Llynfi, flowing into the lake, becomes charged with red silt in time of flood. Llangorse Lake was also said at times to be 'covered and adorned with buildings, pastures, gardens, and orchids'. Archaeology has shown there may be a grain of truth in this story of drowned homesteads.

J. Allan Cash **Fishing in the Usk at Crickh**

On the northern shore a dug-out canoe was discovered, near a stockaded island or 'crannog' settlement like those in the Glastonbury lake village, both of them probably prehistoric. As yet there are no legends attached to the remarkable number of man-made lakes in Breconshire, which outnumber the natural ones. They lie south of the Beacons, from Cray to Pentwyn, and supply water to the crowded industrial towns of South Wales. Cardiff, the Welsh capital, gets its water from reservoirs strung along the Taf Fawr river—Cantref, completed in 1892, Beacons (1879) and Llwyn-onn (1926). The Cardiff–Brecon road runs alongside them; they are fished, and their beauty is enhanced by the larch and pine groves protecting their banks.

Cardiganshire lacks bold mountains. Inland, the wide vistas of bare moorland, most of it over a thousand feet, ascend gently to the brow of Plynlimon (2,468 feet). As though to compensate for this, there is a varied and attractive coastline, at its best where the hard blue grits stand in sheer cliffs, in places 200 feet high. The road from Aberaeron to Aberystwyth, where it follows the very edge of the cliffs, offers superb views out to sea and along the curving sweep of Cardigan Bay. In fact, you will find most of Cardiganshire's scenic attractions on this coast or in the river valleys. No doubt the best known are the gorges and waterfalls hidden in the recesses of the upper Rheidol, a turbulent stream flowing directly into Cardigan Bay. That linguistic buccaneer George Borrow, in the course of his walk through *Wild Wales* in 1854, viewed them at Ponterwyd where he saw a 'deep and awful chasm, at the bottom of which chafed and foamed the Rheidol', as well as at Devil's Bridge, which he thought to be 'one of the most remarkable localities in the world'. You should not miss the narrow gauged railway journey up-valley from Aberystwyth to Devil's Bridge on British Rail's only remaining steam engine. To the native oak-woods clothing the slopes here and along the Ystwyth are now added the darker green blocks of conifers planted by the Forestry Commission. In the reign of Queen Elizabeth I this district yielded a third of all the lead smelted in England and Wales, and Sir Hugh Myddleton, who sank deep mines and kept them dry with water-driven engines, is reputed to have made £2,000 a month from one mine alone. Silver coins were minted for Charles I at Aberystwyth.

The River Teifi is the main artery of Cardiganshire. It is rightly famous among fishermen for its excellent salmon and sewin. The beaver is supposed to have survived later here than on any other Welsh stream. Another survivor you certainly can see today on the Teifi is the coracle, or *cwrwgl* in Welsh, the tiny oval fishing-boats of a design the Romans found in everyday use when they first came to Britain. It has a basket-work frame, formerly covered with rawhide or tarred flannel, and light enough for the fisherman to carry on his back. These ancient craft look perfectly at home on that most lovely stretch of the Teifi down-stream from Lampeter, passing Cenarth Falls and other beauty-spots. Cardigan itself commands the estuary, one of a series of sheltered inlets and bays on this rather wind-swept coast, others with sandy beaches and sailing facilities being Aberporth, New Quay, and Borth. You may hear another legend of submerged villages and farms, a story re-told by Thomas Love Peacock in *The Misfortunes of Elphin*. This fertile 'Lowland Hundred', Cantre'r Gwaelod in Welsh, is supposed to lie beneath the waves in Cardigan Bay, flooded by the sea while the keeper of its dykes slept at his post. Alas for the story, the pebble ridges or *sarnau* running seawards from the shore and thought to be dykes belonging to the old territory, are known to be natural, not man-made.

229

Rheidol valley, north of Devil's Bridge   *Reece Winstone*

Remains of the Norman castle at Hay-on-Wye *J. Allan Cash*

Town and Country, Past and Present

There is much of archaeological and historic interest in the two counties, but you have to search for it. Do not expect the profusion of long and round barrows, hill-forts, Roman roads and towns, fine churches or great houses that we meet in English counties like Dorset, Wiltshire, or Kent. The remoter Welsh uplands were never so thickly populated, the land was more sparing in its yield of crops and stock, the tapestry of its history is patterned with unrest, revolt, and battle. Even so, among the oldest sites that deserve special mention are the New Stone Age dolmens or *cromlechau* – long burial chambers built of huge stones, four to five thousand years ago – grouped together on the north-western flanks of the Breconshire Black Mountains. Cardiganshire has a thick sprinkling of hill-forts, whose earth and stone ramparts and ditches were devised by Iron Age settlers sailing along the Welsh coast from the West Country. Pen Dinas, overlooking Aberystwyth, is a classic example of these hill-forts. Descendants of the fort-builders were a thorn in the flesh of the Romans, who were forced to a strict military control of Wales. To accomplish this, the legions pushed roads along the Usk Valley and through into Cardiganshire. They built one of their largest fortresses at Y Gaer, two miles upstream from Brecon, and another at Llanio.

But the strategic role of the river valleys as natural thoroughfares for invading forces was displayed most vividly in the Anglo-Norman conquest. By 1094 much of Breconshire had fallen into the hands of Bernard Newmarch, who then built himself a castle stronghold on a secure site at Brecon. A long line of castles, symbols of the new power and set out like rooks on a chess-board, sprang up in the Usk lowlands—at Crickhowell, Tretower, Blaen Llynfi, Devynock, with off-shoots at Dinas, Bronllys, and Hay-on-Wye. Those interested in military architecture will want to see and perhaps photograph the unique cluster of round keeps, free-standing towers of early medieval origin, to be found within a radius of thirty miles of Brecon. There are a score of them, the best preserved in Breconshire being at Bronllys, Tretower, and Crickhowell.

Should you find yourself near Builth Wells, you can visit the scene of one of the closing acts in the conquest of Wales. There Llywelyn ap Gruffydd, the last native Prince of Wales, was killed by a spear-thrust in battle with the English on a winter's day in 1282. A monument marks the place, Cefn-y-Bedd in Llanganten. For an altogether happier kind of memorial, and proof that national vitality does not depend solely on political events, go to the ruins of Strata Florida, a Cistercian abbey founded alongside the infant River Teifi in the 12th century. It is the burial-place of Dafydd ap Gwilym (c. 1300–66), the poet whose pure style and fresh lyrical themes struck a new note in Welsh literature. A stone inscribed in Welsh and Latin was placed there in 1951.

Few people in our two counties are far removed from farming and the land. Agriculture is the main industry, ranging from the hill sheep-farmer to the dairyman with his herd of Friesians in the vales, where the milk can be collected by lorry. Whitewashed farmhouses, thick-walled and low-built, shelter in folds in the hillsides. They become fewer each year, for the two counties, like so much of Mid-Wales, have suffered a serious loss of population as families move away to work and live elsewhere. This erosion has gone on for a century, and the 1961 census showed that some rural districts have lost ten per cent of their people since 1951.

Towns are small in this part of Wales. Aberystwyth seems almost a metropolis with a population of just over 10,000, as befits the home of the senior College of the University of Wales (1872), the National Library of Wales, and the County Offices. The resorts between 'Aber' and Cardigan (nominally the county town) were busy ports for coastal and even ocean-going ships in the past century, though their population now rarely tops a thousand or two: they are all the

The Brecon Beacons   *J. Allan Cash*

more restful and refreshing for that. Brecon has always been a town of some consequence. Its prosperity was reflected in events like the formation of a county Agricultural Society in 1755, the first of its kind in Wales. Its social attractions included a theatre: here Roger Kemble brought his travelling company, and at the Shoulder of Mutton in High Street his daughter Sarah was born in 1755. She became the tragic actress Mrs Siddons, queen of the stage at Drury Lane and Covent Garden from 1782 until 1812. Her birthplace is now known as the Siddons Vaults; one of her three actor brothers, Charles, was also born there, in 1775. Brecon became a cathedral city in 1923, when St John's Church, which originated with the Benedictine priory founded soon after 1094, began to serve the new diocese of Swansea and Brecon.

There are counties in Wales with grander mountains, more celebrated coast-lines, and bigger towns than those in Breconshire and Cardiganshire. But if you enjoy unspoiled countryside and pure air, if you camp or sail, walk or fish, then Brycheiniog and Ceredigion – to revert to their Welsh names – will not disappoint you.

Some houses and gardens open to the public

Abercynrig Llanfrynach *Map* DA 22. *Elizabethan manor-house with enclosed rose garden.* W. R. Lloyd, Esq. *Open* by appointment only.

Nanteos 3m SE of Aberystwyth *Map* CF 28, 1m S of A4120. *Georgian mansion with contemporary furniture and pictures.* Mr & Mrs G. R. Bliss.

Tretower Court *Map* DB 22. *One of the earliest and finest fortified medieval manor-houses in Wales. Former home of the great 17th-cent. poet Henry Vaughan, who spent much of his life in the neighbourhood. The grounds adjoin the tower-keep of Tretower Castle.* Ministry of Public Building and Works.

Books for further reading

The 'feel' of Wales

GEORGE BORROW *Wild Wales* 1862
GIRALDUS CAMBRENSIS *Itinerary Through Wales* 1955
B. M. JONES *Tales of Magic and Romance* 1964
D. M. and E. M. LLOYD *A Book of Wales* 1953
T. M. OWEN *Welsh Folk Customs* 1959
HENRY VAUGHAN *The Works of*, ed. by L. C. Martin 2nd edn 1957
D. J. WILLIAMS *The Old Farmhouse* 1961

Scenery, geology, natural history

"Brycheiniog", annual journal published by The Brecknock Society

G. M. HOWE and P. THOMAS *Welsh Landforms and Scenery* 1963
W. N. PHILLIPS *The Birds of Breconshire* 1948
J. H. SALTER *The Flowering Plants and Ferns of Cardiganshire* 1935. Supplement by A. E. Wade 1954

Topography – general

H. L. V. FLETCHER *The Queen's Wales*, Vol. 2: *South Wales* 1956
MAXWELL FRASER *West of Offa's Dyke: South Wales* 1958
DAVID VEREY *Shell Guide to Mid-Wales* 1960
WARD LOCK'S GUIDES *South Wales* 11th edn

Gazetteer

CARDIGANSHIRE AND BRECONSHIRE

Brecon: the Priory Church   Reece Winstone

Aberaeron *Card.* (CE 26). Old fishing port on the rocky Cardigan coast, with a small harbour and shingly beach at the mouth of the Aeron River.

Aberystwyth *Card.* (CF 28) EC Wed (11,227). Seaside resort and university town at the mouth of the conjoined Rheidol and Ystwyth rivers and within reach of beautiful river scenery. The University College of Wales (founded 1872) at present occupies a former hotel on the front near the pier. On the hills behind the town are the modern buildings of the National Library of Wales, various University departments, and Pen Dinas, the site of an important prehistoric hill-fort. Aberystwyth has a small harbour, a shingle and sandy beach, and the remains of a 13th-cent. castle.

Borth *Card.* (CG 28). Some 4 m. of sand extending S from the estuary of the River Dovey. Very popular holiday resort. At low tide remains of a submerged forest are exposed.

Brecon (DA 22) EC Wed (5,800). County town of Breconshire, finely situated in the valley of the Usk where it is joined by the Honddu and the Tarell. The centre of a busy agricultural area. Many excellent Georgian houses. The 13th–14th-cent. red sandstone Priory Church, once administered by the Benedictine monks of Battle Abbey in Sussex, is now the Cathedral

of the diocese of Swansea and Brecon. Remains of a 12th–13th-cent. castle and of old town walls. Good historical and archaeological museum and a military museum in the barracks of the South Wales Borderers. Sarah Siddons (1755–1831) was born in Brecon. Two m. W is the site of a Roman fort, Y Gaer (AM), founded *c.* A.D. 75 and then abandoned in A.D. 140.

Brecon Beacons (DA 22). The highest ground in South Wales, separated from the Black Mountains by the valley of the Usk; on the SE is the deep Glyn Collwyn, and Glyn Tarell is on the W. From the SE the ground gradually rises to the precipitous escarpment on the northern side; here are the three prominent points, the Beacons: Pen-y-Fan (2,906 ft.), Corn-Du and Cribyn, with tremendous views extending to the Malverns and across the Bristol Channel to Exmoor in Somerset.

Bronllys *Brec.* (DB 23). Norman church with a detached tower, and ruins of a 13th-cent. castle.

Brynmawr *Brec.* (DB 21) EC Wed (6,470). On the inhospitable watershed separating pastoral Brecon from

233

The River Usk at Crickhowell

the coal-mining valleys and towns of South Wales. Like them, Brynmawr is now engaged in various other industries.

Builth Wells *Brec.* (DA 25). Where the Wye is joined by the Irfon. Good fishing, and a centre of otter hunting (especially in July). The beauty of the Wye Valley is animated by a succession of rapids just above the town.

Cardigan (CB 24) EC Wed (3,780). Small market town at the mouth of the River Teifi which formerly provided a harbour for larger craft than those now using it. Further N at the mouth of the estuary, enjoying sandy beaches, is the modern resort of Gwbert-on-Sea.

Cenarth Falls (CC 24). Famous beauty spot on the River Teifi, with splendid waterfalls and a salmon leap.

Local fishermen still fish for salmon from coracles. An old bridge crosses the river into Cenarth on the Carmarthenshire bank.

Craig-y-Nos *Brec.* (CJ 21). The castle belonged to Madame Patti, the famous singer, who spent enormous sums in developing and beautifying the estate. It is now a hospital for the Swansea area.

Crickhowell *Brec.* (DC 21). Village in the Usk Valley with remains of a castle built in the 13th cent. on the site of an earlier building. Several Tudor and Georgian houses, and a fine 13th-cent. bridge over the river.

Cwm Einion *Card.* The beautiful 'Artists' Valley', with waterfalls amongst the hills, on the S side of the Dovey Estuary, about 5 m. E of Aberdovey (CG 29). The name of

Devil's Bridge: the three bri

Furnace village is a reminder of the days when there were lead-smelting furnaces in the vicinity. Near by is Bedd Taliesin, the grave of Taliesin, 'The Father of the Bards', said to have been a contemporary of King Arthur.

Devil's Bridge *Card.* (CH 27). One of the finest beauty spots in the whole of Britain. Here the River Mynach enters a deep, wooded gorge, tumbling down over a series of waterfalls. There are three bridges, almost on top of each other, the lowest and oldest of them dating from the 12th cent. (it was built by the monks of **Strata Florida**).

Hay-on-Wye *Brec.* (DC 24). A busy little place on the Wye amid pleasant hill country. Through the town runs the little stream which at this point separates England and Wales; most of Hay is in Wales. The market has been held since 1233. Remains of a Norman castle have been built into a private house. Dominating the skyline to the S is the border summit of Hay Bluff (2,219 ft.), northern sentinel of the Black Mountains.

Lampeter *Card.* (CF 24). Small market town where A482 crosses the Teifi Valley. Long known for its horse fairs (in March) attended by buyers and sellers from all over Britain. St David's College, with its notable neo-Gothic building, is residential and has the unique distinction of being affiliated to both Oxford and Cambridge universities. Salmon and trout fishing in the River Teifi.

The River Ystwyth, south of Devil's Bridge   Reece Winstone

In the Black Mountains, south of Hay-on-Wye   *J. Allan Cash*

Llandysul *Card.* (CE 24) EC Wed (2,450). Small wool town near the junction of the Tweli and the Teifi. Incorporated in the sturdy Norman tower of the church is a 6th-cent. inscribed stone. A good centre for anglers.

Llanelieu *Brec.*, 1½ m. E of Talgarth (DB 23). High up on the slopes of the Black Mountains, a small remote church with a splendid double rood screen still with its original tympanum, original S door and ironwork. Note the pair of 7th–9th-cent. inscribed stones.

Llanfillo *Brec.*, 2 m. W of Talgarth (DB 23). Pleasant village with a church retaining a well-restored 16th-cent. rood screen, a pre-Norman font and other interesting features.

Llangammarch Wells *Brec.* (CK 24). One of the group of three spas of mid-Wales. Now just a village, beautifully situated on the Irfon (fishing).

Llangorse Lake *Brec.* (DB 22). The discovery in this century of an ancient canoe and other remains showed that men fished in this lake (the largest natural lake in South Wales) in prehistoric times.

Llangranrog *Card.* (CD 25). Coastal village in a deep narrow ravine between high cliffs. The N cliff commands fine views up and down the coast.

Llanrhystud *Card.* (CF 26). A stream runs down the street to a sandy beach. Prawn fishing can be rewarding. Five miles inland is Llangwyryfon, with a little old church dedicated to St Ursula and the 11,000 Virgins.

237

Llanwrtyd Wells *Brec.* (CJ 24). On the strength of its chalybeate and sulphur springs, Llanwrtyd Wells set itself up as a spa. But the vogue for such institutions passed, and the village is now a pleasant holiday resort, with fishing in the Irfon and the brooding heights of Mynydd Eppynt to the SE. The Tregaron road runs N up the picturesque Abergwesyn valley.

Llyfnant Valley *Card.* The Llyfnant, which flows into the head of the Dovey Estuary (CH 29), forms part of the boundary between Cardiganshire and Montgomeryshire. There is no road up the valley, but the walk is really worth while. From the upper glen there is a fine view of the waterfall known as Pistyll Llyn (300 ft.), best seen after heavy rains have swollen the river.

Llyswen *Brec.* (DB 23). In the churchyard is the raised tomb of John Macnamara who won the mansion of Llangoed in a bet, to hold as long as he was above ground. The house is splendidly situated beside the Wye. It originated in the 17th cent. but has been virtually rebuilt by Clough Williams-Ellis.

New Quay *Card.* (CD 25). Small seaside resort on steep slopes overlooking Cardigan Bay. Sands, a stone pier and many boats. Magnificent views from the headland on N side of bay.

Partrishow *Brec.* (DC 22). Famed for its secluded church with splendid rood loft and carved screen. Note the 11th-cent. font and its inscription.

Plynlimon Fawr *Card.* (CH 28). The Welsh form of the name is Pumlumon Fawr, which means 'five peaks', but the mountain is in fact a gently rounded moorland devoid of any semblance of peaks, the highest point being 2,468 ft. above sea-level. The most popular walk to the top begins at Eisteddfa Gurig (1,350 ft.), at the point where the A44 crosses the border into Montgomeryshire. The mountain is an important watershed, for it is the source of the Severn, the Wye, the Rheidol and several other rivers.

Ponterwyd *Card.* (CH 28). In ruggedly mountainous scenery, where the A44 crosses the Rheidol on its way down from Plynlimon. There is a waterfall and a striking gorge. Here George Borrow wrote part of *Wild Wales*.

New Quay, Cardigan Bay *J. Allan Cash*

J. Allan Cash **The Rheidol Gorge, near Pont-erw**

Strata Florida: the west doorway

Reece Winstone

Strata Florida Abbey *Card.* (CH 26). Among the hills near the source of the Teifi; the few remains of a once-flourishing Cistercian foundation which in the 12th–13th cent. was the cultural centre of Wales (AM). The ornamental doorway at the W end is notably impressive. The great medieval Welsh poet Dafydd ap Gwilym lies buried somewhere within the walls.

Tregaron *Card.* (CG 25). In summer this little market town among the hills is busy with sheep and cattle fairs and sheep-dog trials. Fishing in the River Teifi. N of the town is the largest peat bog in Wales; in summer the moss is alight with cotton flower. Pony-trekking enquiries: Tel. Tregaron 364.

Tretower *Brec.* (DB 22). Prettily placed village with well-restored remains of a splendid 14th-cent. fortified manor-house, Tretower Court (AM & NT). Adjoining is the keep of the Norman castle with its central round tower (AM).

The Malvern Hills: the view north towards Colwall

HEREFORDSHIRE AND RADNORSHIRE

AN INTRODUCTION BY HARRY SOAN

If you like hills and high moorland, go to Radnorshire; or broad plains, set between hills, then cross the border into Herefordshire. If some time you prefer one and some time the other, or if you can't make up your mind, stay on the border and have at your disposal the best of both worlds.

Herefordshire

Most of the soil of Herefordshire is rich red earth derived from Old Red Sandstone. The more resistant form of this rock is responsible for its hills and for the Black Mountains on its south-western border. Here and there, chiefly by the Malvern Hills on the eastern border, are sandstones and shales of Cambrian and Silurian rocks.

The Herefordshire rivers are Wye, Lugg, Teme, Frome, Arrow, Monnow and Dore – lovely names all of them. The Wye offers salmon; all have trout and some

241

grayling. The principal towns are Hereford, the cathedral city; Ross, from which to explore the beauties of the Wye Valley; Leominster, Ledbury and Bromyard, with their many superb black-and-white timbered houses and inns, and Kington, set amid hills in the valley of the Arrow. Each of them a place to stay in and enjoy slowly, like good wine.

The county's history is a long one. At Dorstone, a fine long barrow, misleadingly called 'Arthur's Stone', takes us back to the New Stone Age. Near Ross-on-Wye, 'King Arthur's Cave' tells of even earlier habitation. The Iron Age comes alive for us in the camp on the Herefordshire Beacon, at the southern end of the Malvern Hills. The Romans have left evidence of a small town at Kenchester. The scanty ruins of Clifford Castle, reputedly the birthplace of 'Fair Rosamund' in about 1140, remind us of the Normans, and the Middle Ages speak in the impressive pile of Goodrich Castle, once the strongest on the Welsh border. Saxons, Angles, Normans, English, Welsh, York and Lancaster, Cavalier and Roundhead all fought their battles in this troubled county, so peaceful today.

Hereford itself dates back to the 7th century, and to Offa, King of Mercia, who had his palace near by at Sutton Walls. Wycliffe's teaching produced Lollards, and a Lollard martyr, Sir John Oldcastle, in Herefordshire. Famous people have been bred here: John Kyrle, the kindly 'Man of Ross', David Garrick, John Masefield, Gilbert Harding – and even, legend says, Nell Gwynn and Dick Whittington.

But all these bare facts, filled in with detail and mulled with imagination, can produce no picture or experience comparable with Herefordshire as it is today. The county's farmers are as hard-headed as farmers anywhere. They don't farm to beautify the countryside; yet that is what they achieve. To see this red earth ploughed in autumn and spring, with jackdaws, rooks, seagulls and piedwagtails following the plough is a sight that, fortunately, leaves most people wordless. The native breed of white-faced Hereford cattle, whose colour is predominantly that of the soil which nourishes them, seen in early morning on the silver dew-sheen of a green pasture or standing in the water of a quiet stretch of the Wye with swallows and martins flighting around them like black lightning, is a microcosm of the beauty of all the earth. Of these cattle, famous wherever beef is grown, you can but adapt the lines of the psalm and say 'Their line is gone out through all the earth and their blood to the end of the world'.

In the fields round Ledbury there are wild daffodils in spring; daffodils so small and lovely as to make the cultivated kinds seem gross and vulgar by comparison and quite properly hidden away in gardens. Round Ledbury, too, are the hop-yards behind tall, wind-breaking hedges. In spring a vast mileage of twine to support the vines is set up by men who look as though they are playing a complicated string game.

Despite the fact that the county is so well farmed, it is yet a land of trees: lone trees, thin coppices, and denser masses like Capler Wood hanging above the Wye near Fownhope. In autumn, when the corn stubbles are weathering and sunlight is a pale gold haze and Michaelmas daisies and dahlias are everywhere in cottage gardens, and leaves are spinning and drifting from the trees – in autumn in Herefordshire there is beauty almost beyond enduring. Oak leaves turning brown as slowly and surely as loaves in an oven, elm leaves floating on many an unnamed brook like fragments of beaten gold and the deep rich red of

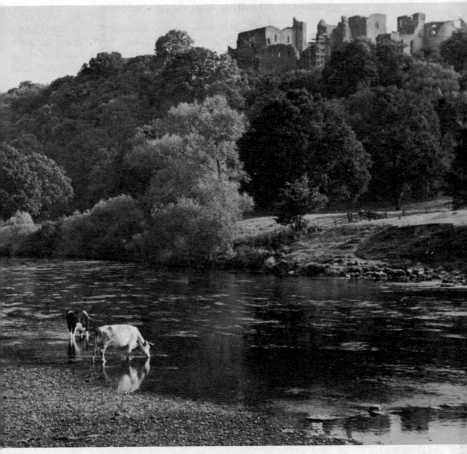

The River Wye, with Goodrich Castle behind

Allan Cash

wild cherry and orchard pear leaves lying on the yellowing grass like spilled wine – these are not sights so much as experiences no man should die without savouring.

Herefordshire villages have to be seen to be believed; each a place marking a spot where, footsore from wandering the county's narrow, sinuous lanes, time has stopped to rest and think, and having eased its mind of a few tentative ideas in black-and-white half-timber, in reddish-grey stone and dim red brick, has passed on, never to return to fashion and shape them. Only in this way can a village like Weobley be accounted for.

The villages and lone farmhouses have nearly all one thing in common, something that writes the word 'home' wherever in the county men work and eat and sleep and when it is all over go at last to rest in the parish churchyard. This is the apple orchard. So many farms have one, covering a handy paddock

243

by the house; the bulk of them cider fruit, many of unknown age, lovely as a woman past her prime whose character has at last got to work on her hitherto merely pretty face; trees that time and neglect and the itching flanks of cattle have twisted and bent and that heavy bearing and gales have broken. Cider today is one of Hereford's principal industries.

Herefordshire in middle spring, with every orchard a haze of bluish-pink, is unbelievably lovely – lovely in sunshine, or against a stormy evening sky. When the apples have been shaken down and the leaves have blown away, the trees

Radnorshire farmland
J. Allan Cash

show their bushy tangled beards of mistletoe. Maybe many's the time you've kissed your wife or girl-friend under a sprig of Herefordshire mistletoe, for tons of it leave the county each December. If ever you want to trace the kiss back to the source of the sprig you had it under, Herefordshire will give you an experience richer than the longest kiss.

Radnorshire

Radnorshire is a Welsh border county that marches with Shropshire and Herefordshire. With a population averaging only thirty-seven people to the square mile you can be almost as alone there as the man in the moon.

The grits, shales and sandstones of rock formation give it its shape. The people who tend its thousands of sheep give it its character. And curlews which come in thousands to its high damp moorlands give it its signature-tune. Their cry, a brief bubbling joy and a long piping lament, describes the realities of Radnorshire life. From hundreds of remote family farms, once bursting at the boundaries with children, the people have now gone. Rural depopulation has swept the county like a plague. Ruins of former farmhouses and buildings moulder in tangles of nettles, bramble and elderbushes. Only a flake or two of whitewash and a few soot-blackened stones indicate that they were once human habitations.

But do not get the idea that this is a county to mourn over, a land that wears its sorrowing heart on its coat-sleeve. What Radnorshire was once like is still embedded in what remains. Though there are some black-and-white timbered buildings, the commonest material is stone – and you'll never look on a style more free of pretence than a white or colour-washed farmhouse with its buildings on a green Radnor hillside. The limewash is a continuing compromise with the economics of bygone hard times. When lime for mortar had to be trundled vast and rough distances, it was used sparingly. The stones of the buildings are bedded chiefly in plain earth dug from the hillside and costing little more than sweat. To prevent rain washing this earth from the slightly pointed joints, limewash is applied annually – usually just before shearing-time, when the neighbours gather to help.

The people are among the friendliest I know. The more people are herded together, the less time they have for each other; the more thinly they are spread, the more they know and appreciate each other. Maybe it is this that has bred a curious classlessness in Radnorshire society. Except in the heyday of the Lords Marchers and the period when Abbeycwmhir – the county's only abbey – flourished, there have been few big and rich estates. When one of Cromwell's officers went to collect fines from Royalist supporters, he composed a verse of descriptive, despairing doggerel:

> Radnorshire, poor Radnorshire,
> Never a park and never a deer,
> Never a squire of five hundred a year
> But Richard Fowler of Abbeycwmhir.

And, so far as I know, there is still no place of obvious opulence in the county; nor, for that matter, of eye-catching poverty. Radnor folk have the kind of equality and independence which is as patent and unassumed as the accent of their speech.

Among the county's churches are some of very ancient foundation and of a

Craig Goch Dam, Elan Valley Reservoirs *Aerofilms*

purely utilitarian simplicity of design. I think of remote Rhulen with its 13th-century church, plain to the point of being primitive, with only two windows and set within a circular churchyard. I cannot imagine setting and structure more perfectly matched than they are here. The old chapel at Maesyronen is a good example of the early dissenters' conventicle. In both cases, four walls and a roof and the intimacy of smallness catch the spirit of a faith which is primarily concerned with the individual and the family.

Radnorshire has only four towns, none of them industrial. Llandrindod Wells, no more than a village a hundred years ago, had by 1886 become a fashionable watering-place through its medicinal springs of saline, sulphur and chalybeate. Today it is the administrative centre for the county, although the little border town of Presteigne, where curfew is still rung, is the county town, and the assizes are still held there. Knighton and Rhayader are busy market towns, but Rhayader is perhaps best known as the gateway to the Elan Valley, that picturesque series of artificial lakes constructed at the beginning of this century to supply the City of Birmingham with water. In recent years Rhayader has become a busy pony-trekking centre.

The county's villages often go unrecognized by English visitors accustomed to the more developed settlement of the typical English village. In Radnorshire, as in much of Wales, the visible village consists of a church, a school and a handful of houses near by: the rest of it is made up of the scattered farms within the parish boundary. How populous the village is you will probably never know unless you attend some winter meeting in the school or hall.

From what the Romans have left in Radnorshire, it seems they had little influence on its inhabitants. Their chief station was at Castell Collen, near Llandrindod Wells. Between the Roman and Norman periods, Offa's Dyke was made from Dee to Severn, and some twelve miles of it are in the county. Following this period of comparative peace came the cruel, bloody and prolonged efforts of the Norman Lords Marchers to subdue the Welsh. That struggle ended in 1282 when Llywelyn ap Gruffydd, the last prince of Wales, got separated from his army by treachery and, after taking refuge in his castle at Aberedw, was killed near Builth in a chance encounter with an English knight. Later Radnorshire was to suffer badly in the 1402 campaign of Owain Glyndŵr, when a large part of the present county was devastated, towns and villages burnt, the Abbey of Cwmhir and several churches severely damaged, and the castle at New Radnor taken and left in ruins. Recovery was slow, and it was not until the age of the Tudors and the Act of Union of 1536, when the present county came into being, that Radnorshire began to see better times.

Radnorshire is a land of brooks that feed rivers well-known to fishermen – the Wye, the Teme and the Arrow, which go to form the county boundary. Then there are the Lugg and the Eithon, which flow right through the county. To follow the Eithon from its source in the Kerry hills down to its confluence with the Wye at Newbridge is to sample the county at its best. The lower reaches of the Eithon, together with the Wye, offer salmon. Both of these and all the others offer trout as well.

I know of no time of the year when Radnorshire is not worth visiting. In the spring it is a land of lambs: except in its four towns, you cannot be out of earshot of their bleating. One of my favourite areas is Radnor Forest, where in almost any valley you can feel yourself in some nameless labyrinth of time. To know how deep and yet how living quietness can be, join the Edw Valley at Hundred House, between Builth and New Radnor, follow it through Cregrina, Rhulen and Llanbadarn-y-garreg to Aberedw, where the river joins the Wye. If, through this narrow way, crossing and re-crossing this lovely river you have not lost the world for a while and found ease of mind, you surely never will.

It is impossible to have known what I can only call the bouquet of peace, more fragrant than any wine, unless you have sat by a Radnorshire brook listening to the water and inhaling the smell of new-mown hay, composed of every grass and herb and coloured with flowers – the harebell, knapweed, clover, milkwort, eye-bright, yellow-rattle, hawkweed and a fox-glove or two and the lovely devil's-bit scabious. In the September harvest-time the little pocket-handkerchief fields of oats stand just below the purple heather line, surrounded by bracken dying in every shade of colour ever seen in fire. If heaven is all that is claimed for it, and if you cherish even the faintest hope of getting there, you should visit Radnorshire to get acclimatized.

Some houses and gardens open to the public

Berrington Hall 3m N of Leominster *Map DE 25. Late 18th-cent. house built by Henry Holland, jun. His decorated ceilings, hall, library, drawing-room and staircase are virtually unaltered. Park of 445 acres.* NT.

Croft Castle *Map DE 26. Norman border castle. See p. 249.* NT.

Dinmore Manor Hope-under-Dinmore *Map DF 25.* C. Ian Murray, Esq. *The house is not open to the public, but visitors may see the 14th-cent. chapel, the music room, the cloisters and the garden.*

Eastnor Castle *Map DH 23. Built c. 1815. Interior by Pugin. Tapestry, armour, pictures. Specimen trees and lovely scenery.* The Hon. Mrs Hervey-Bathurst.

Eye Manor 4m N of Leominster *Map DE 25. Fine Carolean manor-house. Plasterwork ceilings, exhibitions of costume, needlework pictures, private press books, corn dollies, etc.* Christopher Sandford, Esq.

Hellens Much Marcle *Map DG 23. Ancient manor-house of great historic interest, lived in without a break for 600 years.* The Pennington-Mellor-Munthe family.

Hergest Croft Garden 1m W of Kington *Map DC 25. Rhododendrons, azaleas and other flowering trees and shrubs.* Mr & Mrs R. A. Banks. *House not open.*

Kentchurch Court *Map DE 22. Fortified manor-house with 14th-cent. gateway. Carvings by Grinling Gibbons.* Lt-Cdr J. Lucas Scudamore, MBE.

Lower Brockhampton Hall 2½m E of Bromyard *Map DG 25. Small late 14th-cent. moated manor-house in half-timber, with ruins of 12th-cent. chapel.* NT.

Pembridge Castle Welsh Newton *Map DE 21. Moated Norman castle. See p. 256.* R. A. Cooke, Esq.

Books for further reading

Literature

REV. R. F. KILVERT (vicar of Bredwardine 1877–9) *Diaries* ed. by William Plomer 1950
ELIZABETH BARRETT BROWNING, JOHN MASEFIELD, THOMAS TRAHERNE have all made local references in their poems.
H. VAUGHAN *The Battle to the Weak*
F. B. YOUNG *The House under the Water*

Topography – general

H. L. V. FLETCHER *The Queen's Wales: South Wales* 1956; *Herefordshire* (County Books series) 1948; *Portrait of the Wye Valley* 1968
MAXWELL FRASER *West of Offa's Dyke: South Wales* 1958
R. J. W. HAMMOND (ed.) *Hereford and the Wye Valley* 1965
W. H. HOWSE *Radnorshire* 1949; *Historic Hereford*
H. J. MASSINGHAM *The Southern Marches* 1952
ARTHUR MEE (ed.) *Herefordshire* (The King's England series) 1938

DAVID VEREY *The Shell Guide to Herefordshire* 1955; *The Shell Guide to Mid-Wales* 1960
WOOLHOPE CLUB *Transactions* (the archaeology, natural history, etc., of Herefordshire) 1851 to present day

Local interest

H. R. BURROWS *Pictorial History of Hereford Cathedral*
W. H. HOWSE *Old-time Llandrindod* 1952; *Welsh Border Town* (Presteigne) 1950
G. MARSHALL *The Cathedral Church of Hereford* 1949
N. PEVSNER *Herefordshire* 1963
LORD RENNELL OF RODD *Valley on the March* 1958
SID WRIGHT *Up the Claerwen* 1948

Natural history and sport

H. A. GILBERT *The Tale of a Wye Fisherman* 2nd edn 1953; (with W. C. WALKER) *Herefordshire Birds* 2nd edn 1954
INGRAM and SALMON *A Hand List to the Birds of Radnorshire* 1956

Gazetteer

HEREFORDSHIRE AND RADNORSHIRE

Staick House, Eardisland Reece Winstone

Abbeycwmhir *Rad.* (DA 27). 'The abbey of the long valley' was founded in 1143, but the buildings started in the 13th cent. were never finished; the abbey was sacked by Glyndwr in 1402, and little more than the bases of the walls remain.

Abbey Dore★ *Her.* (DD 23). Amid quiet orchards at the S end of the Golden Valley of the River Dore is the loveliest parish church in Herefordshire, once part of a Cistercian abbey, founded in 1147, and restored by Viscount Scudamore in the early 17th cent.

Bromyard *Her.* (DG 25). Small market town in the valley of the River Frome. Many good timber houses, especially the Falcon inn, and good wood carving in the Norman church. Two m. E is Lower Brockhampton Hall (NT).

Colwall *Her.* (DH 24) EC Thurs (2,070). On the western slopes of the Malvern hills. Elizabeth Barrett Browning spent her girlhood at Hope End (but the house no longer exists). On the hills to the SE is an Iron Age camp on **Hereford Beacon** (*see below*).

Croft Castle★ *Her.* (DE 26), 5 m. NW of Leominster. Except for the years 1750–1923, this ancient Welsh border castle, with its four round corner towers in pink stone, has been inhabited by the Croft family since the Norman Conquest. It is now owned by the NT.

Dorstone *Her.* (DD 24). A village at the N end of the Golden Valley. The church was founded by Richard de Brito, one of the knights who murdered Becket. A chalice found in his tomb when it was opened during restoration is now displayed in the church. Note the very good iron candelabra. A near-by prehistoric long barrow known as 'Arthur's Stone' (AM) is yet another of the traditional graves of King Arthur.

Eardisland *Her.*, 5 m. W of Leominster (DE 25). Pretty village with many lovely timbered buildings on the grassy banks of the River Arrow. Note especially the 14th-cent. Staick House and 17th-cent. dovecote. Near the bridge is the old whipping-post.

Eardisley *Her.* (DD 24). The partly Norman church is particularly interesting for its remarkably beautiful 12th-cent. font.

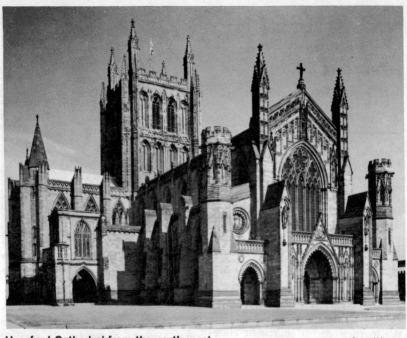

Hereford Cathedral from the north-west

Goodrich* *Her.* (D F 21). Picturesque village beside the Wye, with splendid remains of a 12th–14th-cent. castle, long the home of the Talbots, Earls of Shrewsbury, but left a ruin after its capture by the Parliamentarians in the Civil War (A M). In the church is panelling from the sham 'Gothic castle', Goodrich Court, pulled down in 1950.

Hereford* (D F 23) E C Thurs (46,120). Busy centre of a flourishing agricultural area: hop-yards, fruit orchards, cider factories, and markets on Mon, Wed, Fri. The Cathedral** was begun in 1107, but the process of building and alteration has continued through the centuries. Among its treasures are the *Mappa Mundi* (13th cent.), one of the oldest maps in the world; and one of the world's finest collections of valuable chained books

(another good collection is in All Saints' Church). In centre of city note picturesque timbered 17th-cent. Old House, now a museum. Nell Gwynn is supposed to have been born in Hereford; David Garrick is known to have been. Sarah Siddons and the Kemble family lived here for a time. Nelson was a freeman of the city and is commemorated by a column. The Three Choirs music festival is held at Hereford every third year. In Hereford Museum are most of the finds excavated from the Roman town at **Kenchester** (*see below*).

Hereford Beacon (D H 23). Here, on the county border, the Malvern Hills reach 1,114 ft. above sea-level, and there is an extensive ancient British Camp covering 44 acres. The citadel, about 50 yards in circumference, consists of a thick stone wall

Hereford Cathedral: the n

covered with earth and defended by a deep ditch.

Kenchester *Her*. (DE 24). The site of the important Roman *Castra Magna*, mosaics and other relics from which are in Hereford Museum. The font in Kenchester church was made by Normans from a Roman pillar.

Kilpeck* *Her*. (DE 23). Here is one of the finest small Norman churches in the whole of Britain. Note especially the superb intricately carved S doorway, the huge Norman font under the gallery, the carvings in the chancel reminiscent of Celtic craftsmanship, and the curious Norman stoup with its upper lip clasped by two hands.

Kington *Her*. (DC 25). Small market town close to the Welsh border, noted for its annual September show and autumn sheep sales. Interesting church with good Early English work. In the neighbourhood is a well-preserved section of **Offa's Dyke** (*see below*).

Knighton *Rad*. (DC 27). Pleasant little town on the Teme by the NE boundary of Radnorshire, with wooded hills all around. There is a weekly market; thousands of ewes and lambs are sold at the autumn fairs. On both sides of the town are stretches of **Offa's Dyke** (*see below*).

Ledbury* *Her*. (DH 23) EC Thurs (3,700). Old town on the western approach to the Malvern hills. The 17th-cent. market house is still supported by its original oak posts. Beside it a narrow lane bordered with timbered buildings leads to the large church with its detached tower and tall spire. Ledbury is the birthplace of John Masefield; Elizabeth Barrett Browning's father is buried in the church.

Eastnor Castle (1½ m. E), built in

c. 1815, contains good collections of pictures, armour and tapestries. The splendid park has many specimen trees, including one of the twelve mistletoe oaks in England.

Leominster* *Her*. (DE 25) EC Thurs (6,930). An old wool town among rivers, hop-yards and orchards. It has many lovely timbered buildings and a church remarkable for having three naves built respectively in the 12th, 13th and 14th cent. In the church is kept the ducking stool in which nagging women were placed before being dipped in the river. Five m. NW is **Croft Castle** (*see above*). Berrington Hall and Eye Manor are also notable.

Llandrindod Wells *Rad*. (DA 26) EC Wed (3,250). Benefit is still to be derived from the saline, magnesium, sulphur, lithia and chalybeate springs which first brought the town into notice. Nowadays it is recognized also as a conference centre and a holiday resort, besides being the seat of government of the county. Good fishing in the Eithon. Two m. N is the site of the Roman camp Castell Collen.

Madley *Her*. (DE 23). The large church has developed from a small Norman edifice into a fine example of various styles of Gothic. The Norman N transept now serves as the N porch. In the apsidal chancel is famous early stained glass. More early glass can be seen in the E window of the church at near-by Eaton Bishop.

Much Marcle *Her*. (DG 23). Peaceful village near the Gloucestershire border, with a 13th–15th cent. church rich in interesting monuments, and two fine old houses: Hellens, a manorial house begun in 1292 and

beck Church: the south doorway *Reece Winstone*

with a dovecote dated 1641 and Homme House, shown by appointment only.

New Radnor (DC 26). An ancient borough shorn of its privileges and shrunk to the size of a village. Earthworks of a Norman castle (destroyed during the Civil War) and remains of the old town wall. Here the Somergill river runs underground for a short distance. Radnor Forest rises NW towards the summit of Great Rhos, over 2,000 ft. above sea-level.

Old Radnor, 3 m. SE, has a fine church with an exceptionally fine rood screen, an organ case of Henry VIII's time, medieval tiles, and a large pre-Norman font carved from a single block of stone.

Offa's Dyke. Sections of high earthen banks stretching from the Wye to the Dee, planned by King Offa of Mercia in the 8th cent. to mark the boundary between England and Wales where it was not already marked by natural barriers of river and forest. Sections of it are still to be seen, for example, at **Kington** and **Knighton** (*see above*).

Pembridge *Her.* (DD 25). Large village with picturesque timber houses and a church noted for its detached timber belfry.

Presteigne *Rad.* (DD 26). The county town of Radnorshire, where the county assizes are still held. The church is mainly 11th–15th cent. and the half-timbered Radnorshire Arms is early 17th. The curfew is still rung nightly at 8 from the church tower.

Rhayader *Rad.* (CK 26). Set 700 ft. above sea-level in the Upper Wye Valley, and nearest jumping-off point for the Elan Valley Reservoirs* which provide Birmingham with its water. Drive 4 m. along the SW road out of Rhayader; then follow the road beside the lakes as they wind among the hills for some 8 m. Here is some of the finest lake scenery in Wales. When the lakes are full, the excess water spills magnificently over the great dams. These were completed just after the turn of the century. A recent extension involved the damming of the Claerwen Valley and the creation of a new lake 4 m. long.

Rhulen *Rad.* (DB 24). A little church with an attractive barn-like simplicity and surrounded by a circular churchyard.

Ross-on-Wye* *Her.* (DF 22) EC Wed (6,270). Understandably a centre of tourist attraction at the height of summer owing to its spectacular position on a beautiful curve of the Wye; out of season, a delightful quiet market town centred round its arcaded market hall. Splendid views from The Prospect near the churchyard. 'The Man of Ross' praised by Pope in his essay *On the Use of Riches* was John Kyrle (1637–1724), man of vision and local philanthropist.

Shobdon *Her.* (DD 26). In the mid-18th cent. the second Lord Bateman pulled down the old Norman church, built the present Rococo-Gothic church in its place, and re-erected parts of the original church as 'romantic' embellishments to the grounds of his own house, Shobdon Court, now demolished.

Symond's Yat* *Her.* (DF 21). The word 'yat' means gate or pass. In this well-known beauty spot the Wye flows through a narrow gorge and describes a tremendous loop, taking 5 m. to encompass Huntsham Hill and

254

Ross-on-Wye

J. Allan Cash

curve back to within a few hundred yards of its own earlier course. About 3 m. downstream, in the Doward hills above the river, is 'King Arthur's Cave' in which was discovered relics of inhabitants of 20,000 years ago.

Welsh Newton *Her.* (DE 21). In the churchyard is the grave of John Kemble, martyred in 1679 for saying Mass in the moated 13th-cent. Pembridge Castle, 1 m. NW.

Weobley★ *Her.* (DE 25). Attractive old village, once a borough, with an unusual number of half-timbered houses. The Red Lion dates from the 13th cent. The mainly 14th-cent. church has a splendid spire and several notable monuments. The Jacobean house called The Ley has fine timbers and a priest's hole. John Abel, whom Charles I dubbed 'The King's Carpenter' for his services when Hereford was besieged, is buried in the churchyard at Sarnesfield, 1½ m. W.

Opposite: Detail from the original painting by John Aldridge.
The scene here is a typically undulating Herefordshire landscape with its own breed of cattle, its ciderapple orchards and half-timbered farmhouses, and the Black Mountains of Wales rising on the skyline. Mistletoe is commoner in Herefordshire than in any other county of England.

The bridge across the Teify at Cenarth

G. Douglas Bolton

PEMBROKESHIRE AND CARMARTHENSHIRE

AN INTRODUCTION BY R. M. LOCKLEY

These two counties, anciently known as *Dyfed*, make up with Cardiganshire what is known as West Wales, as distinct from South Wales (which, in the public eye, is chiefly industrial Glamorgan, Monmouthshire and East Carmarthenshire), and from North Wales (counties north of Cardigan and Montgomery shires). Lying in the remote south-west corner of Wales, they have all the beauty and charm which little mountains, narrow valleys and a varied coastline beside a clear Atlantic can yield to the explorer who roves through this beautiful long-settled but thinly inhabited pastoral land. Industry does not intrude – only around Llanelli in the south-east does one see the conical tip and winding-gear of colliery, or the chimney-stack of steel and tinplate works. Elsewhere the landscape is hoary with older history – with ancient tower of Norman or Welsh church, with green-grown outline of prehistoric promontory, fort or burial mound; and everywhere are colour-washed farms and cottages, little human

Opposite: Detail from the original painting by Kenneth Rowntree.

Pembrokeshire lies before us as a county of moorland, cliffs, sea valleys, and hills where neolithic man quarried stone for building. White or colour-washed cottages, as well as the June foxglove, enliven a sometimes melancholy landscape haunted by the curlew.

settlements surrounded with shelter trees and with fields lovingly won from the mountain slopes and the valley bogs. All are Welsh-speaking save in the southern half of Pembrokeshire – 'Little England Beyond Wales' – where, defended by a strong line of Norman castles, the invading Norsemen, Normans and Flemings have for eight hundred years maintained an English colony – the Englisherie – on the sunny plateau of fertile, frost-free farmland.

The contrast is intriguing, as if one were visiting two countries within the one little county of Pembrokeshire. Carmarthenshire, largest of Welsh counties, is gentle and calm and smiling like a beautiful mature woman, with green valleys flowing with milk of a thousand dairy farms; even her coastline is womanly and smooth, with sand and silt. But Pembrokeshire is truly masculine, with great wild cliffs, indented tide-ripped shore, windswept islands and capes resonant with cry of sea-bird and seal, a land ruddy with sandstone rock and soil and manned by a vital race of farmers and fishermen.

The Land

The last ice-sheet covered the central massif of Wales only as far as the northern half of both counties. As it retreated north, it left exposed ice-scarred primitive rocks five hundred million years old; earth-movements had folded and thrust upwards these pre-Cambrian igneous rocks between the younger sedimentary series. This elevated northern part is complicated geologically, ranging from the primary to Cambrian and Silurian exposures, with shales and mudstones forming the northern mountain upfold. The southern coastal plain is simpler, with bands of red sandstone and carboniferous limestone, and the comparatively recent coal-measures.

The relief map shows how the cool wet northern hills yield their water and soil to irrigate and enrich the low placid southern tableland where, only a score miles away, men live kindlier lives in a drier sunnier climate. The lowland plateau is rich in the visible evidence of human history and prehistory.

In both counties the green mountains rise, round and naked, to moderate elevations – to one thousand seven hundred and sixty feet in north Pembrokeshire (Mynydd Presely) and one thousand five hundred and fifteen feet in north Carmarthenshire (Mynydd Mallaen). In the east, the westward thrust of the Brecon Beacons tops the two thousand feet mark, where Carmarthen Van (and its legendary lake), also known as the Black Mountain, towers nobly like some sleeping sentinel above the mining district of Ammanford, on the border.

The coal-measures run from south-east Carmarthenshire along the coast westwards, a thin vein of anthracite continuing under the sea near Saundersfoot and crossing Pembrokeshire to St Brides Bay. The little mines of Pembrokeshire, however, are no longer worked; even the evidence in the form of tips and levels is grown over with nature's kindly cloak, inhabited only by the birds and bats and badgers.

Character of Climate and People

Climate makes people. Part of the charm of the region lies in the contrasts between the harsh sterile mountainous north, with its heavy rainfall and tough Welsh peasant stock, and the fertile plains of the south, inhabited by an easygoing English-speaking people enjoying a mild sunlit climate. Frost is rare and snow rarer in that delectable corner where the Atlantic almost surrounds the peninsula with its thermal jacket. Here the flora has a Lusitanian flavour with

Reece Winstone   **Evening light on a farmstead, Lla**

Laugharne

some half-hardy Mediterranean species. But even in the mountains snow does not lie long: the cyclonic salt westerlies dissolve it as it settles. Rainfall in the south-west corner of Pembrokeshire is only thirty-five inches per annum, but rises rapidly to over eighty inches on moorland above one thousand feet. Spring comes as soon as in Cornwall: along the coast, spring flowers bloom earlier than anywhere on the English mainland. Yet because of this oceanic influence, making for mild winters, summer is never insufferably hot. Along the coast the average July temperature is no more than 16° F above that for January. Great gales in winter drive the salt across the whole region, inviting the visitor either to the headlands to look at the majestic waves, or to the inland *cwms* (valleys) for shelter below the hanging native oakwood. Like the genial character of the native people (who will make you a promise, even if they have no intention of carrying it out, rather than refuse, which would be discourteous), the weather in summer is fickle and inconstant, now a rainstorm, next a radiance of sunlight – nothing is stable and enduring. All is surprise and change, and, if you have a sense of humour, excusable, amusing and not without charm. It is as well to fall in with this happy-go-lucky way of following the mood of the climate, of agreeing to do things tomorrow, if today be wet – and if you feel disposed to do it.

The Welsh Portion

The Welsh-speaking people of the north part are more dour, less forthcoming and more suspicious of the visitor, having suffered English overlordship for centuries, than the smiling southerner who wrested the rich plain from them. They are better singers and scholars than the southerners, more frugal and religious, and largely chapel-goers. They work harder and longer of necessity in their tougher environment, and supply labour to the works and coal-mines of the south-east, doctors and nurses to the hospitals, ministers and teachers to the spiritual and intellectual professions, assistants to the shops, and astute business men to the great cities, especially London, where many a famous trading house will be found to number Western Welshmen among the executives and directors.

There is a great tradition of music and drama, especially in the mining area, expressed at its most fervent in the annual competitions of the Eisteddfodau. The mystic spirit of Wales ascends to its greatest pitch of enthusiasm when two or three are gathered together in choral song – and in rugby football, to which Llanelli has given a notably powerful team.

Industrial Llanelli (30,000) is the largest town; but clean Carmarthen (13,250) is the most central and finest market town, where Welsh farmers meet English dealers, and the main business of West Wales – livestock farming – is conducted. Resonant with Welsh voices and ways, it is a bustling place on Wednesdays and Thursdays, and has a fine covered general market for the housewife and visitor.

Archaeology

The surprising fact that the centre or altar stone, as well as thirty-three rhyolite and dolerite blocks which form the inner ring at Stonehenge on Salisbury Plain, came from Pembrokeshire, argues that the county was sacred to the priesthood of that period – 1600–1400 B.C. No doubt the priests followed and fostered trade; and West Wales was on the sea-route of traders and settlers from Iberia and the Mediterranean. It had lead and copper, as well as gold (at Pumsaint in Carmarthenshire, where the old workings are plain to see); and there was gold in the south-east of Ireland. This was a busy period of fine weather, when small ships studded the western sea, and the huge blocks of stone could make safe voyages in wood and skin boats along the coasts and rivers to Wiltshire.

Both counties are liberally dotted with standing stones, *cromlechau* or dolmens, stone circles, burial mounds, round and long barrows, hill and promontory forts, camps, earthworks and hut circles whose occupation dates from before and some after Stonehenge, and some down past the coming of Christianity and the Dark Age.

Earlier still the limestone caves of the south – Tenby, Caldy and Coygan – have yielded the bones of woolly rhinoceros, hippopotamus, mammoth, giant ox, elk, lion, bear, wolf, hyaena, red deer, reindeer and upper Palaeolithic man.

History

The Romans did not penetrate far into West Wales. Apart from a road to their forts at Carmarthen and Llandovery, with here and there wayside legion camps and some villas, they maintained only a brief and tenuous grip on the native Welsh. Their coins circulated in trade, and have been found in hut dwellings.

The creek at Pembroke
Reece Winstone

They had contact with, but never quite subdued, the fierce yet evangelical Irish Deisi tribe which had invaded and settled and brought the Christian faith to Dyfed. Their influence upon these Irish (Goidelic) Celts is plain in the presence to this day of about a score of 'Ogam' memorial stones bearing a double inscription, one in the Goidelic Ogam alphabet which consisted of strokes along the edge of the stone slab, and the other its translation in Latin.

The power of the Celtic Druids and pagan priests had been crushed under the combined influence of Roman government and Irish hot-gospellers. The patron saint of Wales, as well as that of Ireland, was born, it is said, in *Vallis Rosina*, the narrow glen by the sea, where the present-day cathedral shelters below the world's smallest city, the windswept village of St David's. It was more than once sacked by the Vikings who dominated the coast for centuries during the age of the native Welsh princes. The Viking influence is left in place-names on the coast: Caldy, Skokholm, Skomer, Ramsey, Milford Haven, Haverfordwest, Hubberston, Herbrandston, Haroldston, Hasguard, Studdock, Fishguard. The Welsh held the northern hills and bogs steadfastly, and under a uniform code of law devised by the strong prince Hywel Dda (Howell the Good), the tribes of Wales were combined in an uneasy peace for a while before the coming of the Normans.

'A Welshman loves his brother best when he is dead' – an old saying exemplified in the internecine strife which continued even in the need to combine against the Normans, who seized all these fair lands of the south, drove out the Welsh, and finally settled the plains with their own followers, including two contingents of Flemings rendered homeless by Flanders' floods. Around the perimeter of the fertile 'Englisherie' the Normans built a ring of castles, which today afford the visitor a vivid reminder of their power and the strategic value of these thick-walled defences so mellowed and pleasing to the present eye.

Romantic tales and books have been written about the last invasion of Britain, which took place near Fishguard in 1797, when one thousand two hundred French troops (largely released felons and freebooters) were landed from two frigates. They were ignominiously captured by half that number of the local yeomanry, aided, it is said, by the appearance of Welshwomen masquerading as soldiers in their red shawls.

Living in West Wales

Agriculture is the principal industry, chiefly milk-production in the sheltered inland vales, with sheep pastured on the bare mountain. On the coast, 'horn and corn' (beef-cattle with barley, oats and sugar-beet) is the general rule, with a few thousand acres of the profitable early potatoes where the land is dry and frost-free. The early potato winter chitting-sheds and houses may be used in summer to rear turkeys, a thriving new industry.

Milford is a base for trawlers which go out for a couple of weeks each trip, and bring home hake, ling, whiting and flat fish. Lobsters, crabs and crayfish are taken in pots set along the rocky areas of coast by inshore fishermen.

Llanelli, Ammanford and Burry Port support a varied industry based on the coal-mines, and on steel. But they are really quite small towns, with mountain and countryside pressing hard on the back door.

Milford Haven itself has the deepest water of any British anchorage, and is developing as an ocean terminal for the accommodation of ships and tankers of over fifty thousand tons, with ancillary oil-refineries.

Nature

West Wales is rich in the number of wild species uncommon elsewhere. The rocky islands off the Pembrokeshire coast, hitherto protected only by oceanic gales, are now permanent sanctuaries for thousands of nesting sea-birds: manx shearwaters, puffins, razorbills, guillemots, oyster-catchers and gulls. Grassholm, farthest west and often inaccessible, has twenty-two thousand breeding gannets. Skokholm is a bird observatory, famous for its colony of one thousand storm petrels and for migration studies. Skomer is a national nature reserve. Ramsey is the breeding place of a large colony of Atlantic seals.

On the mainland, buzzards are more numerous than in any other part of Britain. The rare red-billed chough and the peregrine survive along the wild cliffs.

As for flowers, the hedges and lanes glow spectacularly from January onwards, with snowdrops, daffodils, primroses, violets, cowslips, orchids, bluebells and columbines, to name but a few. There are rarer kinds, too, which we need not name so long as collectors of rare plants exist.

Rivers are fished for salmon, trout and 'sewin' (sea-trout), the Teify in the north and the Towy in the east being clear, well-preserved salmon rivers. On both rivers men drift downstream with nets for salmon in small primitive coracles, today made of lath and tarred canvas, which are easily transported on the back for the return walk up-river.

Food for the Gourmet

Carmarthenshire and North Pembrokeshire are famous for farm butter, which, if you can find it, in the remote hill farms, is the tastiest in the world. It's good, too, even in the butter factories which sprinkle West Wales – though ultra-hygiene takes away just a little of the richness. Spread it on 'bara-plank', thin wafer-bread made on a thick iron plate over the fire. 'Cawl', a rich soup prepared

Roch Castle

G. Douglas Bolton

of home-cured bacon with finely chopped vegetables, is also a speciality of the farms and of some inns. Salmon and sewin are delicious.

Pembrokeshire yields a rich harvest of lobsters, sea crayfish and crab, best secured alive in the little seaports, where mackerel, pollack, herring and bass can be bought from the boat in season.

Laver-weed, a parchment-like seaweed, is collected in the far west – Angle and Marloes: after washing and boiling, it is made up into laver-bread cakes with oatmeal, and fried. It is much in demand with the mining fraternity of Glamorganshire to which it is largely exported. It is delicious, with a health-giving tang of iodine.

Some houses and gardens open to the public

Carew Castle 5m NE of Pembroke on A4075 *Map* CA 20. *Fortress, 13th-cent. Plantagenet; N wing added by Sir John Perrot, late 16th cent.*

Kidwelly Castle 9m NW of Llanelli on A484 *Map* CE 20. *Fortress, 12th cent.*

Manorbier Castle 6m S W of Tenby on B4585 *Map* CA 19. *13th cent.; 16th-cent. additions.*

Pembroke Castle At Pembroke *Map* B K 20. *Fortress, 12th–13th cents.; restored by Earls of Pembroke.*

Books for further reading

The 'feel' of Pembroke and Carmarthen

MAXWELL FRASER *Introducing West Wales* 1956
LAWRENCE C. HILL *The Vale of Towy* 1947
DYLAN THOMAS *Under Milk Wood*
RICHARD VAUGHAN Novels, particularly *Moulded in Earth, Who Rideth So Wild, Son of Justin, There Was a River*

Natural history

T. W. BARKER *Handbook to the Natural History of Carmarthenshire* 1905
ROSCOE HOWELLS *The Sounds Between* 1968; *The Cliffs of Freedom* 1961
GEOFFREY C. S. INGRAM and H. MORREY SALMON *A Handlist of the Birds of Carmarthenshire* 1954
R. M. LOCKLEY *The Birds of Pembrokeshire* 1949

History, topography, architecture

An Inventory of Ancient Monuments—County of Pembroke 1925; *County of Carmarthen* 1917

E. H. EDWARDS *Castles and Strongholds of Pembrokeshire* 1909
MARGARET F. DAVIES *Pembrokeshire* 1939
H. L. V. FLETCHER *South Wales* 1956
MIN LEWIS *Laugharne and Dylan Thomas* 1967
J. E. LLOYD *A History of Carmarthenshire* 2 vols 1935
R. M. LOCKLEY *Pembrokeshire* (Regional Books series) 1957
M. and E. LODWICK *The Story of Carmarthen* 1954
A. G. PRYS-JONES *The Story of Carmarthenshire* 1959
VYVYAN REES *Shell Guide to South-West Wales* 1963
W. SPURRELL *Carmarthen and Its Neighbourhood* 1879
M. WRIGHT *Pembrokeshire and the National Park* 1954

Gazetteer

PEMBROKESHIRE AND CARMARTHENSHIRE

Angle *Pemb.* (BJ 20) (320). Charmingly situated at the mouth of Milford Haven, between two Bays, muddy Angle and sandy West Angle. There is a ruined four-storied tower, with a moat and pigeon-house, and a Tudor blockhouse. An oil refinery has been built nearby.

Black Mountain *Carm.* (CH 21). This range of mountains, occupying the whole E end of the county, is separated from the Black Mountain on the Herefordshire border by some 25 m. of mountainous country, culminating in Brecon Beacons, and the valley of the Usk; but all three ranges are now united in a magnificent National Park*. Apart from the road mentioned below (*see* **Brynamman**), much of the area is accessible only by mountain lanes and footpaths. Yet it is worth exploring, and the only considerable lake in the county, Llyn-y-fan Fach, is below the rise to the highest peak, Carmarthen Van (2,632 ft.), which, despite its name, is just over the Brecon border.

Bosherston *Pemb.* (BK 19) EC Wed (90). The main significance of this little village, with its charming lily ponds, is its proximity to the cliffs of St Govan's Head. 1½ m. S is the tiny St Govan's Chapel in a deep hollow of the cliffs, and to the W is Huntsman's Leap. 1 m. E, between St Govan's Head and Stackpole Head is Broad Haven, not to be confused with the Broad Haven on St Bride's Bay (*see under* **Haverfordwest**). 1 m. N of the village is Stackpole (*see below*).

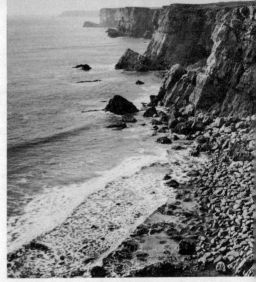

Near Bosherston: the cliffs *G. Douglas Bolton*

Brynamman *Carm.* (CH 21) EC Thurs. A small village about 6 m. E of Ammanford, from which the A4069 starts the climb over the Black Mountain. At the highest point on the road, 1,618 ft., which here passes over the shoulder of Garreg-lwyd (2,028 ft.) there are magnificent views away to Carmarthen Van (2,632 ft.) 7 m. NE.

Caldy Island *Pemb.* (CB 19). 2½ m. S of Tenby; can be visited by motor boat. There is a modern Cistercian priory, and a 12th-cent. Benedictine monastery can be seen. The ancient church contains a stone with an inscription in Latin and Ogam (*see* p. 262).

Carew *Pemb.* (CA 20) EC Wed (760). Ruins of 13th-cent. castle (AM), later a Tudor residence, with a richly carved, 14-ft. Celtic cross (AM) nearby. The church has a fine tower, and monuments of the Carew family, with an unusual chantry chapel in the churchyard. About 1 m. NW, across the river, the 13th-cent. gateway of Upton Castle is still standing.

265

Carew Castle

G. Douglas Bolton

Carmarthen *Carm.* (CE 22) EC Thurs (12,880). County capital and market town; the remains of the Norman castle (AM) occupy the site of the Roman station Maridunum. The church contains the tomb of Sir Rhys ap Thomas, the supporter of Henry VII, and a memorial to Sir Richard Steele, the essayist, who retired to his wife's birthplace in the neighbourhood. At Llanstephan, 7 m. S at the mouth of the R. Towy, where there is a sandy beach, are the gatehouse and keep of a Norman castle and a small Norman church.

Cilgerran *Pemb.* (CB 24) EC Wed (820). Impressive Norman castle (AM & NT), situated above the R. Teify, which here flows through a tree-covered gorge. 3 m. NW, also on the Teify, at St Dogmaels, are the remains of the Benedictine Abbey (AM) founded by Martin of Tours in the 11th cent.

Dale *Pemb.* (BJ 20) (650). Some 12 m. SW of Haverfordwest, at the end of B4321, this village is a good point

from which to explore the southern horn of St Bride's Bay. The modern castle is built on the site of an earlier one; it was near here that Henry Tudor, soon to become Henry VII, landed in 1485. From the top of the unclassified road leading S to St Anne's Head, one can see Milford Haven running due E to Pembroke; and 4 m. out to sea in the opposite direction is Skokholm Island, now a bird sanctuary. 2 m. NW is the village of Marloes, with access to the Marloes Sands; and beyond the village, with fine cliff scenery, is Wooltack Point, looking across to Skomer Island, where hundreds of hut-circles have been found.

Fishguard *Pemb.* (BK 23) EC Wed (4,900). An attractive town, with a port at the foot of a hill, where a French force landed in 1797 and surrendered. 1½ m. W is the little resort of Goodwick, with its harbour for the steamer service to Ireland. These are the only two places in Fishguard Bay where bathing is possible, since rugged cliffs extend from Dinas Head on the E to Strumble Head on the W.

Haverfordwest *Pemb.* (BK 21) E C Thurs (8,870). Handsome market town, with 18th-cent. houses, built on a hill above the W Cleddau River. The keep of the Norman castle remains, and sections of the old town walls. Of its three churches, the most interesting is St Mary's (13th-cent.), with a fine oak roof and carved stalls of later date. 4½ m. E, in its fine park on the banks of the E Cleddau, stands Picton Castle, one of the few castles in Britain to have been lived in continuously from the 13th cent. 6 m. W, on St Bride's Bay, are the attractive little resorts of Broad Haven and Little Haven, reached by picturesque lanes.

Kidwelly *Carm.* (CE 20) E C Wed (2,880). Market town, with small harbour and some sand, at the head of the Gwendraeth estuary. The splendid 13th-cent. castle (AM) replaced an earlier fortress built in 1094 by a follower of Fitz Hammon, the first Norman conqueror of S Wales. The church, with its fine tower, standing beside the river, was originally the chapel of a Benedictine priory.

Lamphey *Pemb.* (CA 20) E C Wed (350). In the grounds of Lamphey Court stand the ruins of the splendid Archbishop's Palace (AM), begun in the 13th cent. and completed by Bishop Gower, who also, between 1328 and 1347, built the still finer Palace at St David's (*see below*).

Laugharne *Carm.* (CD 21) E C Sat (1,010). At the mouth of the R. Taf. This little township, the home and burial-place of Dylan Thomas, has a town hall dating from 1746, and many Georgian houses. From the foreshore is a view of the castle ruins.

Llandeilo *Carm.* (CG 22) E C Thurs (1,930). A market town, with fishing and golf, in the lovely valley of the Towy. Dynevor Castle is modern, and in recent years has become the centre of a summer festival of the arts. In the grounds are the remains of a Norman castle, which may be visited, built on the site of a fortress founded in 870 by Rhodri Mawr, the leader who succeeded in uniting all the princes of Wales. 4 m. SE, perched on a precipitous rock 300 ft. above the R. Cennen, are the ruins of Carreg Cennen Castle (AM) 'the Arthurian castle of one's dreams'; and 6 m. W, on the B4297, the remains of Dryslwyn Castle look across the R. Towy to Paxton's Tower, built in honour of Nelson.

Llandovery *Carm.* (CH 23) E C Thurs (1,990). The name is derived from the Welsh for 'the church amid the waters', through its proximity to the junction of the Rivers Towy, Bran and Gwydderig. There are some remains of a Norman castle, and the college is one of the best-known in Wales. On the right of the Brecon road, some 3 m. E, stands the Mail Coach pillar, with its long, and still relevant, inscription warning drivers against drunkenness. N from the town, an unclassified road, after passing through the village of Cilycwm, bears W under the summit of Mynydd Mallaen (1,515 ft.), before descending to Pumsaint (*see below*). Another by-road leads off the A4069, 2½ m. S of the town, to Myddfai, where there is a double-nave church, with ancient roofs and monuments, standing on the R. Bran.

Llanelli *Carm.* (CF 19) E C Tue (28,730). A manufacturing town, the largest in the county, and owing its development to the industrial revolution in the 19th cent.

Llangadog *Carm.* (CH 22) EC Wed or Sat (1,270). A pleasant village in the valley of the Towy, with an early 19th-cent. mansion, Abermarlais, it is the northern starting point of the road over the Black Mountain, described above (*see* **Brynamman**). 3 m. S, Carn Goch is the largest prehistoric camp in Wales.

Llanstephan Castle *Carm.* (CD 21). *See* **Carmarthen.**

Llawhaden *Pemb.* (CA 21) (400). *See* **Narberth.**

Lydstep *Pemb.* (CA 19). About midway between Lydstep and Sprinkle Havens. The cliffs here, with their caves and views of the coast and out to Caldy Island (*see above*), have been acquired by the NT.

Manorbier *Pemb.* (CA 19) EC Wed (1,010). The moated castle ruins (AM), still partly occupied, stand in a valley, sloping down to the sandy beach of the little bay. Here in 1146 the medieval historian, Giraldus Cambrensis, was born. One of his many works was the *Itinerary Through Wales.*

Milford Haven *Pemb.* (BK 20) EC Thurs (12,800). Situated on one of the finest natural harbours in Britain, the place was already important in the Middle Ages. Most of the existing town, however, dates from the improvements undertaken from the end of the 18th cent. onwards, though the dockyard established at that period was transferred to Pembroke in 1814. It is now a trawler fishing port, with a large oil refinery on the opposite side of the Haven, near the village of Angle.

Narberth *Pemb.* (CB 21) EC Fri (960). An old market town with remains of a Norman castle. Llawhaden, 3 m. NW, has remains of a 13th-cent. Bishop's palace, with a gatehouse, and the church is remarkable for its double tower. At Llaw-

haden, 3 m. farther along the same by-road, is a ruined Norman fortress.

Nevern *Pemb.* (CA 24) EC Wed (740). A picturesquely situated village, on the slope of a hill beside a stream. The present church, though a 6th-cent. foundation, is partly Norman, with a battlemented tower, and the Celtic Cross of St Brynach, near the S door.

Newcastle Emlyn *Carm.* (CD 24) EC Wed (680). There are a few remains of a castle here, and fishing in the R. Teify. At Cenarth, 3 m. W, the river is spanned by a picturesque bridge, with four arches. There we find waterfalls; the local fishermen still use coracles.

Newgale *Pemb.* (BJ 22). At the N end of St Bride's Bay, it can be reached either by the winding coast road from Broadhaven to the S, through Nolton, or by the main road from Haverfordwest to St David's, which passes the still inhabited tower of Roch Castle. Its main attraction is the two miles or so of flat sandy beach, backed by a pebble bank.

Newport *Pemb.* (CA 23) EC Wed (1,190). A golfing and seaside resort, with a sandy beach. The bay is bounded at its W extremity by the 500-ft. cliffs of Dinas Head, which separates it from Fishguard Bay. Parts of the moated Norman castle have been restored as a private house, and may be visited by appointment. The cromlech of Pentre Ifan (AM) is 3 m. SE, and there are further megalithic remains on the slope of 1,000-ft. Carn Ingli, which rises to the S of the town.

Nolton Haven *Pemb.* (BJ 21). A little fishing village in the centre of St Bride's Bay, midway between Newgale (*see above*) to the N and Broad Haven to the S.

Pembroke *Pemb.* (BK 20) EC Wed (12,740). Is dominated by the moated castle (AM), covering an area of 4 acres, and part of the walls (AM) that once encircled the town. Begun as a stone fortress in 1090, it was enlarged in the two succeeding centuries by the earls palatine of Pembroke. The circular vaulted keep, built about 1200, is 75 ft. high with walls 7 ft. thick; the Great Hall is built over the 'Wogan', a subterranean passage leading to the harbour. Opposite the castle, the medieval Monkton Priory was largely rebuilt at the end of the 19th cent. At Pembroke Dock, a small town 1 m. N, though the naval dockyard has been closed, there is still a car ferry to Neyland, and a bridge is under construction.

Penally *Pemb.* (CB 19) EC Wed (510). A small resort, between Lydstep and Tenby (*see below*), with a Celtic cross in the churchyard. There are views across to Caldy Island (*see above*), and to the E are the Pendine Sands, where motor speed trials used to be held.

Llandovery: the River Towy

Reece Winstone

Prescelly Hills *Pemb*. (CB 23). The only considerable range of hills in the county, rising to 1,760 ft. (whence the whole of Pembrokeshire can be seen), this stretch of moors and streams is now a national park. It is rich in prehistoric remains (*see* Introduction p. 261), which have to be explored on foot. Only one motor road from Haverfordwest to Cardigan, the B4329, traverses the area, attaining 1,383 ft. at its summit.

Pumsaint *Carm*. (CG 24) E C Wed and Sat. Near this village in the wild valley of the Cothi is Dolau-Cothi, where in Roman and earlier times mining for gold was carried on – there are still traces of the square-hewn Roman tunnels. The village is now a part of a 2,400-acre N T estate.

St Clears *Carm*. (CC 21) E C Wed and Sat (1,937). Note the fine tower of the partly Norman church. Here Owen Glyndior was defeated in 1406; and in 1843 the little town was one of the centres of the Rebecca Riots, when men disguised as women rode about the S Wales countryside destroying the toll-houses and gates. Though the riot was put down, it achieved its aim, the suppression of toll-gates throughout S Wales.

St David's* *Pemb*. (BH 22) E C Wed (1,500). This cathedral city of only 1,500 inhabitants stands, with its restored market cross, on high ground, so that one's first view of the cathedral is the top of the 116-ft. tower. Only after passing through the S gate does the splendour of the building, built of local purplish sandstone, come into view; but then one can easily believe the story that two pilgrimages to St David's used to be reckoned the equivalent of one to Rome. The main portion of the fabric dates from the 12th cent., and the Lady Chapel, rood-screen and S porch were added during the next century and a half.

The Norman nave, with its roof of Irish oak, is noteworthy, and the interior of the cathedral is of exquisite beauty. Nearby, on the Alun river, are the ruins of St Mary's College, founded by John of Gaunt; and the 14th-cent. Bishop's Palace (AM), built, like Lamphey (*see above*), by Bishop Gower. There is bathing at Caerfai Bay, 1 m. S, and at Whitesands Bay 2 m. NW. This last is bounded to the N by St David's Head, with its prehistoric rampart, hut-circles and rock-shelter. Both there and to the S, where one has a fine view across the sound to Ramsey Island (which can be visited in summer) is splendid rock scenery.

St Dogmaels *Pemb*. (CB 24) E C Wed (1,060). (*See above*, under **Cilgerran**.)

Saundersfoot *Pemb*. (CB 20) E C Wed. Seaside and golfing resort, on a lovely bay. 2 m. E is the tiny village of Amroth, with bathing from a sand and shingle beach, where at low tide a submerged forest is revealed.

Solva *Pemb*. (BJ 22) E C Wed. A delightful village, perched above a winding inlet, which provides anchorage for fishing boats and yachts. The views from the cliffs on either side, S across St Bride's Bay and E to Ramsey Island, are remarkable.

Stackpole *Pemb*. (BK 19) (260). The site of a recently demolished 18th-cent. mansion, standing on parkland on an artificial lake, made by damming the stream. Parts of the house are of an earlier period, and in the church are tombs dating from the 13th and 14th centuries.

Talley *Carm*. (CG 23) E C Wed (410). Near this tiny hill village, in the valley of the Dulais, are the remains of the Benedictine abbey (AM), founded late in the 12th cent. by Rhys-ap-Griffith, Prince of S Wales; the

271

David's Cathedral   *J. Allan Cash*

Tenby, with St Catherine's Island   *G. Douglas Bolton*

central tower and some fragments of the walls have survived.

Tenby* *Pemb.* (CB 20) EC Wed (4,750). The best-known resort in the county, with golf, a harbour and bathing from two separate sandy beaches. The town, with its castle and considerable remains of the town walls (both AM) on a headland overlooking the sea, dates from the 13th cent., but there are many Georgian houses and two notable Tudor buildings, Merchant's House and Plantagenet House on Quay Hill, both

cared for by the NT. There is a small but significant town museum. St Mary's Church has a fine chancel roof and some notable tombs, together with a raised chancel and crypt.

Whitland *Carm.* (CC 21) EC Wed (1,269). This market town is interesting for its long association with the monastic life of S Wales. Here, in the 10th cent., an assembly was summoned to revise the laws for the country; and 1 m. NE can still be seen some remains of the mother house of the Cistercian Order.

The crumbling walls of Montgomery Castle

MONTGOMERYSHIRE AND DENBIGHSHIRE

AN INTRODUCTION BY JEAN WARE

Although Denbigh and Montgomery are both Welsh border counties, Denbigh taking over where Montgomery leaves off along the Shropshire border with Wales, yet no major road leads from one to the other. They meet on the Berwyn Mountains, at a height of two thousand feet, and run alongside down the narrow glen of Rhaiadr. If you want to see the place where one county literally spills over into the other, drive your car up this glen, luxuriantly green in spring, flaming in autumn. Start from the village of Llanrhaiadr-ym-Mochnant, part in Denbigh, part in Montgomery, and travel north-west for four miles, until you can go no further even on foot. Here you gaze up at one of the traditional 'seven wonders of Wales', the Pistyll Rhaiadr, the 'cascaded waterfall', where the Disgynfa river rushes over sheer cliff two hundred and forty feet high, through a natural arch, and into a deep cauldron. I know of no two counties with a more dramatic rendezvous.

273

From England into Denbigh you cross the border with a flourish on the A5 at Chirk. 'Welcome to Wales!' says the roadside sign. 'The last pub in England! Open on Sundays!' From England into Montgomeryshire there is not the same flourish. Indeed, there is a public house in Llanymynech which is half in one land, half in the other. The Border roadways meander companionably in and out of Wales and England; the original of John Bull was a Welshpool man.

MONTGOMERYSHIRE

Montgomeryshire is seven hundred and ninety-seven square miles of moorland plateau, which once formed part of the ancient Principality of Powys. It is divided by a main watershed composed of the Berwyn Mountains, the Vyrnwy mass, and the north Plynlimon plateau, all above a thousand feet, with heavy rainfall and only rough moorland pasture. To the east is the Severn river system, and to the west the fan of tributaries to the Dovey, with their deep valleys lying between the flat plateau surfaces. The county has no coastal strip. It stops two miles west of Machynlleth, in the Dovey estuary. The broader eastern valleys, with smaller rainfall, provide good pasture for winter grazing. Only two east-west roads cut across the county: the A458 from Shrewsbury through Welshpool to Dolgellau, and the A489 from Craven Arms through Newtown to Machynlleth. A branch of the southern part of the old Watling Street entered Wales on the B4393 at Llandrinio, where a farmhouse is still called The Street, and went on to Llangynog and over the Berwyns to Bala.

From the Rodney Pillar on the Breidden hills near Welshpool, in the east, you see Merioneth, Shropshire, Cardigan, Radnor and Denbigh. Here you are on almost the only igneous rock in Montgomeryshire: the rest of the county is of grey shales and sandstones, though on the edge of the forest of Clun the Old Red Sandstone just peeps over the border. You may see it in its glory in the stones of the mediaeval Powys Castle above Welshpool. The only limestone being here on the eastern border, you may find on the Breidden hills rare flora like rock cinquefoil, sticky catchfly, alpine cinquefoil and spiked speedwell. The lack of lime in the rest of the county is the key to the vegetation. The moors, purple with heather, contrast with dark acres of fir and pine, and in the autumn rowans scatter their scarlet berries. In February the valleys smell of leaf-mould and erupt in white, purple and orange patches of snowdrops and crocus; later, wild hyacinths and primroses run riot up the slopes. Montgomeryshire is noted for the beauty of its oaks, especially in the park of Powys Castle. Elms and beeches abound, and all summer the hedges drip with honeysuckle. This is a county of moors, woods and rivers.

The Rivers and Lakes

The great Severn and the Wye have their sources on the windswept flanks of Plynlimon; true to Border give-and-take ('Taffy came to my house, I went to Taffy's house'), the little Camlad, a tributary of the Severn, rises in England and flows into Wales. The two mighty rivers with all their little tributaries sparkle and sing and chatter into England. The Tanat, Vyrnwy, Banwy and Rhiw seam the county with deep valleys, gold and tawny brown as the heather fades. In summer these rivers fill the larders with trout – not large owing to the lack of alkali, but shell-pink of flesh and delicious. Sabrina, goddess of the Severn, flings coloured ribbons of living water across Montgomery from her famous 'amber-dropping hair'. The little Mule cuts a deep, rich dingle in scarlet and yellow;

G. Douglas Bolton   **Sunset on Lake Vy**

The Dee at Llangollen *Reece Winstone*

the Vyrnwy glides through green hills that lounge like dinosaurs in the filtered haze of the uplands; the swift, mischievous Banwy teases with threats of flood; the Rhiw tosses a miniature waterfall into the black-and-white timbered village of Berriew; and the Clywedog, tributary of the Wye, twists and turns down her deep gorge to join the Severn at Llanidloes.

There are a few little lakes above Caersws, where fairy music was heard as late as 1936, near the churchyard of Llanwnog. Here the bard Ceiriog lies buried. ('My heart is in the mountains, with the heather and the little birds.') But the most beautiful stretch of water is Lake Vyrnwy, a reservoir five miles long which supplies Liverpool with water.

Architecture, Language and Politics

Travelling from east to west, you notice that the half-timbered black-and-white houses, at first as numerous as in Hereford or Shropshire, are gradually replaced by stone cottages the nearer you approach the Dovey estuary. Timbered belfries, as at Kerry and Bettws, Newtown Old Church and Llanidloes, are typical of the county. You notice too that Welsh takes the place of English as a first language. Llanidloes, with its timbered market-hall and pitched or cobbled pavements, stands at the blunt edge of the wedge of English speech pushed in from the Border. By the time you reach Machynlleth, you are become so Welsh that even the cows, knee-deep in the Dovey under the shade of the bridge, seem to moo in the 'old tongue'.

This river Dovey is the ancient division between North and Mid Wales – roughly the old Principalities of Gwynedd and Powys. North Wales is contorted by volcanoes, and was a natural fortress for Welsh independence; Mid Wales ends its smoother contours on Plynlimon Fawr (2,468 feet) nine miles south of Machynlleth. Cross the Dovey into Merioneth, and immediately you are in quite another land: the country of the Red Men of Mawddwy, of sea-caves, mountain precipices and lost causes.

Agriculture

Cattle are more important to the economy than sheep, and improved methods of milk-collection have resulted in a change-over from store to dairy cattle. A popular breed is the Welsh Black. But sheep still play a large part. Up to the end of the last century the county was famous for its flannel – indeed, the very word comes from the Welsh word 'gwlanen' meaning 'wool'. Montgomery, Newtown and Welshpool, now market towns, were once great centres of the woollen industry. The breed of sheep distinctive to Montgomeryshire is the Kerry Hills, with white faces and black markings round nose and eyes. Plynlimon sheep, prime mutton of great sweetness, range the uplands, and here too are wild mountain ponies, said to be descended from Roman stock and to have Arab blood. Out of a population of 45,000 there are 7,000 farmers with one or more acres, and their wives and families make up another 10,000 to 15,000. They employ some 3,500 agricultural workers, and most of the remaining population carry, distribute and market.

DENBIGHSHIRE

Denbighshire has a twelve-mile strip of trippery sands on the north-west, a central peaty plateau laced with lush green vales, and coal to the south-east. The six hundred and sixty-nine square miles of this county include the fertile vales of Conway in the west, Clwyd in the east and Llangollen in the south-east. The uplands form a high platform rising to two thousand seven hundred and thirteen feet in Moel Sych, and falling steeply to the vales of Conway and Clwyd.

In the uplands there is rough grazing for sheep; on the lower slopes are cattle, pigs, oats, barley and potatoes. The best agricultural areas are the red sandstone, which in the vale of Clwyd overlays the older limestone. On the hills above Llanrwst the soil is either yellow loam or peat, both dry and boggy; in the valley below, it is clay. Denbighshire is the only county in Wales where alpine wound-wort, downy woundwort and spider orchid may be found. Compared with Montgomery, trees are sparse. Hazels and ash abound, with buckthorn, hawthorn and blackthorn on the uplands.

Industries

Except for the lovely basin of the Ceiriog, tipped towards Montgomeryshire and its mountain frame of the Berwyns, the south-east of Denbigh is industrial. Wrexham, Chirk and Ruabon are the coal-mining centres for the southern half of the North Wales coalfields. (Flintshire lies to the north-east.) Fireclay is mined with the coal, and is used to make bricks and tiles. At Llanddulas are limestone quarries, and there is a large chemical works at Cefn Mawr, near the eastern end of the vale of Llangollen. Various small factories have sprung up round Mochdre, and a toy factory in Llanrwst. There is a biscuit factory in Denbigh, one of the four municipal boroughs, the others being Colwyn Bay (which makes its livelihood with the holiday trade, as do Rhos-on-Sea and Abergele), Ruthin and Wrexham.

The Uplands

Although the valleys of the Conway, Clwyd, Ceiriog and Dee Valley (near

Valle Crucis Abbey

G. Douglas Bolton

Llangollen) are beautiful, and their towns and villages of great historic interest, yet if you want to reach the true heart of this county you must seek out the region known to Welshmen as *Cwm Eithin* from the famous book of that name. Like the Wessex of Hardy's novels, this, the 'gorse glen', is not strictly mapped; but you can take it to include the rural districts of Edeyrnion and Hiraethog and the great moorland of Migneint, with a strip of uplands from Caernarvonshire and Merioneth. This region has bred the eagles among Welshmen, the men of long vision – for no-one can be myopic, either spiritually or physically, if he has been reared here, where he may look daily over the summits of the Berwyns, over to the Merioneth hills of Cader Idris, the Arenig, Yr Aran, over to where the Caernarvonshire giants, Snowdon, Carnedd Dafydd, Carnedd Llywelyn, tower like guardian chieftains.

When you explore these stretches of wild country, shut in by mountains but open at both ends to wide and fertile vales, you may hear again the thunder of the droves of black cattle being driven down the cwms to the English markets. There are stretches of moor above the Conway valley, easily reached from Colwyn Bay on the B5113 moorland road to Llanrwst, which have all the *Cwm Eithin* atmosphere. In May the moors are painted gold and white by broom and black-thorn. Here you may learn about the complicated rules of Welsh poetry from a princely old man in his cabin, listening through his open door to the cry of the curlew 'shepherding the clouds'.

The Valleys

All this is in great contrast to the varied green of the banks of the Conway, Clwyd and Ceiriog, to the sparkling Dee, and the gaiety of Llangollen in July, when thousands of European dancers and singers mingle with the American and Commonwealth teams in the beflagged streets at the International Music Festival. This village of only 3,000 inhabitants has every year since 1947 enter-tained over one hundred and fifty choirs and teams of dancers from all over the world – an enterprise of great vision. Here you may idle in boats on the canal, or

278

scramble up the terraced escarpment of the Eglwyseg rocks, where carboniferous limestone overlies the blue-grey shale which elsewhere forms the hilly structure of this region. Llangollen is as famous now as it was in the early coaching days, when the Ladies of Llangollen, two Irishwomen in masculine attire, entertained the celebrities of the day at Plas Newydd, the black-and-white house you may visit, as they passed through to or from Ireland. The ruined fort (Dinas Bran) and Abbey (Valle Crucis) above the town were built by a thirteenth-century prince of Powys and later fell under the rule of a Marcher Lord – and this is significant, for to this day Llangollen seems far more akin to Montgomeryshire, of the land of Powys, than to Denbighshire, of the land of Gwynedd.

History and Prehistory

Walkers may follow the upland path used by the Beaker folk along the slopes of the Clwydian hills from above Nannerch to Moel Fenlli behind Ruthin. There are some twenty-five Iron Age forts in the county. At Cefn near St Asaph and Plas Heaton near Denbigh you may see good examples of Stone Age caves. Along the eastern border of both Denbigh and Montgomery you may follow the remains of Offa's Dyke, which runs from the estuary of the Dee near Prestatyn (Flintshire) to the Severn estuary at Sedbury Cliffs (Gloucester). You can see it marching south in Denbighshire through Adwy'r Clawdd, Ruabon and Chirk, and in Montgomeryshire through the south-eastern corner. Offa was an 8th-century King of Mercia (middle England) who slew Caradoc, a Welsh princeling, on the marsh between Abergele and Rhuddlan, staining the sea with the blood of both armies. Then he built his dyke to mark the boundary between England and Wales.

A tour of the ruined castles will take you to Ruthin, Holt, Chirk, Rhuddlan and Denbigh (see this by moonlight) and to the sad, green mound at Sycharth, near Llansilin – all that is left of the happy mansion where Owain Glyn Dwr spread his tables with 'linen white' and reared his 'nest of princelings'. In the late 14th century this Welsh nobleman, a man of culture, set up a Parliament for Wales at Machynlleth, and nearly succeeded in ridding Wales of the English yoke. During his risings Ruthin and Llanrwst were burnt to the ground. When he was outlawed and a price set on his head, not one Welshman was found who would betray him. His ghost haunts the hills round Llangollen as surely as Bonnie Prince Charlie haunts the Western Highlands of Scotland.

The Shaking Bridge, Llanrwst   *Reece Winstone*

Some houses and gardens open to the public

Bodnant Garden 4m s of Conway off A496 *Map* CJ 37. *Splendid layout, 19th cent., with 18th-cent. pleasure house.* NT. No dogs or prams admitted. Entrance by the Eglwysbach road.

Chirk Castle nr Wrexham 6m N of Oswestry, off A5. *Map* DC 33. *14th cent., unaltered externally; 17th- to 19th-cent. furnishings.*

Denbigh Castle At Denbigh *Map* DA 36. *13th cent., finely sited; remains of town walls.*

Garthewin nr village of Llanfair Talhaiarn 5m S of Abergele on Abergele–Llanrwst road *Map* CK 36. *18th-cent. Georgian mansion; period furniture, armorial china, family portraits; private chapel; 18th-cent. barn converted into private theatre; overlooks Valley of Elwy.* R. O. F. Wynne, Esq. By appointment only. Tel.: Llanfair Talhaiarn 213.

Gwydir Castle At Llanrwst *Map* CJ 36. *Mainly 12th cent., with period furniture, priests' hiding-hole and a spiral staircase; the garden has over 40 peacocks, and 800-year-old yew tree and centuries-old cedars.* Richard Clegg, Esq.

Llanidloes Old Market Hall 14m SW of Newtown on A492 *Map* CK 28. *Old half-timbered building on open arches; contains noteworthy museum.*

Maesmawr Hall Caersws 6m W of Newtown off A492 *Map* DA 29. *Picturesque old half-timbered house.*

Montgomery Castle At Montgomery *Map* DC 29. *Remains of 13th-cent. castle (AM), above Georgian town in picturesque border countryside.*

Plas Newydd At Llangollen *Map* DC 34. *Picturesque; once the home of the 'Ladies of Llangollen'.*

Powys Castle At Welshpool *Map* DC 30. *Impressive 14th cent., inhabited without interruption 500 yrs.; plasterwork, murals and tapestry. Fine terraced gardens.* NT.

Books for further reading

Local life and customs

S. J. COLEMAN *Legendary Lore of Denbighshire* 1956
S. J. COLEMAN *Legendary Lore of Montgomeryshire* 1956
GERAINT GOODWIN *Watch for the Morning* (a novel) 1938
EILUNED LEWIS *Dew on the Grass* (a novel) 1934
D. PARRY-JONES *Welsh Country Characters* 1952
H. A. E. ROBERTS *Legends and Folk-Lore of North Wales* 1931

Topography and antiquities

A. BLAIR *Rambles in North-East Wales* 1946
M. FRASER *West of Offa's Dyke: N. Wales* 1959
CLEDWYN HUGHES *The Northern Marches* 1953

FRANK PRICE JONES *The Story of Denbighshire through Its Castles* 1951
P. T. JONES *Welsh Border Country* 1946
J. D. K. LLOYD ed. *The Official County Handbook of Montgomeryshire* 1963
W. BESANT LOWE *The Heart of Northern Wales* 2 vols 1912/27
S. O'DWYER *The Roman Roads of Wales: vol. 2 Merioneth and Montgomeryshire* 1934
J. H. B. PEEL *Portrait of the Severn* 1968
Royal Commission on the Ancient and Historical Monuments of Wales vol. IV Denbighshire
DAVID VEREY *The Shell Guide to Mid-Wales* 1960
B. WATERS *Severn Stream* 1949
K. WATSON *North Wales* (Regional Archaeologies) 1965
A. H. WILLIAMS *The Early History of Denbighshire: an Outline* 1950
W. J. WREN *The Tanat Valley: Its Railways and Industrial Archaeology* 1968

Gazetteer

MONTGOMERYSHIRE AND DENBIGHSHIRE

Bodnant Gardens   G. Douglas Bolton

Abergele *Denb*. (CK 37) EC Thurs (7,980). Ancient market town with the little resort of **Pensarn** just to the N, and several old manor houses on the outskirts. The church, like several others in the county, has two parallel naves, and some old glass. 1 m. W, Gwrych Castle, impressively sited, is an imitation antique.

Bodnant *Denb*. (CJ 37). Here, near the little village of Tal-y-Cafn, is the seat of Lord Aberconway, who made over the gardens to the NT in 1949. More than a century old, they are admirably laid out, and can be visited throughout the summer.

Caersws *Mont*. (DA 29). Site of a Roman military station. There is a fine old half-timbered house, Maesmawr; and another, Talgarth, 5 m. W, near Trefeglwys. 2 m. NW, at **Llanwnog**, we find a 15th-cent. roodloft and screen in the village church.

Cerrigydrudion (CK 34) EC Wed (850). 'Rock of the heroes', a small mountain village, by-passed by the main road, with a little church, and almshouses dated 1717. 1 m. SE, to the left of the Corwen road, the remains of an ancient British camp crown the hill of Pen-y-gar, traditionally the spot where Caradog (Caractacus), King of the Britons, was betrayed to the Romans. B4501 runs N past 3-m.-long **Alwen Reservoir**, rising to 1,200 ft. and then dropping down to Denbigh.

Chirk *Denb*. (DC 33) EC Thurs (3,350). Famous for its splendid castle, standing in parkland 2 m. W. Outside walls and towers have scarcely changed since 1310, apart from the insertion of windows; the domestic buildings in the courtyard (rebuilt after purchase by Sir Thomas Myddleton in 1595), with their handsome furniture and decorations, are now shown to the public by his descendents. The church, with its 15th-cent. timbered roof and tower, contains monuments to the Myddletons and Trevors. Nearby, the R. Ceiriog is spanned by Telford's aqueduct, carrying the Shropshire Union Canal, surpassed only by his masterpiece – the even larger aqueduct (1,000 ft. long and 126 ft. high) that crosses the R. Dee on eighteen arches a mile or so N.

Colwyn Bay★ *Denb*. (CJ 37) EC Wed (23,090). The largest resort on the N coast of Wales, with a 3 m. promenade (unfortunately paralleled by the railway), excellent sands, mixed architecture, mild climate, golf and fishing in both sea and river. The promenade is continuous from Old Colwyn on the E to **Rhos-on-Sea** on the W.

Denbigh Castle

Denbigh *Denb*. (DA 36) EC Thurs (8,040). A busy little town overlooking the Vale of Clwyd, best seen from the ruined castle (AM), perched above the town, with the intricate structure of its gateway, between octagonal towers (1382), impressively intact. Within the precincts, the Norman tower of St Hilary's chapel still stands, but the church planned by Leicester 250 years later never rose further than its foundations. Burgesses' Tower (AM) is part of the town walls, another uncompleted project. There is a market cross and, in the yard of the Hawk and Buckle inn, a rare thatched cockpit (AM). The Town Hall, built by Leicester (1572), was enlarged in the late 18th cent. The Church of St Marcella, 1 m. E, with its double nave, has fine hammer-beam roofs,

chancel-screen and 14th-cent. glass, as well as splendid monuments in brass, stone and alabaster. The A453 to Pentrefoelas, after passing **Llyn Bran**, reaches a height of 1,523 ft., then crosses the shoulder of Mynydd Hiraethog between the Alwen Reservoir (*see* **Cerrigydrudion**) and **L. Alled**.

Derwen *Denb*. (DA 35) (410). Tiny hillside village, whose church has one of the finest screens and rood-lofts in the county and a fine churchyard cross (AM), dating respectively from the beginning and end of the 15th cent.

Gresford *Denb*. (DD 35) EC Wed (1,680). The village (where, in 1934, 261 miners lost their lives in a tragic colliery explosion) is situated in the valley of the R. Alun. The peal of twelve bells in the exquisite tower of the church is one of the so-called Seven Wonders of Wales. The carving of the stalls and the monuments in the Trevor Chapel are noteworthy; while the glass in the end windows of the aisles, and the font (both late 15th-cent. and perhaps brought from Basingwerk Abbey), are worthy of one of the finest perpendicular churches in Wales. 4 m. E, an eight-arch medieval bridge crosses the R. Dee at **Holt**, with remains of a castle.

Kerry *Mont.* (DB 29) EC Thurs (1,390). On the R. Mule, whence the wild mountainous sheep country of the Kerry Hills rises to the S. This may be seen from Kerry Pole (1,500 ft.), 1 m. N of the lonely Anchor inn, 5 m. SW of the village on the road to Clun (Salop). The fine Norman

arcades of the church (consecrated in 1176, but rebuilt in the 15th cent.) are worth seeing; so too is its timbered belfry.

Llanarmon-Dyffryn-Ceiriog *Denb.* (DB 33) EC Wed (180). A tiny village near the source of the R. Ceiriog, backed by the Berwyn mountains, with a well-known fisherman's inn, reached by the B4500 from Chirk.

Llanfair Caereinion *Mont.* (DB 30) EC Wed, Sat (1,530). A single-spanned bridge crosses the R. Einion, which is much frequented by fishermen; and there is a notable 14th-cent. effigy in the much-rebuilt church. 5 m. NW, at **Llanerfyl**, the church is remarkable, not only for its contents, but for its circular graveyard, corresponding to an earlier stone circle, and an inscribed Romano-British gravestone.

The Old Market Hall at Llanidloes

Reece Winstone

Llanfair Talhaiarn *Denb*. (CK 36) EC Thurs (840). A small village with fishing in the R. Elwyn. The poet Talhaiarn (John Jones), well-known to Welshman, died here in 1869 and is buried in the churchyard. The fine Georgian house, Garthewin, is open to the public in summer.

Llanfyllin *Mont*. (DB 31) EC Fri (1,250). Little market town in the wooded valley of the Cain, noted for the sweetness of the bells in its 18th-cent. church; and, once, for its ale ('Old ale fills Llanfyllin with young widows').

Llangollen* *Denb*. (DC 34) EC Thurs (3,050). Famous for its Vale, its 'Ladies' and, since 1947, for its festival of international folk song and dance, held each summer. The Ladies of Llangollen were Eleanor Butler (d. 1829) and Sarah Ponsonby (d. 1831), two eccentric recluses who for fifty years never left their home, Plas Newydd, the black-and-white house where they received most of the notabilities of the day, and which now belongs to the town. The 14th-cent. bridge (AM) across the R. Dee, though one of the traditional Seven Wonders of Wales, has been somewhat spoilt by widening. The superb timber roof of St Gollen's, carved with angels, flowers and animals, is said to have been brought from Valle Crucis (*see below*). 1 m. N is **Castell Dinas Bran**, a scanty ruin crowning an isolated hill; and 3 m. further on the manor house, Plas Uchaf. A secondary road leads to **Horseshoe Pass**, 1,300 ft. high, some 2 m. NW.

Llangynog *Mont*. (DA 32) EC Wed (290). Small stone-quarrying village at the junction of the lovely Eirth and Tanat Valleys. 2½ m. W is the lonely little Norman church at **Pennant Melangell**, with early monuments, and 15th-cent. rood-screen (now removed to W Gallery), carved with representations of hares, of whom St Melangell (Monacella) was the patroness. The road to Bala continues up the valley of the Tanat to the top of the wild **Milltir Cerrig Pass** (1,638 ft.).

Llanidloes *Mont*. (CK 28) EC Thurs (2,380). The slate and stone of this little Welsh market town are modified by the painted stucco of one or two buildings in the main street, giving a slightly Georgian impression. The half-timbered Market Hall is now occupied by a museum of local history. The church is notable for its timbered belfry, north arcade and fine hammer-beam roof, these last two brought from Cwmhir Abbey at the time of the Dissolution. The main Aberystwyth road soon leaves the Severn Valley for the much higher valley of the Wye, which it reaches at the pretty village of **Llangurig**, some 900 ft. above sea level, with the hump of Plynlimon (2,469 ft.) away to the NNW. The Clywedog Reservoir is situated on the mountain road that runs N from Llanidloes towards Staylittle and Machynlleth. The actual dam is situated in the Bryntail Gorge about 3 m. from the town of Llanidloes. At 202 ft. high at the crest, it is in fact the highest dam in the United Kingdom.

Llanrhaiadr-Yn-Cinmerch *Denb*. (DA 36) EC Wed (1,080). The perpendicular, double-carved church of this Vale of Clwyd village is remarkable. In addition to the timbered porch and lich-gate and the delicate hammer-beamed chancel roof, there is a Stem of Jesse window (1553), which owes its preservation to having been buried for ten years during the Commonwealth in the parish chest, still kept in the church.

Llanrwst *Denb*. (CJ 36) EC Thurs (2,570). A little town on the R. Conway spanned by three-arch bridge (AM), dated 1636, with Tu Hwnt i'r Bont, an old court house (now NT), at its W end. The church is notable for its screen and roof-loft and the Gwydir Chapel, built by Sir Richard Wynn before the Civil War. This contains family monuments and a great stone coffin, said to be that of Llewelyn ap Iorwerth. Across the river, **Gwydir Castle**, a Tudor mansion burnt in the 'twenties, and partly restored, with its Dutch garden and clipped yews, is open daily. The dower house, Gwydir Uchaf, is a youth hostel: its chapel (AM), noted for its painted ceiling, was built in 1673. Remote in the hills, 2 m. W, the ancient and very primitive church at **Llanrhychwyn** is known as 'Llewelyn's Old Church'.

Machynlleth *Mont.* (CH 30) EC Thurs (1,900). A little town with many old houses, in the lovely valley of the R. Dovey. Now bustling in summer with tourists and fishermen, it was here in 1402 that Owen Glendower summoned his first Parliament to proclaim himself Prince of Wales. The Institute named after him, with its library and museum, is thought to have been the Parliament House. Plas Machynlleth, standing in delightful grounds, now belongs to the town. To the N lie the 17,000 acres of Dovey Forest; and 4 m. SW is the picturesque **Llyfnant Valley.**

Meifod *Mont.* (DB 31) (900). A large village, charmingly situated on the R. Vyrnwy, which here flows through the vale of Meifod, famous for its beauty. The church has Norman arcading and an embattled tower; and across the river stands the fine Regency house, Pen-y-Lan.

Montgomery *Mont.* (DC 29) EC Fri (970). County town only in name, a mile from its own railway station and on no major road, with houses of every period from Elizabethan to Georgian, but none modern, this charming little town sleeps at the foot of the Welsh mountains, almost on the border of England. Above it are the fragmentary walls and towers of the Norman Castle (AM), where the poet George Herbert was born in 1593, and where his elder brother, Lord Herbert of Cherbury, lived through the Civil War. Their father's tomb is in the 14th-cent. church, which also has an early Norman font, carved misericords and a screen, perhaps from the demolished Abbey of Chirbury in Shropshire. The town hall is Georgian. 2 m. SE the B4386 crosses **Offa's Dyke** (*see below*) into England.

Newtown *Mont.* (DB 29) EC Thurs (5,510). Till the beginning of the century one of the main centres of the Welsh flannel industry, this town is now, with Welshpool, one of the two administrative capitals of the county. There are some attractive houses, of which Upper Bryn, half-timbered and dated 1660, is the most impressive. In 1968 the Mid-Wales New Town Development Corporation was established to develop and increase the size of the town. Another new feature is the recently opened Newtown Textile Museum, which will record the historical aspect of the woollen industry which at one time flourished in the town. The main interest for many people will be that Robert Owen, the socialist reformer, was born here in 1771, in the house now occupied by the Midland Bank, the first floor of which is preserved as a museum. When famous, he returned here to die and is buried in the old churchyard near the bridge. The A483, leading S from the town, offers a variety of mountain scenery. Rising sharply, it forks just beyond Dolfor, the main road to Llandrindod

285

Powys Castle   *G. Douglas Bolton*

entering Radnorshire at some 1,200 ft. and following the course of the R. Ithon for many miles. Even better, perhaps, is the left fork, which reaches a height of over 1,500 ft. in the Kerry Hills and continues to Knighton.

Offa's Dyke (DC 29). This great defensive earthwork, consisting of an embankment with a ditch on the Welsh side and running intermittently for 140 miles from the mouth of the Dee to that of the Wye, was built by Offa, king of the Mercians at the end of the 8th cent. to contain the Welsh. It is accompanied for some 40 m., from the Dee to the Severn, by a similar fortification, Watt's Dyke, about 3 m. to the E and following the 400 ft. contour. A footpath, along the line of the Dyke, has been planned. (*See* **Montgomery** and **Ruabon**.)

Pen-y-Bont-Fawr *Mont.* (DA 32) EC Wed. With fishing in the R. Tanat, is a good point from which to visit Lake Vyrnwy (*see below*) 6 m. SW, and the superb waterfall, **Pistyll Rhaiadr**, compared by George Borrow to 'the long tail of a grey courser at furious speed'. From **Llanrhaiadr-Ym-Mochant**, 2½ m. NE, a by-road follows the R. Disgynfa for 3½ m. NE

to where the stream, descending below the Berwyn Hills, is flung over a cliff and through a natural arch from a height of 230 ft.

Pistyll Rhaiadr *Denb.* (DA 32). (*See* **Pen-y-Bont-Fawr.**)

Plynlimon *Mont.* (CH 28). A high, boggy plateau, known as 'the mother of rivers' because both the Wye and the Severn, as well as half a dozen lesser streams, have their source here. The view from its summit, Pen Plynlimon Fawr* (2,468 ft.) just across the Cardiganshire border, which is easily reached by a two-hour walk from Dyffryn Castell inn, 10 m. W of Llangurig (*see under* **Llanidloes**) is impressive in extent.

Rhos-on-Sea *Denb.* (CJ 38) EC Wed (3,430). (*See* **Colwyn Bay.**)

Ruabon *Denb.* (DD 34) EC Wed (3,350). A small manufacturing town (chemicals and terra cotta) in the Denbighshire coalfield. The church contains several monuments to the Wynn family, whose family mansion, Wynnstay, now a school, is nearby. In the large park are the Nant-y-Belan and Waterloo towers, and through it runs a section of Watt's Dyke (*see* **Offa's Dyke**).

Ruthin *Denb.* (DB 35) EC Thurs (3,500). Built on a hill in the Vale of Clwyd, its rather uninviting outskirts conceal an attractive market square. Here are old framed houses with quaint porches; the Maen Huail (AM), an ancient stone block on which, according to tradition, the brother of Gildas the historian was beheaded by order of King Arthur; and the old collegiate church, minus its choir and with a modern spire, but still distinguished by the carved timber roof of Henry VII's time. Christ's Hospital nearby, and the Grammar School, are both Elizabethan foundations; and, also close to the

286

The River Wye

market square, the ruined red sandstone drum towers and curtain-wall of the moated castle (AM) stand in the grounds of a modern mansion, now used as a hotel. The old mother church of Ruthin is 1 m. SE at **Llanrhydd,** where the Hall used to be the home of the novelist Stanley Weyman.

Valle Crucis Abbey* *Denb.* (DC 34). In a remote and lovely dale 1½ m. NW of Llangollen, the ruins of this Cistercian abbey are the most impressive monastic remains in N Wales. Begun in 1202 by Madog, Prince of Powys, the main features of the W end of the ruined church can still be distinguished – its Early English windows and, above them, the later rose window. Of the monastery buildings there remain the 14th-cent. sacristy and chapter house, with the dormitory on the first floor. A quarter of a mile away, standing in a field, is the broken Eliseg's Pillar (AM), erected at the beginning of the 9th cent. by Prince Concenn, in memory of the victory of his great-grandfather Eliseg, Prince of Powys, killed at the battle of Bangor.

Vyrnwy, Lake *Mont.* (CK 32). Formed by damming the R. Vyrnwy 825 ft. above sea level to make a reservoir for Liverpool, this is the largest lake in Wales, 5 m. long and nearly a mile wide. Most easily approached from the SE and (*see* **Pen-y-Bont-Fawr**) it is encircled by a good road; while at the NE end is a rough but magnificent mountain road running over the **Rhiw Hirnant Pass** (1,641 ft.) direct to Bala, 14 m. away. Trout fishing permits may be obtained at the hotel in the model village of **Llanwddyn.**

Welshpool *Mont.* (DC 30) EC Thurs (6,330). The county town, close to the R. Severn, which is here separated from England by the Long Mountain, rising to 1,338 ft. at Beacon Ring.

Built mostly of brick, which is unusual for Wales, many of the houses are Georgian, such as the old post office in Broad Street, originally an inn; but there is a group of timber-framed houses near the castle, one of which has an inscription over the door in nails: 'G— d— old Oliver 1661'. Powys Park, with its lovely woodlands and some of the largest trees in the British Isles, is always open to the public; the castle, bequeathed to the NT by the late Earl of Powys in 1952, is open sometimes. Of this last, the oldest part dates from the later 13th cent., but many of the domestic apartments were added in the 16th; they now contain much fine plaster work and carving, as well as pictures, Georgian furniture and Clive relics. The gardens, modified by Capability Brown, are remarkable. Opposite the door of the parish church (Powys tombs and a fine chancel roof), the Maen Llog, originally a Druid altar, was later used as a throne by the Abbots of Strata Marcella, only the foundations of which are now extant, 3 m. NW. The Powysland Museum has an admirable collection, representing the art and history of the region.

Wrexham *Denb.* (DD 35) EC Wed (35,430). Thanks to its being the centre of an extensive coalfield, this is the largest town in North Wales, though English in speech and appearance. Its chief attraction for the visitor is the five-storied tower of the 14th-cent. parish church, 135 ft. high, splendidly proportioned and richly decorated. Two of the monuments in the church are by Roubiliac; the 18th-cent. wrought iron gates of the churchyard, like those at Ruthin, are the work of the Davies brothers of Bersham; and W of the tower is the tomb of Elihu Yale (d. 1721), the founder of Yale University, USA, whose father emigrated to America from Denbighshire.

Opposite: Detail from the original painting by Thomas Swimmer.

These two Welsh border counties present a wealth of natural beauty, purple with heather and dark with woods. Many of the houses are half-timbered. Objects shown by the picture recall the Welsh bards, the ancient industry of spinning, the grand ruined castles, and the River Severn, which the Romans called Sabrina.

Harlech Castle

CAERNARVONSHIRE, ANGLESEY AND MERIONETH

AN INTRODUCTION BY GEOFFREY BOUMPHREY

If any excuse were needed for grouping these three counties together, history provides it, since their boundaries follow nearly enough those of the ancient Welsh kingdom of Gwynedd. Protected on the north and west by the sea and on the south and east by formidable mountain ranges, the whole region is a natural fortress which for centuries resisted penetration by the invader. When in 1158 the rulers of the other three kingdoms in Wales submitted to Henry II and were reduced to the status of barons, Owen ap Gwynedd, though he would do homage, insisted on bearing the title of prince. In 1267 Llewelyn II, with the acquiescence of Henry III, declared himself Prince of Wales. Not until his death in 1282 did Gwynedd fall. It was then that Edward I declared his own son Prince of Wales, creating a precedent which is still followed. So this is country rich in history, as well as a region of outstanding and varied beauty – of majestic mountain and green valley, of gaunt precipice and tree-hung torrent, of high moorland, plaintive with sheep and curlew, and of coasts where the sea splashes in rocky bays or spreads over smoothing sand.

Opposite: Detail from the original painting by Richard Eurich.

Once *yr ynys dywyll*, the island dark with trees, Anglesey is now a county of little fields, and cliffs, and shell-scattered sands. The picture shows the view across to Puffin Island, where puffins breed and where the monks of St Seiriol's monastery were buried. In the foreground are the Lligwy Burial Chamber of the New Stone Age, the Penmon Cross, and the medieval reliquary sheltering the bones of a saint in Llanidan Church on the Menai Strait.

The Rocks

If traces of human warfare are not hard to find, evidence of nature's struggle is everywhere. The physical 'grain' of the land runs roughly NE – SW. This is the line of the north coast of Caernarvonshire, of the Menai Straits dividing it from Anglesey, and of the Lleyn Peninsula, that long arm of Wales which bounds Cardigan Bay on the north. It is the line, too, of the three river valleys and estuaries that lead into the bay (one of them, the 'Bala fault', extending over twenty miles inland from Barmouth, on the Mawddach Estuary, to Bala Lake) and of the great cleft that splits the length of the Cader Idris Range from Towyn to Tal-y-llyn and further. This noticeable grain is due to the existence of immense corrugations in the underlying Archaean rocks, the most ancient found on the earth's surface – so ancient that they contain no fossil evidence of life. The crest of one corrugation runs north-east from Harlech; the adjoining furrow underlies the most northerly mountains; and, because the whole bed is tilted as well as crumpled, the rise to the next crest is exposed on the surface in several north-east – south-west strips by or near each side of the Menai Straits and on the Lleyn Peninsula. In the six hundred million or more years since the formation of this Archaean sheet, it has been alternately lowered beneath the sea for long periods during which sedimentary rocks would be formed, and raised above the surface for the forces of erosion to do their work. Volcanoes have boiled up, ejecting or injecting flows of lava on it or into it, or spreading vast quantities of volcanic ash to settle in sedimentary beds. And the whole 'club-sandwich' of variegated rocks has been raised, lowered, folded, cracked and subjected to pressures and temperatures that have, in some instances, 'metamorphosed' the original sediments into quite new forms. These are the processes to which we owe the rich variety of rock in the region – the dark grey, almost greenish black of Snowdon and the adjoining ranges, the brown precipices of Aberglaslyn, the green and purple slates of the quarries, or the network of white quartz veining some of the rocks round Llanberis. One other potent force helped to mould the region. About a million years ago a great ice-sheet crept down from the north, following the depression of the Irish Sea and thrusting across the Cheshire plain. In the high mountains of North Wales, too, as the cold deepened, the local glaciers spread and merged into a Welsh ice-cap, powerful enough to deflect the thrust of the main icefield south-westward. The last of the Ice Ages ended less than twenty thousand years ago – and so there still remain in Snowdonia clear and abundant traces of the glaciers' work: valleys deepened and straightened, rocks scored by the flow of ice, 'hanging valleys' gouged out high on the mountain sides (as at Nant Ffrancon); or, conversely, 'moraines' of material loosened and carried down from above, sometimes forming ridges, mounds or flat table-lands, sometimes filling or damming valleys, and even forming lakes (such as the Marchlyns, between Llanberis and Nant Ffrancon).

Snowdonia

The mountains of Snowdonia rise from sea-level; and so their scale and grandeur always come as a surprise to those who know only the continental peaks. Experienced climbers rate them as 'real mountains', for their steep and jagged character, and for the difficulty of many of their ascents. To the Welsh the whole wild region was aptly known as Eryri, the Land of the Eagles. There are four main groups between the county's eastern boundary on the River Conway and the base of the Lleyn Peninsula. First the bluff Carnedd Range, rising steeply from the wide green Conway Valley and once a formidable bastion in Gwynedd's eastern defences. Between this and the narrow precipitous Glyders runs the Nant Ffrancon pass, threaded by Telford's Holyhead road, A5, on its way from Betws-y-Coed to Bangor. Forking left off this at Capel Curig, the A4086 for Caernarvon runs through the next gap, the sombre Pass of Llanberis, with the Glyders now on the right, and on the left Snowdon itself. Viewed from almost any angle, Snowdon is a magnificent mountain, worthy of its rank as the highest peak (3,560 feet) in Wales or England. Its summit forms the apex of six long ridges which radiate from it like flying buttresses. It is these – and one almost sheer precipice – that give the climber such wide scope, from the simple to the very difficult. The view from the top on a clear day is superb. It can be reached by rack-railway from Llanberis; but for those to whom such a course would be sacrilege, there are walking ascents from the two passes mentioned and from the third, Llyn Cwellyn, through which runs the road from Beddgelert to Caernarvon, A487. Beyond this lies our fourth group of mountains, the Hebogs, tapering down to the lower hills of Lleyn. South-east of these four, and spilling over into Merioneth, lie the blunt-topped Moelwyns and sharp-edged Moel Siabod.

Merioneth

Almost the whole of Merioneth lies above the six-hundred-foot contour, and where it joins with Montgomery and Denbigh on the Berwyn mountains its

The Chapel at Capel Curig   *J. Allan Cash*

average height above sea level is about two thousand feet. Yet everything is more genial than in Snowdonia – scenery, vegetation and people. The principal range of mountains, the Rhinogs, runs southwards along the coast from Tremadoc Bay, in the 'armpit' of Lleyn, to Barmouth. Flat-topped, their rolling moorland flanks are spangled with many small lakes. To the south their foothills face the stark precipices of Cader Idris across the Mawddach Estuary, and in turn the southern side of this great mountain (2,927 feet) confronts the slopes of Plynlimon across the Dovey Valley, boundary alike of Gwynedd, of the county, and of North Wales. The Cader Idris range forms the southern end of what has been called 'the Ring of Fire', an S-shaped chain of clearly volcanic mountains whose upper arm is formed by the four Snowdon ranges. The next link to Cader Idris is the sharp-featured Aran range, with peaks of almost three thousand feet. These run on into the Berwyns, which are hardly lower, though smooth and well-rounded – clearly of sedimentary origin. But before meeting the Berwyns, the volcanic chain sweeps north as the Arenigs, with Bala Lake in the cleft of the fork. Arenig Fawr (2,800 feet) is the highest of these. Northwards again (to join eventually with the Moelwyns on the county boundary) is a hilly but swampy region marked Migneint on the map. Its average height above sea level is about one thousand five hundred feet, and since it is crossed by only one main road (B4391) from Bala to Ffestiniog, the walker could hope for nothing better. He can go thirty miles or so north-north-eastwards from Dolgellau to Pentre Foelas, crossing only this one road, climbing six peaks averaging nearly two thousand four hundred feet, and bathing, if he wishes, in mountain lakes.

Lakes and Rivers

Snowdonia is sprinkled with lakes – from Bala, the biggest, four miles long, to innumerable llyns set like jewels among the mountains. There is at least one beside each road through the three great Snowdon passes. High on Migneint lies Llyn Conway, in which that most beautiful river has its source. The Dee, on the other hand, springs from a pallid marsh beneath the frowning precipice of Y Dault (the Black Height), one of the Arenigs. It flows through Bala Lake at the start of its long course to Chester. Snowdonia boasts innumerable 'beauty spots' – the Torrent and the Precipice Walks near Dolgellau, the Fairy Glen and the Conway Falls, near Betws-y-Coed, Pont Aberglaslyn, near Beddgelert – and lovely they are. But these are only a tiny proportion of the beauties to be found by anyone willing to leave the beaten track.

Anglesey

In contrast to the mainland, Anglesey has been almost levelled by erosion and by glacial action. The great ice-sheet left behind it a deposit of boulder-clay on which sprang up a thick forest of scrub oak. As this was gradually cleared, the land proved capable of growing heavy crops of grain. The men of Gwynedd could pasture their animals in the deep mountain valleys; but they needed Anglesey as their granary. Edward I conquered Wales by first taking the island and so starving the mainland of cereals. Until the opening of Telford's fine suspension bridge in 1826, the Menai Straits had to be crossed by ferry, a passage beset with dangerous currents causing whirlpools at certain states of the tide. From the bridge today one can look down on the blue-green water far below and see it streaked viciously with white. The richly wooded banks rising high on either side and the yachts moored off Beaumaris give the scene a Riviera-

Plas Newydd *Edwin Smith*

like quality. Inland, the scenery of Anglesey is not spectacular. But the coast-line is particularly attractive: low cliffs, indented with many small sandy bays, their headlands gay in spring with primrose, white campion, blue squill and sea-pink. The county town, Beaumaris, was founded in 1295, at the same time as its castle – one of the ring of great castles, Rhuddlan, Conway, Harlech and Caernarvon, with which Edward I encircled Gwynedd. Holyhead, the largest town, is much less picturesque. It stands on Holy Island, separated from Anglesey by a narrow estuary-like channel, noisy at low tide with the cries of wading birds. Only on Holy Island, in the cliffs near the South Stack lighthouse, is any grandeur to be found in Anglesey; but everywhere one is conscious of the magnificent backcloth of the mountains of Snowdonia beyond – seen nowhere better than from the domèd summit of Holyhead Mountain (720 feet) with the miniscule pattern of island scenery like a carpet at one's feet.

Industries, Towns and Recreations

Apart from the holiday trade, the main industry of the three counties is sheep farming, the animals being sent down from the mountains to winter in the milder climate and on the more fertile pastures of Anglesey and Lleyn. The woollen mill (or *pandy*) still flourishes in a few places. Roofing-slates are produced at Bethesda, Llanberis, Nantlle and Blaenau Ffestiniog; slab slate for billiard tables at Aberllefenni. A considerable amount of labour is employed by the Forestry Commission, whose activities have displaced many sheep-farms (and

Caernarvon Castle

displeased many beauty-lovers). Dolgellau, the county town of Merioneth, was once of importance for its wool market, situated as it is near the head of the lovely eight-mile Mawddach Estuary and at the junction of two mountain passes and no less than six main roads, including the A487 to Caernarvon and the A494 to Chester (both pioneered by the Romans). The latter goes through Bala, another important wool market and once famous for its stocking-knitters – men as well as women.

On the coast, apart from the four old garrison towns of Conway, Caernarvon, Beaumaris and Harlech, only two seaside resorts have been built to a definite plan – Llandudno and Portmeirion. The former, on a promontory just across the estuary from Conway, is a Victorian pioneer of town-planning; the latter, the fulfilment of a 20th-century architect's dream. Italianate in style, romantic, and beautifully situated in a wide ravine leading down to the sea, it is unique in Britain. Bangor, with its cathedral and University College of North Wales, is a good shopping-town and centre for exploration rather than a seaside resort. For the rest, almost any seaside taste can be satisfied somewhere along the long coastline of the three counties. Golfers will know that the course at Trearddur Bay in Anglesey is one of the best in Wales, and there are many others, not least that at Harlech. Climbers will stay at Llanberis, Capel Curig, Beddgelert, Pen-y-Gwryd or Pen-y-Pass, since all the principal climbs are in the four Snowdon ranges. Lovers of mountain scenery will add to this list such places as

294

CAERNARVONSHIRE, ANGLESEY AND MERIONETH

Dolgellau, Betws-y-Coed and many others. The archaeologist will not – despite Tacitus – expect to find traces of the Druids in Anglesey; but there and elsewhere he can see impressive remains of early man's activities from the Old Stone Age onwards.

As might be expected, the area is rich in wild life – so rich that relatively little can be mentioned here. In high Snowdonia the chough and the raven are to be seen, and the pied fly-catcher breeds in the old oak and birch woods. Redstart, wheatear and ring ousel are by no means uncommon. Among mammals, the beautiful pine marten is said still to exist, with the polecat, the red squirrel and the badger. Otters are plentiful in the large rivers – too plentiful to suit the salmon-fishers. There are brown trout in nearly all the mountain streams and lakes. The gwyniad, a rare member of the salmon family, is found only in Bala Lake, where he is seldom caught except by netting. Among plants, at least one, the Mountain Spiderwort, can be found nowhere else in Britain; while on the high, north-facing rock ledges of Snowdonia grows a wide variety of alpine plants which is presumed to have survived here since the last Ice Age. It includes the Purple and the Mossy Saxifrage, the Moss Campion and the Rose-root. Here, too, though not an alpine, grows the yellow Welsh Poppy. In addition to the Snowdonia National Park, there are two Nature Reserves in Anglesey, five in Caernarvonshire and eight in Merioneth. It is their united purpose to preserve all these beauties for future generations.

Glaslyn and Llyn Llydaw   G. Douglas Bolton

Some houses and gardens open to the public

Beaumaris Castle 7m NE of Bangor on A545 *Map* CG 37. *Moated fortress begun by Edward I; vaulted chapel; small dock for shipping, unaltered.*

Caernarvon Castle At Caernarvon *Map* CE 36. *13th to 14th cent., begun by Edward I; symbol of his authority in N Wales; birthplace of his son, the first Prince of Wales. Has polygonally angled towers. See especially the Eagle Tower and extensive town walls.*

Conway Castle At Conway *Map* CH 37. *13th-cent. triangular fortress; incomplete town walls, flanked by 21 towers and 3 twin-towered gateways.*

Criccieth Castle 7m NE of Pwllheli on A497 *Map* CF 33. *13th cent.; altered externally; notable gatehouse; fine views of Snowdon.*

Dolwyddelan Castle 4m SW of Betws-y-Coed on A496 *Map* CH 35. *12th-cent. keep enclosed with 13th-cent. stone curtain; traditional birthplace of Llewelyn the Great.*

Harlech Castle At Harlech *Map* CF 33. *13th cent., built by Edward I and captured by Owen Glendower; last castle in England & Wales to surrender to the Yorkists; notable gatehouse; extensive views of Snowdon and the Lleyn peninsula.*

Penrhyn Castle 1m E of Bangor off A5 *Map* CF 37. *Rebuilt in 19th cent. of mona marble. Incorporates part of a 15th-cent. fortified tower and is on the site of an 8th-cent. building, the home of the Welsh princes.* NT.

Portmeirion Off main road at Minffordd hamlet *Map* CG 33. *Gardens and original mansion, mid 19th cent. Private village dominated by Arnos Castle colonnade, campanile and domed pantheon.* Clough Williams-Ellis, Esq.

'Smallest' House, Conway. At Conway *Map* CH 37. *So-called 'smallest' house in Britain; mid-Victorian Welsh cottage interior.*

Books for further reading

Local history

T. P. ELLIS *The Story of Two Parishes, Dolgelley and Llanelltyd* 1928
C. J. EVANS *The Story of Caernarvonshire* 1928
E. A. LEWIS *Medieval Boroughs of Snowdonia* 1912
The History of Powys Fadog
H. J. OWEN *The Treasures of the Mawddach* 1950

Topography

H. R. C. CARR and G. A. LISTER *The Mountains of Snowdonia* 1948
W. M. CONDRY *Snowdonia National Park* 1966
H. L. V. WALES *North Wales* 1955

E. HYDE HALL *A Description of Caernarvonshire (1809–1811)* 1952
A. D. LEWIS *Anglesey* (Land of Britain Survey) 1941
J. E. LLOYD *Caernarvonshire* 1914
A. MORRIS *Merionethshire* 1913
R. SCOTT, B. CAMPBELL and F. J. NORTH *Snowdonia* 1949
Snowdonia (H.M.S.O. National Forest Park Guides) 1948

Architecture and Archaeology

An Inventory of Ancient Monuments: Anglesey 1937; *Caernarvonshire: East* 1956, *Central* 1960; *Merioneth* 1921
T. TELFORD *A Description of the Bridge over the Menai Straits*
K. WATSON *Regional Archaeology: North Wales* 1965

Gazetteer

CAERNARVONSHIRE ANGLESEY AND MERIONETH

Conway: Plas Mawr   *G. Douglas Bolton*

Aber *Caern.* (CG 37) (320). ¾ m. from a sandy beach, this unspoilt village is situated at the mouth of one of the loveliest glens* in the county, leading to the Aber Falls 2 m. away. At low tide it is possible to walk out across the Lavan sands almost as far as Beaumaris (*see below*).

Aberdaron *Caern.* (CB 32) EC Wed (1,280). A fishing village and resort, 2½ m. from Braich-y-Pwll, the westernmost extremity of the Lleyn Peninsula, which can be reached by a fine cliff walk. The old house of Y Gegyn Fawr was once a hostel for pilgrims on their way to St Mary's Abbey, the sparse remains of which can still be seen on Bardsey Island, across the Sound.

Aberdovey *Merion.* (CG 29) EC Wed (1,260). A golfing and seaside resort, with extensive sands, just inside the estuary of the R. Dovey, which here forms the boundary with Cardiganshire.

Abersoch *Caern.* (CD 32). *See* **Llanengan.**

Amlwch *Anglesey* (CE 39) EC Wed (2,910). In the first half of the 19th cent., the copper from the Parys mines, already known to the Romans, dominated the copper market of the world. Today the old workings provide a background to this little port, which, with nearby Bull Bay, is developing as a resort, with fishing and bathing. 1½ m. E the village church of **Llaneilian**, with its 12th-cent. tower and spire, has a finely-carved screen and rood-loft, and a curious chapel, connected to the church by a passage.

Bala *Merion.* (CK 33) EC Wed (1,600). A market town, with a Norman castle mound, at the point where the R. Dee issues from the largest natural lake in Wales, 3¾ m. long. At the far end of the lake, **Llanuwchllyn** is a favourite resort for fishermen, and a good point from which to climb the Aran Peaks, 5 m. S, the highest of which is nearly 3,000 ft.

Bangor *Caern.* (CF 37) EC Wed (13,980). City with cathedral and university. The first was once the much restored parish church; the second occupies modern buildings, completed in 1911, in Upper Bangor. In College Road is a museum of Welsh antiquities. 2 m. W is **Menai Bridge** (*see below*); and 1½ m. E is **Penrhyn Castle**, a 19th-cent. imitation of a Norman fortress, and open to the public.

297

Llanberis Pass

J. Allan Cash

Barmouth *Merion.* (CG 31) EC Wed (2,350). A popular resort with bathing, fishing and golf, standing on a narrow strip of land between sea and mountains. Across the lovely Mawddach Estuary is the sandy resort of **Fairbourne**. The church at **Llanaber**, 2 m. N (actually the mother church of Barmouth) is architecturally the most remarkable in Merioneth, having remained almost unaltered since its completion in 1250. Some 4 m. farther on, **Cors-y-Gedol** is the most impressive Tudor mansion in the county, with a fine gateway.

Beaumaris *Anglesey* (CH 37) EC Wed (1,960). Connected to Bangor by ferry, with views* across Conway Bay to the mountains of Caernarvonshire, this is now a dignified little residential town, with yachting and bathing. The County Hall and the Old Bull inn are 17th-cent., and there is a timbered house in Castle Street that dates from 1400. The church is noteworthy for its

monuments and some carved woodwork, but the moated castle (AM) dominates the town. Of its many features, the Great Hall and a little chapel in the central tower are most remarkable. **Penmon Priory** (AM), with its restored Norman church and dovecote, is some 5 m. away, at the extremity of the island.

Beddgelert *Caern.* (CF 34) EC Wed (760). Derives its name from the grave of the hound 'Gelert', slain by the Welsh prince, Llewelyn, in error. At the foot of Moel Hebog, and with Snowdon only 4 m. to the N, the village remains delightfully picturesque despite the summer traffic due to its position at the junction of three important roads. That to the NW climbs 500 ft. on its way to Caernarvon; a second, to the NE, follows the valley of Nant Gwynant, with its twin lakes; while the third leads to the Pass of Aberglaslyn, where the river forges its way to the S between pine-clad crags.

Betws-y-Coed* *Caern.* (CH 35) EC Thurs (780). Though much sought as a beauty spot, the 'Chapel in the Trees' in the valley of the R. Conway is still an enchanting place. The old church has a Norman font and an effigy of the grand-nephew of Llewelyn-ap-Gruffydd; and the bridge by which the Llanrwst road leaves the village has been there since the 15th cent. Three of the most visited spots in the neighbourhood are the Conway and Swallow Falls and the Fairy Glen. At the head of the Gwybernant valley, leading out of the valley of the Lledr, is **Ty Mawr**, the birthplace of Bishop Morgan, the first translator of the Bible into Welsh in the 16th cent. It is open to the public.

Caernarvon *Caern.* (CE 36) EC Thurs (9,000). The county town, but also a yachting centre and resort; it is one of the few places in the kingdom that still retain their city walls and towers (AM) almost intact. The castle, built by Edward I on the Menai Strait and moated on its landward side, covers some 3 acres; little more than the outward shell of its walls remains but its 13 towers and two gateways are impressive. To the SE, the Roman fort of **Segontium** may also be visited.

Capel Curig *Caern.* (CH 35) EC Wed (580). One of the best centres for exploring the mountains** of **Snowdonia**. 4 m. SW at **Pen-y-Gwryd**, and a mile farther on at the highest point of Llanberis Pass (1,169 ft.), are hotels known to rock-climbers throughout the country. From these last, one of the best routes to the top of Snowdon (3,560 ft.) leads past the mile-long Llyn Llydaw to the foot of the main precipices of the mountain. NW from Capel the main Holyhead road follows the rugged Nant Ffrancon Pass, between towering mountains, passing **Llyn Ogwen** and its water-falls at almost 1,000 ft. Here, on the opposite side of the road, a path leads to Llyn Idwal, an eerie spot, with the inaccessible Devil's Kitchen to the S.

Clynnog Fawr *Caern.* (CE 34) EC Wed (1,100). A whitewashed village between sea and mountain; the old collegiate church, rebuilt in the time of Henry VII, is notable for its porch and carved timber roof, rood-screen and stalls. In the N transept is the chest of St Bueno, who founded a monastery here in the 7th cent., and whose remains are in a chapel connected with the church by a passage.

Conway* *Caern.* (CH 37) EC Wed (11,390). One of the most attractive of all Welsh towns, and now a popular resort. From the ramparts of Edward I's romantic castle (AM), with its eight drum towers, are the splendid views of the town and the mouth of the river. The town walls (AM) form a circuit of more than a mile and include the three original gates, the best of which, Porth Uchaf, has both an inner and outer barbican. Of the many old buildings, Plas Mawr, built in 1573 and now headquarters of the Royal Cambrian Academy, has panelling and plaster ceilings, and a picturesque screen. 4½ m. SE, the gardens of the **Bodnant Estate**, beside the R. Conway, are open to the public.

Corwen *Merion.* (DA 34) EC Wed (2,220). On a lovely stretch of the R. Dee, at the northern end of the Vale of Edeyrnion, this little market town was once associated with Owen Glendower. 2 m. E, beyond Carrog station, is a wooded hillock, called Glendower's Mount; and some 200 yds. farther on are the remains of a moated building known as Glendower's Palace. On a hill N of the river from Corwen is Caer Drewyn, one of the best-preserved prehistoric stone ramparts in Wales.

299

Criccieth *Caern.* (CF 33) EC Wed (1,670). A sheltered seaside and golfing resort, facing across Tremadoc Bay to Harlech (*see below*). There are the ruins of a small castle, and Cefn Isaf (AM) is a noteworthy cromlech. At the pretty village of **Llanystumdwy**, 2 m. W, Lloyd George is buried in a mausoleum designed by Clough Williams-Ellis.

Dinas Mawddwy *Merion.* (CJ 31) EC Thurs. Till the time of Henry VIII the capital of the lordship of Mawddwy, this village, with its old pack-horse bridge across the Dovey, is today visited for its mountain scenery, extending to the N to the twin Aran peaks. The main road to Dolgellau climbs the Oerddrws Pass to 1,178 ft.; while a rougher road, leading NE to Bala by way of the Bwlch-y-Groes Pass, attains a height of 1,790 ft. with wonderful views all the way.

Dolgellau *Merion.* (CH 31) EC Wed (2,270). A severe little Welsh town of stone and slate, but magnificently situated in the valley of the Wnion, near the head of the Mawddach Estuary and 3 m. N of Cader Idris (2,937 ft.). Some idea of the splendour of the surroundings* is obtained from the Precipice and Torrent Walks. Of the 12th-cent. Cistercian Abbey of Cymmer, little remains but the restored Norman church. 2 m. SW, Gwernan Lake lies among the mountains; and 5 m. N is the lovely Ganllwyd Glen.

Dolwyddelan *Caern.* (CH 35) EC Thurs (710). The birthplace of Llewelyn the Great in 1194, now an isolated quarryman's village, stands on the R. Ledre, to the S of Moel Siabod (2,860 ft.). In the unrestored 16th-cent. church is a notable brass; farther up the valley the tower of the castle (AM), possibly pre-Norman, matches the ruggedness of the mountain.

Ffestiniog *Merion.* (CH 34) EC Thurs (6,680). Perched above the lovely Vale of Ffestiniog, through which flows the R. Dwyryd, there are a number of waterfalls in the neighbourhood of this village. The slate-quarrying for which the district became famous is mainly carried on at Blaenau Ffestiniog, 3 m. N. A nuclear power station, linked to a hydro-electric reservoir harnessing scheme, is at Trawsfynydd, 3 m. S.

Harlech *Merion.* (CF 33) EC Wed. Once the capital of Merioneth, and one of the historic towns of Welsh nationalism. Yet its splendid castle (AM), built on a rocky spur half a mile from the sea, is a place of lost causes. Though Glendower captured it in 1404, its fall led to his defeat five years later; it was the last place to hold out for the Lancastrians in 1468; and almost 200 years later it was the last Royalist castle in Wales to be captured by the Parliamentary forces. Today Harlech is the home of the adult educational centre, Coleg Harlech, and of the Royal St David's Golf Club.

Holyhead *Anglesey* (CC 38) EC Tue (10,410). The largest town on the island, owing its importance to the mail and passenger service to Ireland, which has been the principal route since prehistoric times. The church of St Cybi has 13th-cent. features, and the wall of the churchyard is probably Roman. Many visitors are drawn here by the cliff scenery near South Stack lighthouse, and the views at the top of Holyhead Mountain.

Llanberis *Caern.* (CF 36) EC Wed (2,330). A quarrying town, beautifully situated along the shore of Lyn Padarn, between which and the smaller Lyn Peris stands the solitary tower of Dolbadarn Castle (AM). At the end of the town is the station for the

Llandudno: the Little Orme

mountain-track railway to the top of Snowdon★ (3,560 ft.), while the road continues past Nant Peris (Old Llanberis), in a picturesque cluster of houses and a church, before starting the ascent through the most awe-inspiring of all the Snowdon passes★.

Llandudno★ *Caern.* (CH 38) EC Wed (17,850). A hundred years ago a mere village, what is today the largest and in some respects the pleasantest seaside resort and residential town in North Wales is splendidly situated on the bay lying between the Great and Little Orme headlands. At the top of the first, 679 ft. above the sea, is the little church of St Tudno; and the Marine Drive curves round the base of the promontory. The town is well laid out, with good shops and the Rappallo House Museum. A mile to the NW are remains of Gogarth Abbey; and 2½ m. E is Penrhyn Old Hall, a fine Tudor building.

Llanengan *Caern.* (CC 32) EC Wed (2,220). Overlooking the sandy beach of Porth Nigel, or Hell's Mouth, the church is worth visiting for its finely-carved screen and rood-loft. The bells are said to have been brought here from Bardsey (*see* **Aberdaron**). 3 m. S is Pencilan Head, the southern tip of the Lleyn Peninsula. 1 m. NE is the little yachting centre of Abersoch, with bathing and golf, from which expeditions can be made to the bird-haunted St Tudwal's Islands.

Llanegryn *Merion.* (CG 30) (590). At the W end of the picturesque Dysynni Valley, the church has a splendid carved rood-loft and screen; and the mansion of Peniarth, 1 m. E, possesses a collection of early Welsh manuscripts. The remarkable 'Bird Rock',Craig-yr-Aderyn, can be reached by an unclassified road, 4 m. NE of the village; and nearby are the foundations of the native Welsh castle, Castell-y-Bere.

Llanfairfechan *Caern.* (CG 37) EC Wed (2,860). A pleasant seaside resort,

in a wooded valley, mountains rising behind. Golf and bathing from sand and shingle beach.

Maentwrog *Merion.* (CG 34) EC Thurs (530). A pretty village in the Vale of Ffestiniog. In the yew-shaded churchyard may be seen the stone (maen) of Twrog, the 6th-cent. saint to whom the church is dedicated. Not far from the station is the Tomen-y-Mur, a castle mound, built by William Rufus within the site of a Roman camp. 3 m. S E, the road runs for some way along the great Trawsfynydd Reservoir, where there is good sport for fishermen.

Menai Bridge* *Anglesey* (CF 37) EC Wed (2,340). Here are two remarkable feats of engineering: Telford's suspension bridge completed in 1826 as a link in the mail-coach service to Holyhead, and widened nearly thirty years ago; and the tubular Britannia Bridge, built by Robt Stephenson in 1850 to carry the railway. The 90-ft. column standing on a hill is to the memory of the first Marquess of Anglesey, who was second-in-command at the battle of Waterloo, where he lost a leg. Plas-Newydd, the later 18th-cent. mansion belonging to the present Marquess, is occasionally open to the public. In the park are two fine dolmens; and 2 m. farther on, to the S W, is the chambered cairn, Bryn Celli Ddu (A M).

Nevin *Caern.* (CD 34) EC Wed (2,250). An ancient little town (Edward I held a tournament here in 1284), and now a seaside resort with bathing and sea-fishing. 4 m. N E are the twin peaks of the Rivals, on the lower slopes of which the road reaches a height of nearly 700 ft. at the quarrying village of **Llithfaen**. The lower of the two mountains (1,591 ft.) is crowned by an iron-age village of more than a hundred hut-circles.

Newborough *Anglesey* (CE 36) (840). Founded by Edward I, the little church here has many attractive features. The sandy warren, stretching southward to the sea, is now a nature reserve, and on the promontory of Llanddwyn Island are a lighthouse and traces of an abbey.

Penmachno *Caern.* (CH 35). The ruined Pandy Mill and nearby Machno Falls are worth visiting; so too is the church for a rare carved stone and what are regarded as the three earliest Christian tombstones.

Penmaenmawr *Caern.* (CH 37) EC Wed (3,750). There is bathing and golf at this resort beneath the great quarried headland of Penmaenmawr, rising 1,500 ft. out of the sea. Nearby is a Druid's circle, Maen Hirion (A M).

Pentraeth *Anglesey* (CF 37) EC Thurs (690). At Red Wharf Bay, a little to the N, are sands and excellent bathing. 4 m. S W the old Manor House of Penmynydd, with 18th-cent. additions, was the birthplace of Owen Tudor, whose grandson became Henry VII. 5 m. N is the unspoiled fishing village of **Moelfre.**

Portmadoc *Caern.* (CF 33) EC Wed (3,420). A small industrial town and slate-shipping port. There are bathing, golf and boating at Borth-y-Gest a mile to the S. At Tremadoc, to the N, Lawrence of Arabia was born at 'Woodlands'. Another attraction is the voluntarily-run light gauge Ffestiniog Railway, oldest of its kind in the world. **Portmeirion,** on a privately owned peninsula at the head of Tremadoc Bay, is a charming holiday resort, created by the architect Clough Williams-Ellis.

Pwllheli *Caern.* (CD 33) EC Thurs (3,640). A popular and growing resort, with golf, bathing and a small harbour.

Rhosneigr *Anglesey* (CD 37). A quiet little resort, with rocks and coves

Portmeirion   *Edwin Smith*

for bathing, a golf course, and sailing on Llyn Maelog. In a bay near **Aberffraw**, another small coastal village 3 m. SE, the tiny church of St Cwyfan stands on an island that is accessible at low tide.

Towyn *Merion*. (CF 30) EC Wed (4,470). The old village is some distance from Morfa Towyn, with its esplanade and miles of sands. The church, though partly modern, has a Norman nave and aisles, and a font of the same period, but its greatest pride is St Cadfan's Stone, seven feet long and inscribed on all four sides with 7th- or 8th-cent. characters that have not yet been fully deciphered. There is a light railway from Towyn to **Abergynolwyn**, some 7 m. NE; from which point the road, on the other side of the river, continues another 5 m. to the pretty lake of Tal-y-Llyn. The village here is an admirable point for the ascent of Cader Idris* (2,937 ft.), one of the grandest mountains in Wales.

Snowdon Range

Edwin Smith

The statue of Eros at Piccadilly Circus   *J. Allan Cash*

CONTENTS

LONDON
City and County

BY R. J. B. WALKER

Though no longer the biggest city in the world, London still holds elements that no other capitals possess.

The Royal Parks, for instance, are huge green spaces in the very heart of the town – 'the Lungs of London', Lord Chatham said. Most of the museums and art galleries are free. The City churches are unique. These range from the Saxon All Hallows-by-the-Tower and the 11th-century foundation of St John's – in the Tower itself, and one of the most perfect examples of Norman architecture in the country – to Wren's City churches, of which only a handful of the original fifty-two survived the War.

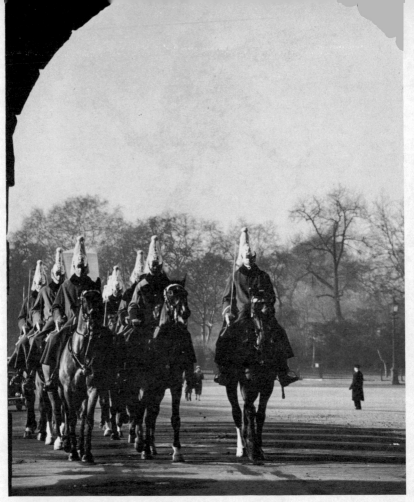

The Horse Guards Parade, Whitehall

Roman London should be explored, if only to see the remains of the Roman Wall.
And I think it is rewarding sometimes to climb to a high place on a fine day and review
the scene from a new angle. The Monument, St Paul's, Westminster Cathedral, the
Shell Centre, all give excellent panoramic views, though some are easier of ascent than
others. The Monument, we find, has 311 steps inside a narrow tube, whereas the
Shell Centre has a lift that shoots up 300 feet in 20 seconds.

London is no cosy market town to be seen in a couple of summer afternoons. It is
immense. Cobbett's description, 'the great wen', applies far more today than in 1821.
But London Transport and the river provide convenient ways of getting about. A
car is ideal for the backwoods of Eltham and Fulham, but, except at weekends, it is
of limited use in central London. The City and such places as the Inns of Court are
best explored on foot – with a 'sensible pair of shoes'. To reach these areas, some may
like to use their cars in spite of the traffic. But, travel as you will, there is much ground
to cover before you can claim, like Sam Weller, that your knowledge of London is
extensive and peculiar.

'Sir,' said Samuel Johnson, 'when a man is tired of London, he is tired of life;
for there is in London all that life can afford.'

Books for further reading

The 'feel' of London

JOHN BETJEMAN *Summoned by Bells* 1960
JAMES BOSWELL *London Journal 1762–3* ed. Pottle 1950
IVOR BROWN *A Book of London* 1961
RICHARD CHURCH *Over the Bridge* 1955; *The Golden Sovereign* 1957
DANIEL DEFOE *Moll Flanders* 1722; *A Tour Through London* 1725
CHARLES DICKENS *Pickwick Papers* 1836–7; *Oliver Twist* 1837–8; *Barnaby Rudge* 1841; etc.
SAMUEL PEPYS *Diary 1660–9* ed. Wheatley 1893–6
PETER QUENNELL ed. *Mayhew's London 1851* 1949
ALAN REEVE-JONES *London Pubs* 1962

Architecture

GERALD COBB *The Old Churches of London* 1948

NIKOLAUS PEVSNER *The Buildings of England: London* 2 vols. 1952–7
JOHN SUMMERSON *Georgian London* 1945

Current guide-books

F. R. BANKS *The Penguin Guide to London* (511 pages)
BLUE GUIDE TO LONDON (269 pages)
H.M. STATIONERY OFFICE *Guide to London Museums and Art Galleries* (128 pages)
WILLIAM KENT *London for Everyman* (270 pages)
WARD LOCK & Co. Ltd. *Red Guide* (287 pages)
LONDON TRANSPORT *Visitor's London* (147 pages)
DENYS PARSONS *What's Where in London* The BP Guide to Shops and Services. You can buy anything in London; this remarkable compilation tells you where.

ANCIENT MONUMENTS AND HISTORIC BUILDINGS

Apsley House, *Hyde Park Corner* (DE 38). Built by Adam for Lord Apsley (1771–8); bought by the Duke of Wellington from his brother in 1817. Contains a collection of Napoleonic War booty: plate, furniture, china, sculpture and pictures.

*The Banqueting House, *Whitehall* (EA 41). Sole fragment of Charles I's proposed Palace of Whitehall. It was designed by Inigo Jones, 1619, and served various uses until in 1890 Queen Victoria lent it to the United Service Museum. It is now being transformed back into a banqueting house.

Carlyle's House, *24 Cheyne Row* (DC 34). Here the Sage of Chelsea wrote most of his major works, 'an old dressing-gown around him, slippers on his feet, his face grim as granite. . . .' (NT).

Greenwich: the Cutty Sark   *J. Allan Cash*

Greenwich (G 3). In or near the Royal Park are: *The Queen's House*, designed by Inigo Jones. It contains part of the National Maritime Museum (*see* p. 314); note also the wrought-iron tulip staircase by Tijou. *The Royal Naval College* standing on the site of 'Placentia', the

**The Houses of Parliament
Clock Tower**   Reece Winstone

birthplace of Henry VIII and Elizabeth I, was made over by William and Mary as a hospital for disabled sailors. Inside are the *Painted Hall* with Thornhill's Baroque ceiling, and the *Chapel* with woodwork from Deptford Dockyard. The *Cutty Sark*, the last of the tea clippers, is now in permanent dry dock at the pier. *The Royal Observatory*, which marks the longitude of zero has been moved to Sussex, but in Greenwich it still contains a collection of early astronomical instruments.

Henry VIII's Wine Cellar, *Whitehall* (EA 41). A priceless survival of the Tudor Palace of Whitehall, with old brickwork and the original brick stillages along each wall.
Visitors require a pass from the Ministry of Public Building and Works, C.I.O. Branch, Lambeth Bridge House, S.E.1.

The Horse Guards, *Whitehall* (DH 41) is the headquarters of the Army London District and is historically associated with the Household Cavalry; the building

was designed by William Kent and completed by John Vardy in 1750–60. Changing of the Guard daily 11 (Sun 10).

*The Houses of Parliament, *Westminster* (EA 38). Known more properly as the New Palace of Westminster. After the Fire of 1834, when the Old Palace was razed to the ground, Barry and Pugin combined to build this masterpiece of the Gothic Revival. The foundation stone was laid in 1840.
Admission to sittings of the Commons is by application to a Member of the Admission Order Office.

The Jewel Tower, *Old Palace Yard* (EA 37). A moated tower (1365–6) forming, with Westminster Hall and St Stephen's Cloister, all that remains of the medieval Palace of Westminster. It was built by Edward III. Lately repaired and the moat stocked with fish.

Kenwood (D 5). Lord Chief Justice Mansfield's country house (Adam *c*. 1767), now contains the Iveagh Bequest of furniture and pictures. In summer the gardens are the scene of open-air concerts.

Lancaster House, *St James's* (DG 38) Begun by Wyatt for the Duke of York, 1825–9 (as York House), and finished by Smirke and Barry for the Duke of Sutherland, *c*. 1841 (as Stafford House). Has a splendid double staircase.

The Mansion House (EF 43). The Palladian residence of the Lord Mayor, built by George Dance, 1739–53.
Admission is by written application to the Lord Mayor's secretary.

Marlborough House, *Pall Mall* (DG 41). Once a royal residence, now the Commonwealth centre for conferences. Begun by Wren in 1709 as a town house for the Duke of Marlborough. It was the home of Queen Mary from 1936 until her death in 1953.

Old St Thomas's Hospital Operating Theatre, near *London Bridge Station* (EF 41). The attic of Southwark Cathedral Chapter House holds the last pre-Lister operating theatre, built in 1821.

Roman London can be studied in the London Museum, the Guildhall and the British Museum. The Temple of Mithras, excavated at Walbrook in 1954, has been moved to Queen Victoria Street; Roman-British tessellated pavements are in the Guildhall and the Crypt of St Bride's; exposed bastions of the Roman wall at the G.P.O., St Giles Cripplegate, the Tower, and W of All Hallows, London Wall.

*Royal Hospital, Chelsea (DD 35). Wren's secular masterpiece, in red brick and Portland stone, was founded by Charles II as a hospital for old soldiers.

**The Tower of London (EH 42). Begun by the Romans, rebuilt at the Conquest, this is a major work of military architecture. The moat is now drained and used as a drill-ground, but the buildings are still guarded by the Beefeaters, the Yeoman Warders of the Tower, in their traditional costume. The White, Beauchamp, and Bloody Towers, the Wakefield Tower (with the Crown Jewels), the Armouries and the Traitors' Gate, should not be missed. Parade service in the Chapel of St Peter ad Vincula on Sundays at 11 a.m.

**Westminster Hall (EA 37). A survival of the Old Palace of Westminster, remodelled by Richard II and his master-builder Henry Yevele (1394–1402). Remarkable timber roof by Hugh Herland, master carpenter to Edward III.

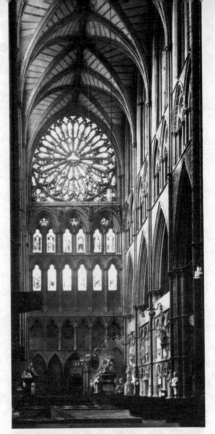

Westminster Abbey, towards the Poets' Corner   *Edwin Smith*

CHURCHES

All Saints', *Margaret Street* (DG 43). Designed by Butterfield and built (1849–59) for the Camden Society.

Brompton Oratory, *Brompton Road* (DC 37). Designed by Gribble and opened in 1884 by Cardinal Manning. Facing Brompton Road is the statue of Cardinal Newman (1801–90).

St Andrew Undershaft, *Leadenhall Street* (EG 43). Mostly early 16th cent., with 17th-cent. glass and a monument to John Stow (d. 1605), author of the first London guide-book.

309

St Anne's, *Limehouse* (F 4). Built by Hawksmoor 1712–24. A landmark for returning seamen. Contains the prize-winning organ from the Great Exhibition.

St Bartholomew-the-Great, *Smithfield* (ED 44). Worth visiting to recapture the atmosphere of a great 12th-cent. priory.

St Bride's, off *Fleet Street* (ED 43). Built by Wren 1670–84, with his most famous spire (1701). Gutted 1940, restored 1957 by W. Godfrey Allen in a style following closely the original intentions of Wren. Shows remains of a Roman burial ground.

St Clement Danes, *Strand* (EB 43). The R.A.F. church, built by Wren, steeple by Gibbs 1719, gutted 1941 and re-constructed 1958. The pavement is studded with badges of the R.A.F.

St Ethelburga's, *Bishopsgate* (EG 43). A tiny 15th-cent. church among the shop-fronts of Bishopsgate.

St Helen's, *Bishopsgate* (EG 43). Now hidden behind towering offices, St Helen's was founded as a Benedictine nunnery in the reign of King John.

St Luke's, *Charlton* (G 3). Near the Charlton Athletic football ground stands this attractive 17th-cent. village church. The grounds of Charlton House nearby are open daily.

St Margaret's, *Westminster* (EA 38). The parish church of the House of Commons, and the scene of many fashionable weddings.

**St Paul's Cathedral (EE 43). One of the great architectural masterpieces of Christendom; till recently its 365-ft. dome dominated London. The foundation stone was laid by Wren in 1675, the last stone by his son in 1710. The view of the interior from the Whispering Gallery reveals the cool spaciousness of Wren's design, the colour of the stone and the delicacy of the carving. Grinling Gib-bons's choir-stalls, the carved organ-case, the door-case in the S transept, Flaxman's statue of Nelson, and the extraordinary monument to Dr John Donne (1631) for which the poet posed in his shroud, are all worthy of attention. In the crypt is Wren's epitaph, *Si monumentum requiris circumspice*—'If you seek his monument, look around you'. Since the wartime air attacks, this famous building has been regarded by Londoners as a symbol of survival.

St Stephen's, *Walbrook* (EF 42). Wren's own model for St Paul's. Completed 1687, gutted 1941, re-consecrated 1954.

Spanish and Portuguese Synagogue, *Bevis Marks* (EG 43). Built in 1700–1 on the plan of the 1675 Sephardic Synagogue in Amsterdam. The interior is ablaze with candelabra and has remarkable furnishings by Wren's craftsmen.

**Westminster Abbey (EA 37), the Collegiate Church of St Peter, was founded, according to legend, by St Peter himself, who appeared to a Thames ferryman and warned him against fishing for salmon on Sundays. Of this foundation, and of Edward the Confessor's (*c.* 1050–65), nothing can be seen. The present building dates chiefly from Henry III (foundation stone 1245), who rebuilt the Confessor's church as a place of coronation and royal burial. Inside, the immediate effect is one of soaring height; the Henry VII Chapel, a triumph of 16th-cent. architecture, has no parallel in London. The Abbey is rich in sculptured monuments, and its Chapel of St Edward the Confessor holds the Coronation Chair, with the Stone of Scone. In the Norman crypt is a remarkable collection of wax funerary effigies representing people buried in the Abbey.

Westminster Cathedral, off *Victoria Street* (DG 37). A period mixture of early Byzantine and Italian Renaissance, by J. F. Bentley 1895–1903. Vast and of magnificent simplicity, it has been considered 'the finest church that has been built for centuries'.

CITY HALLS AND INNS OF COURT

There are 84 Livery Companies in the City. They exist to maintain trade standards at a high level and are all extremely active. The oldest is the Mercers, founded 1393; the newest is the Air Pilots, 1955. Few of the Halls survived the Fires of 1666 and 1940–1, but *Merchant Taylors'* (Threadneedle St) contains an undamaged 14th-cent. crypt, *Apothecaries'* (Blackfriars Lane) has a good 17th-cent. inner courtyard, *Vintners'* (Upper Thames St) an elaborate staircase and *Fishmongers'* (London Bridge) an impressive neo-Greek façade by Roberts and Scott, 1831–4. Permission to enter must be obtained from the Company's Clerk in each case.

The Inns of Court, legal communities originating from about 1300, should be explored at leisure. *Middle Temple* Hall has a double hammer-beam roof (16th cent.), *Temple* church (1185) is one of the five round churches in England built by the Crusaders, *Lincoln's Inn* has 'Paul before Felix' painted for the Old Hall by Hogarth. *Gray's Inn* garden has trees planted by Sir Francis Bacon. *Staple Inn* (no longer connected with the law) has a fine range of Elizabethan half-timbered houses.

The Inns of Court: King's Bench Walk, Temple   *Edwin Smith*

CONCERT HALLS AND EXHIBITIONS

Building Centre, *Store Street* (DH 44). An exhibition for everyone interested in buildings and their equipment.

Craft Centre, *Hay Hill* (DF 42). A constantly renewed exhibition of crafts, such as woodwork, musical instruments, bookbinding, calligraphy and engraved glass.

Design Centre, *Haymarket* (DH 42). The Council of Industrial Design's ever-varied display of goods chosen for their sound design.

Rospa House, *Hyde Park Corner* (DE 38). The Royal Society for the Prevention of Accidents. Models, diagrams, lectures, films – and machines to test your reaction-time as a driver.

Royal Albert Hall, *Kensington* (DB 38). The largest concert hall in London. Designed by Fowke and Scott. Queen Victoria laid the foundation stone in 1867. An annual feature is the promenade concerts, known familiarly as the Proms.

For details of concerts, public meetings, boxing, etc., *see* daily press and theatre agencies.

Royal Festival Hall, *South Bank* (EB 41). Designed by Martin and Matthew and built 1949–51 for the Festival of Britain. Its acoustics and sound insulation are scientifically planned. Good parking arrangements.
For details of concerts, ballets, etc., *see* daily press and theatre agencies.

Royal Horticultural Hall, *Vincent Square* (DH 36). Floral exhibitions are held here fortnightly by the Royal Horticultural Society.

Royal Opera House, *Covent Garden* (EA 43). Near St Paul's church by Inigo Jones stands this reconstruction (1856–8) by E. M. Barry of the old theatre by Smirke. Since 1846 Covent Garden has been used exclusively for opera and ballet.

Sadler's Wells Theatre, *Rosebery Avenue* (EC 46). Built originally on the site of a spring discovered by a Mr Sadler in 1683. The latest theatre, designed by Frank Marcham 1931 and conceived by Lilian Baylis as a North London counterpart to the Old Vic at Waterloo, now specializes in opera and ballet.

Georgian architecture in St James's Street　　　*Edwin Smith*

MARKETS

Food: *Billingsgate* (EG 42), wholesale for fish; *Covent Garden* (EA 42), flowers, fruit and vegetables; *Leadenhall* (EG 43), for poultry, ducks, geese and turkeys; *Smithfield* (ED 44), meat market, formerly the scene of St Bartholomew's Fair; *Spitalfields* (EH 44) and *Berwick Street* (DG 43), for fruit and vegetables.

General: *Borough* (EF 41); *Leather Lane* (EC 44); *Club Row* (EH 46), wkdays for dogs, cats, white mice, guinea pigs; *New Caledonian* (E 4), *North End Road* (C 3); *The Cut, Waterloo* (EC 38), wkdays; *Petticoat Lane* (EH 43); *Portobello Road* (C 4).

MONUMENTS AND OUTDOOR SCULPTURE

Albert Memorial, *Kensington Gardens* (DB 38). Designed by Sir George Gilbert Scott and erected 1863–76. The monument, by J. H. Foley, is to the Prince Consort, whose seated figure holds the catalogue of the Great Exhibition of 1851.

Cenotaph, *Whitehall* (EA 38). Designed by Sir Edwin Lutyens and built 1919–20. A memorial to the fallen of both world wars.

Charles I, *Whitehall* (EA 41). This equestrian statue is by Hubert Le Sueur, 1650; the pedestal is by Joshua Marshall from a design by Wren. Every year on 30th January, the date of Charles's execution outside the Banqueting House (*see* page 307), mourners lay a wreath at its foot.

Charles II, *Chelsea Hospital* (DE 34). This statue, by Grinling Gibbons or Arnold Quellin, is decorated with oak branches every year on Founder's Day, 29th May, to commemorate the Boscobel Oak escape in 1651.

Cleopatra's Needle, *Victoria Embankment* (EB 41). In the time of Thothmes III (*c.* 1500 B.C.) this stood before the Temple

References to London Maps

INNER LONDON

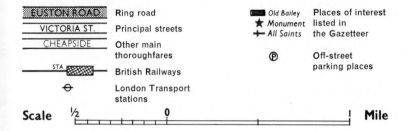

EUSTON ROAD	Ring road
VICTORIA ST.	Principal streets
CHEAPSIDE	Other main thoroughfares
STA	British Railways
⊖	London Transport stations

▬ Old Bailey	Places of interest listed in the Gazetteer
★ Monument	
✚ All Saints	
Ⓟ	Off-street parking places

Scale ½ — 0 — 1 Mile

OUTER LONDON

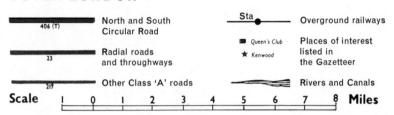

406 (T)	North and South Circular Road
23	Radial roads and throughways
217	Other Class 'A' roads

Sta ●—	Overground railways
▬ Queen's Club	Places of interest listed in the Gazetteer
★ Kenwood	
~~	Rivers and Canals

Scale 1 0 1 2 3 4 5 6 7 8 Miles

MAP REFERENCE SYSTEM

The motorist in London will find that, to guide him along the chief roads, clear signs have been set up by local authorities, the Ministry of Transport, the A.A. and R.A.C. These two maps, which are complementary to each other, give prominence to the sign-marked streets and roads that the motorist will be wise to follow.

All places listed in the Gazetteer are given map references, either two-character (D6) or four-character (DH42). The two-character references occur only in Map 1. All places with four-character references occur in Map 2, and some of these occur also in Map 1. For example:

> Alexandra Palace D6 is in Map 1 only
> Piccadilly Circus DH42 is in Maps 1 and 2
> Madame Tussaud's DE45 is in Map 2 only

PARKING FACILITIES

Central London has over a hundred large car parks and many authorized street parks. Very useful up-to-date leaflets and maps are provided by the A.A. and R.A.C. Free parking is indicated in the streets by a P on a blue background. Parking meters have been installed in many areas of London including Woolwich and Kingston. Garages are listed in the A.A. and R.A.C. publications. Hyde Park Underground Garage is always open. The system of one-way streets is daily subject to revision; the latest information on them can be obtained from the A.A. or R.A.C.

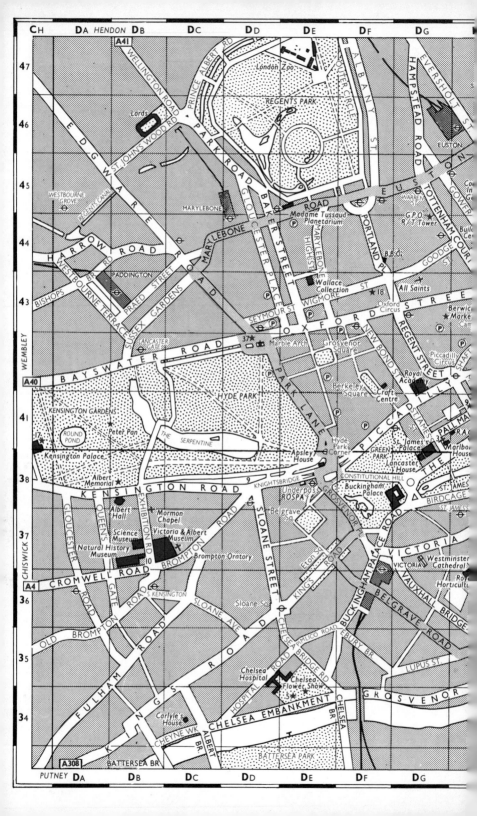

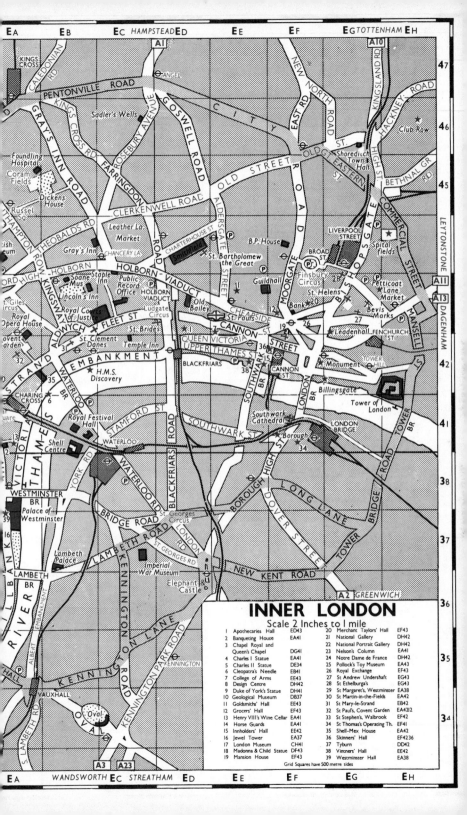

INNER LONDON
Scale 2 Inches to 1 mile

1	Apothecaries Hall	ED43	20	Merchant Taylors' Hall	EF43
2	Banqueting House	EA41	21	National Gallery	DH42
3	Chapel Royal and		22	National Portrait Gallery	DH42
	Queen's Chapel	DG41	23	Nelson's Column	EA41
4	Charles I Statue	EA41	24	Notre Dame de France	DH42
5	Charles II Statue	DE34	25	Pollock's Toy Museum	EA43
6	Cleopatra's Needle	EB41	26	Royal Exchange	EF43
7	College of Arms	EE43	27	St Andrew Undershaft	EG43
8	Design Centre	DH42	28	St Ethelburga's	EG43
9	Duke of York's Statue	DH41	29	St Margaret's, Westminster	EA38
10	Geological Museum	DB37	30	St Martin-in-the-Fields	EA42
11	Goldsmiths' Hall	EE43	31	St Mary-le-Strand	EB42
12	Grocers' Hall	EF43	32	St Paul's, Covent Garden	EA42|2
13	Henry VIII's Wine Cellar	EA41	33	St Stephen's, Walbrook	EF42
14	Horse Guards	EA41	34	St Thomas's Operating Th.	EF41
15	Innholders' Hall	EE42	35	Shell-Mex House	EA42
16	Jewel Tower	EA37	36	Skinners' Hall	EF42|36
17	London Museum	CH41	37	Tyburn	DD42
18	Madonna & Child Statue	DF43	38	Vintners' Hall	EE42
19	Mansion House	EF43	39	Westminster Hall	EA38

Grid Squares have 500 metre sides

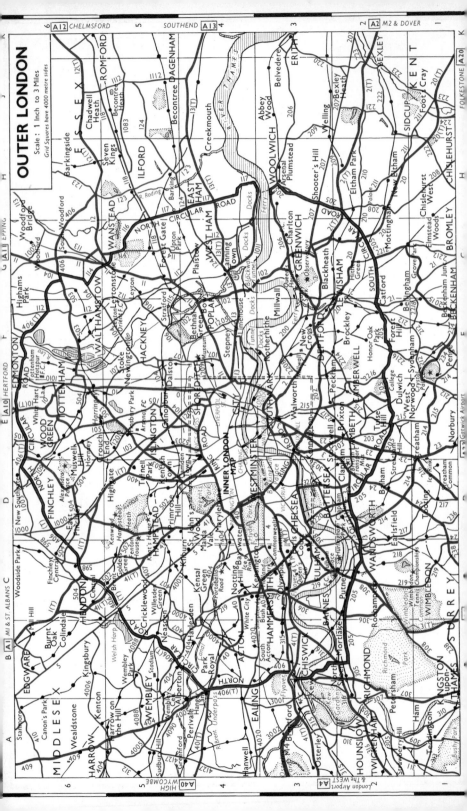

At the foot of Nelson's Column, Trafalgar Square   *Edwin Smith*

at Heliopolis with its companion obelisk, now in New York. Presented to Britain by the Egyptian Government, it was nearly lost in the Bay of Biscay, but was finally erected on its present site in 1878.

Epstein's London Statues are *Rima* (Hyde Park), *Night* (55 Broadway), the *Madonna and Child** in Cavendish Square (Convent of the Holy Child) and the group at Edinburgh Gate, Knightsbridge.

Marble Arch (D D 42), originally Nash's back entrance to Buckingham Palace (1828), was moved to its present position in 1851. The whole area was reconstructed in 1963. Nearby is Speakers' Corner where, at week-ends, orators speak freely on any subject of their choice. For *Tyburn see* this page.

The Monument, *Fish Street Hill* (E G 42). Wren's Doric column (1671–7) near Pudding Lane, where the Fire began in 1666, is 202 ft. high and has 311 steps spiralling to the balcony.

Nelson's Column, *Trafalgar Square* (E A 41). The monument to Admiral Lord Nelson was the result of a compromise made at a competition in 1838, Railton winning first prize with a Corinthian column, Baily second prize with a figure of Nelson. The lions are by Landseer. The monument is 170 ft. 2 in. high.

Tyburn, *Marble Arch* (D D 42). The gallows known as 'Tyburn Tree' was the scene of public executions from 1196 to 1783.

MUSEUMS AND ART GALLERIES

Bethnal Green Museum, *E.2.* (F 4). A branch of the Victoria and Albert Museum (*see* page 315), with a collection of dolls' houses, period costumes and the local Spitalfields silk.

**British Museum (E A 44). Holds the National Library (6,000,000 volumes) and other collections of inexhaustible interest. See especially the Egyptian Galleries, the Elgin Marbles, the King's Library and the Edward VII Gallery. The Reading Room is for use by ticket-holders only, but the public may, on application, view it from the doorway. The Trustees' *Guide to the British Museum*, 2/–, is extremely helpful.

Commonwealth Institute, *Kensington High Street* (C 3). A tent-shaped building by Matthew and Johnson-Marshall, 1962, designed to spread knowledge of life in the Commonwealth. *See Marlborough House,* page 308.

Courtauld Institute Galleries, *Woburn Square* (D H 45), contains Samuel Courtauld's collection of French Impressionists, bequeathed to London University.

Dulwich College Picture Gallery, *Dulwich* (E 2). Designed by Sir John Soane (1814) and set in a garden, it contains an excellent collection of paintings, chiefly English, Flemish and Dutch.

313

National Gallery

Fenton House, *Hampstead Grove* (C 5). A William and Mary brick building, 1693, with a collection of early musical instruments and some fine china (NT).

Foundling Hospital, *40 Brunswick Square* (EA 45). Only the gateway of the original 1739 foundation remains, but in the Court Room (a 1937 copy of the original) are pictures by Hogarth, Reynolds and Gainsborough.

Geological Museum, *Exhibition Road* (DB 37), explains the principles of geology by dioramas representing places in many parts of the world.

Imperial War Museum, *Lambeth Road* (EC 37). Built on the site of Bedlam Hospital, this collection records warfare in all aspects since 1914.

Keats House, *Hampstead* (D 5). John Keats shared this little Regency house with his friend Charles Brown and the family of Fanny Brawne. Under a plum tree in the garden, Keats composed the *Ode to a Nightingale.*

*London Museum, *Kensington Palace* (CH 41). Illustrates the social life of London from flint implements to Queen Victoria's dolls.

**National Gallery, *Trafalgar Square* (DH 42). This incomparable collection represents all schools of European painting from the 13th to the 19th century. Publications include a guide (1/6), a summary catalogue of the collection (5/–) and for each school an admirably detailed volume.

*National Maritime Museum, *Greenwich* (G 3), has a collection of portraits, seascapes, ship models, navigating instruments, books, prints and manuscripts.

*National Portrait Gallery, *St Martin's Place* (DH 42), illustrates British history with a matchless collection of portraits.

Natural History Museum, *Cromwell Road* (DB 37), built by Waterhouse (1865–80), contains the national collection of animals and plants and one of the finest natural history libraries in the world.

Pollock's Toy Museum, *44 Monmouth Street* (EA 43). 'If you love art, folly and the bright eyes of children, speed to Pollock's', wrote R. L. Stevenson in 1887. Pollock's is still a treasure-house of toys.

Public Record Office, *Chancery Lane* (EC 43), is the home of the national

314

archives, accumulated since the Conquest and including *Domesday Book*, two 13th-cent. editions of *Magna Carta* and the log of H.M.S. *Victory* at Trafalgar.

*Queen's Gallery. *See* **Buckingham Palace** this page.

Royal Academy of Arts, *Piccadilly* (DG 42). Founded by George III in 1768, with Reynolds as first President. Summer Exhibition (May–Aug) of works by living artists; Winter Exhibition (Nov–Mar) usually of Old Masters. Special exhibitions in the Diploma Gallery. Admission charges and times vary; they can be seen on the Piccadilly entrance notice board.

Science Museum, *Exhibition Road* (DB 37). The national museum to illustrate, by working models and daily lectures, the growth of physical science and its application to industry.

Soane Museum, *13 Lincoln's Inn Fields* (EB 43). Built by Sir John Soane as his private house (1812–14). It contains Hogarth's *Rake's Progress* and a very large collection of architectural drawings.

*Tate Gallery, *Millbank* (EA 36). The national collection of British and modern foreign painting and modern sculpture. The English schools are strongly represented and include many works by Blake and Turner. Special exhibitions are held almost continuously. *Open* wkdays 10–6, Sun 2–6.

*Victoria and Albert Museum, *Cromwell Road* (DB 37), holds a remarkable collection of applied art from all countries and periods. Still more notable are the Raphael cartoons and the English water-colours. Chamber music concerts are held on Sunday evenings.

*Wallace Collection, *Manchester Square* (DE 43), holds the Hertford family pictures; furniture and porcelain, mostly French; and works by Gainsborough, Reynolds and Bonington.

PALACES AND OTHER ROYAL RESIDENCES

Buckingham Palace (DF 38). Built by the Duke of Buckingham and Chandos on a site occupied by James I's mulberry orchard; bought by George III in 1761; altered by George IV in 1826–30 (Nash), by William IV and Queen Victoria in 1830–47 (Blore) and by George V, who

On parade for Buckingham Palace

J. Allan Cash

refaced the East Front in 1913 (Aston Webb). Queen's Gallery (selection from the Royal Picture Collection). Changing of the Guard daily. Admission to Royal Mews (stables, riding school, state coach), is by written application to the Superintendent.

Eltham Palace, *Court Road* (H 2). A royal residence from Edward II to Henry VIII. Its only remains are the Great Hall with hammer-beam roof (*c.* 1479), the bridge across the moat and a view of the North Downs.

Fulham Palace, *Bishop's Avenue* (C 3). Residence of the Bishops of London since 691. The gardens are sometimes open in summer.

Kensington Palace, *Broad Walk* (CH 41). The elegant brick residence of William and Mary, Queen Anne and the first two Georges. The orangery to the north was built in 1705 by Wren and Vanbrugh.

For **London Museum** *see* page 314.

Battersea Park Fun Fair Edwin Smith

Lambeth Palace, *Lambeth Bridge* (EB 37). London residence of the Archbishops of Canterbury since the early 13th century. Mainly medieval inside, but contains a 17th-cent. hall converted by Blore *c.* 1830 into a library. The gardens are sometimes open in summer.

St James's Palace (DG 41), was built by Henry VIII on the site of a 13th-cent. leper colony, the Sisters of St James in the Fields. The Chapel Royal (ceiling sometimes attributed to Holbein), was the scene of Charles I's last Holy Communion on the morning of his execution in 1649.

The Palace of Westminster. *See* page 308.

PARKS AND GARDENS

Battersea Park (DE 33). The Festival Gardens, designed by John Piper and Osbert Lancaster in 1951, contain a fun fair, a boating lake, open-air sculpture and an illuminated tree-walk.

Green Park (DF 41), a triangle of elm trees and grassy undulations, is bounded by Piccadilly, Hyde Park Corner, Constitution Hill and the Queen's Walk.

Hampstead Heath (D 5), is one of London's highest (440 ft.) and healthiest open spaces. Three famous inns – the Spaniards, Jack Straw's Castle and the Bull and Bush – stand within easy reach. Bank Holiday Fairs on the heath are famous for their Cockney abandon.

Holland Park (C 3) has an orangery and a Dutch garden where concerts are given in summer. The Jacobean house, once the home of Charles James Fox, was bombed in 1941 but has been restored and is now a youth hostel.

Hyde Park and Kensington Gardens (DD 41), form a green expanse between Park Lane and Kensington Palace. *Hyde Park* is named after the Manor of Hyde, a possession of Westminster Abbey from the Conquest to the Dissolution. Beyond the dividing road carried across the Serpentine by the Rennie bridge, *Kensington Gardens* contain the Flower Walk, the Albert Memorial (*see* page 312), the Sunk Garden, the Peter Pan statue and the Round Pond.

Rowing on the Serpentine and swimming in the Lido.

Regent's Park (DE 46), surrounded by terraced houses, is the culmination of Nash's plan to link Primrose Hill to Buckingham Palace. It has boating, bathing, sports, Shakespeare at the open-air theatre, a water-lily pond, Queen Mary's Gardens and the Zoo (*see* page 318).

St James's Park (DH 38), like the Palace (*see* page 316), takes its name from the leper colony that once stood on the banks of the Tyburn. Now, the public roams here among flowers and wildfowl.

SPECIAL ITEMS

B.P. House, *E.C.*2. (EF 44). The head quarters of the world-wide British Petroleum Company.

Members of the public are admitted by special permission only.

A famous inn: the George, Southwark *G. Douglas Bolton*

H.M.S. Discovery, *Victoria Embankment* (EB 42), was launched in 1907, the first British ship to be fitted out exclusively for scientific polar research. Scott took her to the Antarctic for his assault on the South Pole in 1912. She is now recruiting headquarters for the Royal Navy and Royal Marines.

G.P.O. Radio and Television Tower, *Howland Street* (DG 44). 620 ft. to the mast-top. Designed by Eric Bedford, chief architect of the Ministry of Public Building and Works, as part of a national communications scheme. Its revolving restaurant will give a view of London that completes the circle every half hour.

Inns and Public Houses. *The George,* Southwark (NT) is the last galleried inn in London; Shakespeare acted in the courtyard. *The Old Wine Shades,* 6 Martin Lane, is a survival of the Fire of 1666. *The Printer's Devil,* Fetter Lane, has specimens illustrating the history of typography. *The Sherlock Holmes,* Northumberland Street, contains a reconstruction of the Baker Street consulting room. *Ye Olde Cheshire Cheese,* 145 Fleet Street, has Johnson and Goldsmith associations and 'pudding' daily in winter. *The Prospect of Whitby,* Wapping, is an old riverside inn that provides excellent food.

Law Courts (EC 43) and the **Old Bailey** (ED 43). Both Courts are open during sessions, but seating capacity is limited.

Madame Tussaud's, *Marylebone Road* (DE 45). Founded in Paris to portray victims of the French Revolution. Since then it has become an exhibition of waxworks famous everywhere.

The Planetarium, *Marylebone Road* (DE 45). A projector under the dome represents the night sky with an uncanny sense of reality.

Royal Exchange, *Bank* (EF 43). A 16th-cent. foundation. The chimes, restored after the 1939 War, play fourteen English, Scottish or Welsh tunes, 'The Maple Leaf for Ever' and 'Waltzing Matilda'.

Shell Centre, *South Bank* (EB 41), the HQ of the Shell International Petroleum Co. Ltd, rises 351 ft. above street level. From the 25th floor you may see as far as Windsor Castle and even Cambridge.

Shell-Mex House, *Strand* (EB 42). Bearing the biggest clock in London, the HQ of Britain's largest distribution organization, Shell-Mex and B.P. Ltd, contribute a stately landmark to the north bank of the Thames.
Members of the public are admitted by special permission only.

Tours of London. *Coaches* leave Victoria Coach Station daily in summer for guided tours of the West End, the City, London Airport, the East End, and outlying places like Windsor, Knole and Luton Hoo. *River cruises* during the summer leave Westminster Pier for the Tower, Greenwich, Battersea, Kew, Richmond and Hampton Court. Special cruises to the Pool of London area, and round the Docks are made from Tower Pier. Time-tables can be obtained from the Coach Station or Westminster Pier.

The Zoo, *Regent's Park* (DE 47), more properly called the Gardens of the Zoological Society of London, was founded in 1826 by Sir Stamford Raffles and Sir Humphry Davy. Many of the cages and enclosures are being reconstructed to improve the occupants' accommodation and to enhance the appearance of the gardens.
No dogs are allowed inside. There is a car park at the main entrance.

SPORT

For Sport in general the main centres are Alexandra Park (D 6), Crystal Palace (F 1), Earls Court (C 3), Wembley (B 5) and the White City (C 4).

Association Football. The Cup Final has been played at Wembley Stadium since 1923. London professional clubs, with their grounds, are: *Arsenal*, Highbury (E 5); *Brentford*, Griffin Park (A 3); *Charlton Athletic*, The Valley (G 3); *Chelsea*, Stamford Bridge (C 3); *Crystal Palace*, Selhurst Park; *Fulham*, Craven Cottage (C 3); *Leyton Orient*, Brisbane Road (F 5); *Millwall*, New Cross (F 3); *Queen's Park Rangers*, Loftus Road (C 4); *Tottenham Hotspur*, White Hart Lane (F 6); *West Ham United*, Upton Park (G 4).

Athletics. Most of the international matches, the University Sports and the Amateur Athletic Championships, take place at the White City (C 4). Other stadiums are at Chiswick, Motspur Park and Hurlingham (C 2). The 1948 Olympics were held at Wembley.

Cricket. County and Test Matches at Lord's, the M.C.C. and Middlesex C.C. ground (D B 46), and the Oval, the Surrey C.C. ground (E B 34).

Golf. Public 18-hole courses are at Hainault Forest, Mitcham, Richmond Park (B 2) and Beckenham Place Park (G 1).

Greyhound Racing in London is chiefly at Harringay (E 6), New Cross (F 3), Wembley (B 5) and White City (C 4). See the evening papers.

Horse Racing. The chief racecourse near London is at Epsom, where the Derby is run. Other courses are at Alexandra Park, Kempton Park, Ascot, Sandown and Windsor.

318

Rowing. Putney to Mortlake is the principal course. On this are rowed the Oxford and Cambridge Boat Race and the Head of the River Race, both just before Easter, the Wingfield Sculls and the Head of the River Sculls.

Rugby Football. International matches, the University match and the Service championships are played at Twickenham, the headquarters of the Rugby Union (A 2). London Clubs, with their grounds, are: *Harlequins*, Twickenham (A 2); *Blackheath*, Rectory Field (G 3); *Richmond* and *London Scottish*, Richmond (B 2); *London Welsh*, Richmond Old Deer Park (B 2); *Rosslyn Park*, Roehampton (B 2); and *Wasps*, Sudbury (A 5).

Skating at Queensway (C 4), Earls Court (C 3), Richmond, and the Silver Blades at Streatham (D 1).

Swimming. The London Swimming Championships are held at Parliament Hill in July.

Tennis Rackets, etc. The All-England Lawn Tennis Championships have been played at Wimbledon since 1877; on the new ground (C 1) since 1922. Real tennis, and rackets, squash and fives are played at the Queen's Club, Lord's, Hampton Court, Dulwich and many West End clubs.

INDEX

LONDON

Opposite: Detail from the original painting by Rowland Hilder.

Over the myriad lives of London, 'ships, towers, domes, theatres, and temples lie', no longer 'open unto the fields', but open still to the sky's kaleidoscope of greys and blues. From the Shell-Mex building on the Strand, we can gaze down at the bridges of Westminster and Lambeth, and can watch Big Ben shine out the time; nearer, Hungerford footbridge, running beside the railway bridge, leads from Charing Cross to the grounds of the Festival Hall.

ROWLAND HILDER

The Great Bed of Ware

V&A museum

G.B.S.
BY
JOSEPH COPLANS

The Grand Union Canal near Berkhamsted

J. Allan Cash

MIDDLESEX AND HERTFORDSHIRE

AN INTRODUCTION BY MICHAEL ROBBINS

Middlesex and Hertfordshire are natural partners – London's two northern Home Counties. Middlesex is *the* Home County, whose heart was torn out to form the nucleus of the County of London in 1888. More recently, in 1965, it was officially effaced from the map (except as a postal address) by being made part of Greater London. It seems safe to prophesy, however, that Middlesex, after more than a thousand years of existence, will no more be effaced from the minds of Englishmen than was Wessex (which officially disappeared nine hundred years ago). Hertfordshire lies beyond, gently sloping up to the Chiltern escarpment where the land falls away to the great East Midland plain. They go together the more naturally because the border between them corresponds to no strongly-marked geographical feature – indeed, Middlesex was cut back in an artificial and at some places rather puzzling way when the shire of Hertford was created about A.D. 1000.

Fifty years ago the words 'Home Counties' conveyed a picture of undulating country, leafy lanes, cheerful cottages and well-kept big houses, their own local – mainly agricultural – activities encouraged by the spending of money made in the metropolis, in accordance with the centuries-old English practice of putting into the country (some parts of it, at any rate) the profits of commercial

Opposite: Detail from the original painting by S. R. Badmin.

Along the Chiltern side of London lie these two counties, which still have fields and lanes. Suggesting in the foreground Harrow and the Great Bed of Ware, the picture shows, across the Thames, the magnificence of Hampton Court. The centuries are bridged by the likenesses of two acute thinkers: Bacon, who in 1621 was created Viscount St Albans, and Bernard Shaw, whose ashes were scattered in the garden of his house at Ayot St Lawrence.

Syon House, Isleworth

activity in the towns. Today, these counties are more often thought of as mere obstacles which tiresomely separate the city-dweller from countrysides farther away, where ancient peace and the like are not disturbed by suburban nastiness. They get dismissed with a new sneer-word, 'subtopia' – a word as barbarous as the evil it was devised to describe: the mess of brick, concrete, wires and gaudy lights that creeps like an eczema outwards from the great cities of Britain, along the highways, and into the green lanes and little towns that many people choose to regard as the *real* England. This disease has infected parts – far too many parts – of Middlesex and Hertfordshire; but it is silly to dismiss this historic region, where much natural and much man-made beauty is to be found, as a mere suburban muddle, the untidy fringe of the London conurbation – places fit only to be by-passed. On the contrary: there are in them scenes of a special kind which, though they need to be sought out, are just as rewarding as the more obvious natural beauties and rustic retreats of places more distant from London.

The Land

The prime geographical feature of Middlesex and Hertfordshire is that they lie within the Thames basin, on the northern half of the great saucer-like chalk formation that is seen on the surface as the Chiltern Hills in the north and the North Downs to the south. The chalk is overlaid by later deposits – clay, boulders, gravels and alluvium, in that order from north to south – over the southern part of Hertfordshire and virtually all of Middlesex. The Chiltern ridge frowns down from its escarpment that runs from Tring past Dunstable and Hitchin to Royston, with a south-of-England frown that might count elsewhere as a smile. The ancient Icknield Way runs along the foot of the scarp; and the Chiltern line is broken by three significant gaps, near Tring, Luton and Hitchin, all of them used by main roads and railway lines – the Tring gap by the Grand Junction Canal as well. Seen from London, these counties subtend an arc running from Bristol clockwise right round to the Wash; so travellers and goods on their way between London and most of Britain have to pass through one or both of them.

The Chiltern ridge itself has some bold, bare, down-like features; Ivinghoe Beacon is the finest. To the south is a fairly broken country, well wooded, with a pleasing variety of scene, and occasional deeper cuts made by river valleys, which have caused the railways to throw up viaducts – the noble work at Welwyn is all to cross the trifling Mimram stream. Nearer to London comes the clay plain, especially where the Colne flows sluggishly south-west from St Albans and the Lea winds sinuously out past Hertford and Ware. In this part of the region come Hertfordshire's finest monuments – the abbey of St Alban, the country houses of Hatfield, Gorhambury, Moor Park, Panshanger, Brocket, Knebworth.

Clay lies all over north Middlesex, from the line of the Uxbridge Road past Ealing and Southall round to the late-enclosed wilderness of Enfield Chase. The clay is overtopped with hills of Bagshot sands at Harrow and the Hampstead-Highgate ridge which runs out to Wood Green, and there is a long tongue of boulder-material pushed forward in front of the ice-cap running down through Barnet and Finchley. Most of the clay belt was formerly meadow-land, with little arable: hay was the principal Middlesex crop. Farthest south, and latest in geological time, comes the alluvium of the Thames itself. The finest market-garden soil in the country used to be worked on this alluvium in the great loop of the river that stretches from Staines to Isleworth. Later, the brick-earths of the district provided the London stock-bricks with which scores of thousands of London houses, from Buckingham Palace downwards, were built. After that, the south Middlesex plain yielded gravel for mixing into concrete for roads and other requirements of the modern age. Now this wonderful soil grows suburban houses and factories – and an airport; and in between the Roads and Ways and Crescents and Closes lie the three finest Middlesex houses – Hampton Court, Syon and Osterley.

Occupations

Over two and a quarter million people lived in Middlesex and over 881,800 in Hertfordshire at the 1961 census; sixty years before, the figures were almost 800,000 and just over 250,000. More people live in the borough of Harrow than in the city of Plymouth; Middlesex numbers nearly as many people as Wales; Hertfordshire's population has increased by thirty-six and a half per cent – faster than any other county – in the decade 1951–1961.

All this means one thing: rapid change. Development, migration, settlement have been moving on at top speed. This mainly reflects the surge of employment within and close to London during the 20th century. London has never ceased to be the largest industrial centre in Britain (meaning by 'industry' all kinds of productive work, including services, and not confining the word to manu-factures), and people who work in London have been living outside it for many years. What we now call 'commuting' to town was already beginning from some Middlesex villages in the 17th century, though others, like Ruislip in the north-west, were virtually cut off by atrocious roads until much later times. From the arrival of the railways in the 1840s, the provision of houses and services for Londoners became a staple industry for Middlesex; and the flood of houses was slopping over the Hertfordshire fringes, as at Barnet and Rickmansworth, before 1900. Then, between the wars, the garden cities of Letchworth and Welwyn, established in 1903 and 1920, began inroads into Hertfordshire acres which proved a mere curtain-raiser to the New Towns developments of the

1950s: these have dumped three virtually new communities of 60,000 people each at Hemel Hempstead, Stevenage and Hatfield/Welwyn Garden City. These New Towns differ from the earlier 'Garden Suburb' at Hampstead (really in Hendon and Finchley, Middlesex) and the London County Council's housing estates at Tottenham, Burnt Oak and Headstone Lane (Harrow) by trying hard to bring employment with them. Employment in London is the reason why very many people live in the surrounding counties; but they also have large and growing activities on their own soil.

Middlesex has two very large industrial areas: one between Hendon and London Airport, concentrating on many kinds of consumer goods (especially food) and light to medium engineering; the other from Tottenham up the Lea valley and over into Hertfordshire, with many and various industries, especially furniture and metal products. In Hertfordshire, Watford thrives on printing and brewing; Welwyn Garden City has its factory quarter; Stevenage and Hemel Hempstead New Towns can show their due proportion of local industrial employment. Aircraft and their components are an important part of this activity. But agriculture, in its modern mechanized form, holds its important place in Hertfordshire: the most specialized kind of all, market-gardening under glass, has its British origin and centre in the Lea valley round Waltham Cross and Cheshunt. Agriculture as an industry no longer flourishes (indeed, it hardly exists) in Middlesex, though some special garden crops are raised – as they should be in the county that gave Mr Cox's Orange Pippin to the world. But back-gardeners and allotment-holders produce (so it is argued) as much nutriment in the form of fruit and vegetables

Looking downstream at Teddington G. Douglas Bolton

Chiswick House

as was formerly yielded by commercial farming – which must be our consolation for the lost picturesqueness of the hayfield and the harvest-home.

The Record of the Past

What is the historical backdrop of this animated scene? And what has the past left for today's traveller to look at with pleasure and, let us hope, understanding? Prehistoric remains are in museums, and comparatively unimportant. The Iron Age can show three camps – at Wheathampstead, capital of Cassivelaunus, the Belgic king who opposed (and was not defeated by) Caesar in 54 B.C.; its successor at Verulamium, near St Albans; and a settlement at Welwyn. Verulamium, still being excavated, provides the most elaborate Roman site – it was indeed the only *municipium* of Roman Britain. There is also a small villa at Moor Park. In Middlesex, objects of Roman date have been found in some quantities at Brentford and Brockley Hill (Stanmore); but in both counties the roads are the most impressive things the Romans left: the western road from London to Staines; Watling Street, down the Edgware Road to St Albans and Dunstable; Ermine Street, through Tottenham and Enfield to Ware, Buntingford and Royston; Akeman Street, through Berkhamsted and Tring; Stane Street, from Baldock to Bishop's Stortford.

The countryside in between these great roads cannot have been more than very sparsely settled, either in the Roman or the succeeding Saxon age, until the great forward movement of settlement – the unrecorded colonization that filled what we call the Dark Ages – established hamlet and village and manor in a process that we can discern only dimly from place-names, not at all from documents or yet from archaeology. St Albans must have existed in the midst of an uncultivated wilderness of thick woods on waterlogged soil.

History in Buildings
Under the Normans, rebuilding of the abbey church at St Albans was at once begun, and there is Norman work of various quality in both counties. There were motte-and-bailey castles at Berkhamsted and South Mimms (the latter still under excavation); those at Hatfield and Bishop's Stortford have all but disappeared. The 13th century seems to have been a time of little prosperity and only minor building activity; but the later Middle Ages show an abundance of church-building in the Perpendicular style. Most Hertfordshire towns have good churches of this period, like Bishop's Stortford, Hitchin, Ware and Watford; Baldock and Ashwell, somewhat earlier, are both notable, with thin spires. This 'Hertfordshire spike' is a speciality. Middlesex has one excellent church of the latest Perpendicular, at South Mimms, and several good examples of a style of west tower found here and in Kent, with bold buttressed outlines and rectangular windows to the bell-chamber.

Brick building begins, later than in Essex, about 1480, with the Bishop of Ely's house at Hatfield. In the next century, Hampton Court – at once the last great moated dwelling and the first modern country house in England – shows a florescence of brickwork fancy and marks the beginning of the golden age for large and medium-sized houses. Robert Cecil's Hatfield House is the prime Hertfordshire exemplar.

From this time until well into the 19th century, houses great and small were built in the favoured parts of Middlesex and Hertfordshire in such numbers as to excite the admiration of natives like Defoe as well as innumerable foreign visitors. Some of these houses have come and gone, like Cannons near Edgware, the Berkeleys' house at Cranford, and Cassiobury near Watford, seat of the Capels, Earls of Essex. Others remain, like Syon and Osterley in west Middlesex, masterpieces of Robert Adam's art, and the string of great houses in southern Hertfordshire already mentioned.

Smaller houses, many excellent, remain in the towns to delight the passer-by with their elegance, even if they present problems to their inhabitants and others. In Middlesex they are getting few: Chiswick Mall and Twickenham now have the best. In Hertfordshire, enough pleasant houses remain in St Albans, Hitchin, Ware and Hertford to make a walk round the town-centres a pleasure.

The Latest Age
The 19th century's contributions to both counties remain, in sum, disappointing, some railway viaducts apart. The buildings at Harrow School will serve as an example, not unfair, of the muddle that most architects (or, more important, their patrons) made of their chances when challenged by urgent needs for extension. Only in the century's last decade did a lively new style for middle-sized houses make its appearance, with promise for the future – Chorleywood, with C. F. Annesley Voysey's own house, The Orchard, is almost the *locus classicus* of the modern movement in English domestic architecture. J. F. Bentley's Roman Catholic church of the Holy Rood, begun in 1883, in a Watford street, is the best of all the revived Gothic churches.

Since then, so many and so varied buildings have been put up that judgment is bound to remain bemused. Some of them are bad, very bad; but there is much that is good to look at. The old man-made pattern of cottage and lane and hedge-row is disappearing; but a new formal beauty of building and roadway and

Strand-on-the-Green   *G. Douglas Bolton*

landscape can be made to emerge from the welter. There are signs in places that it will do so: the New Towns, though everything is not right about their design, do give reasons for encouragement, especially in the planning of their centres, which respond to the human needs of easy circulation far better than the older towns do.

This introduction has been mainly about buildings, and that is only natural, seeing what the function of Middlesex and Hertfordshire is today and has been for many years. But nature will not be expelled, even with a pitchfork: foxes are still shot from time to time near Kenwood, on the London border of Middlesex, and the reservoirs of the Metropolitan Water Board provide habitats (the ornithologist's word) for birds of marvellously surprising kinds. The oaks and elms, and the hornbeams too, give shelter to wild life in many species.

But the visitor to the two northern Home Counties will be wise if he keeps his eyes open most of the time for the works of man: man seeking how to live close to his fellows, in privacy and community at the same time. He has not yet found *the* answer; but a number of different solutions are assembled in this small territory. It is an area to be avoided by those who can love only the ancient and unchanging in Britain; but people who do not balk at change, in society or in industry or in the larger ordering of life, would be foolish to ignore the good things, as well as the bad, that are happening in Middlesex and Hertfordshire.

Some houses and gardens open to the public

Gorhambury House 2m N of St Albans off A5 *Map* FB 20. *18th-cent. modified classical-style mansion built by Sir Robert Taylor; Sir Francis Bacon's possessions; enamelled glass, Grimston family portraits, Chippendale furniture.* The Earl of Verulam.

Hampton Court Palace 2m W of Kingston-on-Thames on A308 *Map* FB 17. *16th cent. and later, built for Cardinal Wolsey, with additions by Sir Christopher Wren. Notable state apartments, banqueting house and Tudor tennis court. Fine gardens and park near River Thames.*

Hatfield House 20m N of London *Map* FC 20. *Early Jacobean, unaltered. Home of the Marquess of Salisbury, KG. Historic paintings, furniture, armour and relics of Elizabeth I. Adjacent stands one wing of the former Palace of Hatfield, the childhood home of Elizabeth I.*

Hogarth's House Great West Rd Chiswick W4 *Map* FC 17. *18th-cent. house occupied by Wm Hogarth, who did his work here. About 130 prints on exhibit.* London Borough of Hounslow.

Knebworth House Old Knebworth *Map* FC 22. *15th-cent. house embellished in Gothic style in early 19th cent. Banqueting Hall, Minstrel's Gallery, family pictures and pleasant gardens.* Lord Cobbold. Enquiries: Estate Office.

Lockleys ½m from Welwyn off A1 *Map* FC 21. *18th cent. with fine W façade and original panelling. Now a school.*

Salisbury Hall 5m SE of St Albans off A6 *Map* FB 20. *17th-cent. manor house on ancient moated site; many historical associations. Prototype 'Mosquito' aircraft of plywood and paper designed here during Second World War, on show. Lullingstone Silk Farm housed in Nell Gwynne's cottage.* W. J. Goldsmith, Esq.

Syon House At Brentford *Map* FC 17. *16th-cent. house built by Protector Somerset; 17th-cent. repairs by Inigo Jones. Splendid interiors by Robert Adam. Gardens now contain 'The Gardening Centre'.*

The Manor House 6m NE of Berkhamsted, 6m N of Hemel Hempstead off B486 *Map* FA 21. *16th cent. with stone mullioned windows, Elizabethan fireplaces, wall-paintings, and early keyboard instruments; cut yew hedges.* Miss Dorothy Erhart.

Books for further reading

The 'feel' of Middlesex and Hertfordshire

B. GARSIDE *Parish Affairs, Hampton* and others on Hampton
E. GREY *Cottage Life in a Hertfordshire Village*
R. L. HINE *History of Hitchin* 2 vols 1927
G. S. MAXWELL *Highwayman's Heath (Hounslow)* 1949
EDWIN M. WARE *Pinner in the Vale* 1955–7
CHARLES LAMB and IZAAK WALTON were among the many writers who have loved Hertfordshire.

Natural history

JOHN G. DONY *Flora of Hertfordshire* 1967
W. E. GLEGG *History of the Birds of Middlesex* 1935
KENT and LOUSLEY *Handlist of Plants of the London Area* 1951–4
B. L. SAGE *History of the Birds of Hertfordshire* 1959

Topography

N. G. BRETT-JAMES *Middlesex* (County Books series) 1951
ARTHUR MEE's books on both counties 1965
MICHAEL ROBBINS *Middlesex* 1953
SIR W. BEACH THOMAS *Hertfordshire* (County Books series) 1952

Architecture

N. PEVSNER *Hertfordshire* 1953; *Middlesex* 1951
ROYAL COMMISSION on Ancient Monuments: *Herts* 1910; *Middlesex* 1937

A Middlesex bibliography of over 5,000 items is available at Middlesex public libraries; a similar list for Hertfordshire has been started at Hertfordshire County Library.

Gazetteer

MIDDLESEX AND HERTFORDSHIRE

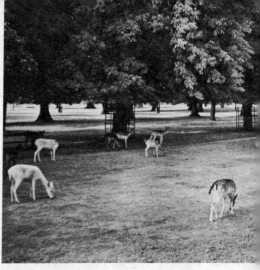

Deer at Bushy Park   *G. Douglas Bolton*

Ashridge Park *Herts*. (EK 21). Originally a monastery for twenty Bonhommes who came over from Normandy, it was later made into a home for the children of Henry VIII. Elizabeth was arrested here on the order of her sister Mary. In the following century, the place was allowed to decay, but in 1808 the 7th Earl of Bridgewater commissioned Wyatt to rebuild. It is now a management college. The gardens are open on Sundays.

Ayot St Lawrence *Herts*. (FB 21). Shaw's Corner, the home of George Bernard Shaw (1856–1950), is kept by the NT exactly as it was in his lifetime.

Silkworms bred in the village contribute to the trousseaux of royal brides.

Baldock *Herts*. (FC 23) EC Thurs (6,820). The 17th-cent. almshouses in the main street have been endowed with funds to maintain them 'to the worldes end'. The church has a 15th-cent. rood-screen extending in three parts across the nave and aisles. The roof-timbers are quaintly carved. John Smith, who is buried here, became Rector after having spent three years deciphering the shorthand of Samuel Pepys's diary, which had lain in Magdalene College, Cambridge, for nearly a century.

Barnet *Herts*. (FC 19) EC Thurs (27,830). The battle of Barnet in the Wars of the Roses brought about the accession to the Throne of Edward IV. Being on the great road between London and the N, this was a regular stopping-place until the needs of modern traffic caused it to be by-passed. The horse fair was one of the last to survive in England.

Berkhamsted *Herts*. (EK 20) EC Wed (15,210). Earthworks and a little masonry are all that remain of the 11th-cent. castle presented by William the Conqueror to his brother. Here stayed Thomas à Becket, Piers Gaveston, Chaucer and three of Henry VIII's wives. The 17th-cent. grammar school, north of the churchyard and greatly enlarged, is famous. William Cowper (1731–1800), poet and hymn-writer, was born in the old rectory, which has been superseded by a more modern one.

Bishop's Stortford *Herts*. (FE 22) EC Wed (21,010). A mound in the public gardens is all that is left of the 11th-cent. castle of Bishop Maurice of London, who was entrusted by William the Conqueror with the security of a ford over the Stort. The church has medieval woodwork. Cecil Rhodes (1853–1902) was born in the old vicarage in South St, which is kept as a museum in his honour, and contains many of his possessions.

Brentford *Middx.* (FB 17) EC Thurs (with Chiswick, 54,830). Often called the county town, though the County Council meetings and the Quarter Sessions were held in the Middlesex Guildhall in Westminster, opposite the Abbey. Though by-passed by the Great West Road, this is a busy built-up area. It retains the Butts, a former archery ground. For the altarpiece in St George's Church, Zoffany used as models the faces of fishermen and friends. Boston Manor (1622) is notable for interior decoration and allegorical subjects executed in plaster on walls and ceilings.

Bushy Park *Middx.* (FB 17). Great park adjoining Hampton Court and begun in 1689; it was intended by William III to rival Le Notre's work at Versailles. The imposing avenue of chestnuts is interspersed with lime trees. In the circular pond, the bronze 'Diana Fountain' is thought to be a statue of Venus bought in Italy by Charles II for the Privy Garden in Hampton Court.

Chiswick *Middx.* (FB 17) (with Brentford, 54,830). The Mall is one of the most beautiful of Thames frontages, and has attracted many artists and eminent people. Walpole House, Thackeray's model for Miss Pinkerton's Academy in *Vanity Fair*, was the home of Barbara Villiers Duchess of Cleveland, mistress of Charles II. The painters Hogarth and Whistler are buried in the churchyard of St Nicholas; so is William Kent, who designed a large part of Chiswick House. In consultation with this young painter, the house was remodelled by the 3rd Earl of Burlington on his return from Italy in 1719, where he had been filled with enthusiasm for Palladio's work, particularly his Villa Capra at Vicenza. Kent supervised the decoration and laid out the gardens. Sir Hans Sloane presented a handsome gateway (1621) by Inigo Jones, Edward VII lived here for a time when Prince of Wales; and here died two Prime Ministers, Charles James Fox and Canning. Sir Joseph Paxton, designer of the Crystal Palace, worked as a youth in the splendid gardens.

Chorley Wood *Herts.* (FA 19) (7,730). William Penn, the founder of Pennsylvania, married Gulielma Springett at King John's Farm in 1672. His portrait shows him in soldier's uniform before he became a Quaker.

Cranford *Middx.* (FB 17) (13,250). The Church of St Dunstan, standing isolated in the parkland of a great house that has been demolished, has notable monuments, the chief of which is that of Sir Roger Aston and his wife, executed in 'alabaster, tuche, rance and black and white marble' by William Cure, Master Mason to James I. He was paid £180.

Edmonton *Middx.* (FD 19) (92,060). Charles Lamb and his sister Mary lived in Bay Cottage (now Lamb's

Hampton Court Palace

Cottage) near All Saints' Church, and are buried in the churchyard, below an inscription by their friend Henry Cary, translator of Dante.

Elstree *Herts*. (FB 19) EC Wed (30,550). The first British film studios were built here in 1913 at a time when a clear atmosphere for outdoor photography had to be found near London.

Enfield *Middx*. (FD 19) EC Wed (109,520). Picturesque and varied cottages in Gentleman's Row have been preserved in a town of very fast growth. Charles Lamb stayed for a time at No. 17. A modern house to the S has an annexe that contains detail from Enfield Palace, including a fireplace of about 1552 carved with Ionic and Corinthian columns and the Royal Arms.

Gorhambury *Herts*. (FB 20). A fine avenue leads from near St Michael's Church in St Albans to the 18th-cent. house of the present Lord Verulam; adjoining this we find the remains of the Elizabethan house of his ancestor, Francis Bacon. He is buried in the chancel of St Michael's. A statue shows him in a characteristic pose: *sic sedebat* – thus he used to sit.

Haileybury *Herts*. (FD 21). The famous public school founded in 1862 occupies buildings originally designed for candidates studying to enter the East India Company.

Hampton Court** *Middx*. (FB 16) EC Wed. When Cardinal Wolsey began building in 1514, he declared that his residence must surpass all others. Fifteen years later it was given by him to Henry VIII, who added the Great Hall and Chapel. At the direction of William III, Sir Christopher Wren designed Fountain Court, Clock Court and a new orangery. This was to be the Versailles of William and Mary. George II was the last king to live here, and nowadays much of the

Palace is allotted 'by grace and favour' to widows and dependents of distinguished servants of the Crown. The historic buildings, which give an insight into the domesticities of Tudor times, and the state apartments with their incomparable collection of pictures and tapestries, are open to the public. So too are the delightful orangeries and the Great Vinery. The extensive grounds, mainly modelled on the work of the French landscape gardener, Le Nôtre, have intimate corners, such as the vestiges of Henry VIII's Privy Garden and a reconstruction of a Tudor knot garden, made entirely from aromatic herbs. The Maze, in that part of the grounds known as the Wilderness, has a fascination of its own.

Harpenden *Herts*. (FB 21) EC Wed (22,020). The flint tower of the church dates from the 15th cent. When Sir John Lawes inherited Rothamsted Park in the early 19th cent., he devoted all his resources to agricultural research. His work continues as Rothamsted Experimental Station in his old home, to which technical visitors are admitted.

Harrow* *Middx*. (FB 18) EC Wed (208,960). The lead spire of St Mary's Church on Harrow Hill (400 ft.) draws attention to the famous public school, rival of Eton. It was founded in the late 16th cent. by John Lyon, a yeoman of the hamlet of Preston, Middx., after obtaining a charter from Queen Elizabeth. The Old Schools (1611) are the earliest part, still in use. The panelling of the Fourth Form Room is scored with the names of past pupils, including Sheridan, Byron, Palmerston, Trollope and, of course, Winston Churchill.

Hatfield *Herts*. (FC 20) EC Thurs (44,180 incl. New Town). The Palace* of Hatfield was originally the home

331

Hatfield House: the Armoury

of the Bishops of Ely, built of beautiful brick at a time in the 15th cent. when stone was unfashionable. Here the children of Henry VIII spent much of their time. The house was given to his sister Elizabeth by Edward VI. Soon after the Queen's death, Robert Cecil accepted it in exchange for his own Theobalds, which James I coveted, and immediately began to build the great house which he did not live to occupy. It is one of the most splendid in the country, and still belongs to the head of the family, the Marquess of Salisbury. The park and the gardens are as memorable as the house and palace with their state rooms, priceless collections, and paintings and relics of Queen Elizabeth.

Hertford *Herts*. (FD 21) EC Thurs (18,660). The county town stands at the point where two smaller rivers meet the Lea. King John of France was imprisoned in the castle in 1359. Hertford Corporation pays half a crown a year in rent to the Marquess of Salisbury for this stronghold at the centre of the town, known to have existed there in early Saxon days.

Hitchin *Herts*. (FB 22) (26,240). The town of Hitchin dates back in its origins to Belgic times and was the site of a monastery in the time of Offa. The ancient church is impressive both in size and appearance. The Priory is a building of unusual merit and its Tuesday and Saturday markets are outstanding attractions.

Isleworth *Middx*. (FB 17) EC Wed (102,890). Syon House*, property of the Duke of Northumberland, was rebuilt by Robert Adam in the middle of the 18th cent. on the site of a Brigittine nunnery founded in 1415 and granted to Protector Somerset at the dissolution of the monasteries. Lady Jane Grey was living here when she was called to the throne in 1553. The façade, surmounted by the lead

Northumberland Lion taken from the family's former town house in London, is seen at its best from Kew Gardens on the Surrey side of the River. The 1st Duke was, according to Adam, 'a person of extensive knowledge and correct taste'. They worked together to build and decorate a house of noble beauty, full of art treasures, and surrounded by parkland and a garden designed by Capability Brown.

Knebworth *Herts.* (FC 22) (2,718). Bulwer Lytton, the 1st Baron (1803–73), wrote many of his novels in the 16th-cent. family home, which was partly demolished and rebuilt into its present fantastic design when he was a boy. The house contains relics of this politician-novelist, as well as admirable paintings and furniture. The gardens are beautiful.

Laleham *Middx.* (FA 16) (3,160). Matthew Arnold (1822–88), poet son of the great Head of Rugby School, was born here and is buried in the churchyard near the Earl of Lucan, who commanded at Balaclava.

Lemsford *Herts.* (FC 21). Two Prime Ministers, Melbourne and Palmerston, died at 18th-cent. Brocket Hall. Capability Brown laid out the splendid garden and widened the River Lea until it formed a lake, now bridged in stone by James Paine.

Letchworth *Herts.* (FC 23) EC Wed (28,110). The first English garden city. It was developed by Ebenezer Howard in 1903 as a result of a campaign for better housing conditions that he conducted in his own paper, *Tomorrow*. His terms of reference, the allotting of zones for industrial, civic and residential usage, have been followed in later new towns.

Mill Hill *Middx.* (FC 19) (24,860). The public school was founded in 1807 for the education of the sons of Non-conformists, but since 1869 it has been open to other denominations. The original buildings, which continue in use, were designed by Sir William Tite.

Moor Park *Herts.* (FA 19). The historic house that had belonged to Cardinal Wolsey underwent a transformation in the 18th cent., when it was rebuilt in the Palladian style, with a grand portico and splendid ceilings and doorways. It is now a golf club.

Osterley Park *Middx.* (FB 17). The original great house was built by Sir Thomas Gresham, the Elizabethan banker. Another banker, Robert Child, commissioned Robert Adam to reconstruct it. The result is the remarkable double portico that, contrary to other neo-classical practice, serves as an entry to the central courtyard and gives lightness to the structure. Much of the furniture was designed by Robert Adam and was acquired by the Victoria and Albert Museum when Lord Jersey presented Osterley Park to the NT in 1949.

St Albans* *Herts.* (FB 20) EC Thurs (52,470). The walls of the Roman city of Verulamium enclosed an area of 200 acres, much of which has been excavated. The Saxons changed its name to St Albans in honour of the first English martyr, who was beaten and beheaded in the 4th cent. for succouring the Christian priest who converted him. A great Benedictine abbey was founded in 793 and rebuilt after the Norman Conquest. Cardinal Wolsey was its 38th abbot.

The nave of the cathedral is 275½ ft. long, a record for a medieval building. Flint, brick and stone taken from the old Roman city are still visible in its walls. Much of the cathedral has been restored, notably by Lord Grimthorpe, who in the 19th cent. spent £140,000 of his private fortune on the work.

The magnificent stone screen, dating from the 15th cent., was shattered during the Reformation, but its stone fragments have been patiently fitted together again. The same is true of the saint's shrine, reconstructed from 2,000 pieces. Note especially the 13th-cent. iron grille on the S side of the saint's chapel, and the vaulting of the presbytery.

The museum is comprehensive. It houses beautiful sections of mosaic, coins found on site, pottery and many other articles that demonstrate the continuous life of the city. A visit is recommended as a preliminary to the Roman remains, which include part of the Roman wall and its bastions, the foundations of the London Gate, a mosaic pavement, and the hypocaust that stored hot air for private baths. The theatre is impressive.

Stanmore *Middx.* (FB 19) EC Thurs (30,750). The highest point (550 ft. above sea level) in the county. A ruined church stands with the newer one in the same churchyard. See the monuments to the two John Wolsten-holmes (1639 and 1669), the Holland family mausoleum and the figure of an angel standing over the grave of W. S. Gilbert.

Stevenage *Herts.* (FC 22) EC Wed (58,690). One of the best-developed modern towns.

Strawberry Hill *Middx.* (FB 17). The eccentric 'Gothick Castle' that grew out of a 'little plaything house' acquired in 1747 by Horace Walpole, who died there fifty years later. It has been enlarged since its occupation by St Mary's Training College for Roman Catholic Teachers.

Facing page: **St Albans Cathedral, West Front**
Verulamium: the Roman theatre

J. Allan Cash
J. Allan Cash

The Thames at Twickenham *Mustograph*

Tring *Herts*. (E K 21) E C Wed (7,990). The parish records go back to 1566 and contain the names of George Washington's ancestors. In Tring Park, Lord Rothschild's Zoological Museum, bequeathed to the British Museum in 1938, shows thousands of rare birds, fish, reptiles and insects, which may be seen free.

Twickenham *Middx*. (FB 17) E C Wed (100,820). Fashionable 18th-cent. village that has retained its residential quality despite rapid growth. Several houses once occupied by famous people have been turned to other uses: York House, where the two last Stuart queens were born (municipal offices); the Octagon Room surviving from Orleans House; Kneller Hall (the Royal Military School of Music); Sandycombe Lodge, home of the painter Turner; and a house in Montpelier Row once occupied by Tennyson. Nearby is the famous Rugby football ground. Eelpie

Island, opposite the public gardens, keeps up its reputation as a pleasure-ground. The house called Pope's Villa is on the site of the poet's villa.

Ware *Herts*. (FD 21) E C Thurs (13,660). The turning point of John Gilpin in Cowper's poem. The Church of St Mary has a magnificent 14th-cent. font with beautiful sculptured figures of the saints. The Great Bed of Ware – mentioned in the plays of Shakespeare, Ben Jonson and Farquhar – came from Ware Park, and is now in the Victoria and Albert Museum, South Kensington.

Welsh Harp *Middx*. (FC 18). A great stretch of water constructed last century to supply the Regent's Canal. Part of the lake and its shores are conserved for public recreation. It is now a yachting centre.

Welwyn Garden City *Herts*. (FC 21) E C Wed (41,460). The second great development by Ebenezer Howard, who promoted the company that chose Letchworth as a pilot plan. Out of his pioneering grew the Town and Country Planning Acts.

Wembley *Middx*. (FB 18) E C Wed (124,840). The stadium, built for the Exhibition of 1924, is the scene of the football Cup Finals and the autumn Horse of the Year Show; the 11th Olympic Games were held there in 1948. The Empire Pool and the Sports Arena were the work of Sir Owen Williams in 1934. The roof, constructed on a system of counterpoise, was revolutionary in its day.

Wheathampstead *Herts*. (FB 21) (3,370). Birthplace of John of Wheathampstead, the 15th-cent. abbot who founded the library of the Abbey of St Albans. The brasses of his parents, Hugh and Margaret Bostock, are among the noteworthy monuments in the church. This village was greatly loved by Charles Lamb.

Finchingfield

ESSEX

AN INTRODUCTION BY K. J. LACE

'This shire is moste fatt, fruitfull and full of profitable things exceding (as far as I can finde) anie other shire for the general commodities and plentie.' So wrote John Norden in 1594: and he might well say the same of Essex today, although he would find it difficult to recognize the county as the place he visited four centuries ago. Essex was perhaps the last of the Home Counties to suffer 'development'; but since 1800, when London began to spread over the county boundary, and in particular during the last fifty years, the southern part of the county has seen the spread of 'Metropolitan Essex'. The expansion of London is now, however, 'cabined, cribbed, confined' by the Green Belt, and building beyond this barrier is being allowed only in a planned and orderly fashion. The plans include the exciting experiment of the 'New Towns' of Harlow and Basildon, and the expansion of places which appear to have changed but little since Norden reported on them. The reorganization of London local government has made 'Metropolitan Essex' a reality; further changes are imminent, and the present is, therefore, a period of change and turmoil. New plans, new roads, new towns and new government will bring great changes in the course of the next few years. Outside this area, however, there remains the Essex of field and river, coast and marsh, village greens and inns: a county rich in history and full of varied scene and interest.

337

Chelmsford Cathedral

G. Douglas Bolton

Essex has, perhaps, the most rapidly rising population of any in England. Almost a quarter of its area is covered with houses. In the south-west and along the Thames, the sprawl of London has engulfed the countryside. Here the county is populous, flourishing, busy with the work of great new industries – motor engineering, board mills, cement, shoes, oil, sugar, medicines – which have been established along the north bank of the river. The new towns of Harlow and Basildon, planned and built within the last fifteen years, are bright and colourful with their modern architecture, green lawns and spacious squares. North of the Green Belt the county is less changed, and here the smaller towns, Ongar, Halstead, Thaxted, Saffron Walden, Epping and Dunmow still look to a rural economy for their support. Amongst the closely cultivated farm lands only the electricity wires and the television aerials suggest that any change has come to the villages in the last two hundred years.

Chelmsford, in the centre of the county, shows the meeting of industrial and rural Essex in bustling harmony. Here you may see a heron fly ponderously over the centre of the town, and the martins still nest under the eaves within a few yards of the busy high street. In the north-east the fashion of holidays by the sea has encouraged the development of the coastal resorts at Clacton, Frinton, Walton and Dovercourt.

ESSEX

No part of Essex rises above five hundred feet. In the coastal plain the roads meander through a tree-lined land of large fields, with unexpected glimpses of silver water or the white sails of small boats where the creeks run farther inland than seems possible. North of the A12 the wayfarer, expecting Essex to be flat, will take pleasure in the wooded vistas of the undulating countryside, and will hardly find a level stretch of road between Saffron Walden and Colchester, Chelmsford or Stansted.

Along the roads, especially in the north, the weather-boarded cottages and timber-framed farmhouses fit quietly and appropriately into the wooded landscape. In the narrow streets of the market towns, and in the villages, such houses and inns lend charm and dignity to the scene. These characteristically English buildings of the 15th and 16th centuries, built when oak, ash and elm (John Norden's 'three building trees') were plentiful, and stone expensive and hard to come by, are indigenous, well built, gracefully proportioned and show the use of local materials to the best advantage. Many of the houses have external beams of oak, weathered to a silvery grey by the passing years, and tastefully carved with floral designs or sometimes, as at Felsted, with the builder's name. The thickness of the plaster applied externally to these half-timbered houses encouraged the decoration of the walls with elaborate patterns or ornaments in high relief. This process, which has shown signs of revival in recent years, known as 'pargeting', may still be seen in its original form on a number of larger buildings and, in simpler form, on cottages up and down the county.

Thatch and plaster at High Roding   *Reece Winstone*

Land and Water

The county lies, as it were, on a great saucer of chalk, its rim exposed in the Saffron Walden area, which conveniently acts as a reservoir for water. Into this saucer at various times have been deposited alluvial and glacial sediments and gravel. First, in a tropical heat the great bed of London clay was laid down. This is exposed in the south and east of the county, and yields fossils of tapir, turtle, shark and the seeds of exotic trees. Next, after a startling change of climate, glacial boulder-clay was left by the retreating ice-cap in a great triangle in the north and west of the county. Today this maintains the great wheat belt of Essex, growing some of the finest wheat in England on a stretch of country which runs north-eastwards across the county for almost twenty miles. On these soils thrives a vigorous farming community, modern in outlook and methods, and thriving as it deserves. In the south-west, from Romford to Leyton, is a great deposit of Valley Gravels. Among these are the remains of elephant, mammoth and elk. At Ilford the number of bones is so large as to suggest that the carcasses of thousands of these beasts were deposited together in a back-water of some great prehistoric river. Along the coast and river estuaries are found alluvial deposits which form the low coastal plain and marshlands. Almost three hundred miles of wall and dyke now defend these from the relentless attack of the sea, since in the last two thousand years the level of the coast has sunk some twelve or thirteen feet and is still sinking. In this unending battle between land and water both sides may claim their victories. The parish church at Walton was engulfed in 1798 and is now deep beneath the sea. In 1953, Foulness Island was evacuated along an ancient road, running parallel to the coast. This is still usable at certain states of the tide, but is now half a mile off-shore. The great tide of 1953 was the latest and most disastrous of many occasions when the sea defences of the county have been breached. On the other hand, the draining of marsh and island at various points along the coast and estuaries has yielded many valuable acres for the use of man since Charles I brought Cornelius Vermuyden from Holland to build the walls which encircle and protect Canvey Island. In spite of the length of the coastline, only at Tilbury, Shellhaven and Harwich is there a sufficient depth of water to allow the establishment of ports for larger ocean-going vessels. In the past, however, the deep indentations of the Thames, Crouch, Blackwater, Colne and Stour, with their creeks and inlets, brought trade, both legal and illegal, to the shores of Essex; and the smaller ports – Leigh, Tollesbury, Maldon, Colchester, Brightlingsea and Manningtree – grew up along the coast. Only yesterday the survivors of the once great fleets of ships – Essex bawleys and Thames barges – plied their trade in this last stronghold of sail.

The Historical Background

Essex has been at the hub of English history since prehistoric times. Its low coastlines and deep-water estuaries allowed seekers after new lands from the east to penetrate far inland. Across the channel, probing northwards over the Thames, came Roman and Norman. The East Saxons left their name on the land and their seaxes in its heraldry. Each wave of invasion left the mark of its success in earthwork, motte and bailey, castle, keep and abbey. Cleared and restored by the archaeologist or preserved in use by successive generations, the record is clearly visible for the discerning eye to see. The church at Greensted with its unique nave of split oak logs is the only Saxon building still in use in

J. Allan Cash   **Saffron Walden : the main st**

England. Elsewhere can be seen the Norman foundation at Waltham Abbey, monasteries at Beeleigh, St Osyth and Prittlewell, castles or earthworks at Hadleigh, Sible Headingham, Colchester, Pleshey and elsewhere, and churches from the Middle Ages, most of them in regular use. Six of these have unusual round towers, and another five have timber belfries. Each in its way reflects another aspect of the Essex story. Monuments to invasions planned but never accomplished also stand plain in the Martello towers and concrete pill-boxes dotted along the sea walls. For those whose interest in the past prompts a deeper study, there is a considerable literature, and there are excellent museums at Stratford, Thurrock, Chelmsford, Colchester and Saffron Walden. The town of Colchester, inhabited since pre-historic times, and the oldest recorded town in Britain, holds within itself a lively record of the changing history of England and of Essex.

The 'Great Essex Road', A12, drives straight and true from London, north-east through Romford, Brentwood and Chelmsford to Colchester and beyond.

The Cliff Gardens at Southend   *G. Douglas Bolton*

ESSEX

The modern traveller in his car follows the road laid down centuries ago by its Roman builders. The pattern of the Roman roads shows clearly on the modern map: A11, A12, A130 and A131 from London to the north, and the great cross-country road from Colchester to the west, A120. Along these roads lumbering wagons followed Queen Elizabeth I on her royal progresses to the stately houses of Ingatestone and Audley End. In the 18th century, stage coaches with names like 'The Chelmsford Machine Fly', 'The Colchester Eclipse' and 'The Norwich Phenomenon' maintained regular timetables. Perhaps the queerest traveller was William Kemp, Shakespeare's original Dogberry, who Morris-danced from London to Norwich in 1599.

Plants and Birds

Within ten miles of Charing Cross, reaching down a green finger from rural Essex into London-over-the-border, is the marvel of Epping Forest. Here, over five thousand five hundred acres of the old Royal forest, remnants of which also remain at Hainault and Hatfield, were preserved by an Act of Parliament in 1878 (after half the area had been rescued from illegal enclosure) for public use for ever. Travelling north, the wayfarer is startled by the dramatic change of scene as he emerges from the fringe of London suburbs straight into the glory of heaths and woodlands which press to the edge of the Cambridge road, stretching unbroken from Woodford to Epping Town itself. Its glades, ponds, wooded valleys and open hilltops are the homes of a great variety of trees, plants, birds, fungi and insects – everything, in fact, of interest to the naturalist.

In the wide marshlands and deep estuaries on the other side of the county the naturalist will also find much to engross his interest. Here Essex is indeed a maritime county. Its creeks and inlets are alive with the movement and colour of a host of wading birds: the knot, dunlin and turnstone on the shallows, tern and cormorant over the waves, and, in due season, the Brent geese winging from the north to the saltings, now overshadowed by the Bradwell atomic power station. A swannery, which rivals that at Abbotsford in Dorset, with hundreds of birds, exists on the estuary of the River Stour, an inland sea ten miles in length from Harwich to Manningtree, between the green fields of Essex and Suffolk.

The Special Flavour

Essex, no less than any other county, has its special points of appeal: its busy yachting centres on the Crouch, Blackwater and Colne; its communities of artists and writers; the 'cathedral' church at Thaxted; rare wild flowers, the Bardfield oxlip, butterfly orchid and leopard's bane; its groups of villages – the Easters, the Lavers, the Tolleshunts; oysters at Colchester; the colours of its miles of wheat at harvest. These things give the county some of its special flavour. But more than these are the contrasts which are, perhaps, nowhere so clearly drawn. The turmoil of the industrial south, and the rural quiet of the countryside, the closely cultivated farms, and the wide desolation of the marshes; the narrow, enclosing streets of the towns, and the wide sweep of the open skies; the buildings which have weathered the centuries, and the modern splendour of the new towns; thatched cottage and tower block; the bustle of towns, and the quiet reaches of the great rivers; the small industries of weaving, lace-making, thatching, boat-building – and the modern mechanization of the Thames Valley. This is the true flavour of Essex. In its diversities lies its essential charm.

Some houses and gardens open to the public

Beeleigh Abbey 1½m W of Maldon off A414 Map FJ 20. *12th cent.; famous library.*

Bradwell Lodge 7m NE of Southminster off B1021 Map FJ 20. *16th and 18th cents.: built by John Johnson, with decorative work attributed to Robert Adam; belvedere used as studio by Gainsborough.* Tom Driberg Esq., MP.

Castle House Dedham 6m from Colchester Map GA 23. *Former home and studios of late Sir Alfred Munnings; collection of paintings and other treasures.*

Colchester Castle At Colchester Map FK 22. *Massive 11th-cent. keep, built largely of Roman bricks; now used as a museum.*

Gosfield Hall 2½m W of Halstead Map FH 23. *Elizabethan gallery and ballroom.* Mutual Households Assocn Ltd.

Hedingham Castle 4½m W of Halstead Map FH 23. *Splendid Norman keep built by Bishop Carboil.* Miss Musette Majendie and Dr Marjery Blackie.

Tewes Little Sampford 1m S of Great Sampford village Map FG 23. *Attractive 15th-cent. manor house with panelling and carved oak beams; part of moat with wild duck.* Mrs Gerald Millar. Entrance through farm.

Books for further reading

The 'feel' of Essex

H. BENHAM *Last Stronghold of Sail* 1948, and *Essex Ballads* 1960
S. L. BENSUSAN *A Marshland Omnibus* 1954
A. CURTIS *A Poacher's Tale* 1960
T. GIRTIN *Come Landlord!* 1957
DAVID SMITH *I Love Life* 1958
F. J. SPEAKMAN *A Keeper's Tale* 1962; *A Forest by Night* 1965; *Out of the Wild* 1967
C. H. WARREN *Content with What I Have* 1967

Fiction

S. BARING-GOULD *Mehala*
V. BRIDGES *It Happened in Essex*
H. PRIESTLEY *The Stranger; Swords over Southdown*

Scenery, architecture

W. ADDISON *Thames Estuary* 1954; *Audley End* 1953

J. A. BRIMBLE *London's Epping Forest* 1968
J. H. COOTE *East Coast Rivers* 1956
H. FORRESTER *Timber-Framed Houses of Essex* 1960
N. PEVSNER *Buildings of England: Essex* 1954

History, topography, general

D. E. BIRCHER *One Village in History* 1966
G. CAUNT *Essex Blood and Thunder* 1967
G. J. COPLEY *Archaeology of S.E. England* 1958
J. C. COX *Essex* (Little Guides series) latest edn
F. DAVIES *Afoot in Essex* 1968
A. C. EDWARDS *History of Essex* 1958
S. M. JARVIS and C. T. HARRISON *In Search of Essex* 1968
G. H. MARTIN *A History of Colchester* 1959
A. MEE *Essex* 1966
N. SCARFE *Essex* (Shell Guide) 1968
C. H. WARREN *Essex* (County Books series) 1950

Gazetteer

ESSEX

Audley End   *J. Allan Cash*

Ashingdon (FJ 19) (1,260). Of great antiquity but now much enlarged by modern building. Scaldhurst Farm is widely accepted as the site of Canute's defeat of Edmund Ironside at the Battle of Assandune. St. Andrew's Church, reputed to have been founded by Canute (1020) in memory of his victory, was restored from a ruinous state in 1949. In *c.*14 a pilgrimage started to a shrine of the Virgin reputed to miraculously cure barrenness. Pilgrims crawled on their knees from Goldencross at the foot of the hill to the church, a distance of one mile. The idea that marriage at Ashingdon was lucky long survived.

Audley End (FF 23). Though smaller in extent than the 'palace' built in 1603 on the ruins of a Benedictine monastery by the first Earl of Suffolk, the present mansion (AM) remains a splendid example of 17th-cent. architecture. It contains a library and pictures, and the stables, at one of the entrances, are an admirable example of Tudor brickwork.

Boreham (FH 20) EC Wed (1,660). Parts of the church, with its battlemented tower, are Norman; and the 16th-cent. S chapel contains fine marble effigies of the period. Boreham House is early 18th-cent. New Hall, 1½ m. W, now a convent, was originally a sumptuous mansion, partly built by Henry VIII.

Bradwell-on-Sea (GA 20). A tiny village, with a sand and shingle beach at the quay (1 m. N). An atomic power station has been built in the neighbourhood. A footpath leads E to the Saxon chapel of St Peter's-on-the-Wall, a small barn-like building, composed of materials from the Roman fort that once occupied the site, which is all that remains of the much greater church, originally built by St Cedd in the 7th cent.

Brightlingsea (GA 21) EC Thurs (4,790). Centre for yachtsmen, with bathing from a beach of sand and mud. There is a timbered Tudor house, Jacob's Hall; and interesting brasses and monuments in the church.

Burnham-on-Crouch (FK 19) EC Wed (4,170). With its pebbly beach and oyster beds, it is a centre for yachtsmen and river craft, and abounds with a variety of wild fowl.

Castle Hedingham (FH 23) EC Thurs (910). A village of old houses and inns, dominated by the keep that is all that remains of the castle (AM), built at the end of the 11th cent. The brick tower of the church is dated 1616, but the nave, with a fine double hammer-beam roof, is Norman, and there is a screen of the 14th century.

Chelmsford (FH 20) EC Wed (49,810). The county town, with an impressive shire hall, built in 1791. The cathedral, until 1914 the parish church, is chiefly of recent date, since most of the original building 'suddenly fell down' in 1800. But the square tower and S porch survived, this last with an interesting parvise, or upper room, containing a 17th-cent. library. A typical Essex building is the weather-boarded mill in Victoria Road. Writtle, 2 m. W, includes a group of charming timbered houses on the green; its church has carved stalls and interesting monuments.

Chignal Smealey (FG 21) (360). In the absence of local stone, many Essex churches contain an unusual amount of flint and brickwork, but the little Tudor church here is unique in that it is entirely constructed of brick, including even the font.

Clacton-on-Sea (GB 21) EC Wed (27,540). Has good sands, a golf-course and all the other amenities of a popular seaside resort.

Coggeshall (FJ 22) EC Wed (2,900). Though this village is celebrated for seed-growing and hand-made lace, its glory is Paycock's House (NT), a great Tudor wool merchant's home, with a wealth of brick-nogging and carved timbers. At nearby Little Coggeshall, fragments of the Cistercian abbey have been built into a private house and its little chapel of St Nicholas has been restored. The brick and weather-boarded Abbey Mill was still working some twenty years ago.

Colchester* (GA 22) EC Thurs (65,070). Camulodunum, where the British under Queen Boadicea harried the legionaries of Claudius, still retains much of the Roman wall, including the fine Balkerne Gate (AM). The Norman castle (AM), its keep the largest in England, is built almost entirely of Roman materials, and houses a notable museum. (Another is maintained in the Georgian mansion Holly Trees, on E Hill.) The ruined nave and W front of St Botolph's Priory (AM) are splendid examples of Norman work; in St John's Abbey,

the beautiful 15th-cent. gateway still stands. The old Siege House is a timbered building, associated with the Revolution; and there are several ancient inns. Bourne Mill (NT), built of materials from the abbey after the Dissolution, is a picturesque building 1 m. S.

Copford (FK 22) (780). In the opinion of Professor Tristram, the medieval wall-paintings in the Norman apse of the church 'rank amongst the finest examples of English workmanship'.

Cressing (FH 22) (810). In the 12th cent., one of the two communities of the Knights Hospitallers in the county. Here, unlike Little Maplestead's (*see below*), the church has long ago disappeared, but near the old Manor House two of the old barns – one for wheat, the other for barley – are amongst the finest in the country. The tiled roofs (each said to weigh 74 tons) are still supported by the original oak timbers; the older of the two roofs dates from 1480.

Danbury (FH 20) EC Wed (2,690). From the hill on which it stands, there are good views out to the Blackwater. In the church, restored since it was bombed during the last war, three effigies of knights are remarkable for being carved out of oak.

Dedham (GA 23) (1,690). In the valley of the Stour, its fine old church tower is still, as in several of Constable's pictures, a notable landmark. The grammar school he attended was built in 1732; and Southfields and Sherman's are examples respectively of Tudor and Georgian houses.

Epping (FE 20) EC Wed (10,000). Lies to the NW of Epping Forest**. This lovely woodland of over 5,500 acres was acquired by the City of London in 1878 as an open space.

Reece Winstone   **Colchester.** *Top:* **Bourne Mill.** *Below:* **The Ca**

Feering (FJ 22) (922). The brick-work in the nave and S porch of the church, with its crocketed pinnacles, shows admirably the use of this material. The church contains a painting by John Constable.

Finchingfield* (FG 23) EC Wed (1,110). With its squat Norman church tower and cluster of attractive houses round the green, crossed by a brook, the village remains unspoilt in spite of its claim to be the loveliest in the county. In Duck End stands an old post windmill; and, 1 m. N, Spain's Hall, with its brick façade, stone-mullioned windows and curved gables, is a beautiful example of Tudor architecture.

Frinton-on-Sea (GC 21) EC Wed (9,570). Combined with Walton-on-the-Naze, is celebrated for its fine sands, fishing and golf. The Naze, 2 m. NE, is the easternmost point in the county and is famous for its fossils.

Great Bardfield (FG 23) EC Wed (900). An attractive village, its houses representing a wide range of architectural periods. The church is worth visiting for the exceptional beauty of its stone screen.

Great Leighs (FH 21). One of the finest of the round flint towers that are to be found in some half-dozen Essex churches. Part of the fabric of the church goes back to the late 10th century. In the N wall of the chancel is a good Easter sepulchre. At Little Leighs, 2 m. NW, the brick gateway is all that now remains of a former Tudor mansion.

Great Waltham (FG 21) (1,630). Nearby are two timbered houses of the 16th cent., Fitzjohn's Farm and lovely Hyde Hall, this last surrounded by a mellow brick wall and a broad moat; while Langleys is a notable house of the 18th century. Some 3 m. to the NW is the sleepy village of Pleshey, where all that remains of the great castle, for 250 years the home of the High Constables of England, is the great mount and the brick arch that once spanned the moat.

Greensted (FF 20) (780). There are three or four other wooden churches in Essex, but Greensted is unique. Not only is it one of the oldest churches in the county, but the nave consists entirely of rough-hewn oak, secured with wooden pins, while the tower is weather-boarded and the spire covered with wooden shingles.

Hadleigh (FJ 18) EC Wed (5,210). The ruins of the 13th-cent. castle were the subject of several studies and a well-known painting by Constable. There are remains of wall-paintings in the Norman church.

Halstead (FJ 23) EC Wed (6,470). There are Bourchier monuments in the flint church, a good example of this Essex building material. Gosfield Hall, 2½ m. SW, with its large courtyard, is one of the county's most imposing mansions; and there is a fine example of pargeting (plaster relief work) at Colneford House, Earls Colne, 3 m. SE.

Hempstead (FG 23) (380). William Harvey, the discoverer of the circulation of the blood, lived here for some time and is buried in the church. Here too, in the parish register, is recorded the baptism of Dick Turpin, the highwayman, in 1705.

High Easter (FG 21). In the neighbourhood are a number of moated, timber-framed farmhouses with brick chimneys. The church has a brick clerestory and fine S porch; the oak roof of the nave is carved with representations of gates, commemorating the Sir Geoffrey Gate who restored it in the 15th cent.

Ingatestone (FG 19) EC Wed (2,470). As at neighbouring Fryerning, the church has a splendid 15th-cent. brick tower; and there are interesting monuments to the Petre family, and a St Christopher wall-painting. The hall is late 16th-cent., and has an 18th-cent. stable block, surmounted by a charming cupola and clock.

Laindon (FG 18) EC Wed (7,810). Very unusual is the two-storied 15th-cent. priest's house built on to the end of the church, itself a simple building with good timbering. There is a 15th-cent. hall, now a farm; and to the S the Langdon Hills – 378 ft., a considerable height for Essex – provide extensive views.

Lawford (GA 23) (1,758). Here is a timber-framed hall, built in 1583, to which a Georgian front was later added. The chancel of the church is unusually fine, and there are some kneeling Waldegrave effigies.

Layer Marney (FK 21) (210). The brickwork of the many-storied gateway, with its towers and twisted chimneys, suggests the splendour of the Tudor mansion that was projected, but never built. The church, reconstructed in the 16th. cent., with its superb Marney tombs, is also remarkable for the beauty of its brick and terra-cotta work.

Little Maplestead (FJ 23) (210). The last to be built, and the smallest, of the four round churches of the Knights Hospitallers that remain in the country (*see above* **Cressing**). The interior, with its circular nave, the roof supported by shafts springing from six piers, is of great interest and has a Norman font of curious design.

Maldon (FJ 20) EC Wed (10,510). Site of the battle against the Danes in 993, described in Byrhtwold's Anglo-Saxon poem, now a busy port at the head of the long Blackwater Estuary, with its islands and mud flats and flocks of wild fowl. The public library was originally designed at the end of the 17th cent. as a grammar school by a Dr Plume, who retained the oak-panelled upper room to house his own collection of 6,000 books, many of them very valuable. All Saints' Church is unique for its 13th-cent. triangular tower. $1\frac{1}{2}$ m. W, the fine chapter house and refectory of Beeleigh Abbey are incorporated in a lovely private house, sometimes open to the public.

Margaretting (FG 20) (770). The church, with its two timbered porches and its tower, is notable for an exceptionally good 'Stem of Jesse' window and a 15th-cent. octagonal font.

Newport (FF 23) EC Wed (2,000). Its single street is lined with attractive houses, some raised on a causeway above it. Crown House has excellent pargeting and a delightful shell porch, but the most remarkable building is Monks Barn, its oriel window supported on an oak base carved with a Coronation of the Virgin. In the church is the finest parish chest in England; curiously carved, it has the inside of the lid decorated with oil paintings, thought to be the earliest of their kind.

Ongar (FF 20) EC Wed (925). All that remains of a once mighty castle at Chipping Ongar is the mound and moat, but it is an attractive village, and the little church is of interest for its wooden turret and the massive timbers supporting the superstructure of the nave. High Ongar Church has Norman work in the door and nave, but more attractive is the tiny church of Norton Mandeville, some 2 m. NE, with its ancient wooden belfry and shingled spire, its well-restored rood-screen and handsomely carved pulpit.

Saffron Walden* (FF 23) EC Thurs (7,810). A very ancient town, as evidenced by the extensive earthworks to the W and S and the discovery of a large Saxon burial ground, and still of great charm. Of its many pargeted houses, the one-time Sun Inn displays what is perhaps the best example of this type of plaster work in the county. Little remains of the 12th-cent. castle, but the museum on Castle Hill is of exceptional interest; and nearby is the so-called Maze, a series of curious circular excavations of unknown origin. The church is a spacious, well-proportioned building, mainly 15th-cent., though much restored and with a spire added in 1831.

St Osyth (GB 21) EC Thurs (1,780). Here, on the site of a Saxon nunnery, an Augustinian priory was built in the 11th cent.; its remains are now incorporated in the present lovely house. The splendid flint gateway, with its two towers and posterns, and the inner gatehouse are both open to the public. The cluster of chimneys, typical of Essex, is a notable feature; and from the 80-ft. tower in the grounds there is a fine view of the neighbouring creeks and marshland. Nearby are three Martello towers. 1 m. SE, Saint Clairs, with its 15th-cent. gateway, is still surrounded by a moat.

Southend-on-Sea (FJ 18) EC Wed (164,980). Now co-extensive with Leigh-on-Sea, Prittlewell and Westcliff, this is a favourite resort of Londoners, providing every kind of entertainment. Its pier is 1½ m. long. There are open-air baths, and to the N of the town is an airfield.

Steeple Bumpstead (FG 24) (770). Moyns Park is a fine example of an Elizabethan moated house, and the village has a half-timbered guildhall built in 1592.

Pre-Norman church at Greensted

G. Douglas Bolton

Thaxted: The Guildhall

Reece Winstone

Thaxted (FG 23) EC Wed (1,830). This little town, at the very heart of Essex and surrounded by charming villages, is dominated by its noble church, justly called the cathedral of Essex, and one of the very few in the county built of stone. It has a variety of houses, Tudor and Georgian, and two fine half-timbered buildings: the Guildhall, whose open ground floor was once a market hall, and another in a cobbled lane nearby that leads to the church. Horham Hall, 2 m. to the SW, is one of the best of the brick Tudor mansions so typical of Essex.

Waltham Abbey⋆ (FD 20) EC Thurs (5,620). Of the great abbey, the gateway and an old bridge remain, and the nave of the abbey church, containing the oldest Norman work in the county (the E end was added in the 19th cent.), is still in use. Here the body of Harold was buried before the high altar after the battle of Hastings, but the tomb has long since been destroyed.

Wimbish (FF 23) (1,380). The restored 12th-cent. church has glass and a screen of the 14th cent., and a curious brass effigy dated 1347. Tiptofts, a moated farmhouse, part of which dates back to 1300, has a unique aisled hall.

Witham (FJ 21) EC Wed (9,460). The town has existed since 913, and is today a rambling place with many old and attractive houses. The church, on nearby Chipping Hill, has interesting monuments and a screen of the 14th cent., but the S porch dates from about 1200, and there is Roman brickwork in the embattled tower. Faulkbourne Hall, 2 m. NW, though restored, is a splendid house, with much of its lovely Tudor brickwork still intact.

Opposite: Detail from the original painting by John Aldridge.
Cornlands slope gently to estuaries, sea-walls, saltings, and white weather-boarded mills, where the wheat is ground. To these coasts came the East Saxons, or 'East Seaxe' (hence the name Essex), some 1,500 years ago. In the foreground we see a coin of King Cunobelinus or Cymbeline; the Silver Oyster of Colchester; and a crystal of sea-salt, the symbol of this county's most ancient industry.

PETER
GRIMES
an
OPERA

AVO

SUTTON HOO BURIAL

The windmill at Thorpeness J.Allan Cash

SUFFOLK

AN INTRODUCTION BY ADRIAN BELL

On one border of Suffolk they plant belts of conifers to stop the soil blowing away; on the other side they plant marram-grass to stop the sea washing the soil away. Erosion is constantly at work. Suffolk is a county of contrasting soils: there are sandy heaths along the coast, and heathlands again in the north-west area around Brandon, called Breckland. But the middle region consists of fertile glacial clay, retentive of water, and this is known as 'high Suffolk'. This is the country of wheat and of oak trees, of thatched and timbered houses, framed with the oak and roofed with the straw of the wheat.

The fertility of high Suffolk depends on a system of pipe-drains and ditches to carry off the winter's rains. The stability of the Breckland soil depends on the afforestation carried out by the Forestry Commission. The battle of the sea-coast is in perpetual crisis: every material has been used, from concrete to

Opposite: Detail from the original painting by John O'Connor.
The South Folk, coming from across the North Sea, gave their name to this county of low shifting coasts, slow rivers, and wide estuaries. From the wealth earned by the medieval cloth trade sprang fine towns and villages. In the picture, we find the flint-panelled tower of a church and the pargeted gable-end of a house. The county's poet is George Crabbe, whose *Peter Grimes* became the subject of the opera by Benjamin Britten, himself a Suffolk man.

marram, to keep the sea at bay. Thus Suffolk as we see it today is a creation of the hand of man, and the face of the county is domestic: you may say it represents a marriage of husbandry and housewifery. The carved and plastered farmhouses speak of a substantial comfort supported by the fields of corn around them. Pastures are few, save in the river valleys. The Stour Valley and the Waveney Valley bound the county to the south and north-east respectively. Here, in contrast to the marram-grass of the east and the conifers of the western areas, you find yourself in a pastoral landscape of willows and green levels full of cattle. The Stour Valley is still the land of Constable's pictures.

But all across Suffolk itself, between Stour and Waveney, are lesser pastoral valleys, dividing the rolling cornland: valleys of streams which for much of their length a horse could jump – the Brett, the Lark, the Blyth and even the Deben. Every small town has its stream or mill brook, as Eye, Framlingham and Lavenham. Windmills were once a feature of every ridge of higher ground, as one would expect in a country of corn. Even forty years ago mill-sails turned in Suffolk without being much remarked on. A few mills have been preserved: a post mill at Saxtead Green, near Framlingham, lately restored by the Ministry of Works, is one of the finest examples of its kind.

Before it was subdued by man, the corn-growing region of high Suffolk was a great oak forest. Even today, if you walk across a late stubble you may see a host of embryo oak-trees sprouting up, twin leaves from acorns dropped from the hedgerow oaks or carried by birds. You realize that in a generation, if men were no more, the oak forest would be on its way again to resume possession of the land.

Farm and Village

The nature of the farming has determined the shape of the villages. Comparatively few compact villages remain – those are the ones which formerly approximated to small towns – Laxfield, Stradbroke, Debenham. These villages included men of every trade required for the amenities of life, from miller and saddler to chemist and glover. The whereabouts of the old compact villages of the open-field system of agriculture may be conjectured from the siting of churches, which are now often some way from the nearest house, and in a number of instances approachable only by a footpath over a cornfield, or across a meadow or through a farmyard.

When high Suffolk was enclosed, a village resolved itself into groups of cottages around the nuclei of the big farms, whose tenants worked on them. The pattern of many of these farmsteads is a house which is Elizabethan at the back, with a Georgian addition in brick of a dining and a drawing room, the two best bedrooms above them. Flanking the farmyard are cottages which were for horseman and stockman, who needed to be close to their charges. With its barns and yards, a large farm whose lay-out belonged to the early 19th century approximated almost to a village itself. There would be several of these farms in a parish, with the lonely church as the only focal point for its population. Footpaths formerly linked these scattered farming hamlets; but with the coming of tarmac and the bicycle, the footpaths have fallen into disuse. To compensate for this, Suffolk has many narrow and winding byways. The few motor-roads crossing the county siphon off the fast traffic; so you may walk or cycle these lanes (which is the only way really to see the country) in peace through the still remote-seeming parishes.

The Abbey gateway, Bury St Edmunds

G. Douglas Bolton

Although the visitor may be unable to discover anything he could call a hill in Suffolk, the county is not flat, but undulating from valley to valley of the small streams that drain it. From a spot on the Cambridgeshire border you can see Ely cathedral like a crumb on the horizon, twenty miles away in the Fens. From the same spot you can also see King's College chapel in Cambridge, thirteen miles away, when a sunbeam lights it up. For there you stand on that chalk ridge which becomes Newmarket Heath – no heath in the sense that Breckland is heath or the country behind Dunwich, but really the eastern end of the Chiltern Hills, which reach here across Bedford and Hertfordshire.

The work of Suffolk is agriculture. It is still the least industrialized of the English counties. Formerly it was the most industrialized. Its prosperity was based on overspill: refugees from religious oppression on the Continent settled here and wove the wool from the great flocks of sheep which the county supported. (Silk-weaving is still a staple industry of Sudbury.) Hence the richly carved houses of Lavenham, a wool-weaving town, and the churches of even smaller villages like Worlingworth, whose font-cover reaches almost to the roof. The same power of money which later was to build Manchester and Birmingham, in an earlier century created lovely little towns like Clare, and embellished churches.

Suffolk Specialities

Suffolk once supplied London with butter from its indigenous Suffolk Dun cow, ancestor of the native Red Poll breed. Suffolk has also bred the Large Black pig, the Black-face sheep and the Suffolk Punch horse. The Suffolk Punch has very little 'feather', i.e. hair about its heels, and was the only horse that could plough the heavy clay without bringing home half a hundredweight of it hanging in gobbets around his hooves. Suffolk people made a fine art of curing the bacon from their Large Black pig, steeping it first in a liquor whose chief ingredient was old Suffolk ale, and then smoking it over a smoulder of oak sawdust. These hams, which once hung in every farmhouse, are now luxuries. On the other hand, the herring bought in Lowestoft is still cheap for these days and is, in flavour, an utterly different thing from the same fish bought in London.

The broad river-estuaries and coastal heaths afford rich opportunities for bird-watchers; but the wild life of mid-Suffolk tends to be there by permission of man. In the neighbourhood of the big estates pheasants are almost as domesticated as poultry. I have even had a partridge nesting under a peony in my garden. But there are derelict aerodromes left over from the war, which are becoming refuges for wild life. Banished by the chemical sprays of modern farming from the cornfields, birds and wild flowers find sanctuary in the wilderness around the ruined buildings.

Buildings

Apart from two small regions of crag and limestone near the coast, Suffolk's only stone for building is flint. One of the most impressive examples of this is Burgh Castle overlooking Breydon Water. Its three great walls and its square bastions, enclosing about four acres of land, still stand much as they did when it was an outpost of the Roman empire. Rough flints and mortar were used to build the round towers of small 11th-century churches, and the effect is a sort of petrified pudding. But dressed flintwork later became a fine art, and was used in chequer designs, interspersed with freestone, or in a series of cuspid forms

Flatford : Willy Lott's cottage

G. Douglas Bolton

around church walls, as at Covehithe. The dark flint cores catch the light flickeringly, like black glass. The nature of Suffolk's chief building materials, wood and plaster, begot a galaxy of talent in carving, in embossing designs on plaster, known as pargeting, and in thatching. The outstanding example of pargeting is the Ancient House at Ipswich, which is a plasterer's fantasy. Barn-building was a trade allied to house-building in this country of abundant corn harvests. Suffolk also abounded once in small brickyards – hence the numerous 'Brick Kiln Farms' in the county. The thatcher's art still flourishes, both in reed and straw.

Great lords lie in effigy in Suffolk's country churches, the Dukes of Suffolk sleeping remote in Wingfield church on a hillside with only two houses near. Lord Bardolph who fought at Agincourt lies in Dennington and the Dukes of Norfolk with their ladies are supine on lofty tombs in Framlingham. It was from Framlingham Castle that Mary marched on London to claim the throne. Blythburgh church, another beauty from the wealth of the wool trade, rides the surrounding heathland like an ark. From here you can walk to Blyford along the bank of the Blyth river, on which the barges used to ply to Halesworth. Wenhaston church nearby contains a famous Doom – a posse of nude lovelies being received into the Devil's maw, their blonde hair and flesh-tints still fresh. You can't help wondering how the monk who painted this warning to his flock knew so accurately the graces of the female figure.

357

Framlingham Castle

Industry Old and New

The Suffolk boundary lies close to the source of man's first tools – flints from the neolithic workings known as Grime's Graves near Brandon. For centuries flints for flintlocks have been knapped in Brandon. Ipswich produces the implements, as well as the fertilizers, for the mechanized farming of today. Sizewell's nuclear power station, in the same county as Brandon, completes the gamut of man as a tool-using animal.

Not far from Sizewell is Aldeburgh, which drains London of its art critics for its festival, where Benjamin Britten's operas have their premières. Architecturally Aldeburgh lacks charm, save for its Moot Hall, once in the town's centre, but now almost on the beach. Southwold, a little to the north of the drowned city of Dunwich, is prettier than Aldeburgh. It is still essentially a cluster of fishermen's whitewashed cottages around a lighthouse, backed by a heath – but cottages which now look as if they were lived in by the ladies of Cranford. There are also some painted ladies in Southwold; but they are figureheads from old ships, refurbished and mounted outside front doors. The winter weather is bitter on the east coast: it would kill a west-countryman; but it stimulates the inhabitants to live almost for ever.

Behind Aldeburgh lies heathland which the poet Crabbe described. Now people play golf where in Crabbe's day gipsies huddled and starved. To read Suffolk's two poets, Crabbe and Robert Bloomfield, is to realize what different feelings the windswept heath of the coast and the rich farmlands of mid-Suffolk could evoke. Crabbe had bitter memories of his boyhood home; Bloomfield had fond ones, although he worked hard as a farmer's boy at Sapiston, and was not strong physically. Crabbe, where he lived, saw

> *Small black-legged sheep devour with hunger keen*
> *The meagre herbage, fleshless, lank and lean.*

But in Bloomfield's country, shepherds and their boys

> *Boast their pastures and the healthful show*
> *Of well-grown lambs, the glory of the spring.*

358

SUFFOLK

Owing to the unstable coastline, there is no continuous coast road in Suffolk. Orford, Aldeburgh, Dunwich, Southwold are all a few miles to the east of the main north–south road, which runs from Ipswich to Lowestoft. The only waterside town that lay on it, Woodbridge, has been by-passed. Woodbridge today is lively, painted and preserved, a place of youth in sailcloth trousers. The Deben estuary is gay with white and blue sails, and glitters at high tide before a background of fields and woods.

Suffolk is a county above all of detail. Unless you travel slowly, you miss many charming glimpses of this domesticated countryside. The fields are nearly always busy: new shapes appear in them, which the machine makes in dealing with the immemorial stuff of harvest. You will see the latest combine-harvester at work, and then perhaps an old harvest wagon, with grass sprouting from its joints, dragged into use once more at need. At Abbot's Hall, Stowmarket, there is housed a museum on rural life. The tools of the horse age are being collected, just before it is too late, and preserved. The collection is continually expanding and is the Folk Museum of the county. Ipswich has in Christchurch Mansion a museum of Suffolk social history, building and personalities. There is also a museum devoted to natural history and archaeology. Although industry and overspill are enlarging the areas of the big towns, Suffolk is still a community that lives chiefly by and on the land – and that is what it still looks like.

Hadleigh *J. Allan Cash*

Some houses and gardens open to the public

Aldeburgh Moot Hall 7m SE of Saxmundham on A1094 *Map* GE 25. *Restored early 16th-cent. timber-framed building of two storeys, with council chamber on upper floor containing old maps and prints, reached by means of external stairway.*

Christchurch Mansion At Ipswich Entry through Soane Street *Map* GB 24. *Furnished as period house (Tudor to Victorian) housing Corporation collection of pictures (including 15th-cent. East Anglian paintings, and works by Gainsborough, Constable, Steer, etc.); applied arts (pottery, porcelain, glass), local history collections, costume, etc.* Ipswich County Borough Council.

Flatford Mill and **Willy Lott's Cottage** East Bergholt 17m SW of Ipswich off B1070 *Map* GA 23. *18th-cent. water-mill and mill house once belonging to John Constable's father. The subject of the 'Hay Wain' and other famous pictures by the painter. Nearby stands the 17th-cent. Willy Lott's Cottage. NT. No access to interiors.*

Framlingham Castle 8m W of Saxmundham on B1119 *Map* GC 26. *Preserves fine curtain walls with thirteen towers, the work of Roger Bigod, between 1177 and 1215. Array of Tudor chimneys. Almshouse built by Pembroke College, Cambridge, in 1639, within inner walls.*

Gainsborough's House Sudbury Gainsborough St *Map* FJ 24. *16th-cent. house with Georgian façade and Strawberry Hill Gothic bow-rooms. Birthplace of Thomas Gainsborough. Gainsborough paintings & contemporary furniture. Modern art exhibitions.*

Hengrave Hall 3m NW of Bury St Edmunds on A1101 *Map* FJ 26. *Splendid early Tudor house of historical interest, with turreted gatehouse and interior courtyard, built by Sir Thomas Kytson. Fine interior panelling. Old glass in chapel. Now a RC convent school. Open medieval church with 11th-cent. tower in grounds.*

Melford Hall Long Melford 3m N of Sudbury on A134 *Map* FJ 24. *Notable Tudor and 18th-cent. mansion (NT), the home of the Hyde Parkers since 1781. Fine porcelain, furniture and paintings.* NT.

Saxtead Green Windmill 2m W of Framlingham off B1115 *Map* GC 26. *Fine 18th-cent. post mill twice altered, the present superstructure dating from 1854.*

Books for further reading

The 'feel' of Suffolk

R. BURN, *et al. The Two Counties of Suffolk; A Pictorial Study*
O. COOK *Suffolk* (Vision of England series) 1948
G. E. EVANS *Pattern under the Plough* 1966
A. JOBSON *A Window in Suffolk* 1962
A. MEE *Suffolk* (King's England series) 1941

Many writers, artists and musicians have settled in Suffolk or are native to it. Notable among their works are the writings of GEORGE CRABBE, EDWARD FITZGERALD, NEIL BELL and ADRIAN BELL; the paintings of CONSTABLE, GAINSBOROUGH and SEAGO; and the music of BENJAMIN BRITTEN (particularly his opera *Peter Grimes*, based upon GEORGE CRABBE'S poem *The Borough*). The local allusions by GILES, the cartoonist, and by PAUL JENNINGS illuminate the scene with humour.

Natural history

W. PAYN *Birds of Suffolk* 1962

Topography and architecture

H. M. CAUTLEY *Suffolk Churches and Their Treasures* 3rd edn 1954
N. PEVSNER *Suffolk* (Buildings of England series) 1961
N. SCARFE *Suffolk: A Shell Guide* 1966
WARD, LOCK & CO. LTD. *Guides to Felixstowe, Lowestoft, Ipswich,* etc.

Gazetteer

SUFFOLK

Aldeburgh (GE 25) EC Wed (2,970). Attractive seaside town; no longer an important harbour as in 15th to 17th cent., from which period dates the much-restored moot house. Birthplace of George Crabbe (1754) and home of Benjamin Britten. The annual musical festival is held in June.

Beccles (GE 28) EC Wed (7,330). Well-placed above R. Waveney, with streets of Georgian houses sloping to the quay, and a yachting centre with annual regatta. The 14th-cent. church has fine porch and a detached campanile. S W of the town, Elizabethan Roos Hall and Leman House, in Ballygate, are both worth seeing.

Blythburgh (GE 27) (650). One of the finest churches in E Anglia, 15th-cent. flint flush-work and stone, the tower 200 years earlier. The spaciousness of the interior is enhanced by a painted roof, with beautifully carved angels.

Bungay (GD 28) EC Wed (3,580). Market town, with boating on R. Waveney, and ruins of Earl Bigod's 12th-cent. castle (AM). A disastrous fire in 1688 accounts for the number of 18th-cent. red-brick houses (some Dutch-gabled). We also find an octagonal butter cross, and Georgian monuments in Holy Trinity. **Mettingham,** 2 m. SE, has the flint-work gatehouse of a 14th-cent. castle, and a moated hall with Dutch gables, built about 1660.

Bury St Edmunds (FJ 26) EC Thurs (21,140). Acquired its present distinctive appearance in 1750–1850, though many of the existing Georgian façades conceal houses of 17th cent. and earlier. Two of the oldest buildings

Kersey *J. Allan Cash*

are in Churchgate St: at one end, Norman House; at the other, Cemetery Gate, serving as bell-tower to St James's, now the Cathedral. Nearby is the early 15th-cent. St Mary's, with a beautiful roof and fine chancel monuments. Of the medieval abbey only scant ruins in Abbey Gardens and the splendid gateway (1347) remain. Outstanding examples of Georgian architecture are the Unitarian Chapel (1711); Angel Corner (1711), now belonging to the NT and open to the public; the Athenaeum Subscription Rooms (1804); the Guildhall (1809) with its 13th-cent. doorway; the Town Hall, originally designed by Robert Adam as a theatre; and the New Theatre, which replaced it in 1819 and is now restored.

Clare (FH 24) EC Wed (1,320). Beautiful little town on the R. Stour, many of the houses with exceptional pargeting; among the best are Nethergate and White House. In the church (fine windows in choir and aisle), is a 17th-cent. gallery pew, and the

361

heraldic glass in the E window is of same period. The villages of **Cavendish** (3 m. E) and **Stoke-by-Clare** (2 m. SW) are both attractive; the first for its colour-washed cottages round the church, its Regency Hall and Tudor chimneyed Blacklands Hall; the second for its lovely 15th-cent. pulpit (only 28 in. in diameter) and the Queen Anne house (now a school) that incorporates parts of a Benedictine monastery.

Debenham (GB 26) (910). Near the source of R. Deben. The church at the top of the village street has a fine nave roof and arcade, and a Lady chapel over W porch. There is a windmill and a moated Elizabethan house, Crowes Hall.

Dennington (GC 26) (520). The restored church is memorable for the beauty of its contents: delicately carved screens and lofts, alabaster tomb of the Lord Bardolph who fought at Agincourt, pyx-canopy before the altar, painted font-cover, and some of the best 15th-cent. carved benches in the county.

Denston (FH 25) (180). Noble 15th-cent. flint-and-stone church, with impressive nave windows and clere-story, containing medieval tiles and glass, carved chancel-stalls and nave-benches, and box-pews from the 18th cent. in the aisles. The rear wing of the Hall is Tudor; the front, fine 18th-century.

Dunwich (GE 27) (140). The 13th-cent. port, with its six churches, lies at the bottom of the sea, which still encroaches. All that is left today is a hamlet of fewer than 150 people, an early 19th-cent. church beside the chapel of the ruined leper hospital, and the remains of a 13th-cent. priory, a small museum, and still crumbling cliffs. 2 m. to the S is the nature reserve of **Westleton Heath**.

East Bergholt (GA 23) (1,720). The birthplace (1776) of Constable, and repeatedly painted by him, it has several old Tudor houses and well-known gardens at East Bergholt Place. The church has an external bell-cage, in which the bells are hung upside down. At **Little Wenham**, 4 m. N, is the 13th-cent. Hall (now AM and unoccupied), one of the best pre-served brick houses of the period in the country; and a church, mainly of the same period, with notable later additions.

Felixstowe (GD 23) EC Wed (17,250). Seaside resort, with golf, two-mile promenade and good bathing. A passenger ferry connects with Harwich, across the estuaries of Stour and Orwell.

Framlingham (GC 26) EC Wed (1,940). Attractive market town, with fine domestic architecture, particularly in Market Hill and Castle St. Remains of gatehouse and external walls of 12th-cent. castle (AM), altered for comfort in Tudor times, when the brick chimneys were added by the Howards, to whose splendour the range of tombs in the parish church bear witness. At **Parham**, 2½ m. SE, is the 16th-cent. Moat Hall, now a farmhouse, as well as Tudor chimneys at Old Hall and decorative brickwork at Parham House.

Fressingfield (GC 27) (730). Well worth visiting for the charm of the carved bench-ends in the church, the Queen Anne rectory and the plaster-and-timber Fox and Goose inn. Whittingham Hall, with its Dutch gables, dates from mid-17th century.

Hadleigh (GA 24) EC Wed (3,460). Market town on a tributary of the Stour, which is crossed by a medieval bridge. The church (Early English, with screen, brasses and lead-covered

Cottages in Lady Street, Lavenham

spire) is one of a group of almost contemporaneous buildings, such as the three-storeyed, timbered Guildhall and the Deanery Tower with its elaborate brickwork. Excellent Tudor and Georgian shops and houses in Market, High and Benton Streets.

Helmingham (GB 25) (210). The quadrangular Tudor Hall, often modified and with 18th-cent. crenellation added by Nash, is surrounded by a moat (the drawbridge is still raised each night) and deer park. Built by the Tollemache family, whose monuments are in the church.

Hengrave (FJ 26) (190). The Hall, now a Catholic convent school, is a magnificent Tudor mansion, built round a quadrangle of white brick and stone. Note the Renaissance carving over the main entrance, and the glass in the chapel. The little church, with its round pre-Norman tower, stands in the park, alongside the house.

Herringfleet (GE 29) (260). The church has an early Norman round tower and thatched roof. Some brick vaulting remains from the 14th cent. at the ruins of St Olave's Priory (AM), and nearby is one of the few smock-mills still working. The village of **Somerleyton** (1 m. SE) and the Hall were entirely reconstructed in 19th century. Visitors are sometimes admitted to this last, with its attractive park. 2 m. NW of Herringfleet is **Fritton**, also with thatched church and still earlier round tower, Norman nave and carved screen. Close at hand is the three-mile Decoy for wildfowl.

Heveningham (GD 27). The Hall is the outstanding Palladian building in the county, with internal decoration by James Wyatt, and park laid out by Capability Brown. The church has a 14th-cent. Heveningham effigy in wood.

363

Ickworth (FJ 26) (80). Ickworth House, with its 200-yd. curved stucco front and central dome, was begun for an Earl of Bristol, who was also Bishop of Derry; but it was not completed till after his death (1803). It contains notable silver and pictures, and was recently acquired, together with the 18,000-acre park (where the Hervey family have lived for 500 years), by the NT.

Ipswich (GB 24) EC Wed (117,330). Industrial town at the head of Orwell Estuary, and largest port between Thames and Humber. Not many of its medieval churches are notable, though the civic church, St Mary-le-Tower, rebuilt in late 19th-cent. Gothic, has a 176-ft. tower and fine carvings, including a pulpit attributed to Grinling Gibbons. The best ecclesiastical building is the Unitarian chapel (1699), with much period detail and box-pews. Wolsey's Gate, red-brick with royal coat of arms, is the only relic of the Cardinal's project to build a college in his birthplace. The Great White Horse is associated with Mr Pickwick's mistake about the number of his room. 16th-cent. Christchurch Mansion is now a museum and picture gallery (works by Constable and Gainsborough), run in conjunction with the museum in High Street. Sparrowe's House, now a bookshop, is a remarkably intact specimen of Jacobean building, with sumptuous pargeting. Two features of the port are the modern granary and the mid-19th-cent. custom house. At **Westerfield**, 2 m. N, the Hall, with formal gardens and Dutch gables, is late 17th-cent.; and the fine hammer-beam roof of the little church is carved with 36 angels.

Kedington (FG 24) (850). Another of the Suffolk churches that, like Dennington, is worth seeing for the loveliness of its interior. The best of the woodwork includes the family pew, the screen (dated 1619), and the three-decker pulpit, complete with canopy, wig-pole and hour-glass.

Kersey (FK 24) (400). Unspoiled village street, intercepted by water-splash and lined with half-timbered cottages. The church, well sited, with flint tower and S porch, has suffered restoration.

Kessingland (GE 28) EC Thurs (1,760). Fishing village, with bathing from sandy beach, and golf. The church has a lofty tower, serving as landmark for sailors, and a thatched roof.

Lakenheath (FH 28). Overlooking great stretch of fenland, now occupied by one of largest US air bases in Britain. Lovely church, of limestone and brick, with a chantry over the W porch. Inside, brick floor, Norman chancel-arch, 14th-cent. wall-paintings and carved bench-ends.

Lavenham (FK 24) EC Wed (1,490). Medieval clothing town, rich in timbered houses (note especially Guild Hall and Wool Hall), and dominated by the church, with a splendid tower and with wood-carving in both chapels and, particularly, in the two chantries.

Laxfield (GC 27) EC Wed (670). Here was born, at Dowsing's Farm (now at peace within its moat), the Puritan iconoclast Wm Dowsing, who did untold damage to the churches of the county in the 17th cent. The Seven Sacrament font and carved bench-heads in his own church were, however, spared. The restored Guild-hall is 15th-cent.

Leiston (GE 26) EC Wed (4,120). With its century-old iron industry, is 2 m. from a lovely stretch of coast, where, at the seaside hamlet of Size-well, a nuclear power station has been built. The church has a fine font and a timbered roof; and, 1 m. N, extensive abbey ruins and an octagonal Tudor tower now serve as a diocesan retreat.

Long Melford (FJ 24) EC Wed (2,410). A spacious village green, 15th-cent. inn, almshouses, two Elizabethan Halls, Melford and Kentwell (the first turreted and with 18th-cent. additions, including a gazebo; the second approached by a lime avenue, and moated; both open to the public), and the finest church in Suffolk. A masterpiece of flush-work and glass (much of it 15th-cent.), it was rebuilt in 1496, largely thanks to a Clopton of Kentwell Hall, whose chantry is one of some thirty monuments and memorials to the family. The Lady chapel, used for a time as a school, is very beautiful.

Lowestoft (GF 29) EC Thurs (45,690). Important harbour and centre of fishing industry, connected by swing-bridge with South Town, a popular resort (bathing, sea and river fishing, and golf). Spacious 15th-cent. parish church, with earlier 140-ft. tower and spire. **The Ness** is the most easterly point in England; to SW, **Lothing Lake** is connected with **Oulton Broad**, a large village and yachting centre.

Lowestoft: heavy seas off Ness Point *G. Douglas Bolton*

Mildenhall (FH 27) EC Thurs (6,740). Market town on R. Lark at the edge of the fen country. Some Georgian buildings, including an almshouse; and an old market cross, wood with lead roof. A fine church, with Lady chapel over beautiful N porch; but its glory is the carving in the roofs.

Nayland-with-Wissington (FK 23). Attractive villages, facing each other across the upper reaches of R. Stour, both with noteworthy churches: the first for carving of roof and gallery, eight painted panels of the 15th cent. and Constable reredos; the second for Norman nave and chancel, and 13th-cent. wall-paintings. At Wissington, near the church, stand a fine mill and the Hall, enlarged at the end of the 18th cent. Alston Court is an early Tudor building, with richly carved timberwork.

Newmarket (FG 26) EC Thurs (11,210). Scene of the first-recorded horse race in 1619, and famous ever since for racing, blood-stock sales and the Jockey Club. Apart from the Rutland Arms and a few houses of the same period, the Georgian atmosphere is fast disappearing. The impressive earthworks, **Devil's Dyke** (AM), which stretch 7 m. across the heath, are actually over the Cambridgeshire border.

Orford (GE 24) EC Wed (650). A fishing and holiday village on the long arm of the R. Ore within the Ness. The fine keep (AM) – all that remains of the castle – has a collection of armour and a splendid view from the roof. The Norman chancel of the church is ruined, but the 14th-cent. nave has a fine font and brasses.

Southwold (GE 27) EC Wed (2,230). Attractive little resort and residential town on cliff top, grouped around greens, from one of which surprisingly

springs a lighthouse. There is a little Dutch-gabled museum. The church, yet another example of East Anglian flint flush-work, with a noble tower, has a hammer-beam roof, screens with much original colouring and a Seven Sacraments font.

Stoke-by-Nayland (FK 23) EC Wed (920). Behind a group of half-timbered cottages rises the 120-ft. tower of the church that Constable so often painted, with its admirable brasses and alabaster monuments, and a notable 17th-cent. library over the S porch. 2 m. NE, Gifford Hall, Tudor, quadrangular, with a gatehouse, contains a fine hammer-beamed hall; and, 2 m. SE, 17th-cent. Thorington Hall (NT) has a fine chimney-stack and period furnishing.

Stowmarket (GA 25) EC Tue (7,790). Market and industrial town, with new I.C.I. factory. The market place still has something of its Regency atmosphere. The church contains a rare wig-stand, some fine monuments and a portrait of Milton's tutor, Dr Young, whom he visited at the Old Vicarage. 2 m. NE, the Manor House – now a farm, Columbine Hall – stands reflected in its moat.

Sudbury (FJ 24) EC Wed (6,640). The Eatanswill of *Pickwick Papers*, with many old houses, including the birthplace of Gainsborough, whose statue stands on Market Hill. Salter's Hall and the Old Moot Hall are 15th-cent.; and all three churches (of which St Gregory's possibly goes back to the 7th cent.) have noteworthy interiors.

Ufford (GC 25) (800). Outside the church, stocks and whipping-post still stand; inside is the superbly carved 18-ft. font-cover (1480), once gilded. Some of the original colour can be seen on the roof; there are painted saints on the S side of the rood-screen. The bench-ends are admirably carved.

Sudbury: the birthplace of Thomas Gainsborough

Reece Winstone

Wingfield (GC 27) (400). The only inhabited castle in Suffolk (unfortunately not shown to the public) is mostly Tudor, but the original 14th-cent. S front is complete, with central gatehouse and corner turrets protected by a moat. The church, of the same period, with chantry chapels adjoining the chancel, is famous for the tombs, both wood and alabaster, of the de la Poles and Wingfields.

Woodbridge (GC 24) EC Wed (5,930). On high ground above the head of Deben estuary, one of the most charming Suffolk towns, with quayside, ancient tide-mill and clustering barns. There are many fine Georgian and earlier houses; the Shire Hall and half-timbered houses in New St are Tudor. The church, with an admirable tower, porch and font of the 15th cent., stands above the town; and

Kyson Hill (NT) is a charming stretch of parkland along the river bank.

Woolpit (FK 26) (810). A village of half-timbered and red-brick houses, whose church has a hammer-beam roof famous for its angels; we find also traceried bench-ends and rood-screens, 17th-cent. chancel-gates and fine monuments.

Yoxford (GD 26) EC Wed (790). A village of charming houses, some timbered and oversailing, some with bow-windows and balconies, surrounded by the parkland of three country houses. Of these, Cockfield Hall is the most beautiful, with its red-brick N wing, stables and gatehouse dating back to the time of Henry VIII, and with a restored central Jacobean block.

368

On the Broads at Potter Heigham   J. Allan Cash

NORFOLK

AN INTRODUCTION BY J. WENTWORTH DAY

Charles II had no use for Norfolk. He said it was fit only to be dug up to make roads for the rest of England. Horace Walpole shuddered when obliged, for family estate reasons, to journey into 'the wilds of Norfolk'. As for Holkham, home of Coke of Norfolk, Earl of Leicester and 'Father of English Farming', that forty-thousand-acre estate when he inherited it in 1776 was so barren 'that two rabbits might often be seen fighting for one blade of grass'.

These are unseemly libels. Norfolk is a county unique. A broad, bright land of high heath and great fir forests; of green marshes and shining broads; of vast barley stubbles that run on to the sky; of moorland purple with heather; and, for contrast, a great city of antiquity, Norwich, proud in ancient beauty yet pulsing with industrial life.

Norfolk has probably the bluest skies in England, the clearest visibility and the least rainfall. Its blue skies, clear distances and that blend of heath and marsh, woodland and stubble, ancient manor house and reed-thatched cottage gave birth to the greatest school of landscape painters in England – the Norwich School. Crome, Cotman, Stark, Stannard, Henry Bright, the Ladbrookes, Lound, Short and, in our day, Munnings, are among its immortals.

369

Norfolk, to be factual, dull and precise, is the fourth largest English county. Yorkshire, Lincolnshire and Devon alone are bigger. It covers 1,302,503 acres. It is an oval, being sixty-seven miles long and forty-three miles wide at extreme points. The North Sea, including the Wash, bounds it on the north and east. Suffolk lies to the south, Cambridgeshire to the west. It is almost an island, for it is cut off from Suffolk by the Rivers Waveney and Little Ouse, and from Cambridgeshire by the Great Ouse and the Nene. Ninety miles of coastline complete the picture.

Norwich had little more than 120,000 inhabitants in 1961, followed by Great Yarmouth with 53,000, King's Lynn with 27,500, and then plenty of little country towns of from 2,000 to 7,000 inhabitants. In the past Norfolk had more than fifty monastic houses, including some of the greatest and most powerful abbeys in England. No other English county can equal this.

The Rocks

The geology of Norfolk is fascinating. Chalk underlies most of it, from the Cambridgeshire Gog Magog Hills through west Norfolk from Thetford to Castle Acre and on to Holme-next-the-Sea. Breckland, that unique wild country of heath, sandy rabbit-warrens and lonely wastes, was the armoury of prehistoric man. Here Neolithic man quarried his flints in at least three hundred and sixty-six pits and underground workings, of which Grime's Graves, near Brandon, are the classic example. His flint axes, arrow-heads, skinning-knives and scrapers were exported all over eastern and midland England.

At Hunstanton one finds carstone, a dark brown, gritty, rather soft 'ginger-bread' stone, much of it lying below Red Chalk. There is also much gault clay. Flint pebbles and cobbles are a ubiquitous material. Faced flints are common as building material. Hence the thousands of flint-built farmhouses, cottages, barns, walls and other buildings.

Links with the Past

Many prehistoric barrows exist; and finds of metals, weapons, ornaments, urns, pottery and other relics of man, dating from 400,000 B.C. to 500 B.C. have been made, the earliest, consisting of pear-shaped axe-handles of the so-called Acheulian type, from the Great Inter-Glacial Period. These have been found at riverside knapping-sites such as Whitlingham.

In Breckland, in the centre of Mickle Mere, are remains of lake-dwellings similar to those of the Somerset lake-villages. Bronze Age swords, gold dress-fasteners and other objects have been found at Caistor St Edmund, Downham Market, in Norwich itself, at Caister by Yarmouth and in a few other places. An interesting early Iron Age settlement was excavated in 1935 at West Harling and its complete plan revealed.

At Brancaster the Romans built the northernmost of their so-called forts of the Saxon shore, which extended as far south as Dover. Although this covered six and a half acres, and once commanded the approaches to the Wash, little remains of it today. Little more can be seen of the once-walled town of Venta Icenorum at Caistor St Edmund, which enclosed thirty-four acres of streets, houses, baths, temples and places of business. A large Anglo-Saxon cemetery is near by.

The outstanding survivals of the Anglo-Saxon period are the remains of a Saxon Cathedral at North Elmham, and the round church-towers which are a

Cley: the windmill J. Allan Cash

distinctive feature of the Norfolk scene. There are just under one hundred and eighty such towers in England, of which Norfolk has one hundred and nineteen. About twenty of them are Anglo-Saxon, the rest probably Norman. But a unique feature of the Saxon period are the Norfolk Broads themselves, many of which are believed to have been formed by extensive peat-digging in Saxon times.

The most splendid example of Norman architecture in the county is Norwich Cathedral. The Normans also built three great abbey churches at Binham, Wymondham and Thetford. Castle Acre, a Cluniac priory, is better worth seeing. A poem of gaunt majestic splendour.

History

Norfolk has played its part in the struggle for freedom. In the Peasants' Revolt of 1381, led by Wat Tyler, Norwich (with London and Bury) was occupied by the rebels. Led by John Litester, they plundered the city, but were finally defeated in a bloody battle at North Walsham.

Nearly two centuries later, Robert Kett, who held the manor of Wymondham, led one of the most pathetic and justifiable revolts in English history. All he asked was that the peasants' common land should not be enclosed, that incompetent priests should be removed, bondmen set free and that every parish should have a teacher to educate 'poor men's children'. Kett raised some 16,000 men and made his headquarters on Mousehold Heath, outside Norwich.

371

There, under a great oak called the Oak of Reformation, he administered justice. In 1549 he captured the city. Twice, the king offered terms of pardon. Twice, they were refused. Eventually the rebels were driven out and slaughtered to the number of 3,500.

'So ended the Norfolk Rebellion,' says Froude the historian, 'remarkable among other things, for the order which was preserved among the people during the seven weeks of lawlessness.' During the Civil War Cromwell garrisoned Norwich, and his men did a lot of damage to the Bishop's Palace and to the Cathedral. Since then the city has had a comparatively peaceful existence.

Norfolk's Golden Age, of sheep, wool and weaving, dated from the arrival of the Flemish weavers in the reign of Edward III. Right up to the mid-18th century, Norfolk throve on the backs of sheep. Hence the great number of ruined churches, and many splendid churches which yet survive, and the older manor-houses which give grace and dignity. When the Industrial Revolution brought in cotton, and caused cloth-making to move to the North of England, the Norfolk wool trade virtually died.

Fortunately, two of its most brilliant aristocratic landowners, 'Turnip' Townshend of Raynham Hall and Coke of Norfolk, of Holkham Hall, the twin fathers of English farming, revolutionized agriculture, then sunk in little better than medieval practices, and brought new and more lasting prosperity to the county. Today, Norfolk farming leads England.

Towns

Norwich is still a city of splendid houses, dominated by the white Norman keep of the castle, called charmingly in medieval times 'Blanche-Flower'. Where there is so much of outstanding interest and beauty it is hard to pick out individual items; but the following cry out for mention: the Cathedral, its close and cloisters, approached through two magnificent gateways, the churches of St Peter Mancroft and St George, Tombland (there are more than thirty old

Blickling Hall   *G. Douglas Bolton*

parish churches, many of note), Suckling House, the Guildhall and the Bridewell (miraculous squared flint-work), Elm Hill (for its old houses) and the Maddermarket Theatre. Among its many old inns, the Maid's Head was where Robert Kett kept open house during the rebellion, and the Dolphin was once a Bishop's palace. Picture-lovers cannot afford to miss the collection of paintings by the members of the Norwich School (Crome, Cotman and the rest), while the collection of civic plate is second only to London's. In short, Norwich preserves more of beauty from the past than almost any other city in England. Its famous citizens have included Sir Thomas Browne, George Borrow, Archbishop Parker, Harriet Martineau and Elizabeth Fry. Today it thrives on the production of mustard, beer, shoes and machinery, and on banking and insurance, among a host of other goods and services.

The city has produced many great men, among them Sir John Fastolf and Sir Thomas Erpingham, and some of the Boleyns and Pastons had houses in the city. The palace of Henry Howard, the poet Earl of Surrey, was in Surrey Street. Matthew Parker, Archbishop of Canterbury, and Doctor Kaye, founder of Caius College, Cambridge, were born there. Sir Thomas Browne came to live in Norwich in 1636 and lived there the rest of his life.

Sir John Fenn, the editor of the 'Paston Letters', was a native, as was Sir James Smith, first President of the Linnean Society, and William Taylor, who translated many famous German works. George Borrow lived in a house still standing in Willow Lane. Crome and Cotman, the artists, were born in Norwich; so, too, were Mrs Opie, Harriet and James Martineau and Elizabeth Fry. Joseph Gurney, the Quaker philanthropist, was born at Earlham.

King's Lynn is an ancient, Dutch-like port on the Wash, with the remote yet bustling air of a provincial capital. Its architecture is quite outstanding – a lot of good Georgian brick (and older), especially in the Tuesday and Saturday market-places, the old Guildhall, with a fine front of chequered flint and stone, the 17th-century Customs House and the Greenland Fishery Building, with early 17th-century wall-paintings. Much of the ancient town-wall survives, with parts of the Greyfriars Monastery and other medieval buildings. Red Mount Chapel, a pilgrim's chapel (c. 1485), is one of the most remarkable Gothic churches in England. St Nicholas Church, from the late 14th and early 15th centuries, is fine. The secular plate, including King John's Cup (mid-14th century) in the Guildhall, is superb, and among other treasures is an almost complete set of Charters signed by Canute and later monarchs. In short, you can spend two days in Lynn and find beauty in every hour of them – and it has some of the finest port-wine cellars in England.

When Defoe described Lynn in the 18th century as having 'more gentry and gaiety' than Norwich or Yarmouth, it was nonetheless a busy port, whose ships, quays and warehouses supplied nine counties. It is busy still – with fruit and vegetable canning, the making of beet sugar and fertilizers, malting barley and brewing beer, in addition to mussel, whelk and shrimp fishing and other more usual maritime activities.

The Broads

The Broads, which include some five thousand acres of water and many miles of rivers, are unique. Annually they attract more than 100,000 visitors. In summer they are overcrowded, noisy and vulgarized. In spring, autumn and winter, this land of marshes and windmills reverts to its old secret

The Fishermen's Hospital, Great Yarmouth

beauty. The peace of slow waters. Wind in the reeds. High clouds sailing like galleons. The chattering of sedge-warblers. Wild duck quacking in the reedbeds. Wild geese chanting under the moon. The bittern booming on indigo nights of spring. Great pike plunging. The sibilant whistle of an otter. Herons fishing like grey ghosts in the shallows. Reed-cutters' barges stacked high with Norfolk reeds – the finest thatching material in England. These are the sounds and faces of beauty.

In spring, a riot of marsh flowers from the rare orchis to kingcups, brassy by the dyke-sides, water-lilies glimmering moonlike, meadowsweet in waves of sweet sickliness, watermint sharp on the air. A botanist's paradise.

Some of the rarest birds in England are found on the Broads. The bittern, once thought extinct, has returned. The rare bearded tits or 'reed-pheasants', climbing like feathered mice through the reeds, ring their tiny bells of song.

The osprey is an occasional splendid visitor. Almost every rare duck on the British list has been recorded and most of the rare waders.

On the coast, with its marching miles of hairy, crested sandhills, miles of shining sands with, at Wells-next-the-Sea and elsewhere, thousands of acres of wigeon-haunted saltings, the sense of lonely, other-worldly beauty persists. That same sense of strange, ineluctable beauty broods over Breckland, the ancient heaths that knew the Ancient Briton and the last of the British great bustards, birds as large as turkeys. Today, some forty thousand acres of dense black, unimaginative Forestry Commission plantations cover these once wild heaths.

Norfolk as a county has produced more than its share of great men: Lord Nelson, Coke of Norfolk, 'Turnip' Townshend, Prime Minister Walpole. It is full of good and splendid houses, Holkham, Houghton, Raynham, Ryston,

374

Binham Priory

G. Douglas Bolton

Rainthorpe, Elsing, Kirstead, Breckles, Morley Old Hall, Blickling, Hunstanton Hall, Oxburgh, East Barsham, Great Cressingham, and a host of others. Castle Rising and Castle Acre are noble ruins. The Peddars Way and the Icknield Way are highroads of pre-history. Today, the rabbit and the homing farm-hand use the ancient trackways of Neolithic man. Many of its old families still survive, and it is heartening that so many of them live on their ancient lands, maintaining the best traditions of good landlordism and 'high farming'. Pre-eminent among private landowners is Her Majesty the Queen at Sandringham. There she owns some fifteen thousand acres or more, which include heathery moorland, rolling farmland, cattle-dotted marshes, great woodlands and model villages. The Sandringham estate was bought in 1861 by Edward VII, as Prince of Wales. It was then only seven thousand acres. It has been steadily enlarged. Today, more than Buckingham Palace or Windsor, it is 'home' to the Royal Family – their own private beloved country estate. Norfolk could receive no more splendid compliment. Sandringham House, a modified Jacobean residence, was built in the '70s.

No man wrote greater truth than old Thomas Fuller, who said of this bold, independent land of the North Folk, which shoulders itself into the North Sea: 'All England may be carved out of Norfolk, represented therein not only to the kind but degree thereof. Here are fens and heaths and light and deep and sand and clay ground and meadow and pasture and arable and woody, and (generally) woodless land, so grateful to this shire in the variety thereof. Thus, as in many men, though perchance this or that part may justly be cavilled at, yet all put together complete a proper person; so Norfolk, collectively taken, hath a sufficient result of pleasure and profit, that being supplied in one part, which is defective in another'.

375

Some houses and gardens open to the public

Caister Hall and **Castle** 3m N of Great Yarmouth, ¾m W Caister-on-Sea *Map* G F 31. *Earliest brick-built castle in Britain (1432), by Sir John Fastolf; later the home of Paston family. New staircase leads to 100-ft. tower with fine views. Vintage cars, motor-cycles, horse-drawn vehicles, etc.* D. A. J. Buxton, Esq.

Castle Rising 5m NE of King's Lynn on A149 *Map* F G 32. *Norman keep surrounded by impressive earthworks (AM). Built probably by the Earl of Arundel.*

Gowthorpe Manor Swardeston 4m SW of Norwich off B1113 *Map* G B 30. *16th-cent. house with porches dated 1574. Late 17th- and early 18th-cent. interiors. Open by appointment only* from Francis Hornor and Son, Old Bank of England Court, Queen St, Norwich. Tel. Norwich 24101.

Holkham Hall 2m W of Wells-on-Sea *Map* F J 34. *18th-cent. yellow-brick Palladian mansion by Wm Kent. Marble hall, State apartments.* The Earl of Leicester.

Norwich Castle At Norwich *Map* G C 30. *Restored 12th-cent. keep. Walls refaced in 1834–9. Castle now used as museum (AM).*

Sandringham House Wolferton 9m NE of King's Lynn on B1440 *Map* F G 32. *Modern Royal Mansion; fine gardens. The grounds shown only when H.M. the Queen or any other member of the Royal Family is not in residence.*

Shell Museum At Glandford *Map* G A 34. *World-wide collection of shells started by Sir Alfred Jodrell; also jewels, pottery, Pompeiian relics, sugar bowl of Elizabeth I. Caretaker:* Leslie Page, Esq, Church House, Glandford, Holt.

Books for further reading

The 'feel' of Norfolk

BRITISH ASSOCIATION *Norwich and Its Region* 1961
R. RAINBIRD CLARKE *East Anglia* (Ancient Peoples and Places series) 1960
A. M. COTMAN and F. W. HANCROFT *Old Norwich: A Collection of Paintings, Prints and Drawings* 1961
J. WENTWORTH DAY *Portrait of the Broads* 1967
LILIAS RIDER HAGGARD and HENRY WILLIAMSON *Norfolk Life* 1943
MICHAEL HOME *Spring Sowing* 1946
R. W. KETTON-CREMER *Country Neighbourhood* 1951
B. KNYVET WILSON *Norfolk Tales and Memories* 1930

Natural history

P. W. BLAKE and others *The Norfolk We Live In* 1964
W. G. CLARKE *In Breckland Wilds* 2nd edn 1937

E. A. ELLIS *The Broads* 1965
R. LUBBOCK *The Fauna of Norfolk* 1879
M. J. SEAGO *Birds of Norfolk* 1967
E. L. SWANN *Flora of Norfolk* 1968

Topography

W. A. DUTT *Norfolk* (Little Guides series) 9th edn 1949
W. HARROD and C. L. S. LINNELL *Shell Guide to Norfolk* 1966
DOREEN WALLACE and R. P. BAGNALL-OAKLEY *Norfolk* (County Books series) 1951

Architecture

H. MUNRO CAUTLEY *Norfolk Churches* 1949
NIKOLAUS PEVSNER *North-East Norfolk and Norwich; North-West and South Norfolk* 2 vols (Buildings of Britain series) 1962
STANLEY J. WEARING *Beautiful Norfolk Buildings* 3 vols 1944–60

Gazetteer

NORFOLK

King's Lynn: the Customs House *G. Douglas Bolton*

Aylsham (GB 32) EC Wed (2,530). On the R. Bure. The church has a gallery, an admirable font (probably a 19th-cent. restoration) and the monument of Bishop Jegon, who built the Manor House in 1608. Abbot's Hall, of the same period, occupies the site of the older house that belonged to the Abbots of Bury St Edmunds. 1½ m. NW is the splendid Jacobean **Blickling Hall** (NT and open to visitors). Anne Boleyn lived here in an earlier house, and her statue, and that of Queen Elizabeth, both in oak, can be seen. There is a fine lake in the park, and the gardens were laid out by Nash's famous associate, Humphrey Repton, who is buried in Aylsham churchyard.

Binham (FK 33) (410). The nave of the Benedictine priory (AM), whose remains, excavated by the Ministry of Works, can be seen nearby, is now the parish church. Mainly Norman, with notable Early English W front and doorway, it contains an octagonal font. **Stiffkey**, a village overlooking salt marshes, lies in a valley 2½ m. N under Warborough Hill (excellent views). The Elizabethan Hall, built by Francis Bacon's brother, can be seen from the churchyard.

Blakeney (GA 34) EC Wed (760). With neighbouring **Cley**, is a favourite yachting and wild-fowling centre. Both villages were anciently seaports, now separated from the sea by salt marshes, 1,100 acres of which belong to the NT. Blakeney Point (and **Salthouse Broad**, 2 m. E) are both famous for their variety of bird life. Blakeney's fine church has two towers, one built as a beacon; Cley's is interesting for its Seven Sacraments font, Jacobean pulpit, misericords and 'Old Maid's Chamber' over the S porch, which is itself the best feature of the church.

Broads, The (*see* Introduction p. 373; *and* **Potter Heigham, Ranworth** *and* **Wroxham**).

Burnhams, The (FJ 34). Domesday Book notes seven Burnhams within a radius of two miles, all 'by Sea' and all with churches, three of which have disappeared, while the sea has receded beyond the marshes. Of these attractive villages, **B. Thorpe** (250) is notable as Nelson's birthplace (church restored in 1890 as memorial); **B. Overy** (540) (Norman church tower, with Jacobean cupola) is a good point from which to visit **Scolt Head**, with its bird sanctuary; **B. Norton**, Norman font, round flint tower and six-sided, painted pulpit (1450); **B. Deepdale**, Saxon tower and an exceptional carved Norman font. 2 m. S of **B. Market** (1,160), **North Creake** Church has the twelve Apostles as well as splendid angels in the roof.

Caistor St Edmund (GC 30) EC Wed (190). Excavations carried out since 1928 indicate that this was originally Venta Icenorum, the capital of the Iceni and later Roman. Materials from the old walls have been used in the medieval church (beautiful font and some wall-paintings) and Old Caister Hall.

Castle Acre (FJ 31) (900). The earthworks (among the finest in England, and with a splendid view of the Nar valley from the top) have been successively occupied by British, Saxons, Romans and Normans. Of the Norman castle (AM) the 13th-cent. gateway remains, overshadowing a village shop. Past the church (painted pulpit panels, fine font-cover) are the most impressive monastic ruins in the county, the 11th-cent. Cluniac priory (AM). Note the Tudor gateway and, especially, the W front, a magnificent example of Norman work. Below is a natural bathing pool in the R. Nar, celebrated for its trout fishing.

Castle Rising (FG 32) (260). This tiny village (it once returned two Members of Parliament), is dominated by the earthworks protecting the castle, whose Norman keep (AM) is exceptionally well-preserved. Opposite the church is Bede House, founded in 1614 for 'twelve spinsters and a governess' (the inmates still wear Jacobean red cloaks and black hats to church on Sundays) and their little chapel, which can be visited on application.

Cawston (GB 32) (1,010). Mellow brick and curved gables add to its other attractions, such as a tree that bears oak, beech and hornbeam leaves, and the 'Duel Stone' (1698), both at the Woodrow Arms; and its remarkable church (graceful tower, painted rood-screen, font-cover and one of the best hammer-beam roofs in the country, with carved angels dating from 1460).

Cromer (GC 34) EC Wed (4,900). Pleasant resort, with cliffs, sands, golf

and fishing, and attractive inland countryside, including the woods and park that surround **Felbrigg Hall** (2½ m. S), and Roughton Heath, with its barrows. (Admission to the park sometimes, and always to the church, but not to the Hall, an elegant Jacobean building with later 17th- and 18th-cent. additions.)

Dereham (FK 31) EC Wed (8,080). Ancient market town, with a few modern factories and many 18th-cent. buildings; one is the Guildhall. The Congregational church stands on the site of the house in which the poet Cowper died (1800). Bonner's cottages, possibly a Tudor guildhall, have the best decorative plaster-work in the county; and immediately behind them is its second largest church (painted roofs in both E transepts, Seven Sacraments font, finely carved 16th-cent. Flemish chest used as altar in one of the chapels, the graves of Cowper and his friend Mrs Unwin, and detached bell-tower). 1½ m. S, at Dumpling Green, is the house in which George Borrow was born (1803).

Elsing (GA 31). On the edge of heathland, a charming village from which to explore the valley of the R. Wensum. The church has a splendid painted and gilt font-cover and one of the best brasses in England; and there is a 15th-cent. moated hall 1 m. SW. At **Swanton Morley,** 12 m. W, one of Abraham Lincoln's ancestors signed his will in what is now the Angel inn (part dating from 1610). This is the country of Parson Woodforde (author of the *Diary of a Country Parson*), who held the living of **Weston Longville** (4 m. SW) at the end of the 18th cent.

Fakenham (FK 32) EC Wed (2,930). Little market town at the junction of seven roads. 2½ m. NE, **East Barsham Manor** is one of the best examples of

Norwich Cathe

Tudor brick and terra-cotta work in England, and has a notable gatehouse. 3 m. SW is the main entrance to magnificent **Raynham Hall**, built by Wm Edge in 1622 and once the home of the great agriculturist 'Turnip' Townsend, Robert Walpole's brother-in-law.

Great Yarmouth★ (GE 30) EC Thurs (51,910). At the mouth of Breydon Water, combines one of our historic herring-fishing ports and a holiday resort with a five-mile promenade and all the fun of the fair. The parish church (recently restored after war damage) is the largest in England. St George's and the Fishermen's Hospital (AM) date from about 1700; and Nathaniel Carter's House on S Quay is now a museum. **Caister-on-Sea** (2 m. N), with a population of 3,000, is a holiday resort; the remains of a 15th-cent. moated castle (AM) are well worth a visit.

Gresham (GB 33) (450). Here are a church (round Norman tower and well-preserved Seven Sacraments font), and the moated site of the manor held by Margaret Paston in 1450. To SW, at **North Barningham** (1½ m.), the church has Palgrave monuments; and farther on, in a fine park, is the nave of a church and **Barningham Hall**, built for Sir Edward Paston in 1612, with dormers, crow-stepped gables and fine brickwork – the S front was remodelled by Repton in 1805.

Grime's Graves, see **Methwold** (FJ 28).

Harpley (FH 32) (390). The church of this village on Massingham Heath has an angel roof, carved pews and 14th-cent. screen. 2 m. N is **Houghton Hall**, the mansion built for Sir Robert Walpole by Kent, Ripley and Campbell, with fireplaces, bas-reliefs, and decoration by the sculptor Rysbrack. 4 m. W is the gateway

(1820–30) of restored Hillington Hall, built in 1627 by Sir Richard Hovel, whose monument is in the church.

Hingham (GA 30) (1,440). Picturesque market town with 18th-cent. houses. In the church is Abraham Lincoln's bust, and the tomb of his ancestor Richard (*see above* under **Elsing**), whose grandson Samuel sailed to America in 1627.

Holkham Hall (FJ 34). The Palladian mansion, surrounded by a great park, designed by Wm Kent in 1734–60 for the Earl of Leicester, whose nephew 'Coke of Norfolk' revolutionized English agriculture. Hall and park are open to the public in summer, and the famous art collection and library may be seen on application to the agent.

Holt (GA 33) EC Thurs (1,950). Largely 18th-cent. rural town, with market place and copies of the original buildings of Gresham's School (founded 1555), rebuilt in 1858. 1 m. NW, **Bayfield Hall** is now a farm; nearby, Letheringsett Hall, with its Regency Doric colonnade, stands where the road crosses the Glaven by a bridge of the same period.

Houghton Hall (*see* **Harpley**).

Hunstanton (FG 34) EC Thurs (4,840). Pleasant resort, with golf, bathing, sands and cliffs, and lavender fields. At Old Hunstanton the church has monuments to the Le Strange family, who used to live at the Old Hall (grounds open to the public).

King's Lynn★ (FG 32) EC Wed (28,370). Though no longer the seaport it once was, it is still a jewel amongst towns. South Gate (AM) is the last remaining town gate; St Margaret's, in Saturday Market, is the largest church still standing (sufficiently notable in itself, but observe the two great brasses); and Greyfriars Tower is the chief memo-

Sandringham House

rial of the dozen monastic institutions that once existed. But in the various streets between Saturday and Tuesday Markets, and especially between King St and the quay, is a host of splendid buildings and merchants' houses, Tudor and Georgian: Greenland Fishery Museum (restored after wartime bombing); Clifton House (tower, splendid doorways and courtyards); Hampton House; St George's Guildhall (now a theatre); the Duke's Head hotel, probably built by Henry Bell, the architect of the splendid 17th-cent. Customs House; and the chequerwork Guildhall, with its many exhibits. The roof of St Nicholas Chapel has carved angels; the upper of the two chapels in the tower on Red Mount has a roof with admirable fan-tracery.

Knapton (GD 33) (290). Situated on rising ground, the fine church tower (vane designed by Cotman) is a well-known landmark. The double hammerbeam roof (1503), carved with 160 figures of saints and angels, is unsurpassed, and the octagonal Purbeck marble font has an early 18th-cent. cover. At **Trunch,** $1\frac{1}{2}$ m. away, the clerestoried church has another magnificent roof, one of the finest painted screens in Norfolk and one of the three carved and crocketed font-covers of their type in England.

Methwold (FH 29) (1,390). Lonely among the heaths, forests and airfields of Breckland, it is a good place from which to visit (via Munford or Weeting) **Grime's Graves,** the prehistoric flint mines, of which the earliest date from 10,000 B.C. Some 360 pits have been counted and 15 excavated; but, to explore the galleries, old clothes and a torch are advisable.

381

North Elmham (FK 32) (900). In the meadow adjoining the rectory gardens are the excavated ruins of a Saxon church, probably the cathedral of East Anglia's oldest bishopric (673–1075); and on a farm beyond the King's Head is the site of a Saxon cemetery.

North Walsham (GC 32) EC Wed (5,010). Here is an octagonal market cross, with clock, cupola and weathervane; the church has a painted screen, a tall font-cover and a 17th-cent. Paston monument; and at the Grammar School of a century later Nelson was a pupil. 3 m. NW, the park of **Gunton Park** is open to motorists, with its great house and the church, built in 1769 with the form of a Roman temple, designed by Robert Adam.

Norwich* (GC 30) EC Thurs (119,900). This historic city (boots and shoes have replaced the medieval clothing industry) revolves around its castle and cathedral. The former, of which Roger Bigod's keep is the most impressive relic, now houses the museum and art gallery (fine collection of the Norwich school of painters). Other notable museums are at Strangers' Hall and the Bridewell. The cathedral, its spire rising to 312 ft., is (excepting only Durham) the most notable example of Norman work in the country, particularly in its nave, S transept and apse. Note the episcopal throne, the 15th-cent. stalls and misericords in the choir, and the vaulted and embossed roof (also in the cloisters, where the bosses are newly coloured and easier to see in detail). In the close, with its old houses, are King Edward's School (1533) and its chapel, and the Erpingham and Ethelbert gateways (both AM). Of the thirty medieval churches still surviving, the largest and most impressive is St Peter Mancroft. Fine individual buildings, Tudor and medieval, are Suckling and Armada Houses, Blackfriars Hall, Samson and Hercules House, Maddermarket Theatre and the chequered flint Guildhall (see pictures and

The ruins of the priory at Thetford

G. Douglas Bolton

exhibits), which shares the new civic centre with the contrasting 20th-cent. City Hall and now with a new library. Elm Hill, Ber, Oak and King Streets all have attractive old houses, while later periods are represented by the Old Meeting House (1693), the Georgian Assembly Rooms and many 18th-cent. private houses.

Outwell (FF 30) (1,150). A marshland village, with neighbouring Upwell, nearly 2 m. long. Beaupre Hall, with its fine gateway, built by a Tudor Speaker of the House of Commons, can be seen from the road; and there are Beaupre monuments in the church, which has a carved-angel roof and three of its original five chapels.

Oxburgh Hall (FH 30). The castellated mansion (NT), surrounded by a moat, was built at the end of the 15th cent. and is still the home of the Bedingfield family. The brick gatehouse is particularly fine; and, though the nearby church was badly damaged by the collapse of the tower in 1948, the Bedingfield chapel and monuments remain unharmed.

Peddar's Way (FG 34, FH 31, FK 28). A prehistoric trackway, later used by Romans, partly metalled, running from a point on the Wash 2½ m. NE of Hunstanton, through Castle Acre, to about 4 m. E of Thetford, but now interrupted by battle ranges.

Potter Heigham (GE 31) EC Wed (690). With its celebrated bridge, this is one of the most popular centres for cruising in the Broads. Upstream the R. Thurne gives access to Martham, Horsey and Hickling Broads. Downstream it flows into the R. Bure, and thence either SE via Breydon Water and the Waveney to Lowestoft, or W through a number of Broads to Wroxham (*see below*).

Ranworth (GD 31) EC Wed (250). A village with its own Broad and, in its church (recently damaged by fire),

one of the finest painted screens in the country. 1½ m. SE, **South Walsham**, another Broads village, has two churches in the same churchyard, one burnt down, except for its tower, and the other with a two-storied porch and 15th-cent. screen and bench-ends.

Sandringham (FG 32) (610). Country home of the Royal family; its park is always open, and visitors are admitted to the gardens when the family is away.

Saxthorpe (GB 33) (660). On the R. Bure, with flint **Manningham Hall**, moated and ghosted, 2 m. NE; and, a mile farther on, **Wolterton Hall**, early 18th-cent. At **Heydon**, 2 m. SW, is the Elizabethan Hall where Bulwer-Lytton wrote many of his novels.

Sheringham (GB 34) EC Wed (4,840). Seaside resort with celebrated golf course. Nearby, on the edge of wooded country, are the ruins of Beeston Priory.

Swaffham (FJ 30) EC Thurs (3,670). Pleasant little town of red-brick 18th-cent. houses on open heathland; market cross erected in 1783. In the church, note the angels in the roof and the unique 'Black Book' and very rare Book of Hours in the priest's chamber.

Tasburgh (GB 29) (310). The church, within earthworks of a Roman site, has a round tower, wall-paintings and the tomb of Elizabeth Baxter, who lived at the lovely old Elizabethan Rainthorpe Hall (1½ m. N).

Terrington St Clement (FF 31) EC Tues (3,020). Among the many marshland churches (**Tilney All Saints**, 3 m. SE, and especially **Walpole St Peter**, 3 m. SW, are also outstanding), here is 'the Cathedral of the Marshes': a cruciform building with clerestory and 81 glazed windows, its tower

Wroxham: the River Bure

G. Douglas Bolton

standing apart from the church. Nearby is the lovely stone and brick mansion, Lovell's Hall.

Thetford (FJ 28) EC Wed (5,400). An immemorial place, once capital of the Iceni and in the 11th cent. one of the half-dozen cities in England. Of its past glory the castle mound survives, and three of its twenty churches, the ruins of a priory and an abbey (AM). But the Guildhall (rebuilt 1909), the King's House, the Bell inn and the Ancient House (with museum) are reminders of Tudor greatness, and there are many 18th-cent. houses, one of them the birthplace of Tom Paine (1737).

Walsingham★ (FK 33) EC Wed (1,180). Set among parks and woodlands, this village of medieval and Georgian houses is among the most beautiful in the country. Until the Reformation, the pilgrimage to the shrine of Our Lady (recently revived, and the shrine rebuilt) was of such importance that men called the Milky Way the 'Walsingham Way'. Today the ruins of the priory, with its 15th-cent. gateway, stand in the grounds of the modern abbey; parts of the ancient Grey Friars can be seen; and there is a fine parish church. 1 m. S W is the Slipper Chapel at **Houghton St Giles**, where pilgrims, whether kings or commoners, had to leave their shoes before approaching the shrine.

Wells-next-the-Sea (FK 34) EC Thurs (2,490). 18th-cent. houses flanking the green and the busy quay show that this little town exists apart from its attractions as a holiday centre: sailing, bathing, some of the best wild-fowling in Norfolk, and a well-sited caravan camp.

Wroxham (GC 31) EC Wed (1,030). On the R. Bure is another popular centre for the Broads, with access to Hoveton, Ranworth and S Walsham Broads; then N by the R. Ant to Barton Broad, or E to join the R. Bure (*see* **Potter Heigham**).

Wymondham (GB 30) EC Wed (6,780). With narrow alleys and old houses clustering round the 17th-cent. two-storied timbered Market Cross (AM), the central splendour of this town is the church, with its two towers. The choir of the original abbey church was destroyed at the Dissolution; and what remains is the superb nave, its Norman arches and triforium surmounted by a 15th-cent. roof of great delicacy. Kett's rebellion started here on the Common; after his defeat, he was hanged from the W tower. 3 m. S W, Elizabethan Morley Old Hall stands within its moat.

Opposite: Detail from the original painting by John Aldridge.

Much of this countryside that was settled by the North Folk the northern group of East Angles, is a covering laid by glaciers on chalk and flints. The light is crisp and the soils are often dry. At Grime's Graves, neolithic miners sought flint with picks of red-deer antlers, making Norfolk one of Britain's first industrial areas. The great men of the county include Nelson, John Sell Cotman, and Sir Thomas Browne.

NELSON

HYDRIOTAPHIA,
URNEBURIALL,
OR,
A Difcourfe of the Sepulchrall
Urnes lately found in
NORFOLK.

Together with
The Garden of CYRUS,
OR THE
Quincunciall, Lozenge, or
Net-work Plantations of the An-
cients, Artificially, Naturally,
Mystically Considered.
With Sundry Obfervations.

By Thomas Browne D. of Phyfick.

LONDON,
at the Signe of the
8.

The Bridge of Sighs, St John's College, Cambridge   *G. Douglas Bolton*

CAMBRIDGESHIRE AND HUNTINGDONSHIRE

AN INTRODUCTION BY J. WENTWORTH DAY

Cambridgeshire, the Isle of Ely and Huntingdonshire are an odd, indivisible trinity. They share one unique natural feature. Today it is their fount of riches – the Great Fen. That once savage, trackless land of shining meres, stinking bogs, half-drowned rough-grazings, waterways and endless rustling reed-beds covered six hundred and eighty thousand acres. It was sixty to seventy miles long from Lincoln to Cambridge, and from twenty to thirty miles wide from Huntingdon to Soham. Today it is the richest, blackest land in England, worth up to £300 or more an acre.

Cambridgeshire, the Isle of Ely and Huntingdonshire produce corn, endless potatoes, carrots, celery, a great deal of canned and fresh fruit, jams, beef, sheep, pigs, bloodstock and, industrially, bricks, cement, artificial manures, electronics, beer, light engineering and a few lesser industries. Agriculture is by far the biggest producer. The Fens proper are a peat topsoil, lying mainly on blue clay, with a rich belt of siltland to the east. This area of some two thousand

Opposite: Detail from the original painting by John Nash.
Under wide skies and on a flattish landscape, this county holds King's College Chapel, the City of Cambridge, and 680 acres of Wicken Fen, a nature reserve maintained as far as possible in its original state. The picture shows the Fenland farmer's strawberries; punts on a dyke or lode; and the image of Sir Roger de Trumpington, set in the Trumpington Church in 1289 and thus the second oldest brass in England.

King's College, Cambridge: the Chapel

square miles has been won from swamp, bog and tidal floods by centuries of hard work, ingenuity and ceaseless vigilance. Once it was little more than a continuation of the Wash, into which the rivers Welland, Witham, Glen, Nene, Cam, Great Ouse and Little Ouse emptied the autumn and winter floods of half central England.

The Romans dreamed of draining it. They built the great Car Dyke to keep out the sea. The Saxons neglected it. The Danes raided it. The Normans forgot it. Elizabeth I made plans to reclaim it. The Stuart Kings really started the work. Francis, Fourth Earl of Bedford, and his band of 'Gentlemen Adventurers' shouldered the burden in 1630 and broke the back of the sullen swamp, which men had said could never be drained.

CAMBRIDGESHIRE

When one considers Cambridgeshire, one regards a county of two utter contrasts. To the south lie the chalk downs and gently rolling hills, bright with corn, rimmed with thin belts of fir trees, the land of the partridge, the extinct great bustard, of barley and rye, beechwoods and cloud-topped elms. Northward lies the black, black, treeless prairie of the endless Fens. Dyke-seamed with roads straight as swords, here and there a lonely farmhouse islanded among willows or whispering poplars. It is a land of sharp winds, autumn fogs, endless horizons, breathtaking sunsets – and black monotony. A farmer's paradise – an aesthete's earthly hell.

Two remnants of the Old Fen survive: Wicken Fen, where this scribe spent an enchanted boyhood, and Wood Walton Fen in Huntingdonshire. We will deal with them later.

First, South Cambridgeshire. Its unique features are the three great defensive earthworks or dykes, Fleam Dyke near Balsham, Bran Ditch by Fowlmere and the mighty Devil's Dyke, seven and a half miles long, from Reach, a Roman inland port, to Wood Ditton. It lies over the Icknield Way and is bisected by the Street Way. Bank and fosse are forty yards wide and the ditch is fifteen feet

Fan-vaulting in the Chapel, King's College, Cambri

deep. The dyke is sixty feet high. These three Early Anglo-Saxon dykes were probably raised by the East Angles to keep out the Middle Angles or Mercians in the 6th, 7th or 8th centuries.

South Cambridgeshire villages, churches, manor houses and farmhouses all have borrowed something from the architectural characteristics of neighbouring Essex, Hertfordshire, Suffolk and Bedfordshire. Cambridgeshire covers no more than five hundred and fifty thousand acres. It is not surprising that it has little definite architectural character of its own, apart from the few remaining lath-and-plaster cottages and farmhouses on the Fen 'islands', still thatched with reed or, more rarely, sedge. The outstanding mansion is Wimpole. Still inhabited, it is the most splendid great house in a county notably deficient in the kind. Here and there one will find old farmhouses, small manor houses, rectories and villages which preserve something of the atmosphere and architectural beauty of earlier centuries. For the most part the county is not blessed with good houses.

Cambridge

The pride and glory of Cambridgeshire is, quite naturally, the University and its superb colleges, churches, chapels, libraries, courtyards, bridges – and that enchanting example of riverside landscaping, the Backs. Cambridge, to my mind, is the loveliest city in England. It is obviously impossible in this short guide to detail its glory and enchantments. Neither a week nor a year is enough in which to appreciate, discover and fall in love with it.

No visitor should miss Trinity, with its superb Great Gate, Great Court, Nevile's Court, the Hall and the rest of this stately college. King's Chapel, a dream of architecture, is without peer. An organ recital or Sunday Service in this chapel, whose foundation stone was laid on July 25th, 1446, is an unforgettable experience. Less obvious are the beauties of the older parts of Queens'; the Library of St. John's and the Combination Room in the same college; the Library at Trinity Hall; the inner courts of Corpus Christi; the grey simple dignity of Peterhouse, oldest of all Cambridge colleges; the Old Court of Pembroke; the cosily charming Hall of Magdalene. Jesus preserves a splendid gatehouse (c. 1500) and parts of the old nunnery of St Rhadegund, suppressed by Bishop Alcock of Ely in 1497, who replaced it with the College. The Nunnery at that time had only two nuns.

In addition to its medieval buildings, Cambridge is splendid with classic architecture: Pembroke Chapel by Wren; Peterhouse Chapel, consecrated in 1632; the Gate of Virtue at Caius, and Trinity College Library, another Wren masterpiece. The Senate House and Fellows' Building at King's, both by James Gibbs (1722–30), are superb examples of the grace and taste of 17th- and 18th-century England. The Fitzwilliam Museum (1837–41); Pembroke New Building; New Court, St John's, heavily Gothic; and Downing College – all preserve canons of good taste.

Ely

The Isle of Ely, for long a Liberty and almost a County Palatine, in which the Bishop had almost the authority of the King, was and still is the heart and centre of Fenland. The Isle became a division of Cambridgeshire as recently as 1826 and rose to the rank of an administrative county in 1888. The glory of Ely is, of course, the magnificent Norman cathedral, one of the most splendid in

ghton Mill on the River Ouse, Huntingdonshire   *J. Allan Cash*

The Horse Shoe
Offord D'Arcy,
Huntingdonshire
J. Allan Cash

England. It dominates the flat fenland for miles around. St Etheldreda began to build a Minster in Ely in A.D. 673. The Danes sacked it in 870. It was reconsecrated one hundred years later. In the last Saxon century it was as mighty as Canterbury or Glastonbury.

Hereward the Wake, Lord of Bourn, 'the Last of the English', held out in the Isle of Ely against William the Conqueror long after the rest of England had surrendered to the Norman power. Today, the great Norman cathedral with its unforgettable nave, its early 14th-century Octagon, the mid-14th-century Lady Chapel and the 13th-century Retrochoir are amongst the best examples of their style in England. Thus, ironically, Norman work utterly dominates that isle which held out longest and last against the armed might of Norman William.

Bishop Alcock's Palace (1486–1501) is notable, as are a few other houses in Ely, including the great South Gatehouse. For the rest, Ely is a bright little city of rather more than 9,000 people. Cambridge requires a week or longer; Ely deserves at least a day.

Wicken Fen is the chief and, indeed, unique natural attraction of Cambridgeshire. It is the last of the old Fen – still undrained. Still a place of dense reedbeds, of sedge jungles, of forests of sallow-bushes and creamy oceans of meadowsweet. But the old village proprietors, the fen owners, who had each their few acres of the wild fen, where they cut their reeds, mowed their sedge, and speared their eels, have sold out. The National Trust owns the fen today, almost to the last acre.

But on Wicken and in a small stranded corner of Burwell Fen there are still butterflies and moths which are rare elsewhere, and which draw, like summer lodestars, entomologists from the four corners of Britain. There are sometimes, in summer, Montagu's harriers, who nest deep among the reeds, hid in the heart of the fen. The fenmen call them by their old English name, 'blue hawks'. There is still, sometimes, in the quiet dusk of a June night, the ghostly note of a bittern. There are grasshopper-warblers, who reel their unending songs through the small hours of the summer nights, when the white sheets and gleaming lamps of the entomologists make ghostly patches of light over pools and sedgy paths where, half a century ago, the will-o'-the-wisp lit his 'corpse candle' and danced his deathly dance. There are little owls on the fen – far too many of them – and barn-owls which float like huge lemon-coloured moths, and kestrels who hover and swing on the summer air-currents under high blue skies, and sparrow-hawks who take the pheasant poults.

There are the wild duck, and teal, and sometimes tufted duck, and, in winter, the wild geese come sparingly on the flooded 'washes' of the Cam – grey-lag, and pink-foot, and white-front. There are the redshank, who nest by the brown dykes and on the cattle pastures of Spinney Fen, and ring their million bells in the green days of spring.

HUNTINGDONSHIRE

Huntingdonshire is a shy, demure county which likes to be left alone. A place of squires and yeomen. It was busy when the coaches ran. Huntingdon and Godmanchester with their lovely houses, Tudor, Stuart, Queen Anne and Georgian, have all the grace and beauty of the older England.

Apart from its memories of Cromwell and Pepys, Huntingdon possessed, until 1851, the largest natural lake in southern England, Whittlesey Mere. One remnant of a lovely wilderness is Wood Walton Fen, now a nature reserve. From the demure Georgian loveliness of Huntingdon, you go over to corn-bright uplands, down a narrow lane, over a 'cock-up bridge' above lily-starred waters where a pike swirls, and suddenly you find – the English jungle.

An old barge up-ended and thatched. A turf-barrow, such as peat-diggers used three hundred years ago. A pile of spits and brotches for thatching. A scythe stuck in a bush. The old tools of the fen greet one. Ahead, a green path runs by the dyke through man-high reeds, sallow-bushes, over-arching oaks and willows. The air is heavy with the scent of meadowsweet. Over all, that ineluctable fen smell of water and wet reeds, fish and damp peat. The old smell of Saxon England. Wood Walton is unique for its insects. The Marsh Moth (*Hydrillula Palustris*), practically unknown elsewhere in Britain, is taken every year. The list of rare plants is botanically mouth-watering. Marsh thistles grow twelve feet high and grass snakes are nearly four feet long!

Holme Wood, once a fen and now a forest, and that great relic of the great Huntingdon Forest, Monks' Wood, are two other outstanding places of natural beauty. In either, a man alone could lose himself. They say that the last kites in England nested in Monks' Wood. Both it and Holme Wood are nature reserves.

There are other, enduring pictures of the Englishness of this shy shire. The broad, sunny High Street of Kimbolton, one of the loveliest villages in England – dominated by the Palladian castle of the Dukes of Manchester. Hounds trotting off across the park to draw Tilbrook Bushes. Houghton Mill, of a splendid homely stateliness, presiding over foam-flecked swirl of waters, a merganser diving in the pool. The winter ring of steel on ice as fen skaters flee over the flooded Port Holme meadows, with swinging strokes, arms going like windmills. Brampton, where Pepys's father lived for several years and walked beside the 'plenteous Ouse'. Cromwellian memories at Hinchingbrooke. The ghost of Charles I being led by John Ferrar of Little Gidding to spend Sunday and sleep a night in that white, thatched farmhouse at Coppingford near Hamerton, which was the King's lodging on May 2nd, 1646, when he went privily across country from Oxford to Stamford and so to join his army at Newark.

Nearly every village has its thatched and plastered cottages, gardens bright with flowers, its moated manor house or manor farm. You can catch great chub, murderous pike, slab-sided bream, highly pugnacious perch and dace, swift as silver arrows, at those happily named river villages, Offord Cluny and Offord D'Arcy. If Izaak Walton looks over your shoulder at Hemingford Grey, you may even land a Pomeranian bream, found in few English rivers.

Some houses and gardens open to the public

Buckden Palace 3m SW of Huntingdon off A1 *Map* FC 26. *Remains of old palace formerly owned by the Bishop of Lincoln but now an RC Retreat House. 15th-cent. tower and gatehouse in red brick.*

Cambridge Colleges *Map* FE 25. *See especially King's College Chapel, Trinity College and the Backs along the river.* The Colleges are open on most days during daylight; slightly restricted access in term time. Admission free.

Cromwell Museum At Huntingdon *Map* FC 27. *Norman building, restored; once a school where Oliver Cromwell and Samuel Pepys were scholars, now a museum of Cromwell relics.*

Elton Hall 5m W of A1 on A605 *Map* FA 29. *15th and 17th cents., with later additions. Fine library including early English Bibles and prayer books; pre-Reformation MSS, Henry VIII's book of prayer with signatures of himself and Mary Tudor. Pictures by Constable, Sir Joshua Reynolds, Franz Hals etc.* Sir Richard Proby.

Kimbolton Castle 11m SW of Huntingdon on A45 *Map* FA 26. *Tudor, 17th cent. and 18th cent. by Vanbrugh; now a school.*

Peckover House At Wisbech *Map* FE 30. *18th cent. on River Nene. Interior decoration in rococo plaster and wood. Lovely Victorian garden.* NT.

Pepys House Brampton 1m SW of Huntingdon on A604 *Map* FC 27. *Gabled house, where for a time Pepys's father lived and where the diarist buried his money in the garden for fear of an invasion by the Dutch.*

Sawston Hall 6½m S of Cambridge on A130. *Map* FE 24. *16th cent. with gallery, priest's hiding-holes, fine furniture and tapestries. Moated gardens, woods and lawns. Occupied by the same family for 500 years.* Capt. R. F. Eyre Huddleston, RN Retd.

Books for further reading

History and topography

J. W. CLARK *A Concise Guide to the Town and University of Cambridge* 1951

OLIVE COOK *Cambridgeshire* 1953

J. WENTWORTH DAY *A History of the Fens* 1954

P. G. M. DICKINSON *Historic Huntingdon* 1944

E. A. R. ENNION *Cambridgeshire, Huntingdonshire and the Isle of Ely* (Hale's County Books series) 1951

SIR CYRIL FOX *The Archaeology of the Cambridge Region* 1949

Huntingdonshire County Guide 1963

Island City of the Fens: the Official Guide to the City of Ely 1963

BRYAN LITTLE *Cambridge Discovered* 1960

JOHN STEEGMAN *Cambridge* 1961

WARD, LOCK & CO. Ltd *Guide to Cambridge and District* 1952

Natural history

J. G. DONY *A Contribution to the Flora of Huntingdonshire* 1940

A. H. EVANS *A Flora of Cambridgeshire* 1939

DAVID LACK *The Birds of Cambridgeshire* 1934

Architecture

B. E. DORMAN *The Story of Ely and Its Cathedral*

NIKOLAUS PEVSNER *Cambridgeshire* (Penguin Buildings of England series) 1954

EDMUND VALE *Cambridge and Its Colleges* (Little Guides series) 1959

Gazetteer

CAMBRIDGESHIRE AND HUNTINGDONSHIRE

Ely Cathedral   *J. Allan Cash*

Alconbury *Hunts.* (FB 27). Large, attractive village with a stream running through its green; the Manor Farm, behind its glowing brick wall, lies alongside the church, 13th-cent. with broached spire. Two nature reserves, Monk's Wood and Wood Walton Fen, lie to NE.

Balsham *Cambs.* (FF 25). Thatched cottages, duckponds and squat-towered brick-and-flint church, remarkable for elaborately carved chancel-stalls and screen. There are two magnificent brasses on the chancel floor, with that rarity, an original 13th-cent. rood-loft and stairs. Near the village is an important section of Fleam Dyke. **Westley Waterless,** 5 m. NNE, has a splendid brass of a knight and his lady, of 1324.

Bottisham *Cambs.* (FF 26). Fine clerestoried church with exceptional 14th-cent. work, including oak parclose, and stone chancel and screens. Also 17th- and 18th-cent. tombs, one to Sir Roger Jenyns, whose family lived at the Hall (rebuilt 1797). The village college, one of those built during the '30s by S. E. Unwin, is unusual in its structure. 1½ m. NW, Anglesey Abbey, hidden among the trees, retains the canons' dormitory, with its vaulted undercroft of a 13th-cent. Augustinian priory.

Bourn *Cambs.* (FD 25) (830). Its post windmill, possibly the oldest in the country, is still standing. The Hall, lovely red-brick Jacobean, is on the site of a Norman castle, with part of the moat still to be seen in the park; and there is considerable Norman work in the church, which has a fine 13th-cent. tower, beneath which is a maze set in the floor. Chancel screen and roof-timbers are 15th-cent., though the angels that look down from these last are modern.

Buckden *Hunts.* (FB 26) (1,160). Charming village, where for centuries the Bishops of Lincoln made their home. Of their palace there are impressive remains (note especially the Great Tower and the fine Tudor gatehouse, with its diapered brickwork). The adjacent church is notable particularly for its wealth of woodcarving (observe the eight 16th-cent. panels in the chancel, with scenes from the Passion). Several bishops are buried here; and here that least bishoply of persons, Laurence Sterne, was ordained in 1736. **Brampton,** 3 m. NE on the banks of the Ouse, has the house where Samuel Pepys's father lived, and a church with 14th-cent. screen and finely carved stalls.

Burwell *Cambs.* (FF 26) EC Wed (2,730). Of the once commanding castle, only the earthworks of moat and keep remain, but the great tower of the church still looks out across the

Godmanchester on the River Ouse

fens; inside, the roofs of the nave and chancel are rich with timber-carving. 2 m. SW, **Swaffham Prior** has two windmills and two churches, these last both in the same churchyard and both with octagonal towers (one ruined); but only one mill and one church are still in use. The winding tree-filled village is uncommonly attractive, and Baldwin Manor is a fine half-timbered house.

Cambridge** *Cambs.* (FE 25) EC Thurs (95,530). Nowhere else in England, perhaps, is there so much of beauty and interest in so small an area. From Emmanuel College to the foot of Castle Hill is barely ¾ m.; turn left into Queen's Road, with the elms and lawns and gardens of the Backs on one side and Clare's new building and the new University Library on the other, and a mile will bring you to the corner of Silver St; turn left again, and ½ m. more brings you back to Emmanuel. Except for the lovely Tudor brickwork of Jesus and the stone classicism of Downing (begun in 1807), practically the whole of historic Cambridge lies within that oblong. Two other thoroughfares traverse it: King's Parade, continuous with Trinity

and St John's Streets; and, best of all, the river, idling between tree-shaded banks and under half-a-dozen bridges – notably Clare and the new footbridge at Garret Hostel Lane, each of which is a starting-point for closer exploration. To catalogue what can be found there is impossible: the fifteen or more colleges, each with its library, chapel and hall, with its courts and gateways and master's lodge, have been built and pulled down and rebuilt over the centuries, sometimes with noble imagination, sometimes imitatively or meanly. The great thing is to wander, and look. The Introduction (*see* p. 389) makes some suggestions. One could add 'And don't neglect the lovely symmetry of Clare, attributed to Inigo Jones; and St Mary the Great; and the Round Church of St Sepulchre, though overrestored, and. . . .' But perhaps more helpfully, as a reminder that what you are looking at is a living and growing community, observe what has been achieved at the Sidgwick site, opposite Newnham (1960); or Sir Basil Spence's new building at Queens'; or Churchill College, out on the Madingley Road, the first post-war college to be erected. (*See also* **Grantchester**.)

Elsworth *Cambs.* (FD 26). A biggish village, with farms and thatched cottages, clustering round a brook, and a beautiful 14th-cent. church on the wooded slopes above it; this last a fine building, with clerestory and pinnacled tower, and poppy-head stalls, with linen-fold backs and curious locker book-rests. 3 m. SE, Childerley Hall is a beautiful Elizabethan house, with chapel, stables and a great barn.

Elton *Hunts.* (FA 29). Tiny village by the R. Nene, with grey 17th-cent. almshouses, a gabled parsonage a century older, and the fine hall, rebuilt about 1660 (its imposing gatehouse is much older), which has noteworthy books and pictures and is open to the public. The church, with its impressive tower, has Proby effigies and two wheel-headed crosses, probably Saxon, in the churchyard. 3 m. N is an earlier, Jacobean hall, finely preserved among other old houses in the village of **Stibbington**.

Ely★ *Cambs.* (FF 28) EC Tue (9,800). From a wooded bluff, above the Ouse and mile upon mile of fenland, rise the great W tower of the cathedral and Alan of Walsingham's octagonal lantern, supported by eight 63-ft. oaks, built to replace the Norman tower that collapsed in 1322. Inside we see a majestic Norman nave, the light from the octagon streaming down on the crossing of the transepts, and beyond it the rich Perpendicular work of the choir and apse; and all around a wealth of carved stalls, chantry chapels and tombs. The King's School stands nearby, incorporating part of the original monastic buildings, notably Prior Crauden's Chapel and Ely Porta. Across the street called the Gallery stands the diapered Bishop's Palace (15th-cent., partly rebuilt in the 18th), and behind it St Mary's Church, with its timbered vicarage, where Cromwell

and his family lived from 1636 to 1647. Apart from this cluster of superb buildings, the town holds little interest, straggling out beyond deserted wharves to the water-filled Roslyn Pit, from which for centuries men have been quarrying clay to puddle the banks of the fenland waterways. Perhaps the finest view of the cathedral is from the hill in the village of **Stuntney**, 1 m. to the SE, where Cromwell once owned a farm.

Godmanchester *Hunts.* (FC 27) EC Wed (8,820 with Huntingdon). Meeting-place of several Roman roads, including the so-called Via Devana to Cambridge; Ermine Street; and another, visible only from the air, and once a small Roman station. To-day a place of charming timbered-and-plastered houses, an Elizabethan grammar school and a large church that contains a set of remarkable 15th-cent. stalls, probably brought from Huntingdon Priory after the Dissolution. The Port Holme meadow, actually in the parish of Brampton, separates Godmanchester from Huntingdon and is noted for its rare wild flowers.

Grantchester★ *Cambs.* (FE 25) (420). A delightful and still unspoilt village, 2 m. upstream from Cambridge, with thatched cottages, Rupert Brooke's vicarage, the Mill Pool, and a church notable for its singularly perfect Decorated chancel. You *can* get there by road; but you *should* go by river. The bridge over the Cam leads to **Trumpington**, another attractive village, though threatened by the London road. A great elm avenue leads to the Hall; the Green Man is a 16th-cent. inn, and Anstey Hall was built about 1700. The restored church, also of the Decorated period and also with a Jacobean pulpit, is best known for the seven-foot brass to Roger de Trumpington, dated 1289, the second oldest in the country.

Guilden Morden *Cambs.* (FC 24) (570). Here among the meadows and orchards on the Hertfordshire border is one of the noblest churches in the county, its spire rising above the pinnacles of a great stepped tower. In the light from ten clerestory windows angels look down from the hammer-beam roof. Beneath the chancel arch stands the unique double rood-screen, and on either side of the entrance are two small enclosed chapels, later used as private pews. 2 m. away to the E, **Abington Pigotts,** on the upper reaches of the Cam, has a charming water-mill among its thatched cottages.

Haslingfield *Cambs.* (FE 25) (850). A pretty village on a bend of the R. Cam, with a rambling wheelwright's shop next door to the smithy, a handsome church and, just to the S, Chapel Hill. Though scarcely 200 ft. high, this is a magnificent viewpoint in the flat landscape, with Ely gleaming from 20 miles away on a clear day, the towers and spires of Cambridge, and dozens of parish churches peeping out among the trees. 2 m. S, **Barrington** is noted for its 30-acre village green; around its border stand many picturesque houses, with a fine church at one end.

Hemingfords, The *Hunts.* (FC 27) (2,060). H. Abbots and H. Grey are two enchanting villages, lying along a loop of the R. Ouse, an ideal spot for exploring this stretch of the river by boat or punt. H. Abbots has a heronry, two lakes, a splendid spire, and angels and figures with musical instruments in the painted roof of the church. H. Grey lost its spire 200 years ago. The Norman manor is probably the oldest inhabited house in England; formerly much larger, it still contains a fireplace, and some windows, from its earliest days.

Hinchingbrooke House* *Hunts.* (FC 27). The outstanding 'great house' of the county, about 1 m. from the county town. At the Dissolution the 11th-cent. nunnery came into the hands of the Cromwell family, who proceeded to rebuild on a lavish scale, incorporating part of the church and chapter house and transporting the magnificent gateway from Ramsey Abbey. When, later, the impoverished Sir Oliver (the Protector's uncle) had had to sell, it passed on to Edward Montagu, ironically enough raised to the peerage as the first Earl of Sandwich for his help in restoring Charles II. He was responsible for laying out the terraced gardens. The present house, which has a great semi-circular window (17th cent.), was badly damaged by a fire in 1830, but was restored. It is not at present open to the public, as it is being restored and will become part of a new comprehensive school.

Houghton-cum-Wyton *Hunts.* (FC 27) (770). Another delightful place for boating, within easy walking distance of the Hemingfords; and for that matter of Godmanchester and St Ives. Here we find attractive examples of thatched houses and a splendid 17th-cent. water-mill (NT), now used as a youth hostel.

Huntingdon *Hunts.* (FC 27) EC Wed (8,820 with Godmanchester). Joined to Roman Godmanchester by its 14th-cent. bridge (AM), and the famous causeway. The Norman castle is now only a series of massive earth-works. Cromwell was born here in 1599; he and Pepys were educated at the grammar school, once a medieval hospital and still retaining its Norman front. Both churches are notable, especially St Mary's for its 17th-cent. work. There are many Stuart and Georgian houses, one of which was the home for two years of the poet Cowper. The town hall was built in 1745. (For **Hinchingbrooke House** *see above*; and for the environs see under

Godmanchester, Hemingfords, Houghton-cum-Wyton and St Ives).

Impington *Cambs.* (FE 26) (1,230). Now getting caught up in the northward spread of Cambridge, is interesting for the church with its half-timbered S porch and its wall-paintings; for the partly Elizabethan red-brick Hall, once the property of the Pepys family, and often visited by the diarist; and for one of the best of the well-known Cambridgeshire village colleges, built by Gropius and Fry (1939).

Kimbolton *Hunts.* (FA 26) EC Wed (820). A large village with many attractive houses flanking both sides of its High Street. At the far end is the church, with its tall spire and noteworthy monuments of the Manchester family. At the other end of the market place is the 18th-cent. gateway to the castle, which stands in a 500-acre park. It is now a school, and is open to the public in the summer. The present building is largely the work of Vanbrugh (18th cent.). In an earlier castle, Catherine of Aragon spent the last four years of her life.

Kirtling *Cambs.* (FG 25) (360). In finely wooded country, with thatched barns, a duckpond and the dried moat of the great Tudor mansion that once entertained Queen Elizabeth, but of which all that remains is the turreted Gate House (AM). Its builder, Henry VIII's Chancellor, Lord North, lies in a painted tomb in the partly Norman church.

Leighton Bromswold *Hunts.* (FB 27) (210). In 1625 George Herbert, the poet, was appointed prebendary here and undertook the rebuilding of the ruined church: to him are due the perfect Jacobean furnishings, which include a twin lectern and pulpit. The curious four-turreted building to the E of the church was formerly a moated gateway for a 16th-cent. castle never finished. (*See* **Little Gidding**.)

Linton *Cambs.* (FF 26) (1,980). Between Furze Hill and the R. Granta runs the mile-long street of this attractive village, with its variety of ancient houses, particularly the half-timbered Trinity Guildhall (now a

Hemingford Grey

J. Allan Cash

private house) beside the church (note the interesting monuments). Here also is another of Unwin's admirable village colleges.

Little Gidding *Hunts.* (FB 28) (30). The house where Nicholas Ferrar, friend of George Herbert, set up the 17th-cent. religious community (described in *John Inglesant*) has disappeared, but the little church, somewhat altered, contains a unique brass font. Leighton Bromswold (*see above*) is some 5 m. S.

March *Cambs.* (FE 29) EC Tue (13,140). One of the largest towns on the Isle of Ely, since the coming of a network of railways just over a century ago, made possible by the last large-scale drainage scheme that brought under cultivation 1,500-acre Whittlesey Mere, 12 m. away to the SW. The old town lies S of the bridge across the former course of the R. Nene (the new river now runs in a straight line to the N, taking most of the water), and is chiefly remarkable for the Church of St Wendreda. A few houses cluster round it, including a thatched farmhouse dated 1658, and it is approached by a fine avenue of elms. The tower is built on two open arches, thus preserving an ancient procession path, and is crowned by a fine spire. There are splendid clerestory windows, set in the flint fabric; but the glory of the place is the double hammer-beam roof, with a host of nearly 200 angels spreading their wings from every vantage point.

Peterborough* *Hunts.* (FB 29) EC Thurs (66,100). Peter's Borough grew up around a Saxon monastery which came into being about 650 on the site which was later occupied by the cathedral. Destroyed by the Danes, rebuilt, burnt, the cathedral as we know it was begun in the 12th cent.

and added to in the 13th and at the turn of the 14th, was sacked by Cromwell, was refurnished in the 19th cent. and given the modern figures of the Apostles on the W front in 1949. This history can be traced from the Saxon foundations, through the Monk's Stone in the choir-aisle (which commemorates those who were massacred by the Danes); the effigies of 12th-cent. Benedictine abbots; the first burial-place of Mary Queen of Scots before her removal to proximity with Queen Elizabeth in Westminster Abbey; and the grave of Catherine of Aragon, showing traces of desecration by the Puritans; down to the figures added in modern times.

The history that can be pursued through the cathedral and its precincts is the history of the city itself, which in modern days has become an industrial town with an accent on railways and brickfields. The museum in Priestgate has exhibits ranging from relics of the Roman occupation to the craftsmanship of French prisoners-of-war during Napoleon's campaigns. The legal profession shows great interest in the 16th-cent. portrait of a judge, the earliest to be painted in traditional robes.

Ramsey *Hunts.* (FC 28) EC Thurs (5,700). Perhaps the oldest of the 7th-cent. foundations that arose along the borders of the fens. Of the abbey, built after the Norman Conquest, the 13th-cent. Lady Chapel now forms part of the Abbey Grammar School. The ruined gatehouse (NT) is 15th cent. Several fires have devastated the town. The church was originally a guest house to the monastery, and was converted to its present use in the 13th cent. It is largely of the late 12th cent., but the tower is post-Reformation. **Warboys**, 4 m. S, is a large fenland village. The church has one of the finest 13th-cent. spires in the county;

adjoining is the 17th-cent. manor house, with an unusual front.

St Ives *Hunts.* (FD 27) EC Thurs (4,080). A busy market town, approached by a fine 15th-cent. bridge, on which stands a single-storey chapel of the period, open to the public. The market square contains a statue of Cromwell; he is said to have farmed here after he left Huntingdon. The quay is noted for its picturesque collection of buildings. To the E is a lovely 10-mile stretch of the Ouse, which flows on past Holywell, the Ferryboat Inn and the Pike and Eel at Overcote Ferry, and **Earith**. (*See also* **Hemingfords** and **Houghton-cum-Wyton**.)

St Neots *Hunts.* (FB 26) EC Tue (5,550). Like St Ives, owes its origin to a monastery now destroyed. It has the finest market square in the county, and its church has a richly-decorated tower. The ancient bridge collapsed some years ago and has been replaced by a concrete one. There are many attractive houses in the town. **Eynesbury**, the mother-parish of St Neots, adjoins on the S side and also has a noteworthy church with a 17th-cent. tower. Paper-making is an old industry; the first machine-made paper was produced here in 1798. The mill still stands on the river.

Sawston *Cambs.* (FE 24) EC Sat (3,380). Here is a modern paper mill, and the first of the village colleges, opened in 1930. Near the partly Norman church (its brasses are remarkable) is the fine mid-16th-cent. Hall, where for a time Mary Tudor took refuge, and where, later, hiding-places were made to conceal Catholic priests. It is open to the public in summer.

Soham *Cambs.* (FF 27) EC Wed (5,080). Here Felix of Burgundy founded his abbey a few years before Etheldreda built hers at Ely, 5 m. away across the Norman causeway; but, unlike hers, his was not rebuilt after the Danes destroyed them both. Part of its church, however, is Norman; though its handsome tower and fine timber chancel screen date from the 15th cent. Orchards now grow in what was then Soham Mere, and at one end of the straggling town are the remains of a windmill. 2 m. SW is the village green of **Wicken**, with the nature reserves of Wicken, Burwell, Adventurer's and St Edmund's Fens, where the primeval fen is carefully preserved, all within easy reach.

Swaffham Prior *Cambs.* (FF 26) (*See under* **Burwell**) (630).

Thorney *Cambs.* (FC 30) EC Thurs (2,140). Northernmost of the fen islands, its thriving oaks and elms form a contrast with the surrounding countryside. Here, again, was a 7th-cent. monastic foundation, destroyed by the Danes; here Hereward the Wake made one of his last stands against the Conqueror; and here the Normans founded another abbey. Little of it remains today except the tall, grey W front and nave of what is now the parish church. Parts of it are incorporated in the 16th- to 17th-cent. abbey house, but 140 tons of its stones were carted off at the Dissolution to build the chapel of Corpus Christi College at Cambridge. Its windmill is dated 1787, but most of the terraced houses were built in the 19th cent. by the fen-draining Duke of Bedford.

Tilbrook *Hunts.* (FA 26) (230). A small village about 2 m. from **Kimbolton**. The church, of Northants type, contains the finest rood-screen (15th cent.) in the county. It retains its vaulted loft and much medieval colouring. There is also a brass to a husband and wife: he has a long dagger, and his feet are on a dog; she has a long buttoned gown and a dog with a collar.

Wimpole *Cambs.* (FD 25) (150). The Hall, a great brick mansion, its central block built in 1632 by Sir Thomas Chichele, its wings and a new front added by Lord Chancellor Hardwick (d. 1764), lies at the end of a magnificent double avenue of elms, more than 2 m. long. It has a collection of old masters, chapel paintings by Thornhill and, in the park, a Gothick folly. Nearby, the church (its brick walls an 18th-cent. restoration, doubtless by the Chancellor) is mainly remarkable for the Chichele Chapel, with its 16th-cent. heraldic glass, a noble Sir Thomas in alabaster, and monuments to two Hardwick Chancellors, and the 3rd Earl in marble.

Wisbech *Cambs.* (FE 30) EC Wed (17,530). Once 4 m., now 11 m., from the sea, and still serving as a port, though, since the coming of the railway over a century ago, the long lines of warehouses along the banks of the R. Nene are less busy with seaborne cargoes. Today the town is the centre for the bulb-, flower- and fruit-growing trade of fenland, and for the canning industry. The Norman castle has long since disappeared, slighted by Thomas Thurloe, Cromwell's Secretary of State, who built himself a new house with the materials. On its site is now a museum, one of the oldest in the country; and nearby an ancient inn. The North and South Brinks, facing the river and the quays, are lined with prosperous Georgian houses, among them Peckover House, belonging to the NT and open to the public. Gilbert Scott's monument to Thomas Clarkson, hero of the fight against the slave trade, stands near the bridge. In passing, the two market places are worth an appreciative glance; while the parish church, notable for its double nave and fine 16th-cent. tower, has the Parke monument and the great Braunston brass. 5 m. NNW is the northernmost village in the county, **Tydd-St-Giles,** famous for its tower, standing 50 ft. from the church, and for the fact that Nicolas Breakspear was once curate here – the only Englishman ever to have become Pope, as Adrian the Fourth.

Wicken Lode

J. Allan Cash

Higham Ferrers: the market square

BEDFORDSHIRE AND NORTHAMPTONSHIRE

AN INTRODUCTION BY W. G. HOSKINS

In Northamptonshire we are in the innermost Midlands. To outsiders, this (and Bedfordshire, which lies to the south-east of it) is very indeterminate country, too often merely a country of passage, since it lies right across most of the main routes out of London to the north and north-west. To the native of either county, each is distinctive and could not be anything else; but it must be confessed that scenically their charms are not easy to see at a glance or to appreciate from a car. A Victorian guide-book summed up Northamptonshire as having 'a quiet beauty that is very refreshing', and this is still true of a good deal of the county, and of much of Bedfordshire.

But one must bring to this (on the whole) green and quiet part of England a greater measure of knowledge – of geology and landscapes, of church and domestic architecture above all, and perhaps of English history in general – than one normally carries about, if its real character is to be enjoyed. Some parts of England reveal their beauties, or appear to, flamboyantly and immediately, and in that way encourage a lazy and superficial visit. Of these

401

The bridge across the Nene at Wansford

G. Douglas Bolton

two counties it would be true to say that visitors who come totally unprepared (save for the well-advertised charms of Woburn Abbey, perhaps) will leave them feeling disappointed except for the occasional pleasant surprise.

Geology and Scenery

The grain of the country runs from south-west to north-east in both counties: that is, across the main lines of movement. Incidentally, one can often achieve happy results in England by noticing any obvious grain like this and deliberately travelling along it rather than across it as the unimaginative or the busy have done for centuries. It is true that this involves the slightly tiresome business of having to cut across busy motor-roads instead of rushing along them; but apart from this minor nuisance there is a lot to be said for such gentle pottering along the line of the grain. It means some intelligent map-reading – but in return one gets a view of a little bit of England that is totally unexpected, of a small piece of country that is homogeneous because of the underlying rocks and the buildings that have come out of them.

So the main grain of Northamptonshire is the Great Oolite, the most beautiful of the limestones (usually called Cotswold stone), and it runs almost the entire seventy miles of the county from the banks of the Cherwell, not far from Oxford, right up to the edge of Peterborough in the Fens. This forms physically the so-called Northamptonshire Uplands, gently undulating country rising to 600 or 700 feet above sea-level in places. Flanking this belt of good building-stone (note the Barnack and Weldon stones) all along its north-western edge is the Middle Lias, better known as marlstone, or occasionally as ironstone since it is rich in iron ore, the quarrying of which is now one of the biggest industries in Northants. This same stone was much used for building in past centuries, ranging in colour from a rich gold in some places to a deep velvety brown in others. So one gets in rural Northants a belt of sheep-grey limestone villages, such as Geddington and Weldon, and a parallel belt of golden or warm brown villages. In some villages the two stones are intermixed in a delightful decorative way. There is another distinctive difference between the Lias and the Oolite, and that is that for centuries the Liassic clays have been under pasture (there are many 'lost villages' in this part of the country, depopulated when the open-field village was turned over to grass for sheep and cattle in the 15th and 16th centuries); whereas the Oolite generally gives a light arable land, more open landscapes, and many pheasants. In the extreme north-east, Northants runs right into the Fens near Crowland – at first sight dull country, but those who live there grow very fond of the great skies, and dark endless fields, and the immense misty views.

Bedfordshire, too, though much smaller and with a very different geology, has a SW–NE grain. In the south, the chalk downs continue the better-known Chilterns and give the greatest heights, usually 600 to 800 feet above the sea. These are perhaps 'the Delectable Mountains' of John Bunyan, who was born, and lived, near Bedford. Then comes a narrow belt of heavy Gault clays (cf. the village named Barton-in-the-Clay), followed in turn by a timbered upland of

Brackley: Winchester House School

Reece Winstone

the Lower Greensand, a light buff-coloured sand producing low wooded hills (but rising to just about 500 feet in one or two places) that die away towards the north-east. Except where mixed with clay, these sands are infertile; and it is no historical accident that along the entire length of the ridge from Woburn on the west to Sandy on the east we get a string of considerable parks and big houses, of which Woburn is the largest and the best known. The fine views from this ridge attracted the builders of country houses, and the stretches of natural heathland made the creation of parks easier than it would have been in a richly-cultivated country. We get the same string of great parks – but on an even grander scale – for the same reason in the so-called Dukeries of Nottingham-shire.

In the centre and north of Bedfordshire the heavy Oxford clays produce a stiff soil, chiefly under grass. It is, however, far from dull scenery: the broad valley of the Great Ouse especially gives some of the most appealing river scenery in the Midlands and much excellent fishing. Bedfordshire is small, and a summary description like this makes it seem smaller and more uniform than it really is. It has to be appreciated rather like chamber music, listened to again and again, unlike the grand and rather obvious symphonic music of counties such as Yorkshire and Devon. Explore it slowly along its various geological grains and you will be rewarded hour after hour. One sees this in the flora, for example, where the variety of soils and sudden changes of elevation produce an exceptionally interesting variety for so small an area: chalk downland, river-meadows, parks and woods, and arable hedgerows. It is also apparent in the farming, for this one small county can show a dozen distinct types of farming – almost a complete miniature of British farming as a whole, with a special emphasis on market-gardening, especially round Sandy and Biggleswade.

Local Industries

Farming is of course the chief occupation in both counties in terms of area; but both are also considerably industrialized. Some districts are best avoided altogether by the visitor, though even they may contain some treasure that is worth the pilgrimage through subtopian brick, such as the modern church of St Mary at Wellingborough, near the railway, which was Comper's masterpiece (1908–30). The interior, still incomplete, is a staggering sight in an English church. But the Northamptonshire boot-and-shoe towns, a score of them, are nearly all dull red brick and painfully uninteresting. The villages of the boot-and-shoe belt are also generally dreary. Northampton, though, as the county town dating from the 10th century, has a good deal of architectural interest. The other important industry in the county is ironstone-working, which has gashed the countryside in enormous ravines – above all, round Corby. This was a pleasant little limestone village thirty years ago: now it is a subtopian town of some 45,000 people, the headquarters of the world-famous Stewarts and Lloyds. Peterborough is chiefly interested in engineering and, apart from its magnificent cathedral (once the abbey church), need not detain the visitor long.

Bedfordshire also has large, profitable and visually dreary industries. Luton is a town of mushroom growth, formerly the centre of the straw-hat industry but now chiefly notable for Vauxhall motors and much other special engineering, as well as for various consumer-goods industries (stockings, electrical goods, etc.). The population has quadrupled since the beginning of the century. The town is of ancient origin, but the new has swamped the old. Many of the Bedfordshire

Reece Winstone   **Earl's Barton Church, Northa**

The triangular lodge at Rushton

villages remain unspoilt and attractive, with thatched cottages and farmhouses amid well-timbered parkland. Brick is the main building material, and the Bedfordshire brick industry is still important. Indeed, the growing brickworks and cement factories are a real problem to lovers of rural Bedfordshire, as they seek to extend their excavations over the clay and chalk of good farmland.

Architecture

The old saying about Northamptonshire is that it is a county of 'spires and squires' – in other words, of fine churches and fine country houses. Archaeologically it follows the same pattern as other East Midland counties in not being visually very exciting; but its churches and country houses put it in the first rank among English counties for interest. Moreover, an exceptional number of the finest houses remain in the hands of their ancient owners – Althorp, Burghley, Boughton, Castle Ashby and Lamport, to name only some of them. Again, as Pevsner rightly says, the country houses of Northants are so numerous and so spread out in time that one could write the architectural history of England between 1560 and 1700 from this county alone. Among the medieval houses, Drayton (from 1328 onwards) is of the highest importance, so too are Northborough and Yardley Hastings. But it is in the Elizabethan period, when many of the great state officials were trying to outbuild each other, that Northamptonshire becomes architecturally the most important region in England. Of these really great houses only Burghley remains intact, still occupied by the Cecils. Holdenby, the largest of them all, survives only as fragments; but Kirby Hall (begun in 1570) remains perhaps the loveliest Elizabethan ruin in all England, especially when one sees it in early summer amid its flowering chestnuts and beeches. Other great houses take the story on into the 18th century. Bedfordshire suffers by any comparison such as this; but it has good things, ducal Woburn, and Wrest Park (with its formal canal garden) among them – and, above all, Luton Hoo, the home of one of the finest private art collections in England (the Wernher collection of paintings, tapestries, ivories, etc.). It is foolish to set up comparisons, but in Northamptonshire one can think only of the pictures at Althorp as in the same class.

The churches of Northamptonshire have been the Mecca of ardent ecclesiologists (or church-crawlers) for over a hundred years. Few counties if any can show so much exciting Saxon work – notably, of course, Brixworth, which has been called the finest monument of the 7th century north of the Alps. The massive chancel-arch at Wittering is also something quite remarkable, and so too are the Anglo-Saxon towers of Brigstock, Barnack and Earls Barton. But how can one do justice to such a county in a page or so, beyond saying that one could write the history of English church-building, from the 7th century to the 20th (St Mary's at Wellingborough, already referred to), from this wonderful county alone? Still, one must mention at least the superb Warmington church (perfect Early English) and noble unfinished Fotheringhay (15th-century) as places of special pilgrimage. And the other thing about the churches is their spires, the broach spires especially, that are so marked a feature of every view in the eastern half of the county.

Once again Bedfordshire suffers by being grouped with Northants. Yet the Bedfordshire churches in general are very interesting, and not as well known as they ought to be. Dunstable priory church (1130 onwards) is famed, of course; so are the magnificent remains – not only of the church, but also of the nunnery and of Hillersden Mansion – at Elstow; so too are Leighton Buzzard church and perhaps the delightful 13th-century church at Eaton Bray. But there are scores of others that ought to be visited by the leisurely motorist making his way, as I have suggested, along the grain of some geological formation, with a one-inch map. Perhaps the small-scale charm of deepest Bedfordshire is epitomized in the unspoilt country interiors of Chalgrave, a few miles north of busy Dunstable, and perfect little Dean, in the extreme north of the county, lost among its trees. The very name is redolent of an older, quieter England – Upper Dean.

For the Gourmet

Alas, the gourmet draws a blank in this part of England, except for the plenty of pheasants on the arable lands and the abundance of pork pies (even more than Leicestershire). The traditional country dishes of Northants and Bedfordshire have, perhaps mercifully, died out; for they were apparently designed to fight the long, hard, damp Midland winters. There is virtually no spring in the East Midlands – a feature of the English climate which never seems to be recorded in the books. One discovers this grim secret by long residence. Hence such a dish as the 'Bedfordshire Clanger', a suet roll filled with meat and onions at one end and passing through other things to jam at the far end, the idea being that one had a complete meal *en route* through the roll. Mercifully, science has found other ways of fighting cold and hunger than this, and the Clanger is now only a folk-memory.

Some houses and gardens open to the public

Aynhoe Park 6m SE of Banbury *Map* EF 23. *16th cent.; rebuilt 17th cent.; remodelled interior by Sir John Soane.* Mutual Households Assocn.

Castle Ashby 7m SE of Northampton adjoining Bedford–Northampton trunk Road off A428 *Map* EJ 25. *16th-cent. mansion with 17th-cent. lettered parapet televised as the typical Elizabethan house; plaster ceilings, oak panelling, staircases, chimney pieces, tapestries and furniture; collection of Italian Renaissance paintings; 19th-cent. terraces and gardens.* The Marquess of Northampton.

Delapre Abbey E side of London Rd, 1m S of Northampton Town Centre *Map* EH 26. *16th- to 19th-cent. house; fine shrubs and rare trees; now the research rooms of the Northants. Record Office and Record Society.* Northampton Corporation.

Luton Hoo 2m S of Luton through Park St gates *Map* FB 21. *18th cent., begun by Robt Adam; remodelled 1903; pictures, tapestries; medieval ivories, porcelain; personal articles of the Russian Imperial Family.* Sir Harold Wernher.

Rockingham Castle 8m N of Kettering 9m E of Market Harborough *Map* EJ 29. *Built by William the Conqueror, used by King John and other English kings as a royal fortress. Elizabethan house and gardens; fine paintings; Dickens associations.* Sir Michael Culme-Seymour.

Sulgrave Manor 7m NW of Brackley off B4525 *Map* EF 24. *16th cent.; associations with George Washington, including personal belongings, portraits; nearby 14th-cent. church with Washington family pew. Set of stocks on village green.* Sulgrave Manor Board.

Woburn Abbey and **Zoo Park** 9m NW of Dunstable on A50 *Map* EK 23. *18th-cent. mansion with £5,000,000 of art treasures. Second largest collection of Canalettos; French and English 18th-cent. furniture; 18th-cent. silver; rare books; 18 state apartments containing many historical family items. The antique market, the recent addition to Woburn's attractions, contains streets of period shops, where antique dealers from all over Europe display fine antiques and objets d'art.* The Duke of Bedford.

Books for further reading

The 'feel' of Bedfordshire and Northamptonshire

P. J. HARRIS and P. W. HARTOP *Northamptonshire, Its Land and People* 1950
GEORGE HARRISON *A Wanderer in Northamptonshire* 1948

History

CANON J. L. CARTWRIGHT *The Pictorial History of Peterborough Cathedral* 1960
J. DYER, *et al. Story of Luton* 1966
C. F. FARRAR *Old Bedford* 1926
C. H. M-D SCOTT *Tales of Northamptonshire* 1936

Natural history

J. G. DONY *Flora of Bedfordshire* 1953
G. C. DRUCE *Flora of Northamptonshire* 1930
LORD LILFORD *Notes on the Birds of Northamptonshire* 1895
P. STREET *Whipsnade* 1953

Topography

A. IRESON *Northamptonshire* (County Books series) 1954
S. LARKMAN *Bedfordshire* 2nd edn 1962
L. MEYNELL *Bedfordshire* (County Books series) 1950
N. PEVSNER *Northamptonshire* (Buildings of England series) 1961; *Bedfordshire Huntingdon and Peterborough* (Buildings of England series) 1968
J. SMITH *Northamptonshire and the Soke of Peterborough* (Shell Guide) 1968

Biography

V. BRITTAIN *In the steps of John Bunyan* 1950
R. FULFORD *Samuel Whitbread, 1764–1815* 1967
G. SCOTT THOMSON *Family Background* 1949; *Woburn and the Russells* 1956
JUNE WILSON *Green Shadows: the Life of John Clare* 1951

Gazetteer

BEDFORDSHIRE AND NORTHAMPTONSHIRE

The statue of John Bunyan at Bedford Reece Winstone

Althorp Park *Northants*. (EG 26). The 16th- to 18th-cent. family seat of Earl Spencer, 6 m. NW of Northampton, and built of grey brick and ironstone. Queen Anne, wife of James I, stayed here on her journey S from Scotland in the wake of her husband. A masque by Ben Jonson was produced in her honour. The house and a priceless collection of furniture and of portraits by Van Dyck, Reynolds and Gainsborough are on view to the public on certain days each week. To the W side of the park, the church at Great Brington contains tombs of the Spencer family from early dates onwards, and brasses commemorating ancestors of George Washington.

Ampthill *Beds*. (FA 23) EC Tues (4,750). This typical country town is at its busiest on Thursdays, when people congregate at the market, which dates back to 1219. The church is of special interest to Americans because it contains a monument to Richard Nicholls (1624–72), the first English Governor of Long Island, New York. Above it is embedded the Dutch cannon-ball that was the instrument both 'of his mortality and immortality'. 17th-cent. Ampthill Park (not open to motor traffic) has trees planted by Lady Holland in imitation of the Almeida in Madrid.

Ashby St Ledgers *Northants*. (EF 26) (170). The conspirators of the Gunpowder Plot (1605) are said to have met in the Manor House.

Aynho *Northants*. (EF 23) (440). It is unusual to find apricots growing on English cottage walls, but here they are. Aynho Park House, open during the season, was designed by Sir John Soane. Its pictures include seven by Murillo.

Barnack *Northants*. (FA 30) (770). Barnack building stone seen *in situ*. The 11th-cent. church tower and later porch and font are particularly worth notice.

Bedford★ *Beds*. (FA 24) EC Thurs (67,300). The county town on the Ouse has since the last war been enlivened by an influx of Italian workers who formed a colony of their own. The river on its slow course to the Wash is ideal for boating and angling.

Visitors will be reminded of the town's associations with John Bunyan (1628–88) by his statue at the north end of the High St, not far from the site of the county gaol, where he was imprisoned following an indictment for 'devilishly and perniciously abstaining from coming to church to hear Divine Service. . . .' Many of his relics are kept at the Bunyan Meeting House,

Fotheringhay Church

built in Mill St in his honour in 1850 on the site of the barn where he preached. The Bunyan Memorial Library Collection is attached to the public library.

Biggleswade *Beds.* (FB 24) EC Thurs (8,700). The centre for market gardens supplying London with vegetables.

Brackley *Northants.* (EF 23) EC Wed (4,040). Magdalen College School, founded in the 16th cent. uses the old chapel of St John's Hospital. Look for the statues in the niches of its tower, similar to those in the parish church.

Brigstock *Northants.* (EK 28) (1,100). A village at the centre of Rockingham Forest where the Woodland Pytchley pack of hounds are kennelled. Portions of the church date from before the Norman Conquest.

Brixworth *Northants.* (EH 27) EC Sat (1,510). The church was built in the late 7th cent. and at two closely related periods afterwards. Roman bricks from a still earlier structure are in its fabric. The Pytchley Hunt's kennels were removed here in 1818.

Burghley House *Northants.* (FA 30). S of Stamford and the river boundary with Lincolnshire. Built for the first great Cecil during the last half of the 16th cent. and considered one of the finest examples of domestic architecture in that flourishing period. Beautiful furniture, Old Masters and carvings by Grinling Gibbons are among the family treasures on view.

Cardington *Beds.* (FA 24) (330). The victims of R.101, the airship which crashed at Beauvais in France on her inaugural flight in 1930, are buried in the churchyard of St Mary's.

Castle Ashby House *Northants.* (EJ 25). Inigo Jones made the inspired alterations and additions to this Elizabethan house, property of the Marquess of Northampton. It has fine furniture, Italian paintings and lovely gardens.

Castor *Northants.* (FB 29) (550). The village takes its name from having been built on the site of a Roman camp. The 12th-cent. church is dedicated to a little-known saint, Kyneburga, who was a Mercian princess. Attention should be given to the magnificently-decorated church tower, and to the 14th-cent. wall-painting of St Catherine.

Charwelton *Northants.* (EF 25) (170). The Cherwell rises in the cellars of an old farmhouse and passes under a 13th-cent. pack-horse bridge.

Cockayne Hatley *Beds.* (FC 24) (120). The wood-carvings of the altar rails came from a monastery in Belgium, and the oak pulpit from Antwerp. The poet W. E. Henley is buried in the churchyard.

Corby *Northants.* (EJ 28) EC Wed (46,580). Open-cast mining has ravaged some of the prettiest scenery in the county, despite attempts at reafforestation, while industrialization has swelled the population of what not much more than thirty years ago was a small village.

Daventry *Northants.* (EF 26) EC Thurs (6,860). Best known in this generation for associations with wireless telegraphy. Charles I stayed here for a week in 1645 before his decisive defeat at the Battle of Naseby.

Deene Park *Northants.* (EK 29). Tudor country house open to the public. The parish church contains a memorial to the Earl of Cardigan, of Light Brigade fame.

Drayton House *Northants.* (EK 28). 'Not a rag in it under forty, fifty or a thousand years old,' said Horace Walpole of a country house with origins and remains dating from the reign of Edward III. 'The rags' include precious china and fine furniture.

Dunstable, *Beds.* (FA 22) EC Thurs (28,940). The town has found other manufacturing outlets since the decline in the straw-plait trade. The Priory Church of St Peter, a truncated fragment of the original Augustinian Priory of which most of the nave survived, is partly Norman and partly Early English, and was restored over a hundred years ago. From its lady chapel, Archbishop Cranmer pronounced sentence of divorce against Catherine of Aragon in 1533. On nearby Dunstable Downs the traditional orange rolling ceremony on Good Friday is an attraction.

Ecton *Northants.* 3 m. NE of Northampton (EJ 26). The father of Benjamin Franklin emigrated from here to New England in 1685.

Elstow *Beds.* (FA 24) (420). Birthplace of Bunyan and, like Bedford, has many associations with him: the cottage in which he lived in 1649, the Moot Hall used by his adherents as a meeting-place and now containing a collection illustrating life in the 17th cent., and the church with the font in which he was baptized. Of special note are the bells in the separate tower of the church, which Bunyan delighted to ring until deterred by scruples.

Finedon *Northants.* (EK 27) EC Thurs (4,370). The 14th-cent. church has an interesting strainer-arch across its nave.

Fotheringhay *Northants.* (FA 29) EC Wed (200). Mary Queen of Scots was tried and executed here. Nothing remains of the castle except a grassy mound. The church has a splendid lantern tower; the chancel was destroyed in the 16th cent. at the dissolution of the chantries.

Geddington *Northants.* (EJ 28) (1,160). A beautiful Eleanor Cross marks one stage of the funeral procession of Queen Eleanor of Castile, which travelled from Harby in Notts. to Westminster Abbey in 1290. The other two Eleanor Crosses that still remain are at Hardingstone and Waltham Cross.

Grafton Regis *Northants.* (EH 24). Edward IV is said to have met his bride, Elizabeth Woodville, under a great oak in Whittlewood Forest, and to have married her here.

Higham Ferrers *Northants.* (EK 26) EC Thurs (4,380). Archbishop Chichele (1362–1443) of Canterbury honoured his birthplace by building a school-house and bede-house in the grounds of the church, as well as a college in what is still called College St. The double nave of the church is an interesting feature.

Holdenby *Northants.* (EG 26) (140). Charles I was kept prisoner for four months in 1647 at Holdenby Hall,

Luton Hoo

G. Douglas Bolton

which was largely demolished in 1651. The present house (built 1873–88) is not open to the public.

Ickwell *Beds.* (FB 24). Birthplace of Thomas Tompion, the most famous English clockmaker, in 1638.

Irthlingborough *Northants.* (EK 27) (5,290). One among the churches typical of this country has a detached bell-tower surmounted by an octagon.

Islip *Northants.* (EK 27). Pretty village on the Nene. The Perpendicular church contains a memorial to a member of the Washington family, and a chancel-screen in remembrance of Mathias Nicoll, Mayor of New York in 1671.

Kettering *Northants.* (EJ 27) EC Thurs (39,270). One of the boot- and shoe-manufacturing centres for which this county is famous, and to which have been added ironworks and other industries. The church's spire makes an outstanding landmark. The Baptist Missionary Society, founded in 1792 by local worthies, met in the house still known as the Mission House.

Leighton Buzzard *Beds.* (EK 22) EC Thurs (18,040). A railway timetable of 1861 records that the journey to London took 63 minutes at a fare of 7s., 1st class single. The Early English church of All Saints has a beautiful broach spire and fascinating gargoyles. The Rothschild Collection of Chinese porcelain can be seen during afternoons April–September, at Ascott House (2½ m.). A very fine 15th-cent. market cross stands in the High Street.

Luton *Beds.* (FA 22) EB Wed (153,820). Though the hat-making industry has outstripped the straw-plait manufacture on which the prosperity of the town was founded, hats and hat-materials are still made by Luton – and many other consumer goods, not least cars. St Mary's Church has some remarkable features, including a rather cumbersome canopied baptistry and a delicate 15th-cent. chapel built around the tomb of William Wenlock (d. 1392), prebendary of St Paul's Cathedral. A visit to modern St Andrew's Church, by Sir Giles Scott, makes an interesting contrast.

Luton Hoo★ *Beds.* (FB 21). Magnificent country house by Robert Adam housing the Wernher Collection of art treasures and the originals of many pictures known in reproduction all over the world.

Naseby *Northants.* (EG 27) (350). Not until 1936 was a column (correcting one raised in 1823) placed to mark the true spot where in 1645 General Fairfax and the Parliamentarians beat the Royalist forces under the command of Charles I and his nephew Prince Rupert. The earlier column still stands where it was put.

Northampton★ *Northants.* (EH 26) EC Thurs (121,890). Few buildings survived the fire that occurred in the town towards the end of the 17th cent. This is a tragedy, since its history is full of events from Saxon and Norman times, right through the Wars of the Roses and the Civil War. Because the town had been disloyal to him, Charles II ordered the castle to be razed to the ground after the Restoration. The attractively named Marefair leads towards most points of interest.

There are only four round churches in England, and St Sepulchre in Sheep St is one of them. It was built in the early 12th cent. in the pattern of the Church of the Holy Sepulchre in Jerusalem.

Oundle *Northants*. (FA 28) EC Wed (3,590). Home of the famous public school. Pleasant country town with good 17th- and 18th-cent. houses. The Talbot Inn contains an oak staircase and other detail brought from Fotheringhay Castle when it was dismantled.

Rockingham *Northants*. (EJ 29). One of the county's stone-built villages. Rockingham Castle, built by William the Conqueror, and the property of the Tudor kings, has a magnificent banqueting hall from the reign of Edward I, and a fine Norman gateway and keep.

Rothwell *Northants*. (EJ 28) EC Thurs (4,760). One of the traditional towns of the footwear industry. The church has interesting brasses and a most unusual ossuary in the crypt. The Market House was begun in 1577 but not completed until 1895.

Rushton Hall *Northants*. (EJ 28). This fine country house, completed in the early 17th cent., has in its demesne a triangular lodge built (1593–5) by Sir Thomas Tresham in veneration of the Holy Trinity. The lodge is open to the public.

Oundle School

J. Allan Cash

Slapton *Northants*. (EG 24). Because wall-paintings in English churches are less common than in other countries, the parish church here should not be overlooked.

Southill *Beds*. (FB 24). Admiral Byng is buried in the family mausoleum of his parish church. He was executed in 1797 for his responsibility in the loss of our colony of Minorca.

Stowe Nine Churches *Northants*. (EG 25). Though it is impossible to locate the sites of the other eight, the surviving church has significant monuments and a fine Saxon tower.

Towcester *Northants*. (EG 24) EC Thurs (2,440). Like other towns with a similar suffix, Towcester has a history that goes back to Roman days. It also possesses literary associations; with Dean Swift, for instance, and as the prototype of 'Eatanswill' in the *Pickwick Papers*.

Warmington *Northants*. (FA 29) (612). The beams and wooden groins in the construction of the Early English church are of the greatest interest.

Weldon *Northants*. (EK 28) (1,650). 2 m. N of the village is Kirby Hall, once the Renaissance home of the Hatton family, and said to have been altered by Inigo Jones in the 17th cent. House and gardens fell into

Peterborough: a cottage built into the arches

Reece Winstone

Rockingham Castle: the Norman gateway

decay, but both have been restored to a limited extent, and are open to the public.

Wellingborough *Northants*. (EJ 26) EC Thurs (33,820). Shoe-making and ironworks are the traditional industries. People with an eye for the antique will admire the misericords in All Hallows Church, but should not neglect the Church of St Mary, a modern masterpiece of ecclesiastical architecture.

Woburn Abbey** *Beds*. (EK 23) The crowds who throng this mos popular ducal seat are given goo value for money, not only a tour of th house and its priceless contents, an of the park with its stately trees an collection of animals, but all the fur of the fair. An antique market ha recently been added.

Yardley Chase *Northants*. (EJ 25) Extensive tract of woodland noted fo fine oak trees, and much loved by th poet William Cowper (1731–1800).

Opposite: Detail from the original painting by Edgar Ainsworth. The shire of the ford across the Ouse, Bedfordshire is a county of winding water and leaning willows, meadowland and park-environed mansions. The picture suggests Bedford's airship and balloon manu facture; its perch, pike, chub, and dace, for which the anglers wait near the fields where marsh marigold and primroses abound.

Market Harborough: the former grammar school

Reece Winstone

LEICESTERSHIRE AND RUTLAND

AN INTRODUCTION BY W. G. HOSKINS

The Midlands tend to get written off as much of a muchness and as generally pretty dull. Few people ever consider going to Leicestershire or Rutland for pleasure, except those rich enough to hunt with the Quorn, the Belvoir, or the Cottesmore in winter. Yet Leicestershire has some beautiful pastoral scenery, especially in the east and south, and above all, to my mind, along the deserted towpaths of the old canals, of which there must be a hundred miles or more. As for Rutland, the smallest of all English counties, it is (next to Dorset) the most unspoilt. For those still capable of moving about slowly, motoring in Rutland is like what it was in England as a whole thirty years ago.

Geology and Scenery

Contrary to another general impression, held by those who know it only from belting along the A6 from London to Manchester, Leicestershire is not flat. As for Rutland, which nestles into it on the eastern side, most of this is a minor version of the Cotswolds, created out of the same oolitic limestone, and is flat only in the sense that the top of the Cotswolds is flat, that is, a country of long undulating slopes and free-flowing winds.

Opposite: Detail from the original painting by Barry Driscoll.

May trees in blossom characterize the smallest of England's counties, Rutland, where foxes are hunted and pheasants are shot, and where the fields have the reddish brown of limestone soil. The map of Rutland leans against the 18th-century gravestone commemorating a stonemason, complete with the tools of his Rutland trade. The ancient turf maze in the middle distance will be found at Wing, not far from Uppingham.

These are two small counties; yet their geology and therefore their scenery cover a very wide range, from the pre-Cambrian rocks of Charnwood Forest, a landscape of crags and splintered rocks and almost moorland scenery in places, to the placid levels of the limestone country in the east.

Heart-shaped, Leicestershire is divided into halves, east and west, by the River Soar on its way to the Trent. The western half, underlain by red Triassic rocks, is generally rather dull – what most people think of as typically Midland. It has its precious little oases, of course; but on the whole it is a landscape that does not vary enough in height to be interesting, and it is dotted with too many red-brick hosiery and boot-and-shoe villages, and even drearier little towns like Hinckley and Coalville. Only the special area of Charnwood is really worth anything as regards scenery. It is very small, about seven miles by five, but most distinctive: wild crags and boulder-strewn slopes, rising to 912 feet at Bardon Hill; and in Bradgate Park it has an almost untouched landscape of the Middle Ages. Bradgate began as a hunting park for some medieval magnate in the 12th century, was taken over for a Tudor nobleman's house about 1500 but never landscaped in the formal sense, and now belongs jointly to the city and county of Leicester, for the use of the public for ever. 'Going out to Bradgate' is a popular excursion for motorists and pedestrians in all the towns around it. Here, in Bradgate and in Charnwood generally, one can still walk on the bracken-covered hills and startle the wild deer.

East of the large city of Leicester, one climbs gradually up into the Liassic uplands. These give a clay country for the most part, usually covered, as in west Leicestershire, with a thick blanket of glacial boulder-clay. On top of this clay again we find islands of sands and gravels, on which most of the villages stand. Ten miles out of Leicester the resistant marlstone breaks through the clays and stands up to some 700 feet; and this higher country rolls away into the western side of Rutland about as far as Uppingham. It is lonely country; for on these uplands many villages perished when enclosures for sheep and cattle pastures were made during the 15th and 16th centuries, and such villages as survive are generally small. Yet this clay country is far from monotonous. It flows away like a green sea for miles in every direction, with little dark spinneys (fox-coverts most of them) dotted about at intervals, and sometimes larger and more ancient woodland, the scene punctuated by dark slender spires. Away from this deserted country, down in the lower levels, we find a landscape largely created by the Enclosure Commissioners of George III's time, crossed by quiet roads with broad grass verges as laid out in those days, and a church spire about every couple of miles.

Half-way across Rutland we come to the broad limestone belt which crosses the whole of England diagonally from Dorset to Yorkshire, the same oolitic limestone that gives us the Cotswolds and all that that word implies – seemly stone-built villages, solid great barns that speak of long-continued arable farming – no longer the green pastures of the Leicestershire clays; stone walls instead of quickset hedges; and the grand towers and spires of the parish churches – loveliest of all at Ketton.

Industries

Rutland has no manufacturing industry except a cement works at Ketton: these are the only tall chimneys one sees anywhere in this part of England. Farming is its great occupation, though of recent years the open-cast workings of the ironstone

The Union Canal below Laughton Hills

LEICESTERSHIRE AND RUTLAND

for ore has extended vastly and is locally important. Leicestershire is basically an industrial county; yet even this remark is misleading, for the eastern and southern thirds of the county are still almost completely rural. In the north-west, bordering Charnwood, is a small coalfield centred on Coalville, a town created in the second half of the 19th century. But the big industries in this western third of the county are hosiery and footwear. These are dull trades but very prosperous. They have not the hard grandeur of the woollen mills, or of the Potteries or the Black Country, the sheer demonic ugliness of these trades that make their landscapes exciting to look at. The two big Leicestershire industries produced scores of extremely dull villages built of red brick and Welsh slate, mostly in the last generation of the 19th century, villages so dull and uniform that a Georgian farmhouse in the main street, left over from a pre-industrial age, beckons like a fountain in a parched desert.

Leicester itself has three main industries – hosiery, footwear and engineering. In the last twenty years, engineering has taken first place over the two historic trades. It is, of course, an industrial city, of some 300,000 people; but since it never went through a real Industrial Revolution (i.e. the filth and power of the Steam Age) it is a town of more or less untarnished red brick. Historically, though, it is outstanding – though one would never expect this, whichever way one came in. But it has major monuments of every age from the Roman period onwards.

The avenue of Clipsham House

Reece Winstone

Archaeology

Neither county has much to offer the eye archaeologically. Not until the Iron Age do we find visible evidence of human occupation, and even then not much. Leicestershire has two impressive Iron Age hill-forts – Burrough Hill and Breedon Hill. Of the Roman period, there are two fine sites: Leicester itself and Great Casterton in Rutland. In the middle of teeming Leicester one can see some of the most impressive Roman remains in this country, the uncovered heart of the Roman town of Ratae Coritanorum. At Great Casterton, excavations during the past dozen years have revealed a site which is an epitome of the history of Roman Britain: a 1st-century fort, a town that was occupied from the 1st century to the 5th, and a villa site occupied from the late 4th century onwards.

It was the Angles and the Scandinavians who filled up Leicestershire and Rutland, founding most of the villages between about A.D. 500 and 1000. Scandinavian place-names abound (scores of -bys and -thorpes), and also sur-names like Gamble, Nutt and Swain over shop windows – all going back to the 9th century when the Danes took over this part of Mercia. Their mark is every-where.

Architecture

Both Leicestershire and Rutland are immensely rewarding for the confirmed church-crawler. Not much of the early periods, though Leicester has the 7th-century church of St Nicholas, and at Breedon are some remarkable Mercian carvings of the 8th century. In the Norman age, St Mary de Castro in Leicester, and Morcott, Tixover and Tickencote in Rutland. Of secular building, the castle hall at Oakham in Rutland (c. 1180–90) is of national importance, a wonderful thing to find in a small country town. The finest medieval churches belong to the years between 1150 and 1350. Here both counties have many first-class parish churches, some of those in Rutland surprisingly grand, like Ketton and Empingham. Visually what one notices is their soaring spires in the wide, open landscapes of the East Midlands: the broach spires (mainly c. 1300) which reach their summit of perfection at Market Harborough, and the later recessed spires (15th century) such as Bottesford and Queniborough and so many others. They always seem particularly appealing in the winter months when, under the dead white sky of a Midland November afternoon, one sees these needles silently piercing the horizon all around. The Midlands in winter have a vast melancholy appeal: those utterly still days when the sky seems to press down on an empty countryside, when the water in the old canals lies leaf-strewn and idle, and the bridle-paths go gently on for mile after mile with no one in sight, past the dark spinneys, the ash-trees and the lonely spires of the deep hunting-country.

Of the Middle Ages, too, are three outstanding secular monuments: the castles of Ashby-de-la-Zouch and Kirby Muxloe, in Leicestershire, both late 15th-century fortified houses rather than true castles; and the Bede House at Lidding-ton in Rutland, once the palace of the medieval bishops of Lincoln. And of a later age there is Staunton Harold church, a complete survival from the Cromwellian period; Brooke church in Rutland (an Elizabethan interior); and Kings Norton in Leicestershire, mid-18th century and deeply appealing to lovers of that age. The church monuments of both counties are also worth looking for: above all those at Bottesford (Leics.), where a series of tombs of the first eight earls of Rutland is one of the finest collections in England; and at Exton in Rutland a more varied collection but equally staggering in its impact.

Leicester: the ruins of Cavendish House

G. Douglas Bolton

The country houses are generally not of the first rank. Only Burley-on-the-Hill in Rutland can be put in the same class as, say, Chatsworth. Nothing vast and Elizabethan, for which one may be thankful, but many medium-sized and excellent houses, like Quenby (1620–30). The grandest pile in Leicestershire (and pile for once describes the general effect) is Belvoir Castle, on a magnificent site and very romantic-looking at a distance (rebuilt in the early 19th century). Mostly, though, the country houses are more homely, not shut off in enormous parks, but visible from the village road and often in the village itself. Peasant building in both counties is also very rewarding. The red brick of 18th-century Leicestershire can be most attractive, with roofs of the rough-hewn Swithland slate from Charnwood; while on the Stone Belt one gets houses of ironstone or limestone, finished off with the velvety brown, stone slates from Colly Weston. Also one should examine in town and village churchyards the beautifully lettered and carved headstones, of Swithland slate in Leicestershire and of Ketton stone in Rutland, some of them remarkable examples of popular art before it degenerated in the early 19th century.

Flora and Fauna

The characteristic trees are the ash, planted at intervals in the hedgerows, and the flowering hawthorn, which was universally used in the enclosures of the Georgian period (1760–1820) to produce a quick-growing fence, now the delight

Leicester: St Nicholas Church, the Roman Forum and the Jewry Wall

G. Douglas Bolton

of the hunters. These quickset hedges, and the biggish square fields, the long, easy, exhilarating slopes, the small willow-fringed streams at the bottom – all these ingredients have produced the most famous hunting country in England. So the fox is to be found everywhere; and there are wild deer at Bradgate Park (not hunted) which probably descended from those brought there when the park was created some eight hundred years ago. Fishing in the numerous 18th-century canals is a common sport, and a characteristic sight on a Saturday afternoon. These canals, otherwise hardly used at all today, provide some of the pleasantest scenery in Leicestershire. Walking along their crumbling towpaths one passes nothing more for hours than the bicycle of some hopeful fisherman.

For the Gourmet

Leicestershire has long been notable for two good things to eat: pork pies and cheese. Most people have heard of Melton pies, first created for the hunting people for whom Melton is spelt Mecca; but I myself think the best pork pies in England are made in Leicester. As for cheese, Stilton was first created in a Leicestershire country house in the early 17th century. When it was transported to the Great North Road, to the Bell Inn at Stilton, it got a national reputation and a new and false name. It is too late to alter that now; but in south Leicestershire an excellent red cheese is still made and named after the county. This, at its best, is one of the great regional cheeses of England.

423

Some houses and gardens open to the public

Ashby-de-la-Zouch Castle 9m SE of Burton upon Trent on A50 *Map* ED 31. *14th cent.; 15th-cent. tower by Lord Hastings; a Royalist stronghold during the Civil War.*

Belgrave Hall At Leicester *Map* EF 30. *18th cent.; now a museum containing furniture, pictures and an agricultural collection.*

Belvoir Castle 7m W of Grantham, 12m N of Melton Mowbray *Map* EJ 33. *Originally 11th cent., rebuilt 19th cent.; picturesque hilltop setting overlooking Vale of Belvoir. Magnificent state rooms, objets d'art and armoury, collection of paintings.* The Duke of Rutland.

Kirby Muxloe Castle 5m W of Leicester off B5380 *Map* EF 30. *Moated 15th-cent. fortified brick manor house, in ruins.*

Oakham Castle At Oakham *Map* EJ 30. *Splendid Norman Hall with unique collection of horseshoes.*

Prestwold Hall 3m NE of Loughborough off A60 *Map* EF 32. *Mid-Georgian, enlarged by Wm Burn; painted marble halls, Chippendale furniture, family portraits; extensive gardens.* Mr and Mrs David Babington Smith.

Stanford Hall Swindon 7½m NE of Rugby off A427 *Map* EF 27. *17th cent.; built by Smiths of Warwick; fine collection of Stuart pictures, family costumes; replica of Percy Pilcher's flying machine of 1898; motor-cycle museum.* Lord Braye.

Stapleford Park 5m E of Melton Mowbray off B676 *Map* EH 31. *16th cent., with later extension; old wing has sculptures depicting religious, historical and legendary scenes; pictures, furniture. Church contains 15th-cent. brass and Rysbrack tomb. Lake with heronry and geese; miniature steam passenger railway.* Lord Gretton.

Books for further reading

Local life and customs

COLIN D. B. ELLIS *Leicestershire and the Quorn Hunt* 1951

BERNARD NEWMAN *Portrait of the Shires* 1968

J. and A. E. STOKES *Just Rutland* 1953 (with separate chapters on Oakham and Uppingham schools)

History, topography, architecture

COLIN D. B. ELLIS *History in Leicester 55 B.C.–A.D. 1900* 1969

C. N. HADFIELD *Charnwood Forest: a Survey* 1952

W. G. HOSKINS *Leicestershire: an illustrated Essay on the History of the Landscape* 1957; *Rutland: A Shell Guide* 1963

ARTHUR MEE *Leicestershire and Rutland* (King's England series) 1967

GUY PAGET and LIONEL IRVINE *Leicestershire* (County Books series) 1950

NIKOLAUS PEVSNER *Leicestershire and Rutland* (Buildings of England series) 1960

FLORENCE E. SKILLINGTON *The Plain Man's History of Leicester* 1950

Gazetteer

LEICESTERSHIRE AND RUTLAND

Belvoir Castle *J. Allan Cash*

Ashby-de-la-Zouch *Leics*. (ED 31) EC Wed (7,770). Readers of Sir Walter Scott's *Ivanhoe* will remember the scenes of pageantry in the Tournament Ground here. Though the chivalrous episodes are fictional, such a field exists not far away. The present fortress was built on the site of an earlier Norman stronghold, but was 'slighted' – that is, disarmed and partly demolished – in the Civil War. The most impressive portions that remain are the Great Hall and the kitchen. The chapel is ruined. Near it stands the Solar, the sun parlour occupied for a short time by Mary Queen of Scots.

The church has family tombs, an effigy of a 15th-cent. pilgrim, and a finger-pillory believed to have been used on those people whose behaviour was offensive in church!

Bardon Hill *Leics*. (EE 31). Vantage-point 912 ft. above sea-level looking across Charnwood Forest towards Derbyshire and the Welsh Marches. It was a Bronze Age settlement, covered with primeval forest, but quarries have now cut into the hillside.

Belvoir Castle *Leics*. (EJ 33). Seat of the Dukes of Rutland, rebuilt in 1816 after a fire, at a period early enough to escape the worst of 19th-cent. taste. The view from the terraces is remarkable, and the gardens with their classical statuary are beautifully landscaped.

The galleries contain paintings by Dutch and Flemish masters – Rembrandt and Rubens among them – and portraits by great English painters. Other treasures on view include Gobelin tapestries, armour, fine furniture and relics of that Marquis of Granby who gave his name to so many English inns.

Bottesford *Leics*. (EJ 33) EC Wed (1,874). A most attractive Early Perpendicular church noted for the tombs and monuments of the Manners family, the owners of Belvoir Castle; the inscriptions read like a history book. The spire, 210 ft. high, is a landmark pointing to this wealth of decoration.

Bradgate Park *Leics*. (EF 30). Adjoining the city of Leicester, the park is open to motorists on Wednesdays and Thursdays during the summer; otherwise it is reserved for walkers. Lady Jane Grey, the proclaimed Queen of England for so pathetically short a time, was born in the house (*see* p. 418) in 1537.

Breedon-on-the-Hill *Leics*. (EE 32) (529). The church incorporates in its fabric many fragments of a sculptured frieze that have survived from some building of the Saxon period. The figures – a lion, with saints and strange beasts – are surrounded by an interlaced pattern of curves and spirals.

425

Exton: the park gates

Brooke *Rutland* (EJ 30). The interior of the church is full of beautiful Elizabethan woodwork, unrestored.

Brooksby *Leics.* (EG 31). George Villiers, 1st Duke of Buckingham, was born in this Tudor manor house, which, despite its charms, he quickly outgrew at the Court of James I.

Burley-on-the-Hill *Rutland* (EJ 31). To a grander mansion came George, Duke of Buckingham, and here was staged a masque by Ben Jonson. The house has twice been destroyed and twice rebuilt, and now has a beautiful N front of columns and Doric capitals. The Norman church contains a 15th-cent. font, a carved reredos, and the alabaster figures of a knight and his lady whose dress places them as having died not later than the early 15th cent.

Castle Donington *Leics.* (EE 32) EC Wed (4,311). A small attractive town, with a gabled and timbered keyhouse. The stone pulpit in the church is made of memorial slabs taken from the floor. See also the brasses of Robert de Staunton and his wife with their children and pet dogs. An earlier carving, *c.* 1320, shows a monk laid out in elaborate vestments.

Nearby, the East Midlands Airport is of interest, and King's Mills on the Trent is most picturesque, with weirs, water-wheel and cottages.

Charnwood Forest *Leics.* (EF 31). Wild scenery on miniature scale to the NW of Leicester.

Clipsham *Rutland* (EK 31). From local quarries came much of the stone that makes this county's little-known villages as delightful as those of the Cotswolds. It can be seen at its best in Clipsham Hall, which also has a fine yew hedge.

Cottesmore *Rutland* (EK 31) (3,100). The chapel on the N side of the church is a memorial to the men of the British and American Air Forces who were stationed here in the Second World War. Bronze Age and subsequent early burial-places have been excavated nearby.

Exton *Rutland* (EK 31) (630). The church stands in parkland, and contains a noteworthy collection of monuments, mostly of the Noel and Harington families, from the 14th cent. to the present day. The angel seated at the organ on the Tower Screen should not be missed.

Great Casterton *Rutland* (EK 30) EC Wed (310). In addition to the newly discovered Roman remains mentioned in the Introduction, visitors should see the church for an example of 13th-cent. architecture untouched by restorers. The square Norman font, decorated roughly in diamond pattern, is quite exceptional. Note too the Elizabethan pulpit, the ironwork on the door of the church and, of course, the Norman arches.

Kegworth *Leics.* (EE 32) EC Wed (2,889). This town on the R. Soar has a beautiful church of the Late Decorated period, with two aisles, carved figures in the roof and stone angels supporting the chancel. The stained glass, some of it 600 years old, is set in tracery and finely matches the general design.

Ketton *Rutland* (EK 30) (1,455). The 14th-cent. church with earlier tower does not allow itself to be dwarfed by the cement works or by the factory chimneys that make a landmark in this flattish countryside. Ketton was once famous for the stone that forms part of many important buildings far afield.

Kirby Muxloe *Leics.* (EF 30) EC Wed (3,860). Ruins of a moated and fortified country house built in the late 15th cent. The stone gatehouse and brick façade survive, though the interior has crumbled. Open all the year round.

Leicester* *Leics.* (EG 30) EC Thurs (282,800). Industrial city still following the traditional manufacture of hosiery and footwear, while having expanded in other directions, especially in engineering.

At the Roman period the city was fortified. Remains of that occupation are preserved in the Jewry Wall, a mass of masonry demonstrating the brick courses used by the Romans, and retaining four arched alcoves. This adjoins the Forum, near which are Roman baths of a slightly later date. Pieces of Roman pavement are preserved also in the town, and others are exhibited at the museum.

In the 13th cent., Simon de Montfort was Earl of Leicester, and despite his political interests he became concerned for the welfare of the town. His statue takes pride of place among three others in the 19th-cent. clock tower at the city's centre, where the main streets cross. Richard III slept in the town before the battle of Bosworth Field. A house near Bow Bridge over the Soar can claim that his body rested here after the defeat of his forces, and was later brought back after having been thrown into the river. Prince Rupert captured Leicester in 1645 after a three day's engagement that John Bunyan saw, but it was promptly reoccupied by the Parliamentarians following their decisive win at Naseby.

But perhaps the event that has had the greatest effect on Leicester was the discovery of the stocking-frame in the late 17th cent. And modern travellers will remember that Thomas Cook inaugurated his tours in 1841 by a railway excursion from Leicester to Loughborough and back.

St Nicholas is the most ancient of the city churches. In its structure, Roman and Saxon building materials are evident. The Norman tower and the Saxon nave give additional interest to interior and exterior design. Not far away, and adjoining the Castle to which it belongs, stands the Church of St Mary de Castro. Its unusual design is due to the addition of a chancel in the 12th cent. and later still a wide nave and a tower. The roof of this later nave (on the S side) and the 13th-cent. font are among the church's main beauties.

The façade of the Castle Hall, where the Judge of Assize sits, consists of 18th-cent. brickwork, overlaying the original Norman materials; but the interior, especially the roof, is imposing. The river and the surrounding lawns make it a perfect setting at the heart of the city. On the way out through the gateway into the Newarke, and beyond Trinity Hospital, some famous houses have been formed into the Newarke Houses Museum; they contain collections that illustrate graphically the industrial history of Leicester. The Newarke Gate leads out from what was once a walled enclosure extending to four acres.

St Martin's Church, near the Guildhall, has been the Cathedral since 1919, when Leicester recovered her status as a city. The Bishop's Throne is particularly fine, and shows carved birds and animals as amusing as those on a chair in the sanctuary, which enact a hunting misadventure that could take place at any time in the shires.

A passage separates St Martin's and the Guildhall, a timbered building begun in the 14th cent.; it was the scene of a feast to celebrate the defeat of the Spanish Armada. Adjoining the hall is the Mayor's Parlour, with a splendid chimney-piece and a chair in which Prince Rupert once sat.

Liddington *Rutland* (EJ 29) (310). Thomas Cecil, son of Queen Elizabeth's Lord Burleigh, transformed a medieval archiepiscopal palace into a verandahed bede-house for twelve men and two women – a proportion

fixed perhaps to ensure that a modicum of housework was done for the men! The upper floor keeps some of its panel-work, a fine ceiling and handsome windows in what was originally the banqueting hall, though the whole structure has had to be restored.

Lindley Hall *Leics.* (ED 29). Birthplace of Robert Burton, author of *The Anatomy of Melancholy*, in 1577. Best known nowadays as a testing centre for motor industry research.

Loughborough *Leics.* (EF 31) EC Wed (39,580). Another of the traditional towns of the hosiery trade that have added engineering to their occupations. It has an important Institute of Technology. The War Memorial Tower,* built in 1923 to commemorate the dead of the 1914 War, is memorable for the carillon from which bell-music was broadcast for the first time. Bells have been part of Loughborough since the arrival of John Taylor in the last century. He came to recast the bells of the parish church, and stayed, setting up a bell-foundry that has become world-famous. Great Paul of St Paul's Cathedral was cast here – the biggest bell in England, nine feet tall and over sixteen tons in weight.

Lutterworth *Leics.* (EF 28) EC Wed (4,682). John Wycliffe was rector here for twenty years until his death in 1384. Thirty years later his writings were condemned by the Council of Constance, and his remains were disinterred, burnt and scattered into the Swift – by which, according to his doctrine, they were dispersed across the world. He is now chiefly remembered for having promoted the first translation of the Bible into the common tongue. St Mary's Church contains relics that are of interest through their age, though they cannot with any certainty be attributed to the great reformer.

John Wycliffe's church at Lutterworth

Oakham, Rutland

J. Allan Cash

Market Bosworth *Leics.* (EE 30) (1,570). It may be difficult to imagine Dr Johnson as a humble usher at Market Bosworth Grammar School. But the defeat and death in 1485 of Richard III on Bosworth Field, 2 m. S, is readily visualized through Shakespeare's play.

Market Harborough *Leics.* (EH 28) EC Thurs (12,880). A neighbourhood famous in fox-hunting tradition for the Pytchley, Quorn and Fernie hounds. The early 17th-cent. Grammar School in the market place, and the spire of St Dionysius, are worthy of attention.

Market Overton *Rutland* (EJ 31) (420). Roman and Saxon treasure has been found near here, including a primitive clock run on a principle, known to the Egyptians, by which a pierced vessel sinks in a quantity of water.

Melton Mowbray* *Leics.* (EH 31) EC Thurs (18,040). Fox-hunting again, but now more in retrospect after the day's chase, at inns where Melton Mowbray pork pies and Stilton cheese are served near their place of origin. The Church of St Mary is remarkable for its W porch and a clerestory of 48 windows added to the nave and transepts in the 16th cent.

Oakham *Rutland* (EJ 30) EC Thurs (5,730). The county town epitomizes the county: settled, beautiful, unhurried. The Norman banqueting hall of the Castle, in reality a manor house on the grand scale, is handsome and beautifully ornamented. On its walls, in accordance with a custom that goes back beyond memory, hang horseshoes nailed there by visiting royalty and the nobility. These shoes ～ge from the tiny to the enormous, ～ most are inscribed with historic ～es.

Above the church perches Cock Peter, one of the oldest weather-vanes in England. Inside is kept the Oakham Bible, contemporary with Magna Carta. The Grammar School, founded in the 16th cent., and sharing its founder with Uppingham, has outgrown its original buildings, but these still stand. The Butter Cross and the town stock are in the square. Titus Oates (1649–1705), who was responsible for the Popish Plot, was born here; so was Jeffery Hudson, the dwarf knighted by Charles II. He hopped out of a piping hot pie and succeeded in amusing his royal master.

Quorn *Leics.* (EF 31) EC Wed (3,334). The hounds of the famous Quorn Hunt (whose kennels are now at Barrow-on-Soar) take their name from the village that was once known as Quorndon. The church has two unusual stone screens, and a 14th-cent. chapel full of memorials to the Farnham family; one of these was an Elizabethan gentleman who, 'descended of an ancient house, with honours led his life', to the extent of winning a pension from his Queen.

Rothley *Leics.* (EH 31) EC Wed (3,714). Lord Macaulay was born at Rothley Temple, an Elizabethan house with a chapel that originally belonged to an affiliated order of the Knights Templar. It is not open to the public.

Shawell *Leics.* (EF 27). After the death of his friend Arthur Hallam, Lord Tennyson wrote *In Memoriam* while he was staying at the Rectory.

Staunton Harold *Leics.* (ED 31) (182). One of the rare churches built in the Commonwealth period; hence its inscriptions are worthy of note. For instance, over the doorway appears the record that 'In the year 1653, when all things sacred were throughout the nation either demolished or profaned, Sir Robert Shirley, Baronet, founded this church, whose singular praise it is to have done the best things in the worst times and hoped them in the most calamitous'.

Stoke Golding *Leics.* (EE 29). The detail in the village church is very beautiful, especially the tracery of the windows and the clustered pillars with elaborate capitals.

Tickencote *Rutland* (EK 31) (80). The church has a late Norman arch over the chancel, in five curved patterns, some of them unique. The vaulting of the roof over the choir resembles that of Canterbury. Note also the square 13th-cent. font.

Uppingham *Rutland* (EJ 29) EC Thurs (2,410). The school founded towards the end of the 16th cent. has become one of England's most famous institutions. It is based on a very attractive town.

Waltham-on-the-Wolds *Leics.* (EJ 32) EC Tue (712). At the centre of Leicestershire's little-known Wolds.

Wanlip *Leics.* (EG 31) (75). Site of a Roman villa. Admirers of brasses should not miss that of Sir Thomas Walsh, the church's founder; he has a lion at his feet, while his wife obviously prefers the two dogs at hers. Dated 1393, this piece presents the earliest English prose inscription on brass known in England.

Uppingham School

J. Allan Cash

Stoneleigh Abbey

WARWICKSHIRE

AN INTRODUCTION BY JOHN MOORE

The pleasant and charmingly-named village of Meriden, which lies between Birmingham and Coventry in what was once the Forest of Arden, considers itself to be the geographical centre of England. It is very proud of this, and also of being the headquarters of the oldest body of archers in Great Britain, 'The Woodmen of Arden'. In fact, all Warwickshire is boastful of being 'the county closest to England's heart'. And indeed you feel you are at the very heart of our land when you drive through the lush green dairy-farm countryside: everywhere the elm tree, which is called the Weed of Warwickshire, everywhere the unhurrying water-courses running down to the slow rivers, and the English villages with aristocratic double-barrelled names, such as Baddesley Clinton, Wellesbourne Hastings, Temple Grafton, Wootton Wawen, Radford Semele – even Bishop's Itchington, though that sounds less aristocratic.

The great Forest of Arden originally covered most of the county lying northwest of the Avon; a forest neither dark nor formidable if we may draw conclusions from *As You Like It*: 'Here shall you see no enemy but winter and rough weather.' The fragments of it which still remain give the impression of a high wood broken up by many clearings which let in the sun.

Shakespeare's Country

Where the forest fringe touched the River Avon at Stratford, Shakespeare was born, appropriately on St George's Day, 1564; and there by a happy coincidence, if we can believe the legend, he died also upon St George's Day, in 1616. For sentimental as well as practical reasons Stratford is the proper centre and starting-point for any tour of Warwickshire. It is said that 200,000 people every year visit the birthplace in Henley Street, a delightful timber-framed house

433

which was probably about fifty years old when Shakespeare was but a little tiny boy there. Presumably most of these multitudinous pilgrims also visit the poet's grave in Holy Trinity Church beside the river; New Place, the home of his last years, with its enchanting Elizabethan garden and its mulberry tree (grown from a slip of a mulberry which in turn was grown from a slip of Shakespeare's own tree); and Hall's Croft, the beautiful house of his son-in-law, the physician John Hall, whose famous casebook was called *Selected Observations on English Bodies or Cures both Empiricall and Historicall, performed upon very eminent Persons in desperate diseases.* He left no account of Shakespeare's last illness: perhaps because he failed to cure it.

A still vaster horde of pilgrims, according to Stratford statisticians, visit the theatre to see the plays: some 300,000 per annum, coming from every country under the sun. It is an excellent modern brick building, rising sheer from the river bank, flood-lit at night during the season and delightfully reflected in the water, where its glowing image is generally rippled by a dozen snowy swans.

At Shottery, a mile from Stratford, is 'Anne Hathaway's Cottage' (in fact it is not a cottage at all but the very handsome farmhouse which belonged to Anne's yeoman father) where Shakespeare courted the girl, much older than he was, whom he married after a bit of a schemozzle by special licence when she was already three months gone with child. There is a footpath way to it from Stratford, and going along it you are certainly treading where Shakespeare trod. But whichever way you go from Stratford-upon-Avon you are following in his footsteps. They will lead you to the villages round about, to which he is supposed to have given their epithets in the old jingle – Piping Pebworth, Dancing Marston, Haunted Hillboro', Drunken Bidford and so on. The legend of Bidford's drunkenness rests upon a tale, probably apocryphal, of Shakespeare's drinking-bout there a little time before he died. Michael Drayton, the Warwickshire poet who wrote *Poly-Olbion*, is said to have been his companion, in some versions of this story. Drayton loved his native Warwickshire and especially its River Avon: he was probably thinking of its alternating pools and swift shallow reaches at Bidford when he wrote of 'Ev'ry pearl-pav'd ford and ev'ry blue-ey'd deep'. Luckily the river here is not deep enough for motor boats and so it remains unspoilt all the way from Evesham, through Stratford and beyond Kenilworth. Indeed, it is probably little changed from the time when Shakespeare leaned upon the lovely Clopton Bridge at Stratford, which has a parapet that is most accommodating to elbows, and watched the perch swimming among the lily-pads, which later turned up as 'tawny finn'd fishes' in *Antony and Cleopatra*. He certainly must have walked upstream along the river bank to Charlecote, the home of the Lucy family where he is supposed to have poached one of Sir Thomas Lucy's deer. This got him into trouble (so the tale runs) for which he took an immortal revenge, if indeed Sir Thomas, the local magistrate, is portrayed as the doddering Justice Shallow. The whole story is discounted by the scholars; but the fallow deer still graze in Charlecote Park.

Round about here the Avon runs the sweetest course of any river I know, between its willows and its water-meadows, by delightful old mills, and through the villages which have grown up about them. Upstream lies Warwick with its most majestic castle – 'the fairest monument of ancient and chivalrous splendour,' wrote Sir Walter Scott, 'which yet remains uninjured by time'. It is matched in splendour by the church of St Mary, rebuilt many times, with a Wren tower magnificently looming over the whole ancient town. Its Lady Chapel contains the marvellous

Welford-on-Avon: cottages on the village g

tomb of Richard Beauchamp, Earl of Warwick. Elizabeth's Leicester has his monument in the church, and 11,445 less famous men are commemorated by a memorial to those of the Royal Warwickshire Regiment who were killed in the First World War; a considerable sacrifice, out of the heart of England!

Above Warwick, and still only a long day's walk from Stratford, is Leicester's own castle, Kenilworth. In 1575 the Queen made a progress thither and there were great junketings in her honour, which cost her favourite a thousand pounds a day; a minor item in the bill represented the cost of 38,400 gallons of beer. It is likely that young Shakespeare, then aged eleven, may have had his first glimpse of the Queen there, and his first awe-stricken sight of the great lords and ladies whom one day he would write about with such familiar ease.

Cotswold Country

South-west of Stratford you gradually come out of the rich, green, elm-dotted, mixed-farming country, as you approach the foothills of Cotswold. Cattle give way to sheep; meadows to cropped turf; meandering streams to swifter ones. The river here is the Stour, which winds down off the hills through charming villages and hamlets built mostly out of the greyish-brown stone from the local quarries: Clifford Chambers, Atherstone-on-Stour, Preston-on-Stour, Alderminster, Newbold (which its inhabitants call Nobbled), Tredington, Honington and Shipston, the 'sheep's town' long famous for its fleeces and its flocks.

The highroad from Shipston to Chipping Norton runs along a fine ridge from which you look down at good Cotswold country on either side. This is a borderland between four counties; the nearby Four Shires Stone marks what used to be the meeting-point of Warwickshire, Worcestershire, Oxfordshire and Gloucestershire. It was a meeting-place for people too – horse-copers and hucksters used to foregather there, wrestlers and prize-fighters, with the crowds that cheered them on. Today only three counties meet at the Four Shires Stone; the bureaucrats have re-drawn the boundaries and from the neighbourly get-together of English counties Worcestershire has been excluded.

Villages near here include Long Compton, Little Compton and Compton Verney, and there is even Compton Scorpion, where Sir Thomas Overbury was born. But the most famous of the Comptons is, of course, Compton Wynyates, the seat of the Marquis of Northampton, tucked under the scarp of Edge Hill close to the Oxfordshire border. It is perhaps the most splendid of all the great houses in the West Midlands. It was begun in 1480 by Edmund Compton, and finished in 1520 by his son William. It has had an exciting history: Henry VIII, Queen Elizabeth and James I, all stayed under its roof. James ennobled the second William Compton, making him Earl of Northampton; the second Earl naturally took the King's side in the Civil War: he and his three sons, all of whom were knighted, fought right on their home ground as it were, in the battle of Edgehill. That was in 1642; and the Earl was killed next year at Hopton Heath. In 1644 Compton Wynyates was taken by the Parliament troops after a brief siege, but the Northampton family got it back two years later by paying a fine of £20,000, and promising to fill in the moat and dismantle the fortifications.

The name Wynyates means 'wind gate' – a gap in the hills through which the wind blows. (In the old days they called the place less elegantly 'Compton-in-the-Hole'.) The Tudor house is built of rosy-pink brick which glows most wonderfully in the sun, set off by the pitch-black timbers.

Wootton Wawen Church

G. Douglas Bolton

Charlecote Manor on the River Avon

Towns and Industries

The antiquary Camden, writing of Warwickshire during the reign of Queen Elizabeth, divided the county into two parts: the Feldon, or meadow-land, and the Woodland, which, of course, included the great Forest of Arden. Most of the northern half of the county was woodland; and Shakespeare probably thought it a pretty uncivilized place compared with the cultivated and well-farmed district round about Stratford-upon-Avon. Today, of course, this once wild waste is one of the most highly industrialized parts of Britain.

Rugby lies at the eastern edge of it, a nice-looking market town with its great school, of which Dr Arnold was the famous headmaster and which counts among its famous pupils Matthew Arnold, Arthur Hugh Clough, Rupert Brooke, Wyndham Lewis, C. L. Dodgson ('Lewis Carroll'), Thomas Hughes, who wrote *Tom Brown's Schooldays*, and W. S. Landor, whose schooldays were terminated by his expulsion from Rugby school. Rugby town is a betwixt-and-between place; a centre both of foxhunting and engineering; they seem to get on together quite well. Coventry is the chief centre of the motor-car and cycle industry in Britain. It sends the products of its skills all over the world, earning a substantial part of Britain's living thereby. But it possesses older associations which will probably be remembered for as long as its industrial fame. Its medieval Mystery Plays have a secure place in our literature. Its Godiva story, whether true or not, has become part of our folklore and of our history too, though the historians insist on spelling the name of Leofric's wife 'Godyfu'. Its destruction by the Germans on the 14th November 1940 lit a blaze of British defiance at which we warmed ourselves through a bleak winter. And lastly its rising again, with a new cathedral, city centre, theatre and railway station, is a post-war story to uplift the spirit and match the heroics of 1940. Sir Basil Spence's cathedral stands against the grim ruins of the old one in the midst of the city of motor-cars and big business: an imaginative juxtaposition. And here we find, among the works of many artists and craftsmen, Epstein's fine St Michael in bronze, John Piper's eighty-foot-high window in all its rainbow splendour, and Graham Sutherland's huge tapestry, the largest ever woven in one piece.

West of Coventry, among the disintegrated and vanishing fragments of Arden, is Meriden, that middle-of-England village so proud of its closeness to the country's heart. About it there is a little bit of pastoral land which probably won't remain so much longer, and then you come to Elmdon Airport and the approaches to Birmingham, that sprawling city of a thousand trades and crafts and sciences, the second biggest in Britain, eighty square miles of it, getting on for one and a quarter million people, appalling suburbs ever creeping outwards to eat up its green belt.

Its industrial history is a fairly long one. It has been, as old Leland put it, 'mayntayned by smithes' ever since the year 1500 or so, when the metal-workers began to get their iron and coal in quantity from the Stafford and North Warwickshire mines. At the time of the Civil War it was important enough to hammer out no less than 15,000 sword-blades for the Parliament men, on whose side its sympathies lay. In Shakespeare's day it was, presumably, merely a market town with many blacksmiths, lying on the farther side of Arden, possibly unknown to him. At the time of the making of the Domesday Book its inconsiderable Manor was sold to a vassal of Baron FitzAnsculf; it 'was and is', according to the documents, 'worth twenty shillings'.

Some houses and gardens open to the public

Anne Hathaway's Cottage Shottery 1m w of Stratford-on-Avon off A422 *Map* EB 25. *Thatched Elizabethan cottage; birthplace of Shakespeare's wife.*

Aston Hall 2½m from the centre of Birmingham in Aston Park *Map* EA 28. *Jacobean mansion built by Sir Thomas Holte; plasterwork ceilings; friezes, carved fireplaces; furnishings, including needlework hangings by Mary Holte; Great Hall.* Corporation of Birmingham.

Charlecote Park 5m NE of Stratford-on-Avon off B4086 *Map* EC 25. *Elizabethan; restored with picturesque gatehouse* (NT). *The deer park has Shakespearian associations.*

Kenilworth Castle 1m W of Kenilworth off B4103 *Map* EC 27. *Norman foundations with additions by John of Gaunt; 16th-cent. gatehouse; historic associations.*

Ragley Hall 2m SW of Alcester off A435 *Map* EA 25. *17th-cent. home of the Seymours; magnificent Baroque entrance hall designed by James Gibbs; paintings, porcelain, furniture; gardens and park with lake.* The Marquess of Hertford.

Shakespeare's Birthplace At Stratford-on-Avon *Map* EC 25. *16th cent.; half-timbered house, birthplace of the poet; numerous relics.*

Warwick Castle At Warwick *Map* EC 26. *14th cent.; overlooking River Avon; Guy's Tower and Caesar's Tower; imposing gatehouse; Great Hall; state rooms, armoury and objets d'art.*

Books for further reading

Local life and customs

J. H. BLOOM *Folk Lore, Old Customs and Superstitions in Shakespeare Land* 1929

Natural history

J. E. BAGNALL *The Flora of Warwickshire* 1891

C. A. NORRIS *Notes on the Birds of Warwickshire* 1947

Topography

F. R. BANKS *Warwickshire and the Shakespeare Country* (Penguin) 1960

J. H. BLOOM *Warwickshire* (Cambridge County Geographies) 1916

A. BURGESS *Warwickshire* (County Books series) 1950

J. C. COX *Warwickshire* (Little Guides series) 3rd edn, rev. 1930

T. EDWARDS *Warwickshire* (Vision of England series) 1950

J. FLEMING *Shakespeare's Country in Colour* 1960

L. FOX *The Borough Town of Stratford-on-Avon* 1953

A. MEE ed. *Warwickshire* (King's England series) 1966

WARD, LOCK & CO. LTD. *Guide to Leamington Spa, Warwick, Kenilworth, Stratford on Avon, and Shakespeare's Warwickshire* 1962

Biography

U. BLOOM *Rosemary for Stratford-on-Avon* 1966

M. ECCLES *Shakespeare in Warwickshire* 1961

A. FAIRFAX-LUCY *Charlecote and the Lucys* 1958

E. HAMILTON *The Mordaunts* 1965

A. PARKER *Great Men of Warwickshire* 1966

Gazetteer

WARWICKSHIRE

Alcester (EA 25) EC Thurs (3,456). A market town notable for the number and variety of its ancient houses. The Old Malt House (about 1500) and other timber-framed buildings of the period, as well as 17th- and 18th-cent. ones, can be seen in Henley St; at one end is the picturesque Town Hall. 1½ m. SE, Ragley Hall and its park are open to the public: this 17th- and 18th-cent. mansion contains pictures and period furniture, and there is sailing on the lake.

Arbury Hall (ED 28). Standing in a 300-acre park that overlooks a chain of lakes, the house, originally Elizabethan but transformed at the end of the 18th cent., is an example of the Gothic style, though the stables, with their Flemish-type work (the central gable was designed by Wren), are 100 years older. It is the 'Cheverel Manor' described in *Scenes of Clerical Life*: George Eliot was born at South Farm on the estate where her father was agent, and later lived at Griff House nearby. **Astley**, adjoining one of the entrances to the park, has a noteworthy church, with 15th-cent. choir-stalls and misericords; and the castle, NE of the church, is a fortified manor house of the 13th cent., restored in the time of Mary Tudor.

Aston Hall (EA 28). Now controlled by Birmingham City Museum and Art Gallery, this is one of the most splendid Jacobean mansions in the country, and contains a collection of English furniture and some valuable pictures. The parish church, completely rebuilt in the 19th cent., is

Chesterton Mill   *Reece Winstone*

worth visiting for its wealth of medieval monuments.

Berkswell (EC 27) EC Thurs (2,400). The church is remarkable not only for the almost unaltered Norman chancel, but for the two connecting crypts with their groined vaulting and original stone seats, and the half-timbered chamber over the 16th-cent. porch. There is a medieval cross outside the church, and on the green, close to the original well, are the village stocks.

Birmingham★ (EA 28) EC Thurs and Sat (1,107,187). Slightly larger than Glasgow, Birmingham is the second biggest city in Britain, but its suburbs extend into Worcestershire and are continuous with the Black Country in Staffordshire. Described as early as 1538 by Leland as being largely 'mayntayned by smithes', it owes its greatest expansion to the Industrial Revolution, continued in the present century by the development of the motor-car and allied industries. Thus, while large areas are today undergoing reconstruction, the

441

Compton Wynyates

principal civic buildings, grouped around Victoria Square, are 19th-cent. work. The Town Hall (1834), with seating capacity for 2,000 people and one of the finest organs in the country, has been the centre of the city's musical life since Mendelssohn conducted the first performance of *Elijah* there in 1847. The City Museum and Art Gallery, one of the best outside London, possesses an outstanding collection of English water colours. The Corporation is also responsible for the nearby Museum of Science and Industry, established in 1950; Aston Hall (*see above*); and Blakeley Hall, Yardley, a restored 18th-cent. house, now a museum of local history. The other important artistic centre is the Barber Institute of Fine Arts, founded in 1932 and situated, like most of the buildings of Birmingham University to which it is attached, at Edgbaston. Here are a fine concert hall and an expanding

collection of pictures. Of the city's churches, the most memorable are: St Philip's (since 1905 the Cathedral), built in 1711–15, with four windows designed by Burne-Jones and executed by William Morris; St Paul's (1779), with box-pews and an octagonal spire; and St Martin's, which, though rebuilt in the 19th cent. on the site of the Norman parish church, contains the 14th-cent. tombs of the de Berminghams. Places open to visitors in outer Birmingham are Messrs Cadbury's works and the garden suburb of Bournville; the Botanical Gardens at Harborne; and the Soho Foundry at Winson Green, where the partnership of Matthew Boulton, James Watt and William Murdoch started in 1796.

Brinklow (EE 27) (1,144). Noteworthy by archaeologists for one of the finest Norman motte-and-bailey castles in the country. Combe Abbey,

3 m. W, a large 17th-cent. house, incorporating some remains of a Cistercian foundation of 1150, stands in a timbered park, containing the largest lake in the county, Combe Pool, but is not open to the public.

Burton Dassett (ED 25). All that remains of a once flourishing village is a farm, the vicarage and one of the most attractive churches in Warwickshire. Except for its porch and tower, most of the work is Norman and earlier; and, being built on a hill, the altar is almost on a level with the capitals of the nave. From the top of the hill (692 ft.) there are splendid views, S to Edge Hill and W over the Avon valley.

Castle Bromwich (EB 28) EC Wed (9,205). Interesting for its early Jacobean mansion, with 18th-cent. additions; and for the brick Georgian church (1726–31), all of whose furniture, including the three-decker pulpit, is elegantly of the period.

Charlecote Park (EC 25). Home of the Lucy family since the 12th cent., the present house is a typical 16th-cent. mansion; its charming gatehouse has been attributed to John of Padua, architect to Henry VIII. Both house and park, with its herd of fallow deer, are administered by the NT and are open to the public. The church, standing at one of the entrances, has Lucy effigies dressed in Elizabethan costume.

Coleshill (EC 28) EC Thurs (7,900). Situated on a steep hill, the town is dominated by the church, one of the most interesting in the county for its monuments. Outside the old market house the combined pillory, whipping-post and stocks may still be seen. 1½ m. E is **Maxstoke Castle**, a red sandstone structure dating from the 14th cent., built on a square plan, with curtain-walls, angle-towers and parapets, and surrounded by a moat. The Great Hall of 1345 has survived. 2 m. S of the castle are the remains of the priory founded in 1342.

Compton Wynyates (ED 24) (47). Situated in a valley SW of Edge Hill, this Tudor mansion, scarcely changed since its completion in 1520, is one of the most beautiful in England. Built round a courtyard, of mellow brickwork and black timbers, it contains splendid period furniture and plaster ceilings, and some tapestries and pictures, including a Giorgione. House and gardens are open to the public.

Coughton Court (EA 25). This, the home of the Throckmorton family for 5½ centuries, is now the property of the NT. Its outstanding feature is the battlemented gatehouse, dating from early in the 16th cent., the Gothic wings on either side having been added in the 18th cent. The house, which is open to the public, contains valuable furniture and relics, particularly some connected with the Gunpowder Plot in 1605, in which the Throckmortons played a leading part. The parish church, just S of the house, has family tombs and brasses.

Coventry* (ED 27) EC Thurs (331,270). Established under the protection of a Saxon convent in the 7th cent., the fourth city of England and centre of the cloth-weaving industry from the 14th to the end of the 17th cent. and, today, of the motor-car and cycle industries, Coventry has always been important. Despite savage bombing in the 1939 War, various historic buildings have survived, including St Mary's Hall (AM), built in 1360 for the local trade guilds; parts of the city wall; two of the original twelve gates (AM); and that admirable half-timbered building, Ford's Hospital. Of the principal churches, two

443

escaped disaster; one of these was Holy Trinity. The Cathedral Church of St Michael on the other hand, was completely destroyed, except for the 300-ft. spire and some external walls. Here, in 1962, the most controversial of modern cathedrals was completed, to the design of Sir Basil Spence and with outstanding works by Epstein, Piper, Sutherland and other artists. In other respects too the city has led the work of post-war reconstruction, by building the fine new shopping precinct and the Belgrade Theatre.

Henley-in-Arden (EB 26) EC Thurs (2,015). A charming market town in the heart of the one-time Forest of Arden, its single street lined with 15th- to 17th-cent. houses, many of them timber-framed. Adjoining the church is the 15th-cent. Guildhall, and farther N the steps and shaft of the 15th-cent. market cross. **Beaudesert** Church, on the other side of the R. Alne, built at the end of the 12th cent., contains much fine Norman work.

Kenilworth (EC 27) EC Thurs (20,450). Standing on a mound, formerly surrounded by a lake, are the remains of the red sandstone castle (AM) described in Scott's novel. The oldest part is the keep, completed in about 1180; John of Gaunt built the Great Hall and State Apartments; while further additions, including the gatehouse, were made by Queen Elizabeth's favourite, the Earl of Leicester, to whom she presented the castle. The rich Norman work of the W doorway of the church was probably brought there from the abbey, whose remains may still be seen a little to the SW.

Knowle (EB 27) EC Thurs (4,610). Distinguished particularly by its church, the best example of the Perpendicular style in the county, with carved stalls and misericords. Opposite the church is the 15th-cent. timbered Guildhall; and ½ m. NE, Grimshaw Hall, a lovely house of the same style and period, whose gardens are sometimes open. 4 m. SE, off the A41, are the church and ruins of **Wroxall Priory**; to the W of which, in secluded country, is **Baddesley Clinton Hall**, a 14th-cent. fortified manor house, largely rebuilt in the 15th cent., but still surrounded by its moat.

Leamington Spa (ED 26) EC Thurs (44,860). Known for its medicinal waters since the end of the 18th cent., the town is spaciously laid out with Regency and early Victorian buildings. Now mainly residential, its position and hotels make it an excellent touring centre.

Maxstoke Castle and Priory (*see* **Coleshill**).

Merevale Abbey (EC 29). The main surviving part of this Cistercian foundation is the large and beautiful 'chapel without the gates', still, from medieval times, serving as the parish church. The S chapel, with its E window, dating from about 1340 and filled with glass of the period, is noteworthy.

Meriden (EC 28) (2,750). According to tradition, the medieval cross on the village green marks the centre of England. 2 m. NW, **Packington Hall**, a mansion in the classical style, stands surrounded by a wooded park, which contains a herd of black fallow deer; it is not open to the public. ¾ m. NE of this is the Old Hall, where Charles II stayed after escaping from the battle of Worcester.

Packwood House (EB 27). A lovely Tudor timber-framed house, with brick moulding, oak-panelled rooms and period furniture. The gardens (like the house, open to the public) are charming, in particular the Yew Garden, planned to represent the Sermon on the Mount.

Polesworth (EC 30) EC Wed (4,020). Of the Benedictine nunnery little remains except the 14th-cent. gatehouse and the nave of the church. An impressive monument in this is the sculptured effigy of an abbess, probably the only one still to be seen in England. Pooley Hall, NW of the village on the opposite side of the R. Anker, has a fortified tower to the NE, and a chapel to the S of the house.

Rugby (EE 27) EC Wed (56,450). With important railway and engineering works, is best known for its school, made famous by the reforms of the 19th cent. Its Head at that time, Dr Arnold, was described by one of his pupils, Thomas Hughes, in *Tom Brown's Schooldays*. E of the town are the 820-ft. masts of the GPO Radio Station.

Shipston-on-Stour (EC 24) EC Thurs (2,007). A pleasant agricultural town in the Vale of Red Horse, midway between the two northern spurs of the Cotswolds. An unclassified road leads NW through the village of Ilmington to the highest point in the county, **Ilmington Down** (854 ft.), with a splendid view, including the isolated Meon Hill, crowned by Iron Age earthworks. 4 m. E of the town, at **Upper Brailes**, another unclassified road forks left to **Edge Hill** (705 ft.), some 6 m. NE, with its octagonal Gothic tower. In the little village of **Lower Brailes**, the church, so imposing that it is known as 'the Cathedral of the Feldon' should not be missed.

Stoneleigh (ED 27) EC Thurs (1,296). The village has a fine manor house, a church containing Norman work, and a green surrounded by cottages. Stoneleigh Abbey, to the S, is an Italianate mansion, completed in

Kenilworth Castle: the Norman keep

Stratford-upon-Avon: Holy Trinity Church

1726, with an Elizabethan wing, and the 14th-cent. gatehouse of the original monastery. It contains admirable portraits and furniture. In the grounds of the Abbey are the National Agricultural Centre and the permanent site of the Royal Agricultural Society's Show.

Stratford-upon-Avon (EC 25) EC Thurs (18,600). Famous as the town where Shakespeare was born and to which he retired. His birthplace in Henley St has been restored; it contains many relics. Adjoining is the new Shakespeare Centre, which was opened in 1964. The Guildhall has for its upper storey the grammar school, where Shakespeare was pro-

bably educated. Holy Trinity Church, notable in itself, is more especially so for his grave and bust and the registers of his baptism and burial. Nash's House adjoins the garden of New Place, the house in which Shakespeare spent his retirement; and nearby lies the lovely Knot Garden, where he is said to have written the *Tempest*. The Royal Shakespeare Theatre, rebuilt in 1932 to replace an earlier one, is in Waterside, where we find also the Library, the Picture Gallery and the Museum, all rich in Shakespeariana. A short walk away can be seen Anne Hathaway's cottage at Shottery, a still unspoilt example of an Elizabethan yeoman's farmhouse; Wilmcote, the home of Shakespeare's mother, who was married in the church; and Clopton House, built in Shakespeare's time but remodelled in the 18th cent., and displaying period furniture and paintings by Reynolds, Romney and others.

Sutton Coldfield (E B 29) E C Thurs (81,630). Now mainly residential, it still holds reminders of the medieval town round the church, which contains the tomb of the town's great benefactor, Bishop Vesey of Exeter, who died in 1554 aged 102. A modern hall, with a public park and golf course, occupy the site of the mansion he built for himself at Moor Hall. The chief attraction of the town, however, is 2,400-acre Sutton Park* to the W, controlled by the Corporation and largely preserved in its natural state. 1½ m. SE is the medieval mansion, **New Hall**, one of the oldest inhabited houses in the country, surrounded by its moat.

Upton House (E D 24). This charming 17th-cent. mansion, enlarged in 1927, stands high to the S of Edge Hill. Now belonging to the N T, the house contains English china and 18th-cent. furniture, and one of the finest private collections of pictures in the country.

Warmington (E E 24) (328). Built round a green, with views of Edge Hill and across the valley to the beacon tower on The Burton Hills, it has a fine Elizabethan manor, and a 14th-cent. church with one very unusual feature: a priest's chamber, with its original door, fireplace and sanitary accommodation built over a chapel.

Shakespeare's birthplace at Stratford-upon-Avon   *G. Douglas Bolton*

Warwick* (EC 26) EC Thurs (17,700). Owes its distinctive character to the town's having been largely rebuilt by the brothers Smith after a fire in 1694. High St and Northgate St give admirable examples of the result; the Court House, Landor House and Shire Hall are from that period. Tudor architecture is well represented by Mill St, Oken House and Lord Leycester's Hospital; while two of the medieval town gateways, both with their chapels, are still almost intact. Of the collegiate Church of St Mary, only the Norman crypt and the later chancel and Beauchamp chapel (with its magnificent Warwick tombs) survived the fire, the nave and transepts having been rebuilt, as well as the tower designed by Wren. The castle, on a cliff above the Avon, is one of the most imposing medieval fortresses in the country and, unlike its rival Kenilworth, is admirably preserved and still in occupation. The state apartments, with an impressive collection of armour, furniture and pictures, are open to the public.

Warwick Castle

J. Allan Cash

Opposite: Detail from the original painting by Rowland Hilder.

Shakespeare's county is geographically the centre of England. Michael Drayton, whose poems celebrate the Forest of Arden and Warwickshire's nightingales, was born in 1563, the son of a tanner, at Hartshill. In 1819 'George Eliot' was born at Arbury Farm Chilvers Coton; her *Middlemarch* and *Adam Bede* are alive with scenes and people characteristic of the county. And at Warwick in 1775 was born Walter Savage Landor.

SHAKESPEARE

GEORGE
ELIOT

MICHAEL
DRAYTON

WALTER
SAVAGE
LANDOR

HILDER

Eckington Bridge over the River Avon

J. Allan Cash

WORCESTERSHIRE

AN INTRODUCTION BY JOHN MOORE

Three rivers impose their personalities upon the Worcestershire scene: the strong Severn and its tributaries, the swift-running temperamental Teme and the slow meandering Avon. We may thus divide the county into three watersheds, and find a distinctive character in each. But this arrangement leaves out the most populous part of Worcestershire, the wealthiest and the most unprepossessing, which we will discuss first.

The Industrial North-East

This extends from Kidderminster in the west – affectionately known to its inhabitants as 'Kiddie', and famous all the world over for its carpets – to Redditch in the east, equally famous for fishing-tackle; and from Bromsgrove in the south to the outskirts of Birmingham and to Dudley in the north. Dudley manufactures chains and anchors – a surprising speciality for a town situated about as far inland as it is possible in this island to be. It can be called the 'capital' of the Black Country conurbation, which includes Stourbridge – as well known for its glass as 'Kiddie' is for carpets – and Halesowen, the birthplace of Francis Brett Young, who used it as a background for some of his tales.

Opposite: Detail from the original painting by Ian Henderson.

Encircling the cherry-orchards of the Teme, Worcestershire unites the industrial with the rural across a stretch of country sometimes mellow, sometimes bright with red soil. In the background of the picture loom the Malvern Hills. Inset is the effigy of King John that, with its sinister expression, rests upon his tomb in Worcester cathedral.

The Abbey, Pershore

Reece Winstone

(It looks very different today.) Other manufactures of the Black Country, which extends, of course, into Staffordshire, are hardware, boilers, chemicals (especially at Warley), springs, tubes, nuts and bolts. The ugliness of this Black Country is simply demonic, and has to be seen to be believed.

To the north and east of the district the smoke thins; but the enormous, sprawling city of Birmingham inevitably imparts its spirit to this part of the county, and will shortly spill over into the few agricultural areas which precariously survive. The hills of Clent and Lickey provide some good walks still, and among the ling there you seem a long way from the second biggest city in Britain – though from 1,000 feet or so you have a terrifying view of the extent of the smoke-cover, an industrial haze covering 270 square miles and hanging over the heads of two and a quarter million people.

There is some good farming country between Bromsgrove and Redditch, which incidentally manufactured pins before it thought of bending them into fishhooks. Its hook-makers have naturally extended the range of their manufactures to include beautiful split-cane trout rods and delicately feathered dry-flies.

The Severn Valley

Seeking the open country, people who live and work under the Black Country's canopy of evil-smelling smoke turn west towards Bewdley, high up on the Severn (the birthplace and home of a Prime Minister, Earl Baldwin) and to the Wyre Forest lying beyond it, against the Shropshire Border. Wyre consists mainly of birchscrub mixed with oak, hazel and buckthorn; the rock beneath is Old Red Sandstone. From the naturalist's point of view it is interesting, as one of the very few localities in England where the big terra-cotta moth called the Kentish Glory still survives. The caterpillars feed in companies on the birch trees, and the moths fly swift as swallows over the heaths in the early April sun.

The Severn goes down through a dairy-farming land by way of Stourport, Holt and Hallow. It grows deeper, wider and more murmurous as it comes in sight of Worcester's Cathedral tower. In some of these reaches above the city the angler has a chance of catching a salmon. Below Worcester, for some reason which has never been satisfactorily explained, the salmon won't take; and the banks are lined every week-end with coarse-fishermen from the industrial Midlands.

Worcester, with its noble Cathedral (overlooking one of the most delightful cricket grounds in England) has the air of a country town, but possesses some old and new industries. Among other things it makes the famous Worcester porcelain and the equally famous Worcestershire sauce. Its battle, on the 3rd September 1651, was Cromwell's 'crowning mercy', and the Faithful City saw the King's downfall and the triumph of the hated Roundheads. It has always had a great reputation for loyalty to our Kings; as it happens, the worst of them, King John, is buried in its Cathedral. In the remarkable effigy upon his tomb you meet him, as it were, at close quarters; and are dismayed, even horrified, by what Sir Arthur Bryant described as his 'sly vulpine face, and deceptive geniality'.

The Teme Valley

In flood-time the brown Severn runs brick-red, tomato-soup-colour for a little way below Powick, where the Teme comes into it out of the red sandstone country to the west. This sandstone is rather soft, so that the Teme has cut itself a deep channel; and wears away a little more every flood. It is a river of moods, up-and-down very quickly. The gently-rippled pools, dimpled with the rises of grayling, may be changed within an hour to raging torrents in which no human swimmer could survive.

The Teme Valley, from Ludlow and Tenbury Wells to the junction with the Severn, is a vivid place of bright red soil and the lushest green grass. In summer everything is colourful here: purple loosestrife and yellow skull-cap along the river banks, the river itself speckled with water-crowfoot as a lawn is with daisies, buttercups decking out every May meadow as a Field of the Cloth of Gold. If you care for the humbler and rarer plants you can find Twayblade and Butterfly Orchis and the two scarce ferns, the Adder's Tongue and the quaint delicate Moonwort.

This is a cherry-country, such as A. E. Housman wrote about, and in fact there are more of the orchards in Worcestershire than there are in the Shropshire-lad district above Tenbury Wells. But Teme-side farming is more mixed than most, and the orchards, of damson and apple as well as cherry, alternate with pastures and hayfields, patches of soft fruit, corn and hops. The hopyards lie along the Teme and to the west of it, towards Bromyard; Worcestershire comes third to Kent and Hereford as a hop-growing county. The great Hereford cattle, which match the soil, are seen in the Teme meadows. The old, large, half-timbered farm houses give to this land an air of graciousness and prosperity; and indeed it is a rich countryside, where a man may successfully grow almost anything he has a mind to, from Clun sheep to cider-apples – or even cricket-bat willows, which are successfully grown in some of the meadows beside the Teme.

451

The Avon Valley

Shakespeare's Avon (and therefore to some of us a Sacred River, like Alph in *Kubla Khan*!) enters Worcestershire near Priors Salford, close to its junction with the Arrow. The willows hang over it, the yellow flags process beside it, and except at flood-time it goes slowly upon its meandering way:

> *The current that with gentle murmur glides,*
> *Thou knowst being stopped, impatiently doth rage;*
> *But when his fair course is not hindered,*
> *He makes sweet music with th' enamell'd stones,*
> *Giving a gentle kiss to every sedge*
> *He overtaketh in his pilgrimage.*

The 'tawny-finn'd fishes' which Shakespeare had in mind when he was writing *Antony and Cleopatra* were probably perch, and swam in Avon, not in Nile! Chub, roach and bream are the other fishes which give sport to the anglers in these favourite stretches between Bidford and Evesham town.

The country round Evesham is flat, almost treeless, and is given over to market-gardening. The black earth grows the best asparagus in the world; and the tawny asparagus-fern or 'bower' in early autumn imparts its brightness to what is otherwise one of the bleakest landscapes in the Midlands, a kind of agricultural slum, nearly as gloomy in its own way as Dudley's industrial dreariness. The fields, denuded of hedgerow timber and nowadays, indeed, of hedgerows too, are not so much fields as vegetable-factories. They produce, as well as the asparagus, a succession of lettuces, radishes, sprouts, cabbages, spring onions, peas, runner beans. Tumbledown sheds with corrugated tin roofs are scattered over the holdings.

There are, however, belts of plum orchards to alleviate this dismal spectacle. The Vale of Evesham is almost as famous for its Pershore plums as it is for asparagus. About three springs in five, the blossom comes before the leaf; and then on 'blossom Sunday', which sometimes happily coincides with Eastertide, the motorists drive out from the towns to tour the orchard districts, where the black boughs are dressed with the delicate white petals like a late sprinkle of snow. Alas, the blossom lasts not much longer than an April snow! One day the Vale seems to wear its bridal gown; next day the myriad petals, blown by a chill wind, put you in mind of confetti on the day after the wedding.

The plum-picking, generally in August, is almost as busy a time in these parts as the Teme-side hop-picking in September. Yellow egg-plums, Prolifics, purple Pershores and Victorias are reckoned by the ton and sent by train and lorry all over Britain. When the harvest is over there is only time for the briefest of holidays before the market-gardeners are busy picking their sprouts.

The Avon flows discursively as good talk, devious, leisurely, catching Evesham in a big loop like a bight in the middle of a rope. In this noose poor Simon de Montfort was caught too, when he unwisely chose to stand and fight against the Lord Edward, son of Henry III, and Gilbert De Clare on the 4th August 1265. There he died as bravely as he had lived. It was the last battle of the Barons' War; as decisive as Cromwell's victory at Worcester and the Yorkists' at Tewkesbury – both places within fifteen miles of Evesham. So within a little triangle of country much history has been made.

To the east of Evesham is some stone-walled country, which in spirit seems to belong to Gloucestershire rather than Worcestershire: with Broadway somewhat self-consciously beautiful, amid inspiriting North-Cotswold slopes. But even here some of the big fields which used to pasture sheep, and which in war-time grew corn, have been turned over to market-gardening; and, close to Campden, sprouts by the hundred acre disfigure a landscape that was surely destined for grander things.

By way of Cropthorne (where at Craycombe House Francis Brett Young wrote his later Worcestershire novels), the Avon with many twists and turns flows down to Pershore, a sleepy place which the jets from a neighbouring experimental aerodrome irritate no more than bluebottles annoy a slumberous cow. An old-fashioned town, contented among its plum-orchards (with a notable parish church that once formed part of a Benedictine Abbey), and nowadays a Festival of Arts each summer – before plum-picking begins!

South of Pershore the river, still wriggling like an eel, passes close to a big wood called Tiddesley, mixed timber but mainly oak, where the lovely White Admiral butterfly recently established itself. Then through farmland and more market-gardens the river's sweet will takes it down to Eckington and under the beautiful Eckington Bridge, upon which Sir Arthur Quiller-Couch wrote a poem; and so to the foot of Bredon Hill, celebrated by another poet:

> *Here of a Sunday morning*
> *My love and I would lie,*
> *And see the coloured counties*
> *And hear the larks so high*
> *About us in the sky.*

Cottages at Kempsey   *Reece Winstone*

Childs Wickham Church

There is no evidence that A. E. Housman knew Bredon Hill; his reference in the second verse to 'the springing thyme', which is by no means characteristic of Bredon, suggests that he didn't know it at all, but wrote his very depressing piece on the strength of a view of the hill from the train, on his way up to Shropshire.

You can, however, on a clear day see a great many coloured counties from the top of Bredon Hill: nine or ten, it is said, but that is a matter for argument. It is an outlying piece of the Cotswolds, formed of the same oolitic rock, in which the skeletons of ichthyosaurs have been found. Delightful villages, some built of the local stone, some black-and-white half-timbered, stand in a ring about its lower slopes, Bredon's Norton, the Combertons, Elmley Castle (where the Park maintains an ancient herd of fallow deer), Ashton-under-Hill, Beckford, Overbury, Kemerton. A tour of the narrow lanes which run right round the hill is well worth making. Close to the summit there was an iron-age fort, which seems to have been the scene of a great fight or massacre. The hill is 991 feet high, but a Folly built at the very top adds the necessary 9 feet to make up the 1,000.

This Folly gives you a splendid view over the plain of Malvern. You look down on the Avon easing itself round the lower slopes of the hill and traipsing, as they would say in Worcestershire, lazily through the enormous meadows or 'hams' which are still held in common: the owners of other land in the adjacent village have a right to pasture cattle on the ham's aftermath.

Across the plain, which is fifteen miles wide, rises the magnificent ridge of the Malverns: 'old as the hills' is the word, for this pre-Cambrian rock is more than five hundred million years old. At the foot of the hills there was once a forest – Malvern Chase, which gave its name to a romantic tale by the Rev. W. S. Symonds, a rector of nearby Pendock; this book and its companion,

454

Hanley Castle, are still sought after, though long out of print. What was once 'A chace for royal deer' now forms a series of commons which merge into the brackeny, furzy, lower slopes of the Malverns. Higher up, the soil grows thin and the ancient rock outcrops through it here and there. The highest hill, the Worcestershire Beacon, is 1,395 feet. You can walk south from its summit by a tremendous saddleback nine miles long until you reach the 'British Camp' or Herefordshire Beacon (1,114 feet) – the ridge of the Malverns forms the county boundary. From the trenches and parapets running round the British Camp a platoon could still hold the hill against a battalion: it must have been a formidable fortress, guarding the pass over the hills. South of it, at the end of the range, is the quaintly named Ragged Stone Hill, which possesses a Midsummer Night's Legend: you must take care to walk clear of the stone's shadow when the sun first strikes it at first light on Midsummer morning, or some fearful fate will befall!

Malvern, tucked under the ridge, sheltered from west winds but denied the late afternoon sun, is known for its schools and its Waters, for the good stained-glass in its Priory Church, and for its annual Festival, which in pre-war days was given over chiefly to performing the plays of George Bernard Shaw. Indeed, the town was almost a second home to him; and each summer he was to be seen, lanky, bearded and prophetic, striding over those tall bare hills, from which according to his mood a man may look west into the wildness of Wales, or eastwards upon the assured agricultural landscape of Worcestershire, with its air of custom and continuity. Almost smug, you might say – but remember that these fields have been cultivated continuously for more than a thousand, possibly for nearly two thousand, years. The Worcestershire place-names, pretty thick on the map, are sometimes Celtic, often Saxon: occasionally a bit of both. The Romans came, the Saxons, the Normans; the fields were ploughed in turn by sweating men with the breast-plough, by the heaving oxen, by the heavy-hoofed horses, with wooden share, with the sharp steel; by Celt, Saxon, Frenchman, serf, peasant, by the servants of monks and lords, by tenant-farmers and owner-farmers, by German and Italian prisoners-of-war. This Worcestershire land is the very heart of England. Our conflicts and our battles, our king-making and king-breaking, our conquests and our disasters, have never interrupted the rhythm of ploughing and planting for long. History has passed like the cloud-shadows which dapple the fields on a changeable day; but the grass and the corn have kept on growing.

Cropthorne: the post office *Reece Winstone*

Some houses and gardens open to the public

The Almonry At Evesham *Map* E A 24. *14th-cent. half-timbered building, formerly the Almonry of the Benedictine Abbey, now a local history museum portraying the life, culture and industry of Evesham and its Vale from Prehistoric times to the present day.*

Dowles Manor Bewdley 3m W of Kidderminster off B4194 *Map* D H 27. *11th- to 16th-cent. house with notable murals and furniture. Open by appointment only.*

Dudley Castle 6m SE of Wolverhampton on A461 *Map* D K 28. *Remains of 14th-cent. stronghold, now part of Dudley Zoo. Open daily from 10. Castle & Zoo 3/–, 1/6 child.; Wed 2/–, 9d. child.*

The Greyfriars Friar St, Worcester *Map* D J 25. *15th-cent. timber-framed house built for the then adjoining Franciscan Friary.* N T.

Tenant: Matley Moore, Esq. *2/–; parties over 20, 1/–.*

Harvington Hall Chaddesley Corbett 4½m SE of Kidderminster on A448 *Map* D J 27. *Moated Tudor house with secret hiding places; Elizabethan wall paintings.* The RC Archdiocese of Birmingham.

Holt Castle Holt Heath 6m N of Worcester off A443 *Map* D J 26. *Restored, preserving 14th-cent. tower and later medieval work with 18th-cent. panelling.*

Spetchley Park 3m E of Worcester on A422 *Map* D J 25. *19th-cent. mansion surrounded by fine gardens and park.*

Worcester Guildhall At Worcester *Map* D J 25. *Restored 18th cent., built by Thomas White; paintings in Assembly Room, ceiling restored 1964; 'scold's bridle' in Lower Hall.*

Books for further reading

The 'feel' of Worcestershire

M. FRASER *Companion into Worcestershire* 1949
J. NOAKE *The Rambler in Worcestershire* 3 vols 1848–54
N. PEVSNER *Worcestershire* 1968
I. L. WEDLEY *'Twixt Severn and Teme: Story of a Delightful Country* 1928

Natural history

J. AMPHLETT and C. REA *The Botany of Worcestershire* 1909
J. G. HARRISON *Handbook of Birds of the Malvern District* 1941
A. J. HARTHAN *Birds of Worcestershire* 1961
SIR C. HASTINGS *Illustrations of the Natural History of Worcestershire* 1834

E. LEES *The Botany of Worcestershire* 1867
TREES IN WORCESTERSHIRE 1957

History, topography, architecture

W. DREGHORN *Geology explained in the Severn Vale and the Cotswolds* 1967
F. T. S. HOUGHTON *Worcestershire* (Little Guides series) 1952
W. M. INGEMANN *Minor Architecture of Worcestershire* 1938
T. NASH *Collection for the History of Worcestershire* 2 vols 1781
W. NIVEN *Illustrations of Old Worcestershire Houses* 1873
L. T. C. ROLT *Worcestershire* (County Books series) 1951
B. SMITH *A History of Malvern* 1964
Victoria County History of Worcestershire 4 vols and index 1906–26

Gazetteer

WORCESTERSHIRE

Broadway: the beacon tower on Fish Hill *Reece Winstone*

Abberley (DH 26). Together with a 19th-cent. church, the ruins of a Norman one beside the rectory, and a 160-ft. clock tower, its distinctions are an unchanging charm and the Abberley Hills, rising in a curve to the S. 1 m. S, **Great Witley** lies beneath Woodbury Hill (904 ft.), crowned with an ancient British camp. Here are a Georgian hundred-house (now a hotel) and an 18th-cent. church, with rich rococo decoration and Rysbrack's giant memorial to the family of its builder, the first Lord Foley (d. 1732). He also built Witley Court (a 19th-cent. Earl of Dudley spent £250,000 on enlarging it), which, in its 500-acre park, was burnt down in 1937.

Besford (DK 24) (270). The church has unusual 14th-cent. timber work. The W window is of oak, as also are the traceried windows in the bell-tower, which is timber-framed like the nave. The wainscoting here is made from old pews, but the rood-loft is a rare pre-Reformation example. Noteworthy too is an Elizabethan painted triptych.

Bewdley (DH 27) EC Wed (5,610). Perched above the Severn, on the fringe of Wyre Forest, the town recalls by its heraldic anchor its one-time importance as a river harbour. Tudor and Jacobean houses (notably Wyre Court, Recorder's House in High St and a three-gabled building in Load St), the 18th-cent. church and the predominantly Georgian character of the town as a whole bear witness to its days of prosperity. The original parish church, 1 m. S in the park of Ribbesford House (presented to George Herbert and his brothers by Charles I, but rebuilt in 1820), is remarkable for its Norman tympanum, the rare 14th-cent. oak arches of the S arcade, and a window by Burne-Jones and Wm Morris. Standing above the town is Tickenhill House, its brick façade of 1738 encasing the remains of a Tudor royal palace. The folk museum it contains – one of the finest in the country – has been removed to the County Museum at Hartlebury Castle.

Birtsmorton (DJ 23). The Court is an admirable example of a 14th- to 15th-cent. manor house, with a timbered quadrangle; moated, and approached by a bridge and a massive turreted gateway. It was presented by Henry VI to Sir R. Nanfan, whose tutor here was Wolsey and who is buried in a tomb of Purbeck marble in the church.

Bredon (DK 23) EC Thurs (1,400). Large, picturesque village on the Avon, at the foot of **Bredon Hill** (991 ft.) 3½ m. to the NE, at the top of which are fine views, Romano-British earthworks and a 200-year-old tower,

457

The River Avon at Fladbury

Parson's Folly. In the village, timbered houses and a splendid tithe barn (N T) lie beside the river, and a slender 14th-cent. spire reaches 160 ft. The nave and two-storied tower, with original vaulting, are Norman; the Mitton chapel is 13th-cent., and the chancel and its armorial tiles 14th-cent., with memorials of several periods, including the canopied monument to the Reeds (1611), who founded the almshouses in the centre of the village.

Bretforton (E A 24) (970). Largest and most accessible of a 5-m. string of villages, all watered by Avon tributaries, all with gabled manor houses, timbered dovecotes and cottages, and medieval churches. To the N, the three **Littletons**: South (manor rebuilt 1721, clipped yews, church with Norman door and old pews); and Middle and North (lovely grouping of

14th-cent. manor, tithe barn, and a dovecote and the church, with fine Norman front, 16th-cent. pews, embattled Smith chapel over porch and monuments); and **Cleeve Prior** (broad streets, Kings Arms, manor with great yew hedge). Bretforton itself has no fewer than six dovecotes, of varied architecture, and the half-timbered Golden Fleece. To the S lie Badsey (a 17th-cent. monument in the restored church); and the loveliest of all, **Wickhamford** (many-gabled manor beside a stream, looking over lawn to the lake; church with Jacobean linenfold box-pews, chancel-gates and altar-rails, and fine canopied alabaster monuments).

Broadway (E A 23) E C Thurs (2,795). Considered the finest Cotswold village in Worcestershire; its main street and its green are lined with stone cottages and great houses, amongst which are

Abbots Grange (with chapel and hall), Tudor House and the Lygon Arms. The old church, not much used, has some Norman work and a rare palimpsest brass; the new one is 19th-cent. The road to Stow winds up to the top of **Fish Hill** (1,024 ft.) with Beacon Tower and fine views at the top.

Bromsgrove (DK 27) EC Thurs (36,500). An ancient industrial town, by-passed by the M5 but with an overspill from Birmingham, less than 15 m. N. Its old buildings include part of the grammar school; the Council House of mellow brick, Dutch gabled and mullioned; and nearby, the church, approached by an ascent of many steps, with its 15th-cent. steeple rising to 200 ft. and, inside, restored black-and-white roof lighted by clerestory, and Talbot monuments. Their ancient manor, with its Tudor chapel and lake, stands at the end of a lane, 2 m. SW. Largely rebuilt after a fire in 1710, the W front, with its stepped gables and the fluted columns of its Renaissance porch, survived.

Chaddesley Corbett (DJ 27) (1,517). In its wide street of black-and-white cottages, the old Talbot Inn faces the church (Norman arcade and font, and 18th-cent. tower and spire). 1 m. NW, **Harvington Hall** rambles many-gabled within its moat, opening to a lake. Tudor, with wall-paintings and secret passages and hides, much modified in 18th cent. and since restored, the Hall is open to the public almost daily.

Cleeve Prior (*see* **Bretforton**).

Cotheridge (DH 25). A double avenue of limes, half a mile long and nearly 300 years old, leads to Court and church, which (largely 12th cent., with massive timber-framed tower, box-pews and altar-rails of later period) faces the great house, Georgian, with remains of earlier gabled building.

Cropthorne (EA 24) (610). Cottages and church (wall-painting, Saxon cross recovered from chancel-wall, and Dingley tombs) sloping to the

The Malvern Hills

Avon; and N across the river, past Charlton Hall, **Fladbury**, with its landing-stage, inn, water-mill and church, surrounded by yew trees and containing notable brasses.

Dormston 2 m. W of **Inkberrow** (EA 25) (80). A tiny hamlet, in which Moat Farm, with its dovecotes and lantern, and the fine church tower, make a delightful group of black and white.

Droitwich (DJ 26) EC Thurs (8,970). Well-known residential spa, with golf and good hotels, a few old houses and three churches, of which one (R.C.) is noted for its modern mosaics; and three great houses within reach. Salwarpe Court ($2\frac{1}{2}$ m. SW), the 16th-cent. timber-framed home of the Talbots, is now a farmhouse. $1\frac{1}{2}$ m. E stands brick-built, stone-mullioned Westwood House, Jacobean with a gatehouse; and 5 m. SE, Elizabethan Huddington Court, with latticed windows, twisted chimneys, swans on the moat and dovecotes on the lawn.

Dudley (DK 28) EC Wed (63,820). Islanded in Staffordshire, the one notable castle ruin (AM) of Worcestershire looks out from its hill across nine counties and the grim splendour of the Black Country. In the grounds is a well-known zoo; nearby stand some ruins of a priory and, to the NW, Wren's Nest Hill, with its fossil caves, is now a nature reserve. But the town's fame still rests on its iron works as it did in the 17th cent., when, for the first time, coal was used by Dud Dudley for smelting instead of wood.

Eckington (DK 24) (900). Approached by a fine old bridge across the Avon, the village church has a Norman doorway and S arcade, an ancient dug-out chest and the Hanford tomb, Tudor husband and wife with their thirteen children beneath a canopy. 2 m. E, on the slopes of Bredon Hill

(*see above*) is Elizabethan Woollas Hall; 2 m. S, at **Bredons Norton**, the Manor gateway is dated 1585.

Elmley Castle (DK 24) (350). No longer any sign of the castle, but a lovely village street, and a medieval church worth visiting for its 13th-cent. dragons, writhing beneath the eight carved sides of the font; and for its monuments, especially the sculptured figures of the Savage tomb.

Evesham (EA 24) EC Wed (13,140). Built on both sides of the Avon, in the centre of the orchards of its Vale, the town has an air of elegance and prosperity. A few timber-framed, and more Georgian, buildings; and, at its heart, the precincts of the ruined abbey (AM) running to the river bank. Here, side by side, are two noble churches, both much rebuilt in the 16th cent. and since restored, both containing chantries with superb fan-vaulting built by the last Abbot, Clement Lichfield, who also completed the fine bell-tower just before the Dissolution swept away the remainder of his abbey.

Fladbury (*see* **Cropthorne**).

Hagley (DK 28) EC Thurs (5,650). At the foot of the Clent Hills, it is not the large village one goes to see but the Lyttletons' Palladian Hall in its landscaped park, complete with rotunda, Ionic temple and Gothic ruins. Visitors are admitted to admire the Italian plasterworks and Chippendale furniture.

Halesowen (DK 28) EC Thurs (50,390). Manufacturing town, with collieries and steel works, on the fringe of Birmingham and the Black Country. The impressive church, still dominating the town if only by its size and position, has notable monuments, including that to the poet Wm Shenstone. 1 m. SE, the ruins of its

The old cross, Ombersley

Reece Winstone

once great abbey can be seen in a farmyard.

Hanbury (DK 26) (834). An attractively sited village, its much-restored church holds the succession of monuments to the Vernons (from 1627 to the 1920 window), one of whom in 1701 built the Hall (which is to be opened by the NT). Of local brick, with stone quoins, it is an exquisitely proportioned example of its period. Lovely **Mere Hall**, E-shaped and timber-framed, is 2 m. SSW, at the end of the avenue of elms.

Harvington Hall (*see* **Chaddesley Corbett**).

Kidderminster (DJ 27) EC Wed (45,510). Still making carpets as it has done for 200 years, still looking up to St Mary's on the hill above the R. Stour. Much rebuilt in the 18th and 19th cents., the church is noteworthy for its monuments, and as the place where Richard Baxter (d. 1691), the Nonconformist preacher, had to build five galleries to accommodate his audiences.

Littletons, North, Middle and South (*see* **Bretforton**).

Malvern, Great* (DH 24) EC Wed (28,630). Inland resort and residential

461

town, noted for its drama festival and public school, it is beautifully situated on the slopes of the Malvern Hills (*see below*). Its chief beauty is the majestic priory church, the Norman arcades of the nave enclosed in a 15th-cent. building, with wonderful glass of the period, especially in the E window. At **Little Malvern**, 3 m. S, the tower and choir of another priory church remain, also with good medieval glass. 2 m. NE, Madresfield Court stands behind its moat in a large park, with an avenue of trees a mile long.

Malvern Hills (DH 24). The most impressive range in the county, extending for nine miles along the Herefordshire border, with super-lative views* (fourteen counties, it is said, can be seen on a clear day) from the Worcestershire and Herefordshire Beacons (1,395 and 1,114 ft. respec-tively). On the latter are the almost perfect remains of an ancient British camp, some 44 acres in extent.

Martley (DH 25) (1,022). A neat village, with a fine 300-year-old rectory and a grey-and-red sandstone church, visited for its well-preserved wall-paintings, largely 13th-cent., but partly 15th-cent. To the S, **Berrow Hill** rises 602 ft., with views of the Teme Valley.

Ombersley (DJ 26) EC Thurs (2,130). An attractive place, with many elaborately timbered houses, includ-ing the pleasant King's Arms; and the Court, an early 18th-cent. house, since refronted.

Pershore (DK 24) EC Thurs (5,620). A medieval stone bridge of six arches crosses the Avon to this market town, with its 18th-cent. houses and two churches. The greater of the two is only a part of the mighty abbey church that once stood here, but what remains beneath the lantern tower is of rare

beauty, especially the Norman arches that support the tower, the presbytery and the vaulted roof.

Pirton (DJ 24) (130). Two contrast-ing qualities of its black-and-white timbering are the simplicity of the church tower and, half a mile away, the elaborate work of Pirton Court.

Ripple (DJ 23) EC Thurs (620). An attractive village, grouped round the slender cross on the green, it is worthy of its treasure: the set of misericords in the church, carved to show the activities appropriate to the months.

Rous Lench (EA 25) (266). A small but lovely village, the black-and-white cottages culminating in historic Lench Court, with its clipped yews and seven acres of terraced gardens. The church too is impressive, with Norman work, canopied altar and one of its chapels that contains a series of Rous monuments.

Severn Stoke (DJ 24) (610). A pleasant village by the river, with the folly known as Dunstall Castle nearby, and one of Capability Brown's master-pieces 2 m. E at Croome d'Abitot. Here he not only laid out the grounds, with grottoes, statues and artificial lake, but is also said to have designed and built the mansion, with church and village to match.

Shelsley Walsh (DH 26) (50). Tiny hamlet in the Teme Valley, amongst hop fields and kilns. The court house is good Jacobean, timber-framed; the restored church noted for one of the finest chancel screens in the county and a rare wooden tomb (1596). The road to **Clifton** (2 m. S) reaches a height of more than 600 ft.; a private road nearby has been used for hill climbs since 1906. At **Hanley William** (3½ m. NW), standing considerably higher, the church has a timber turret, Norman font and a pulpit hewn in one

J. Allan Cash   **Worcester Cathedral on the River Se**

piece from the trunk of a tree and beautifully carved.

Stourbridge (DJ 28) EC Thurs (51,300). Industrial town at the gateway to the Black Country, with large iron and glass works, some of them still employing traditional methods. St Thomas's is an 18th-cent. church, with plaster vaulting and balconies; and at Old Swinford, the most ancient part of the town, the restored church has timbering and a large balcony. The Blue Coat School was founded by Thomas Foley in 1667; and Dr Johnson was a pupil at the older Grammar School in High St.

Stourport (DJ 27) EC Wed (14,610). Nothing was here but a small hamlet until in 1766 James Brindley built his canal linking the Severn and the Trent. Within thirty years it had become a major inland port, complete with quays, warehouses and bridge, much of which can still be seen, though falling into disuse. Today iron and carpets are its staple industries. Gilbert Scott built the church in the 19th cent.; its Methodist chapel is noted for the richness of its marbles and alabaster; there is a fine public park; boat trips on the Severn; and at the outskirts, Old Mitton Mill mentioned in the Doomsday Book. 2 m. E is **Hartlebury** with its church, old grammar school and castle. This last, which is of red sandstone, mainly rebuilt in the 18th cent., but still surrounded by its moat, has for centuries been the palace of the Bishops of Worcester.

Strensham (DK 23) (200). The church of this tiny hamlet (birthplace of the poet Samuel Butler in 1612) looks out across the Avon to Bredon Hill. Besides its painted gallery and two-decker pulpit, it is noted for its effigies of the Russells from the 14th to the 18th cent.; some are brasses (including the oldest in the county), others are of marble.

Tenbury Wells (DF 26) EC Thurs (2,070). A little market town, with pump room, hotels and excellent trout fishing in the Teme. At **Burford** (1 m. W) - which, though in Shropshire, forms a 'suburb' of Tenbury - the church is noted for its monument and a fine Elizabethan triptych.

Wickhamford (*see* **Bretforton**).

Worcester★ (DJ 25) EC Thurs (70,230). For centuries the Cathedral City, and today an industrial town with one of the Severn power stations, and celebrated for glove-making and china. (The Royal Porcelain Works, founded in 1750, and its museum, can be inspected by appointment.) Old Tudor timbered houses can be seen to advantage in New, Fish and Friar Streets. Among 18th-cent. buildings are Britannia House, the Berkeley Hospital, St Swithin's, the spire of St Andrews, and, exceedingly handsome, the Guildhall (designed by Thos White, a pupil of Wren's), with statues of Charles I and II on its façade. Of the seven or eight medieval churches, the cathedral is outstanding. The Edgar Tower leads to College Green, with the King's School (still using the monk's refectory), circular chapter house, cloisters and, overlooking the river, the cathedral. Originally Norman (the magnificent crypt remains) and much restored in the last century, the major part of the building dates from the 14th cent. Its glory is the choir, with innumerable monuments, including Prince Henry's delicately wrought chantry and King John's effigy and tomb. Nearby, the Commandery is a Tudor house, built on the site of an earlier hospital of St Wulstan. In the City Art Gallery is a collection of 28 paintings by David Cox. Once every three years the Three Choirs Festival is held in the cathedral.

The Pump Room, Matlock Bath

DERBYSHIRE AND STAFFORDSHIRE

AN INTRODUCTION BY PHIL DRABBLE

Derbyshire and Staffordshire must be two of the least publicized, least known and least appreciated counties in England. They stretch from the Pennines in the north to the industrial clamour of the Black Country in the south, and the country varies from the bleak stone-wall mountain scenery in the north of Derbyshire to some of the richest dairying country in England, in the Uttoxeter area.

The main road from West Bromwich, in the south, through Stafford and Stoke, passes through some of the dullest – but most important – industrial areas in the land. Yet only a few miles to the east, the road through Lichfield, across Needwood Forest to Sudbury and Ashbourne to Bakewell might almost be in another country: Needwood is famous for its oaks, and the whole route is well wooded until one climbs the stone-walled hills of Derbyshire.

The lovely River Dove divides the two counties, and Dovedale, shared between them, has scenery rugged and wild enough to give a wonderful sense

465

of solitude even in this bustling, crowded age. Indeed, its characteristic mood can be very awe-inspiring. Black clouds often crown its glowering peaks; and when the thunder groans and belches and roars to crescendo, the echoes buffet from rock-face to rock-face down the valley until they magnify the difference between Nature and puny Man. This Peak District, the northern tip of Staffordshire and north-western part of Derbyshire, is a National Park that is worth exploring times without number.

The red marls and gravels and sandstone of Staffordshire and South Derbyshire give way to the typical limes and millstone grits of Derbyshire. Beresford Dale, where Charles Cotton so often played host to his friend Isaac Walton, has been the object of pilgrimages by fishermen ever since – nor is it only associations that draw them: it is the excitement of the scenery too.

Although it is such a wonderful country to explore, some of its best parts can be reached only on foot. Such as Milldale, with its little stone bridge, built for packhorses but scarce wide enough for men, and the wild stone-wall country above, with craggy hills where nothing disturbs the peace but sheep and the soulful cries of the curlew. With the car left on the road below, there are rocks to be climbed and unforgettable views as reward for the effort. Even in the summer the breeze is drawn up the valleys, as if in a chimney-stack, giving freshness to the most sultry day. In the winter the road from Chapel-en-le-Frith through Castleton to Hope is an adventure. To leave the main road there and potter up the by-road to the north till it peters out at Edale or Upper Booth is a lesson on the superficiality of Progress.

The Cat and Fiddle Inn, just inside Cheshire on the Buxton-Macclesfield road, boasts that, at 1,690 feet, it is the highest in England. Certainly it is the coldest and bleakest – which makes the warmth and hospitality of the folk who live in these harsh hills more charming by contrast. To the south of the Peak District, where Derbyshire runs into Staffordshire, one might be in another land, though the Roches, grim rocks tumbling down the hills outside Leek, are as wild as anything Derbyshire can show. It is still a stone-wall country of lonely farms and dewponds, the last filled by double the rainfall of the Midland Plain a few miles to the south. From the Cheshire border, in the west, across to Ashbourne in Derbyshire and down to Uttoxeter and Abbots Bromley, in Staffordshire, stretches a tract of superb dairying and stock-feeding country. Between the Stafford-Cannock and Stafford-Rugeley roads, Cannock Chase is a huge sixteen-square-mile lung for the teeming industrial population of the Black Country, in the south, and of Stafford and the Potteries in the north. Half of the Chase is afforested with egregious foreign conifers; but half is lovely open moorland and natural woods of silver birch and oak. There are grouse and deer to be seen by those who will park at Milford Common or Sherbrook Valley and walk a mile or so from the milling thousands who enjoy themselves there at weekends.

Even the industrial south is an area of surprise worth investigating. Going north from Dudley along the Dudley-Wolverhampton New Road, a wooded hill stands a few hundred yards to the west. Housing estates cluster right to the foot of Wren's Nest Hill, and one's first inclination might well be to escape with all speed. But the hill is honeycombed with caves left from the lime-workings of the Industrial Revolution. Tunnels dip steep into the earth to a canal which runs hundreds of feet below; and these workings are a veritable paradise for all who are interested in fossils. They are exceptionally rich in variety, but world-famous in particular for trilobites or 'Dudley Bugs' – fossilized crustaceans, up

G. Douglas Bolton   **Lichfield Cath**

to four inches long, which once swam over the area like gigantic marine wood-lice. Wren's Nest, in spite of its urban surroundings, has been made a Nature Reserve because of its exceptional fossil wealth.

Customs

Staffordshire and Derbyshire are particularly rich in customs which still continue from ancient days. At Abbots Bromley, on the Lichfield-Uttoxeter road, the ancient Horn Dance is still performed in September to commemorate the hunting rights which were once enjoyed in adjacent Needwood Forest. The ceremony is a remarkable example of the way in which the church frequently took over the traditional pagan customs. In this case the process is not complete. The horns, huge reindeer horns mounted on handles, are kept in the church (where they may be seen at any time), and they must not be taken outside the parish; but there the vicar's jurisdiction over them ends. Although they are housed in the church, it is the dancers who control them. For generations the horn dancers have mostly been members of one family, and they choose their own team.

At Tissington, in Derbyshire, between the Ashbourne-Buxton and Ashbourne-Winster roads, the wells are 'dressed' on Ascension Day. Although it is a public holiday, attracting visitors as well as natives, it really perpetuates a pagan ceremony of propitiation to the gods of water. This has been absorbed into the church to a greater extent than the Horn Dance. It is thought by some to commemorate the survival of the villagers from the Black Death of 1350, in which the purity of their well may have played a part – but the real origins are possibly very much older.

At Ashbourne they have a Shrovetide Football Match in which any of the inhabitants may participate, Sturston Mill and Clifton Mill, at each end of the town, being 'goals'. The players play towards the goal nearest their own homes, and the ball has to be struck against the mill-wheel after being taken up the mill-race. The player so scoring a 'goal' keeps the ball and is a hero for a year. The game is not recommended for those of a delicate constitution.

History

Derbyshire is a lucrative hunting ground for the prehistorian. Ploughing has never been practicable on the rocky uplands, and so ancient remains have been disturbed unusually little. In the Hartington area, especially, tumuli of great importance remain. High Low, Lean Low, Carder Low and, most famous of all, Arbor Low, are well worth visiting. Ditches, vallums and stones, dating from the period of Stonehenge or earlier, are still as they have always been. At Arbor Low, stones like giant figures round a sundial lie stark and lonely. It is seen at its best on a blustery spring afternoon, when the sense of solitude there is almost tangible and the curlews cry like lost souls pleading to the priests of a religion long dead.

Both counties are rich, too, in Roman remains. Ryknield Street and Watling Street cross at Wall, where the Roman town of Letocetum once stood. There were baths here for the garrison; and the hypocausts, a complicated system of flues for heating the floors, are still clearly visible – to provide food for thought for all whose modern systems of central heating may well seem less efficient. At Buxton, in Derbyshire, there was a bath heated naturally by water gushing, as it does today, hot from the belly of the earth. It may well have been thought the only warm place in 'bitter Buxton' on a winter's day.

village pond at Tissington   *Reece Winstone*

At nearby Castleton an amethystine fluor-spar, known as Blue John, is a lovely translucent stone which can be worked into beautiful ornaments. It does not appear to have been mined between the 18th century and Roman times; but Pliny mentions a vase made from Blue John for which Petronius is said to have given the equivalent of £30,000; while Nero, characteristically, is said to have paid twice the price for another.

Industry

Buxton was built on the profits of its lime industry – 100,000 tons have been dislodged in a single blasting operation. But the famous Crescent, one of the most gracefully dignified streets in England, is said to owe its existence to copper, the Fifth Duke of Devonshire having built it in 1780 from the profits of one year's working of his copper-mines at Ecton. Since then the population has multiplied twentyfold to about 19,000.

The main industries of Staffordshire and Derbyshire, apart from the quarrying and farming mentioned, and brewing at Burton, are bound up with coal and iron. There are coalfields scattered from south Staffordshire and Cannock Chase to North Staffordshire and Derbyshire. In the north of Staffordshire are the Potteries, described in many of Arnold Bennett's novels and for ever associated

The sheep-wash bridge at Ashford

Reece Winstone

The twisted spire of Chesterfield church *Reece Winstone*

with the name of Josiah Wedgwood. In the south-west corner of the county, the Black Country became famous in the Industrial Revolution and has remained famous ever since. Each town has seemed to specialize in a different craft: Cradley for chains, Willenhall for locks, Darlaston for nuts and bolts and so on. Famous men who have changed history are associated with the area. Boulton and Watt, Wilkinson and Murdoch make the Black Country as memorable for material success as Dr Johnson, of Lichfield, for matters of the mind. And, because of the immense variety of trades, the area is not only prosperous in booms, but far more resilient than most when times are harder.

Derbyshire, too, spreads its interests widely. Although it is not nowadays of industrial significance, lead mining has been practised in Derbyshire at least from Roman times, and there are many old workings. As well as Buxton's lime, Derbyshire is much concerned with iron-smelting, heavy and general engineering and textile manufacture, including rayon. These last two are especially centred round Derby itself, which can also claim to be the birthplace of the most famous motor-car in the world, the Rolls Royce, and of many of the aero-engines which power the world's aircraft.

Some houses and gardens open to the public

Chatsworth 5m NE of Bakewell on A623 *Map* EC 37. *17th cent.; 19th-cent. additions by Wyatville, State apartments with wood-carvings and painted ceilings; pictures, drawings, sculpture, furniture and library with early MSS. Garden with cascade and one of the highest fountains in Europe.* Trustees of the Chatsworth Settlement.

Chillington Hall Brewood 8m NW of Wolverhampton between A5 and A449 *Map* DJ 30. *12th cent., ancestral home of Giffards; rebuilt 18th cent. by Sir John Soane; grounds by Capability Brown; associations with the flight of Charles II after battle of Worcester.*

Dr Johnson's House At Lichfield *Map* EB 30. *Birthplace of Dr Johnson in 1709; now a museum.*

Hardwick Hall 6m W of Mansfield off B6039 *Map* EE 36. *Elizabethan mansion, built by Bess of Hardwick; home of the Dowager Duchess of Devonshire; tapestries, portraits and notable High Great Chamber* NT.

Izaak Walton's Cottage Shallowford 5m NW of Stafford, between Norton Br and Gt Bridgford off A520 *Map* DJ 32. *Restored cottage, where Izaak Walton was born in 1593; now a museum.*

Kedleston Hall 4½m NW of Derby between A6 and A52 *Map* ED 34. *18th-cent. mansion, home of Viscount Scarsdale, in 500-acre park; south front by Robert Adam; magnificent marble hall; pictures.*

Melbourne Hall 8m S of Derby on A514 *Map* ED 32. *18th cent.; home of Queen Victoria's first Prime Minister, Lord Melbourne. Notable pictures and wrought-iron pergola.* The Marquess of Lothian.

Moseley Old Hall 4m NE of Wolverhampton off A460 *Map* DK 30. *Originally Elizabethan half-timbered, now 19th-cent. brick; panelled rooms served as refuge of Charles II after battle of Worcester in 1651. Garden in 17th-cent. style.*

Peveril (or **Peak**) **Castle** Castleton 9m NE of Buxton on A625 *Map* EB 37. *Built by Henry II on impregnable position. Norman keep associated with Sir Walter Scott; 13th-cent. round towers.*

Trentham Gardens on SW edge of Stoke-on-Trent on A34 *Map* DJ 34. *Beautiful rose and Italian gardens in picturesque setting; ballroom, boating and swimming pool. Former mansion of the Duke of Sutherland was demolished in 1910.*

Books for further reading

Local life and customs

S. J. COLEMAN *Staffordshire Folk-Lore* 1955
C. PORTEOUS *The Ancient Customs of Derbyshire* 1690

Staffordshire is described in the novels of ARNOLD BENNETT; Derbyshire in those of CRICHTON PORTEOUS.

History, architecture and topography

P. DRABBLE *The Black Country* (Regional Books series) 1952; *Staffordshire* (County Books series) 1948
K. C. EDWARDS and others *The Peak District* (New Naturalist series) 1961
N. W. GREENSLADE and D. G. STUART *History of Staffordshire* 1965

M. JONES *Potbank* (Britain Alive series) 1961
A. MEE ed. *Derbyshire: the Peak Country* (King's England series) 1937; *Staffordshire: Beauty and the Black Country* (King's England series) 1937
NATIONAL PARKS COMMISSION *Peak District* (National Park Guide No. 3) 1960
N. PEVSNER *Derbyshire* (Penguin, Buildings of England series) 1953
C. PORTEOUS *Derbyshire* (County Books series) 1950; *Peakland* (Regional Books series) 1954; *Portrait of Peakland* 1963
T. L. TUDOR *Derbyshire* (Little Guides Series) 5th edn by E. C. Williams 1950
WARD, LOCK AND CO. *Matlock, Dovedale, etc.* (Red Guides series) 4th edn 1963

Gazetteer

DERBYSHIRE AND STAFFORDSHIRE

Bakewell on the River Wye Reece Winstone

Abbot's Bromley *Staffs*. (E A 32) E C Wed (1,190). An attractive village of black-and-white houses (notably Church House and Goat's Head Inn, with a butter cross in the market place), where the Horn Dance is still performed every September. **Blithfield Hall** (open in summer) is 3 m. S W across a large lake. The ruins of **Chartley Castle**, in its great park with an 18th-cent. manor house, are 5 m. N W.

Alton *Staffs*. (E A 34) E C Thurs (1,290). On a rock to one side of the Churnet Valley stand the tower of a medieval castle and a 19th-cent. convent (chapel by Pugin); to the other, we find Alton Towers, 19th-cent. Gothic, with park and splendid gardens (public admitted in summer).

Ashbourne *Derby*. (E B 34) E C Wed (5,660). Good access to Dovedale and the Manifold Valley, with its handsome Church St (16th-cent. grammar school, 17th-cent. Owlfield and Peg's Almshouses; and Georgian mansion house, clergymen's widows' almshouse and Green Man Hotel, where Johnson and Boswell stayed several times); and one of the finest churches in the county, mainly 13th to 14th cent., with 212-ft. spire and numerous monuments, particularly Thos Banks's white marble Penelope Boothby.

Bakewell *Derby*. (E C 36) E C Thurs (4,040). Handsome little town on R. Wye, crossed by medieval bridge, and convenient for visiting Haddon and Chatsworth (*see below*), with **Monsal**

Dale 4 m. N W. Several stone houses of 17th and 18th cents. (Market and Town Halls, Catcliffe and Bath Houses, Holme Hall and others). Cruciform church, typical of this county, 12th–14th cents. (fine effigies in Vernon chapel, stump of Saxon Cross in churchyard).

Betley *Staffs*. (D H 34) E C Wed (633). Half-timbered houses beside an attractive mere. But the chief interest lies in the church. Not only is the whole supported by octagonal oak pillars, but the arches of the nave, clerestory and roof are all of finely worked timber.

Biddulph *Staffs*. (D J 35) .E C Wed (16,100). On the edge of its moor (1,100 ft.) near the source of the R. Trent and the ancient Bride Stones. Here are the ruins of the Old Hall, destroyed during the Civil War; and a later one of the 17th and 18th cents. In the church, note the Norman font, sandstone altar-rails and Flemish glass in one window.

Black Country, The. A great conurbation, continuous with Birmingham, running N W from **West Bromwich** to **Wolverhampton** and S W from **Walsall** to **Stourbridge**, and still growing. Though hardly 'tourist country', it is an essential part of Britain, and provides a unique landscape. This may be seen from **Wednesbury** parish church, a fine building 700 ft. above sea level with a fighting-cock lectern.

473

Buxton: the Crescent

J. Allan Cash

Bolsover *Derby*. (EE 37) EC Wed (11,820). The castle (open to the public), standing on a steep hill above the chimneys and pit-heads of the valley, is a Jacobean building on the site of Peveril's Norman keep, and is being restored. Built by two generations of the Cavendishes (the younger entertained Charles I here at a cost of £15,000, which included a Ben Jonson masque), family monuments may be found in the Cavendish chapel, which survived when fire gutted the church in 1897.

Broughton *Staffs*. (DH 33) (300). Amongst the woods that still remain from Blore Forest, both church and hall were built by Thos Broughton in mid-17th cent. The first has high oak pews and period glass; the second is a gabled house with richly carved timbers.

Burton-upon-Trent *Staffs*. (EC 32) EC Wed (50,220). A County Borough on the R. Trent and the Trent and Mersey Canal, 10 m. SW of Derby and 21 m. NE of Walsall and Black Country. Famous for brewing, an industry originally started by the monks of Burton Abbey after they had discovered that the water of Burton made beer clear and sparkling. The Abbey was founded in 1002 and became a collegiate church after the Dissolution. A few relics of the Abbey remain near St Modwen's Church, Parish Church of Burton.

Buxton★ *Derby*. (EA 37) EC Wed (19,730). Standing nearly 1,000 ft. above sea level, a centre for exploring the Peak District (*see below*). Spa waters known to Romans and Mary Queen of Scots, but developed by the 5th Duke of Devonshire, who built the Crescent, Assembly Room (now the Clinic) and stables about 1790. These last, with 19th-cent. additions (including the great dome) are now the Devonshire Royal Hospital. A good viewpoint is the tower on Grin Low (1,450 ft.), with the Goyt Valley 3½ m. to the W and Axe Edge, with its inn, the Traveller's Rest (1,535 ft.), to the S.

Cannock *Staffs*. (DK 31) EC Thurs (42,190). A large mining town at the edge of the 30,000-acre **Cannock Chase**, which, much of it wildly beautiful, rises to 800 ft. at prehistoric Castle Ring. 4 m. SW, moated Hilton Hall stands in a fine park.

Castleton *Derby*. (EB 38) EC Wed (670). A magnificent situation★★ at the W end of the Hope Valley, separated from **Kinder Scout** (2,083 ft.) and **Kinder Low** (2,077 ft.), 5 m. NW, by Lose Hill, Back Tor, Mam Tor and the Vale of Edale. Just above the village is the Norman keep of ruined Peveril Castle (AM). The church has a Norman chancel-arch and box-pews. The neighbourhood abounds in caves. 1½ m. W, **Mam Tor** (NT) is an Iron Age hill-fort.

Caverswall *Staffs*. (DK 34) EC Thurs (5,200). The castle, now a convent, is a turreted Jacobean building standing within the dried-up moat of the medieval original. In the church, the kneeling figure of Lady St Vincent is by Chantrey (1816), and there is a Jacobean altar table.

Chatsworth★ *Derby*. (EC 37) (30). With Haddon and Hardwick, one of the three great Derbyshire mansions, its grounds among the most notable in the country. Of the original Elizabethan buildings, the Hunting Tower and Queen Mary's Bower in the grounds survive, but the old house was replaced by the present one between 1687 and 1705 by the 1st Duke of Devonshire (architect, Talman), while in the early 19th cent. the 6th Duke employed Sir Jeffrey Wyatville to add a new NE wing. The interior is decorated with sumptuous painting, carving and plaster-work.

Cheadle *Staffs*. (EA 34) EC Wed (8,130). On the edge of a wild moor leading to the Weaver Hills stands a group of timbered and gabled Elizabethan houses near the 19th-cent. church. The other church, with its 200-ft. spire and rich internal decoration, is one of Pugin's masterpieces. 2 m. NE is the Hawksmoor nature reserve, 200 acres of woodlands, moors and marshes.

Chesterfield *Derby*. (ED 37) EC Wed (70,020). Coal and iron centre, famous for its 228-ft. spire, warped out of the perpendicular by its lead and timber covering. Mainly 14th cent., but much restored, the church is notable for the number of chapels (once belonging to guilds) and the series, some very good, of Foljambe monuments. There is a museum at **Old Whittington**, about 3 m. N, in Revolution House.

Clifton Campville *Staffs*. (EC 31) (460). The mainly 14th-cent. church, one of the finest in the county, has a spire 189 ft. high, with flying buttresses. Above the chapel in the N transept is a priest's chamber with fireplace and 13th-cent. windows. There are five screens, and carved stalls and misericords, a Rysbrack monument and a fine Tudor table-tomb of alabaster. 3 m. W, Haselour Hall is a gabled building not to be missed.

Cromford *Derby*. (EC 35) EC Thurs (1,250). The Old Mill (1771) is where Richard Arkwright first used water-power to drive a cotton mill. In the village street stands the Georgian Greyhound Inn and the church built by Arkwright. The 15th-cent. bridge has rounded arches on one side and pointed on the other. At the S end are the remains of a bridge chapel. Willersley Castle is the house Arkwright built for himself in the late 18th-cent. classical manner.

Croxall *Staffs*. (EB 31). Three-storied Oakley farmhouse, to the S, was the manor of the Stanley family 500 years ago. The gabled brick hall was for many generations the home of the Curzons, to whom there is a remarkable series of tombstones in the church. But the most interesting memorial here is to Sir Robert Wilmot-Horton and his wife: of her, Byron wrote, 'She walks in beauty like the night. . . .' Sir Robert was responsible for the decision to burn the M S. of the poet's memoirs.

Dale Abbey *Derby.* (EE 33) (1,240). Part of the gatehouse, some vaulting in a cow-house and the great arch of the E window are all that remain of a 12th-cent. foundation, situated beneath sandstone cliffs. The village church, only 26 × 25 ft. and under the same roof as a dwelling house, is, however, one of the most curious in the country. It is filled with box-pews, a gallery and a 1634 pulpit; and it has 13th-cent. wall-paintings. The Cat and Fiddle Mill is in working order.

Derby★ *Derby.* (ED 33) EC Wed (217,500). A prosperous trading town in the Middle Ages; industrialization began with the introduction of the country's first silk mill in 1717, hence the preponderance of 18th-cent. domestic architecture that typifies the centre of the town (Market Place, Irongate, King and Queen St and, especially, Friargate). Growth of engineering in the 20th cent., including railways, has more than doubled the population. The tower of All Saints (parish church, raised to cathedral in 1927) is 16th cent., although the siting of the power station detracts from its beauty. The church itself, rebuilt by Gibbs (1725), the architect of St Martin-in-the-Fields, is a splendid example of its period, with numerous monuments and splendid wrought-iron screens and communion-rails by Thos Bakewell. The most significant municipal buildings are County Hall (1660) and the Assembly Rooms (1764) recently damaged by fire, though the façade is being restored. The rare, but considerably restored, Bridge Chapel is 15th cent. **Littleover Church,** 1 m. W, has a Norman porch with 14th-cent. windows.

Dovedale★★ *Derby.* (EB 35). A lovely stretch of the valley of the R. Dove (famous trout stream); a steeply wooded limestone ravine with crags and caves, running some 7 m. N from Thorpe to **Hartington** (*see below*) and continuing into Wolfscote and Beresford Dales. (*See also* **Ashbourne** and **Ilam.**)

Dudley *Staffs.* (DK 28) EC Wed (63,820). The town, recently declared to be within the boundaries of Staffordshire, is mentioned in the chapter on Worcestershire (*see* p. 460).

Elford *Staffs.* (EB 31) (370). Charming little village in the Tame Valley, with an old tall-chimneyed hall, a cluster of picturesque cottages and a lime avenue leading to the church, which, much restored in the last century, contains a sculptured gallery, modern wood-carving and medieval alabaster tombs.

Ellastone *Staffs.* (EB 34) (274). Near the R. Dove, at the foot of the Weaver Hills, which rise to 1,000 ft., it is the 'Hayslope' of George Eliot's *Adam Bede;* her father, the model for the hero of the novel, spent his youth here in a thatched house that is still standing. 2 m. W, Wootton Lodge, splendidly situated, is a 17th-cent. mansion, though the Old Hall, where Rousseau wrote his *Confessions*, has gone.

Enville *Staffs.* (DJ 28) (600). The tower of the church is modern, the nave-arcades Norman, the chancel (carved misericords) rebuilt in the 14th cent. by Roger de Birmingham, who is buried here. Nearby stands the Hall (fine collection of pictures) in charming grounds designed by the poet Shenstone. **Kinver Edge** (NT), a viewpoint 2 m. S E, is crowned by an ancient camp, and there is a rock-dwelling known as Holy Austin Rock.

Eyam *Derby*. (EC 37) (990). 800 ft. above sea level, with White Edge (1,156 ft.) 3 m. away to E. There is a 9th-cent. Saxon cross (AM) in the churchyard, which is surrounded by pleasant houses, including the Georgian Rectory. The Hall is Jacobean, stone with mullioned windows. 2 m. N, on Eyam Moor, Wet-Withens is a Bronze Age circle of 16 stones, still standing within a bank of earth.

Haddon Hall* *Derby*. (EC 36). Wonderfully sited, among trees and fields sloping to the R. Wye, is one of the most romantic places in the county. Mainly constructed in the 16th and 17th cents., but on the foundations of a Norman stronghold (it was not lived in between 1700 and 1900; then it was admirably restored), its beauty is the result of growth rather than design; e.g. it is typical that the Norman font in the chapel has a Jacobean cover, and that both seem in place. Furnishings, pictures and gardens are full of interest.

Hardwick Hall *Derby*. (EE 36). Some 15 m. E of Haddon but, unlike it, far from having merely grown, it took its present shape in 1591–97, by the direction of a woman who was over seventy when she began and yet managed to live the last ten years of her life there. The formidable Bess of Hardwick, having married from the Old Hall (its ruins stand close by) at 13 and outlived four wealthy husbands, started her project at the age of 71. The result was the Elizabethan mansion that we see today, with its presence chamber and most of the original decoration, hangings and furniture.

Hartington *Derby*. (EB 36) EC Wed (400). Attractive little town near the entrance to Beresford Dale, with cottages and 19th-cent. town hall in the market place; gabled and mullioned 14th-cent. hall rebuilt 1611; and

Fishing in the River Dove   Reece Winstone

church with monuments and two-storied porch.

Hathersage *Derby*. (EC 38) EC Tues (1,520). A Peak village 3 m. S of High Neb (1,500 ft.) with Carl Wark, an Iron Age hill-fort, to the E, it is the 'Morton' of *Jane Eyre*. There are two early 19th-cent. mills and Rock House near the Derwent Bridge, and a 16th-cent. hall with 19th-cent. front; Robin Hood's Little John is by tradition buried in the churchyard; and the church has brasses and tombs of the Eyre family, who lived at North Lees, 1½ m. N, a small but impressive 16th-cent. manor house. In September the Longshaw sheepdog trials are held near here.

Ilam *Staffs*. (EB 35) (130). Near the entrance to Dovedale, on the R. Manifold, which is partly subterranean and has a lovely valley (ruins of Jacobean Throwley Hall; and Thor's Cave, near Wetton Mill). J. Watt-Russell rebuilt the village and Tudor hall (where Congreve wrote *The Old Bachelor*) in the 19th cent. There are two Saxon crosses in the churchyard; the church contains a probably Saxon font and an octagonal chapel and tomb designed by Chantrey. The shrine of St Bertram is in the grounds of the Hall.

Ingestre *Staffs.* (DK 32) (170). In a fine park bounded by the R. Trent, a hamlet, with 17th-cent. hall, rebuilt in Regency Gothic after a fire, and church (1677) usually a-scribed to Wren.

Kedleston *Derby.* (ED 34) (70). The Hall is the finest Georgian house in the county, with splendid grounds and lake (admission in summer). The N front is by James Paine (1761), but Robert Adam built the more elegant S front, the great hall, the rotunda, the music-room, some of the furnishings and the bridge. The church, 13th-cent. cruciform, has box-pews, font and communion-rails of about 1700; effigies of Curzon knights, and, as one would expect, an ambitious monument to the late Lord Curzon of Kedleston.

Leek *Staffs.* (DK 35) EC Thurs (19,100). An ancient town, its prosperity founded on the silk industry and situated in the upper Churnet Valley amongst moors and mountains; the rugged Staffordshire Roaches, rising to 1,500 ft., are some 6 m. to N beyond Rudyard Lake. Little remains of Dieu-le-Cresses Abbey, 1¼ m. N.

Lichfield* *Staffs.* (EB 30) EC Wed (22,100). The red sandstone cathedral, with its three spires, splendid front choir and chapter house, is an out-standing example of early English and Decorated work. Monuments and decoration were savaged during the Civil War, but restoration was carried out by Bishop Hacket (1662) and again in the 19th cent., when much of the carving on the W front was done. The 16th-cent. Herkenrode windows in the Lady Chapel were brought from Belgium in 1803; stalls and Bishop's throne were carved in 1860 by George Eliot's uncle, Samuel Evans, the original Seth Bede. A lovely view of the Cathedral can be gained from across the 17-acre Stowe Pool. Dr Johnson was born in a house in the market place, now a museum; there is a well-restored timbered house in Bore St and a city museum. At **Wall**, 3 m. SW on Watling St, the excavated remains of the Roman city of Letocetum (NT) can be seen.

Matlock *Derby.* (ED 36) EC Thurs (19,560). An inland spa, mainly developed through the 19th cent., in the valley of the Derwent, with the Heights of Abraham rising to 1,100 ft. At Riber, the 19th-cent. castle is now a zoo; the Hall and Manor House of two centuries earlier stand in pleasing contrast. At **South Wingfield**, 5 m. SE, are the historic ruins of the Manor House (note the tower and vaulted crypt), begun in 1440 and originally larger than Haddon, where Mary Queen of Scots was long imprisoned.

Melbourne *Derby.* (ED 32) EC Thurs (3,640). Despite its three towers, the exterior of the church is largely masked by a tithe barn, but inside we find magnificent clerestoried Norman nave and crossing. The Hall (16th cent., enlarged and considerably redesigned in the 18th) and its splendid grounds are open in summer.

Peak District* *Derby.* (EB 39). See Introduction p. 466 and **Buxton, Castleton, Hathersage** and **Tideswell**.

Potteries, The *Staffs.* (DJ 34). The potter's craft has been practised here from the 17th cent. to the present day; and Arnold Bennett's Five Towns – **Stoke, Burslem, Longton, Hanley** and **Tunstall** – were made famous, long before he wrote about them, by Wedgwood, Spode, Copeland and

Minton; specimens of their work may be seen in the Minton Museum. At **Trentham**, 1 m. S W of Longton, the 1,000-acre park with its lake and garden is now open to the public, though the 19th-cent. Sutherland mansion (the 'Brentham' of Disraeli's *Lothair*) was demolished in 1905.

Repton *Derby*. (ED 32) EC Wed (1,850). Remains of the ruined 12th-cent. priory are incorporated in the famous school, the most important being Prior Overton's Tower, now part of the Headmaster's House. The late Saxon crypt of St Wystan's Church should not be missed. **Foremark Hall**, 2 m. E, is a Palladian house of 1760; the church, a century older and externally Gothic, has kept intact its original Jacobean furnishings, box-pews, three-decker pulpit and rood-screen.

Stafford *Staffs*. (DK 32) EC Wed (52,560). Still famous for boots and shoes as it was in the 18th cent., when its M.P., Richard Brinsley Sheridan, said 'May its trade be trod underfoot by all the world'. He used to stay at Chetwynd House (now the P.O.); and in the same Greengate St are two Tudor houses: High House and the Swan. St Mary's has a great octagonal tower, rare in this country, a spacious 13th-cent. interior, a Norman font, and a bust of Izaak Walton, who was baptized here. Tucked away nearby, St Chad's has a Norman nave with clerestory, and a superb chancel-arch, with five orders of almost unimpaired Norman carving.

Stoke (*see* **Potteries**).

Sudbury *Derby*. (EB 33) EC Wed (1,000). A pretty brick village, with a notable inn (1671) and a 17th-cent. hall, containing a wealth of plaster-work and carving, unfortunately not on view. The restored church is remarkable chiefly for the Vernon

Repton: the Saxon crypt   Reece Winstone

effigies. **Somershall Herbert Hall** 2½ m. NW, has Elizabethan half-timbering.

Tamworth *Staffs*. (EC 30) EC Wed (34,600). An imposing castle, with Saxon and Norman work in the keep and curtain-wall, which encloses Tudor and Jacobean domestic buildings, now a museum. It stands on a 130-ft. mound, raised by Alfred's daughter

Ethelfleda (d. 918), and overlooks the junction of the Tame and the Anker. The church has a unique feature: twin spiral stairs leading to the roof of the Norman tower. It also has windows by Ford Madox Brown and Wm Morris. The town hall (AM) was built in 1701 by Thos Guy, founder of Guy's Hospital.

Tideswell *Derby*. (EB 37) EC Tues (1,760). This small town, with Miller's Dale 2 m. S and the mountains of the Peak District rising to the N, is noteworthy for one of the outstanding churches of the county, a 14th-cent. structure with a four-turreted tower. 2 m. NE are the well-known round barrows, Tideslow and Tup Low.

Tutbury *Staffs*. (EC 32) EC Wed (2,470). A pleasant little town on the R. Dove, with a timbered inn. On the hill below the ruins of the castle stands the church, with Norman arcades, clerestory and triforium, and the magnificent S front.

Youlgreave *Derby*. (EC 36) EC Thurs (1,310). The restored church contains much Norman work, including the font, and a 15th-cent. tower. Alabaster effigies of Cokaynes and Gylberts can be seen; the E window in the chancel is by Burne-Jones and Wm Morris. Old Hall Farm (1630) and Old Hall (1650) lie to the NW. **Arbor Low**, 3½ m. W, a Bronze Age circle of stone about 250 ft. across, is the most famous Derbyshire antiquity; and nearby is the large round barrow, Gib Hill.

John of Gaunt's castle at Tutbury

Reece Winstone

Opposite: Detail from the original painting by Julian Trevelyan.
Surrounded by grimy furnaces stands the Potteries Museum, Stoke-on-Trent, as the symbol of the more refined products for which Staffordshire is famous. On the right is the bust of Josiah Wedgewood, next to a blue jasper-ware vase and a mug of 'spit ware', decorated by spitting tobacco-juice at the wet glaze. The county's prosperity was largely founded on the Grand Trunk Canal.

Ellesmere

SHROPSHIRE

AN INTRODUCTION BY PHIL DRABBLE

Shropshire is about fifty miles long by forty wide and is roughly divided in half by the River Severn, which is the longest river in England and Wales. Its western boundary is the border between England and Wales, and memories of the raids and skirmishes, bloodshed and hates that have rattled round the marches through the centuries are still green – so much so that it can be taken as a slight to hint that a Shropshire man was born 'the wrong side of the border.' Looking down on all this turmoil, and on everything in history and pre-history that happened before, is Shropshire's most famous mountain, the Wrekin, whose volcanic rock is the oldest in England. The Watling Street runs just below it; but if you turn off and follow the lanes at its foot until you return to the Watling Street again, you will have seen peerless scenery – and covered a surprisingly long distance. Indeed, the Midland expression designed to bring a verbose speaker to the point is 'Stop going all round the Wrekin.'

To the west of the county the hills lift range upon range into Wales; south of the Severn are the uplands of Shropshire, and to the north is the rich dairy and arable country which has made Shropshire farming famous. In the north of the

Opposite: Detail from the original painting by S. R. Badmin.

This is a county of black-and-white houses and of long blue hills. In the picture, we see the half-timbered medieval church at Melverley; clay pipes from Broseley; the Iron Bridge (1779) over the Severn; a plate in the original willow pattern designed by Thomas Minton; a teapot from the Coalport pottery, and in it a Salop flower, Touch-Me-Not. Milton's *Comus* was first performed at Ludlow Castle.

Haughmond Abbey

G. Douglas Bolton

county, too, lie the Shropshire meres, six huge sheets of water which are paradise for the naturalist and botanist. By contrast, the Long Mynd, towering above the Shrewsbury-Ludlow road, is quite out of context with the rest of the county. It is a heather-covered plateau of grit and shale, rising to 1,674 feet, almost as old as the rock of the Wrekin. The bleak, wild central area is shared by wild ponies and grouse, and to the west the hill falls suddenly away, so that the prevailing winds provide a constant surge of eddies and up-currents which account for its popularity as a centre for gliding.

Leaving the Long Mynd, the road from Church Stretton to Much Wenlock runs along the narrow spine of Wenlock Edge, famous for its views and its lime-quarries. In parts the Edge is so narrow that it is possible to look out either side and see the country dissected beneath like a specimen on an anatomist's table. Much Wenlock, with its ancient Priory and Guildhall, welcomes travellers along the Edge with an unchanging, almost medieval, hospitality. The limestone core of the Edge is as much in contrast with the grit of Long Mynd as it is with the rugged glacial gorge at Ironbridge, or the rich red sandstone of basalt-capped Clee Hill.

The south of the county is as soft and beautiful as the north-west is wild. Lovely Corvedale, from Ludlow to Bridgnorth, is well-wooded and rich,

482

wonderful country for game, and every glade is resonant with crowing pheasants at dusk and brilliant with them in the setting sun.

History and Towns

Watling Street, entering Shropshire from Staffordshire at Weston-under-Lizard, passes near Wroxeter, which is on the site of the Roman settlement of Uriconium, once the fourth Roman city in Britain. You can still see remnants of the original paving, of shops and of the lawcourt, the whole enclosed, originally, by a wall two miles long. There are, too, remnants of the baths (used also as brothels in those days), of the forum and of various workshops. A multitude of personal belongings have been dug up and are to be seen in the museum at Shrewsbury. The later history of Shropshire is inextricably interwoven with the history of Wales. Offa, King of the Mercians, built his dyke, in the 8th century, from the Dee to the Wye. A great deal of the earthworks, ditches and ramparts, twenty or thirty feet high, still remain and will be an irresistible attraction to anyone in tune with the romance of the past. The best stretch is in the Clun and Mainstone area. From Norman times onwards, a string of castles, ranging in importance from fortified manor houses to major works of war, was built to keep the Welsh under control.

Ludlow is perhaps the most enthralling town in the county, either for the historian or for the lover of beautiful things. Perched on a commanding hill, moated by the River Teme, its castle dominates the whole countryside around with a power that the centuries have never clipped. It still preserves its priceless half-timbered buildings and the crooked alleys that grew instead of being planned. The market square is the finest in the country and the Norman castle has been enlarged and strengthened through the ages till it seems to have grown with English history. Here were raised the tragic young princes who perished in the Tower of London.

But Ludlow Castle is not unique: there are castles, in varying stages of repair, at Whittington (one of the many legendary origins of Dick Whittington) and Bridgnorth, Clun, Moreton Corbet, Stokesay, Hopton and Shrewsbury, among others. Shrewsbury Castle is not particularly attractive, because it was so 'modernized' by Thomas Telford when he was appointed surveyor of public works in Shropshire in 1788. He is more happily remembered for his canals, aqueducts and roads. It was at Shrewsbury in 1403 that Henry IV conquered Hotspur and the rebels who had plagued the English along the Welsh Marches, an episode immortalized by Shakespeare. During the Civil War in 1645 the town was captured simply and easily by the Roundheads, who persuaded a sympathizer to let them in by the Water Gate. The town itself lies within a loop of the meandering Severn and is full of wonderful timbered houses and surprising vistas round every other corner. Much of the stonework for the buildings came from the Quarry, now the centrepiece of the town's fine park. This is jewelled with a superb flower-garden, called the Dingle. The original Shrewsbury School faced the ancient castle; but now it has been moved to imposing buildings facing the Dingle across the Severn, into what is said to have been the 18th-century foundling hospital.

Bridgnorth is another of Shropshire's riverside fortified towns. Indeed it regards itself as *two* towns, High Town and Low Town, the latter being two hundred feet below, right at the edge of the river. A steeply winding road connects them, helped by steps and alleyways and the steepest cliff-railway in

The church and banqueting hall, Stokesay

J. Allan Cash

England. A tower is perched on the hill, overlooking the town. It is the keep of the Norman castle, and it leans three times as much out of true as the Tower of Pisa – but it has stood safely there for 800 years and shows every sign of being there for as long again. Its hour of greatest danger was in the Civil War when a Roundhead tunnelled into the rock beneath. He had almost got underneath the powder-magazine when the defenders discovered the plan and surrendered. The town is notable, too, for ancient caves in the rock on which the castle stood. The Hermitage was an ancient cave-chapel, and Ethelred, brother of England's first king Athelstan, is said to have lived here as a hermit.

The county was as famous for men of God as for men of war. Much Wenlock Priory was founded by Mercian King Penda's granddaughter Milburga. It was destroyed by the Danes; but Lady Godiva restored it. Again it was destroyed – to be restored once more by the Norman Roger de Montgomery. Finally it was sacked by Henry VIII. The ruins are well worth visiting, as is the rest of the town with its unspoiled medieval buildings. There were other religious houses at Lilleshall and Haughmond; but the most famous of all is at Buildwas. Roger de Clinton, crusader and Bishop of Chester, built it 800 years ago, and like so many others it was razed by the infamous Thomas Cromwell on the orders of Henry VIII. It is still a vast impressive monument to the religious fervour of olden times. The great pillars support seven pairs of the finest Norman arches in England, and the crypt and cloisters still remain. The abbot's house has been made into a private riverside residence. Incongruously enough, the ruins of this peaceful riverside abbey are now dominated by a clinically functional power-station.

485

esay Castle   *G. Douglas Bolton*

Industry

Thinking of the Clun Forest sheep that make such spectacles of the sales at Craven Arms, or of the rich dairying land to the north, on the Cheshire border, most people consider Shropshire an agricultural county. But the story of the Ironbridge Gorge is of the greatest interest either to the historian or to the student of the rise and fall of our prosperity. Today the whole scene along the Severn banks of Coalbrookdale is derelict and decayed where, two centuries ago, it was throbbing with industry. The town of Ironbridge clings to the steep banks of the Gorge like grimy starlings clinging to a cliff. It got its name, as well as its prosperity, from the iron bridge which spans the river. This was built by the ironmaster Abraham Darby in 1779, the first bridge in the world to be made of iron, symbol of the prosperity that iron was to bring to this remote and pastoral valley, ground by glaciers from the land in the Ice Age. It had to wait for the second Iron Age, the Industrial Revolution, to get rich. Wilkinson, another ironmaster so wrapt in his craft that even his coffin was of iron, confounded the sceptics by building a boat of iron – which to their amazement floated! At about the same time, the district became as famous for the delicacy of its Coalport China as for its heavier industry.

Farmland from the Long Mynd   J. Allan Cash

Ironbridge, Salop

Success had come to Coalbrookdale; but – alas – success ate into the supply of raw materials, and the prosperity evaporated like the capital of an over-reaching man. Visitors there can read the story of the last two centuries of boom and slump on the face of the land as clearly as phrenologists can read the bumps on heads. Since 1967, however, the scars of old enterprise are being covered by the great new town of Telford, which is being built to bring prosperous industry to the area again. For the rest of the county, Shrewsbury, as well as being an important market town, is, like Wellington, much engaged in engineering, both agricultural and general.

Famous People

The great ironmasters Wilkinson and Darby made their impact not only on Shropshire history and prosperity but on the country as a whole. Clive of India lived at Walcot Hall, near Lydbury North, with its wonderful parkland and lakes. He went to school at Market Drayton and his family home was Styche Hall at Moreton Say. Charles Darwin was born and educated in Shrewsbury. Mary Webb's novels fired popular imagination the more because of the vivid pictures of Shropshire life they contained. She lived, at various times, at Stanton and Pontesbury and Meole Brace and Leighton. But the writer who has perhaps done most to make Shropshire known to readers all over the world was a Worcestershire man – A. E. Housman, author of *A Shropshire Lad*.

487

Some houses and gardens open to the public

Burford House Gardens 9m from Ludlow, 1m W of Tenbury Wells on A456 *Map* D F 26. *18th cent.; in beautiful setting on banks of River Teme; nurseries, clematis, trees, shrubs and plants.* J. Treasure, Esq. Dogs not allowed.

Hodnet Hall Gardens 12m NE of Shrewsbury on A53 *Map* D G 32. *60-acre garden with rare shrubs, ornamental lakes and pools.* Mr & The Hon Mrs A. Heber Percy. *Enquiries:* H. F. Dodson, Hodnet 202.

Ludlow Castle At Ludlow *Map* D F 27. *11th-cent. foundations by Roger de Lacy; 12th-cent. circular chapel; 12th- to 16th-cent. tower, great hall and chamber. First performance of Milton's Comus held here in 1634.*

Shipton Hall 6m SW of Much Wenlock at junction of B4368 and B4378 *Map* D F 29. *Elizabethan manor house in picturesque Corvedale setting; notable 18th-cent. interior work and stable block.*

Shrewsbury Castle At Shrewsbury *Map* DE 31. *12th cent., with later additions; 18th-cent. alterations by Thomas Telford; historic associations.* Presented to the Corporation in 1924.

Stokesay Castle Craven Arms 8½m S of Church Stretton on A49 *Map* D E 27. *One of the oldest 13th-cent. fortified manor houses in England; Castle last occupied in 18th cent.; Elizabethan gatehouse.* Lady Magnus-Allcroft.

Wenlock Abbey Much Wenlock 8m NW of Bridgnorth on A458 *Map* D G 29. *Pre-Conquest foundations of Cluniac monastery of St Milburga, privately maintained as a garden; 11th- to 15th-cent. priory; remains of 13th-cent. abbey nearby with chapter house.* Ministry of Public Building & Works.

Wroxeter Roman Town 5m SE of Shrewsbury on B4380 *Map* D F 30. *Remains of Roman Town of Uriconium A.D. 140–150; public baths and colonnade.*

Books for further reading

Local life and customs

S. EVANS *Shropshire Days and Shropshire Ways* 1938
ALFRED EDWARD HOUSMAN *The Shropshire Lad,* various edns
MARY WEBB *The Shropshire novels: Golden Arrow, Gone to Earth, House in Dormer Forest, Precious Bane,* and *Seven for a Secret*

Natural history

H. E. FORREST *Fauna of Shropshire* 1899
W. A. LEIGHTON *Flora of Shropshire* 1841

History and topography

THOMAS AUDEN *Shrewsbury: a Historical and Topographical Account of the Town* 2nd edn 1923; *Shropshire* (Oxford County Histories) 1912
M. HERRING *Shropshire* (Vision of England series) 1949
P. T. JONES *Welsh Border Country* 3rd edn 1949
ARTHUR MEE *Shropshire* (King's England series) 1968
J. B. OLDHAM *A History of Shrewsbury School 1552–1952* 1952
NIKOLAUS PEVSNER *Shropshire* (Buildings of England series) 1958
JOHN PIPER and JOHN BETJEMAN *Shropshire* (Shell Guides series) 1951
EDMUND VALE *Shropshire* (The County Books series) 1949
DOROTHY P. H. WRENN *Shrewsbury and Shropshire* 1968

Gazetteer

SHROPSHIRE

Bromfield　　　　　*G. Douglas Bolton*

Acton Burnell (DF 30) (230). The Georgian hall stands in a hilly park, with folly and two lakes; and, nearby, the ruined fortified manor house (AM), visited by Edward I in 1283, and built at the same time as the church by Robert Burnell, Bishop of Bath and Wells. To S, **Langley Chapel** (early 17th cent., with period furnishings) stands close by the walls and gatehouse of Langley Hall.

Alberbury (DD 31) (960). Church (Norman to 15th cent., with saddle-back tower and magnificent roof) connected by a wall to a ruined tower; Loton Park, Jacobean with additions; 2 m. SW, Braggington Manor, now a farm, 17th cent.; and, 2 m. S, the red sandstone tower of **Wattlesborough Castle** is incorporated in a farm, with moated garden.

Atcham (DF 30) EC Sat (390). Small village in a bend of the Severn, with concrete bridge carrying main Holyhead road, alongside earlier one of 1768. The Mytton and Mermaid Inn was previously a dower-house. Across the river, 1 m. to S, Cronkhill is a country house by John Nash. To N a drive leads from village to Attingham Park (NT and open to public), late 18th-cent., with period plaster ceilings and decoration, in grounds improved by Repton.

Battlefield (DF 31) EC Sat. Here, in 1403, Henry IV defeated Hotspur. So great was the slaughter that Robert Ive, rector of nearby Albright Hussey, built the church (1410) to commemorate the slain, together with an adjoining college for five chaplains and a master. This last, like his own church, has disappeared, and the chantry has taken its place. Albright Hussey Manor (timber and brick of 16th and 17th cents.) still stands within its dry moat.

Bishop's Castle (DD 28) EC Wed (1,230). Hilly borough in attractive Clun Forest country. The timbered 'House on Crotches' dates from 1573; the best 18th-cent. buildings are the town hall, the market house and the Castle Hotel (on the site of the vanished castle). Road to N leaves Stiperstones to the E and follows Hope Valley to **Minsterly**, 10 m. away, with attractive brick-and-stone church (1690), period pulpit and maids' garlands.

Bitterley (DF 27) (860). Pretty village at the foot of **Titterstone Clee Hill**, with **Brown Clee Hill** 6 m. away NNW, both over 1,700 ft. and both crowned with ancient British camps; here are fine views over Herefordshire to Radnor Forest. There is a church-yard cross, and the church has a Norman font, a Jacobean pulpit and monuments.

489

The Reader's House, Ludlow

Bridgnorth (DH 29) EC Thurs (7,550). Busy Low Town on the banks of the Severn (Thomas Percy, Bishop of Dromore, Ireland, famous for editing the *Percy Reliques*, was born in 1729 in the black-and-white house, built about 1580, that stands across the bridge by the old quay) is connected with enchanting High Town by a funicular railway and roundabout road. Here the half-timbered town hall (AM) divides High Street, with the restored north gate (now a museum) at one end, and the Georgian houses of East Castle Street at the other, which takes us to the leaning tower, sole relic of the Norman castle (AM), and, nearby, to St Mary Magdalene church, built by Telford in 1794. The charm of the place lies in the medieval atmosphere that pervades its streets of black-and-white houses, well viewed from the funicular. (*See* p. 483.)

Bromfield (DE 27) (420). At the junction of the Onny and Teme rivers, with a broad waterfall beside the footpath through Oakley Park. There is the stone, timbered gatehouse of a former priory, the nave of whose church now serves the village. (Note the great entrance porch, and the 17th-cent. painted chancel ceiling.) Near the station is Ludlow's racecourse.

Buildwas (DG 30) (240). The ruins of the 12th-cent. abbey are now AM; the six chimneys of the power station stand in contrast. (*See* p. 485.) Beside the Severn are a lido and a camping ground.

Burford (DF 26). Attractively situated in Teme Valley on Worcestershire border, with 18th-cent. red-brick rectory and restored church noteworthy for 15th-cent. Cornwalle monuments, including an earlier brass and later triptych by Melchior Salaboss, removed from altar to N wall of chancel.

Chirbury (DC 29) (910). Charming brick-and-stone village, with half-timbered school and church surrounded by yews. **Corndon Hill** (1,640 ft.) is 3 m. to E and Montgomery 2 m. in the other direction, across the border. **Marrington Hall,** one of the finest black-and-white buildings in the county, lies 1 m. to S E on the edge of Marrington Gorge.

Church Stretton (DE 29) EC Wed (2,170). An inland resort since end of last century. The neighbouring country is superb. A 2 m. walk up lovely **Cardingmill Valley** leads to Robin Hood's Butts (1,461 ft.) at the top of **Long Mynd,** a 10-m. stretch of moorland. 1½ m. N, **All Stretton** has a 16th-cent. manor and black-and-white cottages. **Acton Scott,** 3 m. S, has a fine brick Elizabethan hall in an attractive park.

Claverley (DH 29) (1,310). Half-timbered cottages and red sandstone church (Norman to Perpendicular, restored; with 13th-cent. wall-paintings, two fonts and an alabaster tomb). 1 m. NE, moated Ludstone Hall, restored Jacobean with formal gardens; 2 m. S, Georgian Gatacre Hall (home of Gatacre family since time of Edward the Confessor) and, beyond, Victorian-Elizabethan Gatacre Park on site of earlier Elizabethan mansion.

Cleobury Mortimer (DG 27) EC Thurs (1,190). Charming little town of timbered and Georgian houses, with very little building since mid-19th cent., except Gilbert Scott's restoration of the church. Fishing in the R. Rea, walking in Wyre Forest to E or on **Clee Hill,** which rises to over 1,600 ft. 6 m. W. 1 m. SE, Mawley Hall, a Georgian house, stands on a hill in a well-timbered park, with notable RC chapel.

Clun (DD 28) EC Wed (1,570). Market town, with stone bridge over R. Clun, and Clun Forest (no trees, but mile upon mile of rounded hills up to 1,300 ft., famous for sheep) to NW. Here are the ruins of the moated Norman castle once a stronghold in the Marches and still formidable; and the church, mainly of the same date, has later angels in the roof of the N aisle and a two-storied porch. The town hall was built in 1780; Trinity Hospital almshouses a century earlier, with wooden lantern, trim quadrangles and chapel. 9 m. W, running N and S of **Newcastle,** there is a stretch of the famous Offa's Dyke (*see* p. 483).

Coalbrookdale (*see* **Ironbridge**).

Condover 5 m. S of **Shrewsbury** (DF 30) EC Wed (950). Church originally Norman, but mainly 17th cent., pinkish stone with monuments from 1587 to 1868, one by G. F. Watts. Several old houses, but principally the fine Elizabethan hall, of the same stone as the church, gabled and mullioned, with a yew garden in the large park. Now a school for the blind, it may be seen by appointment in August. 3 m. SE, **Pitchford Hall** (16th cent.), the outstanding timbered house of the county, was occupied by 13 generations of the Ottley family, the first having bought the estate in 1473 and the last dying there in 1807. The church, adjacent to the house, mainly 13th cent. with 17th-cent. furnishings and, most impressive, an effigy of a medieval knight carved in oak.

Craven Arms (DE 28) EC Wed. Famous among sheep farmers for its sales; but to others for the countryside roundabout and **Stokesay Castle** (AM), an example of a 13th-cent. fortified manor house, with well-preserved Elizabethan gatehouse. The church here, largely rebuilt after damage in the Civil War, has 17th-cent.

furnishings, almost intact. Norton Camp is a Celtic camp on a wooded hill 2 m. SE. At **Onibury**, 2½ m. SSE, the interior of the little Norman church was attractively restored by craftsmen in 1902.

Diddlebury (DF 28). In Corvedale, at foot of **Wenlock Edge** (*see* Introduction p. 482), it has a Georgian hall with a park, and pre-Norman work in the church. 1¼ m. SW, Elsich Manor, timber and brick, has a moat. 3 m. E, 800 ft. up Brown Clee, the small **Heath Chapel**, lonely in a field, is perhaps the outstanding Norman structure in the county.

Ellesmere (DD 33) EC Thurs (2,250). All around are small lakes or 'meres'; the largest of them (113 acres), with boating and plenty of pike, comes right up to the town. Across it one glimpses rebuilt Ottley Park, with fallow deer that browse at the water's edge. Hardwick Hall is a red-brick building (1733) 1¾ m. W. At **St Martin's**, 3½ m. farther on, are Regency almshouses and one of the most remarkable churches in the county (13th cent. with much later tower), because of its pews, gallery and three-decker pulpit, which still has its velvet hangings.

High Ercall (DF 31). The last place except Ludlow to hold out against Parliament in the Civil War; the Hall (built 1608) was the Royalist HQ. In the course of the fighting, the church tower was badly damaged. The almshouses were built in 1694. 4 m. W, the Shrewsbury road passes the ruins of **Haughmond Abbey**, grey-green amongst ponds and woods. The Norman chapter house, with three fine arches, is complete; parts of the kitchen and the abbot's lodge also exist; and beyond stretches the great demesne of Sundorne Park (Jas Wyatt, 1800), on the edge of its 60-acre lake.

Hodnet (DG 32) EC Thurs (1,600). Main-road village, with black-and-white houses. The church has Norman priest's door, octagonal tower, monuments and chained books. The Hall (fine gardens open to the public) was built in 1870 to house the large family of Bishop Heber ('From Greenland's Icy Mountains'). 2 m. NW at **Hawkstone** is an attractive landscaped park, with a Queen Anne mansion (now housing RC students), a folly, grotto and lake, as well as a hotel and golf course.

Hopton Castle (DD 27) (100). Tiny half-timbered village, dominated by Norman keep of ruined castle beside a stream, with Hopton Titterhill rising 1,300 ft. behind.

Ironbridge (DG 30) EC Wed (1,810). Here, in this Severn gorge, was the centre of the 18th-cent. iron industry, whose secret is proclaimed by the names of neighbouring Coalbrookdale and Coalport. (*See* fuller account in Introduction p. 486.) 2 m. SW at **Benthall** is a well-restored late 17th-cent. church (box-pews and gallery), and the magnificent Hall (NT), built in 1535 of grey stone, with mullioned windows.

Kinlet (DH 28) (500). To N of Wyre Forest, its hall (1729) stands in a fine park; so also does the Norman to 14th-cent. church, with notable monuments, and some glass of the later period in the E window.

Leebotwood (DE 29) EC Thurs (210). Picturesque Pound Inn and black-and-white houses on the slopes of Lawley Hill. The church, not to be missed, is on a hill ½ m. off main road; lit by clear glass, there are box-pews, gallery and double-decker pulpit, quite unspoilt. Similar furnishings will be found at 13th-cent. **Longnor** Church, 2 m. N, where there is also a fine brick house of the 17th cent. (*See also* **Condover**.)

Lilleshall (DH 31) (8,000). Obelisk to first Duke of Sutherland (1833) on crag, and Leveson monument (1764) in restored 13th-cent. church. 12th-cent. abbey ruins (note carved Norman arch) crumbling by a stream 1 m. SE, at the edge of the park, where the modern Tudor hall (Wyatville, 1830) is now a national recreation centre. E across the main road, 7 m. away, at **Preston-on-the-Weald Moors,** a fine brick-and-stone hospital, flanked by lodges, stands behind elegant iron gates at the end of an avenue of trees.

Llan-y-blodwell (DC 32) (720). Pretty little inn beside the rushing Tanat, much favoured by anglers; but everyone can enjoy the lovely scenery from the hills above it. The church was rebuilt in the 19th cent., when the 15th-cent. screen was repainted. The hall, now a farm, has an 18th-cent. garden house.

Longville-in-the-Dale (DF 29). An Apedale village, with Wilderhope (NT) higher up the slopes of Wenlock Edge, an early 17th-cent. stone house now a youth hostel (can be viewed). 3 m. NE, Lutwyche Hall, part Elizabethan, part Queen Anne, is a handsome brick house standing in a park.

Ludlow★ (DF 27) EC Thurs (6,770). (*See* Introduction p. 483.) The pink sandstone castle, for centuries the seat of the President of the Council of the Marches, is a splendid ruin with a splendid viewpoint. Here Milton's *Comus* was performed in 1634; here

A wall of the chapter house, Much Wenlock priory

Edwin Smith

also Butler's *Hudibras* was written. Broad Street, leading through Broad Gate, and flanked with fine Georgian houses, takes us to Butter Cross, which stands among timbered black-and-white houses. The church is one of the noblest parish churches in the country, with carved screen and stalls and a magnificent window. In the church-yard are the ashes of A. E. Housman, author of *A Shropshire Lad*.

Lydbury North (DD 28) EC Wed (640). Pretty village below Clun Forest. The church has battlemented tower, a 15th-cent. screen and loft, and Plowden chapel. (Elizabethan Plowden Hall, with its own chapel and numerous hiding places, is 2 m. E.) Across the dammed-up stream, in a great park, Walcot, an 18th-cent. house, was bought by Clive of India, a Shropshireman, for his retirement.

Much Wenlock (DG 29) EC Wed (2,370). An attractively situated little town on the NE tip of Wenlock Edge, with Georgian houses and inns, some half-timbered: notably Raynald's Mansion, with its galleries; Guildhall (moveable stocks and panelled rooms); and Manor House (1577). The abbey ruins (AM) are considerable, mainly Early English, but the outstanding features are the interlaced Norman arches and doorways in the chapter-house wall. (*See also* Introduction on p. 482.)

Munslow (DF 28) EC Wed (374). A pretty lane leads from the main road to a group of limestone cottages, with Georgian rectory and medieval church of the same material (16th-cent. glass and timbered porch). Beyond, Milli-chope Park is a classical Regency House, with a lake and grounds. 3 m. E, **Broncroft Castle**, local red sandstone, 14th cent, with 19th-cent. additions, is still inhabited. (*See also* **Diddlebury** and **Rushbury**, both nearby.)

Oswestry (DC 32) EC Thurs (11,190). Situation rather than architecture distinguishes this busy town (Lloyd Mansion is the best of several half-timbered houses, and the Headmaster's House of the ancient grammer school is 18th cent.): the road rises to over 1,000 ft. in less than 2 m., with mountain views from the old race-course. A little to the N, Old Oswestry has an Iron Age hill-fort. (For **Whittington**, 2 m. E, *see below*.)

Preston Brockhurst (DF 32). Main-road village with little of interest except the 17th-cent. manor: but 2 m. W is Clive Hall, birthplace of Wm Wycherley; and, 2 m. SE, its quiet disturbed by an airfield, **Moreton Corbet** has ruins of late 16th-cent. castle (AM) and, nearby, much more impressive ruins of a mansion begun in 1606 but burnt before completion.

Shifnal (DH 30) EC Thurs (3,640). Attractive town, gradually losing to industrialization, but with fine houses in the neighbourhood: Haughton Hall (1718) beside its lake to NW; Aston Hall, classical 18th-cent., in park to E; and, 1 m. S beside a stream, moated and terraced Shifnal Manor, now a farm.

Shipton (DF 29) (126). Lovely Corvedale village, the inn, church and cottages making a group with the fine Elizabethan manor and 18th-cent. stables.

Shrewsbury* (DE 31) EC Thurs (49,730). Wonderfully situated, on a hill almost islanded by the Severn, which is crossed by two classic bridges (English and Welsh), and on its landward side is guarded by the castle (pink sandstone, notable for Telford's conversion to a private dwelling, now used by the Corporation). Its wealth of half-timbered buildings stands with fine 18th- and 19th-cent. work. The first are to be found everywhere, in

The bridge over the River Severn, Shrewsbury

Reece Winstone

alleys and side streets and particularly in Frankwell. Among the most admirable are: Henry VII's house and the Unicorn in Wyle Cop; Council House gateway; Whitehall, with gatehouse and dovecote; the Market Hall and Drapers' Guildhall; Ireland's, Owen's and Rowley's mansions (the last a museum and much restored); and houses in Grope Lane and Butcher Row. The outstanding structure of the 18th cent. is new St Chad's (1792), which looks out across the Quarry (*see* Introduction p. 483) and the river to Shrewsbury School, removed from the 1630 grammar school buildings (now public library, art gallery and museum). There are many Georgian town houses, for whose owners the Lion Hotel, an old posting-house with decorated ballroom, once catered; and Allat's School, Bowdler's School and Millington Hospital are all fine 18th-cent. classical buildings. St Mary's Church has wonderful 15th-cent. glass, and an older Jesse window in the E end; St Alkmund's spire is nearly 200 ft. high, and its interior 1795 Gothic; the inside of St Julian's was redesigned in 1748; but the Abbey Church, by the English Bridge, though over-restored, is mainly late Norman and Early English. (*See also* **Atcham, Battlefield** and **Condover**, all nearby.)

Telford (DG 30). This new town, to house eventually 200,000 people, is being created on land between Bridgnorth, Dawley and Wellington, and will incorporate the two latter towns and Oakengates. The first neighbourhood, Sutton Hill (8,000) with its pedestrian ways and traffic-free shopping centre is in existence, and the old village of Madeley will have a redesigned traffic-free shopping centre catering for 26,000 people by the spring of 1969.

Tong* (DH 30) (5,850). Justifiably one of the show places of the county. Its church, with unusual spire, was converted to a collegiate foundation in 1410 by Elizabeth de Pembruge, whose effigy lies with her husband's near the choir-screen. These are only two from a remarkable collection of tombs (mostly of the Vernon family) that, together with the fan-vaulting of the Golden Chantry and much fine timber-carving, make the place unique. **Boscobel House** (AM), Charles II's hiding place, is $3\frac{1}{2}$ m. E;

495

and, beyond, 18th-cent. Chillington Hall stands in its 1,000-acre park, looking out over its Great Pool.

Wellington (DG 31) EC Wed (13,630). The most distinguished feature of this mainly industrial town is the parish church built in 1790 by George Steuart. Just out of town to the S, the trees start to climb the Wrekin (1,335 ft.; *see* Introduction p. 482). Apley Castle, a Georgian brick house, stands in its park to the N. 5 m. W, at **Wroxeter**, is a church with coloured effigies and 17th-cent. furnishings, and nearby the excavated remains of Roman Uriconium (*see* Introduction p. 483).

Whitchurch (DF 34) EC Wed (7,160). A seemly little town, with many Georgian houses and Higginson's Almshouse, founded in 1647. The church was rebuilt in 1715; but, though there are noteworthy monuments, particularly the 15th-cent. Talbot tomb, much of the period beauty of the interior has been spoilt by restoration. To the S W stretches the primeval peat-bog known as **Fenn's Moss,** extending into **Flintshire.**

Whittington (DD 33) EC Thurs (2,471). 2 m. NE of Oswestry (*see above*), this village has romantic ruins where, beneath ivy-covered masonry, swans frequent the water-filled moat; the turreted twin towers of the gatehouse are splendidly intact and house the local library. The brick church, with its 1747 tower and nave rebuilt in 1804, is attractive from without.

Worfield (DH 29) EC Wed (4,680). Half-timbered village, with a fine church (spired tower and screen, both Perpendicular). Davenport House, a brick-and-stone building of 1726–7, stands adjacent in a pleasant park.

Worthen (DD 30) (1,960). With fishing in Rea Brook, and stone cottages and houses, as becomes a village so near the Welsh border. Its very wide church is filled with Elizabethan benches and Jacobean box-pews. 1½ m. NW, Hampton Hall is a 17th-cent. red-brick house, hidden in a valley on the slopes of Long Mountain.

The church at Tong   *Edwin Smith*

Moreton Old Hall

Reece Winstone

CHESHIRE AND FLINTSHIRE

AN INTRODUCTION BY FRANK SINGLETON

Despite its strong identity, Cheshire is one of those regions which tend to be thought of, superficially, as 'the gateway to . . .' – whether the south or north depends quite literally on the point of view. Bounded by Yorkshire, Derbyshire, Staffordshire, Shropshire, Denbighshire and Flintshire, any affinities it has are with Flintshire. It is least like Lancashire, with which, for so many purposes, it is popularly associated. It is possible to say 'We're Cheshire', with overtones which refuse to vibrate from 'We're Lancashire'. Anybody in Lancashire likely to say 'We visit on the other side' would not mean of the Pennines but of the Mersey. Cheshire is urbane, smart; and lots of lovely Manchester money has surrounded the pretty meres in the north with expensive attractive modern houses, their beautiful gardens in settings of woodland and water.

The county is a hollow plain, lying between the uplands of the Pennines and of North Wales. Here, as everywhere, the scenery and buildings indicate the nature of what lies beneath the surface of the earth. The varieties of Red Sandstone make Cheshire a plain, not uniformly flat, but diversified by gently rolling country, a rural, warm, red landscape in contrast to the greys and browns of Lancashire, as is its domestic architecture, black-and-white, to brick or stone. The climate is warmer, drier and sunnier than that part of the plain which stretches north into Lancashire. Such the county is essentially; but with characteristic English eccentricity it has an anomalous addition. To the north-east there stretches up beyond Stockport, thrusting up high into the Yorkshire Pennines, between Lancashire and the Peak district, a wild and alien arm, as unexpectedly out of character as would be the arm of one of the witches of Macbeth if suddenly skinned out by some soignée society beauty.

FLINTSHIRE

It is much easier to think of Flintshire, the smallest Welsh county, as a western extension into the Border country, which is here predominently English. The same undulating plain country, where sheep graze, stretches to the cattle-raising uplands. Flintshire, too, is so bounded on the south by Shropshire and Denbighshire as to contribute idiosyncracy to the map in the shape of a small enclave, known as Part of Flint. ('We're Flint.' 'We're Part of Flint.' Any overtones?) Flint and Cheshire also share the low and sandy coast with estuarine flats along the River Dee, across whose sands we seem for ever to hear Kingsley urging Mary to go and call the cattle home. The silting of this sand has reduced what was once busy shipping to the small craft of today, and has contributed the fine beaches which are among the amenities of the holiday resort, Rhyl, which was chosen as the starting-point for the world's first commercial hovercraft service. Passengers were swept on a bed of foam across the Dee estuary to Wallasey in twenty-five minutes, a journey which takes some hours by land. The service was an experimental one, but one hopes that the lessons learnt from it may make a hover from Rhyl to Wallasey a durable attraction on this coast.

This westward extension of the plain ends in Flintshire's steep limestone escarpment, which rises to 1,800 feet facing north behind Prestatyn, Rhyl's only rival as a holiday resort. The line of the hills along the south-west boundary is dominated by Moel Fammau, visible on clear days from the Lancashire moors. The Snowdon range, as a whole, standing as it does in the course of the prevailing south-westerly winds, shelters Flintshire, Cheshire and indeed Lancashire as far north as the Ribble from the heavier rainfalls elsewhere. The upland looks down for several miles on the picturesque Vale of Clwyd, and this, together with Watt's and Offa's dykes which traverse the county, bring reminders that this is border country and that beyond the mountains when the sun goes down it is 'evening on the olden, the golden sea of Wales'.

In Flintshire itself the English have managed to predominate: only a minority of the people speak Welsh. The small city of St Asaph has, appropriately, one of the smallest cathedrals. Mainly Decorated in style, it is a plain cruciform red-sandstone structure, rebuilt in 1284 and restored between 1867 and 1874. Also in Flintshire is Hawarden, where long into the evening of his days Mr Gladstone wielded his axe, felling trees and pondering Homer, theology or the necessity of forming yet another administration. 'Stop here or gently pass.'

Agriculture and Industry

Agriculture still thrives in Flintshire. Dairy and arable farming predominate in areas where the soil is rich, while poorer quality higher land is given over to sheep farming. Modernization and mechanization of the county's farming industry has been greatly assisted by the manufacture of agricultural machinery at Mold and the training facilities of the horticultural institute at Northup, under the auspices of the County Education Authority. There is evidence of forestry and timber industry in Flintshire, which can best be seen in the conifer woods of the inland uplands of the county.

Flintshire, despite its small area, plays a major role in the industrial life of Wales. Important mineral deposits found in Flintshire are lead, coal, limestone, boulder clay and fireclay, all of which have fostered significant local industries. The county's largest industrial concerns are now steel works at Shotton, textile works at Flint and Greenfield, and aircraft factories at Broughton. The College of Technology at Connah's Quay, which receives financial support from the local industries, assists with the instruction of young people in the skills and techniques necessary for the maintenance of the established industries. The new glass factory at St Asaph typifies the mode of recent advance of industry in Flintshire.

· CHESHIRE

Agriculture and Towns

Cheshire continues northwards to include other estuarine resources; for between the mouths of Dee and Mersey there thrusts out, north-westwards into the Irish Sea, the wedge of the Wirral Peninsula. This is a ridge-and-vale country, presenting a typical Cheshire landscape of grass, arable, heath and mixed-farming country with distant views of the Welsh hills. The northern coast has become a dormitory area for Birkenhead, Cheshire's big-city equivalent to Liverpool, across the Mersey. This expansion of Liverpool's activities boasts not only great docks and ship-building yards but continuously expanding residential amenities, especially on the rising ground leading to Bidston, Oxton and Prenton hills. Wirral, beloved of the bird-watchers, ends just short of Chester, greatest and most beautiful of the county's towns. Along Merseyside and hugging the conurbation of greater Manchester are Cheshire's chief suburban centres. The heart of the county is mainly rural and agricultural. Potatoes and milk are the main products. The pastures are carefully tended: the grazing season for high-yielding cows is long. Farm buildings are well-planned and well-built.

The traveller, newly arrived at Liverpool, sees the evidence of this from the train, as the green, grassy landscape, the rich pastures for the grazing cattle, roll gently up to the first slopes of the Pennines on the east. 'How lush and lusty the grass looks – how green!'

Industry

Cheshire's industrial resources have not ruined the agricultural scene; but they are still there, and valuable. The only coalfield is a narrow strip along the Pennines – really an extension of Lancashire, as are the textile manufactures of

The estuary, Rhyl

the adjacent towns of Stockport, Macclesfield (famous for its silk manufacture), Hyde, Dukinfield and Congleton. Besides coal, Cheshire has beneath the soil another source of wealth more peculiar to her – salt. Under the rich grasslands run the salt deposits, liable to subside at times. Here and there a church spire leaning at a strange angle is a reminder. The ancient industry of salt-mining is responsible for some of Cheshire's most characteristic features. All around Nantwich, which has famous brine baths, are little meres caused by the subsidence of stretches of land which have been mined below. Here, and at Middlewich and Northwich, conveniently placed for distributing their products to the many businesses who use them so widely, are the famous alkali works where Sir John Brunner and Dr Ludwig Mond established a thriving concern from which grew Imperial Chemical Industries.

Not far away is Crewe, a paradise for train-spotters and all interested in railways, which were the sole begetters of this home of 50,000 people, many connected in some way with the great locomotive works. A modern town of great charm and interest is Port Sunlight, which Lord Leverhulme created by the estuary of the Mersey. He started by reclaiming the great area of swamp; and then built the town that not only includes all the miracles of industrial science but expresses his belief that nothing need be ugly. Every amenity serves the community. Its crowning glory is the Lady Lever Art Gallery.

Mirror of the Plain

Alderley Edge is a woodland district on the western side of the ridge which runs through mid-Cheshire, and which, like any ground that presumes to rise in a plain, enjoys disproportionate advantages.

The plain and the rich variety of what it contains can be seen, as well as anywhere, from the heights which, by contrast, seem to rise abruptly. On a summer day you look over a changing scene of green fields, black-and-white farms and houses, woodlands, the meres gleaming through the trees, and rivulets and little rivers winding across the rich meadows. In the Middle Ages this was a great area of natural woodland. Today there are extensive plantations of conifers. From Eddisbury hill you can see far, and all around they have built sanatoria at heights by no means impressive to Lancashire, which can see some of them from heights twice their measure. This Cheshire plain has mirrored the changing history of the county since earliest times, through Cheshire's part in each chapter of the island story. The crowning glory of Cheshire is Chester, which is indeed one of the glories of England.

History

Castra – a camp. And what a camp! – guarding the coastal gate of the road into England that avoided the mountains of Wales, and the sea-gate through which invaders from the River Dee came, until in the 15th century the sands, so ruinous in other ways, in this case provided protection. There are many remains of Roman occupation and traces of Roman roads. Every year more relics of Rome are raised from below the town built over the ruins in the Middle Ages. Today Chester is largely a medieval city assailed by strangling problems of traffic; but in so many ways it is unchanging. It is full of beguiling black-and-white houses and other buildings. One of its most famous features is the Rows, which convert the pathways into shadowed corridors along their length – a medieval arrangement which, for once, affords the pedestrian some refuge from the roaring

Tatton Park, near Knutsford *J. Allan Cash*

Elizabethan farmhouse, Henbury, Cheshire   *J. Allan Cash*

traffic. The castle looms up on its height. The cathedral glows rosily in sandstone. Grey and slender church pinnacles, big doll's house structures with bulging windows, the old bridge spanning the slow river, make the place a sort of magic, fairytale setting for all the events of the crowded past, not always so gentle as it may seem, not including in the story, war, plague and scarcity. J. Cuming Walters, most charming of writers on the county, gives a good account (particularly of the Rows) in what he calls 'one of the most picturesque of cities where we can set our feet on fragments of Watling Street, can enter crypts which have never yielded up the secret of their origin and purpose, linger in the arched stone corridors, the Rows, and, leaning over the balconies, muse why these balustraded passages were ever constructed. For there is nothing like them elsewhere. These Rows run parallel with the streets, the front portions of their second storeys forming a paved promenade reached by steps from the paths below. The galleries are open in front – beneath are the shops and warehouses. Was this a device to secure the wares of the merchandise against possible Welsh marauders?'

At Domesday, Cheshire included the parts of Lancashire between Mersey and Ribble, as well as parts of what is now called Flintshire, and was raised to the status of county palatine, a dignity much diminished by Henry the Third. Prince Edward (later Edward the First) was, however, created Earl of Chester, a title which has generally been borne by the Prince of Wales. The Middle Ages are epitomized in Chester and its cathedral, the Tudor period in the many examples of domestic black-and-white architecture – some, such as Moreton Old Hall, Bramall and Gawsworth rectory, among the finest in the country.

Cheshire has originated many great and famous families. For those who cherish a love of Mrs Gaskell's *Cranford*, the increasingly modernizing town of Knutsford cannot entirely dispel the shades of Miss Mattie and Miss Pole and their well-loved associates.

Food

Dairy farming enabled Cheshire to produce a famous cheese, less crumbly than Lancashire, not so hard as Double Gloucester. George Borrow's dictum that if you would enjoy the famous Cheshire cheese do not look for it in Chester is probably no longer true. If it is, you may find it anywhere else in the county. Cheshire's greatest delicacy is perhaps not so famous; but there is no doubt the best shrimps in the world are from Parkgate, on the estuary of the Dee – nothing more delicious than a pot of parkgaters. You can find residents with whom you can leave a pound and they will post shrimps to you, once a week or what have you.

Cheshire is a good place for eating out, often in picturesque surroundings in country villages, and Flintshire can muscle in here with pleasant inns which are often good for the salmon which the Dee very acceptably yields.

Lewis Carroll window in Daresbury church

Reece Winstone

Some houses and gardens open to the public

Adlington Hall 5m N of Macclesfield off A523 *Map* D K 38. *Partly Elizabethan 'Black & White', partly 18th cent.; Handel associations and 'Bernard Smith' organ, restored 1959.*

Beeston Castle 3m S of Tarporley off A49 *Map* D F 35. *13th-cent. stronghold built by the 6th Earl of Chester, on a steep hill.*

Bramall Hall Bramhall 2m S of Stockport off A5102 *Map* D J 38. *15th-cent. half-timbered building.*

Chester Castle At Chester *Map* D E 36. *19th cent., preserving ancient Agricola Tower, which now houses museum of the Cheshire Regiment.*

Flint Castle At Flint *Map* D C 37. *13th cent., built by Edward I; in ruins; detached circular keep surrounded by moat.*

Hawarden Castle 7m W of Chester *Map* D D 36. *Ruined castle, visited by Henry VII and twice besieged during 17th-cent. Civil Wars.*

Lyme Hall Disley 7m SE of Stockport off A6 *Map* D K 38. *Elizabethan, with 18th- & 19th-cent. additions, Palladian façade, Jacobean rooms, pictures and furnishings. Noted for its tapestries, period furniture and Grinling Gibbons carvings.*

Little Moreton Old Hall 4m SW of Congleton on A34 *Map* D J 35 *Surrounded by a moat with access across a stone bridge, Little Moreton Hall is a fine example of 16th c. half-timbered construction with bold black and white patterns. The house is a complex of overhangs, irregular lines and seemingly dangerous though picturesque angles.*

Rhuddlan Castle 3m S of Rhyl off A547 *Map* D A 37. *13th cent., built by Edward I; round towers, gatehouses and 9-ft-thick curtain walls. Excellent preserved moat.*

Tatton Park 3½m NE of Knutsford *Map* D H 38. *Entrance on Ashley Road, 1½m NE of junction of A5034 with A50. 18th-cent. Georgian house by Samuel and Lewis Wyatt. Gardens and park (2,000 acres) landscaped by Humphrey Repton.* NT property leased to Cheshire County Council.

Books for further reading

The 'feel' of Cheshire and Flintshire

S. J. COLEMAN *Lore and Legend of Flintshire* 1956
ELIZABETH GASKELL *Cranford*
CHRISTINA HOLE *Traditions and Customs of Cheshire* 1937
H. HUGHES *Cheshire and its Welsh Border* 1966
J. H. INGRAM *Companion into Cheshire* 1947
J. MORLEY *Life of Gladstone* 1903
J. C. WALTERS *Romantic Cheshire* 1930
H. WILLIAMS *They Lived in Flintshire* 1960

Natural history

A. W. BOYD *The Country Diary of a Cheshire Man* 1946
T. A. COWARD *The Fauna of Cheshire* 2 vols. 1910
J. B. L. WARREN *The Flora of Cheshire* 1899

FLINTSHIRE ORNITHOLOGICAL SOCIETY *The Birds of Flintshire* 1968

History and topography

CHESHIRE COMMUNITY COUNCIL *A History of Cheshire*
E. DAVIES *Flintshire Place-Names* 1959; *Prehistoric and Roman Remains of Flintshire* 1949
SIR J. G. EDWARDS *The Building of Flint* (Flintshire Historical Publications vol. 12)
N. F. ELLISON *The Wirral Peninsula* 1955
FLINTSHIRE COUNTY LIBRARY *Guides to the Castles of Ewloe, Flint and Rhuddlan and to the Abbey of Basingwerk*
W. M. GALLICHAN *Cheshire* 1957
H. HUGHES *Cheshire and its Welsh Border* 1966
ARTHUR MEE *Cheshire* 1950
C. R. WILLIAMS ed. *History of Flintshire* vol. I 1961

Gazetteer

CHESHIRE AND FLINTSHIRE

Adlington Hall *Ches.* (DK 38). One wing of this half-timbered house was built in 1581, but the Legh family lived here before then. The Great Hall contains an 18th-cent. organ which Handel is said to have played.

Alderley Edge *Ches.* (DJ 37) EC Wed (3,620). 'The Edge' is a cliff making a viewpoint over comparatively low country. Alderley Old Mill (1½ m.) is NT property.

Basingwerk Abbey *Flints.* (DC 37). A religious house founded in 1132 for the Savigniac Order but in 1147 transferred to the Cistercians. Parts of the church and monastic buildings have survived.

Beeston Castle *Ches.* (DF 35) (280). The ruins of a 13th-cent. castle, modelled from a Saracen fortress, stand on an outcrop of red sandstone and give a remarkable view of the county.

Birkenhead *Ches.* (DC 39) EC Thurs (141,680). Keeps its identity, though mainly dependent on its docks, which were amalgamated with Liverpool's in 1847. The physical links with Liverpool on the other side of the river are the Mersey tunnel and the ferry-boats. Little survives from before the Industrial Revolution except the ruins of a 12th-cent. Benedictine priory, which include the chapter-house, the crypt and part of the refectory. This absence of ancient monuments is explained by the fact that a hundred and fifty years ago Birkenhead was a small village.

Chester Cathedral   *J. Allan Cash*

Bramall Hall *Ches.* (DJ 38). In the Domesday Book, Bramhall village appears as Bramale, but neither spelling is accepted by the owners of the Hall. It is an admirable example of the timber-and-plaster construction of the late 16th cent., incorporating earlier work. The contents are equally fine.

Cat and Fiddle Inn *Ches.* (EA 37). The second highest licensed premises in England (1,690 ft.) make a base★ for moorland walks towards Macclesfield Forest.

Chester★★ (DE 36) EC Wed (59,280). Though they follow the line of the Roman fortifications on two sides, the town walls are mainly medieval, built of local red sandstone and varying in height from 12 to 40 ft. There are many towers – King Charles's Tower from which he watched the Battle of Rowton Moor, Pemberton's Parlour and Bonewaldesthorne's Tower are a few of them – and many gates. All differ in form and history.

Of the Roman remains, the amphi-theatre is the most remarkable. It

505

The old Dee Bridge at Chester

may well have had provision for 9,000 spectators, although much of it has still to be excavated.

The cathedral is built of the same red sandstone as the city walls. It began as a college for canons and then became a Benedictine abbey. A large amount of rebuilding was done in the 14th and 15th cents., but not until after the Reformation did the abbey church become a cathedral. Comprehensive restoration work was undertaken in the last half of the 19th cent. The 14th-cent. stalls repay close scrutiny. The Spanish ironwork of the gates into the choir aisles is exceptional; so too are the Early English Lady Chapel and the reconstructed shrine of St Werburgh. The detail in the cathedral is enhanced by a rosy light reflected from the stone.

The bridge over the Dee, built in the 13th and 14th cents. is unusually picturesque through the lack of symmetry in its seven arches. The Rows have been mentioned in the Introduction. There are also many town houses, inns, alleys and churches, of which the best is St John's, partly ruined, on an incomparable site above the Dee.

Clwyd, Vale of *Flints*. (DA 37). Fertile land bounded by mountains: an approach to more grandiose Welsh scenery.

Combermere Abbey *Ches*. (DF 34). Site of a Cistercian foundation. It is said that submerged bells can be heard from the depths of the lake.

Congleton *Ches*. (DJ 36) EC Wed (16,800). Traditionally a silk-manufacturing town, which cherishes many customs including 'St Peter's Chains' or 'The Sweep's Bells': these were strapped to acolytes who danced through the streets on the eve of the feast of St Peter to proclaim the forthcoming wakes.

Crewe *Ches*. (DH 35) EC Wed (53,390). The railway junction takes about 600 trains each day; the population is mainly engaged at the locomotive works.

Daresbury *Ches*. (DF 38) EC Thurs (280). Birthplace of the Rev. C. L. Dodgson (Lewis Carroll), author of *Alice in Wonderland* and inventor of the Cheshire Cat.

Doddington *Ches*. (DH 34). The hall is late 18th-cent., but the tower in the grounds was built in 1364. Near the balustraded steps leading to it are four statues; one of them represents Lord Audley, the hero of Poictiers.

Dyserth *Flints*. (DA 37) (1,630). In the church, the Jesse window (one illustrating the genealogy of Christ) and a very early cross should not be missed. Dr Johnson 'trudged unwillingly' to a nearby waterfall, which he was delighted to find dry.

Eaton Hall *Ches*. (DE 36). Once the family seat of the Duke of Westminster, it has been almost entirely demolished.

Ellesmere Port *Ches*. (DE 37) EC Wed (44,710). One of the first steam-ferry ports, where the Ellesmere Canal joins the Ship Canal and the Mersey. A fuel-saving experiment, with horses working a treadmill on board, did not survive its pilot scheme.

Ewloe *Flints*. (DC 36) EC Wed. The castle was a stronghold of Llewelyn ap Gruffydd, and later witnessed the defeat of Henry II. The apsidal Welsh tower and the circular one to the W were built in the 13th century.

Farndon *Ches*. (DE 35) (810). Birthplace of the cartographer John Speed (1552–1629).

Flint *Flints*. (DC 37) EC Wed (14,290). With its Great Tower, the plan of the castle is unique in Britain, though it has parallels in France. The English building, begun by Edward I, is a melancholy place washed by shallow tides.

Gawsworth *Ches*. (DJ 36) EC Wed (1,370). Though the church of this picturesque village was impaired by Victorian restorers who objected to the 'popishness' of the pre-Reformation works of art, the timbered rectory and the hall escaped. Here lived Mary Fitton, thought by some to be the 'dark lady' of Shakespeare's sonnets.

Havanna *Ches*. (DJ 36). Once occupied in the manufacture of cigars.

Hawarden *Flints*. (DD 36) EC Wed (19,140). The home for 60 years of William Ewart Gladstone (1809–98) is not open to the public, but the old castle in the grounds may be visited on certain afternoons. The circular keep and the remains of the banqueting hall are imposing and command a fine view. In the church is a stained-glass window by Burne-Jones to commemorate the statesman.

Holywell *Flints*. (DB 37) EC Wed (8,610). The Well of St Winefride has been diverted by mining operations, and is now fed from a reservoir into the original bath in the crypt of a chapel built in 1480 by the mother of Henry VII. Legend proclaims that water burst out of the ground at the spot where the saint's head rolled after being severed by Prince Caradoc, whose advances she spurned. Since earliest times this has been a place of pilgrims, a hospice for whom was erected as late as 1870.

Hoylake *Ches*. (DC 38) EC Wed (32,270). Nowadays a seaside resort with a famous golf course, but previously a harbour, 'The Hoyle

Gawsworth Old Hall

G. Douglas Bolton

Lake', from which William III set out for Ireland in 1689 to fight the Battle of the Boyne, and where ships lightened their cargoes before sailing up the Mersey.

Knutsford★ *Ches.* (DH 37) EC Wed (9,390). Mrs Gaskell, who wrote of this small town as *Cranford*, is buried in the Unitarian graveyard. A local custom was to sand the streets for a wedding and to make designs at the entrance to the bride's home.

Leasowe *Ches.* (DC 38). The original purpose of the castle, now a railwaymen's convalescent home, is obscure, though it is more likely to have been defensive than to have made a grandstand for races, as some authorities declare. In Commonwealth days, when the Stanley family to whom it belonged became unpopular, it was known as Mockbeggar Hall.

Little Moreton *Ches.* (DJ 35).

Moreton Old Hall★, with its moat, is one of the most perfect examples of this county's Tudor and Elizabethan manor houses. An inscription at the Great Hall tells us how 'Rycharde Dale Carpeder' made the magnificent windows in 1559 'by the grac of god'.

Llanasa *Flints.* (DB 38). The church has windows, set up from 1501 to 1520, depicting the instruments of Christ's crucifixion: a cock and the hand of Judas grasping a bag of money.

Longdendale *Ches.* (EA 39). Running into Yorkshire and Derbyshire, this was formerly marsh but now is a string of reservoirs.

Lyme Hall *Ches.* (DK 38). An Elizabethan house, twice altered, where Mary Queen of Scots stayed when, though in captivity, she was allowed to take the waters at Buxton as a cure for rheumatism. A herd

508

of indigenous red deer have been bred here for centuries by the Legh family.

Lymm *Ches.* (DG 38) EC Wed (7,330). The age of the market cross, which stands on a sandstone dais, has baffled experts. It is surmounted by a weathercock, and has two stocks at its foot.

Macclesfield *Ches.* (DK 37) EC Wed (37,580). Some of the street names of this traditionally silk-manufacturing town are clues to its earlier plan: Jordansgate, Chestergate. The 13th-cent. St Michael's (a church which has been well restored) has fragments of crosses taken from some earlier building. The Legh and Savage Chapels contain memorials of both these families; the most notable is the fragmentary 'Pardon Brass' of Roger Legh, who died in 1506.

Moel Fammau *Flints.* (DB 36). The highest point (1,820 ft.) in the Clwyd Mountains, surmounted by the remains of a tower erected on George III's Jubilee in 1820, but later blown down. The views towards Derbyshire and Snowdonia are magnificent.

Mold *Flints.* (DC 36) EC Thurs (7,730). The county town containing a new Civic Centre, comprising Shire Hall, Law Courts and County Library Headquarters, erected in parkland surroundings on the outskirts of the town. Mold has a fine 15th-cent. church where the painter Richard Wilson is buried. The foremost Welsh novelist, Daniel Owen, is the town's most famous son, commemorated by a statue near the town centre.

Offa's Dyke (DC 36). This originally ran from Prestatyn to the estuary of the Severn, and acted as a defence against the Welsh.

Parkgate *Ches.* (DC 37) EC Wed (with Neston, 11,830). Once the starting-point of the Dublin packet, used by many famous persons, including Handel.

Port Sunlight *Ches.* (DD 38) EC Thurs (3,740). Lord Leverhulme built this as a new town for his employees, complete with public buildings and the Lady Lever Art Gallery.

Prestatyn *Flints.* (DA 38) EC Thurs (13,200). The county's second holiday resort.

Port Sunlight

Edwin Smith

Deer in Lyme Park

G. Douglas Bolton

Rhuddlan *Flints*. (DA 37) EC Thurs (2,600). A castle built in the last half of the 13th cent. to guard the mouth of the Clwyd and the coastal route to Wales. Richard II was imprisoned here. It was 'slighted' by the Parliamentarians in 1646.

Rhyl *Flints*. (DA 38) EC Thurs (21,370). Popular seaside resort, with tides that recede far across the sands.

Runcorn *Ches*. (DF 38) EC Wed (26,030). The Cheshire end of the Runcorn-Widnes bridge, with a span of 1,082 ft. of steel, is the largest arch in Europe, third largest in the world.

St Asaph *Flints*. (DA 37) EC Thurs (2,552). In this 'village city' the most notable building is the small cathedral (182 ft. long, 65 ft. wide and 108 ft. across the transepts). It was destroyed by the English in 1282 and rebuilt; its woodwork was burnt by Owen Glendower, its tower overthrown by a storm, but it has survived with many treasures, including a collection of early Bibles and prayer-books kept at the chapter-house.

Sandbach *Ches*. (DH 36) EC Tues (9,860). A 17th-cent. writer proclaimed that 'the scituation of the Town is very delightsome', and this remains true. Two tall crosses in the market place have been shattered, removed piecemeal, defaced, and used as garden ornaments before finally being restored to their site and reconstructed.

Stockport *Ches*. (DK 39) EC Thurs (142,470). A manufacturing town that developed a sideline in top-hats. A statue of Richard Cobden (1804–65), who was MP for Stockport and engaged in the repeal of the Corn Laws, stands in St Peter's Square.

Tabley Hall *Ches*. (DH 37). The Old Hall is on an island in the grounds of the newer 18th-cent. house. Its great hall, staircase and gallery are threatened

Rhuddlan Castle

G. *Douglas Bolton*

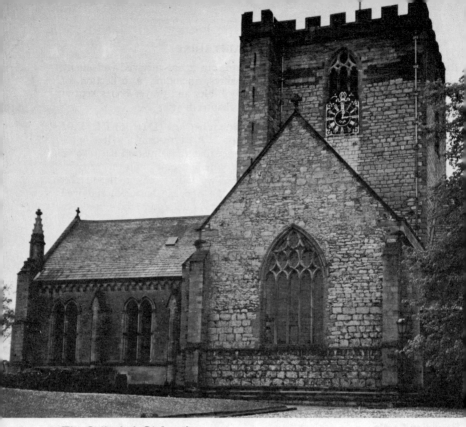

The Cathedral, St Asaph

G. Douglas Bolton

by subsidence through brine-pumping. A little church has been removed from the island to the greater security of the park.

Upton *Ches.* (DE 36) EC Wed (7,700). Zoological gardens 2 m. N of Chester, showing animals in naturalistic surroundings: a smaller Whipsnade.

Vale Royal *Ches.* (DG 36). A hotel and country club occupy the site of a Cistercian abbey built of Eddisbury stone in Edward I's reign. The foundations mark it as having had a greater length (421 ft.) than even Fountains Abbey.

Wallasey *Ches.* (DC 39) EC Wed (103,210). A county borough of six townships across the Great Float

(docks and ship-building) at the NE corner of the Wirral peninsula.

West Kirby *Ches.* (DC 38) EC Wed. Seaside town overlooking Hilbre Island (once an important telegraph station) and the mountains of Wales. There is known to have been a church at 'Cherchebie' before the Norman Conquest.

Wirral, *Ches.* (DD 38) (21,850). The peninsula between the Mersey and the Dee was originally an extensive Royal forest and game-preserve – and the home of outlaws.

Woodhead *Ches.* (EA 39). Here the railway emerges from the Pennine 'backbone of England' after a three-mile short cut underground from Yorkshire.

Opposite: Detail from the original painting by Thomas Swimmer.

Between the Pennines and the hills of North Wales, Cheshire lies in a plain, sharing with Flintshire the coastal flats along the Dee. Here we find many half-timbered houses, such as Moreton Old Hall. On a more modern note, we remember that Crewe takes 600 trains a day. The picture reminds us also of fishing and shrimping, and the famous Cheshire cheese. Hawarden, in Flintshire, was for most of his life the home of Gladstone.

THE ROWS, CHESTER

FINEST PARKGATE SHRIMPS

SONS
AND
LOVERS

D. H. LAWRENCE

Nottingham Castle

NOTTINGHAMSHIRE

AN INTRODUCTION BY M. W. BARLEY

In this motor-car age, many people know England well enough to pick out a coastal county by its resorts and coastal scenery, but would find it much more difficult to signalize the character of a midland county. Yet Nottinghamshire has its own pattern of scenery, distinct and attractive, if the traveller has the eye and patience to find it.

The Rock Beneath

In this county more than in most the scenery grows out of the rock, and one cannot be seen clearly without understanding the other. The bony structure, as it were, is a fairly simple one. Successive layers of sedimentary rock were later tilted down to the east, so that as one drives from Mansfield through Newark towards the east coast, one crosses first the sandstones of Sherwood Forest, then clays beginning at Ollerton, and eventually (east of the Trent) the lias limestone. Each zone has its distinctive scenery and has given character to its part of the county. In the west the narrow band of magnesian limestone, hard and very good for building, has the hilliest scenery of the county. In the gently rolling county of the sandstones, the fields are sometimes covered with pebbles,

Opposite: Detail from the original painting by David Gentleman.

In this county stands Byron's ancestral home, Newstead. Against the monument that Byron set up to his dog Boatswain we see the landscape painter Bonington, the son of a Nottingham lace merchant. D. H. Lawrence, another Nottinghamshire man, expressed in his *Sons and Lovers* the county's blend of coal and leaf On the left is a painted water-can from a barge on the Trent, set upon a shawl of Nottingham lace.

The castle gateway, Nottingham

Reece Winstone

and the soil is so sandy and poor that until modern times farmers could do little with it: the area was royal forest, reserved for hunting. The sandstone soaks up water like a sponge, so that while farmers are short of it on the surface, the lower levels have great supplies, which modern engineers can pump up to supply Nottingham, Newark and other towns. The rock is easily cut, and underneath Nottingham's buildings there is a fantastic honeycomb of caves, wells and passages, some of which may be a thousand years old; while Mansfield's rock-dwellings were inhabited until quite recently.

The clays, stretching from the Trent at Radcliffe to the northern boundary at Gringley on the Hill, form a plateau in the centre of the county, its edges cut by valleys and 'dumbles' in the Southwell-Farnsfield area; the steep slopes of red soil and tree-lined valleys are as attractive as any part of the county.

It is easy for the traveller to tell where he passes from one formation to another, because each western edge forms a pronounced scarp. The road from Nottingham through Ollerton runs on the sandstone (because it is dry) and the clay scarp of the Keuper Marl lies in view to the east. Going from Ollerton to Tuxford, the short hill in Kirton takes the road up on to the Keuper Marl plateau; so does the road from Retford to Gainsborough at Clarborough. The next pronounced step, going eastwards, lies just outside the county boundary but frames its scenery: the Belvoir Hills to the south-east and the limestone ridge of south Lincolnshire stretching from Barrowby Hill to Lincoln.

NOTTINGHAMSHIRE

Overlying this simple pattern, and complicating it somewhat, are rivers, geologically new, and other deposits made during or since the Ice Age. The River Trent, which once flowed east from Nottingham, now curves north past Newark; it has cut its way through the red clays of the Keuper Marl (Radcliffe on Trent, Clifton) so that at Gunthorpe and Hazelford there are steep, tree-covered bluffs visible on the other bank. The Trent has also laid down a wide band of gravel and other alluvial deposits all the way from Attenborough to the Lincolnshire boundary. In the south-east, the Nottinghamshire Wolds consist of boulder-clays laid down during the Ice Age; they were once wooded (hence *wolds*), but are now mostly under grass.

To someone attached to, say, the Yorkshire Dales or the Lake District, the Vale of Trent and the Vale of Belvoir may seem undistinguished; but, seen from vantage points like East Bridgford, the high ground north of Tuxford, or Broughton Hill on the Melton Mowbray road, the immense sweeps of wood and field with silver rivers, church spires and power-stations seen through a misty air have a strong charm of their own.

Local Industry

For two thousand years man has been busy taking what he needed from these soils and changing the landscape. On the western boundary the River Erewash cuts through the coal measures, which must have been worked in Roman times, judging from the coal found on Roman sites in the east midlands. Wollaton Hall, one of the grandest Elizabethan mansions in England, now within the boundaries of Nottingham, was built in 1588 from the profits of coal. Now the Nottinghamshire-Derbyshire-Yorkshire coalfield is the most productive in

Thoresby Park   J. Allan Cash

England. Those who choose to explore the western band of the county can discern, through the chaotic scatter of mining, old and new, and the villages which it has created, untouched pockets of beautiful country: the winding lanes, deep valleys and small woods round Teversal, or the more open but very secluded farmland round the site of Beauvale Priory. As techniques have improved, new mines have been sunk to greater depths and farther east, including the first south of the Trent, at Cotgrave. These modern mines regenerate old villages, but remain otherwise quite unobtrusive.

The gypsum found in the Keuper Marl also created an old industry – quarrying alabaster for church monuments and furniture, which were made up in Nottingham, and, more recently, working its softer forms to make plaster for floors and walls. All the older houses in the county have plaster floors; and since 1946 new quarries and mines have been opened at Staunton near Newark and at Gotham south of Nottingham for the production of plaster-board in great quantities. At Barnstone, at the foot of the Belvoir Hills, the lias limestone is quarried for cement.

Modern industry has an immense appetite for gravel and concrete; and great lagoons have been created in the Trent Valley, at Attenborough, Hoveringham and north of Newark. They have added a new element to the scene – sailing-boats. They have also filled local museums with prehistoric dug-out canoes and many other finds. The newest industry of all is electricity. Power-stations line the Trent and the Soar (Wilford, Staythorpe, High Marnham, West Burton and Ratcliffe-on-Soar), using local coal, river-water for cooling and some of the gravel-lagoons as ash-dumps. The great cooling-towers are strikingly impressive at a distance; but near at hand the acres of railway sidings and the power-lines crossing every field make a mess of the landscape. Nevertheless, the Nottinghamshire scene is everywhere, rural and predominantly clean.

One local industry has altered villages and created towns without directly affecting the landscape. William Lee, an Elizabethan parson born at Calverton, invented a machine for knitting stockings. Eventually Nottingham and nearby villages became famous for its stockings; thousands of cottages had frames in them, and the last framework knitters are still living. The frames were usually in an upstairs room and lighted by a long window, examples of which can still occasionally be seen.

Old Routes and New

The traveller, whether hurrying on business or exploring with his wife and family on a Sunday afternoon, ought to give a thought to the age of the routes he uses. The enterprising can put a boat on the Trent, as man has done from earliest times. Modern man has canalized it (locks at Gunthorpe, Newark, Cromwell and elsewhere), deepened its course and confined it between flood banks.

One Roman road cuts through Nottinghamshire, the Fosse Way on its course from Axminster through Bath and Leicester to Lincoln, and another, from Lincoln to Doncaster, crosses the northern part of the county. There are other, far older roads. They either follow high ground, such as the Soar and Trent banks, or else make for crossings of the Trent. The Soar ridge-way above Thrumpton gives fine views over the river and the Gotham Hills; the Trent ridge-way from Radcliffe through East Bridgford commands the most characteristic view of the Trent. The modern A1 follows from Grantham the course of

Southwell Minster   *G. Douglas Bolton*

a prehistoric track making for the Trent crossing at Newark. The great knob of sandstone on which Nottingham Castle stands must have been a landmark for prehistoric travellers, and several lanes from the Belvoir Hills, such as the road by Harby and Colston Bassett towards Nottingham, aim at a river crossing.

The great North Road of Norman times was the road through Nottingham and Ollerton to Blyth. After struggling through the clay of Tuxford, the medieval traveller was glad to get to the sandy ground west of Retford. Later the road was diverted to pass through Retford for the sake of its coaching inns; but the Ministry of Transport has now put the road back on its medieval line. The M1 cuts through the western side of the county and follows the Nottinghamshire–Derbyshire boundaries.

Sherwood Forest

First legends, then facts. Legends about Robin Hood and his fellow outlaws were popular even in the Middle Ages; but no historian has been able to prove

517

that he actually existed. Nevertheless, the stories are a valid commentary on the rich and the poor of medieval England, and on the unpopularity of laws with a class bias. Now facts. The poor, sandy land of central Nottinghamshire, thinly settled and difficult to get a living from, was used for hunting by the men of the Shire (Shire-wood). Then Norman kings took it over as a royal forest, defining its boundaries carefully, and built a hunting lodge at Clipstone, near Edwinstowe. Sherwood Forest ran north from the walls of Nottingham as far as Warsop, and the River Leen was its western boundary. The Nottingham-Ollerton road was its eastern boundary. Within this vast area, special courts administered special laws, to preserve the beasts of chase and the forest and the undergrowth in which they flourished. Land was cleared only by royal concession. Most of Nottinghamshire's medieval monasteries – Welbeck, Newstead, Rufford, etc. – were planted within its bounds by feudal landowners, who alone had the land to give – land not already settled and farmed – and could get the necessary licenses.

The ruins of Newark Castle  *J. Allan Cash*

There is little left of what children imagine as Sherwood Forest. It must always have been a region of glades and open tracts, rather than dense woodland. Most of the oak has gone, for building castles, abbeys, churches and ships, or for charcoal. The Forestry Commission's regular plantations surround the new mining-villages such as Clipstone. The glades of oak and silver birch near Ollerton (Bilhagh and Birklands) still give the best impression of a medieval forest, and some giant oaks still stand.

The Dukeries

When the monasteries disappeared, in 1536–40, dukes took over, or reassumed what their ancestors had given. Great aristocratic mansions were created at Worksop, Welbeck, Rufford and Newstead out of monastic buildings, and a new site was developed at Thoresby. The old roads through the forest became private drives, flanked by ornamental planting and entered by monumental gateways. Streams were dammed to make lakes, or monastic waterworks improved; derelict woods were replanted and intervening fields improved. An 18th-century commentator said that half Nottinghamshire held no more than 'four Dukes, two Lords and three rabbit-warrens'. Now, except for the Duke of Portland, the peers have gone; the deer are confined to a few parks (Wollaton, Thoresby and Welbeck) and the rabbit-warrens are empty. Only Welbeck and Thoresby remain of the mansions, neither of them used as a home. Modern farming and forestry methods are making the most of poor soil. There remain open spaces – woods and valleys, secluded lanes and diversified views – which serve as a lung for the people of mining-towns and villages nearby.

Byron and Lawrence

Newstead Priory (not Abbey), the home of the Byron family from 1539, was the poet's residence for a short time from 1808, and many places nearby have associations: his grave at Hucknall, Annesley Hall where his Mary Chaworth lived, Holme Pierrepont where he visited, and the Clinton Arms Hotel at Newark where he stayed while a Newark printer was producing a volume of his poems. But Greece meant more to him, just as his grave is a place of pilgrimage for Greeks.

D. H. Lawrence was, in a much more real sense, a Nottinghamshire man. Though he left the county early in life, his first novels, stories and poems are set in the mixed mining and farming round Eastwood, north-west from Nottingham, of which he knew every inch, and whose essential flavour he could convey.

Why come to Nottinghamshire?

For views – from the Belvoir Hills or the Trent Hills. For scenery of great variety: the sweeping woodland of Sherwood Forest, or the secluded valleys round it; the great sweep of the Trent Valley or the fascinating marshland on the northern fringe of the county, now reclaimed and drained. For churches – rich town churches (Nottingham and Newark), a great minster (Southwell) and good village churches. For castles (Nottingham, Newark), county houses and charming villages built of red brick with pantiled roofs. For sailing, on the Trent or the gravel-lagoons; for coarse fishing, again in the Trent, in old canals and lagoons. Even for birds – for the Nottingham Corporation's sewage works at Stoke Bardolph is well known to ornithologists. The pleasures and rewards of the county, if not flamboyant, are very real and remarkably varied.

Some houses and gardens open to the public

Newark Castle At Newark-on-Trent. *Map EJ 35. 12th to 15th cent.; fine gatehouse. King John died here in 1216; castle besieged during Civil War. Enquiries for parties:* Museum Curator, Appleton Gate, Newark, Tel. 2358.

Newstead Abbey 4½m s of Mansfield on A60 *Map EF 35. 12th-cent. Abbey converted into a house at the 16th-cent. dissolution; Byron associations.* Corporation of Nottingham.

Nottingham Castle At Nottingham *Map EF 33. 17th cent.; restored 14th-cent. gateway; now a museum and art gallery.*

Thoresby Park 3m N of Ollerton, 1½m NE of Budby off A614 *Map EG 37. 19th-cent. palatial Dukeries mansion in Sherwood Forest.*

Wollaton Hall 2½m w of City centre *Map EF 33. 16th-cent. mansion; now a natural history museum; deer park, lake. The residence of the Willoughby family from 1588 to 1925. Francis Willoughby (1635 to 1672), the noted naturalist and friend and patron of John Ray (1627 to 1705), did much of his work here.* Corporation of Nottingham. *Enquiries for conducted tours to parts of hall not normally open:* Curator, Tel. Nottm. 281333.

Books for further reading

The 'feel' of Nottinghamshire

SAMUEL BUTLER *The Way of All Flesh*
GRAHAM GREENE *A Gun for Sale*
FRED KITCHEN *Songs of Sherwood* 1948
D. H. LAWRENCE *Sons and Lovers, White Peacock*
HILDA LEWIS *Penny Lace*
STANLEY MIDDLETON *A Short Answer*
CECIL ROBERTS *A Terrace in the Sun*
ALAN SILLITOE *Saturday Night and Sunday Morning*

History and topography

DUNCAN GRAY *Nottingham Through 500 years* 2nd edn 1960

W. G. HOSKINS *Midland England: a Survey of the Country Between the Chilterns and the Trent* (The Face of Britain series) 1949
J. H. INGRAM *North Midland Country* (The Face of Britain series) 1948 and *The River Trent* 1955
PETER LORD *Portrait of the River Trent* 1968
CHRISTOPHER MARSDEN *Nottinghamshire* (County Books series) 1953
ARTHUR MEE *Nottinghamshire: the Midland Stronghold* (King's England series) 1949
NIKOLAUS PEVSNER *The Leaves of Southwell* (King Penguin Books) 1945 and *Nottinghamshire* (Buildings of England series) 1951
A. C. WOOD *A History of Nottinghamshire* 1948

Gazetteer

NOTTINGHAMSHIRE

Clumber Park   *J. Allan Cash*

Annesley (EF 35) EC Wed (912). Mary Chaworth, who inherited Annesley Hall, was the first love of Lord Byron; both were in their 'teens. She, however, married Jack Musters, thus uniting two local land-owning families.

Arnold (EF 34) EC Thurs (30,640). A village now almost swallowed up by Nottingham, but at one time closely associated with the Luddites, the weavers who fought the Industrial Revolution by smashing the machines that threatened their livelihood. Richard Parkes Bonington (1802–28), the landscape painter, was born at 79 High St, but did most of his work in France. He died at the age of 26 from 'brain fever' caused by exposure to the sun while sketching.

Aslockton (EH 34) (707). Archbishop Cranmer was born in a manor house that no longer exists. He was able to spend only the shortest periods at home between his 14th year and his martyrdom, but from the earthwork known as Cranmer's Mound he 'surveyed the face of the country and listened to the tuneable bells of Whatton'.

Attenborough (EF 33) EC Thurs. The church, in which Cromwell's horses were stabled, has one of the oldest doors in England, grotesque carvings and beautiful glass. The baptism of Henry Ireton is recorded in the parish register for 1611. He fought on the Parliamentary side at Edgehill and Marston Moor, married Cromwell's daughter, died of plague and was buried in Westminster Abbey. After the Restoration his body was exhumed and hanged at Tyburn.

Beauvale Priory (EE 34). Agricultural buildings have assimilated the remains of the 14th-cent. Carthusian priory that fell victim to Henry VIII's dissolution of the monasteries.

Beeston (EF 33) EC Thurs (62,070). Centre for the manufacture of drugs and toilet preparations which grew from the business genius of Jesse Boot, 1st Lord Trent, who started work at the age of 14 in his mother's small herbal shop in Nottingham.

Bingham (EH 33) EC Wed (4,704). The Early English and Perpendicular-style Church of All Saints has a notable lancet window set into the thickness of the wall at the W end, carvings of the Seven Deadly Sins, and a sequence of memorials dating from every century since the church's foundation and culminating in the wooden figure of Ann Harrison, the fish-seller who died in 1928 when nearing her hundredth year, and who gave most of her earnings to the church.

Blyth (EG 38) EC Wed (992). Part of the church has early Norman work similar to that done on the Continent before the Conquest. Much of this has been crowded out by Early English and Perpendicular additions.

Budby (EG 36) (289). The 1st Earl Manvers built this model neo-Gothic village in 1807 for workers on his Thoresby estate.

Bunny (EF 32) EC Wed (627). With the exception of the 14th-cent. church, everything in this village bears the stamp of Sir Thomas Parkyns, who was known as the Wrestling Baronet. The hall was designed by him, and took on much of his eccentricity; he commissioned a school and an alms-house, which fared rather better. He wrote a treatise on wrestling, *The Cornish Hugg*, which he dedicated to King George I; he also designed his own monument in the church, which depicts a tiny figure laid low by Time.

Calverton (EG 34) EC Wed (6,670). Believed to be the birthplace of William Lee, the Elizabethan parson who invented a stocking-frame. The Queen was disappointed that it could not make silk stockings, and the frame was eventually developed in France. Nevertheless it is due to Lee's invention that the hosiery industry flourishes in this county.

Clipstone (EG 36) EC Wed (3,968). Very little remains of what is known as King John's Palace but that part which dates from before his reign. It continued to be the royal hunting lodge of the Tudors before passing to the nobility. The eccentric 5th Duke of Portland built a gatehouse on the way to Edwinstowe. It is similar to the one at Worksop Priory, and is embellished with representations of Robin Hood and his band.

Clumber (EG 37). This great seat of the Dukes of Newcastle was built in

Kingston-on-Soar: Babington Chantry in St Wilfred's Church   *J. Allan Cash*

1770 and demolished in 1937. The grounds were taken over by the military during the 1939 War and used as an ammunition dump. They suffered greatly. The public is now allowed to visit the park with its plantations, rides and avenues, inaccessible between the wars. The Duke of Newcastle's collection of pictures from the house are on exhibition in Nottingham Castle Museum.

Creswell Crags (EF 37). Caves in a ravine on the Derbyshire boundary have yielded some of the earliest known artifacts by ancient Britons.

Dukeries, The (EG 37). The three stately homes of Welbeck, Clumber and Thoresby are dealt with separately. Their deer-parks, woodlands, gardens and lakes cover 7 sq. m.

East Leake, 3 m. SSE of **Gotham** (EF 32) EC Wed (4,230). In addition to noteworthy architectural detail, the church has a 'shawn' or tin trumpet which measures 10 ft. when extended. This was used by the bass singer until the middle of the 19th cent., and is one of the six surviving in England.

East Stoke (EH 34) EC Wed (198). Where Lambert Simnel, having been 'crowned King of England' in Dublin, was captured by Henry VII in 1487.

Eastwood (EE 34) EC Wed (11,330). Birthplace of D. H. Lawrence (1885–1930). The town figures memorably as 'Bestwood' in *Sons and Lovers*.

Edwinstowe (EG 36) EC Wed (4,152). Centre for Birklands and Bilhagh, two stretches of Sherwood Forest. Some trees are so striking that they have been given individual names. The hollow Major Oak is said to be 1,400 years old. Another tradition is that Robin Hood married Maid Marian in Edwinstowe church.

Gotham (EF 32) EC Wed (1,662). Though mining and plaster works are the village's industries, a more lasting product may be the medieval Merry Tales, in which the Wise Men of Gotham did various idiotic things, such as building a hedge around a cuckoo to prevent it from flying away; they also attempted to drown an eel, and set a barn on fire to destroy a wasp's nest. Note the sign of the Cuckoo Bush inn.

Harby (EJ 37) (265). Eleanor of Castile, wife of Edward I, died here in 1290. Beautiful 'Eleanor crosses' were erected at every stage where her funeral procession halted on its journey to Westminster Abbey.

Hawton (EH 35) (74). The church is visited chiefly for its magnificent Easter Sepulchre on which is carved the story of the Resurrection. From Good Friday until Easter Sunday the church's crucifix was placed in a niche and guarded by watchers dressed as Pilate's soldiers.

Holme (EJ 35) (83). John Barton, who made a fortune out of the wool trade with Calais, rebuilt the church in the late 15th cent. Above the porch is a room known as Nanny Scott's Chamber, where an old woman immured herself against the plague, but died from sorrow at having to witness the burial of all her friends.

Hucknall Torkard (EF 34) EC Wed (25,270). Lord Byron's body was brought here from Greece when his relatives found that permission for burial in Poet's Corner at Westminster was unlikely to be granted. His bust is in the chancel, a lamp burns in his name, and a brass wreath of laurels is set into stone sent to England by the King of Greece.

Kelham (EH 35) EC Tues (245). The Hall, now a theological college, was built in the middle of the 19th cent. by Gilbert Scott in the neo-Gothic style. It has a new chapel containing forceful sculptures by Charles Sergeant Jagger.

Kingston-on-Soar (EF 32) (247). Rebuilding the church of St Wilfred in 1900 employed as far as possible the materials from the earlier structure, and preserved within it the Babington Chantry (c. 1550). This is one of the most important church monuments in the county, and has been described by Sacheverell Sitwell as being 'somewhat of Portuguese-Indian influence'. It has columns covered with a hexagonal pattern, and a wealth of other decoration including some two hundred figures of infants in barrels – a pun on the family name of Babington.

Langar (EH 33) EC Wed (456). The recumbent figures of Thomas, Lord Scroope and his wife Philadelphia are watched over by the smaller alabaster effigy of their son in the family chapel within the church. The detail of their robes is worth studying. Admiral Howe (d. 1799) is buried in the churchyard, and Samuel Butler (1835–1902), author of *The Way of All Flesh*, was born in the rectory adjoining the church.

Linby (EF 35) (280). One of the two crosses in the village has a very old medieval base. But Linby is best known for Castle Mill, a battlemented building where James Watt set up his first machine for the spinning of cotton and flax. The toll of young lives is chronicled in the churchyard by 163 graves of child apprentices killed by labour conditions.

Mansfield (EF 36) EC Wed (55,540). The market town adjoining Sherwood Forest has grown into an industrial centre. It was the legendary Miller of Mansfield who dared to entertain

Henry II with venison poached from his own preserves.

Newark (EH 35) EC Thurs (25,030). Long before the town's prosperity was founded on wool shipped down the Trent to the merchants of Calais and Flanders, it was a stronghold on the way to the N. The castle, in which King John died in 1216, was dismantled in 1646 on the collapse of the Royalist cause, and is now a splendid ruin.

The Church of St Mary Magdalen has unusual proportions, its spire being 22 ft. higher than the length of the church. The oldest parts are four central piers and the crypt. The wide nave dates from the reign of Edward II. Because of their slight stonework, the windows in the transepts are especially noteworthy. See also Robert Markham's chantry chapel, which has a peephole and a crudely painted Dance of Death.

Newstead Abbey* (EF 35). Byron and his mother were too poor to live at Newstead when he inherited the property, but after he left Cambridge he moved in, despite heavy debts, until obliged to sell six years later. The house was originally a 12th-cent. Augustinian priory. It was converted by a Byron ancestor in 1540, and presented to the City of Nottingham by Sir Julian Cahn in 1931. It has a beautiful west front, and romantically landscaped gardens. The magnificent rooms contain the poet's possessions, including furniture, portraits and rare editions of his work.

Nottingham* (EF 33) EC Thurs (313,000). Though not lacking in history, this town, because of its good planning, appears to be modern. The proud civic buildings include a Council House (1929) designed with a dome and pediment that derive from St Paul's Cathedral.

Newstead Abbey

G. Douglas Bolton

The town of Snotingaham was occupied by the Danes in 868, and the imposing castle was built on its present rock site after the Norman Conquest. A Royal Charter was granted by Henry II. Having been held by the Royalists, the castle was demolished in 1651, but rebuilt in an Italianate style by the 1st Duke of Newcastle, only to be burned by Luddite rioters in the 19th cent., and later restored. The castle is now leased by the Duke of Newcastle to the Corporation, which has converted it into a museum and art gallery. Bronzes of Robin Hood and his men by a local sculptor have been set below the castle wall. The Corporation has also acquired Elizabethan Wollaton Hall as well as Byron's home.

The famous annual Goose Fair, traditionally held in the market place, now spreads its stalls and amusements over a less restricted site at the edge of the forest. The market place has been planted with trees and flowers, and the market itself put under cover.

Though Nottingham was originally celebrated for lace curtains and carvings in alabaster, both now out of fashion, the city has kept up with the times, aided undoubtedly by its central position and by the navigable Trent on which it stands.

525

Retford (EH 38) EC Wed (18,770). The two parts of this mainly Victorian town are joined by a bridge across the River Idle. The cruciform church of St Swithun is largely 15th-cent., though the central tower collapsed in 1651 and was rebuilt on its four 13th-cent. arches.

Rufford Abbey (EG 36). The home of Arabella Stuart, who came to a tragic end because she was close in succession to James I. The Elizabethan and Jacobean house is set among parkland and ornamental water at the head of an avenue of limes leading from the gates. It is in the hands of the Ministry of Works, which is safeguarding the most important parts of its construction, including the vaulted undercroft that is part of a 12th-cent. Cistercian foundation.

Scrooby (EG 38) (375). From this inland village on the small River Ryton the *Mayflower* was launched. William Brewster, one of the two leaders of the Pilgrim Fathers, worshipped in the church, which contains a pew known as Brewster's Pew. It has handsome wood carvings and a 15th-cent. bench-end.

Sherwood Forest,* largely between Ollerton (EG 36) and Worksop (EF 37). Whether or no Robin Hood is mythical, this area was once a strictly preserved royal forest. Including the Dukeries, which have formed three great enclosures, it still measures 20 m. by 5–10 m. Much of it is heath, but there are many fine trees – oaks as well as birches – in Birkdale and Bilhagh.

Southwell (EG 35) EC Thurs (5,125). Charles I stayed at the Saracen's Head (at that time the King's Head) in 1646 before being taken into the captivity that ended in his execution.

The Minster, though possibly the least visited of English cathedrals, makes Southwell notable. The town itself is also less seen than it deserves. The Minster was begun in the early 12th cent.; yet the transepts and nave of the first building period are still standing. Of the three Norman towers, two have the pyramidal roofs of their original design, despite rebuilding after fire in 1711, and further work in 1880. The glass in the E window was brought from the Chapel of the Knights Templar in Paris, where Marie Antoinette worshipped. The brass lectern was reclaimed from the lake at Newstead Abbey, where it had been thrown at the time of the Dissolution of the Monastries. The Chapter House, built at the end of the 13th cent., is exceptionally graceful, owing much to its construction without the usual central pillar. Its door, which has a centre shaft, is one of the most beautiful in England. Throughout the Minster, carved foliage, with every leaf different and never stylized, appears over doorways, around seats and on the capitals of pillars.

Thoresby Park (EG 70). The seat of Earl Manvers, lacking the long history of Welbeck and Rufford. It was enclosed out of the Forest in 1683. The present residence dates from 1864–75, and has all the impressive qualities of that Victorian period. It is set in a splendid park through which runs a public road, and the damming of the River Meden has produced beautiful ornamental waters. It is open to the public at certain times of the year.

Welbeck (EF 70). Though the history of the abbey goes back to a 12th-cent. Premonstratensian monastery, the existing structure is architecturally mixed. It combines mainly 18th-cent. work linked with restorations that followed a fire in 1900. Its chief fame is the complex of

Silver birches in Sherwood Forest

Reece Winstone

underground buildings constructed for the eccentric 5th Duke of Portland. These included a ballroom and an extraordinary glass-roofed riding school known as the Tan Gallop. The many rooms were linked by tunnels and served by a miniature underground railway. The Tan Gallop has been demolished, but alongside it is a giant covered riding school in cast iron. The house and grounds are not open to the public. The Duke lives at Welbeck Woodhouse.

Wollaton Hall, (E F 33) 2½ m. W of the city centre. One of the most grandiose though not the most beautiful of Elizabethan houses, now the property of the City of Nottingham, and con-

taining a natural history museum. The first English greenhouse is said to have been built in these gardens in the 17th cent. A high standard of horticulture is maintained.

Worksop (E F 37) E C Thurs (35,580). The 12th-cent. priory church originally resembled Southwell Minster, having twin Norman towers with wooden spires and mouldings of foliage in the interior. But only the shell remained until between the wars, when the church and lady chapel were restored and civic buildings were grouped around them. The gatehouse S of the Priory was originally the entrance to the monastic buildings.

Wollaton Hall

J. Allan Cash

Lincoln Cathedral

LINCOLNSHIRE

AN INTRODUCTION BY M. W. BARLEY

Some people are faddy about food, others about scenery. Lincolnshire is an acquired taste. Those who do not already know it would be sensible to try it. The second largest county in England, it is probably the least known and one of the least regarded. Yet it has scenery and a coastline as distinctive as any; as grand a collection of churches as any, set in villages of great variety; woodland, open upland and marsh, and a county town distinguished by one of the most impressive cathedrals in England.

The county has been divided, throughout historic times, into three parts. Lindsey, roughly the northern half, was an independent Kingdom in Saxon times. Kesteven comprises the southern half, except for the low ground around the Wash, known as Holland. The last-named has nothing to do with the Dutch Holland, but is an entirely independent name, meaning *overlooked by high ground* – that is, by the Wolds and the Heath.

The Rock Beneath

Seventy miles long and forty miles wide, the scale of the scenery is Lincolnshire's most distinctive characteristic. Bounded on the north by an impressive

529

Michaelgate, Lincoln *Reece Winstone*

estuary, the Humber; containing on the west the River Trent at its widest; holding, on the south, the largest expanse of absolutely flat (and immensely fertile) farmland in England; giving, from its vantage points, the widest views of earth and sky – Lincolnshire calls for a taste for the grandiose.

The rock frame is a simple one. Layers tilted up to the west and gently down to the east provide a succession of steps or scarps. The most pronounced, a ridge of limestone, runs all the way from the Humber's brink at Whitton and Alkborough through Lincoln to the Leicestershire boundary. Only a mile or so wide at the north, it is known as the Cliff; it broadens south of Lincoln into a plateau called the Heath, wide enough for airfields. The next step to the east is of chalk, severed from the Yorkshire Wolds by the Humber.

From the edge of the cut, above South Ferriby, is the best view of the wide Humber estuary, great enough to dwarf the barges passing up to Goole and Gainsborough. A prehistoric ridge-way follows the scarp of the Wolds south, and from the high points on it there are more immense views, with Lincoln Minster and Boston Stump, the Humber and the Wash as their farthest landmark. The smooth curves of chalk landscape are everywhere under the plough (unlike the Downs of Southern England) so that, in Tennyson's words, the summer corn 'clothes the Wold and meets the sky'.

530

Reece Winstone **Lincoln: the High Bridge over the River With**

Fen and Marsh

Along with the Cliff, the Heath and the Wold, Fen and Marsh are essential ingredients of the Lincolnshire landscape. In no part of England has man so revolutionized the face, and the use, of the land. The Fen is a wide band of low ground surrounding the Wash and running south into Cambridgeshire, which persistent effort, spread over a thousand years, has reclaimed from the sea and protected from river floods. It is criss-crossed by flood-banks and water-channels of every age from Saxon times to the 1950s (the new channel for the Welland round Spalding). Its safety has long depended on pumping – first windmills, which can still be seen at Waltham, Heckington, Alford, and Burgh le Marsh, then beam-engines driven by steam, and now the immensely successful electric pumps, such as that at the mouth of the Black Sluice at Boston. Inland from the villages the soil is peaty – black to the eye, rich to the farmer in the most favourable seasons, but a wasting asset, for it dries as it shrinks, and even blows away.

The marshland lies between the Wolds and the sea. It, too, has been reclaimed over the past thousand years, but from salt-marsh and not from peat fen. Behind the seaside resorts of Cleethorpes and Mablethorpe, and as far south as Skegness, lies a band of rich grazing land.

The Past

Prehistoric man has left his mark on the county. First there are prehistoric roads, most of them still in use. The best is the road from Scunthorpe south to Lincoln, clinging to the edge of the limestone ridge: you can pick it up again south of Lincoln running through Wellingore. From the Humber at South Ferriby another follows the western edge of the chalk wolds, above Horkstow, to Melton Ross, Caistor, Donington on Bain and Scamblesby to Ulceby Cross. Still another ancient road runs on the east side of the Wolds through Brocklesby and Louth. On the high Wolds there are the long barrows or burial mounds of Stone Age man, such as the Dead Men's Graves, Skendleby.

There are small hill-forts of the Iron Age at Honington, overlooking the Ancaster Gap, and at Round Hills, between Ingoldsby and Boothby Pagnell. In the area of sand-dunes, pines and heather, south of Scunthorpe, prehistoric settlements were thick on the ground; and Scunthorpe Museum has one of the best collections of flint implements.

The Roman conquest left very distinctive traces. Apart from Lincoln itself, which was the Roman city of *Lindum Colonia*, a centre for retired soldiers, the market towns of Caistor and Horncastle have traces of their Roman walls; and at Ancaster, the line of the wall and ditch can be clearly seen. The motorist can enjoy, driving along Ermine Street both south and north of Lincoln, the most impressive stretches of Roman road in Britain. The Foss Dyke, the canal joining the Trent at Torksey with the Witham at Brayford, still carries barge-loads of corn, as it did in Roman times. Salt was made on the coast at Ingoldmells. Nor does archaeology end with the departure of the Roman armies: one of the county's most distinctive types of monument is the deserted village, of which there are scores of examples, such as West Wykeham and South Cadeby, both near Louth, and Ingleby, between Saxilby and Sturton. Most of these villages died between four and five hundred years ago. Now all that remain are banks and mounds in grass fields, showing where lanes once ran and farmhouses stood. Several Norman castles have been deserted, too, and have left impressive

Burghley House, Stamford

earthworks behind them, as at Castle Bytham, Old Bolingbroke and Owston Ferry on the Trent.

Coast and River

Thousands of people from Midland towns hurry through these parts of the county to get to the coast, because it really is 'so bracing', as the old Skegness poster said. There is room for all of them, and more, on the immense stretches of firm sand, sheltered by sand-dunes covered with sea buckthorn and marram grass. Behind the sandhills one sees, inevitably, a spread of bungalows and caravans; but once on the beach one ceases to be aware of anything but the great expanse of sea, sand and sky.

At any week-end in the season, the waterways of Lincolnshire are lined with fishermen from Yorkshire and Midland towns. The main Trent and the Roman Foss Dyke, and more especially the Witham, the Ancholme, the Welland and the South Forty Foot provide the most comfortable fishing in England for those who like a day out with the family. The Witham is the main centre for match angling.

Local Industry

One of the county's most valuable industries deals with the harvest gathered in the North Sea, the Atlantic and even as far away as the Arctic: the fishing industry. Grimsby is one of the largest fishing-ports in the world, and the fish docks are worth a visit. From Cleethorpes you can watch the trawlers leaving

533

and entering the mouth of the Humber. At Boston trawlers tie up at wharves in the centre of the town. A large industrial estate extends along the Humber bank between Immingham and Grimsby. Immingham is a busy port, with deep-water docks, which is also developing as a passenger port.

The oldest Lincolnshire industry is agriculture: today it is certainly the most highly developed. Wherever you look you cannot see an acre unused. The typical large farmstead now has a lofty glasshouse, for bringing on seed potatoes in the spring; a corn drier, running for twenty-four hours daily in harvest time; perhaps a short-wave radio station for communicating with neighbouring farms under the same management; or even a landing ground for the farmer's light aircraft. From farming stems the canning industry – vegetable and fruit at Boston and Spalding. One industry is now a matter of history – or indeed of archaeology: salt-making, using brine from salt-impregnated clay from the marsh, preparing a solution and evaporating it in clay pans over turf fires. The waste product of

Church and sundial cottage at West Deeping   Reece Winstone

this industry, which went on until Elizabethan times, was soil washed free of salt. It was stacked round the kilns; and you may still see, both in the Marshland and in the Fens, mounds which might appear natural but are really as artificial as the tip-heaps round a coalmine. Pottery and other débris of the salt industry of Roman times can sometimes be found at low tide at Ingoldmells, and the mounds are particularly obvious near Bicker, by the Welland below Spalding.

One industry of ancient origin still continues: iron-working. The ironstone of Kesteven (near Castle Bytham, Colsterworth, etc.) was worked in Roman times, and probably before, but on a small scale. Now immense machines eat through whole fields in a season, and the ore is taken miles by rail to Corby or to Ilkeston. In North Lindsey, the ore quarried round Scunthorpe goes to the local steel works: the chimneys smoking by day and the furnaces glowing by night are a familiar landmark.

At South Ferriby the chalk and clay are quarried for cement, and in the extreme south, quarrying for sand and gravel in Tallington and nearby parishes is steadily turning cornfields into lagoons – and, incidentally, taking land in which there are many buried traces of prehistoric man.

One unique industry draws each year thousands of visitors in April or May: the growing of spring flowers, tulips in particular, round Spalding. Only the richest soil can be used for such a crop. Fields with stripes of the most brilliant colours are spread over many miles; but the most unusual sight is a carefully arranged carpet, perhaps outside a farmhouse, made of the heads of tulips cut off because it is the bulbs that are wanted and not the blooms.

Tennyson's Lincolnshire

Visitors to Lincoln itself will see the bronze statue of the Lincolnshire poet standing by the Minster; but his home was many miles away, in the southern Wolds. He was born in the rectory at Somersby, and he knew the country round and the people well enough for them to leave a strong mark on his poetry. If you explore Tennyson's country, you are bound to notice the strange names of nearby villages – Salmonby, Bag Enderby, Fulletby, Skendleby and the like. Names ending in -by are more common in Lincolnshire than in any other county. They were given by the Danes, who settled a thousand years ago. They also bequeathed to us Hogsthorpe, Mablethorpe and all the other names ending in -thorpe. In Lincolnshire towns you may find street-names like Kirk Gate, which is simply the Danish version of Church Street. Most counties have place-names of distinctive character; and here that character is Danish.

Wild Life

Lincolnshire naturalists have had great success in preserving remnants of the once extensive tracts of wild country. Recently, over 90 acres of washland on the River Glen was acquired for the purpose of developing a winter wildfowl refuge. The biggest nature reserve in the county is the splendid expanse of sand-dunes and salt-marsh between Skegness and Gibraltar Point. A field station and bird observatory are maintained there, and bird-watching is rewarding both for the casual visitor and for the serious student. There are also reserves in the sandhills and marshes at Saltfleetby and Theddlethorpe. Linwood Warren, near Market Rasen, and Scotton Common, near Scunthorpe, are reserves of heathland with birch, pine, heather and rare birds. Epworth and Haxey Turbaries, in the Isle of Axholme, show what Fenland used to be like.

Lincolnshire Food

Whatever Melton Mowbray may claim, I aver there is no doubt that Lincolnshire makes the best pork pies and that Lincolnshire haslet is better than Yorkshire. Some bakeries make plum bread nearly as well as the Lincolnshire farmer's wife – I know of a shop in Spilsby worth visiting for that reason alone.

Some houses and gardens open to the public

Allington Manor 5m NW of Grantham off A52 *Map EJ 34. 17th cent.; Dutch-gabled; original dog-leg staircase.*

Boston Guildhall At Boston *Map* FD 34. *15th cent.; Borough art gallery and museum; associations with Pilgrim Fathers, many of whom were imprisoned in the cells.*

Doddington Hall 6m SW of Lincoln on B1120 *Map EK 37. Elizabethan mansion approached by picturesque gabled gatehouse; fine china and furnishings; notable gardens.*

Gainsborough Old Hall At Gainsborough *Map EJ 38. 15th- to 16th-cent. manor house in brick, stone and half-timber; period rooms and furniture; Great Hall and medieval kitchen.*

Greyfriars City and **County Museum** At Lincoln *Map EK 37. 13th-cent. friary; fine barrel roof in upper room; used as a school; now a museum of local antiquities and natural history.*

Lincoln Castle At Lincoln *Map EK 37. 11th cent. with later additions; founded by William the Conqueror; Norman bailey and two motte hills. County gaol (c. 1780) now houses the Lincolnshire Records Office.*

Tattershall Castle 3½m SE of Woodhall Spa on A153 *Map FC 35. 15th cent.; red brick; restored.*

Thornton Abbey 4m SE of Barton-upon-Humber off A160 *Map FA 41. 14th-cent. gateway; dry moat spanned by long bridge with arcaded walls and circular towers.*

Books for further reading

The 'feel' of Lincolnshire

ALAN BLOOM *The Skaters of the Fens* 1958; *History and Anecdotes of the Sport of the Fens*

J. N. CLARKE *Country Gleanings: From the Lincolnshire Wolds* 1954

MABEL PEACOCK *Lincolnshire Tales, and North Lincolnshire Dialect: Tales and Rhymes in the Lindsey Folkspeech* 1886

ETHEL H. RUDKIN *Lincolnshire Folklore* 1936

J. E. SWABY *The Marksmen: Tales of the Lincolnshire Marshes*

Natural history

JOHN CORDEAUX *Birds of the Humber District* 1872

E. A. R. ENNION *Adventurers Fen* 1949

A. E. SMITH and R. K. CORNWALLIS *The Birds of Lincolnshire* 1955

History and topography

M. W. BARLEY *Lincolnshire and the Fens* (Face of Britain series) 1952

T. A. BEVIS *A Guide to the Fens and Fenland Churches* 1967

C. BREARS *A Short History of Lincolnshire* 1927

JOHN BYGOTT *Lincolnshire* (County Books series) 1952

D. C. DUNLOP *Pictorial History of Lincoln Cathedral* (Pride of Britain series) 1959

R. L. HILLS *Machines, Mills and Uncountable Costly Necessities: A Short History of the Drainage of the Fens* 1967

ARTHUR MEE *Lincolnshire* (King's England series) 1949

J. WENTWORTH-DAY *A History of the Fens: Being an Account of their Swamps, Meres, Men, Sports, Duck Decoys, Drainage, Riots, Floods, Legends, Fish and Fowl* 1954

Gazetteer

LINCOLNSHIRE

Alkborough (EJ 42) (460). York Minster is visible from this height above the confluence of the Ouse, Trent and Humber. In addition to the 11th-cent. church, there are two unusual sights: a Roman camp, incongruously named the Countess Close after Countess Lucy, wife of Ivo Tailbois, Norman Lord of the Manor; and, cut in the turf, a maze. Of this last, a plan in black and white stone is set into the floor of the south porch of the church.

Ancaster (EK 34) (722). A hoard of coins and other remains uncovered on the 9-acre site of the Roman camp on Ermine Street is shown in Grantham Museum. The famous Ancaster stone has the quality of hardening immediately after being quarried.

Ashby Puerorum (SD 37). So called because a local bequest contributes to the support of the choirboys of Lincoln Cathedral.

Bardney (FB 36) EC Wed (1,835). The great Benedictine abbey N of the town is believed to have been founded by Ethelred, King of Mercia, in the 7th cent. The foundations of its church have been excavated, and stonework from the ruins is preserved in the parish church of St Lawrence.

Barton-upon-Humber (FA 42) EC Thurs (6,590). Small port, which had a prosperous ferry trade across the river mouth. The lower part of the Saxon tower of St Peter's Church has beautiful arcading, round-headed below and triangular above, continuing deep into the structure.

Boston: the 'Stump'   *Edwin Smith*

Belton Park (EK 33). Generations of the Brownlow family have devoted themselves to enriching their home and planting their estates. The H-shaped house took on its Palladian aspect in the 18th cent. when a cupola by Wren was removed. Some of the rooms, and the private chapel, are festooned with carvings by Grinling Gibbons. The main drive of the park is open to the public. The church is filled with Brownlow memorials, and has a Norman font.

Blyton (EJ 39) EC Wed (959). The chancel of the church is hung with flags of the Allies, donated by kings, Heads of Government and famous men of the 1914 War – a collection initiated by a mother whose son died in France.

Bolingbroke (FD 36). The stronghold, which was owned by John of Gaunt and was the birthplace of Henry IV in 1367, suffered demolition by the Parliamentarians in 1643.

Boston* (FD 34) EC Thurs (25,150). Merchants built the church of St

537

Grantham House, Grantham

Reece Winstone

Botolph in the 14th–15th cents. when this was one of Britain's chief ports. In the 17th cent. the Corporation petitioned that their borough 'might be put among the decayed towns'. The famous church spire known as the Boston Stump has for centuries shown a guiding light for travellers on land and sea.

Boston, Massachusetts, was founded by men who sailed from here to New England in 1630 in the wake of the Pilgrim Fathers. The link has been perpetuated. Fydell House (1726), occupied by a branch of Nottingham University, sets aside a room for transatlantic Bostonians. St Mary's Guildhall contains the Court to which Brewster and others who later embarked on the *Mayflower* were brought from the cells below. The SW chapel of St Botolph was restored in the middle of the last century by New Englanders in memory of John Cotton, who was vicar here before leaving for America in 1633. The lower section of the church tower has a tablet inscribed with the names of five men who became Governors of Massachusetts.

Bourne (FA 31) EC Wed (5,640). Birthplace of Robert Manning (1288–1338), the Gilbertine monk who pioneered writing in language that could be understood by the common people. White Bread Meadow is auctioned annually for charity during the time taken by schoolboys racing over a measured distance.

Caistor (FB 40) EC Wed (1,894). A well in the citadel of the Roman camp on the site of an ancient British hillfort is still used. It is near the church, which has evidence of Norman, Saxon and medieval building in its tower.

Castle Bytham (EK 31) (553). The cruciform church treasures an 18th-cent. sundial inscribed with the pun 'Bee in Thyme'; a brass candelabra of the early 19th cent.; and the village maypole, which was later used as a ladder to the belfry. The earthworks of the Norman castle are across the stream that flows into the River Glen.

Cleethorpes (FD 40) EC Thurs (33,760). Holiday resort, which developed from small fishing hamlets.

538

Its attractions include a pier and an open-air swimming pool.

Coningsby (FC 35) EC Wed (2,629). The dial of the clock in the church tower measures 16½ ft. and has a single hand, typical of the early 17th-cent. clocks. The mechanism includes a pendulum suspended independently in the tower wall, and clockweights of stone.

Corby (EK 32). Beautiful medieval wall-paintings were discovered in 1939 under the plastered and whitewashed interior of the church.

Crowland (FC 31) EC Wed (2,835). The Benedictine abbey was built in the 8th cent. by King Ethelbald over the hermitage of St Guthlac, whose wisdom had attracted numerous followers. The monastic buildings were partly destroyed and rebuilt many times, but the N aisle (used now as the parish church) survives; so does the tower at the W end, to which has been added a two-storied porch and a blunt spire. The remainder of the ruined but still magnificent W front has five tiers of statues representing saints, apostles and personages associated with the early history of the Abbey. A statue of Christ holding the World, believed to have come from the missing W gable, surmounts the extraordinary triangular bridge in the centre of the town. This bridge of three semicircles meeting at an apex was built in the 13th cent. when the streets were waterways.

Donington (FC 33) EC Tues (1,967). Formerly a centre for flax and hemp; it still has an important horse and cattle fair. The church contains a memorial to Matthew Flinders (b. 1774), who surveyed the unknown coasts of Australia.

Dunston (FA 36). A pillar 92 ft. high was set up on the Heath in 1751 by the eccentric Francis Dashwood of the Hellfire Club, to act as a land lighthouse for travellers. To commemorate his Jubilee, the lantern was replaced by a statue of George III, but it had to be removed when it became a danger to low-flying aircraft.

Edenham (FA 32) EC Wed (416). The church has effigies of 14th-cent. knights, and an arcaded 12th-cent. font on shafts of Purbeck marble. The monuments of the Bertie family, Earls of Lindsey and Dukes of Ancaster, show an unbroken line since the time of Charles I. The family seat, Grimsthorpe Castle, is palatial, with a 13th-cent. tower, Elizabethan wings and a N front built in 1722 by Vanbrugh. Its rooms contain treasures, such as the clothes worn by Charles I when sitting to Van Dyck for his portrait; this painting itself is there too, and a collection of coronation robes, furniture and ceremonial plate – the perquisites of successive Lord Great Chamberlains.

Epworth (EH 40) EC Wed (1,975). John Wesley (1703–91) and his brother Charles (1707–88) were born in the Rectory, which was burnt down when they were children by a mob objecting to their father's political sympathies. A chapel, manse and school were erected in 1889 in memory of the brothers.

Gainsborough (EJ 38) EC Wed (17,470). The descriptive passages in *The Mill on the Floss* by George Eliot, who used this town as a prototype for her St Ogg's, are still identifiable. King Alfred was married here in 868, and Sweyne, King of the Danes and father of Canute, died at his camp at Thonock Park in 1014. Many years later the town was a frequent battleground between Royalist and Parliamentarian troops. The Old Hall, part of a medieval manor rebuilt in the late 15th cent., has a fine roof, a stone oriel window and a kitchen with great ovens and fireplaces.

Grantham* (EK 33) EC Wed (26,030). A perfect view of St Wulfram's magnificent Church is obtained from Swinegate. Above the S porch, in a room formerly occupied by the priest, is kept the library (some of the books still chained), which was left to the church in 1598. The 14th-cent. crypts are remarkable. Grantham House has a 14th-cent. hall used in 1503 by Princess Margaret, daughter of Henry VII, on her journey N for her wedding to James IV of Scotland. The statue opposite the Guildhall honours Sir Isaac Newton (1642–1727), a pupil of the Grammar School. An 18th-cent. landlord of the Angel Inn, the medieval hostelry established by the Knights Templar, bequeathed an annual sum for the preaching of a sermon against drunkenness.

Grimsby (FC 40) EC Thurs (95,030). The 14th-cent. *Lay of Havelock the Dane* tells us how Grim the Fisherman rescued the King's son and landed with him at what was to become the foremost fishing port in Europe. The docks and the fish market should be noted.

Heckington (FB 34) EC Wed (2,020). The 8-sailed windmill is well preserved. The third church on the site was built in the 14th cent. by the Abbey of Bardney. Richness is expressed in its design and decoration, notably in the Easter Sepulchre of Richard de Potesgrave, vicar of this church and chaplain to Edward III.

Holbeach (FD 32) EC Wed (6,620). Market town mentioned in Domesday, and now the centre of a bulb-growing district. Birthplace of Susannah Centlivre, wife of Queen Anne's cook, who wrote 18 comedies, in one of which David Garrick played the lead. The Late Decorated and

Early Perpendicular N porch of the church has a traceried arch.

Horncastle (FC 36) EC Wed (3,950). Site of the Roman fort, Banovallum. The town's horse fair is described by George Borrow in *The Romany Rye*. The church has a brass depicting the King's Champion of 1519 (*see* **Scrivelsby**), an inscription to Sir Ingram Hopton who 'paid his debt to nature' at Winceby in 1643, and a collection of scythes said to have been used as weapons at that battle.

Immingham (FB 41) EC Wed (5,500). A Saxon village which has developed into a port and industrial centre. The Pilgrims' Memorial marks the spot from which the Pilgrim Fathers originally set sail for Holland in 1608. The Norman parish church of St Andrew has six unusual 18th-cent. paintings of the Apostles.

Kingerby (FA 39). The 19th-cent. hall stands on a circular mound surrounded by fosse and embankment, where Stone Age implements and skeletons of early Britons have been discovered below Roman works.

Kirkstead (FB 36) (85). The beautiful chapel of St Leonard, erected for the use of lay persons, has survived the Cistercian abbey to which it was attached. Note the 13th-cent. timber screens, the second oldest in England.

Knaith (EJ 38). Thomas Sutton, founder of Charterhouse School and Hospital in London, was born at the Hall in 1532.

Lincoln** (EK 37) EC Wed (76,720). The Norman bishop Remigius built his church on rising ground to be 'as strong as the place was strong and as fair as the place was fair'. It developed after fire and earthquake into the present triple-towered cathedral. The Early English work of Bishop Hugh of

Somersby Rectory, the birthplace of Tennyson   Reece Winstone

Avalon (d. 1200) in the aisled choir, apse and transept was continued by his successors, resulting in one of the most magnificent of the English cathedrals. Lincoln's copy of Magna Carta is preserved in the chantry of Bishop Longland. Stephen Langton, the Archbishop of Canterbury who played a leading part in the struggle with King John, was born in the county.

Among many remarkable sights, the city has a castle founded by William the Conqueror, two well-preserved Norman domestic buildings (the Jew's House and another misleadingly known as 'The House of Aaron the Jew'), a gateway that has been in use since Roman times, the High Bridge with medieval houses built over the arch, and a river frontage at Brayford Pool.

Louth (FD 38) EC Thurs (11,400). The crocketed spire of the 15th-cent. church is attached to the tower by flying buttresses. The grammar school founded by Edward VI existed as an endowed school three hundred years earlier. Its scholars include Governor Eyre of Jamaica, Sir John Franklin, Captain John Smith (first President of Virginia) and Alfred, Lord Tennyson.

Mablethorpe (FF 38) EC Thurs (5,550). Now a pleasant seaside resort, this, in Tennyson's boyhood, was a village with lonely sand-dunes where he and Charles played and read their joint masterpiece *Poems of Two Brothers*, published by a Louth book-seller.

Pickworth (FA 33) (113). Bomb damage in the 1939 War led to the discovery of 14th-cent. wall-paintings in the church.

Revesby (FD 36) EC Thurs (305). Sir Joseph Banks (1743–1820), the naturalist who sailed with Captain Cook, was born on the site of what is now the Victorian building of Revesby Abbey. His forestry and drainage work in the district are a lasting memorial.

541

Scrivelsby (FC 36) (40). Home of the Dymoke family, traditional holders of the title of King's Champion, conferred on an ancestor by William the Conqueror. Their privilege was to ride in full armour into Westminster Hall at the time of the Coronation, challenging to single combat all who denied the King's sovereignty. This demonstration of chivalry was last performed at the coronation of George IV.

Scunthorpe (EJ 41) (70,000). Among some interesting sights are the early 14th-cent. parish church, Brumby Hall, a 17th–18th-cent. mansion and Normanby Hall, furnished in Regency style. The town houses the regional Museum and Art Gallery for North Lincolnshire. Two miles north of Scunthorpe, at Dragonby, a large Iron Age and Roman-British settlement is being excavated.

Skegness (FF 36) EC Thurs (12,610). Holiday resort with bracing air, a pier 1,843 ft. long and all manner of entertainments.

Skirbeck (FD 34). The old mill, the last in England to grind woad, ceased work in 1932. One of the treasures in the church of St Nicholas is an Elizabethan pulpit with a desk supported by six strange birds carved in wood.

Sleaford (FA 34) EC Thurs (7,940). Market town that owes its prosperity to road and rail communications. In the cathedral-like church of St Denis, note particularly the tracery of the windows, the oak rood-screen (early 15th cent.), a tapestry pulpit-cushion worked in Warwickshire, and the needlework altar-carpet (framed). The two last are of the 17th cent.

Somersby (FD 37) (118). Alfred, Lord Tennyson (1809–92), was born at the old rectory. 'The well-beloved place, where first we gazed upon the sky' brings many reminders of his early poems.

Somerton Castle (EK 35). Two ruined towers (one attached to an Elizabethan farmhouse), and a moat full of water, are part of the great fortified manor house, 2 m. W of Boothby Graffoe, where the captive King John of France was entertained in 1360.

Spalding (FC 32) EC Thurs (15,550). Fenland town, a centre for agriculture and bulb production. A visit in springtime is delightful, when a tulip festival is held at the height of the bulb season. Ayscoughfee Hall, restored in the 18th cent., was the home of Maurice Johnson, who in 1710 founded the still extant 'Gentlemen's Society of Spalding' to which Newton, Addison, Pope, Sir Hans Sloane and other men of letters and science belonged. The museum of the Society, and an ornithological collection, are housed in Broad St.

Spilsby (FE 36) EC Tues (1,665). A statue of Sir John Franklin, born here in 1786, stands in the market place. Memorials in the 14th-cent. church and in Westminster Abbey commemorate the explorer, whose body has never been found.

Stamford (FA 30) EC Thurs (12,910). An archway known as Brasenose Gateway recalls the students who seceded from Oxford and in the 14th cent. set up a rival seat of learning. The town is celebrated for its architecture; examples are Browne's Hospital, built by a wealthy merchant in the reign of Henry VII, the Town Hall, Stamford School (founded in 1532), the ruined chapel of St Leonard's Priory and six ancient churches. Sir Malcolm Sargent was a pupil at Stamford School.

The entrance to the park of Burghley

J. Allan Cash **The tulip fields near Spa**

Landmark in the fens: the ruin, Woodhall Spa

Reece Winstone

House, home of Elizabeth I's statesman (1520–98), is near St Martin's Church, where he is buried. His splendid house contains paintings, furniture and carvings, and is open to the public on certain days of the week.

Stow (EJ 38) EC Thurs (375). The cruciform church, built *c.* 1040 under the patronage of Leofric of Mercia and his wife Lady Godiva, is remarkable for being mainly of that century except for the 15th-cent. tower and minor architectural detail.

Swineshead (FC 34) EC Wed (2,087). A farmhouse has absorbed the materials of the 12th-cent. Cistercian abbey where King John lodged in 1216 after the incident when he lost his baggage in the Wash. The battlemented tower of the parish church, the stocks in the war memorial garden and the tolling curfew in winter months are unusual survivals.

Tattershall Castle★ (FC 35). After Agincourt, Ralph Cromwell transformed an old Norman castle into a home of medieval brickwork, with a quadrangular tower standing over the moat, and four storeys topped by octagonal turrets, from which there is a

remarkable view. The guard house is a museum, and the property belongs to the NT. A row of 17th-cent. almshouses north of the church was restored in 1967.

Wainfleet (FF 35) EC Thurs (1,184). Birthplace of William of Waynflete, the Bishop of Winchester who founded Magdalen College, Oxford, and in 1484 gave Magdalen College School to this town.

Willoughby (FE 37) (541). Boyhood home of John Smith (1579–1631), the penniless local boy who became President of Virginia and Admiral of New England, and whose life was saved by Pocahontas, the Red Indian princess, who died at Gravesend in 1617.

Woodhall Spa (FC 36) EC Wed (2,310). Health-giving bromo-iodine springs were discovered accidentally during an unsuccessful attempt to find coal.

Woolsthorpe (EJ 33) (581). The stone-built Manor House was the birthplace of Sir Isaac Newton in 1642; adjoining it is the orchard where he is said to have discovered the law of gravity.

Opposite: Detail from the original painting by Kenneth Rowntree.

Above sea and fen and windmill, Lincolnshire is the rolling farmland of the wolds. Lincoln itself climbs steeply to the cathedral, a monument of surpassing grandeur. To the north-west runs Foss Dyke; to the south, the fields of tulips glow round Spalding; and over the shire browse the Lincolnshire Longwools. Isaac Newton, suggested in the foreground, was born in Colsterworth parish, south of Grantham.

Tarn Hows

LANCASHIRE
and the Isle of Man

AN INTRODUCTION BY FRANK SINGLETON

'A county that gives itself the airs of a continent' was somebody's comment about Lancashire, and there is more than a little truth in it.

As much as England itself, the most densely populated county provides within its boundaries the most remarkable contrasts – great cities such as Manchester and Liverpool, lovely mountains, picturesque villages, industrial towns, rich farmlands, bare moorlands, beautiful rivers such as the Lune and, in their upper reaches, the Ribble and the Hodder, as well as rivers like the Irwell and the Mersey which have yielded to industry even the memory of country origins. The bewildering variety may, however, be broken down into some broad categories. The industrial and agricultural plain is an extension northwards of the New Red Sandstone of Cheshire. It grows narrower but is discernible around the coast, broadening out again to the north where, meeting the eruption of the

Opposite: Detail from the original painting by Derek Hyatt.

A county of contrasts, of fell and plain, of lake and sea, of dirt and the placid loveliness of Coniston Water, Lancashire is associated with industry, but we should not forget that it is also a county of much beautiful countryside, of wild bluebells, and the landscape paintings of George Stubbs, perhaps better known for his pictures of horses.

limestone, which has come down from the Yorkshire dales and the Pennines, it contributes to the beautiful and contrasting scenery around the great sweep of Morecambe Bay.

Rock and Soil

Scenery and, to some extent, buildings are always conditioned by the nature of the crust of the earth beneath. The plain lies to the west of a line drawn from Lancaster to Warrington. It is agricultural, with some of the most rewarding soil of the county, often broken in the south by coal-mining activities. Between the Ribble and the Lune, and behind Blackpool, the plain is known as the Fylde, from the old English gefilde, a plain or field. Until recently it was a land of windmills, and still has many old white-washed villages. It must have one of the highest poultry populations in the country.

To the east of this line is a moorland district with more rain, poor soil and, particularly south of the Ribble, manufactures. Here are the great industrial towns in an area roughly square, with its corners at Preston, Blackburn, Bolton and Oldham. Moorland and mill-town one might call this part. The hills of north Lancashire run up to the Pennines, which stretch almost to Scotland.

In the south the stone of the Pennines is largely millstone grit. The beauty of the northern uplands, rising to mountain height, springs largely from carboniferous limestone. Then, surprisingly to many people, Lancashire claims a large and beautiful area in the Lake District, which includes one shore of Windermere, all Coniston, and runs into the upper reaches of the Duddon Valley where the counties of Lancashire, Westmorland and Cumberland meet on the summit of the fells.

Cartmel and Furness

The railways run across the wide estuary of the River Kent and part of Morecambe Bay to Lancashire-across-the-sands, which was formerly reached by travellers crossing the bay on foot at low-tide, often disastrously. It consists of two contrasting peninsulas. Cartmel, whose name is Norse in origin, meaning 'sandbank by the rocky ground', is the most aloof of the regions of Lancashire, largely because the Industrial Revolution passed it by. Everywhere one sees a patchwork of fields knit together by the thin lines of stone walls and green hedges. Shapely, wooded hills come down close to the sea. The Priory which serves Cark as parish church, one of the few escapees from the Dissolution, is interesting with a square tower curiously set at a diagonal. Here you may see a first edition of *The Faery Queen*. Spenser had many associations with this and other parts of Lancashire.

Furness, the remotest part of Lancashire, contrasts in history and appearance. Here sandstone and limestone meet, lightly scattered with glacial deposits. Both rocks may be seen in the building material of the churches, field boundaries, farmhouses and barns. Warm-coloured red sandstone was used when in 1127 Furness Abbey, the greatest of the Benedictine houses in these north-western counties, was founded in the Vale of Nightshade by Stephen, Count of Boulogne, Lord of Lancaster, later King of England. The monks mined the rich ores, manufactured iron and engaged in similar activities until the middle of the Second World War, when the hawthorn began to conceal the disused workings.

This is the most rewarding part of Lancashire for the archaeologists, who increase continuously. Here the chipping-floors of a flint-tool factory have been

The Manchester Ship Canal *J. Allan Cash*

discovered among the sand-dunes of Walney Island; there are important stone circles and Iron Age camps, on the green fell-tops, close cropped by the black-faced Herdwick sheep. The distance is blue and craggy, rocks are strewn among the bracken, curlews call and circle in a sky far distant from the smoke-laden air of the manufacturing south.

Architecture

Lancashire has not a good record for caring for its old buildings. It avails not to bewail what has gone. Much still remains. Throughout the northern area peel-towers, and the general architecture of fortified houses, farms and even churches are constant reminders of the persistence after the Norman settlement of the marauding Scot, the enemy from the north. The grim stone castles kept watch through Plantagenet and feudal times – sometimes up to the Civil War. Some, like Clitheroe, embarked on a second career as romantic ruins. Lancaster Castle still lives, dominating the county town, a splendid setting for the assizes and the pageantry of the law. From the keeps the peel-towers were copied for smaller

547

The Promenade, Douglas, in the Isle of Man

residences, as at Wraysholme near Kent's Bank, Borwick Hall, near Carnforth. With the Renaissance came fine houses such as Hoghton Tower and many smaller manor houses and farms. Speke Hall, near the Liverpool airfield, and Hall i'th' Wood, Bolton, now a folk museum, were gifts by Bolton's great son, Lord Leverhulme. An important survivor is Chetham's Hospital, the famous blue-coat school in Manchester. Among manor houses Rufford Hall is notable. The Stanleys great house, Knowsley, was much enlarged during the 18th century and diminished in the 20th, and a number of interesting small churches remain from the 17th and 18th centuries, as at Tarleton, Edenfield, Holy Trinity, Warrington and the attractive and quite unspoilt Presbyterian (now Unitarian) chapel at Rivington.

Some of the best early 19th-century Classic architecture is to be found in the great public buildings in Liverpool. The Gothic revival and the Victorian church-building era left, on Lancashire, the mark that perhaps is the dominant impression of the manufacturing towns. Pugin, Scott, Street, Waterhouse, and later Sir Ninian Comper, and Sir Giles Scott did their best and worst. Gothic, Gothic, everywhere – banks, gas-offices, grocers, lodging-houses, insurance companies, public houses, town halls, public baths, in villas in the suburbs – and in the grand house at Scarisbrick Lancashire possesses the maddest fantasia of all by Pugin and the Scarisbricks. The best modern architecture is to be seen in the houses and flats being built by certain municipalities, in the sky-scrapers

548

of Manchester and Liverpool – where the modern cathedral continues its slow but splendid progress.

The late Haslam Mills, the author of the charge that Lancashire gave itself the airs of a continent, pointed out that disparity, contrast, variation, are the most striking characteristics of the county throughout town and countryside. The traveller from Liverpool to Manchester may have noted, as he did, what he called 'the peculiar vacancy of the view from the carriage window as the train travels across fields which seem to have no purpose except to hold the earth together and grow celery. . . . It is a frontier between the two cities of Manchester and Liverpool, two cities which are not and never really have been on speaking terms!' Despite the miracles of communication that have been achieved, from canals and railways to airways and the arterial East Lancashire road, it remains a curious fact that the last tolerable train from Liverpool to Manchester was lately 9.10 p.m. and that the two cities are entirely different. And so it is, as he points out, with ever-widening variations throughout the county, 'One of the boundaries of Lancashire on the north is the River Duddon, which runs in a veritable viaduct of sonnets by Wordsworth, while its south-eastern boundary is the River

Hornby Castle   *G. Douglas Bolton*

Tame, the waters of which are black with the blackness which does not come of depth, and very likely, if anyone were bold enough to lap them, are warm'. At any rate, I seem to remember having seen a wisp of steam over its course, and, though the Tame is still a melodious stream and goes over a shallow fall between Ashton-under-Lyne and Dukinfield which fills the night hours with a loud music, its song has come to sound as though it were all about cops, and twists, and counts, and effluents: I can imagine it laughing merrily because somehow up its course it left a limited company 'stopped for bobbins'.

And again, it would still be possible to cause the reader, by merely reciting a list of place-names, such a violent change of idea and association as would be quite impossible in Somerset or Westmorland or even in Yorkshire. Thus there is the North Shore at Blackpool. There used to be a peremptory frontier at Blackpool between north and south, those who promenaded and conversed and flirted to music of a band keeping to the north and regarding the south, where in the open air they danced to music in couples, as slightly infected – but in our own times distinctions like this have been obliterated.

Next to Blackpool we might place the Jesuit country round Stonyhurst, and next to Stonyhurst, Strangeways, where Saturday is quite universally the first day in the week and a somewhat historic Nonconformist chapel was some time ago converted into a synagogue, the tapering portion of the spire being removed to signalize the change from the New Testament to the Old. And almost next door to Strangeways there is Kersal, where conversation is largely carried on in modern Greek, and where the Greek Prime Minister might easily be staying for the week-end without any of the rest of us being any the wiser; and from Kersal, with its Egyptian cigarettes and its Balkan politics, we might jump to Fleetwood, where I believe they go fishing in the direction of Iceland.

'But it would still', as Mr Mills says, 'be Lancashire, and, when we had brought all these places within our ambit, and had included farther Union Street, Oldham, and the shores of Lake Windermere, we should find that we had still forgotten much matter of further diversity – Southport, for instance, where good Lancashire people go before they die.'

Off the west coast of Lancashire, in the Irish Sea, lies the Isle of Man. It displays many of the same characteristics of the county, which is not surprising, as it is the annual pleasure-ground of the occupants of the crowded industrial areas. It has also many Royal associations, since from the beginning of the 15th century until the middle of the 18th – the Derbys, who occupy a position in Lancashire comparable with that of the Royal Family, were lords of Man.

The title of Bishop of Sodor and Man (the Sodories are islands off the west coast of Scotland) is a reminder that in its earlier history Man was the most southern of the Hebrides, and it has received influences, as well, from all the other islands that surround it – Northern Ireland and Cumbria, as well as from the Lancastrian lowlands.

The island consists of a high plateau running north-east to south-west, in which the major rivers have cut deep glens, which figure prominently in the programmes of the sightseers. The coastal scenery on all sides of the southern part of the island is bold and picturesque, especially in the neighbourhood of Spanish Head and the islet off the south coast known as the Calf of Man.

The climate is equable, with mild winters and cool summers, and garden hedges of fuchsia are everywhere a colourful feature, even in winter.

The Royal Liver Building, Liverpool

J. Allan Cash

There is an old saying which speaks of Liverpool gentlemen, Manchester men and Bolton chaps. The human qualities which make most southerners, whatever they may think of the climate and other conditions, pronounce enthusiastically for the friendliness of the people, are found in all three categories. The gourmet, however, will do best who can rid himself of prejudice in the matter of food, for the most characteristic of dishes are the ones most generally enjoyed by the chaps and their lasses. It is a land of cakes. Nelson and Eccles cram them with currants. From Bury come Simnel cakes and Bury puddings – delicious kidney-shaped concoctions, these last, that can vie with any haggis for flavour, and are utterly superior to the fat-less hoops of insipid filling known in the south as 'black puddings'. From near Preston an over-sweet, but popular confection, Goosnargh cake. There is a great consumption, too, of what, during the war, the Government off-puttingly referred to as 'edible offals'. Tripe here is already cooked, not, as in the south, requiring several hours preparation. Cowheels, lamb's trotters, pigs' feet, chitterlings do not reach the tables of the genteel, except the more discriminating. To sample them you should ask for them in France where that nation of gourmets shows discrimination in offering them as delicacies. Those who shrink from the delicious nutrition of a pig's nose will enjoy it as 'museau' in a dish of hors-d'œuvres in Paris. Greatest of all is a well-made Lancashire hot-pot. Lancashire cheese is good and the best of all cooking cheeses. Morecambe Bay shrimps are famous. Towards the end of June begin the staggered holidays, or Wakes, of the industrial Lancashire towns. The stay-at-homes are remembered by their friends who send them the delicious Manx kippers. The fame of these has now found them a market in America, to which they are regularly flown.

Some houses and gardens open to the public

Castle Rushen At Castletown *Map CC 46. 12th- to 14th-cent. stronghold; state apartments, Norman keep flanked by towers; one-hand clock given by Elizabeth I.*

Chetham's Hospital and **Library** At Manchester *Map DJ 39. 15th cent. with modern additions; now used as school; library is claimed to be the first public one in Europe. Open by appointment with the Governor.*

Heaton Hall 4m N of Manchester on A665 *Map DJ 40. Georgian house by James Wyatt; contemporary furnishings and 18th-cent. organ.*

Lancaster Castle At Lancaster *Map DE 46. Norman, much-restored castle.*

Manx Village Folk Museum Cregneash 6½m W of Castletown *Map CC 46. Number of thatched cottages and workshops (including Harry Kelly's Cottage) illustrating traditional Manx life.*

Old Parsonage (Fletcher Moss Museum) Didsbury 5m S of Manchester off A34 *Map DJ 39. 19th cent.; now the Fletcher Moss Museum of water-colours and porcelain.*

Peel Castle 12m NW of Douglas facing Peel Bay *Map CC 48. 14th cent.; captured by the Manxmen in 17th cent.; associations with Sir Walter Scott's* Peveril of the Peak *and* Lay of the Last Minstrel.

Pitt Hall 2m S of Manchester off A34 *Map DH 39. 18th cent.; Georgian mansion; Gallery of English Costume.*

Witchcraft Museum Witches Mill. At Castletown *Map CC 46. Museum of curious objects connected with magic and witchcraft.*

Wythenshawe Hall 6m S of Manchester off A560 *Map DJ 39. 16th- to 19th-cent. half-timbered, restored; 17th-cent. furnishings.*

Books for further reading

The 'feel' of Lancashire and the Isle of Man

W. H. AINSWORTH *Lancashire Witches*

S. L. CORBRIDGE *It's an Old Lancashire Custom* 1952

R. NEILL *Mist Over Pendle* and *Moon In Scorpio* (novels)

E. H. STENNING *Portrait of the Isle of Man* 1958

T. THOMPSON Short stories and anecdotes in dialect, particularly *Lancashire Laughter* 1951 and *Under the Barber's Pole* 1949

E. WAUGH Various volumes of poems and tales, particularly *Sketches of Lancashire Life and Localities* 1856

Natural history

R. K. GRESSWELL *Sandy Shores in South Lancashire* 1953

C. OAKES *The Birds of Lancashire* 1953

R. MILLWARD *Lancashire* (Making of the English Landscape series) 1955

P. G. RALFE *Birds of the Isle of Man*

Architecture and topography

H. C. COLLINS *The Roof of Lancashire* 1951

P. FLEETWOOD-HESKETH *Lancashire Architectural Guide* 1955

W. GREENWOOD *Lancashire* (County Books series) 1951

J. LOFTHOUSE *Lancashire Countrygoer* 1962

S. MOORHOUSE *Holiday Lancashire* (Regional Books series) 1955

F. SINGLETON *Lancashire and the Pennines* (Face of Britain series) 1952

E. H. STENNING *Isle of Man* (County Books series)

WARD LOCK & CO. LTD. *The Isle of Man* (Red Guides series) 1968

Gazetteer

LANCASHIRE
and the Isle of Man

Blackpool *Fox Photo*

Ashton-under-Lyne *Lancs.* (D K 41) E C Tues (50,170). Fine 15th-cent. glass in the church pictures Sir John Ashton and his family, and five other beautiful windows give the history of St Helena and her discovery of the True Cross.

Ballasalla *I. o. M.* (CC 47) E C Thurs. Rushen Abbey, an early off-shoot of Furness Abbey in Lancashire, has been a ruin since the 17th cent. The Crossag of Monk's packhorse bridge over the Silverburn is one of the most picturesque sights in the island. Built in the 14th cent. it is now the only medieval bridge on the island. Half a mile along the river is Silverdale, Manx National Glen, which contains swings, a roundabout, boating lake, and car park.

Barrow-in-Furness *Lancs.* (D C 46) E C Thurs (64,820). The red sand-stone Furness Abbey, situated in the 'Vale of Deadly Nightshade' on the outskirts of this shipbuilding town, was founded in 1127 by a small group of monks. The layout of the ruined monastic buildings is clear, and sub-stantial portions of the church towers, walls and architectural detail have sur-vived. Note especially the treasures in the Chapter House, the rows of stone seats in the Sanctuary, and the effigies of 12th-cent. knights in the Infirmary Chapel.

Blackburn *Lancs.* (D G 42) E C Thurs (106,110). From here James Hargreaves (d. 1778) was expelled by a mob who feared redundancy through his inven-tion of the spinning jenny. But the true effects are best illustrated by the spread of the town (which can be effectively seen from the top of Blackmoor) and in the Lewis Textile Museum.

Blackpool★ *Lancs.* (D D 43) E C Wed (152,130). The peak season of this most popular and populous northern resort is during the annual Wakes, when mills and factories close. It has every form of entertainment.

Blackstone Edge *Lancs.* (D K 41). Part of the exposed Roman road into Yorkshire is sound pavement with curbs and a central groove thought to have been worn by some primitive braking system.

Bleasdale *Lancs.* (D F 44). Remark-able circle of wooden posts similar to Woodhenge, which preceded Stone-henge in antiquity. When exposure to air threatened them with disintegra-tion, they had to be removed to Preston Museum, and concrete posts of identical dimensions substituted. Yet the site is fascinating, and not only to archaeologists.

Bolton *Lancs.* (D H 40) E C Wed (160,890). Birthplace of Samuel Crompton, whose spinning-mule (1779) changed the face of Lancashire. He lived in a tenement in the then decaying half-timbered Tudor Hall-i'-th'-Wood, which later was rescued by the 1st Lord Leverhulme, another native of the town, and converted into a noteworthy folk museum.

553

Braddan Old Kirk *I. o. M.* (CD 47). Outdoor summer services attract thousands of worshippers to the 18th-cent. church and the runic crosses in its graveyard.

Burnley *Lancs.* (DJ 43) EC Tues (80,590). The ancestral fortified home of the Towneley family, Towneley Hall, combines beauty of house and garden with a museum and art gallery, all the property of the Corporation. Note the medieval vestments from Whalley Abbey in the anteroom of the chapel, and the domestic apparatus of the huge kitchen. Edmund Spenser lived in a cottage at Hurstwood (3¼ m. N).

Bury *Lancs.* (DJ 41) EC Tues (59,980). Birthplace of Sir Robert Peel (1788–1850). His bronze statue is in the market place. Wrigley Collection of water-colours and engravings is on view in the Art Gallery.

Calf of Man *I. o. M.* (CB 46). Island bird-sanctuary at the SW tip of the coast, presented to the Manx nation in 1937.

Cartmel *Lancs.* (DD 47) EC Wed. The 12th-cent. Priory Church was unroofed at the Dissolution. Some fine bench-ends show the effect of weathering before the church was restored and provided with a black oak screen of Flemish workmanship – the rarest of its great possessions. Note also the tomb of Sir John Harrington (*c.* 1380) and an umbrella used for centuries to shelter the vicar officiating at burials. Elizabethan Cark Hall (2 m. SW) and Holker Hall (pictures, gardens and fallow deer) are full of interest. Kent's Bank was the northern end of the 7-mile route across Morecambe Sands used by coaches and horsemen before the coming of steam.

Castletown *I. o. M.* (CC 46) EC Thurs (1,750). Original capital of the island. The tidal harbour is dominated by Castle Rushen, the axis of Manx history. Its square tower, partly destroyed by Bruce in 1313, but soon rebuilt and added to, is the focus of concentric fortifications. Former use as a prison, mental hospital, barracks and legislative buildings has resulted in certain adaptations. It now contains the Deemsters' Court, and the Court of the Magistrates and High Bailiff. Part of a Celtic crucifix brought here from the Calf of Man is one of the island's greatest treasures.

Chorley *Lancs.* (DF 41) EC Wed (31,260). Cotton and engineering town, the birthplace of Henry Tate in 1819. He founded a sugar empire and endowed the Tate Gallery in London. Miles Standish (1584–1656) of *Mayflower* fame was born at Duxbury Hall (1½ m. S). Astley Hall (¾ m. NW), an Elizabethan mansion reconstructed in 1666, contains fine pottery, furniture, tapestries and pictures, the property of the Corporation.

Clitheroe *Lancs.* (DH 44) EC Wed (12,150). The ancient keep of the stronghold of the de Laceys, perched on a limestone crag above the town, witnessed bitter fighting in the Civil War. From Pendle Hill, the rumoured meeting place of witches, it is often possible to see York Minster, Whalley Abbey and the Irish Sea.

Coniston* *Lancs.* (DD 49) EC Sat (1,100). Village made famous by John Ruskin (1819–1900), who lived at Brantwood, the house now kept by the Education Trust as his memorial. He took great interest in the museum, which has since been given his name and contains many of his possessions. Coniston Old Man (2,635 ft.) can be climbed in under two hours. The lake, a smaller edition of Windermere, to which it lies parallel, is celebrated for the water speed records of Donald

Coniston Water, near Nibthwaite Woods   G. Douglas Bolton

Campbell. It can be best viewed from Tarn Hows, part of a large tract of NT land.

Cregneish *I. o. M.* (CB 46). This picturesquely situated village of thatched cottages contains the island's Folk Museum, which enshrines an earlier age. Furniture, domestic utensils, farm implements and a hand-loom used by the last of a family of weavers, are kept together in workday order. The Chasms, fissures of great depth, lie on the north side of the village.

Dalton-in-Furness *Lancs.* (DC 47) EC Wed (10,320). Birthplace of Romney (1734–1802), who is perhaps best known for his portraits of Emma, Lady Hamilton. Though his wife and children did not share his fashionable London life, he returned to them after 37 years, and is buried here.

Douglas* *I. o. M.* (CD 47) EC Thurs (20,290). In 1869 this town replaced Castletown as the island's capital through having a superior harbour. It

has since developed tourist attractions such as large dance halls and a promenade 2 m. long. The Legislative Buildings, which include the Keys Chamber and the Tynwald Court, are notable in view of the island's distinctive form of Government. The Manx Museum illustrates all phases of Manx history, by means of such treasures as the Cronk-yn-How pictured stone and the medieval Sword of State used on Tynwald Day.

Duddon Valley *Lancs.* (DC 49). Wordsworth's sonnets describe this beautiful scenery with the utmost fidelity.

Fleetwood *Lancs.* (DD 44) EC Wed (27,760). Fishing port and seaside resort at the mouth of the Wyre. It was developed last century by the founder of Rossall School, whose buildings overlook Morecambe Bay.

Hale *Lancs.* (DE 38) (2,410). Village extolled by Jane Carlyle (1801–66) as the 'beautifullest in all England'. John

Cottages at Hawkshead

Middleton, a giant of 9 ft. 3 in. known as the Childe of Hale, is buried in the churchyard. He won brief fame as a wrestler at the Court of James I. Speke Hall, 2 m. W, on the perimeter of Liverpool Airport, and probably the finest black-and-white house in the county, is leased from the NT by Liverpool Corporation.

Hawkshead *Lancs*. (DD 49) EC Thurs (630). Wordsworth lodged at Ann Tyson's Cottage (note its quaint outside staircase) while he was attending the grammar school, where he carved his name on his desk. The medieval gatehouse of Hawkshead Hall and the Elizabethan church, together with the curious alleys and archways of the little town, are worth a leisured visit.

Heysham *Lancs*. (DE 46) EC Wed (with Morecambe, 40,100). Steamers from Belfast use the landing place of St Patrick's missionaries, who built a chapel in his honour; round it grew a strange rock-hewn graveyard. Near the later (12th- to 14th-cent.) church there is a good example of a Viking Hogback tombstone and the shaft of a 9th-cent. cross.

Kirk Maughold *I. o. M*. (CE 49). Large churchyard containing 42 Celtic and Viking crosses in the Cross House. The church font is of a size generally used for total immersion. The grave of Sir Hall Caine is here.

Kirk Michael *I. o. M*. (CD 49). Largest village in NW of island. Church with Runic crosses and monuments and the tombs of several bishops of Sodor and Man. Bishopscourt, the seat of the Bishop of Sodor and Man, lies 1 mile N of Kirk Michael. The bishop's glen is now Manx National Trust property and may be entered free of charge.

Knowsley Hall *Lancs*. (DE 39). The Stanley family, the Earls of Derby, have occupied their estates since the 14th cent. The great irregular house has been added to in almost every period since the original battlemented tower was built for the mother of Henry VI. The rooms, with their decoration, furniture and pictures, are superb.

Lancaster *Lancs.* (DE 46) EC Wed (48,890). The place that has given its name to a dynasty, an energetic county and a royal duchy remains the county town despite its industrial rivals. In 1322 Robert Bruce burnt the castle and town to the ground, but both were rebuilt by John of Gaunt and enlarged and restored by Elizabeth I as a defence against the Armada. The Norman-style keep in the court-yard has the Queen's initials carved on its battlements, and a turret known as John of Gaunt's Chair was added at the same time to serve as a lookout – a function that it still fulfils. John of Gaunt's Gateway Tower is one of the finest in England. The 15th-cent. Church of St Mary has beautiful choir-stalls that originated in Cocker-sand Abbey.

Laxey *I. o. M.* (CE 48) EC Thurs (1,340). Bathing resort with a Great Wheel, the Lady Isabella 72½ ft. in diameter that formed part of the machinery for local lead mines. Terminus of the Snaefell Electric Railway.

Lindale *Lancs.* (DE 48) EC Thurs. The first model iron ship to confute the experts completed successful trials in 1786 on a reach of the Winster bordered by country famous for iron since Roman times.

Liverpool* *Lancs.* (DD 39) EC Wed, Sat (747,490). Industrial and shipping city, imaginatively rebuilt after air-raid damage. Merseyside and the Docks, and the commercial and civic buildings, are of outstanding interest.

The Walker Gallery and the Picton and Hornby Libraries (for the Kelmscott Chaucer, a 14th-cent. Book of Hours and many literary treasures) form part of a group dedicated to the Arts. The new RC cathedral, begun in 1933 from drawings by Lutyens, but now being completed from designs by Gibberd, and the even newer conception of Sir Giles Gilbert Scott (though begun in 1904) for the C of E cathedral, can be compared. The great docks, where one-fifth of UK tonnage is registered, provide excitement in conjunction with the surface life of the Mersey, and the road tunnel that supplements ferryboat links with Birkenhead and the Wirral.

Manchester* *Lancs.* (DJ 39) EC Wed, Sat (661,040). Headquarters of the cotton industry; between 1887 and 1894 the town was converted by the construction of the 35½-m. Manchester Ship Canal from an inland place into a seaport. The cathedral, formerly the parish church, is mainly Perpendicular in style, and was built between 1422 and 1520. The E end was bombed in 1940. Chetham's Hospital, originally a manor house, became a college for priests in the 15th cent., and is now a school housing the oldest free library in England, with valuable early books and MSS. The John Rylands Library, built in 1899, has achieved a great reputation, and the Central Reference Library is one of the finest of its kind in Britain. The main art collections are in the City Art Gallery and the Whitworth Gallery; this last is remarkable for its English water-colours, including many by J. M. W. Turner. Wythenshawe Hall (for furniture, paintings and architecture dating from the 16th cent.), Georgian Platt Hall (for the Museum of Costume) and Heaton Hall (designed by Wyatt) are Corporation property.

Morecambe *Lancs.* (DE 46) EC Wed (with Heysham, 40,000). The sweep of its bay gives this town great individuality. The shrimps are still caught from horse-drawn carts fitted with nets, and the sands may be crossed at low tide by recognized routes.

Oldham *Lancs.* (DK 40) EC Tues (118,300). The town's Wakes, which begin when mills and factories close on the last-but-one Saturday of June, are the most famous of these Lancashire holiday periods. The design of the Town Hall holds closely to the classic style.

Ormskirk *Lancs.* (DE 40) EC Wed (21,450). The church spire is accompanied by a tower built to house the bells from Burscough Priory when it became ruinous. The Derby Chapel contains Stanley monuments.

Peel *I. o. M.* (CC 48). The best of Manx kippers are cured at this fishing port, which has managed to withstand the more insistent claims of tourism. The castle on St Patrick's Isle is reached by a causeway. The ruined cathedral of St German's, thought to have been founded by a disciple of St Patrick, the smallest cathedral of the Church of England, the Old Palace of the Bishops, Fenella's Tower, the 'Irish' Round Tower, St Patrick's Chapel (*c.* 9th cent.) and the coast in each direction – all these have features of outstanding interest.

Point of Ayre *I. o. M.* (CE 50). Extreme northern point of Island. Wide expanse of heath land with interesting bird life and plants. Lighthouse which may be inspected at the head keeper's discretion.

Port Erin *I. o. M.* (CB 46) EC Thurs (1,440). Fishing port S of Bradda Head, from which the Calf of Man can be visited when the weather and the birds' breeding season permit. The Marine Biological Station has a fascinating aquarium open to the public. Popular family resort, good bathing beach with deep sands, open-air bath.

Port St Mary *I. o. M.* (CC 46) EC Thurs (1,400). Steep small town over a delightful harbour. Very good bathing beach and yachting centre.

Prescot *Lancs.* (DE 39) EC Thurs (13,080). Nicholas Hawksmore, a pupil of Sir Christopher Wren, added a tower and a spire to the church, which was already famous for its black-and-white roof.

Preston *Lancs.* (DF 43) EC Thurs (113,210). The town was sacked by Robert the Bruce in 1323, occupied by the Old Pretender in 1715 and by his son in 1745. At Hoghton Tower (6 m. SE), a fine example of a fortified manor house, James I knighted a joint of beef that pleased him – hence the sirloin.

Ramsey *I. o. M.* (CE 49) EC Thurs (4,610). To the delight of townsmen, Queen Victoria was able to land here in 1847 when rough weather made Douglas unsafe. Mooragh Park's Marine Lake is the chief pleasure-ground of this family resort.

Rivington *Lancs.*, 2 m. N of Horwich (DG 41) (150). Reservoirs under Rivington Pike (1,190 ft.) supply Liverpool with some of its water. The beautiful 400-acre Lever Park was presented to the public by the 1st Lord Leverhulme. The charming stone-roofed chapel (1703) retains its original fittings.

Rochdale *Lancs.* (DK 41) EC Tues (85,790). John Bright (1811–89), the Quaker reformer, is buried in the graveyard of the Friends' Meeting House. Some historians suggest that the Society of Equitable Pioneers,

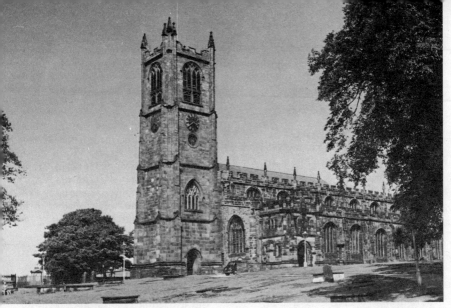

Lancaster: the Parish Church

G. Douglas Bolton

founded here in 1844, was the forerunner of the Co-operative movement.

Rufford Old Hall *Lancs.* (DE 41). Property of the NT, and housing the Philip Ashcroft Museum. The banqueting hall of this beautiful timber-and-plaster house has a very rare 15th-cent. screen and a hammerbeam roof.

Salford *Lancs.* (DH 39). An ancient borough now the hub of that group of industrial towns called South East Lancashire, but which the Saxons and the Middle Ages called Salfordshire. Though separated from Manchester by the Irwell, the two towns are so closely joined that they appear as one. The docks of the Ship Canal are here, and it is a centre of the many industries which have now been added to that of cotton.

Samlesbury *Lancs.* (DG 43) EC Wed (1,200). The Higher Hall, which succeeded a fortified mansion destroyed by the Scots after Bannockburn, was owned by the family of the Blessed John Southworth (1592–1654), the Jesuit martyr.

Sawrey *Lancs.* (DD 49). Beatrix Potter (1866–1943), who has delighted generations of children with her books, lived at 17th-cent. Hill Top Farm, preserved by the NT.

Scarisbrick *Lancs.* (DD 41) EC Wed (8,170). The Hall, built by Augustus Pugin and his son, is an excellent example of Victorian taste.

Sefton *Lancs.* (DD 40) (480). The 15th-cent. church known as the Queen of Lancashire has a chancel-screen with delicate carvings, and some brasses of the Molyneux family.

Snaefell★ *I. o. M.* (CE 48). The highest Manx mountain (2,034 ft.) can be climbed by electric railway for a view on clear days of the peaks of Wales, Ulster, the Lake District and Scotland.

Southport *Lancs.* (DD 41). A beautiful resort by the Irish Sea with a great expanse of sand and tree-shaded streets, the chief of which, Lord Street, with gardens, broad pavements, fashionable shops, is

559

regarded as one of the finest thorough-fares in the world. It was the earliest garden city in the country.

Speke (D E 38). *See* **Hale.**

Stonyhurst *Lancs.* (D G 43). In 1794 the Jesuit school was moved from St Omer to the ancestral home of the Shireburn family. Treasures in the library include a 7th-cent. Gospel of St John, a copy of Froissart's *Chronicles*, Caxton's *Golden Legende* and a Book of Hours owned by Mary Stuart at the time of her death.

Tunstall *Lancs.* (D G 47) (90). The 'Brocklebridge' of Charlotte Brontë's *Jane Eyre*. Here in real life the sisters walked to church, taking dinner to eat in the room over the porch.

Tynwald Hill *I. o. M.* (CC 48). Every 5th of July a great concourse hears new laws promulgated in the Manx language and English from the summit of this three-tiered mound, 12 ft. in height, near the centre of the island. The ceremony begins with a service at the Church of St John the Baptist, followed by a procession and ritual formulated by ancient Scandinavian custom. Tynwald Court is then held in the church.

Warrington *Lancs.* (D G 38) EC Thurs (75,530). This historic place, standing near the ford of the Mersey at Latchford, knew battles from Roman days until 1648, when Cromwell entered the city after his victory at Preston. His bronze statue is near the bridge. The library claims to be first in England to be supported by the rates (1848).

Whalley *Lancs.* (D H 43) EC Wed (3,810). Two medieval gateways and part of the chapter house are the best of the abbey's remains. The last abbot was hanged in 1537 for his part in the Pilgrimage of Grace – that unavailing protest against the Dissolution. The canopied stalls, and the brass of Ralph Catterall (d. 1515) with his wife and twenty children, are two of the treasures in the parish church.

Wycoller Hall *Lancs.* (D K 43). The ruin of the house that inspired Charlotte Brontë to repopulate it as Ferndean Manor in *Jane Eyre*.

Rufford Old Hall

G. Douglas Bolton

Bolton Abbey

Allan Cash

YORKSHIRE, THE WEST RIDING

AN INTRODUCTION BY PHYLLIS BENTLEY

Yorkshire is the largest county in England, and the West Riding of Yorkshire, with its 2,777 square miles, is by itself the next largest. Its shape has been compared with that of a leg of mutton, the shank-bone lying to the north-west, the meaty portion spreading diagonally south-east across England to the Humber. Its landscape is diverse, lacking only a sea-coast to complete its variety.

Traces of early man are widely scattered throughout the Riding, but are not especially notable, except the huge neolithic monoliths of millstone grit, called the Devil's Arrows, near Boroughbridge on the north-eastern boundary.

A glance at the history of the Riding shows first invasion and then frequent rebellion. Britons, Romans, Angles, Danes, Normans – the list of invaders is familiar in English history; but here the Danes have a special importance. The fierce Vikings sailed up the River Ouse into the Riding in the 9th century, and founded a Danish kingdom which lasted nearly a hundred years before it was

561

The Choir, York Minster

Edwin Smith

at last absorbed into England. Dialect words and place-name terminations of
Danish origin, such as *thwaite, thorp, kirk, by*, still remain from this Danish
occupation. After the Norman Conquest the North rebelled, and William the
Conqueror put the rebellion down with fire and sword; the terrible results
appear in Domesday Book (1086) where entry upon entry shows the severe drop
in value of all West Riding lands after the conquest. The Norman barons built
castles – the ruins of Pontefract, Conisbrough, Skipton still remain – here as
elsewhere, but did not penetrate into the wild hilly west. During the Wars of
the Roses in the 15th century the West Riding barons were actively engaged on
both sides; the Yorkist white rose and the Lancastrian red rose became identified
later as the emblems of the two counties. In the Civil War of the 17th century
the West Riding was divided in opinion; the west was for Parliament, the east
for the King, and not only political but religious differences tore the Riding in
half. Later John Wesley (1703–91) preached frequently in the western part of
the Riding, and the population has remained largely Nonconformist, as the
numerous chapels throughout the Riding show. The coming of the Industrial
Revolution caused riots and even murder on the part of the textile operatives,

562

particularly in Huddersfield and Halifax. These rebellious 'Luddites' were betrayed by one of their number, tried at York Castle and hanged.

It was under the Danish kings that the land between the Tees and the Humber which we now know as Yorkshire was divided for administrative purposes into 'thryddings' or thirdings, third parts. These thirdings remain today as Ridings, North, East and West.

There are four great physical facts which have made the West Riding what it is today: the Pennine Chain; the innumerable streams flowing down eastwards from its heights; a great coalfield; a deposit of iron ore.

The Pennine Chain in the West Riding is not a long thin ridge of mountains, but a turbulent mass of interlocking hills spreading from the west over two-thirds of its entire area. As they roll east the hills gradually diminish in height until they sink into the Vale of York, where two minor gravel ridges are to be found. The climate of the Riding follows the trend of the hills. In the west the weather is apt to be rainy, cold and at all times windy, for the great winds which have crossed the Atlantic beat against the Pennine slopes and the clouds

York Minster: the West Front *J. Allan Cash*

are condensed into driving rain. In its passage across the county the weather mellows – the average annual rainfall is 70 inches in the Pennines compared with 20–25 inches in York.

The Pennines in the West Riding are diverse in structure. In the northern part of the Riding they are of carboniferous limestone; then along the River Aire there is a geological 'fault' known as the Aire Gap; to the south the Pennines are of millstone grit. The limestone hills are grey-white, grow short, sweet, very green grass, and abound in caves and 'pot-holes', where streams flow underground. They contain the highest peaks in the West Riding: Pen-y-Ghent (2,273 feet), Whernside (2,414 feet) and Ingleborough (2,373 feet). But these are not 'peaks' in the ordinary sense of the word, for they have huge flat tops, like truncated cones. The horizontal strata characteristic of carboniferous limestone produce strange and striking formations of cliff and cave: Kilnsey Crag, Gordale Scar, Malham Cove. The most important of the underground caves are the Victoria Caves, discovered on the day of Queen Victoria's coronation, a huge system of connected underground caverns within Ingleborough, where stalactites and stalagmites can be seen, and bones and flints and other relics tell the story of early man. The north-west corner of the Riding certainly offers its most beautiful landscape, with its towering pale grey rocks, bright green grass and silver rivers, its fields divided by the tall 'dry', i.e. mortarless, grey walls. The valley of the River Wharfe is particularly picturesque and beautiful.

Millstone grit landscape is different. The hills show dark, very hard rock covered with moors of purple heather and stretches of bracken and long, rough grass; the streams do not plunge underground but tumble briskly down, limeless. Here too the fields are divided by dry walls, but their stones are less spiky and less elaborately arranged than in the more northerly country. Many large reservoirs feeding neighbouring towns lie high up in these hills, ruffled into waves like mountain tarns. These millstone grit hills are perhaps bare, bleak and wild; but they have a sombre, massive beauty very dear to West Riding hearts. Both limestone and millstone grit hills afford pasture to sheep, but on the millstone hills, with their scantier pasture, the breeding of sheep is no longer the important occupation it has remained on the limestone.

In neither part is the West Riding at present well forested. The Pennine summits are above the tree line, and industrial smoke has bared many hill slopes. Oak and ash were the indigenous trees, to which other deciduous trees (not very tall) and sometimes firs and larches have been added. The flora and fauna differ little from those of other counties, but purple heather and ling, bilberries and white-bolled cotton grass are found on the moors, while the mauve-blue harebell brings its delicate colouring and slender stem to the grass. In the wilder parts of the Riding, curlew with their long pointed beaks and melancholy cry are to be seen and heard by the rivers, the acrobatic peewit loops above the grass, the grouse calls *go-back go-back* on the moors.

Rivers

The five main rivers of the West Riding are often compared with the fingers of a hand. Nidd, Wharfe, Aire, Calder and Don, they all rise in the Pennines and make their way, south and east for the three northerly streams, north-east for the Don, becoming the River Ouse as they join each other and two North Riding rivers, and falling eventually into the Humber and so to the North Sea. One river, the Ribble, rising in the Pennines, is prevented from following an easterly

The Shambles, York

course by an outlying spur of hills, and strays away (as all Yorkshiremen feel) westwards into Lancashire.

Coal

A considerable coalfield, fringing the hills, lies beneath the surface of the millstone grit West Riding, north to south from Castleford to Sheffield, west to east from Barnsley to Doncaster and on under the North Sea.

A deposit of iron ore, now exhausted, originally lay under the hilly country around Sheffield.

The plain of York, once long ago a marsh, is now from the silt of the rivers fertile farming country, growing barley and oats and affording ample pasture to milk-cows and cattle. It is here that we find the 'broad acres' of the Riding.

These physical facts made possible the steel and wool-textile industries.

Sheep and limeless streams provide wool, and soft water kind to fabric, both essential features in wool-textile manufacture; tumbling water provides easy water-power; iron provides the material for machinery and steam-engine boilers; coal provides the steam. The wool-textile trade has a well documented history of at least six hundred years, for contemporary tax records show that 974 pieces of woollen cloth were manufactured in 1396 in the West Riding, and from then onwards historical records are abundant. First located chiefly in York, the hand cloth industry presently took great hold in the Pennines, where it supplemented the produce of the infertile land as a livelihood; when water-power, machinery and steam-power were one by one invented, the Pennines had the materials necessary for these close at hand. Today the area roughly enclosed between Bradford, Leeds, Batley, Huddersfield and Halifax produces some four hundred million square yards of woollen and worsted cloth a year. The landscape of these industrial towns is a dramatic if 'satanic' landscape of interlocking hills, forested by innumerable mill chimneys springing from various levels, with rows of small houses clinging, at times it seems precariously, to the hillside slopes, and the Pennines looming close around. Other industries now add their own ingredients to this thickly populated and powerfully productive area, teeming with vigorous life.

Combined with neighbouring supplies of coal, some other necessary ingredients and (again) water, the deposit of iron ore led to the great steel industry of Sheffield. The city's history of cutlery-manufacture goes back for at least six hundred years. Chaucer in his *Canterbury Tales* (*c.* 1387) says of the Miller of Trumpington: 'A Sheffield thwitel baar he in his hose' – a thwitel or whittle being an ancestor of our small knife. Begun as a domestic industry, Sheffield steel now occupies many huge forges and rolling-mills; the tipping of a molten cauldron and the rolling of the red-hot steel provide superb though alarming spectacles. The Sheffield mark is known all over the world as indicating excellence, and standards are regulated by the Cutlers' Company, headed by the elected Master Cutler.

Architecture

In architecture the city of York, situated at the point where the three Ridings meet, is the show-piece, though in fact York belongs to none of the Ridings, but to itself alone. It administers its own affairs, is both a city and a county and therefore has both a Lord Mayor and a Sheriff. In York the architecture of every century is to be found: Roman walls, medieval gateways, twenty churches and the superb Minster, which among other beauties boasts the Five Sisters, a magnificent stained-glass window of five enormous slender lancets, in *grisaille*. The York Museum, which takes you into lifesize reconstructions of old York streets, faithfully modelled with shops, vehicles and inhabitants, is justly renowned.

The huge ruins of Fountains Abbey, near Ripon, are among the largest and most beautiful monastic remains in England. Such a wealth of old parish churches, Norman castles, and fine nobility houses exist in the Riding that only a small proportion of them can be listed even in the Gazetteer. Of special local interest are the yeoman clothiers' houses of the 17th century, and the old weavers' cottages with their long row of windows in the 'loom-chamber' in the second storey, which are to be found in numbers in the upland folds of the hills round Halifax and Huddersfield.

Recreations

Pot-holing, the exploration of the underground caves in the north-west, dangerous because of the sudden influx of water caused by unexpected rain, is followed with fervour by a devoted few, in whose adventures all take an interest. The old West Riding game of knur and spell is now no longer played except as a folk-lore revival.

No county has a more glorious record on the cricket field than Yorkshire, which in the past century has won the county championship twenty-seven times outright, and to this result West Riding players have largely contributed. To football also, especially Rugby Union and Rugby League, the Riding is devoted. The St Leger race at Doncaster in September and the York races are widely known, but the hilly character of the Riding is not encouraging to horsemanship sports except in the east. Pigeon-racing and whippet-racing, especially by miners, are popular sports.

Of intellectual recreations, music is the West Riding's prime interest. The many choral societies are justly famed, and Huddersfield's yearly performance of Handel's *Messiah* under the conductorship of Sir Malcolm Sargent has gained a nation-wide reputation on radio and television. Musical societies of all kinds flourish, including those for the amateur performance of musical comedies. The brass band is a homelier but very genuine witness to the popular love of music, and bands from West Riding mills often win the national championship.

A comparatively new intellectual pursuit is amateur drama. The Huddersfield Thespians, the Bradford Civic Theatre and the Halifax Thespians (the last two of which own their own theatres) put on eight or ten productions every year of very high amateur standard, while innumerable smaller groups strive in emulation.

Food

Yorkshire pudding, a delicious fluffy batter baked in the oven till it achieves a crisp, light-brown surface, eaten with gravy as a course by itself, is strongly to be recommended, as is the rich, brown, treacly parkin. York hams are well known. 'High tea', a 'knife and fork' meal eaten between five-thirty and six-thirty, usually comprises ham, with every possible variety of bread, scone, teacake, sweet cake, parkin and pastry. West Riding women are good providers and expect their guests to make a hearty meal.

Character

The West Riding character is robust, shrewd, stubborn, sardonically cheerful though not optimistic, plain-spoken when speaking at all, warm-hearted and extremely independent. Perhaps because of their long history as earners in skilled industries, the West Riding people are accustomed to regard themselves as everyone's equal; indeed they think so well of themselves that a stranger has to prove his worth before he is considered an equal. Once he is admitted to friendship, however, he is a friend for life. Tenacity of feeling is preferred in the West Riding to expressiveness, and any affectation of effusiveness or superior manners is despised. A broad humour, laconically uttered, a considerable respect for that formidable and competent housewife the Yorkshirewoman, a slightly excessive interest in 'brass'; and, again – and again – obstinacy: these complete the portrait.

The number of celebrated persons born in the West Riding is so considerable that no account of them can be given here: reference should be made to the appropriate volumes. The three Brontë sisters, of Irish and Cornish parents, are the most famous writers; their home in Haworth near Keighley, now the Brontë Parsonage Museum, should certainly be visited. Within this century two strong groups of West Riding novelists have given vigorous if rather sardonic pictures of the life of their native Riding: the 'feel' of the Riding will be found best in their works.

Some houses and gardens open to the public

Abbey House Museum Kirkstall Abbey 2½m NW of Leeds on A65 *Map* EC 43. *Original gatehouse of ruined Cistercian Abbey; occupied continuously for 800 years; now a folk museum with three streets of houses, shops and craft workshops and collections of pottery, costume, toys and games.*

Brontë Parsonage Museum Haworth 4m SW of Keighley on A6033 *Map* EA 43. *Brontë relics.*

Cliffords Tower At York *Map* EG 45. *Partly 13th cent.; two-storeyed keep built on an 11th-cent. motte raised by William the Conqueror.*

Fountains Hall 3m SW of Ripon off B6265 *Map* EC 46. *17th cent.; in grounds of famous Abbey.*

Harewood House 7m S of Harrogate on A61 *Map* ED 44. *Home of H.R.H. the Earl & Countess of Harewood; 18th-cent. exterior by John Carr and interior by Robt Adam; State rooms; pictures, Chippendale furniture, and Sèvres porcelain; park designed by Capability Brown.*

Knaresborough Castle 3m E of Harrogate on A59 *Map* ED 45. *14th cent.; ruins including keep, two baileys and gatehouse with porter's lodge; above River Nidd.*

Newby Hall 4m SE of Ripon off B6265 *Map* ED 46. *18th-cent. Adam House and gardens; fine statues, Gobelin tapestry.*

Pontefract Castle At Pontefract *Map* EE 42. *Norman stronghold in ruins; small museum of local relics, Roman pottery and coins.*

Books for further reading

The 'feel' of Yorkshire

JOHN and RICHARD FAIRFAX-BLAKE-BOROUGH *The Spirit of Yorkshire* 1954

HERBERT LESLIE GEE *Tales They Tell in Yorkshire* 1954

HARRY J. SCOTT *The Changeless Dales* 1946

Among the many Yorkshire novels are THOMAS ARMSTRONG's *The Crowthers of Bankdam* and *Pilling Always Pays;* PHYLLIS BENTLEY's *Take Courage, Manhold, Inheritance* and *Love and Money;* the BRONTES' (ANNE's *The Tenant of Wildfell Hall*, EMILY's *Wuthering Heights*, CHARLOTTE's *Shirley* and *Jane Eyre*); and WILLIAM RILEY's *Windyridge.*

History and topography

GEOFFREY DOUGLAS BOLTON *Yorkshire Revealed* 1955

LETTICE COOPER *Yorkshire: West Riding* (County Books series) 1950

MARIE HARTLEY and JOAN INGILBY *The Wonders of Yorkshire* 1959

CUCHLAINE A. M. KING *The Yorkshire Dales* (British Landscape Through Maps series) 1960

WILLIAM T. PALMER *Wanderings in the Pennines* 1951

ARTHUR RAISTRICK and JOHN L. ILLING-WORTH *The Face of North-West Yorkshire* 1949

WARD, LOCK & CO. LTD. *The Yorkshire Dales.* 5th edn (Red Guides series) 1960

Architecture

JOHN L. ILLINGWORTH *Yorkshire's Ruined Castles* 1938

NIKOLAUS PEVSNER *Yorkshire: the West Riding* (Buildings of England series) 1959

ELLA PONTEFRACT *The Charm of Yorkshire Churches* 1936

BENJAMIN WADE *Yorkshire's Ruined Abbeys* 1938

BERNARD G. WOOD *Historic Homes of Yorkshire* 1957

Gazetteer

YORKSHIRE, THE WEST RIDING

Fountains Abbey: the cellarium   *Edwin Smith*

Adel (EC 44) EC Wed (6,110). Small Norman church, perfect of its period, with a sculptured S doorway and chancel-arch.

Aldborough (EE 46) (790). Site of the Roman city of Isurium, where the consuls and governors of York had villas. The form of their civic buildings and lines of defence are clear. A stone panel (*c.* 100) to the god Mercury is built into the N aisle of the church, three sections of mosaic are nearby, and the ground plan of a basilica measuring 52 ft. by 24 ft. contains fragments of tesselated pavement. The museum has Roman works of art and domestic articles found on the site.

Austerfield (EG 39) EC Thurs (480). William Bradford, eventual Governor of Plymouth, New England, who kept a log of the *Mayflower* on her journey to the New World, lived in the modest yeoman's house preserved in his memory.

Barnsley (ED 40) EC Thurs (74,650). Impressive civic buildings do much to relieve the severity of the town, a centre for the iron and coal industries. 40-acre Locke Park was presented to the town in memory of Joseph Locke, who aided the development of the steam engine after his apprenticeship to George Stephenson.

Birstall (EC 42) EC Tue (6,700). Charlotte Brontë, who came here on visits to her friend Ellen Nussey, describes Elizabethan Oakwell Hall in *Shirley*. The house is little changed.

Bolton Abbey* (EA 45) EC Wed (160). Beautiful ruins where the Wharfe spreads out into a valley. The priory was founded in the early 12th cent. for black canons of the Augustinian Order who, unlike monks, came under the jurisdiction of bishops. The nave of their church was spared during the Dissolution of the Monasteries, and is to this day used for services, but the front, which was to have been crowned by a tower, had to be left uncompleted. Most of the monastic buildings have been razed to the ground.

Boroughbridge (EE 46) EC Thurs (1,850). Where Edward II won his victory over the Duke of Lancaster in 1322. The Devil's Arrows west of the town, so-called in the belief that they were bolts which were 'shot at ancient cities and therewith overthrew them', are three megaliths comparable with those at Stonehenge. 3,000 years old, they may have influenced the Romans when they chose a site for Isurium (*see* **Aldborough**).

Bradford (EB 43) EC Wed (295,770). Centre of the worsted trade. Cartwright Memorial Hall was erected as an Art Gallery in 1904 in honour of Edmund Cartwright (1743–1823), the inventor of the power loom. St Peter's

Shadows over Fountains Abbey

Church, mainly of the 14th and 15th cents., with a fine roof and a long nave, became the Cathedral in 1920. A museum illustrating the city's domestic and social life is housed in Bolling Hall, the SW part of which was built *c.* 1330. It has mullioned windows, plaster ceilings and a Jacobean garden laid out by the Corporation. It belonged to the ancestors of President Woodrow Wilson's wife, Edith Bolling Galt.

Bramham Park (EE 44). This Queen Anne House, after being partly destroyed by fire in 1828, had to wait until this century for restoration, during which a horseshoe staircase modelled on the one at the Palace of Fontainebleau was added to the W front. A collection of paintings hangs in splendid rooms. The stable block and an oratory overlooking the lake were designed by James Paine. The French gardens, with their ingenious use of running water, make this estate unique.

Brimham Rocks (EC 46). Outcrops of millstone grit weathered into grotesque shapes. They have descriptive names such as Yoke of Oxen, Baboon Rock, the Dancing Bear, etc. The 200-ton Idol Rock balances on a stalk 12 in. in diameter. The loneliness of their situation on Brimham Moor makes them a weird sight.

Cawood (EF 43) (970). Site of the palace to which Cardinal Wolsey retired in 1530, vainly hoping to end his life enlarging and enriching it to rival Hampton Court, which he had given to Henry VIII. Though the palace was demolished in 1646, the graceful 15th-cent. gatehouse was spared, complete with oriel windows and the vaulted archway through which many royal personages rode.

Clapham (DH 46) EC Thurs (610). Centre for walking, climbing and potholing, convenient for waterfalls, an ascent of Ingleborough (2,373 ft.) and a maze of limestone caves crowded with stalactites and stalagmites deep in the mountain.

Conisbrough Castle (EF 39) EC Thurs (17,500). Cylindrical keep, supported by six buttresses and standing high above the Don. These reinforcements, which taper towards the top, were originally capped with turrets. The living quarters and a hexagonal oratory are on the second and third storeys behind walls 15 ft. thick. Sir Walter Scott set a scene in *Ivanhoe* here.

Doncaster (EF 40) EC Thurs (86,400). The town's charter was granted by Richard Coeur de Lion in 1194. Its pride is the Mansion House, designed by Paine in the 18th cent., and the Church of St George, the work of Sir Gilbert Scott. Mining country lies to the W. The St Leger, the last of the year's racing classics and senior to the Derby by four years, is run on Town Moor.

Farnley Hall (EC 44). A house of 1581 with an 18th-cent. addition houses the Fawkes family's Cromwellian relics and also works by J. M. W. Turner, who was a frequent visitor. Various of the treasures have had to be sold in payment of death duties. Admission by arrangement.

Fountains Abbey★★ (EC 46). The loveliest of England's ruins was founded by Archbishop Thurstan in the early 12th cent. for twelve Benedictine monks who decided to embrace the Cistercian rule. The abbey grew in size and wealth through the wool trade and ownership of land, but in 1539 the treasure was scattered and the roofs dismantled. The nave with eleven bays, and the Chapel of the Nine Altars at the end, are special features. Note also the chapter-house, the double avenue of arches in the cellarium, and the foundations of the

infirmary, which was built in part over the Skell. Nearby Fountains Hall (*c.* 1610) was constructed of stones taken from the Abbey. It has an imposing hall and minstrels' gallery, panelled bedrooms and superb furniture and works of art.

Goole (EH 42) EC Thurs (18,800). Port with extensive docks, though situated fifty miles from the sea. The Don meets the Yorkshire Ouse via the Dutch River, a canal cut by Vermuyden, a Dutch engineer employed by Charles I.

Guiseley (EB 44) (6,650). Maintaining tradition, a pageant to depict the life of the saint is staged on the Saturday after St Oswald's Day (August 6th) in the grounds of the delightful Elizabethan Rectory.

Halifax (EA 42) EC Thurs (96,070). Industrial centre that specializes in the clothing trade. Bankfield museum, housed in a splendid Italianate mansion, has many art treasures, including a set of tapestries made by machinery, and exhibits of local interest, among which is a gibbet on which men guilty of stealing cloth in excess of 13½d. were executed. The town hall was designed in 1859 by the architect of the Houses of Parliament, Sir Charles Barry. A fine view is obtained from Beacon Hill and from the 250-ft. Wainhouse Tower, which has a narrow internal staircase in what was intended to be a chimney. St John's Church is one of the few remaining old buildings in the town centre. The West Yorkshire folk museum is in medieval Shibden Hall, which is a half-timbered house with stone additions and furnished in period style, set in 55 acres of lovely grounds.

Harewood House (ED 44). Present home of H.R.H. the Princess Royal and the Earl and Countess of Harewood:

a mansion completed in 1771 by John Carr, with decorations by Robert Adam, plasterwork by Zucchi, murals by Angelica Kauffman, furniture designed by Adam and made by Chippendale, and a great collection of pictures and porcelain. Additions in 1843 altered the classical balance of the design. The gardens by Capability Brown are landscaped to provide each vista with a distant natural landmark. The formal Terrace Gardens are later additions. In all, the park extends to 1,800 acres.

Harrogate* (ED 45) EC Wed (56,330). Inland watering place, an ideal centre for tourists and much favoured for conferences. The properties of the waters were discovered in the 16th cent. when a traveller noticed their resemblance to those of continental spas. In all there are 88 springs of sulphur and iron, and the Royal Baths, administered by Leeds Regional Hospital Board, can provide more than 1,000 treatments daily. The Royal Pump Room, over the main sulphur spring, is now a museum. From the observatory tower on Harlow Hill you can view this spacious town of hotels, fine houses and impressive gardens, as well as catching glimpses of the Tees and Humber, York and Ripon.

Haworth (EA 43) EC Tues (4,160). In some lights the town appears as bleak and windswept as the moors. Both contribute to understanding the strange genius of the Brontë family. The Parsonage, to which they moved in 1820, is maintained by the Brontë Society. Here is the sofa upon which Emily died, Charlotte's work-basket just as she left it, and the books, barely an inch square, that the children wrote in secret; they now belong to the Bonnell Collection of MSS brought from America. The cramped rooms express frugality,

while the darker side of the family's natures is reflected by the graveyard and the moors that were Emily's respite from family troubles.

Huddersfield (EB 41) EC Wed (130,300). Well-planned town, noted for textiles. The Tolson Memorial Museum has a collection of exhibits illustrating the development of the cloth industry.

Ilkley (EB 44) EC Wed (18,520). As Roman Olicana, and as an early religious stronghold, the town has many items of historical interest, though it is chiefly regarded as a gateway to Upper Wharfedale,* the centre for touring and walking over Ilkley Moor in quest of the great stones, ancient bridges and splendid vantage-points in an untrammelled countryside.

Ingleton (D G 47) EC Thurs (1,890). The ravines down which plunge the Doe and the Twiss form a chain of waterfalls that can be followed on foot. Thornton Force and Beezley Falls are most impressive after rain. White Scar Caves, discovered in 1923, present a complication of rock chambers. This paradise for pot-holers should not be explored without expert guidance.

Knaresborough (ED 45) EC Thurs (9,310). Attractive town on the R. Nidd, possessing many 18th-cent. houses. The 14th-cent. keep is the best-preserved part of John of Gaunt's castle, where Richard II was held captive in 1399. Two famous local sights are the Dropping Well, a waterfall that trickles as if through a giant sieve, and has petrifying properties; and the Wishing Well of Mother Shipton, the mythical Yorkshire prophetess. The manor house, with its chequerboard walls, was presented by James I to his son

Charles as a fishing lodge.

Leeds (ED 43) EC Wed (510,600). The University specializes in science and technology, and has a beautiful circular library. Notable are the markets, the Town Hall and Civic Hall, and Headingley cricket ground, where Test Matches are played. Kirkstall Abbey*, founded in 1152, is a sister house to Fountains Abbey. Temple Newsam, the 'Hampton Court of the North', a house of mellow brick, is filled with treasures, and set in gardens famous for their roses.

Malham (DJ 46) EC Thurs (170). The R. Aire bursts from a subterranean course into Malham Cove. Gordale Scar to the E is part of the same geological fault, and produces a ravine with a magnificent succession of waterfalls.

Markenfield Hall (ED 46). Early 14th-cent. moated manor house. The drawbridge has been replaced by a stone structure.

Marston Moor (EE 45). Scene of Cromwell's decisive victory over the Royalists in 1644.

Nidderdale (EA 47). Beautiful scenery opens up below Bradford's reservoirs at Angram and Scar Head.

Pontefract (EE 42) EC Thurs (27,110). The castle where Richard II was murdered or starved to death in 1400 was 'slighted' in 1649, and nothing remains but ruins on a splendid site. The Church of All Saints combines restoration and disrepair. Pontefract cakes are lozenges flavoured with liquorice, which is a Mediterranean plant believed to have been imported by the Romans.

Ripon* (ED 47) EC Wed (10,490). Ranks with York and Beverley as an original centre of Christianity. The cathedral (or minster) is small, but of importance because it embodies a diversity of architectural styles. The 13th-cent. Wakeman's House was the home of the medieval official pledged to make good all losses from theft during the hours of curfew. The Wakeman's Horn is still blown at 9 p.m.

Rotherham (EE 39) EC Thurs (85,350). Coal and iron town possessing a fine Perpendicular-style church with a crocketed spire. The chantry is built into the 15th-cent. bridge over the Don.

Sedbergh (D G 49) E C Thurs (2,330). The famous public school was founded in the early 16th cent. by Roger Lupton, Provost of Eton. A building

Gardens at Harrogate

G. Douglas Bolton

that dates from 1716 contains the library and museum. The narrow main street was part of the turnpike between Kendal and Kirkby Stephen. Note the charming 17th-cent. Friends' meeting house, where George Fox, the founder of the Society, is said to have preached beneath a yew tree.

Selby (EG 43) EC Thurs (9,870). Believed to be the birthplace of Henry I (1068–1135), the only English-born son of the Conqueror. Navigation of the Ouse so far inland is possible by small steamers. The Abbey Church of the Virgin and St Germanus is considered one of the most splendid monastic churches in England. It was damaged by fire in 1906, but has been well restored; additions were made to the towers in 1935. The Norman W doorway, the E windows, and the screens and sedilia are of special interest.

Settle (DJ 46) EC Wed (2,297). Old-world town high in the hills and characterized by gabled houses with oriel windows and turrets. The local museum contains bones and artefacts found in Victoria Cave (reached from Langcliffe), some of which date from the Ice Age.

Sheffield (ED 38) EC Thurs (493,950). The prosperous industrial city now celebrated throughout the world for cutlery. It was made here in Chaucer's day. In 1720 a Lincolnshire clockmaker, Benjamin Huntsman, started a series of experiments that resulted in the discovery of crucible steel, on which the present industry's reputation was founded. The cruciform church of St Peter and St Paul, dating from the 14th cent., became the cathedral of the bishopric founded in 1913. The Graves Art Gallery has a fine collection of pictures, including Constables, Cotmans and Turners.

The city is within easy reach of wonderful moorland country* and the Derbyshire Peak District.

Skipton (DK 45) EC Tues (12,990). Market town in the centre of Craven, which has wild scenery extending into Lancashire. The castle, founded by Robert de Romillé in Norman times, came into the hands of the Clifford family in 1269. Their motto 'Désormais' is sculptured in great letters on the parapet over the gateway. The older parts of the castle, including the dungeon, are open to the public. One of its beauties is the situation high on a rock above its moat, which now forms part of the canal.

Studley Royal (ED 46). The deer park and pleasure gardens make a perfect approach on foot to Fountains Abbey (*see above*), past avenues and hedges, temples and statuary and Italian and Dutch gardens that have brought the R. Skell into ponds and fountains. The church is an extraordinary product of 1871 in the style of the 14th cent., decorated with carvings, glass and ironwork, walls of Egyptian alabaster and a painted roof. At Robin Hood's Well, the outlaw is said to have been thrown into the brook by the Curtal Friar.

Swillington (ED 42). The church has a curious black tower that contrasts with the local stone in the remainder of the building.

Wakefield (ED 42) EC Wed (61,590). County town of the West Riding, situated on the R. Calder. The crocketed spire (247 ft.) of the cathedral is the tallest in Yorkshire. Note the woodwork in the chancel and the gilding of the High Altar. The city has many Georgian houses, and a chantry chapel (restored) originally erected in the reign of Edward III, against the old bridge across the river.

Knaresborough

G. Douglas Bolton

Wharfedale* (EA 45). One of the most beautiful valleys in England, with a combination of villages and ruins, peaceful and wild landscapes. The Strid, above Bolton Abbey, is approached from the car park at Cavendish Pavilion and beyond the Meeting of the Waters, where the river is divided by numerous small islands. At the Strid the water runs through a narrow channel at some points 30 ft. deep, and may be crossed in a stride – though this is dangerous, and the return step is made more so by overhanging rock.

Wragby (EE 41) (500). The church, with its medieval glass brought from Switzerland, stands surrounded by yews in the park of Nostell Priory (home of the Winn family), which has been acquired by the NT. The splendid façade of the house is by James Paine, and a wing was added by Robert Adam. It is a treasure-house of historic objects, but chiefly celebrated for a collection of Chippen-

dale furniture and a remarkable portrait gallery.

York** (EF 45) EC Wed (104,470). The capital of the North, unique for the completeness of its walls and the preservation of antiquities from prehistoric times onwards, and situated at the junction of the three Ridings of Yorkshire, to none of which it belongs. 'Winchester was, London is, York shall be, the finest of the three' is a prophecy of Mother Shipton. Caer Ebrauc to the British, Eboracum to the Romans, Jorvik to the Danes – the titles are an illustration of early history. William the Conqueror built two castles here, facing each other across the Ouse. The most noteworthy survival on these sites is Clifford's Tower, built in the 13th cent. by Henry III in a quatrefoil plan high on a mound. It was saved centuries later from demolition when the citizens of York pleaded that it was exceeded only by the Minster as an adornment to their city. The rest

575

Towards Ripley, from Addingham High Moor *Edwin Smith*

of the castle has been mainly replaced by the Assize Courts and the Castle Museum, containing among its treasures a reconstruction of a York street in the 18th and 19th centuries.

The Minster is the largest cathedral built in England in the Middle Ages (60,952 sq. ft.). It grew on the site of four earlier churches, taking two and a half centuries to complete after a beginning in 1220; thus it combines the best of the Early English, Decorated and Perpendicular periods. By the orders of Sir Thomas Fairfax after the battle of Marston Moor, the fabric was spared destruction at the hands of the victorious Parliamentarians. The crypt incorporates a pillar of the Roman praetorium and parts of two earlier churches. Among the treasures of the chapter-house are Saxon gospels dating from 982, illuminated missals, and the Ivory Horn of Ulphus presented in 950 by a Saxon nobleman. But it is for medieval glass that the Minster is justly world-famous, its sole rival being Chartres.

Of the 125 windows, the E Window and the Five Sisters Window (restored in 1925 as a memorial to the women who died in the 1914 War) are perhaps the best known, but throughout the cathedral are superb examples of the local glassmakers' art in the three periods during which the Minster was built. This wealth of craftsmanship was removed for safety in the 1939 War. This has produced unrivalled opportunities for restoration, and the consequent cleaning, releading and assembly into their original form has brought the windows back to pristine perfection.

The city has many features of architectural interest, and deserves to be explored on foot and at leisure, taking in the great medieval walls and 'bars' or gates, the Assembly Rooms and the medieval Shambles, where shops lean precariously across a narrow street. But we must not forget that this is also a modern city, glorying in the past, yet living and thriving in the activities of our time.

Opposite: Detail from the original painting by S. R. Badmin.
Within its great expanse, Yorkshire has wild dales, barren moors, and also a wonderful richness of soil. Ruined abbeys abound. Yorkshire was the home of the Brontës and the setting for some of their novels. Not the least of the county's institutions is one shown by the picture: a Yorkshire high tea. This, we see, is composed of scones, apple-pie, parkin, Wensleydale cheese, and ham.

WUTHERING
HEIGHTS

EMILY
BRONTË
1847

1818—1848

S. R. Badmin

YORK

GRETA BRIDGE   J.S. COTMAN

MULTANGULAR TOWER
RIEVAULX ABBEY
FOUNTAINS ABBEY
RICHMOND CASTLE
KIRKHAM PRIORY

The harbour, Whitby

YORKSHIRE, THE EAST AND NORTH RIDINGS

AN INTRODUCTION BY MARIE HARTLEY AND JOAN INGILBY

A peace and quiet that have been lost to many parts of England are to be enjoyed in both the East and North Ridings. There is, to begin with, plenty of room. The East Riding compares in size with many other English counties, and the North Riding, twice its size, contains one National Park (the North York Moors) and half another (the Yorkshire Dales). Add to this that there exist only two areas with major industries, those on the perimeter round Hull and Middlesbrough, and it will be obvious what a vast area of unspoilt country the Ridings contain. Villages tucked under hillsides, farms covering the plains, mansions sheltered by woodlands and headlands overlooking bays, merge into one harmonious landscape after another.

Beside the western dales and the north-eastern moorlands (the latter alone cover 1,000 square miles) there are the Yorkshire Wolds, the Howardian Hills, the great Plain of York, many miles wide, and other vales such as those of Pickering, Mowbray and Cleveland.

Opposite: Detail from the original painting by S. R. Badmin.

The largest of England's counties, Yorkshire is endowed not only with dales and moorlands, but also with fertile plains now used for agriculture. The coastline, with its beautiful bays and long stretches of firm sand, has both large holiday resorts and quiet seaside towns. In Captain Cook, Yorkshire gave the world one of its most famous explorers.

Troutsdale

G. Douglas Bolton

The coast, roughly divided between the two Ridings, runs for almost a hundred miles, from north of the highest cliffs in England, at Boulby, to the low-lying shore of Holderness. Large holiday resorts, quiet seaside towns and former fishing villages, preserving their individual charms, face lovely bays and firm extensive sands.

The Shape of the Land

As would be true elsewhere, the different underlying rocks have affected the scene and also the way of life of the people of the East and North Ridings. The region falls geologically into three principal divisions: the rocks of the Carboniferous age in the Yorkshire Dales, those of the Jurassic system in the North York Moors and chalk in the East Riding.

The various strata of the Carboniferous series – the limestones, shales and sandstones, which weather differently – have given the characteristic stepped shapes to the hills of the Yorkshire Dales. Swift powerful rivers spanned by graceful bridges flow down the three main dales of the North Riding – Wensleydale, Swaledale and Teesdale – and cleave the Pennines, which rise to well above 2,000 feet. Waterfalls offer grand spectacles, especially at High Force in Teesdale, where the Whin Sill, a rock of volcanic origin, has thrust up to form a great bastion. Hardraw Force, two miles from Hawes, is the highest single drop waterfall in the country. The hard water, resulting from the limestone, discouraged the establishment of industries such as textiles; so that these dales remain sparsely populated, green and pastoral, where sheep and cattle are reared, and where grey stone villages, linked by stone walls, merge into a scene that is harmonious from valley bottom to fell top.

From this hilly country we must traverse the Plain of York to reach the North York Moors. The great vale, almost wholly devoted to farming, forms the link between the different regions of Yorkshire. Up it a narrow strip of magnesian limestone makes a ridge along which the Roman legions tramped towards Hadrian's Wall and where now modern traffic ceaselessly roars on the double trackway of the A1 trunk road.

Across the vale rises the escarpment of the Hambleton Hills, with beyond them the Cleveland Hills – in other words the area known as the North York Moors. Here we find the same rock-system, the Jurassic, that underlies the Cotswolds; so that, as there, a fine durable limestone has been quarried to build castles, abbeys, mansions, houses in village streets and piers of harbours. Also, the presence of clays encouraged the making of tiles and bricks. Buildings are characterized by the warm hue of the limestone and the mellow tone of red pantile roofs.

Rivers and valleys, chief of which are Bilsdale and Ryedale, are numerous and small in scale. Patches of arable land, and, in places, bosky dells in deep-set dales adjoin the flat tabular hills, clad with mile after mile of heather. Parkland and some of the most delightful villages in England stretch from the moors to the Howardian Hills, so named after the family at Castle Howard. Around Whitby, in the Lias, the lower strata of the Jurassic rocks, are found the well-known fossils, ammonites and belemnites.

The third geological division, the chalk, underlies most of the East Riding. Although of a harder nature, it is part of the same chalk belt that runs up England from Dorset and the Channel. It has given us the headland of Flamborough with ocean-washed caves, pillars and white-cliffed little bays with pebbly beaches.

The main chalk mass, the Yorkshire Wolds, rises to 800 feet. Dry uplands, intersected by steep-sided dales, swept by fierce winds and covered with a thin soil, they were once a huge sheep-walk. Reclaimed gradually by local landlords in the eighteenth century, they have been converted into fruitful cornlands, planted with trees and laid out with roads. Here the landscape is in an altogether lighter key than those of the two other regions. Besides the white chalk, exposed in cliffs, quarries and old lanes, the bright light from the sea is reflected from windy skies on to a land that in August and September surges away to distant horizons – an expanse of waving corn.

Farther south, east of Hull, lies another division of the East Riding, Holderness, where chalk, much lower, has been overlaid by alluvial soil left after the Ice Age, and is now some of the richest land in Britain. The low cliffs of boulder-clay offer little resistance to the tides that wear them away at a rate of over four feet a year. They end at Spurn Head, a spit of sand three miles long.

Early Man and the Romans

For those who wish to study the prehistory of Yorkshire, visits to the British Museum and to museums at Hull, Scarborough, Whitby and York are essential. At Hull we ourselves find the Mortimer collection of objects from tumuli on the Wolds quite fascinating. The bones of the kind of animals – lion, hippopotamus, elephant – that lived in a warm climate before the Ice Age have been found in Kirkdale Cave near Kirby Moorside and at the foot of some of the cliffs on the coast.

Early men first appeared over 9,000 years ago, living on rafts on the swamps of the Vale of Pickering and the coastal region, when a land mass stretched across the North Sea to Denmark. Bronze Age man, at first avoiding the high hills, found dry sites for habitation on the Wolds, and dwelt all along the ridge of corallian limestone of the Jurassic rocks, which still provide sunny sites for villages, on the northern margin of the Vale of Pickering. Eventually some of these men – the Urn people – were driven on to the North York Moors, where, except for a few standing stones, ruined habitations are hard to find amongst the bracken and heather. In time their place was taken by the Iron Age folk, of whom the Parisii, the same people who gave their name to Paris, distinguished by their chariot burials, settled on the Wolds, whilst a poorer folk, the Brigantes, penetrated into the Yorkshire Dales.

If the Romans interest you most, Yorkshire, where many forts, stations and roads were required for subduing the fierce Brigantes, offers a wealth of material. Especially at York Museum may be seen inscribed stones, tombstones and tesselated pavements. In 1959, Catterick, the Roman capital of North Yorkshire, was excavated before the A1 trunk road was driven across it; and each summer the fort at Bainbridge in Wensleydale is explored by archaeologists from Leeds University. From Roman Malton, next in importance to York as a road centre, the road northwards, passing through Cawthorn Camps, now extensive bracken-covered earthworks, is well seen near Goathland. Another feature of Roman Yorkshire is the signal stations spaced along the coast.

Castles, Abbeys, Churches and Great Houses

For a fine summer's day we can think of no more rewarding sightseeing than to visit a ruined abbey or castle; and nowhere in the country is there to be found a greater wealth of medieval building in a similar area. If, for instance, from a point half-way between Leyburn and Richmond we describe a circle only eight miles in diameter, we take in three castles – Richmond, Middleham and Bolton, and three abbeys – Easby, Jervaulx and Coverham.

In these wild and remote regions the Norman earls built castles from which to protect their lands, and the Cistercians founded their abbeys, which, gradually enlarged and beautified, stood in splendid settings by the rivers. The ruins of Rievaulx and Byland at the edge of the North York Moors, no more than six miles from each other, rival those of Fountains and Tintern for beauty. In them history and architecture unite in a unique appeal. Whitby reminds us of religion in Saxon times and the first English poet Caedmon. The first monastery was linked with others at Hackness and Lastingham in the North York Moors; and at Kirkdale church in the same region is to be seen a famous Saxon sundial. Goodmanham church, in the East Riding, is connected with the conversion of King Edwin of Northumbria.

But if we wish to see the perfection of mediěval architecture, then Beverley Minster in the East Riding is at hand. Many people prefer it to York. Almost every village church of the Ridings is worth visiting for some architectural feature – especially the elaborate Norman doorways at Riccall, Kirkburn, North Newbald and elsewhere. If we had to pick out two, the Early English church at Skelton near York and the Decorated at Patrington in Holderness would be our choice.

As well as two architectural treasures – Castle Howard and Burton Agnes Hall – several of the great houses of the two Ridings are regularly on view. In the East Riding, the home of Wilberforce, the emancipator, a fine Georgian house in Hull, is now a museum open to the public. In the North Riding, there are one or two houses at Whitby and Staithes connected with Captain Cook.

For those who like to make literary pilgrimages, there are Wood End, the home of the Sitwells, now partially a natural history museum, at Scarborough,

Newby Hall, Skelton (near Ripon, West Riding)

G. Douglas Bolton

and Shandy Hall, at Coxwold, where Lawrence Sterne wrote part of *Tristram Shandy*. But nothing except the village itself, Winestead in Holderness, reminds us of the birthplace of Andrew Marvell.

Industries Past and Present

In the Yorkshire Dales, lead-bearing veins gave rise to an industry that began with the Romans and faded away, because of the imports of cheap foreign lead, at the end of the 19th century. Ruined smelt-mills and spoil-heaps, long grassed over, lend an interest, if but a sad one, to remote dales. Similarly, alum and jet were once mined along the coast and on the Cleveland Hills. The jet gave rise to Whitby jet ornaments and carvings, which, developed by skilled craftsmen, flourished in Victorian times. The craft is now carried on by only one or two men. Development of potash deposits has recently begun at Boulby, near Whitby, and may soon begin at Hawsker, south of Whitby. Other prospecting is in progress in the Egton area. Several light industrial trading estates are being established in the county, such as those at Catterick Bridge, Richmond and Huntington.

Close to the coast, ironstone used to be mined in Cleveland, and is the origin of the now colossal steel works of Teesside, which, together with the works of the Imperial Chemical Industries, occupy the banks of the Tees near its mouth. The other industrial area round Hull, the third largest port in the country, consists largely of docks and the big milling concerns making flour and cattle-cake. Some ship-building is carried on at Whitby, and sail-planes are made at Kirkbymoorside. Elsewhere farming is all important. The horned

Swaledale sheep and Cleveland bays (bought for the Royal Mews) are specialities. It is a commentary on the times that the Fylingdales ballistic missile early-warning station has been built within the North York Moors National Park.

Flowers and Woodland

Naturally, with such a diversity of rock and geographical features, the flora to be found in the two Ridings is very varied. Pride of place must be given to the Alpine flowers, relics of the Ice Age, on the hills of Teesdale, amongst which the spring gentian is pre-eminent. Unfortunately, part of the area in which they grow will be submerged when a new reservoir, at present under construction at Cow Green, is completed and filled. Perhaps the wild daffodils in Farndale make the finest botanical sight, for they stretch for nine golden miles along the banks of the River Dove. Along the coast grow plants such as sea-holly. In the Yorkshire Dales, the meadows easily rival those in the Alps for profusion of flowers, and especially in Upper Swaledale the pastures are sprinkled with mountain pansies. On the moors and in the gills many mosses and ferns occur.

Here and there, as round High Force and in Upper Swaledale, hazel woods are remains of the forest land that once covered the dales, whilst in Teesdale and Swaledale juniper claims only a fraction of the acreage of former times. Magnificent trees grace many parks, and large tracts of Teesdale and the North

Hornsea Mere

G. Douglas Bolton

Rievaulx Abbey

J. Allan Cash

York Moors have been taken over for the State Forests and planted with conifers by the Forestry Commission.

Sport and Food

When every kind of sporting facility abounds in the county, small wonder that Yorkshiremen are regarded as great sportsmen. Many are the famous Yorkshire packs in the annals of hunting. Every river, from the Ure in the west to the Whitby Esk in the east, provides excellent trout fishing, and the Driffield Beck is a nationally known chalk-stream. As for grouse moors, Yorkshire possesses some of the best shoots in Britain. Winners of races from the Derby to the Grand National have been trained at Malton and Middleham and racing in Yorkshire is at Teesside Park, Stockton, Teesside, Redcar, Thirsk, Catterick Bridge and York. Not only are there miles of glorious walking country, but Scarborough has a cricket and a lawn-tennis week, and Ganton a famous golf course. At Sutton Bank is the headquarters of the Yorkshire Gliding Club. Usually at the Scarborough cricket week the current Yorkshire eleven plays the rest of England. Whitby Marina, started in 1965, is a centre for sea sports, and a water-skiing club has been established at Lake Semerwater.

Sport and food are, not surprisingly, linked together: grouse and trout may be had at the appropriate seasons. Yorkshire pudding, light as a feather, cheesecakes, a speciality of farmhouses all over the Ridings, tasty York ham, tender moorland lamb and most kinds of fish, freshly caught by local fishing fleets, make mouth-watering dishes, not to mention the Wensleydale cheese, made from the milk of cows pastured in the dales.

583

Some houses and gardens open to the public

Bolton Castle 4m NE of Aysgarth off A684 *Map EA 49. 14th cent.; picturesque Wensleydale setting; prison of Mary Queen of Scots in 1568–9; captured by Parliamentary forces in 1645.*

Burton Agnes Hall 6m SW of Bridlington, 18m S of Scarborough on A166 *Map FB 46. Elizabethan house containing fine furniture, a large collection of French Impressionist pictures, Oriental porcelain. Café, free car park.*

Burton Agnes Norman Manor House 6m SW of Bridlington, 18m S of Scarborough on A166 *Map FB 46. 12th cent.; original Norman piers and groined roof of lower chamber. Old donkey water-wheel.*

Castle Howard 6m W of Malton off A64 *Map EH 47. 18th cent.; designed by Vanbrugh; pictures, statuary and furniture. Fine park.*

Kirkham Priory 5m SW of Malton on A64 *Map EH 46. By River Derwent; notable 13th-cent. sculptured gatehouse.*

Pickering Castle 8m N of Malton on A169 *Map EH 48. Large shell keep on mound between two baileys, partly 12th cent.*

Richmond Castle At Richmond *Map EB 50. 11th to 12th cent.; rectangular keep overlooking River Swale.*

Scarborough Castle At Scarborough *Map FA 48. 12th cent.; fortified by Earl of Albemarle with additions by Henry II; damaged during the Civil War and the First World War.*

Wilberforce House At Hull *Map FA 42. Elizabethan house; birthplace of Wm Wilberforce, now the Wilberforce Historical Museum.*

Books for further reading

The 'feel' of the East and North Ridings

E. GUTCH ed. *Examples of Printed Folklore: North Riding* 1901, *East Riding* 1912
MARIE HARTLEY and JOAN INGILBY *Yorkshire Village* 1953; *Life and Tradition in the Yorkshire Dales* 1968
WINIFRED HOLTBY *South Riding; Anderby Wold* and other novels
STANLEY WILLIAMSON and KENNETH BROWN eds *The North Countryman* 1957

Natural history

R. CHISLETT *Yorkshire Birds* 1952
J. F. ROBINSON *The Flora of the East Riding of Yorkshire* 1902
SCARBOROUGH FIELD NATURALISTS' SOCIETY *The Natural History of the Scarborough District* 1953–6

History and topography

A. J. BROWN *Fair North Riding* 1952
H. B. BROWNE *The Story of the East Riding of Yorkshire* 1912

A. G. DICKENS *The East Riding of Yorkshire with Hull and York* 1955
WILLIAM EDWARDS *The Early History of the North Riding* 1924
O. HARLAND *Yorkshire, North Riding* 1951
J. H. INGRAM *Companion into North Riding* 1952
C. A. M. KING *The Yorkshire Dales* 1960
C. B. KNIGHT *This is York* 1951
ARTHUR MEE ed. *Yorkshire: East Riding and York City* 1941; *North Riding* (King's England series) 1941
J. E. MORRIS *East Riding* 1932; *North Riding* 1931; *York* (Little Guides series) 1924
N. PEVSNER *Yorkshire, North Riding* (Buildings of England series) 1966
VICTORIA COUNTY HISTORIES *North Riding* 1914–25; *City of York* 1961
WARD LOCK & CO. LTD. *The Yorkshire Coast* (Red Guides series; also issued with alternative titles *Bridlington, Filey, Scarborough, Whitby*)
G. B. WOOD *Yorkshire* 1967

Gazetteer

YORKSHIRE, THE EAST AND NORTH RIDINGS

Ampleforth (EF 47) (810). The public school, which originated in 1802 when English Benedictine monks returned from exile in France, is laid out to give a magnificent view over its playing fields. The modern church by Sir Giles Gilbert Scott has an interior of green stone and many fine carvings.

Aysgarth (EA 48) EC Wed (260). A single-arched Elizabethan bridge spans the Ure, which is famous for its cataracts that pour over limestone terraces.

Bedale (EC 48) EC Thurs (1,120). The tower of the Church of St Gregory in this market town at the centre of hunting country was used as a defensive position against Scottish raiders, with access through a portcullis. Note the arcading in the church and the fresco of St George and the Dragon. Snape Castle (3 m. S), a medieval stronghold, was the home of Catherine Parr, who outlived Henry VIII.

Beverley* (FA 43) EC Thurs (16,020). Chief town of the E Riding. The North Bar, a brick structure with stepped battlements, is the survivor of the town's five gates. The market cross in Saturday Market, and the courtroom in the Georgian guildhall, are noteworthy. In the height of its tower, the Church of St Mary rivals Beverley Minster. Note the minstrel's pillar in the nave and the panelled chancel-ceiling with portraits of early kings. From the twin

Flamborough Head   *Edwin Smith*

towers of the minster a modern clock strikes the hours in the S tower and the quarters in the N. A double set of transepts is a feature of the interior. Observe the Percy Shrine's Gothic canopy and the plain frid stool near the High Altar. It dates from the days of King Athelstan, and conferred on fugitives a degree of immunity from the law.

Bowes (DK 51) EC Wed (550). There are three unusual survivals inside the limits of a Roman camp: remains of the Rere Cross, thought to have marked the frontier between Scotland and the Kingdom of Northumbria, a bath 27 ft. by 18 ft., built for the legionaries, and a massive 12th-cent. keep with walls so thick that rooms were built into them.

Bridlington (FB 46) EC Thurs, suspended June–Sept (26,010). A resort that combines new and old, the old exemplified by the fine priory church founded in the reign of Henry I, and the great Bayle Gate, dating from about 1388, which is now a museum and courtroom. When Queen Henrietta Maria, wife of Charles I, landed in 1643 with arms purchased

585

from the proceeds of the Crown Jewels, the harbour was bombarded and she retreated to Boynton Hall (*c.* 1550). This arrival embarrassed the owner, a Parliamentarian.

Brough (EK 42). Roman station of Petuaria where Ermine St crossed the Humber. An inscribed stone now in the Mortimer Museum, Hull, records the gift of a theatre by Marcus Ulpius Ianuarius about A.D. 160.

Burton Agnes (FB 46) (640). 'We enter under a Gate house built with 4 large towers into a Court, which is large, in the middle is a Bowling green palisado'd round' – so wrote a visitor in 1697, and it is the first impression on arriving today at this late-Elizabethan manor house. The plaster-work in ceilings and overmantels, the oak staircase and the present owner's collection of French Impressionist paintings are special features. The house's Norman forerunner, to the W, offers a contrast.

Castle Howard (EH 47). Home of the Howard family, begun by Vanbrugh in 1702 and continued while he was working on Blenheim Palace. His central cupola was destroyed by fire in 1940. Magnificent rooms at the ends of corridors flanked by hidden staircases contain a wealth of art treasures. The grounds, set off by ornamental water and the Temple of the Four Winds by Vanbrugh, complete the splendour of the place.

Catterick Camp (EB 49). The 'Aldershot of the North'.

Coverham Abbey (EB 48). Most of the 12th-cent. foundation of Helewisia de Glanville has been enclosed in a private garden. Two arches and part of the transept survive, also sculptured coffin-lids and the effigies in stone of two knights, believed to be the foundress's son and grandson.

Coxwold (EF 47) (210). The church where Laurence Sterne preached between 1760 and 1768 has a rare octagonal tower. In the gabled house which he named Shandy Hall he wrote *A Sentimental Journey* and *Tristram Shandy*. Newburgh Priory, to the S, has a small room closed at one end; it is believed to have contained the body of Oliver Cromwell brought here secretly by his daughter Mary. Byland Abbey (1½ m. NE), founded 1177, is notable for an unusual façade and S transept to the ruined abbey church, and fine medieval floor tiles.

Egglestone Abbey (EA 51). 1½ m. SE of **Barnard Castle** (*Durham*), this abbey ruin is worth visiting.

Filey (FB 48) EC Wed, suspended during season (4,710). The seashore is characterized by Filey Brigg, a mile-long reef of oolite rock which juts into the sea. The receding tide exposes hundreds of rock pools. St Oswald's Church, once cut off from the town by the boundary between the E and N Ridings, has now been returned to the E.

Flamborough Head (FC 47). Chalk headland (250 ft.), which caused innumerable wrecks until the lighthouse was built in 1818 to replace an octagonal tower. Fine observation-point for shipping, seabirds and stack rocks, within reach of many caves.

Gilling Castle (EG 47). This lovely house, built in the 16th and 18th cents., was acquired in 1929 for use as a preparatory school to Ampleforth College. The Elizabethan dining-room known as the Great Chamber has pendentive ceilings. The original frieze, oak-panelling and stained glass were salvaged from the estate of William Randolph Hurst, the American millionaire, who had removed them to a London warehouse. The terraced gardens below are open to the public, and the house can be seen by arrangement.

Goodmanham (EK 44). The 12th-cent. church is believed to occupy the site of a pagan temple destroyed by Coifi, its high priest, when he was converted in 627.

Great Ayton (EF 51). Picturesque village at the foot of the Cleveland Hills. Captain Cook went to school here and the school room has been preserved as a museum and memorial to him.

Guisborough (EG 51) EC Wed (12,080). The ruins of the great Augustinian priory founded by Robert the Bruce in 1119 stand in the grounds of the 19th-cent. Guisborough Hall, but the monument known as Bruce Cenotaph, rescued from the priory at the Dissolution of the Monasteries, is in St Nicholas Church in the old town that was the capital of Cleveland.

Hedon (FB 42) EC Thurs (2,340). Port superseded by Hull. A beautiful mace of the reign of Henry V, believed to be the oldest in England, may be seen at the town hall. The church known as the King of Holderness (begun *c.* 1180) has a glorious

N front, two tiers of traceried windows and a magnificent tower.

Helmsley (EG 48) EC Wed (1,290). The 12th-cent. castle, once owned by George Villiers, 1st Duke of Buckingham, fell into disuse when Sir Charles Duncombe, a London banker, commissioned Vanbrugh to build the great house known as Duncombe Park and now occupied by a girl's school.

Hornsea Mere (FC 44). Largest freshwater lake in the county, 12 ft. above sea-level, ¾ m. from the sea and originally formed by glacial deposits. It has fishing, sailing, a sanctuary for birds and a breeding spot for herons.

Howden (EH 42) EC Wed (1,930). Cobbled market town possessing a medieval church with a dominating tower and W front. The ruined choir and chapter-house, best seen at first from the market place, are particularly beautiful.

Hull★ (FA 42) EC Thurs (303,270). A seaport created and laid out by Edward I at the end of the 13th cent., which was to become the third seaport in England. Since the reign of Henry VI the Lord Mayor has ranked also as 'Admiral of the Humber'. Trinity House began in 1369 as a guild and developed into an institution for the relief of distressed mariners,

Hutton-le-Hole

G. Douglas Bolton

The ruins of Jervaulx Abbey

and the oldest navigational school in the country. It is now housed in a dignified Georgian building, where the practice of strewing rushes in the board room is continued. Holy Trinity Church (272 ft. long) is one of the largest in England. This is a town of museums, including the Mortimer collection, now in the Transport Museum, famous for prehistoric, Saxon and Roman antiquities, the Museum of Fisheries and Shipping (see the whaling exhibits) and Wilberforce House, where the great abolitionist of slavery was born in 1759. Visitors to the dockyards should get a permit from British Transport Docks.

Hutton-le-Hole (E H 49) (200). Picturesque village built round a green and watered by a stream crossed by foot-bridges. The Ryedale Folk Museum at Hutton-le-Hole illustrates the way of life from remote times onwards of the people of Ryedale.

Jervaulx Abbey (E B 48). The destruction of this great Cistercian abbey at the Dissolution was thorough, but the ground plan can be sufficiently well traced to give an impression of the day-to-day life in a monastic house.

Kilburn (E F 47) E C Wed (260). The great white horse on Roulston Scar was cut by the village schoolmaster and a band of helpers in 1857. Robert Thompson (d. 1955), who was famous throughout England for woodwork that rivalled medieval craftmanship (he signed it with the drawing of a mouse), had his workshop in a timbered house on the green.

Kirkbymoorside (E G 48) E C Thurs (2,070). The parish register records the death of Charles II's favourite, 'Georges Viluas, Lord Dooke of Bookingham', who died here in 1687 after a hunting trip.

Kirkdale (E G 48). The church combines Saxon, Norman and Early English architecture and is crowned with a 19th-cent. tower. A Saxon sundial over the porch records that Orm the son of Gamal bought St Gregory's Church when it was 'all to brocan and to falan' and caused it to be made anew from the ground and dedicated to Christ and St Gregory in the days of Edward the King and Earl Tosti (the Confessor and the brother of King Harold).

Kirkham Priory (E H 46). Religious house endowed by Walter l'Espec *c.* 1130 after a fatal accident to his son. It is beautifully situated by the R. Derwent. The Norman doorway to the refectory, the cloister lavatorium where the monks washed before meals, and the fine 13th-cent. sculptured gatehouse still stand erect.

Lastingham (E H 49) E C Wed (140). The early Norman crypt built in 1078 over the grave of St Cedd is reached by steps inside the present church. It forms a complete church with chancel, nave, aisles, vaulted roof of squat pillars and an ancient altar stone.

Malton (E H 47) E C Thurs (4,430). Market town on the Derwent, and central in corn-producing country. St Michael's is a fine late Norman church with a perpendicular tower. The museum has many personal possessions of Roman legionaries, brought to light during excavations. A cross in Orchard Field marks the site of their camp. Malton is also a famous centre for training race horses.

Marton in Cleveland (E F 51). A monument high on Easby Moor draws attention to the village where Captain Cook (1728–1779), the famous explorer, was born.

Meaux Abbey (F B 43). The great Cistercian monastic house which ranged over sixty acres was dismantled by order of Henry VIII. Its stones were used for strengthening Hull's defences. Some fragments, including tiles, have been preserved by the owner of the land.

Middleham (E B 48) E C Thurs (640). The ancient stronghold of the Neville family was taken over by the Crown after the Battle of Barnet in 1471. It was dismantled in 1646 and became a source of building material for the town, but the splendid keep and walls of what was one of the greatest castles in the N manage to remain imposing. The Swine Cross in the town, the Well of St Alkelda – the Saxon princess who shares the dedication of the church – and the church itself should be visited, and a watchful eye kept in the neighbourhood for horses in training in this Newmarket of the N.

Middlesbrough (E E 51) E C Wed (157,310). Port on the S of the Tees estuary, noted for pig iron, steel and chemical industries, and for having produced the material for some of the world's most famous engineering structures, such as Sydney Harbour Bridge and the Storstroem Bridge in Denmark. The town's own remarkable bridges, the Transporter, which can carry nine vehicles and 600 persons, and the Newport Bridge, which operates on a system of vertical lift and can rise 100 ft. in 45 seconds, are reminders of this town's achievements.

Mount Grace Priory.(E E 49). Most complete of Carthusian priories in England, founded by Thomas Holland in 1397 for twenty monks, who lived in separate cells according to their strict rule. Though sharing the common fate of monasteries under Henry VIII, part was made habitable as a private house in 1654, and enlarged in 1901. It now belongs to the N T.

Northallerton (E D 49) E C Thurs (6,720). County town of the N Riding, with an inn that charmed Charles Dickens. A small brick almshouse is known as Maison Dieu. The English destroyed 12,000 Scots at the Battle of the Standard in 1138. A bronze shield on the modern obelisk (2 m. N) illustrates the strange components of the successful standard.

Norton Conyers (ED 47). The Tudor mansion with Dutch gables in its beautiful façade served Charlotte Brontë as a model for the home of Rochester in *Jane Eyre*. The Great Hall has entertained many kings and famous people. Its chief treasure is a marquetry table surviving from a chapel in the park founded in memory of those that died at Agincourt.

Patrington (FD 42) EC Wed (1,410). The church known as the Queen of Holderness, a fine example of the Decorated period, has a 189-ft. spire incorporating an arcaded belfry. The S transept, the Easter Sepulchre and the modern gilded reredos are features of a cathedral-like church.

Pickering (EH 48) EC Wed (4,193). Market town in a prosperous valley which in early days was flooded, and has yielded lake dwellings and Bronze Age relics. Richard II was held prisoner in the moat-and-bailey castle before his death at Pontefract in 1400. The dungeon, chapel, postern gate and three towers in the outer walls still stand. Lovely mural paintings of the 15th cent. were discovered in the nave of the church under a coat of whitewash.

Richmond* (EB 50) EC Wed (5,760). The town selected in 1945 by the British Council as typically English. It has ancient alleys known as wynds, and a large market place. Holy Trinity Church (1150) has shops and offices built into its walls, and is now used as the Grammar School chapel. The curfew bell is rung nightly. The 11th-cent. castle was impregnable on three sides, with the fourth side protected by the keep. It was never attacked. The town is best viewed from the top of this keep, and the castle from across the R. Swale.

The Theatre Royal (1788) is the second oldest theatre in England. A riverside walk leads to Easby Abbey, founded in the early 12th cent. for Premonstratensian canons. Little is left of its church, but the monastic buildings are extensive. The Green Howards Museum contains uniforms, medals, campaign relics, etc. from the 17th cent. onwards.

Rievaulx Abbey* (EF 48). The chapter-house with its unusual apse and the shrine of the 1st Abbot are of special interest in this romantically-situated Cistercian house founded by Walter l'Espec in 1131. A glorious view of the dales is obtained from Rievaulx Terrace, high above the ruins to the east.

Robin Hood's Bay (EK 50) EC Wed. Picturesque fishing village once notorious as the haunt of smugglers. The crowded buildings are said to be due as much to the reluctance of young couples to move far from their in-laws as to the steepness of the site. Leeds University has established the Wellcome Marine Laboratory in the village.

Scarborough* (FA 48) EC Wed (42,590). 'Scarthaborg' was burned by Harald Hardrada in 1066 as a reprisal for its resistance to his aims. The keep of the castle dates from the 12th cent. The barbican, approached across the moat, was built 100 years later. This town has a reputation as a spa and is a seaside resort with residential qualifications. It is seen best from Oliver's Mount, 500 ft. above sea-level. Anne Bronte is buried in the graveyard of St Mary's Church, badly damaged in the Civil War. The autobiographical works of Sir Osbert Sitwell and *Before the Bombardment* give the flavour of this delightful place in the beginning of this century.

Stamford Bridge (EH 45) EC Sat (580). Scene of the last great Saxon

Wensleydale, near Hawes

J. Allan Cash

victory, when in 1066 Harold defeated his brother Tostig and Harald Hardrada, King of Norway, after they sailed up the Humber at the head of powerful forces.

Thirsk (EE 48) EC Wed (2,670). Market town with an attractive square that once contained a bull ring. The market cross can be seen at 18th-cent. Thirsk Hall. The 15th-cent. church has an impressive oak roof and fine glass in the E window. Good centre for touring the Hambleton Hills.

Wensleydale (EA 48). The R. Ure runs for sixty miles through the largest and least industrialized of the Yorkshire dales before joining the Swale.

Whitby (EJ 51) EC Wed (11,660). The Esk makes a division between the old and new parts of a resort with a seashore running E and W. The best view is obtained from the incongruously named Khyber Pass. A synod held in Whitby in 664 consolidated Christianity in the land, besides settling the date of Easter. Whitby Abbey, founded in 657, was destroyed a century later by the Danes. The remains of the rebuilding are Early English. Captain Cook served his apprenticeship in a house in Grape Lane, now an antique shop. The W front was bombarded during the 1914 War. Once a great whaling station, the port is still busy with fishing, and the local jet that found favour with Queen Victoria continues to be polished by a few remaining craftsmen.

592

Hadrian's Wall

DURHAM AND NORTHUMBERLAND

AN INTRODUCTION BY SID CHAPLIN

These two counties are divided by the Tyne and its tributary the Derwent, except for one small knuckle of Durham. But the Northumbrian burr crosses the waters of Tyne and is spoken by Durham men from Ryton to Derwenthaugh; and the inhabitants also share a dialect rooted in Norse and preserved by long use in the older industries and occupations. Whether in ships, sheep or coal, the two counties have much in common, beside their east and west boundaries on the North Sea and Pennine Range respectively. In both, industry is confined to the river mouths and the coast. The Roman roads and settlements bonded the region together, and the warm, wide dales – Teesdale, Weardale, North and South Tyne and Coquet – are united in more than the rich arable land and pastures of their 'bottoms', or great sheep-runs where sheep are not counted to to the acre, but acres to the sheep.

From the old priory of Lindisfarne we can trace that Celtic Christianity which drew its piety and strength from St Cuthbert, its love of learning from the

Venerable Bede, and which flowered again in the Methodism that conquered the mining villages and penetrated to every valley head. Here is a splendour of language as well as of landscape and architecture. The border ballads are no longer sung; but a love of good conversation prevails.

The Rocks Beneath

The record of the rocks in our two counties make relatively easy reading. The land is built, essentially, of those rocks of the Carboniferous age, including the Carboniferous Limestone series and the Millstone Grit, which form the rolling moors of the north and the extensive heather-clad fells of the Pennines. Included also are the massive Fell Sandstones which rise in the Rothbury Hills and their extensions to form a girdle of high ground about the Cheviots.

Eastwards, these rocks pass beneath the Coal Measures, which every year provide about thirty million tons of steam and coking coals. Eastwards again, the coal-bearing measures in their turn disappear beneath the newer Permian rocks, of which the most important member – the magnesian Limestone – provides those unlikely hills, cliffs, caverns and sea-shore sculptures of the Durham coastline. A little farther down the coast the 'white mines' of anhydrite form the basis of a great chemical industry at Billingham. Marsden offers the treat of a descent by lift down into the dining-room or bar of an inn excavated from the cliffs, and there the visitor can view (and hear) the turbulent colonies of fulmar petrels, kittiwakes and cormorants on the splendid Gothic pinnacle of Marsden Rock with its sea-worn arches and weathered, blind windows.

Whin Sill and Cheviots

The rocks I have mentioned constitute the main body of the land. Intruded into them as a once-molten sheet of magma is the Whin Sill, to which we owe High Force, Cauldron Snout and the Farne Islands, as well as the dramatic plinth of Hadrian's Wall about Housesteads, such sea-castles as Dunstanburgh, Bamburgh and Lindisfarne, and many miles of drystone walling.

Lastly, there are the roots of one great volcano in the Cheviots, that elevated tract which is, in effect, the deeply dissected graveyard of past plutonic activity whose immense outpourings of lava still cover an area of nearly 300 square miles. In the heart of this was intruded our only exposed mass of ancient granite. A crease in the heather marks the Salter's Road which runs from Tynemouth to Scotland. Here, amidst a prehistoric empire of hilltop villages, man is most aware of an alien rock. Here he still warms his hands at a peat fire, keeps company with the fishing heron and sees (if patient) one of those elusive herds of goats, not truly wild but gone wild once more within the most remote – and most rewarding – of all the Marches.

The Romans

In the Museum of Antiquities, University of Newcastle upon Tyne, there is a superb reconstruction of a temple of Mithras, the Persian sun-god worshipped by the legions. It is rich in colour and decoration. On the altar lie the implements used to carry and kindle the specially-imported fir-cones. At *Corstopitum*, that Roman city within the Wall near Corbridge, we can see in plan the foundations of their granaries, temples, military quarters, aqueducts and drains. The garrison strong room, as deep and narrow as a mausoleum, is now open to the sky. In the museum we can see coins, tools, fragments of armour, pottery,

jewellery – treasure and trivia of which the sum total has less power to move than the grooves made by waggon wheels at Housesteads, or a piece of coal recovered from the abandoned coal-hole of a Roman-British settlement at Bolam Lake.

The Wall

From Newcastle westwards, the Roman Wall may be easily discovered from the Military Road (B6318). Much of the Military Road was constructed by General Wade, after the Rebellion of 1745, from the demolished stones of the Wall and often built over its foundations or those of the road that ran within it. Hence the story of an encounter with the apparition of a Roman officer on horseback, lopped short because he was riding along the *old* road below! In its final form the Wall was of stone from six to eight feet broad and too high to be scaled by one man on another man's shoulders. It was protected by a ditch. Within the Wall ran a road, and, some distance behind it, a great flat-bottomed ditch known as the Vallum, used to delimit the military zone when the Wall was built by Hadrian about A.D. 122.

The Wall was pierced by gateways, called milecastles because they are about one mile apart, with watch-towers at intervals between, and further strengthened by seventeen fortresses, like Housesteads and Chesters, each manned by auxiliary regiments.

If you would see the Wall at its best, go to Housesteads. There is a car-park on the Military Road, and a pleasant walk over pasture land leads to the southern gateway of the fortress. Outside the gateway is a cluster of buildings which may have been shops or taverns, or the posts of traders who dealt with the people

The bridge over the River Coquet, Felton

G. Douglas Bolton

Marsden Rock

G. Douglas Bolton

of the country beyond the Wall. Within the fortress itself are the foundations of the commandant's house, the regimental shrine and latrine, and the inevitable granaries.

Near Housesteads the Wall overlooks a cluster of little lakes, the Northumbrian loughs, and undulates like a snake of stone over rolling hills, to crown sheer cliffs and plunge headlong down steep ravines – in Camden's words, 'riding over the high pitches and steep descents, wonderfully rising and falling'. The feel of the country can only come from walking to Twice Brewed, or better still, if you are in good heart and can spare the time, to the Nine Nicks of Thirlwall, so-named because it was there that the tribes once breached or 'thirled' the Wall.

Birds, Beasts and Flowers

St Cuthbert, it is said, loved the birds and beasts. The grey seals, which still inhabit the outer Farnes, kept vigil with him. Legend has it that he once gave his breakfast to an eagle, and that he taught the eider-ducks their gentle ways. They may still be seen riding the waves near Dunstanburgh, their brood following in a single line. The Lindisfarne Gospels are full of wild creatures and seabirds, perhaps a better guide to the Celtic imagination than to the living creatures. Thomas Bewick, in his illustrations and tailpieces to *British Birds and Quadrupeds*, is true to life, and adds affection to accuracy. He worked all his life in Newcastle, but retained his roots in the countryside.

His walks must often have taken him past the cottage at Wylam where George Stephenson was born. There is every opportunity to compare his art (woodcuts and superb water-colours collected in the Newcastle Central

597

Library and the Hancock Museum) with the life of his native countryside; but one must voyage farther afield to see his raven ranging the Cheviot hilltops, or his wild white bull and the last wild herd of English cattle in the park at Chillingham Castle. Of all the gibbets which so obsessed him there remains only one, on the moors near Elsdon. As one would expect in a region where at any given time the sheep will outnumber the human population, most of the birds – nearly two-thirds of those recorded in Britain – are to be found, and so are most of the British beasts. Tweed and Coquet are great salmon rivers in the season that opens with a riot of rowan berries: the troutfisher's line still cuts the crystal air in these and the remainder of our streams and rivers.

In Teesdale, on Widdybank Fell, with its bell-heather and juniper, are such rarities as the spring gentian, the bog-sandwort and the mealy primrose. In the Cheviot valleys, I am told, there are for the seeking star saxifrage, the dwarf cornel and pyrola secunda. But most of us will be content with the purple spread of heather over hills and fells; the cuckoo-pints and bluebells of Castle Eden and other denes; the waterside array of mint and kingcup along the waters of the Tyne. Or with the pansies of Weardale, the red and gold of butcher's broom on the Derwent slopes, and sand-dune treasure in harebells, campion, valerian and thyme.

Bamburgh

Edwin Smith

A Choice of Buildings

I admit a preference for the odd and unconsidered works of man: the web of drystone walling, for instance, with its variations in technique and patterns of lichen, or those tiny chain-factories of Winlaton with their double hearths and stone water-troughs. There is nothing much of architectural interest, I suppose, in Heighington, in Durham; but the village with its watch-dog of a church and succession of greens is all of a piece; and there is pleasure in 'tasting', first Belsay, then Bywell, in Northumberland, one for its Italianate arcades and quiet dignity and the other for its unexpected riches of two churches, a castle and a market-cross in a meadow. The visitor who calls at the Palace of Bishop Auckland would be lacking in enterprise if he failed to deviate a mile or two to see the Saxon Church of Escomb, tall and narrow with some of the original floor of naked cobble still intact, before continuing to Durham and the Romanesque splendour which surrounds the shrine of St Cuthbert. He should look at the peel-towers of Corbridge and Doddington as well as the castle of Alnwick, and walk a colliery wagonway as well as a Roman road. At Causey Arch, East Tanfield, in Durham, is a bridge built in 1727 to carry the wooden rails of one of those early railways over a deep ravine – a forerunner of Robert Stephenson's High Level at Newcastle and Royal Border Bridge at Berwick-upon-Tweed. There is a curious link between Causey Arch and Seaton Delaval Hall, in Northumberland, built by Sir John Vanbrugh: in the old kitchen, now a sitting-room, a model of the type of dandy-wagon which ran over the Arch serves as a coal-scuttle. There could be no more appropriate reminder that beauty as well as spoil came from the mining of coal.

The Flavour of the Land

Castle, minster and ancient church – these are listed in the Gazetteer which follows. But there is much else. The gourmet will remember to sample 'caller herrin'' baked in rolls, and Craster kippers, as well as fresh salmon; but he will have to make friends with mining folk to enjoy 'singin' hinnies', spice loaf and stotty cake. The cult of the giant leek is followed from Bishop Auckland to Amble: on a September evening the visitor might do worse than call at a leek show, and sample afterwards the free bowl of soup that goes with local ale.

If he should wish to return with other souvenirs than violet crystals of fluor-spar, or a handful of barytes fragments in green, yellow, white and blue, there are casts of a Roman blacksmith or Celtic god to be had at *Corstopitum*, tweed at Otterburn, or paintings of the Border school from the Stone and other Newcastle galleries.

With these would go memories and impressions, indelible pictures in the mind – of sheep flowing like a stream by the abandoned smelt-mill at Ramshaw, or folk gossiping in the square at nearby Blanchland. There would be the velvet lawns and jackdaws of Durham – or that token of cruel times, the grotesque, foliated face of the Sanctuary door knocker. There would be herdsmen driving cattle through the streets of Alnwick and Hexham, miners marching with banners and brass bands to their Durham 'Big Meeting', and an immaculate and dazzling ship passing on her first trial through Tynemouth piers into the open sea. Above all there would be the ring of voices, voices of shepherds, miners and ship-builders, farm-hands and steel-workers, different in shades of dialect but full of that warmth, that feeling for the 'hyam', or home, which lies between Tees and Tweed.

Some houses and gardens open to the public

Alnwick Castle At Alnwick *Map* EB 61. *Norman, restored; great park; keep, armoury and main apartments with treasures; famous border fortress of the Percy family.*

Barnard Castle At Barnard Castle *Map* EA 51. *11th- to 13th-cent. ruins; three-storeyed circular keep.*

Bowes Museum At Barnard Castle *Map* EA 51. *Modelled on the grandeur of a French palace; fine art collection.*

Durham Castle At Durham *Map* EC 54. *Norman 14th cent.; fine hall, notable crypt chapel, carved doorway; used since 1837 by the University of Durham. Free car park.*

Lindisfarne Castle Holy Island 5m E of Beal across sands *Map* EB 64. *16th cent.; restored in 1900* NT.

Newcastle Castle and **Black Gate** At Newcastle upon Tyne *Map* EC 56. *12th-cent. three-storeyed keep; gate tower; south postern; houses a small museum.*

Norham Castle 7m SW of Berwick-upon-Tweed on B6470 *Map* DJ 64. *12th-cent. keep built by Bishop Hugh Puiset; associations with Scott's Marmion; Norman church nearby.*

Warkworth Castle 8m SE of Alnwick on A1068 *Map* EC 60. *Splendid ruins of 12th-cent. castle; gatehouse, hall and keep; castle figures in Shakespeare's Henry IV.*

Washington Old Hall 6m SE of Gateshead on A182 *Map* ED 55. *17th cent.; ancestral home of George Washington; now Washington museum* NT.

Books for further reading

The 'feel' of Durham and Northumberland

ARTHUR BARTON *Two Lamps in Our Street* 1967
FREDERICK GRICE *Bonny Pit Laddie* 1960
SYDNEY MOORHOUSE *Companion into Northumberland* 1953
W. W. TOMLINSON *Comprehensive Guide to the County of Northumberland* 1968
GEORGE M. TREVELYAN *The Middle Marches* (In *Clio, a Muse—and Other Essays*) 1934

Natural history

GEORGE BOLAM *Birds of Northumberland* 1912
RICHARD PERRY *A Naturalist on Lindisfarne* 1946
HENRY TEGNER *Beasts of the North Country* 1961; *A Border County: an Account of Its Wild Life* 1955

History, topography, architecture

B. ALLSOPP *Historic Architecture of Newcastle upon Tyne* 1967
BERTRAM COLGRAVE *Durham Castle* (Great Houses series) 1953
SIR TIMOTHY EDEN *Durham* 2 vols (County Books series) 1949
HERBERT L. HONEYMAN *Northumberland* (County Books series) 1949
B. LONG *Castles of Northumberland* 1967
ARTHUR MEE *Northumberland* (King's England series) 1964; *Durham* (King's England series) 1969
NIKOLAUS PEVSNER *County Durham* (Buildings of England series) 1953; *Northumberland* (Buildings of England series) 1957
THOMAS SHARP *Northumberland: A Shell Guide* 1954
C. J. STRANKS *Durham Cathedral* (Pride of Britain series)

Gazetteer

DURHAM AND NORTHUMBERLAND

Barnard Castle and the River Tees   *Reece Winstone*

Alnwick *Nthmb*. (EB 61) EC Wed (7,610). Attractive stone town, dominated by Alnwick Castle (Norman, but restored in 18th and re-restored by Salvin in 19th cent.), high above the river. Of the two town gates, the one with the Percy lion is 15th-cent., and the gatehouse of the medieval abbey has survived. Both bridges, the town hall and lofty Brislaw Tower are all 18th-cent. **Hulne Priory**, incorporating work of the 13th cent., lies in a lovely park, 3 m. NW, beyond the remains of Alnwick Abbey. **Alnmouth**, 4 m. SE, is a pleasant resort, quiet, with sands and golf.

Bamburgh *Nthmb*. (EB 63) EC Wed (558). Unspoilt little resort, with golf and bathing. Lancelot eloped to the Castle (AM) with Arthur's Guinevere, but the imposing Norman building one now sees is largely the result of restoration in the 18th and 19th cents. The church is remarkable for a fine 13th-cent. crypt and chancel. Grace Darling is buried in the churchyard, and a museum is dedicated to her. To the N, beyond Budle Bay, is Lindisfarne (*see below*), 4 m. off the scattered Farne Islands, unexcelled for bird-watching, and with a tower and monastic remains on one of them. **Seahouses** and **Beadnell**, attractive seaside resorts, are to the SE.

Barnard Castle *Durham* (EA 51) EC Thurs (5,400). A good centre for Teesdale, its ruined castle (AM) standing impressively above the river. Blagrove's House (now a café) is Elizabethan; the town hall dates from 1747; the Bowes Museum has important collections, especially of Spanish paintings. 1½ m. SE are the ruins of Egglestone Abbey (AM). **Staindrop** (5 m. NE) has a church with fine Neville monuments; and nearby at **Raby** is the largest and most impressive castle in the county.

Berwick-upon-Tweed *Nthmb*. (EA 65) EC Thurs (12,170). Having changed hands 13 times in 300 years, this border town is now English: a resort with sands, golf and fishing instead of fighting. Of its three bridges, the handsomest is the 17th-cent. one of 15 arches; the Royal Border was built in 1850 by Robert Stephenson; and the last, when opened in 1928, was the longest road-bridge in the country. The castle is now mainly a railway station; the extensive Elizabethan town walls (AM) set the fashion for European fortifications in their day. The 18th-cent. barracks have been disfigured, but there are period houses between them and the quay; and the town hall (1754) is a building well worth a visit.

Blanchland *Nthmb*. (DK 55) EC Thurs (170). Exquisitely situated on the Derwent, with the moor rising to 1,170 ft. at Dukesfield Fell (3 m. N),

Blanchland on the moors *Edwin Smith*

and Hangman's Hill, over 1,400 ft., some 7 m. to the W, this stone-built village remains unspoilt. There is a medieval gatehouse, and the church incorporates part of the 12th-cent. Abbey church. Nearby lies the newly created Derwent Reservoir.

Brancepeth *Durham* (EC 53) EC Wed (300). Approached from the S, the castle is an impressive sight, but it turns out to be mainly a 19th-cent. reconstruction. The nearby church, however, contains remarkable Jacobean timber-work (pews, choir-stalls, pulpit, screen, roof and font-cover), and Neville effigies.

Bywell *Nthmb.* (EA 56) (140). Charmingly situated on the Tyne. Small, but with evidence of greater days: a medieval market cross, a fine gateway-keep, a castle, an 18th-cent.

hall and two early but restored churches side by side – St Andrew's (with a Saxon W tower) and St Peter's. **Ovingham**, 3 m. NE, has a similar tower, and the vicarage is partly medieval, partly Jacobean. Across the river at **Prudhoe**, EC Wed (10,660), are the ruins of a castle, built in the 12th cent.

Chester-le-Street *Durham* (EC 55) EC Wed (20,300). Formerly a mining town, its parish church, with partly octagonal tower, noteworthy for a series of 14 effigies of his family removed thither in 1594 by the then Lord Lumley. **Lumley Castle**, 1 m. E, a splendid quadrangular building, with towers at each corner, only slightly modified since it was built at the end of the 14th cent., is now an annexe of Durham University.

Lambton Castle, on the other hand, 1½ m. NE, is essentially 19th cent., though its battlements and turrets, seen across the R. Wear, are extremely picturesque.

Chillingham *Nthmb.* (EA 62). A village of neat cottages by the great park in which stands the 14th-cent. Chillingham Castle, ancestral home of the Earls of Tankerville. The famous herd of completely white cattle roams, as it has for 700 years, over 600 acres of the park.

Chollerford *Nthmb.* (DK 57). On the N Tyne river, and near the Roman Wall (*see* Introduction) that runs through Chesters Park, where one of the important forts has been partly excavated. (There is an excellent museum.) Nearby is Chesters, a fine 18th-cent. country house. 3 m. N, **Haughton Castle**, in its lovely park, is a 13th- to 14th-cent. castellated mansion.

Corbridge *Nthmb.* (DK 56) EC Thurs (2,430). A small Tyneside town: the bridge is 17th cent., the church has a Saxon tower and a pele tower alongside. 1½ m. W, at Corstopitum (AM), the foundations of a Roman town have been excavated, and there is a museum. 1½ m. NE, **Aydon** has an unusually fine 13th-cent. fortified house. To the SW, the Devil's Water flows through lovely woods, past ruined **Dilston Castle**, 1½ m. away.

Darlington *Durham* (EC 51) EC Wed (84,700). Most of the town is the product of the railway age (Stephenson's first locomotive can be seen at Bank Top station). The outstanding exception is the Early English collegiate Church of St Cuthbert, now hemmed in, but of great beauty (note the stone rood-screen, carved misericords and stalls, and spectacular font cover). **Cockerton**, with its pleasant green and 18th-cent. hall, is now a

suburb. 5 m. NW, **Walworth Castle**, dating from about 1600, is impressive.

Dunstanburgh Castle *Nthmb.* (EC 62). Superbly situated on the cliffs at the S end of Embleton Bay, this great castle (AM), built in the 14th cent., has been decaying since the 16th, but is still magnificent. **Embleton** village, standing back from the sea, has a fine church, and the pele tower of the vicarage is 15th cent. 2 m. S is the fishing village of **Craster**, with a fine house also incorporating a pele tower; and 2 m. farther still, beyond the cliffs of Cullernose, is the village of **Howick**, with its harbour and 18th-cent. hall.

Durham** *Durham* (EC 54) EC Wed (24,400). The old city of Durham was originally confined to the rocky peninsula that is almost enclosed within a loop of the Wear, and was dominated by its cathedral, monastery and castle. Today it is essentially unchanged. Though since 1837 the University has taken over parts of the two last, the superb 12th-cent. buildings remain, scarcely changed in outward appearance, and one of the grandest sights in the country. Aspects of it can be well seen from the 18th-cent. Prebend's Bridge, Gilesgate and South Street. The cathedral can be fully appreciated only with a guide, but its splendour is attributable to the fact that its basic structure – nave, chancel and transepts – were created in a single period, roughly 1070–1140. After that, the two principal additions were Bishop Pudsey's Galilee, about 1170 (the Lady Chapel was built at the W end, possibly because it followed the tradition of keeping women at a distance from the chancel); and, 60 years later, the Chapel of the Nine Altars behind the high altar. Neither of them detracts from the majesty of Bishop Flambard's nave. The same two bishops played a major part in the construction of the castle, whose Great Hall is now the dining hall for University College students. This last can, and should, be visited; as also the fine monks' dormitory, now the Cathedral Museum, which contains St Cuthbert's coffin, with his pectoral cross and stole, as well as superb illuminated MSS. Palace Green, with its mainly 17th-cent. buildings, is delightful; while N and S Bailey, with attractive old houses, remind us by their name that these were once part of the city's fortifications.

Finchale *Durham* (E C 54). Here, 2 m. N E of the village of Pity Me, are the ruins of a 13th-cent. priory (AM). Not only are these the most important remains in the county, but they lie in a lovely curve of the R. Wear, with a background formed by trees.

Ford *Nthmb.* (D K 63) E C Wed (780), and neighbouring **Etal**, both charming villages on the R. Till, with the Cheviots rising 5 m. to the S, and both with castles of the first half of the 14th cent. Ford was Gothicized by Robert Adam in the 18th and drastically modified in the 19th cent.; the other is a picturesque ruin. At **Etal** there is also an 18th-cent. manor among thatched cottages. **Duddo**, some 3 m. N, has a group of prehistoric standing stones.

Gainford *Durham* (E B 51) E C Wed (1,100). A grey stone village above the R. Tees, with an attractive green. The beautiful 13th-cent. church (Jacobean font cover and a Middleton monument) stands close by the river, and the hall is Elizabethan, well restored in 19th cent. At **Winston**, 2 m. W, is another Teesside village, with a fine single-span bridge and Jacobean Westholme Hall, an excellent example of its period, dated 1606.

Gibside *Durham* (E B 55). Here, on the Derwent, 3 m. S W of Whickham, is a notable 18th-cent. estate, unfortunately falling into ruins. In grounds landscaped by Capability Brown, the W front of the Elizabethan hall, overlooking the river, was added in 1805; but the orangery, stables and detached banqueting house, an admirable example of the Gothic revival, were designed by Paine, about 1760. He also built the classical mausoleum (converted into a church 50 years later and still in use), which is perfectly furnished with period three-decker pulpit and sounding board, and box pews.

Haltwhistle *Nthmb.* (D H 56) E C Wed (7,490). A town wonderfully situated in the S Tyne valley, where the Caw Burn flows down from Greenlee Lough, beyond the Roman Wall (*see* Introduction). Just outside the town are the ruins of **Bellister Castle**; **Blenkinsopp Castle** (1339) is 3 m. W, and 1 m. farther on are the ruins of **Thirlwall Castle**, itself built with stones robbed from the Wall. Most attractive of all is **Featherstone**, a Jacobean rebuilding of a medieval castle, 3½ m. S W, in its wooded park above the river.

Hexham* *Nthmb.* (D K 56) E C Thurs (9,900). Perhaps the most romantic of all Northumbrian towns. Seen from the Tyne bridge, the priory ruins and church, the 15th-cent. moot hall and still earlier manor office (or gaol) stand out against a distant background of trees. There are a few Tudor, and more Georgian houses; parts of an Elizabethan grammar school; and the curious market piazza (1766). But the chief building is the priory church (only fragments of the monastic buildings remain). Here we find a remarkable pre-Conquest crypt, though the choir and transepts were rebuilt in the 13th cent., and the nave was not completed till 1908. Among its treasures are the fine pulpitum, the frid-stool (anyone seated on it could claim sanctuary) and the Acca cross.

Houghton-le-Spring *Durham* (ED 55) EC Wed (31,600). Until recently a mining town, with all that is interesting centred round the 13th-cent. church (note the detached Guild Chapel, two storied and embattled). Here are the Kepier Grammar School (1574), the 17th-cent. almshouses and Jacobean Houghton Hall, a square building now used as a social club.

Housesteads *Nthmb.* (DH 56). A craggy section of the Roman Wall, with picturesque lakes to the N. This was the fort of Vercovicium, and the NT maintains a museum, open daily.

Ingram *Nthmb.* (EA 61) (230). An angler's village on the Breamish, where it comes tumbling down from Cushat Law, Comb Fell and Hedgehope Hill, all over 2,000 ft. (with Cheviot itself, 2,676 ft., just behind them). Near the waterfall of Linhope Spout, the prehistoric village of **Greaves Ash** covers some 20 acres.

Lanchester *Durham* (EB 54) EC Tues (4,000). A Norman 13th-cent. church, with fine carving in chancel (tympanum and corbel heads), and three pieces of 13th-cent. stained glass. In the porch is a Roman altar to the goddess Garmangabis, probably from the Roman fort ½ m. SW, which was in use till the end of the 4th cent.

Lindisfarne *Nthmb.* (EB 64) (240). Or Holy Island (since it was from here that St Aidan began the reconversion of England in the 7th cent.) is less than 2 m. by 2 m. in extent, yet it has a village, a public house, a 16th-cent. castle (in private ownership, but open on certain days), and the ruins of an 11th-cent. Benedictine monastery. At low tide, the island can be reached on foot or by car across the 3 m. of sand that separate it from **Beal**, a small seaside and golfing resort.

Middleton - in - Teesdale *Durham* (DK 52) EC Wed (1,500). An attractive village in the SW corner of the county where the R. Lune, flowing down from

Finchale Priory

G. Douglas Bolton

Outberry Plain (2,143 ft.) joins the Tees, continuing over the Yorkshire boundary into Lune Dale. 5 m. NW is the impressive High Force waterfall, where the Tees drops 70 ft.

Morpeth *Nthmb.* (EB 58) EC Thurs (14,150). In the lovely Wansbeck Valley, the clock tower, once a prison, still nightly sounds the curfew. The church, largely 14th cent., has some fine glass, and there are ruins of a castle; but most of the town dates from the fire in the 17th cent., including Vanbrugh's modified town hall (1714). **Mitford**, 1 m. W, is a village with an ancient church, a pretty vicarage and a castle, sited on a rocky hill. Nearby, on the right bank of the Wansbeck, are the ruins of **Newminster Abbey**. 3 m. downstream, **Bothal** has a restored 14th-cent. gateway to its castle, and a church with an angel roof and the fine Ogle tomb.

Newcastle upon Tyne* *Nthmb.* (EC 56) EC Wed (269,390). Once a station on the Roman Wall, now a large regional capital spreading in all directions, the city preserves at its centre a high sense of civic dignity. This is largely due to the initiative of a builder called Grainger, who planned and rebuilt a series of fine streets and squares in the first half of the 19th cent., entrusting the plan to John Dobson. Grey Street and Eldon Square are two of the best results, and Dobson also designed the fine Central Station. From earlier periods, examples are the well-preserved Norman keep of the castle, which, with the adjoining Black Gate, now houses a fine collection of Roman antiquities; surviving sections of the turreted town walls; and the cathedral, with its crypt and rare 'crown' spire. The most noteworthy of the other churches is perhaps All Saints, rebuilt in classical style in the 18th cent., with an elegant spire, and preserving a rare Flemish brass. The Guildhall, given a new front in 1796, retains its 17th-cent. interior; and the Holy Jesus Hospital and Trinity House, with its hall and chapel, are of the same period. Sandhill, by the quayside, has 17th-cent. domestic architecture, notably the fine Surtees House; and the

Newcastle: the River Tyne

J. Allan Cash

city is remarkable for its open spaces, among them the 1,000-acre Town Moor and picturesque Jesmond Dene Park. In the north of the city the new buildings of the University and the Civic Centre dominate the skyline.

Norham *Nthmb.* (DJ 64) EC Wed (640). A grey little village on the Tweed, with a pleasant vicarage beside the church (fine Norman chancel) at one end and, on higher ground at the other, the keep of the Norman castle (AM), associated with Scott's *Marmion*.

Ponteland *Nthmb.* (EB 57). A main road village on the R. Pont, with a pele tower, a medieval church (some 14th-cent. glass) and the Blackbird Inn, incorporating part of a castle, sacked in 1388. 5 m. NW we reach **Belsay**, an attractive village, with Grecian mansion, designed by Dobson in the early 19th cent., standing in fine gardens; and two 14th-cent. towers of the ruined castle, carefully preserved.

Rothbury *Nthmb.* (EA 60) EC Wed (1,650). A charming village in the heart of Coquetdale, with stepping-stones across the river, and Simonside (1,409 ft.) towering up to the S. Cragside and Whitton Grange are two pleasant modern houses (the gardens of the first are open to the public); and the rectory, incorporating part of a 14th-cent. tower, is now a home. 3½ m. NW are the ruins of **Cartington Castle**; and 4 m. downstream stands **Brinkburn Priory**, wonderfully situated by the river, its church very well restored in the 19th cent.

Ryton *Durham* (EB 56) (14,700). Most attractive of Tyneside villages, with its green, its 18th-cent. houses and cottages and the broach spire of Holy Cross (17th-cent. screen and stalls) rising from the trees.

Seaton Delaval *Nthmb.* (ED 57) EC Wed (5,673). A small township; but 2 m. ENE is the Hall, Vanbrugh's masterpiece and one of the outstanding secular buildings in the county, with its gardens, orangery, obelisks and statues. (Open to the public.)

Sedgefield *Durham* (ED 52) EC Wed (4,900). Grouped around the green are the early 18th-cent. almshouses, rectory and manor (now RDC), and the notable Early English church (fine stone carving in chancel, and 17th-cent. woodwork). Hardwick Hall, 1 m. W, is an 18th-cent. house, with Gothic buildings by Jas Paine (gatehouse, banqueting house and temple) in the grounds, unfortunately falling into decay.

Stanhope *Durham* (DK 53) EC Wed (2,000). An attractive little Weardale town, 700 ft. up and with fells all around, rising to over 2,000 ft. in the SW. There is a medieval church, some 18th-cent. houses, a Jacobean hall and a 1798 castle. Across the old bridge, Unthank Hall, now a farm, is a handsome building with porch and mullioned windows. Nearby is the limestone Heathery Burn Cave, extending for 500 ft., in which was discovered a hoard of Iron Age weapons, tools and ornaments.

Sunderland *Durham* (ED 55) EC Wed (220,000). The main commercial, industrial and cultural centre of the county. Among historical attractions are the 7th-cent. monastery of Monkwearmouth, still in use as a church, and the 15th-cent. Hylton Castle. There is a museum which traces the history of England's largest shipbuilding town back to the 14th cent. and includes a priceless collection of the town's historic glassware.

Tynemouth *Nthmb.* (ED 56) EC Wed (with N Shields, 72,400). A seaside resort, with golf, and bathing at Prior's Haven. The ruins of the priory and castle (both AM) are impressively sited, overlooking the sea. Nearby, to the N, are **Cullercoats** and **Whitley Bay**; both are golfing and seaside resorts.

Wallington Hall *Nthmb.* (EA 58). Near the village of **Cambo** (associated with Capability Brown), the hall is one of the finest in the county, standing in its great park, with the moors rising to over 1,000 ft. beyond. It was built in the 17th cent., its central courtyard was later converted into a picture gallery, which is now, with the rest of the house and its splendid contents, open to the public.

Wark-on-Tyne *Nthmb.* (DJ 57) EC Thurs (690). Charmingly situated on the N Tyne river, with picturesque **Chipchase Castle** (Jacobean additions to an ancient pele tower); an 18th-cent. chapel in the park 2 m. SE.

Warkworth *Nthmb.* (EC 60) EC Thurs (920). On the tidal waters of the Coquet, with golf and a sandy beach 1 m. away. The Norman church is one of two in the county with a stone spire; the ancient bridge has a tower at one end. The hermitage is an AM, and so is the castle, with its impressive keep, gatehouse and hall. Open to the public.

Whittingham *Nthmb.* (EA 61). A pretty village on the Aln. It has a modernized pele tower, and a pre-Conquest church, whose size testifies to the importance of the place when the main western route to Scotland crossed the river here, before it was diverted to Coldstream. The village has two notable mansions: Eslington Hall, built in 1720, and extended in 1797; and Callally Castle, containing work of eleven periods, including some fine 18th-cent. stucco.

The village of Rothbury

J. Allan Cash

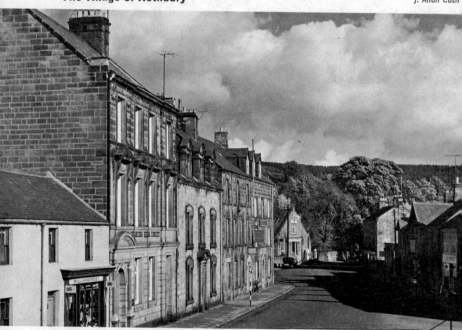

Opposite: Detail from the original painting by Barry Driscoll.
Primitive in hill and moor, Northumberland forms a border not only between England and Scotland, but between the present and the past. Alnwick Castle has, we see, stone figures and a barbican. With the coming of a later age, George Stephenson served in the county's coal-pits as an engineer. Its fauna include trout and salmon, and the 'wild' cattle of Chillingham Castle. From its flora is shown the sea-pink.

Brotherswater from Kirkstone Pass

CUMBERLAND AND WESTMORLAND ('CUMBRIA')

AN INTRODUCTION BY MARGUERITE STEEN

The counties of Cumberland and Westmorland are bounded on the north by the green estuary of Solway and the foothills of the Cheviots. Westward lies the slate-grey Irish Sea and eastward the Pennines, with the River Eden following their chain along a broad and fertile valley, eventually to empty itself into the Solway Firth.

The southern borderline zigzags north-south-north-south, tracing both shores of Lake Windermere, and crosses the Kent estuary at the head of Morecambe Bay to loop as far south as Kirby Lonsdale, over which broods the table-top of Ingleborough. Across the Bay, Lancashire pushes out a blunt spur into the Cumbrian peninsula which is known as Lancashire north of the sands, to its inhabitants as Furness and Cartmel, and to all as part of the 'Lake District'. The coastline of Cumberland comes right down to the head of the Furness block; that of Westmorland barely spans the Kent estuary.

Opposite: Detail from the original painting by Claud Harrison.

In Westmorland, the 'land of the dwellers west of the moors', we watch fells, dales, and lakes recede into the distance. Across the foreground a beck slides clear and cold. On the grass, a pair of wrestlers are at grips; hounds stand eager for the aniseed trail; and girls carry rushes and flowers in the August ceremony of rush-bearing.

CUMBERLAND AND WESTMORLAND

The unifying feature of the counties is the beauty of the scene, the purity of the light and the dramatic variations of colour and contour, which become progressively exciting as one penetrates inland, leaving the flat coastal strip with the river-mouths of Kent, Leven, Duddon, Esk and Derwent for the mountains, purple with heather and flaming with bracken in autumn, bejewelled with lakes and tarns, each holding its own colouring of purple, blue, green or near-black.

Rock and Rain

Over millions of years volcanic eruptions, floods, frosts, snows and rains shaped what today is known as the Lake District. The traces of glaciers are left on its rocks, its milder contours indicate what once were moraines, its small, savage screes are survivals of the Ice, Stone, Bronze and Iron Ages. Glaciated igneous rocks form its core, with small outcrops of limestone, printed with fossils. At Kentmere lie the post-glacial deposits known as diatomite. Fault lines have influenced the pattern of its valleys, winds and warfare its dark, uncompromising architecture.

The climate (admitted, even by residents, to be a little formidable) is largely responsible for the notable beauty of the region. Cumberland and Westmorland receive the western, rain-bearing winds direct from the sea; the hills enjoy the heaviest rainfall in England – hence the soft air, the delicacy of the colouring, the luxuriance of trees and herbage. Lakelanders say with truth that to know the full glory of their country is to visit during the winter months, when the

Wordsworth's cottage, Grasmere

J. Allan Cash

mountain tops are lost in low-rolling cloud, when the lakes overflow (on rare occasions Bassenthwaite and Derwentwater, Buttermere and Crummock, become two instead of four), and fearsome sunrises are succeeded by no less fearsome sunsets. It is under these conditions that the traveller may come closest to appreciation of the local character, with its toughness and resilience – for himself, he may be excused for preferring the mild spring and summer, or the glowing autumn.

Towns and Industries

Of the two counties, Cumberland, the larger, is industrially the more important, though its coalfields, extending southwards from Aspatria and far under the sea, are now declining. Of its two sizeable ports, Whitehaven imports grain, timber, aluminium and phosphate rock, its exports being coal and detergent materials; Workington imports iron ore, and exports coal, iron and steel rails. Whitehaven has an important chemical industry, established between the wars. After the Second World War the coastal regions of Cumberland were scheduled as 'development areas'. The first atomic research centre in Great Britain was established near Sellafield and, in 1956, the first atomic energy power station was opened at Calder Hall. Behind the coastal strip, little sign of industry meets the eye, except for a few slate or granite quarries. However, the city of Carlisle has many expanding industries, and there is a new Rocket Research Establishment at Spadeadam in North Cumberland. The Solway Firth continues to supply bowling and putting greens with its inimitable turf.

Kendal

The town of Kendal gathers into its small compass of broad streets, of bridges, yards and courts, of heavy limestone buildings and grey-green slated roofs, the essence of Cumbrian architecture. Border raids, fires, floods and the Black Death are part of its legend. Apart from its aesthetic and historical importance, Kendal was the pioneer town of the great English woollen industry; in 1331 Edward III granted a letter of protection to a Flemish weaver, who established the trade which flourished for six hundred years. In *Henry IV* Shakespeare referred to the 'Kendal green', as famous in its epoch as the hodden grey, a similar stout woollen weave. Kendal Brown Snuff became famous under the Georges, and is manufactured today by descendants of the original inventor. The present prosperity of small Kendal owes much to one of the finest boot and shoe industries in the country, but the factories have done little to disturb the essentially Tudor atmosphere of the town, over which brood the ruins of Queen Katherine Parr's castle from its green eminence above the river.

Set on the A6, although it has not the advantage of being placed on a lake, Kendal is a good centre from which to explore Cumbria. It has good inns, some dating back to the 17th century. The old towns of Appleby, Carlisle, Cockermouth, Keswick and Penrith are also of historic interest; but apart from these, the little seaside towns of Seascale, Silloth and St Bees, and the holiday centre of Alston, high up in the Pennines, with an unrivalled view (on clear days) of the distant sea, there is little of urban interest in Cumbria to detain the traveller. He will make for the mountains and lakes.

The paramount rural industry, equally distributed between the two counties, is sheep-farming. Ancestors of the little dark Herdwicks were, according to a highly dubious legend, washed ashore from the wreck of a Dutch East-Indiaman, and established themselves on the loose shale and thin turf of the hillsides. From their fleece was made the famous hodden grey, a coarse, hard-wearing tweed admirably handled by Lakeland tailors. John Peel 'with his coat so grey' is buried in Caldbeck churchyard. The Herdwick sheep tend today to be replaced by Swaledales – heavier, better mothers and economically more satisfactory.

Next to sheep, tourism is the major industry and, as such, now taken seriously. Cumbria has suffered little from the so-called progress which has invaded less remote regions. It is expensive to drive new roads into the mountains. The television mast does not bristle from every roof-tree, because reception is none of the best in the valleys. Very few farms are still without the benefits of electricity since the N W Electricity Board completed its rural lakeland electrification programme in 1965.

Some Tours

For the motorist, making his preliminary survey of the district, there are certain 'musts'. One is the good road from Newby Bridge, skirting Windermere, north by Ambleside, the quiet waters of Rydal and Grasmere, over Dunmail Raise, by Thirlmere (unfortunately masked in forestry) to Keswick at the head of Derwentwater; thence following Bassenthwaite and the Derwent Valley to Carlisle. This route affords an inimitable panorama of the better-known lakes and, at a distance, of Helvellyn, Skiddaw and Blencathra, giants of the Lakeland mountains. From Kendal one may break off over the beautiful desolation of Shap Fell, with its eery light and eerier legends, to Penrith and the Scottish border; alternatively there is the road over Kirkstone Pass and by Ullswater, which brings one to the same destination. Westward from Kendal, skirting the Langdale Pikes which like slumbering elephants, trunk to trunk, dominate the horizon, an adventurous driver can reach Wastwater, most dramatic of the lakes with its dark water and plunging screes. Having made these considerable journeys, the motorist has no more than scratched the local surface, unless he has at some moment abandoned his four wheels, to climb to the tarns, such as small, bleak Goats' Water. None but the walker can claim more than superficial acquaintance with the Lake District.

Flora and Fauna

Both counties were formerly rich in wild flowers. Pesticides and agricultural mechanization have now robbed the hedgerows and accessible woodlands of many of their treasures; but in the more distant reaches may still be found such rarities as the bee orchis, pink sundew, bird's-eye primrose, bog asphodel, various saxifrages and parnassus grass. On the limestone flourishes the rock rose, in all its varieties of colour, and wild scabious. Daffodil, primrose, briar rose and bracken are commonplace in the wild garden of the Lakes.

Fauna include the usual small rodents and mammals; ermine (the white-coated, winter stoat) has been seen above Wastwater; red deer, fox and otter. Trout and salmon, formerly free to local fishermen, now require a licence. A little game is strictly preserved. Free to the eye and camera of the naturalist are goosander and great crested grebe, winter visitors. Occasionally osprey, great grey shrike, waxwing and rock dove – even, rarely, the golden eagle. Peregrine, buzzard, woodpecker and wood-warbler, breed locally. The heron is a familiar figure on the fringes of lakes and estuaries. Curlew, plover and gull nest in bogs.

Elterwater, Westmorland (near Skelwith, Lancashire) *Edwin Smith*

The roar of the red deer, the bark of the fox, contribute to the local music of waterfall, curlew and that shy, occasional visitant, the whooper swan, while Old Brock, the badger, lumbers about his business.

The Past

The Stone Age men who tamed the wild goat, grew corn and made the querns in which to grind it would be surprised today to find their troughs used as bird baths in private gardens. The Roman invasion under Agricola swept north through Westmorland and Cumberland and left its traces in the western terminus of Hadrian's Wall at Bowness on Solway, and in forts and villas such as those at Hardknott and Ravenglass. It was not until 1157 that Cumberland became part of England. After the Roman invasion and the Norman conquest it still belonged to the Scottish kingdom of Strathclyde. Hence some of the names: Blencathra, Helvellyn, Glaramara, Skiddaw. Runic and Celtic relics in the form of fonts or crosses survived the long Border warfare, which ended in the battle of Clifton Moor, near Penrith, in 1745. During those belligerent years were built the numerous castles and fortified churches (notably Salkeld) and all the little yards and courts in which the peaceful population took refuge from the marauders. In 1745 Prince Charles Edward advanced from Carlisle with his army of Highlanders on what was to prove a disastrous expedition and was beaten back along the same track from Derby. 'Here the Pretender stabled his troops' is a common label along the line of that dolorous pilgrimage, which may be traced today in a rusted stirrup, a scrap of chain armour, or even the armoured corpse of one of Charles Edward's troopers, reclaimed (as the writer saw) from the peat which preserved it.

You may fish, swim, shoot, sail and glide. Beagling is a favoured sport, Sheep-farming and fox-hunting run together: the footpacks of the Blencathra

Wastwater, Cumberland

J. Allan Cash

and Melbreak hounds are strongly supported by farmers, shepherds, quarrymen and others. There is a variety of climbing, some of the climbs rated 'Vee Diff' in mountaineering vocabulary. The famous Tophet Bastion offers hazards which are regarded respectfully even by alpinists.

Of spectator sports there is endless variety. Sheepdog Trials take in Hound Trails and Terrier Shows. Sheepdogs are the leading event and attract competitors from across the Yorkshire and Scottish borders. The Hound Trail has peculiar fascination for the stranger: specially bred hounds hunt a drag of oil and aniseed and are heavily backed by the local fancy. As for the Lakeland terrier, his section of the show is invariably popular – a tough, courageous little character, equal to tackling a fox in its earth. After the Trials, Grasmere Sports is the leading event of the season, and here Cumberland wrestling takes pride of place. There are fell-racing and point-to-points. The winter visitor has fine skating or curling on the tarns and good ski-ing on the slopes of Helvellyn.

The Mary Wakefield Westmorland Musical Festival, held biennially in Kendal, was the forerunner of many of its kind which, in the last half century, have sprung up all over the country. Fifty years ago it was attracting musicians and singers of world-wide renown to the little town and it is still a notable local event.

Famous Figures

Cumberland and Westmorland, for all their beauty, have attracted writers rather than painters. The Lakes conspicuously lack a Constable. Of the Lakeland Poets, Wordsworth, the indigenous one, was born at Cockermouth, educated at Hawkshead, lived at Grasmere and Rydal, and is buried in Grasmere churchyard. Southey lived for forty years at Greta Hall, near Keswick, and is buried at Crosthwaite; Thomas de Quincey lived at Nab Cottage on Rydal Water.

Of modern writers, Constance Holme rates as the Mary Webb of the Lakes; she lived at Milnthorpe, the so-called 'lost seaport' of Westmorland on the Kent estuary. After Graham Sutton's less well-known work, one turns for the Cumbrian scene to Hugh Walpole's Herries saga. The four big romantic novels, written at 'Brackenburn' on the shores of Derwentwater, range from the early 18th century to the present day. Beatrix Potter's house at Sawrey ('Lakes', though just in Lancashire) attracts an average of 10,000 visitors every year. The creator of 'Peter Rabbit' devoted a handsome share of her royalties to the purchase of some 4,000 acres of land which she left to the National Trust.

Brougham Castle, Westmorland   *G. Douglas Bolton*

Some houses and gardens open to the public

Abbot Hall At Kendal *Map* D F 49. *18th cent.; Georgian house converted into an art gallery and cultural centre.*

Carlisle Castle At Carlisle *Map* D D 55. *12th-cent. restored, preserving dungeons, and used partly as barracks.*

Cockermouth Castle 8m E of Workington on A594 *Map* D B 53. *Ruins of Norman castle besieged and dismantled during Civil War; gatehouse and upper ward overlooking River Derwent.*

Corby Castle Wetheral 6m E of Carlisle off B6263 *Map* D E 55. *17th cent. & 19th cent.; 18th-cent. grounds with forest trees by River Eden. Grounds open; house closed to public.*

Dove Cottage and **Wordsworth Museum** At Grasmere *Map* D D 50. *Former home of*

Wordsworth and De Quincey. Rooms furnished as in Wordsworth's time.

Levens Hall 5m S of Kendal on A6 *Map* D E 48. *Elizabethan house; notable interior fittings; topiary gardens laid out by Beaumont.*

Muncaster Castle Ravenglass 6m SE of Gosforth on A595 *Map* D A 49. *Partly ancient mansion; refuge of Henry VI; terrace overlooking Lake District fells.*

Sizergh Castle 3m S of Kendal on A6 *Map* D F 49. *15th to 18th cent. with 14th-cent. pele tower NT. Tudor Great Hall, Jacobite relics, fine panelling, old English furniture.*

Wordsworth House At Cockermouth *Map* D B 53. *18th cent.; birthplace of the poet in 1770 NT.*

Books for further reading

The 'feel' of the area

A. H. GRIFFIN *In Search of the Real Lakeland* 1961; *In Mountain Lakeland* 1963
W. R. MITCHELL *Men of Lakeland* 1966
G. S. SANDILANDS *The Lakes: an Anthology of Lakeland Life and Landscape* n. edn 1950
GRAHAM SUTTON *Smoke across the Fells; Shepherds' Warning; Fell Days* 1946–8
H. H. SYMONDS *Walking in the Lake District* revised S. Johnson 1962
HUGH WALPOLE Rogue Herries novels: *Rogue Herries; Judith Paris; The Fortress; Vanessa* 1930–3

Natural history

W. HODGSON *Flora of Cumberland* 1898
H. A. MACPHERSON *Vertebrate Fauna of Lakeland* 1892
J. E. MARR *Geology of the Lake District* 1968
R. STOKOE *The Birds of the Lake Counties* 1933

History and topography

M. J. B. BADDELEY (comp.) *Baddeley's Guide to the Lake District* 23rd edn 1964
F. G. BRABANT *The English Lakes* 4th edn revised B. L. Thompson (Methuen Little Guides series)
W. G. COLLINGWOOD *Lake District History* 2nd edn 1928; *The Lake Counties* n. edn 1949
W. HEATON COOPER *The Hills of Lakeland* 1938
S. JENNET *The Lake District* 1965
M. LEFEBURE *The English Lake District* 1964
NORMAN NICHOLSON *Portrait of the Lakes* 1963
N. PEVSNER *Cumberland and Westmorland* 1967
W. A. POUCHER *The Lakeland Peaks* 1960
W. ROLLINSON *A History of Man in the Lake District* 1967
FRANK SINGLETON *The English Lakes* 1954
W. H. THOMPSON and G. CLARK *The Lakeland Landscape* 1938

Gazetteer

CUMBERLAND AND WESTMORLAND

Ambleside *Westm.* (DD 50) EC Thurs (2,390). A sheltered situation under Wansfell and within 1 m. of Lake Windermere provides excellent walking (to Loughrigg Terrace and Jenkin Crag for views), for ascents of Wansfell Pike (1,587 ft.) and Loughrigg Fell (1,101 ft.) and for touring the Langdales. The fascinating 17th-cent. Bridge House, once a summer house surrounded by orchards, is an information centre for the NT. A picturesque ceremony takes place every July when children come in procession to strew the floor of St Mary's Church with rushes. The extensive Roman fort of Galava, at Borrans Field at the head of the lake, shows signs of having been rebuilt after flooding.

Appleby *Westm.* (DG 52) EC Thurs (1,860). This claims to be the smallest county and assize town in England, with a population greatly declined since the Middle Ages. Its high st rises steeply from the Eden Valley. The castle, which was captured by the Saxons in 1388, was held for Charles Stuart by the Lady Anne Clifford whose marble monument is in the church of St Lawrence. The Norman keep is surrounded by beautiful lawns. At the June Horse Fair, gypsies foregather on the outskirts of the town.

Bewcastle *Cumb.* (DF 57) (520). Remote moorland village which was the site of a Roman fort with a ruined castle revealing material taken from Hadrian's Wall. It has also the shaft of a cross (7th–8th cent.) sculptured on all four sides and standing in the churchyard.

At Grange in Borrowdale   *J. Allan Cash*

Birdoswald *Cumb.* (DG 56). The turf continuation of Hadrian's Wall runs to the N of this Roman camp. Its remains include a stone wall, a corn-drying kiln, and stones showing the marks of Roman chisels have been used for building nearby farmhouses. Smaller discoveries can be seen in Carlisle Museum.

Blencathra *Cumb.* (DD 52). Mountain E of Skiddaw also known as Saddleback (2,847 ft.). It should be climbed from Threlkeld or following the ridge from Scales.

Bolton *Westm.* (DG 52). Pretty church with two Norman doorways, unusual stonework and a geometrical chancel-screen.

Borrowdale** *Cumb.* (DC 51) EC Wed (720). Perhaps the most beautiful of the Lakeland valleys, situated above Derwentwater on the road from

617

Keswick. Castle Crag, an ancient fort between the Jaws of Borrowdale, and the arrestingly balanced Bowder Stone are features of note.

Bowness *Cumb.* (DC 56) EC Wed. Site of the Roman camp at the western extremity of Hadrian's Wall. The bells in the church porch were stolen from Scotland as a reprisal after a border raid in which the church's own bells were lost in Solway Firth.

Brampton *Cumb.* (DF 56) EC Thurs (3,130). Market town within reach of the Wall, a pretty lake known as Talkin Tarn, and the Written Rock above the R. Gelt, where a Roman standard-bearer has carved a moving inscription. Lanercost Priory (2½ m. NE) stands in the beautiful meadowland bordering the Irthing. The Early English nave is still used for worship. Note the Lanercost Cross (1214) in the aisle, the clerestory arches, and the 12th-cent. gatehouse where Edward I was three times received by the monks.

Burgh-by-Sands *Cumb.* (DD 56) EC Tues (790). King Edward I, who died within sight of Scotland on his way N against Robert the Bruce, was brought back to lie in state in this fortified church. The 12th-cent. tower, embattled and without ornamentation, has the appearance of a Norman keep. A monument to Edward I stands near the village.

Buttermere *Cumb.* (DB 51) (60). The village, built on a level site, is finely situated between the lakes of Buttermere and Crummock Water.

Caldbeck *Cumb.* (DD 54) (740). John Peel lies in the graveyard surrounded by the fells where he hunted on foot with his hounds for fifty-five years. The rousing song was written in the huntsman's lifetime by his friend J. W. Graves.

Carlisle★ *Cumb.* (DD 55) EC Thurs (71,110). County town where licensed houses have been State-owned since an experiment in the 1914 War. Always a border stronghold against the Scots, the town never surrendered until 1745, when the Young Pretender rode in on a white horse preceded by a hundred pipers – very soon to return beaten and dispirited after the retreat from Derby. The cathedral suffered partial destruction in 1645 at the hands of General Leslie. Its proportions have been affected, though some Norman work of 1123 and much detail have been spared. Note the E window, which has glass as beautiful as any in York Minster.

The castle, founded in 1092, has in its inner ward a Norman keep, at the top of which is a windowless cell named after MacIvor, Sir Walter Scott's hero in *Waverley*; the walls and door are covered by drawings made by prisoners. The Queen of Scots was imprisoned in Queen Mary's Tower for two months in 1568, a bitter introduction to English prison life.

Castlerigg Circle *Cumb.* (DC 52). Ring of 48 standing stones, the biggest nearly 8 ft. high, which is assumed to be Keats' 'dismal cirque of Druid stones upon a forlorn moor'.

Cockermouth *Cumb.* (DB 53) EC Thurs (5,820). The house where William Wordsworth (1770–1850) and his sister Dorothy were born is kept by the NT as a place of literary pilgrimage.

Debatable Land, The *Cumb.* (DD 57). Tract from the Sark to the Esk, long disputed between Scotland and England.

Derwentwater★ *Cumb.* (DC 52). This lovely lake, 3 m. long, has scenery of wonderful variety; behind it Skiddaw rises to the N. Its islands are the property of the NT. The Falls

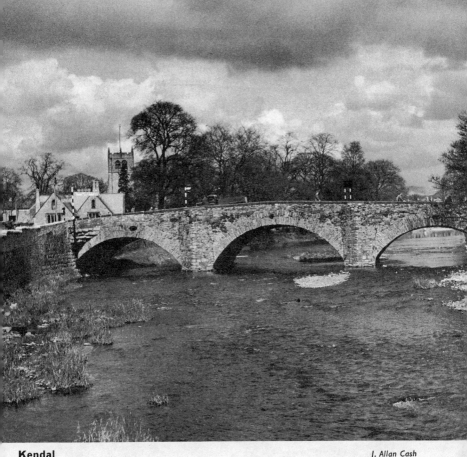

Kendal

of Lodore, extolled by Southey, are at their most impressive after heavy rain. A memorial to John Ruskin (1819–1900) stands on Friars Crag above the E shore of the lake.

Edenhall *Cumb.* (DF 53) EC Wed. According to Longfellow's ballad, the luck of the House of Musgrave would fail if the precious medieval 'fairy' cup in the family's possession were shattered. As it happens, the house has been demolished, and the 700-year-old cup of exquisite Syrian or Persian enamelwork is kept safely in London. The Norman church, on Saxon foundations, contains numerous Musgrave monuments.

Ennerdale Water *Cumb.* (DB 51). Stern mountains encircle the least frequented of Cumberland's lakes, and promote an individual but rather sombre atmosphere.

Eskdale *Cumb.* (DC 50). Lakeless valley noted for waterfalls and ascended by a light-gauge railway. Walkers should make for Hardknott Pass with its Roman fort and tremendous view* of Scafell Pike.

Gilsland *Cumb.* (DG 56). Two altars, with inscriptions still legible, are reminders of the Roman forces who manned this part of the Wall. Sir Walter Scott, who described the village in *Guy Mannering*, met his future wife, Charlotte Charpentier, here in 1797.

Gosforth *Cumb.* (DA 50) EC Sat (770). The tall slender cross is judged to be a relic of Scandinavian settlement before the Norman Conquest. Its carving shows a combination of early Christian and Nordic pagan symbolism.

Grasmere* *Westm.* (DD 50) EC Thurs (1,040). Wordsworth lived for ten years at Dove Cottage, near the almost circular little lake. It is open to the public. He and his wife and his sister Dorothy are buried in the churchyard of St Oswald's. De Quincey (1785–1859) took on the cottage from him. The local museum has many relics of Lakeland poets and their eminent visitors, but the natural scenery is best commemorated by their poetry.

Great Salkeld *Cumb.* (DF 53). The embattled church tower is entered through a cunningly-devised gate of 14th-cent. ironwork, and contains two vaulted rooms and a dungeon connected by a spiral staircase. The

Friar's Crag, Keswick

Reece Winstone

Roman altar, now in the porch, was discovered in 1890.

Hadrian's Wall *Cumb.* (DF 56). This is the fortified line dating back to Roman days, stretching from Wallsend to Solway Firth (73½ m.), comprising a wide ditch, the 15-ft. wall (built of turf W of Gilsland, later succeeded by stones), and the Vallum, which was intended as a southern defence. The Wall, built A.D. 122–26 under Aulus Platorius Nepos, had regularly spaced mile-castles about 1,620 yards apart with interspaced turrets, which were supplied by garrisons from sixteen forts.

Helvellyn★ *Cumb. & Westm.* (DD 51). Three routes from Patterdale lead to the summit of the third highest mountain in the Lake District (3,118 ft.). The most popular is from Wythburn.

Kendal *Westm.* (DF 49) EC Thurs (19,140). Woollen goods are still a local industry, though the Kendal Green of Shakespeare's day is no longer in production. Catherine Parr, the last of Henry VIII's wives, was born in the castle, which is now ruined. Her minute prayerbook has been acquired by the Corporation and is kept in the Mayor's Parlour. Among other valuable possessions, the town hall has portraits by Romney, who left his wife and family here while for forty years he worked in London. The church, with noteworthy double aisles, contains many historical relics. The quaint alleys of this town should be explored on foot.

Keswick *Cumb.* (DC 52) EC Wed (4,750). One of the best centres★ for Lakeland. A visit to the model of the Lake District in the museum notably helps excursions; apart from the interest of the other exhibits, which include MSS. of the poets and Sir Hugh Walpole. Coleridge lived at Greta Hall between 1800 and 1809, and Southey during 1803–43. Crosthwaite Church (¾ m.) on a site chosen by St Kentigern in 553, has a complete set of consecration crosses. Here Canon H. D. Rawnsley (1851–1920) is buried. As one of the founders of the NT, he ensured the preservation of large tracts of country. In summer, the town is host to the Keswick Theatre Festival.

Kirkby Lonsdale *Westm.* (DG 47) EC Wed (1,240). In the words of John Ruskin, here are moorland, sweet river and English forest at their best. The town also has Georgian houses and a 15th-cent. bridge across the Lune.

Kirkby Stephen *Westm.* (DH 50) EC Thurs (1,720). Market town among high mountains. The church, of cathedral-like proportions, has carvings and also memorials of the Musgraves and Whartons, who lived at Wharton Hall (1¾ m. S), now mainly a farmhouse.

Kirkoswald *Cumb.* (DF 54) EC Wed (790). The moated castle ruins consist mainly of dungeons and one fine turret. The church has a tower set 200 yards away from its main body, and a stream flowing from under its nave. The great house of the Fetherstonhaugh family, known as the College, is a private residence.

Kirkstone Pass★ *Westm.* (DE 50). The inn between Caudale Moor and Red Screes on the road from Windermere to Ullswater is the highest in the Lake District.

Levens Hall *Westm.* (DE 48). The Elizabethan house grew from a peel-tower refuge against the Scots. More famous even than the house's carved fireplaces are its gardens.

621

Shap Abbey

Edwin Smith

Long Meg and Her Daughters *Cumb*. (DF 53). Stone circle near Little Salkeld, comparable with Stonehenge.

Lowther *Westm*. (DF 52). The remains of the castle stand in an imposing 3,000-acre park. Of the house, with its 500-ft. terrace and ramparts, only a portion of one tower is 13th-cent., the rest having been destroyed and rebuilt many times, including the rooms where Mary Queen of Scots enjoyed the hospitality of Sir Richard Lowther.

Mallerstang *Westm*. (DH 49). Pendragon Castle, reputed to have been built by the father of King Arthur, is in a remote valley near the Yorkshire border.

Maryport *Cumb*. (DA 53) EC Wed (12,330). Formerly a seaport based on the coal and iron industries, this town now has a new industrial estate not centred on iron and coal. An unprecedented discovery of Roman altars at Netherhall was made in the 19th cent., and there have also been more recent discoveries.

Muncaster Castle *Cumb*. (DB 49). From the terrace of the Pennington family seat there is a famous view of the mountains above Eskdale. Among many treasures, the family cherishes the enamelled bowl known as the 'Luck of Muncaster', presented by Henry VI when he was in flight after his defeat at Hexham, and a piece of the *Fighting Temeraire* set into panelling – a relic of the great sailing ship painted by Turner.

Naworth Castle *Cumb*. (DF 56). Imposing 14th-cent. castle built around a central courtyard. It is the private residence of the Earl of Carlisle.

Penrith *Cumb*. (DF 53) EC Wed (10,930). Original capital of Cumbria, for centuries engaged in border strife; now has a ruined castle. Richard III slept in a wainscoted room in the Gloucester Arms. A feature of the churchyard is a group of 'hogback' stones, little houses for the dead dating from before the Conquest.

Ponsonby *Cumb*. (DA 50). Moated church with 13th-cent. remains.

Ravenglass *Cumb*. (DA 49). Harbour of declined importance. Walls Castle, one of the greatest Roman survivals in the N, shows signs of having been a villa or bath connected with a fort at Muncaster. A famous breeding-place for gulls and terns may be visited by boat.

Rydal★ *Westm*. (DD 50) EC Thurs (530). The village on the smallest of the Lakes, where Wordsworth lived at Rydal Mount between 1813 and 1850, and where he died. He planted Dora's Field with daffodils and gave it to his daughter, and from a rock known as Wordsworth's Seat he sat and surveyed the view that was so much part of his life and poetry. Three other famous men chose to live near: Dr Arnold of Rugby, Thomas de Quincey and Hartley Coleridge.

St Bees *Cumb*. (CK 51) EC Thurs (1,040). A priory was built on the site of the nunnery founded by a legendary Irish princess of the 7th cent., who was granted 'as much land as was covered by snow on Midsummer Day', and of which one carved stone endures. The school was founded by Archbishop Grindal in 1583.

Scafell★ *Cumb*. (DC 50). May be ascended from Wasdale Head or, by cragsmen, combined with Scafell Pike (3,210 ft.) via Mickledore Ridge.

Seascale *Cumb*. (DA 50) EC Thurs (2,000). Small seaside resort making a good base for Wastwater and the high mountains to the E. The 19th-cent. church has a wealth of carved oak and fine glass.

Shap *Westm*. (DF 51) EC Thurs (1,150). High village famous for quarry stone, and for the remains of a 16th-cent. abbey. Keld Chapel (1 m. SW) is NT property.

Sizergh Castle *Westm*. (DE 48). The Strickland family have enjoyed occupation of their castle since 1239. It has a 14th-cent. pele tower flanked by Elizabethan wings, and a room occupied by Catherine Parr after Henry VIII's death. The chapel contains a portable altar of painted Italian leather, a licence for which was granted to Sir Thomas Strickland over 500 years ago.

Solway Moss *Cumb*. (DD 57). Fluid mass of mud and decayed vegetation, 7 m. in circumference, scene of the defeat of the Scots in 1542, and of a great natural disaster in 1771.

Temple Sowerby Manor *Westm*. (DG 52). Gardens famous for roses, and open to the public.

Ullswater★★ *Cumb. & Westm*. (DE 52). Great lake in three reaches which increase in grandeur to the N, it is bordered by Gowbarrow Park (NT), associated with Wordsworth's 'Daffodils'.

Vale of St John *Cumb*. (D D 52). Romantic valley flanked by Wanthwaite Crags and the Dodds of Helvellyn. Watson's Dodd, a strange rock formation, was Scott's fairy castle in his poem *The Bridal of Triermain*.

Wasdale Head* *Cumb*. (D B 50) EC Thurs. Chief British centre for climbing rock, snow and ice. England's highest mountain, Scafell Pike, towers above Wastwater, her deepest lake.

Whitehaven *Cumb*. (CK 51) EC Wed (26,250). In the 17th cent., the development of coal mines and port facilities were fostered by the Lowther family, so that in sixty years a hamlet became a seaport. In 1788 Paul Jones sailed into the harbour in *Ranger*, his privateer, but failed to capture it. The town was bombarded by a German submarine in 1915.

Windermere* *Westm*. (DE 49) EC Thurs (6,880). Town combined with the older Bowness on the largest English lake, which is narrow and beautiful, with wooded banks, and splendid views of the fells. There is a summer steamer service. The wooden equestrian statue of St Martin, in the church of which he is the patron saint, is of a very rare kind and may have been carved locally in the early 17th cent.

Workington *Cumb*. (DA 52) EC Thurs. (29,210). Steel is notable as one of the main industries; coal lies under the sea. Workington Hall has been largely rebuilt since Mary Queen of Scots stayed there and wrote her letter of appeal to Elizabeth before being escorted to Bolton Castle.

Wreay *Cumb*. (DE 54). Sarah Losh, a wealthy 19th-cent. recluse, built two schools, a cemetery chapel and a church in the style of a Roman basilica, designing them herself and employing a local mason. The pulpit, lectern and reading desk are of prehistoric bog oak.

Ullswater: the pier near Pooley Bridge   G. Douglas Bolton

The Mull of Galloway

J. Allan Cash

THE
SOUTH-WEST
LOWLANDS

Wigtown, Kirkcudbright, Ayr, Dumfries

AN INTRODUCTION BY GEORGE SCOTT-MONCRIEFF

Scotland's four south-westernmost counties are by no means homogeneous. Ayrshire is by far the most thickly populated, serving to some degree as a dormitory and to a large degree as a holiday-place for the people of Glasgow, and is the only one to have known much industrial development. Dumfriesshire includes part of the hill country along the English Border, then stretches north and west through more open, fertile land into the central Lowland hills, whence it may be approached by one of two dramatic entrances: the Devil's Beef Tub,

The Devil's Beef Tub, near Moffat

whose road descends on the old spa of Moffat, or through the great green lumps of the hills flanking the Dalveen Pass. Only Kirkcudbrightshire and Wigtownshire, lying along the northern coast of the Solway Firth, have much in common, originally forming (along with Carrick, the hill-country to the south of Ayrshire) the Pictish province of Galloway, and retaining much of that earlier unity despite their modern division into counties.

Industry

Scotland's Klondyke came to Ayrshire with the working of its seams of coal and iron ore in the 19th century. It has largely receded, leaving scars along the northern part of the county. But before then there were many local industries, now largely in desuetude with the growth of mass-production and centralisation. Ayrshire has, in consequence, a number of old towns, some of which retain modern variants of earlier industries. Other crafts have gone entirely. In the days when the headgear of the common man was a 'bonnet', Kilmarnock gave its name to the most popular style: an outsize beret with a toorie in the middle, knitted by the women in their own homes. Kilmarnock is now noted for its carpets. Mauchline provided snuff-boxes for Scottish noses, very neatly made of wood with close-fitting hinges and lids, and attractively decorated: they, and other products of the craft, are now collectors' pieces. Stout country boots still claim with pride their genesis in Maybole, and there are modern shoe factories.

626

Ailsa Craig, the great bald rock off the Ayrshire coast, once more provides granite for the best curling-stones. At Prestwick there is an aircraft industry associated with this, the most fog-free airport in Britain, from which there are regular services to northern Europe and America.

Industry has receded much more markedly from the Galloway towns. The little burgh of Gatehouse-of-Fleet, for example, that could once boast brewery, tannery, soapery, cotton-mills, a boat-building yard and a bobbin-factory, has now none of these. In the 18th century, after the developing laird, having built his mansion which is now a hotel, canalised the River Fleet, the port of Gatehouse even offered some rivalry to that of Glasgow. Like other Galloway harbours it no longer sees any craft bigger than the occasional yacht. Even Portpatrick, so near Ireland it once served as a Gretna Green for runaway Irish couples, is now but a fishing harbour. Only the sheltered port of Stranraer maintains a regular mail and passenger service with Ireland. Tweedmills and a distillery are virtually all the industry in the area apart from such as is directly associated with agriculture. The historic old towns of Dumfriesshire—Annan, Lochmaben, Langholm, Sanquhar, even Dumfries itself—are relatively quiet and peaceful places.

Dumfries: the River Nith and the Old Bridge   *J. Allan Cash*

The landscape

The Lowland belt of grey-brown shale runs right across Dumfriesshire and Galloway and provides whinstone from which most of the older houses are built. But Dumfriesshire has a good deal of sandstone, usually of a rather dark, even liverish, red, which latterly provided a more tractable material. There is granite in Galloway, at Dalbeattie and Creetown and the hills behind, of a delicate silvery brightness, which provides finer houses. To the north, near Sanquhar, Dumfriesshire has coal-bearing rock. But it is in Ayrshire that we come to the main coalfields. Here the rock formations are extremely mixed, with shale, some granite and many different sandstones besides volcanic intrusions. Out to sea, Ailsa Craig is a massive lump of greenish granite.

Heather hills lie all the way inland from the rugged cliffs and sandy bays and wildfowl-noisy estuaries of Galloway's beautiful Solway coastline. The hills cross the border some distance into Ayrshire. They include The Merrick, at 2,764 feet the highest hill of southern Scotland, rising in fine remote country where also lies in a bare bed of granite remote Loch Enoch, itself 1,650 feet above sea-level and containing an island with another loch in the middle.

The little fields of Galloway, carved out amongst stony outcrops and homely trees, bounded by stone dykes, rise quickly into the heather hills. It is a countryside on a wonderfully satisfying scale, small enough to be intimate, bold enough to be exciting, always with a rise and fall in the ground to lure one farther.

To the north the hill country becomes increasingly noble and rugged, with great lonely stretches by deep Glentrool, the Cauldron of the Dungeon and the Back Hill of the Bush, places that do not belie their romantic names. The wilderness overflows into the Carrick country of Ayrshire around the big water of Loch Doon, and a little way into Dumfriesshire before it gives place to the fertile fields of Nithsdale and Annandale. Dumfriesshire includes to the east the typical Border hill country of Eskdale and Liddesdale, and to the north part of the Lowther Hills, that 'vast expanse covered with thick, short, tawny grass and moss' that stretches across the central Lowlands. All over the southwest there is a plenitude of lovely country, hill and coast, with friendly little towns and villages.

North of Carrick, Ayrshire flattens out gradually, with wide rivers and good golf-courses, the farmland broken into by patches of moor. At Alloway is the thatched cottage where Robert Burns was born. Near by is the shell of Kirk Alloway where Tam o' Shanter watched the witches dance, and the ancient humpbacked bridge across which he escaped from the clutch of Cutty Sark in that hugely humorous poem in which Burns celebrated the character of his own people and their land.

The people

While in early times both Ayrshire and Dumfriesshire became part of the kingdom of the Britons of Strathclyde, Galloway remained a Pictish province, isolated from the kingdoms of the northern and southern Picts which occupied the greater part of Scotland. The degree of Roman penetration is disputed: it was certainly not great, although Ayr marked the terminus of a Roman road; but through it, indirectly, a Romanised Pict became the first Christian missionary to Scotland.

THE SOUTH-WEST LOWLANDS

St Ninian seems actually to have spent some time in Rome before he established his *Candida Casa* on the peninsular Isle of Whithorn about the year 393. On the coast at Glasserton is the cave which he used as an oratory before building his stone chapel. It was to Whithorn Priory that the Scottish kings made their pilgrimages for many centuries: the last royal pilgrimage being that of Mary Queen of Scots in 1563.

Coastal Ayrshire and Galloway had their share of Viking incursions, and a final overlay of Dalriadic Scots who left their Gaelic language to linger longer in the south-west than anywhere else in the Lowlands. Probably there were Galloway hill-folk of the last century who used Gaelic words, and there are still those who pronounce their Gaelic place-names correctly.

The Gallowegians long maintained considerable independence, sometimes siding with the English and giving Robert the Bruce a hard time in subduing them.

Stone and lime

Inscribed stones, one in the museum at Whithorn and two in the church at Kirkmadrine, go back almost to Ninian's day and are perhaps the oldest Christian relics of British origin. The Kirkmadrine stones have been described as menhirs christened with the Chi-Ro symbol. The famous richly-carved 7th-century cross

Ancient crosses and inscribed stones in the Whithorn Museum *J. Allan Cash*

Dundrennan Abbey

J. Allan Cash

in Ruthwell Church, to the south of Dumfriesshire, is one of the finest examples of European art to survive from the Dark Ages (*see page* S.15).

The church of New Abbey, better known as Sweetheart Abbey, is, although roofless, relatively intact. At Dundrennan, farther along the Solway coast, the Abbey ruins are singularly beautiful. West again, little but the fine chapter-house of Glenluce Abbey survives. In Ayrshire, Crossraguel Abbey is an ampler ruin.

Galloway was a great stronghold of the Covenanters, the Presbyterians who opposed Episcopacy in the 17th century. Tombstones of slaughtered Covenanters in the old churchyards bear epitaphs in vigorous rhyme. The little kirks of the period are of an architectural austerity and simplicity now better appreciated than they once were. There is a good example at Mochrum, with outside stairs and a carved oak pulpit surmounted by a sounding-board. The only ornament permitted was in the 'laird's loft', the gallery from which the local bigwig might listen to the sermon. Kilbirnie kirk in Ayrshire has a superb loft, ornate with coats-of-arms.

The later medieval castles of Scotland in many ways represent the most individual and characteristic examples of native architecture. Some delightful castles survive in Ayrshire: Cassillis, Dean, Maybole, Kelburn, Rowallan, amongst them. Galloway has Mochrum and the cottage-size castle of Craig-caffie. Outstanding amongst several Dumfriesshire castles is Amisfield Tower, in which the tradition may be seen at its fullest flowering in the south, austerity enriched both in appearance and comfort by the skilful projecting of upper chambers.

Dumfriesshire also has in Drumlanrig a splendid late 17th-century anachronistic castle. Only a little later, Dumfries House (in Ayrshire despite its name) was being built by William, the father of the Adam brothers, as an entirely peaceful mansion; while at Culzean, Robert, the greatest of the Adams, returned to anachronism with an elegant interior enfolded within great towers – the effect much happier within than without.

630

Beasts and flowers

Galloway once had its own breed of sheep, and its native ponies were famous for their hardiness and mettle. The sheep have long been replaced by the coarser-woolled blackface breed. But Galloway cattle are still much to the fore, a popular beef breed, and the 'beltie', black with a clean white cummerbund round the middle, is pleasing to see. The brown-and-white, piebald Ayrshires are a dairy breed, able to yield good quality milk on rough grazing. And from Ayrshire comes the best of Scottish cheeses: Dunlop.

Moorland and shore birds are to be seen in rich variety – even, on occasion, the golden eagle. There are great stretches of grouse-moor, and Wigtownshire has some of the best partridge-shooting in Britain. Ailsa Craig has its gannetry, and a new colony has been started on the Scar Rock in the Solway. There is good salmon and trout fishing in the many rivers, burns and lochs.

The mild climate of the south-west makes for a lush vegetation. It is a little surprising to see palm trees amongst the cabbages in cottage gardens on the Mull of Galloway. Here at Logan is a famous garden with many exotic and semi-tropical trees, plants and shrubs. On the Ayrshire coast the fine gardens of Culzean provide one of the most visited places in the country.

Men and books

Born near Ayr and dying in Dumfries, making friends and writing poems in Galloway, Robert Burns belongs to the south-west. His first and last homes are pilgrim places. Thomas Carlyle's birthplace at Ecclefechan in Dumfriesshire, an attractive white house built by his master-mason family, is in the keeping of the National Trust for Scotland. *Guy Mannering*, one of Scott's best novels, is set in Galloway, and the cave of his smuggler villain, Dirk Hatteraick, may be found (not without difficulty) below the cliffs at Ravenshall. Stevenson set *The Master of Ballantrae* in Galloway. John Galt, contemporary of Scott and the author of some delightful novels of Ayrshire life, was born at Irvine.

Paul Jones, father of the American Navy, was born in the gamekeeper's cottage at Arbigland, near Kirkbean. Many Galloway names are to be found in the Arctic, bequeathed by two early explorers, Sir John and James Ross, whose family home of Balsarroch deserved preservation both for its association and its architecture. Galloway also provided a background for the 'kailyaird' novelist, S. R. Crockett, for some of John Buchan's stories and for Dorothy Sayers' thriller, *Five Red Herrings*. Langholm is the Dumfriesshire birthplace of the contemporary poet, Hugh MacDiarmid.

The three Faed brothers from Gatehouse were Victorian artists whose remarkable virtuosity merits them some return to favour. More recently, its charming old houses and water-girt setting have made Kirkcudbright the home of many artists.

It is said that Queen Victoria once asked Carlyle what he thought was the most beautiful scenery in Scotland, to which he replied, 'The road from Gatehouse to Creetown'. She tried again, hoping he would mention her own Deeside: what did he think was the second most beautiful scenery? 'The road from Creetown to Gatehouse', he told her firmly.

Although many people share Carlyle's feelings for the scenery of the south-west, it still remains a countryside largely unspoilt and uncluttered, where solitude – especially in the Galloway hills – is freely to be found.

Some houses and gardens open to the public

Burns's Cottage Alloway *Map* CD 61. *Birthplace of Robert Burns, with museum.* Burns Monument Trust.

Carlyle's Birthplace Ecclefechan *Map* DB 57. *Thomas Carlyle was born here in 1795. Carlyle relics and MS letters.* NT for Scot.

Culzean Castle *Map* CC 60. *Magnificently-situated 18th-cent. castle designed by Robert Adam. Paintings, furniture, plasterwork. See the Oval Staircase and the Round Drawing Room. Walled garden, aviary, swan pond. See also p. 640.* NT for Scot.

Lochinch and **Castle Kennedy Gardens** *Map* CB 56. *Beautiful gardens on a loch-girt peninsula, with magnolias, azaleas, rhododendrons, etc.* The Earl and Countess of Stair. *Gardens only open.*

Logan Gardens 1m s of Ardwell *Map* CB 54. *Nearly 100 years' devotion have produced these remarkable sub-tropical gardens on the Mull of Galloway. Many exotic trees and shrubs, and in spring carpets of primulas from China and the Himalayas.* Trustees of the Logan Gardens Estate.

Logan Gardens

Books for further reading

General

S. R. CROCKETT *Raiderland: All About Grey Galloway – Its Stories, Traditions, Characters, Humours* 1904

C. H. DICK *Highways and Byways in Galloway and Carrick* 1916

FORESTRY COMMISSION *Glen Trool: National Forest Park Guide* 2nd edn 1954

THEO LANG *Glasgow, Kyle and Galloway* (The Queen's Scotland series) 1953

ANDREW MCCORMICK *Galloway: The Spell of its Hills and Glens* new edn 1947

NEIL MUNRO *Ayrshire Idylls* 1912

C. S. DOUGALL *The Burns Country* 1904

JOHN MCVIE *The Burns Country* 1962

J. A. RUSSELL *The Book of Galloway* 1962

J. F. ROBERTSON *The Story of Galloway* 1963

J. E. SHAW *Ayrshire 1745–1950* 1953

DAVID L. SMITH *Tales of the Glasgow and South Western Railway* 1962

In Literature

GEORGE DOUGLAS BROWN *The House with the Green Shutters* 1901

ROBERT BURNS *The Poems of*

S. R. CROCKETT *The Raiders* 1894

JOHN GALT *Annals of the Parish* 1821, *The Provost* 1822

DOROTHY L. SAYERS *Five Red Herrings* 1931

SIR WALTER SCOTT *Red gauntlet* 1824

Gazetteer

THE SOUTH-WEST LOWLANDS

Wigtown, Kirkcudbright, Ayr, Dumfries

Burns's Cottage, Alloway   *Scottish Tourist Board*

Alloway (CD 61). *See* **Ayr.**

Annan *Dumf.* (DB 56) EC Wed (5,856). Market town near the mouth of the river of the same name. About a century ago a railway viaduct was built across the Solway Firth, about 1½ m. wide at this point, connecting Annan to the Cumberland coast, but the viaduct was removed after suffering severe damage from masses of floating ice in the estuary in January 1881.

Ardrossan *Ayr.* (CC 64) EC Wed (9,568). Busy port, 1 m. from popular seaside resort of **Saltcoats**, and starting-point for steamer trips in Firth of Clyde.

Auchinleck *Ayr.* (CF 62) (4,800). See **Cumnock.**

Ayr★ (CD 62) EC Wed (46,747). Seaport and county town of great historic interest, and centre of the 'Burns country'. Wallace Tower in the High St. (1852) replaces an earlier building of the same name from which the clock and bells were transferred. Note the 'Twa Brigs' of Burns: the Auld Brig, now closed to traffic, dates from the end of the 13th cent.; the New Brig (1788) fulfilled Burns's prophecy, when it was swept away in 1877 and had to be rebuilt. At Alloway, a suburb 2 m. S, the 'auld clay biggin' in which Burns was born (1759), and the adjoining cottage, are now a museum (*see p.* s.8). The Grecian monument to the poet near by contains Thom's figures of Tam o' Shanter and Souter Johnnie. Prestwick 3 m. N, well-known watering place with excellent golf course, is now an important airport.

Ballantrae *Ayr.* (CA 58). Fishing village, with golf links; views across the North Channel to Kintyre and Ireland.

Beattock *Dumf.* (DA 60). From here the A74, rising to 1,014 ft., runs alongside the railway over the Lowther Hills into Lanarkshire.

Caerlaverock Castle★ *Dum.* (DA 56). Originally built in the 13th cent., within a double moat and entered by a drawbridge, the castle has been subsequently much altered. The fine 17th-cent. range of buildings was added when it became a residence rather than a fortress. It is claimed to be the 'Ellangowan' of Scott's *Guy Mannering.* (AM)

Cairnryan *Wig.* (CA 56). Fishing village on E shore of Loch Ryan, with an early 18th-cent. house (Lochryan) set in attractive gardens. To NW is the beginning of the beautiful Glen App.

Canonbie *Dumf.* (DD 57). Angling village on a bend of R. Esk. Hollows Tower, 2 m. N, recalls Johnnie Armstrong, the 16th-cent. Border raider, feared for his exploits as far away as Newcastle.

Carronbridge *Dumfries.* (CJ 59). Starting-point of the splendid Dalveen Pass (where A702 reaches 1,105 ft.) over the Lowther Hills, past Ballencleuch Law to S and Greenlowther (2,404 ft.) to N. Just to the NW of the village is Drumlanrig Castle* (1675–88), built by first Duke of Queensberry, who was so horrified by the cost that he never lived there; it is now one of the seats of the Duke of Buccleuch.

Carsphairn *Kirk.* (CF 59). The A713, running SE from Ayr to New Galloway and Castle Douglas, here reaches 800 ft. above sea-level, making the village an excellent centre for walking. Within a radius of 6 m. the highest points are Corserine (2,669 ft.) to SW and Cairnsmore (2,613 ft.) to NE; while less than 5 m. to the NW Loch Doon is the starting-point of a long chain of hydro-electric stations.

Castle Douglas *Kirk.* (CH 56) EC Thurs (3,250). A busy little town on Carlingwark Loch, a haunt of wild fowl. On an island in the R. Dee, 2 m. W, are the grim ruins of Threave Castle, with walls 8 ft. thick and 70 ft. high, once a stronghold of the Douglas family.

Castle Kennedy *Wig.* (CB 56). Between the Black and White Lochs, 3 m. E of Stranraer, are the ruins of Castle Kennedy (1607) and the modern Lochinch Castle, whose beautiful gardens* are open to the public.

Crossraguel Abbey (CC 60). *See* **Kirkoswald.**

Culzean Castle (CC 60). *See* **Turnberry.**

Cumnock *Ayr.* (CF 61) EC Wed (5,822). Mining town on the Lugar Water, with a good 18th-cent. Mercat Cross.† James Keir Hardie, founder of the Independent Labour Party, lived here for many years, and his bust stands in front of the Town Hall. In the churchyard of the neighbouring town of Auchinleck is the grave of Dr Johnson's biographer, James Boswell. Near by is Auchinleck House, built by Boswell's father, Lord Auchinleck, a judge of the Court of Session, shortly before his death in 1782. Another well-known 18th-cent. figure, the inventor William Murdoch (1754–1839), was born in the same parish. The most important of his inventions was the use of coal gas for lighting purposes, the first experiments for which were carried out in a cave that is still shown here.

Dalbeattie *Kirk.* (CJ 56) EC Thurs (3,221). The town, on the Urr Water, owes its origin (1780) to its impressive granite quarries. 2½ m. NNW is the notable Mote of Urr, an 80-ft. mound surrounded by a fosse; while 1 m. W are the ruins of the castle of Buittle or Botel, once the home of John de Baliol, founder of Balliol College, Oxford, in the 13th cent.

Darvel *Ayr.* (CF 63) EC Wed (3,173). Lace-making town in the Irvine valley near Loudoun Hill. Birthplace of Sir Alexander Fleming (1881–1955), discoverer of penicillin.

Dumfries* (CK 57) EC Thurs (27,988). Historic town, the centre of a road network at the lowest crossing of the R. Nith, which here ripples over a weir. The town was made a

---

† Market cross or proclamation place.

royal burgh by William the Lion and its oldest existing charter was granted by Robert II in 1395. Robert Burns spent the last five years of his life here (1791–6) in a house, now a museum, in Burns St., and was buried in the churchyard of St Michael's. The old town hall in the middle of the market place, known as the Mid Steeple, was built in 1708. The Old Bridge, now reserved for foot passengers, was built in 1208 by Devorguila, the wife of John de Baliol. One and a half m. N are the ruins of Lincluden Abbey, founded as a convent in the 12th cent.

Dundrennan (CH 54). *See* **Kirkcudbright.**

Dunure *Ayr.* (CC 61). Small coastal village, with ruins of a castle and an ancient 'beehive' dovecot. Croy Brae, 2 m. S on the Girvan road, is the famous 'Electric Brae', where, owing to the lie of the land, the road appears to go downhill, whereas in fact it is ascending.

Ecclefechan *Dumf.* (DB 57). The historian Thomas Carlyle was born here and is buried in the churchyard. The family's house is now a museum (NT for Scot.).

Fairlie *Ayr.* (CC 65). Holiday resort on Firth of Clyde, famous for its boatbuilding. A ferry service runs between Fairlie and the island of Bute.

Gatehouse of Fleet *Kirk.* (CF 55). This small village, 2 m. from the head of a narrow bay, is a good centre for exploring the Fleet Water and a number of castles in the neighbourhood. Of these, Cardoness Castle, 1 m. SW, has a good 15th-cent. tower.

Girvan *Ayr.* (CB 59). EC Wed (6,475). Harbour and holiday resort, with sandy beach and good fishing. Ten m. out to sea the famous Ailsa Craig rises sheer from the water to a height of over 1,000 ft. The unusual type of granite, of which the island rock mainly consists, is much favoured

Ailsa Craig

Aerofilms

for curling-stones. The rock can only be ascended from the E side, where scanty grass affords subsistence to rabbits and goats. The other sides, which are precipitous, provide extensive breeding-grounds for sea birds, especially gannets. The lighthouse on the S side can be seen for 13 m.

Glenluce* *Wig.* (CC 55). The ruined 12th-cent. Abbey, with its 15th-cent. Chapter House, is of unusual interest. Castle of Park, a castellated house 1 m. S dates from 1590; and 2 m. NE are the remains of the earlier castle of Carscreugh.

Gretna Green *Dumf.* (DD 56) EC Wed (2,050). Separated from England only by the R. Sark, the smithy and the toll-house were once famous as the scene of runaway marriages, which were put an end to by legislation of 1856 and 1940.

Irvine *Ayr.* (CD 63) EC Wed (20,421). One of the oldest royal burghs of Scotland, and at one time the port for Glasgow; now a busy industrial town. The ruined Seagate Castle dates from the 14th cent.

Kilmarnock *Ayr.* (CE 63) EC Wed (47,722). A busy manufacturing town. In Kay Park the Burns Museum contains many important MSS. of the poet. The first edition of his poems was published here in 1786.

Kilwinning *Ayr.* (CC 64) EC Wed (7,849). By tradition the cradle of Freemasonry in Scotland. A curious local festival is celebrated annually on the first Saturday of July, when the Kilwinning Archers shoot at the 'papingo' or popinjay suspended from the steeple of the ruined 12th-cent. abbey (see the opening scenes of Scott's *Old Mortality*).

Kippford *Kirk.* (CJ 55). Sailing and golfing resort on the Urr Estuary at the point where it widens into the Rough Firth. Rough Island is a bird sanctuary.

Kirkbean *Kirk.* (CK 55). Birthplace of John Paul Jones (1747–92), regarded as a founder of the American Navy. At one time also he was commissioned by Catherine the Great as a Russian Admiral. A memorial font was presented to the Church by the U.S. Navy in 1945.

Kirkcudbright* (CG 55) EC Thurs (2,687). A prosperous little town at the mouth of the R. Dee where it flows into Kirkcudbright Bay. It contains much good 18th-cent. architecture, and a fine 16th–17th-cent. Tolbooth. At the top of the town stands the imposing ruin of the castle built by Sir Thomas Maclellan of Bombie. Four and a half m. SE the transept and choir of Dundrennan Abbey* are all that remain of the Cistercian Monastery founded by Fergus of Galloway in the 12th cent.; Mary Queen of Scots is said to have spent her last night in Scotland here.

Kirkoswald *Ayr.* (CC 60). Here Robert Burns attended the school, and two of his best-known characters, Tam o' Shanter and Souter Johnnie (whose real names were Douglas Graham and John Davidson) are buried in the churchyard. The latter's cottage is now the property of the NT for Scot. Two m. E is Crossraguel Abbey* (founded 12th cent.), with an imposing gatehouse, a curious dovecote, and several other buildings still in a good state of preservation (AM).

Langholm *Dumf.* (DD 58) EC Wed (2,369). Neat little town, with cobbled streets and busy tweed mills. Much favoured by fishermen, as it stands at the junction of the Wauchope and

J. Allan Cash **Doorway in Glenluce Ab**

Ewes Waters with the R. Esk. The conspicuous monument on White Hill commemorates Sir J. Malcolm (1769–1833), a Governor of Bombay.

Largs *Ayr.* (CC 65) EC Wed (8,854). Attractive seaside resort, with fine beach and lovely views across to Bute. Skelmorlie Aisle, with its painted roof, is all that remains of the old Parish church of St Columba; it was converted into a mausoleum in 1636. Near by a mound covers remains, possibly those of Norwegians who fell in the battle (1263) between Alexander III and Haco, King of Norway.

Lochmaben* *Dum.* (DA58). Delightful holiday resort, with several lakes and rivers in the neighbourhood. The ruined castle is one of the reputed birthplaces of Robert the Bruce (1274–1329), who was certainly closely associated with the town. A good statue of him stands in front of the Town Hall. The Castle Loch is the only fresh water in Scotland, possibly in the British Isles, to contain vendace, which are netted in August; tradition has it the fish were introduced by Mary Queen of Scots.

Lockerbie *Dumf.* (DB 58) EC Tues (2,820). Agricultural town with attractive houses and noted for its sheep sales, especially the great August lamb fair. The gardens of Castle Milk (3 m. S) are worth visiting, and on a hill SE of the town is an interesting Roman camp.

Mauchline *Ayr.* (CE 62) EC Wed (3,800). Many associations with Robert Burns. Here, in the house of Gavin Hamilton, still standing, he married Jean Armour; 'Poosie Nansie's', where the 'Jolly Beggars' met, though much altered, is still an Inn; the churchyard was the scene of the 'Holy Fair'; and 'Holy Willie' was an Elder of the Kirk.

Maybole *Ayr.* (CD 60) EC Wed (4,586). The 'capital' of Carrick, the southernmost division of Ayrshire. Near the middle of the town is the Castle*, the town house of the Kennedys of the Cassillis and Ailsa family; one of the strongest and finest of its class and still inhabited.

Moffat *Dumf.* (DA 60) A holiday resort, that has been famous since the 18th cent. for its sulphur and saline springs. The old spa building remains and many good houses. John Macadam (1756–1836), the father of modern road building, is buried in the churchyard. Five m. N, as the A701 into Peeblesshire approaches its highest point (1,334 ft.), the Devil's Beef Tub may be seen to the right of the road, a huge hollow 500 ft. deep.

Moniaive *Dumf.* (CH 59). Three rivers and three roads meet in this attractive village, associated with Annie Laurie, whose family owned Maxwelton House, 3 m. SE. After her marriage, she lived in Craigdarroch, 2½ m. W, an 18th-cent. Adam house with attractive gardens, where she died.

New Galloway *Kirk.* (CG 57). Golfing and angling village at N end of Loch Ken, through which flows R. Dee. In the churchyard at Kells, ½ m. N, are curious carvings and inscriptions. NW is Glenlee hydroelectric power station; SW are Clatteringshaws Reservoir and Cairn Edward Forest.

Newton Stewart *Wig.* (CE 56) EC Wed (1,873). Attractive golfing, fishing and touring centre on R. Cree. Opposite is the village of Minnigaff, with ruined church and carved tombstones. Four m. S is Wigtown Bay. From Bargrennan, 7 m. N, a township for foresters working in Glen Trool National Forest Park, a road leads to

Loch Trool, high in the hills with fine views. A cairn near the E end commemorates the victory over the English by Robert the Bruce in 1307.

Port Logan *Wig*. (CA 54). Small fishing village and resort on the Rhinns of Galloway, about 7 m. from the Mull of Galloway with its lighthouse and magnificent views. In the village is a sea-water pond noted for its tame fish; and the sub-tropical gardens of Logan House⋆ (2 m. N) are open to visitors.

Portpatrick *Wig*. (BK 55). Another resort on the Rhinns of Galloway, which, prior to the development of Stranraer, was the port for mail boats to N. Ireland. In the bay at the foot of the cliff are the remains of the harbour built in 1821.

Prestwick *Ayr*. (CD 62) EC Wed (13,139). *See* **Ayr**.

Ruthwell⋆ *Dumf*. (DA 56). The church contains, in an apse specially built for it, one of the two most celebrated Runic Crosses of Anglo-Saxon times (the other is at Bewcastle in Cumberland). It stands 18 ft. high and probably dates from the 8th cent.

Saltcoats *Ayr*. (CC 64) EC Wed (14,085). *See* **Ardrossan**.

Sanquhar *Dumf*. (CH 60) EC Thurs (2,065). Historic little town with memories of Covenanters who renounced allegiance to Charles II in 1680 and, similarly, objected to the 'Usurpation of James VII' in 1685. Note characteristic 18th-cent. Tolbooth.

Detail from the Runic Cross in Ruthwell Church   *J. Allan Cash*

Stranraer *Wig.* (CA 56) EC Wed (9,304). Situated at the head of Loch Ryan, its harbour is the starting-point for the short sea route (39 m.) to Larne in N. Ireland. In the centre of the town are the ruins of a 15th-cent. castle.

Sweetheart Abbey* *Dumf.* (CK 56). So called because Devorguila (the daughter of Alan, last 'king' of Galloway, and wife of John de Baliol), who founded a Cistercian Abbey here in the 13th-cent., ordered that her husband's heart should be buried with her before the High Altar. From the summit of Criffel (1,866 ft.), SW of the Abbey ruins, magnificent views extend across the Solway Firth to the Fells of the Lake district.

Sweetheart Abbey   *J. Allan Cash*

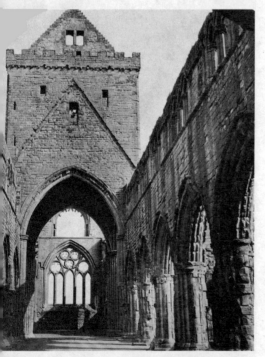

Symington *Ayr.* (CD 63). An attractive village with a Norman church founded in 1163.

Troon *Ayr.* (CD 63) EC Wed (10,611). Holiday and residential resort, with good sands and well-known golf course. Lady Isle, 3 m. offshore in the Firth of Clyde, is now a bird sanctuary.

Turnberry *Ayr.* (CB 60). Seaside and golfing resort, with ruins of castle, another reputed birthplace of Robert the Bruce (*see* **Lochmaben**). Two m. NE, perched on a tree-clad cliff amidst lovely gardens, is Culzean Castle,* one of the finest Adam buildings in Scotland (NT for Scot.); the upper part was presented to General Eisenhower in 1946.

Wanlockhead *Dumf.* (CJ 61). One of the highest villages in Britain, at the head of the Mennock Pass (1,380 ft.). Formerly a lead-mining centre.

Whithorn* *Wig.* (CE 54). The ruins of St Ninian's Priory (12th cent.), of which the transept served as Parish Church as late as 1822, are approached through an archway known as the Pend. A museum contains a good collection of stone crosses. In 396 Ninian, the first Christian missionary to Scotland, landed at the so-called Isle of Whithorn to the SE, where he built a chapel.

Wigtown (CE 55). Two stone crosses stand in the wide main street, which also contains modern County Council buildings. In the churchyard are the graves of the Wigtown Martyrs, two women Covenanters who, in 1685, were bound to stakes on the shore and left to drown in the rising tide. A small monument marks the site of the crime. Two m. NW are the Standing Stones of Torhouse, a perfect Bronze Age circle about 60 ft. in diameter.

Opposite: Detail from the original painting by Barry Driscoll.

Gannets breed on the granite island-hump of Ailsa Craig; the barnacle goose is a regular winter visitor to the Solway Firth. Shown here is a champion Ayrshire cow. Conspicuous to right and left are the ruins of Dundrennan Abbey, and prehistoric sculptured stones from Dornoch near Annan.

The Eildon Hills

THE
SOUTH-EAST LOWLANDS

Roxburgh, Berwick, Selkirk, Peebles

AN INTRODUCTION BY GEORGE SCOTT-MONCRIEFF

The four south-eastern counties, those of Roxburgh, Berwick, Selkirk and Peebles, include most of the Scottish Border with England. Chiefly this is hilly country; but towards the lower reaches of the Tweed it levels down to an undulating plain in the old province of the Merse, whose early history was more closely linked with that of the rich lands of Lothian to the north. Indeed, the visitor from England, coming by way of the Cheviot Hills, is liable to feel that 'Caledonia stern and wild' is a myth when he first looks down upon the more fertile Merse. It is to the south-west, in Roxburgh and Selkirk, that we find the characteristic Border country of hills rising to well over 2,000 feet with narrow

Opposite: Detail from the original painting by Julian Trevelyan.
Near the banks of the Tweed stand the romantic ruins of Melrose Abbey, beloved of Sir Walter Scott, who built his mansion of Abbotsford not far away. His bust by Chantrey is shown here. In the distance the fertile land rises towards the triple peaks of the Eildon Hills.

valleys and wandering mountain streams, interspersed with woods and patches of arable land. To the north-west, Upper Tweeddale, the county of Peebles, presents hills even more lofty and somewhat different in character from those lying nearer the English Border. Peeblesshire, in fact, has a higher mean altitude than any of the Highland counties, for it nowhere comes down to sea-level.

Industry

Visiting the peaceful, unspoilt Border countryside today, it is hard to realise that in medieval times it contained two of Scotland's four richest and busiest towns – perhaps the most flourishing of them all. They stood one at each end of the Merse, and neither exists on Scottish soil today. Roxburgh, after repeatedly falling into English hands, was razed to the ground by the Scots to prevent further enemy occupation, and leaves not a stone above the turf. Berwick and half-a-dozen square miles on the north bank of the mouth of the Tweed is the only trophy remaining of the many bloody campaigns made by the English in their efforts to annex Southern Scotland. When, long years later, the Industrial Age arrived, the Border counties were almost unaffected, since there was neither coal nor iron to exploit. In fact they might have been given over entirely to agriculture (and there were some notable agricultural improvers of the last century amongst the Berwickshire farmers in particular) and to the tourists brought to the countryside by Sir Walter Scott's poems and novels, had it not been for the enterprise of the men who developed weaving on a new basis.

The Border hills had long provided sheep-runs, and the weaving of tweeds had likewise a long tradition; but they now began to be produced not by single weavers working in their own cottages, but on a bigger scale, with the establishing of mills in Hawick, Galashiels, Walkerburn, Innerleithen, and the older towns themselves. None of the other native crafts of Scotland has shown itself so vigorous in maintaining quality and a sense of design within the framework of large-scale production. Now, using many of the finer imported wools as well as the local product, the Border mills are famous throughout the world for their output, which includes knitted as well as woven goods.

The Berwickshire coast is rocky and inhospitable, with few harbours. Only Eyemouth, once a great haunt of smugglers, is sufficiently sheltered to maintain a large fishing-fleet, although St Abbs has a few boats in its picturesque harbour, and crabs and lobsters are fished from Burnmouth. Agriculture remains the chief activity of the area, but, with increasing mechanisation, does not prevent a fairly steady decline in population. Shepherds from the Border, whose dogs work for them with an uncanny wisdom wonderful to see, can find employment in far parts of the world: Australia, New Zealand and South America.

The rock

The heather-covered Border hills are formed almost entirely of brown or grey flags and shales. In fact Selkirkshire is geologically the only really homogeneous county in Scotland, a country whose great mixture of stirred-up geological formations inspired much of the pioneer work in the science. To the north of Peeblesshire, however, there is a more mixed rock that includes sandstone and a little coal on the Lothian edge. On the east of Roxburghshire there is a red sandstone, and in the richer arable land of southern Berwickshire we come into the limestone belt that continues far south into the coalfields of the north of

Rounding up sheep in the Border country

J. Allan Cash

England. St Abbs Head offers the most interesting geological study, with contorted rocks worn smooth by glacial action. Here the junction of different formations is pierced with many caves inaccessible by land along the 300-foot high precipice of Petticowick.

Sandstone, both red and cream-coloured, provided the building material for the older houses in the Merse, giving place to grey whinstone in the hill country. At Stobo in Peeblesshire a thick, dark attractive slate was formerly worked, and may still be seen on many Border roofs.

The people

The Picts are the earliest people of Scotland of whom much is known. In the south-east some Pictish place-names survive, but more are of Brythonic origin. The Brythonic Celts, or Britons, who came into the south of Scotland, left it one Arthurian romance: Lyonnesse derives from Lothian, while the wizard Merlin is supposedly buried in a mound at Drummelzier in Peeblesshire. The great

643

days of the Northumbrian kingdom, that at one time seemed to be achieving the consolidation of Britain with a capital in York, left Anglo-Saxon names in Berwickshire and Lothian. The collapse of Northumbria, which followed the Pictish victory of Nectansmere in the year 685, opened the way to a final settlement of the area – that of the Scottish Celts, who came originally from Ireland, bringing their own Gaelic nomenclature.

Although the northern end of Watling Street came up through Roxburghshire by Melrose, and the Romans built walls both to the north and south of the four counties, they made no important settlements here. The earlier artefacts, remains of hill-fortresses, burial tumuli and occasional inarticulate standing-stones, date from both before and after Roman times.

The four abbeys

The beginning of Scottish Border history as we know it dates from the foundation of four great abbeys whose ruins have inspired prose, poetry and paint, and are still cynosures for the visitor. All four were founded during the reign of David I (1124–53). As elsewhere, the monks developed agriculture, industry and the civilised arts, despite the fact that their situation near the English frontier left them open to constant raids. Each of the abbeys was several times sacked and burnt, but was constantly rebuilt until, after 400 years, the Reformation brought Nemesis. It was the monks who first established Border wool as an important export that fetched a high price on the Continental market.

The ruins of Melrose Abbey are the most substantial and interesting, retaining much finely carved detail. Dryburgh, where Sir Walter Scott chose to be buried, has the most beautiful site, set amongst big trees on a spur of land in a curve of the River Tweed. Jedburgh, although only the shell of the church survives, gives a fair sense of its former glory in both Romanesque and Gothic arcading. Kelso retains little more than the battered western tower in which the last monks were put to the sword by Spanish mercenaries during Hertford's raid of 1545: the tower is now surrounded by the houses of the kindly market-town that grew up beside the Abbey after the obliteration of Roxburgh on the opposite bank of the Tweed.

The Border reivers

The decline of the abbeys saw the rise of the Border reivers (or plunderers). The countryside passed into a state of anarchy in which only family loyalties held, and Scotts, Douglases, Armstrongs, Elliots and Grahams raided each other or joined forces to cross the Border and raid the English. When food grew scarce at Harden House the beautiful wife of Auld Wat Scott served a dish at table containing only a pair of spurs, implying that it was time to ride again:

> Then there was riding, riding in haste,
> And a cracking of whips out owre the lee,

as the ballads tell.

Jedburgh gave its name to 'Jeddart Justice', which meant hanging without the tedious preliminaries of a trial. A Scottish Act of Parliament ordered every landowner to fortify his house. In all the Border country little towers were built, often hardly more capacious than a cottage, but strongholds none the less. Most of these are ruinous today; but the survivors show a surprising and delightful

645

River Tweed near Kelso   *J. Allan Cash*

architectural sense, finely matched to the countryside. Details of corbelling, machicolation and parapet seem to blossom from the austere and solid stone walls like the windswept trees and wildflowers that decorate the surrounding hillsides.

Larger castles are older: the most massive is Hermitage, whose great grim shell stands in barren country near Newcastleton. Much kindlier, Ferniehirst, south of Jedburgh, is now a Youth Hostel. Traquair in Tweeddale is the most romantic home in Scotland, a fairy castle breaking into history, with its memories of Mary Queen of Scots, of Montrose and Prince Charlie.

Of the little towers, Darnick, near Melrose, is one of the best, happily preserved. Smailholm Tower stands wonderfully austere against the background of the shapely Eildon Hills. Harden is still a Scott home, rising above a deep gully, 'Auld Wat's meat-safe'.

For some reason the best ballads come from north of the Border, recording in rough-hewn words the days when rough courage was a principal virtue. Even the most bloodthirsty reiver remained a hero to the Borderers, and, if he were brought to justice, was lamented in haunting rhyme. Outlaws they might be, but law was at a discount, while lawless exploits lay at the heart of Border life.

Sir Walter Scott

Sir Walter Scott gave a new gloss to Scotland's history and made its Border, home of his ancestors, the first great tourist resort of Britain. His house of Abbotsford became a place of pilgrimage in his lifetime and has remained one ever since. Architecturally it is a somewhat preposterous pastiche with none of the authenticity of his novels; but it contains many relics, in the collecting of which he was a pioneer. Besides his writings, his personality was infectious in setting value upon tradition and things old and historic.

A contemporary of Scott whom he befriended was the rustic poet, James Hogg, the Ettrick Shepherd, whose memorial stands by St Mary's Loch in the old Ettrick Forest, hunting-place of the Scottish kings, that is now Selkirkshire. Lionised in Edinburgh and London in his own day, Hogg is now perhaps most appreciatively remembered for a work that was then totally ignored, his remarkable *Confessions of a Justified Sinner*, acclaimed by André Gide as the first of all 'psychological' novels.

Today

In Scott's day the ruins of the four abbeys were ivy-shrouded and tree-sprouting, fitting to be romantically admired, especially by moonlight. Today they are cleaned up, their tottering walls cemented, and maintained in the good care of the Ministry of Works. But they are still attractive and interesting, and Dryburgh is beautiful in its landscape.

The little Border towns are friendly places, and the people are beginning to appreciate and preserve their modest but characteristic houses. Many of these, like the rural steadings and cottages, are built of whinstone rubble, a hard, intractable stone, beautifully jointed by the handiwork of a great tradition of masons.

The Berwickshire coast is without good beaches for sunbathers. The visitor to the Border is more likely to find his way into the hills. Here there is much land lovely and remote, even secluded glens rarely seen by men, that offer the walker

Angling near Traquair

a refreshing solitude not readily to be found today. There are many drove-roads and rights of way, and generally the wayfarer can walk where he will if he uses his discretion and his manners are good: odious only are the litter-louts, the dyke-breakers, the gate-leavers-open and the casual incendiaries. The Forestry Commission has planted much woodland, liable to be monotonously coniferous; but older woods are more varied.

There is excellent salmon fishing in the Tweed, and trout to be taken from its many tributaries. The heather hills provide shooting with grouse and blackgame, and the blue mountain hare that turns white in winter: elsewhere there are common hares, partridges and pheasants. There is a little fox-hunting ; but Border foxes are liable to live in wild and rocky fastnesses in the hills. Otters, badgers and roe-deer are shy creatures sometimes to be seen. The annual Common Ridings of the Border towns are loyal and lively celebrations, genuine local occasions conducted with no self-conscious eye upon the tourist. Hedgerow and moorland plants and flowers of all the usual kinds abound; but there are few Alpines.

Except for the Selkirk bun, Border catering offers few specialities. It compensates with the quality of its basic ingredients: salmon and trout from clear streams, hill-fed mutton and prime beef. Homemade oatcakes, if you can get them, are better fare than any wheaten bread.

Some houses and gardens open to the public

Abbotsford House 3m W of Melrose *Map* D F 63. *The home of Sir Walter Scott from 1812–32. His rooms unchanged since his lifetime, including the study where he wrote the Waverley Novels.* Mrs Maxwell-Scott.

Mellerstain 3m S of Gordon *Map* D G 64. *Important and unique example of the work of William and Robert Adam. Exquisite ceilings,* notable paintings and furniture. Magnificent view from terrace: lake, lawns, wooded parkland. The Lord Binning. *Teas.*

Traquair House nr Innerleithen *Map* D D 63. *Romantic and historic mansion, the oldest inhabited house in Scotland. Mary Queen of Scots and Darnley stayed here in 1566. Many historic treasures.* P. Maxwell Stuart, Esq.

Books for further reading

The history and romance of the Borders

MICHAEL BRANDON *Ho For The Borders* 1964
SIR G. DOUGLAS *History of the Border Counties (Roxburgh, Selkirk, Peebles)* 1899
MADGE ELDER *Tell the Towers Thereof* (The Ancient Border Story) 1956
H. DRUMMOND GAULD *Brave Borderland* 1922
WILL GRANT *Tweedale* 1948
JEAN LANG *A Land of Romance* (The Border, its History and Legends) 1938
SIR WALTER SCOTT *Minstrelsy of the Scottish Borders*
JOHN WILSON *Tales of the Borders* 1948

Topography

FRANCIS R. BANKS *Scottish Border Country* 1951
JAMES BAIKIE *The Charm of the Scott Country* 1927

W. S. CROCKETT *The Scott Country* 1930
THEO LANG ed. *The Border Counties* (The Queen's Scotland) 1957
JAMES L. MACK *The Border Line* 1926

Scenery and architecture

JOHN GEDDIE *The Scott Country* 1922
G. BURNETT *Companion to Tweed* 1938
ROBERT HUGILL *Borderland Castles and Peles* 1939

Angling and natural history

W. H. LAWRIE *Border River Angling* 1939
WM. SCROPE *Days and Nights of Salmon Fishing in the River Tweed* 1921
G. JOHNSTON *The Natural History of the Eastern Borders* 1853
A. H. EVANS *A Fauna of the Tweed Area* 1911

Gazetteer

THE SOUTH-EAST LOWLANDS

Roxburgh, Berwick, Selkirk, Peebles

Abbotsford   *J. Allan Cash*

Abbey St Bathans *Berw.* (DH 66). Small village, beautifully situated on the Whiteadder, near the Lammermuir Hills – Heart Law (1,283 ft.) to NW. The church contains the tomb of a prioress from the long-vanished Abbey Church. At Edinshall, 2 m. SE, on the slopes of Cockburn Law (1,065 ft.), is one of the few Pictish brochs, or towers, in S Scotland.

Abbotsford* *Selk.* (DF 63). The mansion, built in 1817 by Sir Walter Scott in imitation Scottish Baronial style, contains numerous historical and personal relics, a fine collection of arms and armour, and Scott's study, still much as he left it.

Burnmouth *Berw.* (DK 66). Picturesque fishing village at the foot of steep cliffs, with magnificent coastal scenery on either hand.

Clovenfords *Selk.* (DE 63). Remarkable for its 6 acres of glass-houses, filled with grape vines. Across the Tweed is Ashiestiel, Scott's home before he built Abbotsford.

Cockburnspath *Berw.* (DH 67). Here the A1 road skirts the Lammermuirs, with glimpses of the rocky coast below. The village has a 17th-cent. Mercat Cross† and a 14th-cent. church,

---

†Market cross or proclamation place.

though the curious round tower is considerably later. The cove contains a tiny harbour and good sands; while at the S end of adjacent Pease Sands are remains of the Norman Church of St Helen's.

Coldingham *Berw.* (DK 66). Hilltop village, near St Abbs Head, where in the 7th cent. a church was founded by St Ebba. The 12th-cent. choir of the priory which replaced this church is now incorporated in the Parish Church (note good arcading). Nearby Coldingham Bay, with its sandy beach, is a popular resort.

Coldstream *Berw.* (DJ 63). On N side of the Tweed, which is here spanned by Smeaton's fine 18th-cent. bridge leading into England. Though less popular than Gretna Green, the little Toll House was the scene of many runaway marriages until legislation in the last century prohibited them. Here, in 1659, General Monk raised the famous regiment of Foot Guards, an event marked by a tablet

649

Dryburgh Abbey

J. Allan Cash

in the market place. On the English side of the river, 6 m. NE, are the remains of Norham Castle, made famous by Scott's *Marmion*.

Dryburgh Abbey ** *Berw.* (D F63). One of the loveliest ruins in Scotland, set amongst lawns and trees on the bank of the Tweed. Founded in 1150, the Abbey repeatedly suffered damage at the hands of the English, and from the 16th cent. no further attempt to repair or rebuild it was made until it was taken over by the Ministry of Works. Here, according to his wish,

Sir Walter Scott was buried, with other members of his family; also F-M Earl Haig, to whom the nation presented, in 1925, the ancestral home of Bemerside, 1 m. to N.

Duns *Berw.* (D H 65) EC Wed (1,840). Small market town, built after the old town on the slopes of Duns Law had been burned by the English in 1545. There is a Mercat Cross in a Park on the S side of the town; and the Covenanters' Stone on Duns Law (713 ft.) recalls the encampment of Leslie's army in 1639. W of the town is the modern Duns Castle, with its 14th-cent. tower and a fine avenue of limes in the grounds.

Earlston *Berw.* (DF 63). Formerly *Ercildoune*, which was closely associated with the semi-legendary 13th-cent. prophet and poet of Scottish folk lore, Thomas the Rhymer. A tablet in the church bears the words: 'Auld Rymer's Race Lyes in this Place'.

Eildon Hills★ *Roxb.* (DF 63). These lovely triple peaks, the highest of them 1,387 ft., command superb views of the countryside beloved of Sir Walter Scott (an indicator points out the places of special interest). At near-by Newstead, on Leaderfoot Hill, a monument marks the site of the important Roman camp of Trimontium, where a number of important finds, now in the Museum of Antiquities in Edinburgh, were made during excavations in 1910.

Ettrick *Selk.* (DC 61). The little church stands on the Ettrick Water, in a valley dominated by Ettrick Pen (2,270 ft.). James Hogg, 'the Ettrick Shepherd', who became well known as a poet, was baptized and buried here (1835). A little to the E a monument marks the cottage where he was born. 5 m. N the well-known fishermen's inn, Tibbie Shiels, stands between St Mary's Loch and the Loch of the Lowes.

Eyemouth *Berw.* (DK 66) EC Thurs (2,160). Fishing port and popular resort at the head of a rockbound bay, where the numerous caves were formerly used by smugglers. Wonderful coast scenery. Robert Burns was made a Royal Arch Mason in the town during his Border Tour, 1787.

Dryburgh Abbey: memorial to James II of Scotland *Reece Winstone*

Galashiels *Selk*. (DE 63) EC Wed (12,370). Tweed and woollen manufacturing town in the valley of the Gala Water. Among interesting monuments are a 17th-cent. Mercat Cross and Sir R. Lorimer's 1914–18 War Memorial. The 17th-cent. Gala House, with its painted ceilings, is now an Arts Centre; and a Border Musical Festival is held here each May. The town crest on the Municipal Buildings, with its motto 'Sour Plums', commemorates the capture of some English raiders, caught robbing a plum tree in 1337.

Greenlaw *Berw*. (DH 64). A small town on the Blackadder, with a good market cross (1696) and a tall-towered 18th-cent. church. 3 m. S are the ruins of Hume Castle (600 ft.), with fine views of the surrounding countryside.

Hawick *Roxb*. (DF 61) EC Tue (16,200). In the heart of Teviotdale, where the Slitrig Water joins the Teviot, this is one of the most important Border towns, noted for woollen and hosiery manufactures. The Mote Hill, possibly the mound of a Norman castle, was more probably the meeting place for the town Moot or Court of the Manor. The town is noted for the picturesque 'Riding of the Common', which takes place annually in June to commemorate a defeat of the English by some young townsmen at Hornshole Bridge (2 m. NE), in revenge for the harrying of the town by the English after their victory at Flodden in the previous year, 1513. 2 m. SW is the massive peel tower of Goldielands; and, 1 m. farther on, Branxholm Hall, the tower of which dates from the 16th cent.

Hermitage Castle* *Roxb*. (DE 59). Once a stronghold of the Douglases, the four towers and connecting walls of this immensely strong 14th-cent.

Hermitage Castle *J. Allan Cash*

fortress are still almost perfect; inside are the remains of a still earlier tower. The scene of many grim events, the castle was visited in 1566 by Mary, Queen of Scots, who nearly died of a fever after riding the 40 miles from Jedburgh and back to see Bothwell.

Innerleithen *Peebles* (DD 63) EC Tue (2,300). Woollen town, with golf course and mineral springs, where the Leithen Water joins the Tweed. 5 m. to NE rises Windlestraw Law (2,162 ft.), with many hill forts in the vicinity. Traquair House*, 1 m. S, where William the Lion held court in 1209 and Mary, Queen of Scots stayed with Darnley in 1566, is probably the oldest inhabited mansion in Scotland; though most of the present building dates from the 17th cent.

Jedburgh* *Roxb*. (DG 62) EC Thurs (3,650). One of the most attractive towns in the Lowlands, dominated by the ruins of the great red-sandstone Abbey* founded in the 12th cent. and frequently added to and rebuilt. The nave and the rose window are splendid. Queen Mary's House, like the three-span bridge built in the 16th cent., is

now a museum. Ferniehirst Castle, perched on a rock above the River Jed some 2 m. S, with its great hall and fireplace, is now a youth hostel.

Kelso* *Roxb.* (DH 63) EC Wed (3,960). A pleasant town in a bend of the Tweed, near its junction with the Teviot. Each night a curfew is sounded from the Court House in the spacious market place. Of the 12th-cent. abbey, once the greatest on the Border, the main portions still standing are the W tower and transepts. The five-arched bridge was built by Rennie in 1803. From it, there is an excellent view of Floors Castle, the vast 18th-cent. mansion originally designed by Vanbrugh, but later added to by Playfair. Mellerstain House*, a notable example of the work of the Adam brothers, with its fine gardens, is 6 m. NW. The Kelso Ram Sales, which take place in September, attract buyers from all over the world.

Ladykirk *Berw.* (DJ 64). The little stone-vaulted church was built about 1500 by James IV as a thank-offering for his escape from drowning in the Tweed, though the tower, with its charming cupola, was probably completed by William Adam in 1743. On the English side of the river are the ruins of Norham Castle.

Lauder *Berw.* (DF 64). The only Royal Burgh in the County, with good fishing in the Leader. Note the quaint little Tolbooth, with its flight of steps; and the 16th-cent. church, which may be partly the work of Sir Wm. Bruce. Thirlestane Castle, incorporating a 14th-cent. stronghold, contains portraits by Lely, Romney and Aikman. A fine road over the moors to the W reaches a height of 1,100 ft., before descending to the Gala Water.

Melrose** *Roxb.* (DF 63) EC Thurs (2,130). Perhaps the finest and most beautifully situated of all the ruined Scottish abbeys, the 'Kennaquhair' of Scott's *Monastery*. The red-sandstone Cistercian Abbey was frequently ravaged by the English, but part of the nave and choir still show some of the finest 14th-cent. work in the country. Now an AM, it has been carefully repaired, and practically the whole of the ground-site has been excavated. Note the fine five-light window on S transept, and the museum. The heart

Floors Castle, Kelso

Scottish Tourist Board

Melrose Abbey

Radio Times Hulton Picture Library

of Robert the Bruce is said to have been buried beneath the E window.

Morebattle *Roxb.* (D H 62). Pleasant fishing village almost surrounded by the Kale Water. 2½ m. S W are the ruins of Cessford Castle, with its 14-ft.-thick walls; while across the Border rises the Cheviot (2,676 ft.), the highest point in the whole range.

Newstead (D F 63). *See* **Eildon Hills** *above.*

Peebles (D C 64) E C Wed (5,540). Busy shopping centre, well known for its tweed mills. A good centre for fishing and touring. Queensberry Lodging, now incorporated in the Chambers Institute, which houses an interesting museum, was the birthplace of the notorious 18th-cent. Marquess, 'Old Q'. 1 m. W of the town, beautifully situated on the Tweed, is one of the most memorable of the smaller Border castles, Neidpath.

Polwarth *Berw.* (D H 65). A village of great antiquity 4 m. S W of Duns. It is the 'Polwarth-on-the-Green' of Allan Ramsay's famous ballad and a descendant of the famous Thorn Tree still flourishes. The Parish Church, which dates from 900, has an interesting 'Laird's pew' and the family vault of the Lairds of Polwarth. It was in this vault that Sir Patrick Hume of Polwarth hid to escape arrest for his alleged complicity in the 1684 Rye House Plot, his food being brought to him by night by his daughter Grisell from near-by Redbraes Castle.

Roxburgh (D G 63). Now a small village. The old town, which in the 13th cent. was one of the four Royal Burghs, has completely disappeared, and little remains of the castle, some 3 m. to N W.

St Abbs *Berw.* (D K 66). A small, sandy fishing-harbour and resort, beneath 300-ft. cliffs, with many caves once used for smuggling. N W from St Abbs Head, from which there are fine views of the rocky coast, are the grim ruins of Fast Castle, the 'Wolf's Crag' of Scott's *Bride of Lammermuir*.

Selkirk (D E 62) E C Thurs (5,630). Built round a small square, on the

St Abbs: the harbour

slopes of a hill beside the Ettrick Water, the Royal Burgh of Selkirk is now noted for its tweed mills, but in the old days it was famous for its 'souters', or shoemakers. Their gallantry at Flodden Field is commemorated by a monument, and by the ceremonial 'Riding of the Marches' that takes place each June. From the 110-ft. spire of the Town Hall a curfew is still rung each night. Note the statue of Mungo Park, the African explorer, born near Selkirk. In front of the Old Court House stands a statue of Sir Walter Scott, sheriff of the county for 32 years. An interesting little museum in Halliwell's Close is worth a visit. About 4 m. SW a Roman fort of the 1st cent. was discovered at Oakwood.

Smailholm *Roxb.* (DG 63). The fine 16th-cent. peel tower, romantically situated on a rock to the SW, is mentioned in *Marmion* and the *Eve of St John*; while Scott himself spent some years of his childhood at the near-by farm of Sandyknowe.

Stobo *Peebles* (DB 63). Norman church, with good 13th-cent. doorway. In the barrel-vaulted porch still hang the 'jougs', an iron collar by which wrong-doers were chained to the wall. See also the interesting 'laird's loft', or pew. On the opposite side of the Tweed, Dawyck Woods are famous for their great variety of trees, this being the first place in Britain to which the larch was introduced, in 1725.

Yarrow *Selk.* (DE 62). This classic valley is true ballad country. Newark Castle, built about 1466 as a hunting seat for James II, was the scene for the recital of 'The Lay of the Last Minstrel' by Sir Walter Scott. Across the stream from Newark, at Foulsheils, stands the ruined cottage where Mungo Park, the African explorer was born in 1771. The Kirk of Yarrow, erected in 1640, replaced the more famous Kirk of St Mary of the Lowes, at St Mary's Loch. At the head of this loch stands a statue of James Hogg, the Ettrick Shepherd.

Loch Lomond near Rowardennan Scottish Tourist Board

THE
GLASGOW
LOWLANDS

Renfrew, Lanark, Dunbarton, Stirling

AN INTRODUCTION BY JACK HOUSE

The population of Scotland is just over five million souls. Of that five million, half at least dwell in the Lowlands, in and around the city of Glasgow.

Why should Glasgow and its environs be so populous? The answer is simple. First of all, the River Clyde. Second, the deposits of coal and iron on its banks. The River Clyde is more than 100 miles long. Its source is a little spring in the Lowther Hills at the extreme south end of the County of Lanark, the biggest county in Scotland. At its source it is known as the Daer (pronounced 'Dahr') Water, and once it flowed down the Daer valley to Watermeetings, where it

657

met the Potrail Water and was joined after a mile or two by the Clydes Burn to become the Clyde. But now it goes first into the Daer Dam, providing water for much of Lanarkshire and is also noted for good fishing. Coming to the confluence of Watermeetings, the river is known as the Clyde. Famous for salmon and trout, it runs shallow through southern Lanarkshire, an area of placid beauty in the English style, with soft hills, orchards, fertile farms and good hotels. No one, seeing the Clyde hereabouts, could imagine that on its waters the world's biggest ships have been launched. There are pleasant little villages on its banks, and only the existence of a main trunk road gives any indication that an industrial belt lies ahead. The first signs are at the Falls of Clyde, near the county town of Lanark: unless there has been very heavy rain, they look only a shadow of their former selves, because they have been harnessed for a hydro-electric supply.

It is well worth taking the steep road up to Lanark, which keeps its ancient air very well. Here in June is one of the outstanding festivals of Scotland – Lanimer Day. The whole town goes *en fête* for a week, and the climax is 'The Lanimers', when an enormous fancy-dress parade of children goes through the town to the Wallace Monument (Sir William Wallace, Scottish hero, lived in Lanark), and the Lanimer Queen is crowned.

For several miles the Clyde still wanders through delightful orchard country, and then there is a sudden and dramatic change. On the heights above the glen through which the river flows are the industrial towns of Motherwell and Wishaw, and then the Royal Burgh of Hamilton. We have come from vegetables and fruit into iron and coal, and although steel-works have replaced the iron, and many of the mines are now derelict, the area is still highly industrialised. But there are still many pleasant patches of countryside, and Hamilton itself is full of picturesque little town scenes – to say nothing of the famous Mausoleum of the Dukes of Hamilton, set in the grounds of what was once Hamilton Palace. It has one of the most remarkable echo chambers in the world.

By this time the Clyde, as well as the scene, has changed. The river, too, has become industrial, and though optimistic anglers still whip the water they are amazed if they catch anything. The river winds in and out by Bothwell, passing the ruins of Bothwell Castle and the birthplace of David Livingstone, by Cambuslang, the 'biggest village in Scotland', and the Royal Burgh of Rutherglen, which claims to be older than Glasgow and resists all attempts at amalgamation with the city. The ground of the Clyde Football Club is on the boundary, and it is possible for a player to kick the ball in Rutherglen and score a goal in Glasgow.

Glasgow

And now the river comes to Glasgow Green, the park where Bonnie Prince Charlie reviewed his Highland Army in 1745. In coming to the Green, the river also comes to Glasgow, the biggest, the oldest, the most maligned and best liked town in Scotland. Perhaps I should qualify that final superlative by adding that it is best liked by Glaswegians.

Saint Mungo, patron saint of the city, settled in Glasgow in the year A.D. 543. But there was a settlement by the Clyde before that, and the place was well known to the Romans, who seldom ventured north of Glasgow because the natives were hostile. The first Glasgow Cathedral was built in 1124. Glasgow University was established in 1451. In the 18th century Daniel Defoe described

Glasgow and the River Clyde *Aerofilms*

Glasgow as 'the most beautiful little city in Europe'. In the 20th century John Betjeman described Glasgow as 'the finest Victorian city in the world'.

Despite all this, Glasgow has had a bad reputation among people who have never visited it. It is, in fact, a lively, friendly place and many English, French, Canadian, Polish and American servicemen who landed in Glasgow during the war keep coming back for holidays. It has historical buildings, fifty-five principal parks (one of them, Queen's, has more flowers in it than the five Royal Parks of Paris put together), five theatres, many cinemas (one is the largest in Europe), more than 1,000 pubs, good restaurants and tea rooms, five senior football clubs (including Hampden Park, the second biggest football stadium in the world), and the Gorbals. This famous former slum is now being turned into the show-piece of Glasgow.

Glasgow is known to its inhabitants as 'a great place to get out of'. This somewhat double-edged statement really means that Glasgow is especially suit-able as a tourist centre. Within one hour, by road or rail, you can be in the Highlands, or in the Burns Country, or on the bonny, bonny banks of Loch Lomond, or on the breathtaking Firth of Clyde, or in Stirling, where Robert the Bruce defeated the English Army at the Battle of Bannockburn in 1314. Within an hour you can even be in Edinburgh, the Capital of Scotland – but you should be warned that Glaswegians consider Edinburgh rather a foreign place. Edinburghers think that Glaswegians are jealous. Glasgow's reply is that 'Edinburgh is the Capital, but Glasgow has the capital!'

The Clyde flows through Glasgow and there are fourteen miles of docks in the harbour. The local saying is, 'Glasgow made the Clyde, and the Clyde made

Loch Lomond

J. Allan Cash

Glasgow'. The city has spent more than £20,000,000 in deepening the river and making it navigable. Ships from all parts of the world can sail into the centre of the city.

One of the best ways to see the Firth of Clyde is to sail down the river from Bridge Wharf, in the middle of Glasgow. You sail on the *Queen Mary II*, which is really the *Queen Mary I* – but the steamer graciously gave up her title when the liner *Queen Mary* was launched at Clydebank. Here is one of the world's greatest concentrations of shipbuilding yards. During the Second World War more ships were launched on the Clyde than in all the shipyards of the U.S.A. put together.

As the steamer reaches Renfrew Ferry, you sail out of Glasgow and see Renfrewshire to the south and Dunbartonshire to the north. From this point on it is true to say that the south is in the Lowlands, while the north is in the Highlands. This is the case all the way down the Firth of Clyde – and some parts of the Highlands are very much lower than the Lowlands!

Renfrewshire and Dunbartonshire

Renfrewshire is an agricultural county with a number of industrial towns. Its capital is the Royal Burgh of Renfrew, and one of the titles of the Prince of Wales is Baron Renfrew. The main town is Paisley, on the banks of the River Cart, a tributary of the Clyde. It is famous for its shawls, thread, marmalade and poets. Renfrewshire has its own group of shipbuilding yards at Port Glasgow and Greenock. Port Glasgow was built by the city of Glasgow in the 17th century to be its harbour; but the deepening of the Clyde changed all the plans. From Port Glasgow in 1812 the *Comet*, the first practical steamship in Europe, was launched by Henry Bell. Some 150 years later a replica of the *Comet* was built and sailed on the river. It is now on show at Port Glasgow. Greenock has the oldest shipbuilding yard in the world, Scott's, started in 1771. It has also sugar-refineries and a rope-works which makes 'big tops' for some world-famous circuses. From Gourock down the coast to Wemyss Bay, Renfrewshire is residential and is made for holidays.

Dunbartonshire on the north follows the same pattern. Once the *Queen Mary II* sails over the invisible Glasgow boundary, you see Yoker with its enormous power-station, and then John Brown's shipyard, where the *Queen Mary*, the *Queen Elizabeth*, the *Vanguard* and other famous ships were built and launched. Incidentally, these enormous ships could not be launched if it were not for the fact that the mouth of the River Cart is just opposite John Brown's. The Clyde is so narrow here that it was described by an envious English shipbuilder as 'that trout stream'; big ships are launched diagonally across the river so that the stern goes up into the River Cart.

In the distance you can see Ben Lomond from the deck of the steamer; but the nearer scene is very industrial indeed, with yards, factories, oil-depots, and the world's biggest grain-distillery. The distillery is at Dumbarton, just beside Dumbarton Rock (which looks remarkably like Gibraltar in miniature). Denny's shipyard, where the *Queen Mary II* was built, is in the lee of the Rock; nowadays they also build 'hovercraft' there.

From Dumbarton onwards it is a succession of holiday places, with Helensburgh, Rhu and Garelochhead outstanding. From Dumbarton or Helensburgh it is a mere step to Loch Lomond, the largest stretch of inland water in Britain.

John Brown's shipyard, Clydebank *Scottish Tourist Board*

Loch Lomond is so near to salt water that geologists consider it a freak. At Tarbet, for example, it is only a mile from Arrochar, on the sea fiord of Loch Long. When a Viking leader named Magnus sailed up Loch Long, he made his men pull the galleys across that mile and refloated them on Loch Lomond, so that he could burn and pillage the loch-side villages to his heart's content.

Loch Lomond is beautiful, but suffers terribly from tourist traffic. It is best seen in spring or autumn. A favourite local conundrum is, 'What piece of water in Scotland surrounds a foot?' The answer is, 'Loch Lomond, because it has twelve inches in it'. Inch is the Scottish word for island, and at the south of Loch Lomond there is a group of islands with such names as Inchmurrin, Inch Cailloch, Inch Tavannach and Inch Lonaig. There are actually thirty islands in Loch Lomond.

Stirlingshire

The west and south of the loch are in Dunbartonshire. Ben Lomond and the east are in Stirlingshire, and between Ben Lomond and Stirling, the county capital, stretches the Rob Roy country. Rob Roy, the Scottish Robin Hood, was immortalised by Sir Walter Scott in his novel; but he was a very real man, and everywhere you go in the district you see places connected with his name. Truth is mixed with fiction, however, and at Aberfoyle you will see the poker, chained to a tree, which was used by Bailie Nicol Jarvie to defend himself against attack. The worthy Bailie existed only in the mind of Scott – but his poker is there all the same!

Between Aberfoyle and Stirling lies Scotland's only lake, the Lake of Menteith: all the other lakes are called lochs. This is the Highland way into Stirling, the Gateway to the Highlands. The Lowland way, a trunk road from Glasgow,

663

passes through a mainly industrial region, with bits of countryside clinging desperately to the scene.

Although Stirling is only some 25 miles from Glasgow, it is in a different ambience. The shallow river you have seen at Aberfoyle is the Forth, and at Stirling it becomes deeper and slowly broadens into the Firth of Forth. From Stirling Castle on a clear day you can see the Forth Bridge, and even, if your eyes are very sharp, Edinburgh Castle.

Stirling was the capital of Scotland long before Edinburgh, and although very much smaller, retains a certain dignity. The buildings around the castle have been well preserved. For its size, the town is particularly well served with hotels and restaurants. Although Stirling would prefer to consider itself part of the Highlands, the aspect you see from the Castle Rock is that of the Lowlands, with coal-mines and industrial towns amid the fields and hills. North of Stirling, just as north and north-west of Glasgow, you reach some of the grandest scenery in the world. But in these Lowland counties rests what there is of Scotland's prosperity.

Some houses and gardens open to the public

The Botanic Gardens Gt Western Rd, Glasgow *Map* CF 66. *Outstanding collections of tree ferns, orchids, begonias and other glasshouse plants. Herb garden, chronological border, etc.* The Corporation of Glasgow.

Pollock House Pollokshaws, sw of Glasgow *Map* CF 66. *Baronial mansion built by William Adam in 1752. Paintings by Goya, Hogarth, El Greco, etc. Extensive gardens.* The Corporation of Glasgow.

Provan Hall nr Stepps, NE of Glasgow *Map* CG 66. *15th-cent. mansion which has been described as the most perfect example of a simple pre-Reformation house remaining in Scotland.* NT for Scot.

Stirling Castle *Map* CH 69. *Ancient and historic castle in a commanding situation with far-ranging views. Kings and queens have lived, died and been born here.* Ministry of Works.

Books for further reading

Fiction

The novels of DOT ALLAN, GEORGE BLAKE, CLIFFORD HANLEY, GUY MCCRONE, NANCY BRYSSON MORRISON. *Lighter* aspects of Glasgow life in COLM BROGAN *The Glasgow Story* 1952 and CLIFFORD HANLEY *Dancing in the Streets* 1958

Scenery and geology

BRITISH ASSOCIATION *The Glasgow Region* 1958
GEORGE BLAKE *The Firth of Clyde* 1952

JACK HOUSE *Down the Clyde* 1960
MAURICE LINDSAY *Clyde Waters* 1958 and *The Lowlands of Scotland* 1953
ROBIN SMALL *Doon The Watter, the Firth of Clyde* 1962

Topography and history

J. HOUSE *The Heart of Glasgow* 1965
C. A. OAKLEY *The Second City* 1967
J. M. REID *Glasgow* 1956
WARD LOCK'S RED GUIDES *Glasgow and the Clyde* 15th edn 1965; *Western Scotland* 16th edn 1966

Gazetteer

THE GLASGOW LOWLANDS

Renfrew, Lanark, Dunbarton, Stirling

Airth *Stirling*. (CJ 68). 1 m. N of road bridge over Forth to Kincardine. Note Mercat Cross† with two sundials; and Wallace's Tower (14th cent.), part of modern castle.

Ardlui *Dunb*. (CD 71). Village at N end of L. Lomond, in picturesque mountain setting, with Ben Vorlich (3,092 ft.) to SW. Terminus of steamer trip from **Balloch** (*see below*).

Arrochar *Dunb*. (CC 70). Busy road centre at head of L. Long and 2 m. W of Tarbet on L. Lomond. The road to Inveraray and Campbeltown passes through Glen Croe and the Argyll National Forest Park amidst wonderful mountain scenery.

Balloch *Dunb*. (CD 68). A popular resort on L. Lomond, and departure-point for loch steamers. Here the R. Leven flows from the loch into the Clyde, through an area busy with bleaching, dyeing and calico-printing.

Bannockburn *Stirling* (CJ 69) EC Wed (4,760). A mining village, 1 m. E of the battlefield where Robert the Bruce defeated Edward II in 1314, thus achieving Scotland's independence. The site of the battle has been taken over by the NT for Scotland. Note the Borestone, on which Bruce is said to have set up his standard. To

---

† Market cross or proclamation place.

---

the S is site of battle of Sauchieburn (1488), where James III was defeated and killed by his own nobles. Bannockburn House was the headquarters of Prince Charles Edward in 1746.

Blantyre *Lanark*. (CG 65) (16,850). Mining town. Birthplace of David Livingstone (1813) in Shuttle Row, now a museum. 2 m. N are remains of a 13th-cent. priory.

Bothwell *Lanark*. (CH 65) EC Wed (3,180). The Collegiate Church, partly 14th cent., is noted for its pointed barrel vault, and contains monuments to the Douglas family. The pride of the town is the impressive Douglas stronghold, Bothwell Castle* to the NW, whose great tower (begun in 13th cent.) took 36 years to complete.

Bowling *Dunb*. (CE 67). Western terminus of the 38-mile Forth and Clyde Canal, built by Smeaton in 1790. Symington's *Charlotte Dundas*, the first working steamboat, was launched here in 1802; and, in 1812, Bell's *Comet*, first of the Clyde passenger steamers.

Bridge of Allan *Stirling*. (CH 69) EC Wed (4,060). Quiet inland resort on Allan Water, near its junction with the Forth. Modern spa with medicinal waters. Chopin stayed at Keir House, whose woods shelter the village, in 1848; and R. L. Stevenson was a frequent visitor.

Cambuskenneth Abbey *Stirling*. (CJ 69). 1 m. NE of Stirling are the remains of the 12th-cent. abbey where, in 1326, Robert the Bruce held his Parliament, and where James III and his queen were buried in 1488.

Campsie Glen *Stirling*. (CG 67). Village at the foot of the glen, from which the road crosses the Campsie Fells to **Fintry** (*see below*). Splendid views from the top of the road (1,064 ft.).

665

Carfin *Lanark.*, 1½ miles NE of Motherwell (CH 65). A mining village, where a grotto, dedicated to Our Lady of Lourdes in 1922, attracts thousands of pilgrims every year.

Crawford *Lanark.* (CK 62). This Clydesdale village is a good centre for the Lowland hill country. Tower Lindsay is all that remains of a once important castle.

Crookston Castle *Renf.* (CF 66) *See* **Paisley** *below.*

Crossford *Lanark.* (CJ 64). A little village set amongst orchards, near the junction of the Nethan with the Clyde. 1 m. SW is the interesting and well-preserved 16th-cent. Craig Nethan Castle, the 'Tillietudlem Castle' of Scott's *Old Mortality*. Hallbar Tower is 1 m. NE on the Fiddler's Burn.

Cumbernauld *Dunb.* (CH 67). One of the most interesting of Britain's 'New Towns', laid out along a ridge W of the old village, planned to have local industries and a population of 50,000.

Douglas *Lanark.* (CJ 63) EC Wed (2,260). The restored chancel of St Bride's Church contains the tomb of the Earl of Angus (died 1514), known as 'Bell-the-Cat', and a fine range of Douglas tombs, as well as some early French stained glass. All that remains of Douglas Castle is the chapel and porch. Note the two 17th-cent. towers in the town; one containing a clock presented by Mary, Queen of Scots; the other commemorating the raising of the Cameronian Regiment.

Dumbarton *Dunb.* (CD 67) EC Wed (26,115). Busy shipbuilding town, dominated by the 250-ft. rock on which stands the castle, with panoramic views.★

Eaglesham *Renf.* (CF 65). Interesting 18th-cent. village built by an Earl of Eglinton. The B764 Kilmarnock road climbs nearly 1,000 ft. to the SW, with good views of the surrounding hills. Rudolf Hess landed near here in 1941 after his surprising flight from Germany.

East Kilbride *Lanark.* (CG 65) EC Wed (53,463). The new town here is designed eventually to accommodate 90,000 people with local employment. The first meeting of Scottish Quakers took place at East Kilbride in 1653. 1 m. N is the restored 16th-cent. Mains Castle.

Elvanfoot *Lanark.* (CK 61). In a setting of mountains and streams, the village is the starting-point of two passes, Dalveen and Mennock, which cross the Lowther Hills to the SW. Both roads ascend to over 1,000 ft.; while a third to the SE passes Beattock Summit (1,029 ft.).

Falkirk *Stirling.* (CJ 68) EC Wed (38,060). Important for coal-mining and the great Carron ironworks. Well-preserved sections of the **Roman Wall** (*see below*) can be seen in the grounds of the fine Callendar House E of the town; while 2 m. W is the best-preserved of the Roman forts, known as Rough Castle.

Fintry *Stirling.* (CG 68). In the Lennox country between Campsie Fells and Fintry Hills. 3 miles E is the Loup of Fintry, a 100-ft. waterfall, and beyond this Carron reservoir. The ancient Culcreuch Tower lies a little to the N.

Garelochhead *Dunb.* (CC 69) EC Wed (2,890). Well-known resort and yachting centre. A stiff climb takes the road from sea-level to Whistlefield, at the foot of Beinn Chaorach (2,338 ft.), with views of L. Long and L. Goil.

Gartocharn *Dunb.* (CE 68). A quiet village from which to explore the SE of L. Lomond and its wooded islands. To NW stands Ross Priory in its lovely parkland.

Glasgow★ *Lanark*. (CF 66) EC Tue (960,527). 'Glasgow made the Clyde and the Clyde made Glasgow'; and the consequent generations of ship-builders, merchants and manufacturers made the handsome streets and squares of 18th–19th-cent. houses – but were also responsible for the Gorbals. Indeed, though its cathedral dates from the 12th cent., Glasgow is mainly a product of the past 200 years, when the dredging of the Clyde improved navigation. Prior to this, the city covered only a small area at the E end of the present vast conurbation, and it is here that the most ancient buildings are to be found. The cathedral★ is the finest unmutilated Gothic church in Scotland: note particularly the 12th-cent. crypt and 13th-cent. choir and tower. The oldest house in Glasgow is near-by Provand's Lordship (1471), built as a hospital but now a museum. (*See also* **Provan Hall**.) Note the Merchants' Hall, Crown and Tron steeples, all of the 16th cent. The University, founded in 1451 and the oldest in Scotland, is now housed in Victorian Gothic buildings in Kelvin-grove Park, designed by Sir Gilbert Scott. Near by are the important art gallery and museum with the famous Burrell Collection, as well as a comprehensive collection of Dutch, French and Scottish paintings. The Mitchell Library, a modern building in North Street, is the largest free library in Scotland, with an important collection of Burnsiana.

Three m. W of the city is the new

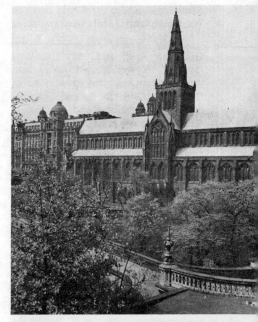

J. Allan Cash

Glasgow Cathedral (*above*) **and the University Buildings**

road tunnel under the Clyde between Whiteinch and Linthouse, replacing the old ferry.

Gourock *Renf.* (CC 67) EC Wed (10,367). A well-known resort and yachting centre on the great bend of the Clyde, with far-spreading views of Cowal, L. Long and the Argyll Hills. There is a car ferry to Dunoon, and steamer trips to all parts of the Firth and the Kyles of Bute. 2½ m. SW, near the Cloch Lighthouse, the ruins of Levan Castle stand amongst woods.

Grangemouth *Stirling.* (CK 68) EC Wed (22,000). Busy port and BP oil refinery on the estuary of the Forth; the E terminus of the Forth and Clyde Canal.

Greenock *Renf.* (CC 67) EC Wed (72,388). Important industrial and shipbuilding town on the Clyde. On the waterfront near the W Pier is the old West Kirk (1591), the first to be built after the Reformation, and removed hither from its original site. James Watt (1736–1819), the famous engineer, was born here, and Chantrey's statue of him now stands in the Watt Library and Institute.

Hamilton *Lanark.* (CH 65) EC Wed (46,370). Centre of important mining district. Owing to subsidence, Hamil-

ton Palace had to be demolished, but the mausoleum (on which the Ducal family spent £150,000 in 1850) still stands in Low Parks. Most interesting building in the town is the octagonal parish church, built by Wm. Adam in 1732, in front of which stands the Celtic Netherton Cross. To the S are the ruins of Cadzow Castle, with its unique herd of wild, white cattle. On the opposite side of the R. Avon is Chatelherault Lodge, designed by Wm. Adam. Barncluith with its Dutch gardens, constructed on a series of terraces overlooking the Avon, was planned by John Hamilton in 1583.

Helensburgh *Dunb.* (CC 68) EC Wed (11,221). Holiday and residential resort at mouth of the Gare Loch, with views across the Clyde to the Renfrew Hills. J. Logie Baird, the television inventor, was born here, and Henry Bell was Provost at the time when he launched the *Comet* (*see* **Bowling**), the fly-wheel of which is preserved in Hermitage Park.

Inversnaid *Stirling.* (CD 70). Port of call for steamers on E shore of L. Lomond, at the end of the Aberfoyle Road. The waterfall caused by the outfall from L. Arklet is associated with Wordsworth's *Highland Girl*; and a road to N leads to Rob Roy's

View across the Clyde from the Cloch Lighthouse

Ben Lomond from Luss

Cave, mentioned in Dorothy Wordsworth's Journal. The village is surrounded by the most magnificent mountains.

Kilmacolm *Renf.* (CD 66) EC Wed (2,650). Small inland residential and golfing resort. 2 m. SE are the ruined church and holy well of St Filan and the rock on which he is said to have sat while he was baptizing children.

Kippen *Stirling.* (CG 69). An attractive village in the Forth Valley.

Kirkintilloch *Dunb.* (CG 67) EC Wed (23,226). Originally known as Caerpentulach, one of the forts on the **Roman Wall** (*see below*).

Lanark *Lanark.* (CJ 64) EC Thurs (8,500). The parish church has a conspicuous tower with a statue of Wallace over the doorway. The walls of the 12th-cent. church of St Kentigern can still be seen. S of the town are the textile mills of New Lanark, the model town built by the great socialist reformer Robert Owen in 1784. Beyond this are the Cora Linn Falls, some 90 ft. high, and above them the remains of Corehouse Castle.

Leadhills *Lanark.* (CJ 61). The height of this attractive village, 1,350 ft., is exceeded only by that of neighbouring Wanlockhead (1,380 ft.). These are the two highest villages in Scotland. Now a golfing and walking

669

resort, the district was until recently noted for its lead, though in the 12th cent. there was also extensive gold and silver mining.

Loch Lomond★★ *Dunb.* (CD 69). Famous for its fishing and its steamer cruises, the 'Queen of Scottish Lakes' is the largest in Britain: 24 m. long, 5 m. at its widest point. At the S end are a number of islands, on one of which, Inchmurrin, stands ruined Lennox Castle. A fine road runs the whole length of the W shore, beneath a range of mountains over 2,000 ft. high; across the loch, Ben Lomond towers to a height of 3,192 ft. (*see also* **Balloch, Inversnaid, Luss** and **Tarbet**).

Luss *Dunb.* (CD 69). Pretty village, facing the beautiful islands of L. Lomond. Coleridge, Wordsworth and his sister stayed here in 1803.

Motherwell *Lanark.* (CH 65) EC Wed (76,300). Famous for its coal, steel and engineering. Here, in 1871, David Colville founded the Dalzell Works. To N is the ancient tower of Jerviston House, whilst to the SE 17th-cent. Dalzell House incorporates a much older tower.

Paisley *Renf.* (CE 66) EC Tue (95,527). Once famous for its shawls, now the biggest thread-producing centre in the world. The parish church, largely restored in the 15th cent., was once the nave of a great Cluniac Abbey, part of which, the Place of Paisley, has been restored as a War Memorial. 2 m. S are the Braes of Gleniffer, and 3 m. E the remains of 14th-cent. Crookston Castle.

Pollokshaws *Lanark.* (CF 66). Now a suburb of Glasgow. The fine mansion of Pollok House★, designed by Wm. Adam and standing in spacious

grounds above the White Cart river, contains paintings by Goya, Hogarth, Raphael, etc.

Port Glasgow *Renf.* (CD 67) EC Wed (22,316). The main port for Glasgow until the 18th-cent. dredging of the Clyde. Newark Castle, with its courtyard, hall and stepped gables, is a fine example of 16th-cent. building.

Provan Hall★ *Lanark.* near **Stepps** (CG 66). Probably the most perfect pre-Reformation mansion in Scotland, standing in acres of woodland. (NT for Scot.

Renfrew (CF 66) EC Wed (18,797). Industrial and shipbuilding centre, with a car ferry across the Clyde to Yoker. Glasgow airport lies S of the town, off the Paisley road.

Roman Wall. Usually known as the Antonine Wall (or as Graham's or Grime's Dyke), this was constructed in AD 140 as the northern frontier of Roman Britain—a function it fulfilled for less than half a century. Consisting of a turf rampart with a ditch in front and a military road behind, it spanned the waist of Scotland from Bowling (CE 67) on the Clyde to Bo'ness (CK 68) on the Forth, linking a line of forts built by Agricola 60 years earlier. Little of it remains today. The best-preserved forts are Kirkintilloch and Rough Castle (near Falkirk); and sections of the wall can be seen at Callendar House (*see* **Falkirk**), and particularly to the NW and NE of the town of Bearsden (CF 67).

Rosneath *Dunb.* (CC 68). Resort and yachting centre on Gare Loch, with the quiet waterside villages of Kilcreggan and Cove near by. N. of the latter, built over the dungeons of an old tower, is Knockderry Castle, the

Stirling C

'Knock Dunder' of Scott's *Heart of Midlothian*.

Rowardennan *Stirling*. (CD 69). Terminus of road on E side of L. Lomond and starting-point of one route up Ben Lomond (3,192 ft.). In summer a passenger ferry connects it with Inverbeg.

Stirling* (CH 69) EC Wed (28,243). Here the Old Bridge, dating from 1400, was once 'the gateway to the Highlands'. The town is dominated by its fine castle*, alternately fortress and Royal residence. Built between 13th and 17th cents., it contains a splendid Parliament Hall, the Chapel Royal, with 17th-cent. wall paintings, and the Douglas Room, containing many interesting relics. The approach to the castle passes the Church of the Holy Rood, in which Mary was crowned Queen of Scots at the age of 9 months; and an incomplete house, Mar's Wark, begun by the Regent Mar in 1570. Argyll's Lodging, a splendid 17th-cent. house, is now a hospital. 1 m. E the Wallace Monument, 220 ft. high and standing on Abbey Craig (362 ft.), provides stupendous views.

Strathblane *Stirling*. (CF 67). Golfing resort at the foot of Strathblane Hills and Campsie Fells – an area of great geological interest. 1 m. NE is the waterfall, Spout of Ballagan. Duntreath Castle, 2 m. NW, preserves its dungeons and medieval stocks.

Tarbet *Dunb*. (CD 70). A busy road junction with a steamer pier on the W shore of L. Lomond, and only 1½ m. from Arrochar on L. Long. Some 4 m. N is the power station of the L. Sloy hydro-electric scheme.

The Wallace Monument, Stirling

Opposite: Detail from the original painting by John Elwyn.
The Clyde is one of the great waterways of the world, providing anchorage for the largest ships, many of which were built in the shipyards of Glasgow and Greenock. In the foreground are representations of two historic ships launched on the Clyde, Bell's *Comet* of 1812 and the *Queen Elizabeth*; and of James Watt, the steam-engineer born in Greenock. On the northern horizon loom Ben Lomond and other outposts of the Highlands.

Edinburgh Castle from the Grassmarket   *J. Allan Cash*

THE
EDINBURGH
LOWLANDS

Fife, Kinross, Clackmannan, The Lothians

AN INTRODUCTION BY MORAY MCLAREN

This area has been called 'The Cradle of Scotland'. Its deep historic interest stems from the fact that through it there flows the River Forth, opening out into the Forth Estuary, which appears on the map to cut Scotland almost in two. South of the estuary lie the Lothians; north of it, Fife and Clackmannanshire, with Kinross beyond. All who approached Scotland in friendly enterprise from Europe had to do so by means of the Firth of Forth. In or near this area the Scottish Wars of Independence were fought or moved towards their climax. But today its importance rests on the fact that upon the southern shores of the Firth of Forth there lies the City of Edinburgh.

Opposite: Detail from the original painting by Leonard Rosoman.

Silhouetted against the Firth of Forth and the distant coastline of Fife, Edinburgh clusters about its Castle Rock, seen here from the Pentland Hills. In the foreground is a portrait by Landseer of Sir Walter Scott, born in the city in 1771. A landscape of contrasts: roughness and sophistication, crag and pavement, great 18th-century houses and small villages, golf-courses and mines.

Edinburgh

For half a millennium Edinburgh has been the capital (I hesitate to say the chief town) of Scotland. She has been praised as 'the Athens of the North', and abused, not so much for her smoke ('Auld Reekie') as for her greyness. The precipitate tumbling and climbing quality of Edinburgh is the first thing visitors notice about her. She is built around a central rock, and from that castellated rock she steps down to the sea or, elsewhere, upwards towards her surrounding hills, the Pentlands. So large and upstanding is 'Arthur's Seat', a huge rocky projection in the centre of the city, that you might justly call it (though not so high as the Pentlands) a mountain. The Water of Leith, a small river which tumbles through the gorges of Edinburgh's descent to the sea, contains brown trout, to angle for which you pay the sum of 5s. per year. Edinburgh is the one capital city of Europe which has within its borders a mountain, a trout river and, on the slopes of its Pentland Hills, grouse and mountain hare. But she has much else besides.

Edinburgh's chief glory lies in her dramatic contrasts of appearance. There is a great greyness – and a sudden profusion of colour; there is height – and yet vista; above all, there is the contrast of romantic and classical building. The romantic, in the Castle and Old Town, is obvious. But the visitor is implored not to neglect the finest example of neo-Georgian town-planning in Europe, the late 18th- or early 19th-century New Town, lying between the splendour of Charlotte Square to the south-west and the gracious amplitude of Drummond Place to the north-east.

There is not much danger of the visitor neglecting the romantic side of Edinburgh. The 1,000-year-old Castle stands upon its rock in the very heart of the city, visible from every quarter of Edinburgh. On one side the rock is sheer, and has been scaled only three times in history. To the east the Castle Rock slopes down more gradually, and on it is built the Old Town and 'Royal Mile', through which has flowed the stream of Scottish history – Mary Stuart, John Knox, Montrose, Boswell, all the Stuart kings and innumerable others. In the centre of it there is the High Kirk of St Giles, sometimes called a cathedral – which it never was. These black old buildings on the Castle slope cannot strictly be called beautiful; but they reek with interest. To the English visitor they look extremely 'foreign'.

'Foreign' too is the Palace of Holyroodhouse, which lies at the foot of the Royal Mile and at the other end from the Castle. Partly French in style, it has been added to by Scottish sovereigns for the last 500 years before and since the Union of Crowns. It is still a Royal Residence; but you can make a tour of its interior when the Royal Family is not in residence. Before Holyrood became a palace it was an abbey. You may see the delicate tracery of the Abbey Church beside the Palace. The rage of the Reformers and the neglect of the ensuing centuries have not destroyed all its beauty.

Princes Street is one of the most famous thoroughfares in Europe. North of Princes Street Gardens (once a loch), it runs parallel to the Royal Mile. It has only one side; but from that side you can look south up into the Old Town and the sun – one of the most romantic prospects in Europe. Apart from its incomparable view, it has the merit of being a fine street to stroll in, to shop in and to feel the ebb and flow of life in. In the neo-Gothic Walter Scott monument it can boast the largest memorial to a man of letters in the world. The Floral Clock, too, is famous. And at the east end is the Calton Hill, where is set the

Edinburgh

Aerofilms

City Observatory. Stevenson (and many agree with him) considered the view of Edinburgh from 'The Calton' the finest of all.

This hard core of the essential Edinburgh (the Old and the New Town) is built out of satisfyingly massive stone. On any fine day this greyness makes a superb foil for the colours in the wide and spacious gardens, the wide, long vistas to the sea and to the hills. Edinburgh is a city, above all, of space and height and varying polychrome set on a noble architectural frame of delicate grey. It must be one of the finest settings for a city in the world. It most certainly is a superb setting for the famous International Festival of Music and

675

The Bass Rock seen from Tantallon Castle

Drama and the Arts which takes place annually in the last two weeks of August and the first week of September. This Festival, first held in 1947, goes from strength to strength.

Outside the centre of Edinburgh there are many places of interest: the Royal Botanic Garden, the Zoo, the village of Cramond with its memories of Robert Louis Stevenson, the many University departments (all stemming from the fine Adam's 'Old Quad' near the Old Town), and, of course, the Forth Bridges. These are down by Queensferry, and connect Edinburgh with the north of Scotland by leaping over the Firth of Forth. Until recently only one bridge was in operation – that near-seventy-year-old miracle of functional beauty as of engineering, the rail bridge. This should certainly be seen. Beautiful, too, is the new Forth Road Bridge, opened by H.M. Queen Elizabeth on 4th September, 1964.

The Lothians

Edinburgh is the chief town of the old province of Lothian, as well as being the capital of Scotland. Lothian, which once stretched down to Berwick and the English border, is now reduced and divided into three counties, East Lothian,

Midlothian and West Lothian. Of these, the last is mainly industrial; while Midlothian, a partly agricultural, partly mining county under the shadow of the hills, is chiefly distinguished by the fact that nearly half of its area is taken up by Edinburgh. Of the three, the most distinctive is East Lothian. This rich agricultural county seems to mark out its own borders for itself by the immediate presence of red soil and the red sandstone buildings. When Cromwell's soldiers came there they found 'the greatest quantity of corn they ever saw'.

Its county town is Haddington, which is, after Edinburgh, one of the most interesting and charming towns in Scotland. Its charm lies in its beautiful, wide 18th-century streets; its interest in the fact that the Town Council has wisely preserved its character.

To the south of it there rise the beautifully rounded contours of the Lammermuir Hills. Though not 'grand' in the accepted Scottish scenic sense, they are wild moorland, filled with grouse and with small trout streams where most of the fishing is free. The beautiful little white and black village of Gifford lies upon the ascent to them. Farther up the hills is the historic 17th-century Castle of Nunraw, which Scott chose as the setting for *The Bride of Lammermoor*. It is now a Cistercian Monastery, to which visitors are warmly welcomed.

In the Lammermuirs East Lothian presents the full wild moorland effect, in its lower stretches a rich farming land (one of the richest in Scotland), and on its coastline a grim determined outlook facing north-east. The Bass Rock stands severely sentinel out to sea just beyond North Berwick. By North Berwick is Tantallon Castle, also built of red sandstone, once a stronghold of the Douglases. Gullane, Luffness, Muirfield, North Berwick – all these are associated with some of the finest golf-links in the world. The reason for their excellence lies in the incomparable springy sandy turf on which they have been laid out. It is the same quality of turf which you shall find in Fife across the waters of the Forth.

Fife

Fife has been called 'A beggar's mantle fringed with gold'. The beggar's mantle part of it is Central and West Fife, given over to a rather severe form of agriculture in the minor uplands and to coal-mining. The fringe of gold is that lovely sandy coastline which stretches eastwards from Aberdour right up to St Andrews, with Crail, Pittenweem, Anstruther and St Monance between. The 'Scottish Riviera' it has been called, and the claim is not too fanciful. It is just as beautiful a coastline as its *vis-à-vis* in East Lothian, and it has one great advantage: it faces south, displaying in the clear sunshine its colours of blue, green and gold.

Fife, bounded on the north by the wide estuary of the River Tay, on the south by the even wider Firth of Forth and on the east by the North Sea, is three parts an island. It is one of the chief boasts of Scotland that it encourages individuality in its children and in its own scenery. Fife has always kept up its individuality; and it is even said that some of the older folk there, when asked for their nationality, will say 'Fifer' rather than Scottish – and, most certainly, rather than 'British'.

St Andrews, all in all, is an entrancing little city. It has the most famous golf-links in the world. There are some fine 18th-century and neo-Georgian architecture, some spacious streets, some exhilarating if rather austerely cold bathing, and many attractions for the holidaymaker and the scholar of antiquities. It is the seat of the oldest University in Scotland.

It is difficult to imagine that this was once the setting for martyrdom and assassination – until we see the bottle dungeons from which no prisoner ever escaped. St Andrews is a haunted town of delicate and intimate beauty; but the ghosts who haunt it come from a time too remote to affect, still less frighten us. There is nothing in Britain to compare with this small city of gaunt bare ruins, gracious little Regency streets, wide golf-links and golden sands, grey and blue sea, and the scarlet gowns of the students to remind us of the blood that was shed here.

Falkland Palace

Scottish Tourist Board

Fife also contains the almost perfectly preserved little 16th-century town of Culross, delicate in its grey stone (silver almost) and pink pantile roofs. In Fife, too, is the historic town of Dunfermline where St Margaret, Queen of Scotland, lies buried and where Robert the Bruce was also interred. Grey, green and proud Dunfermline is one of the many places in Scotland which has historic claims to be the capital. Falkland Palace, with its memories of Mary Queen of Scots, is very well worth a visit. So too is Cupar, the county town of Fife.

Kinross and Clackmannan

When you come into Kinross, which lies between Fife and Perthshire, you begin to sniff the north. The first Highland hills are visible; and there are the Ochil Hills as well as the sweep of the small hill range above Loch Leven within the county itself. An agricultural county as yet not much touched by this age, its predominant colour is green, the green of close-cropped turf under the shadow of the northern mountains. The chief glory of Kinross-shire is, however, Loch Leven. This large, almost perfectly rounded lake lies under the steep slopes of the Lomond Hills and is probably the most famous piece of trouting water in the world. With its silver mail and deep pink flesh, the Loch Leven trout has unrivalled qualities as a sporting and fighting fish, and it is for this reason that international trouting competitions from all over the world are held here. Loch Leven has its romantic side, too. On one of its four islands there is a ruined castle where Mary Queen of Scots was imprisoned, and from which she escaped. It is a unique sheet of water in Scotland, seldom disturbed by storms, and possessing a quiet beauty.

Clackmannanshire, adjoining Kinross, is easily the smallest county in Scotland. The whole place, particularly the little town of Clackmannan itself, has a kind of miniscule charm. It was from Clackmannan Hill that Robert Bruce first saw the Scottish host assemble at his orders before Bannockburn. It was from the same vantage-point that he saw the dust of Edward II's huge army approaching. You, too, can go there and look down upon the field of one of the ten decisive battles of history. You will see where the Bannockburn joins the Forth and where, between these two, the huge English host was caught and entrapped to its doom. You will see Stirling Castle which Edward II failed to relieve, and behind it the great bulk of Highland Scotland which Edward never subdued, never reached. Well – the English reach it today and get a more friendly welcome!

Some houses and gardens open to the public

Culross Palace Map CK 68. *Early 17th cent., with painted walls and ceilings.* Ministry of Public Building and Works.

Edinburgh Castle. Map DC 67. *See p.* 683 Ministry of Public Building and Works.

Falkland Palace Map DC 70. *Splendid and historic hunting palace of the Stuart Kings. Still the property of the Sovereign, now administered by the* NT *for Scot. Gardens contain original Royal Tennis Court.*

Gladstone's Land 483 Lawnmarket, Edinburgh Map DC 67. *Interesting 17th-cent. house with unusual painted wooden ceilings. Headquarters of Saltire Society.* NT for Scot.

Hopetoun House nr S. Queensferry Map DB 67. *Scotland's most imposing Adam mansion. Fine interior decoration, paintings, etc. Red deer in magnificent parkland.* The Marquess of Linlithgow.

The House of the Binns 3½m E of Linlithgow Map DA 67. *Dates from the 15th cent. and contains early 17th-cent. plaster ceilings. Fine view of the Forth estuary.* NT for Scot.

Huntly House Canongate, Edinburgh Map DC 67. *16th-cent. house. Museum of local history; Edinburgh glass, Scottish pottery.* City and Royal Burgh of Edinburgh.

Lady Stair's House Lawnmarket, Edinburgh Map DC 67. *Built in 1622; relics of Burns, Scott, Stevenson.* City and Royal Burgh of Edinburgh.

Lauriston Castle nr Cramond Map DB 67. *Built 1583, with 1827 extension. Furniture, etc. Fine views over Forth estuary.* City and Royal Burgh of Edinburgh.

Linlithgow Palace Map CK 67. *Ruined former Royal Palace where Mary Queen of Scots was born in 1542. See p.* 684. Ministry of Public Building and Works.

Palace of Holyroodhouse Edinburgh Map DC 67. *Historic palace and the official residence of H.M. The Queen when in Scotland. See also p.* 683. Ministry of Public Building and Works. *Open only in the absence of the Royal Family and the Lord High Commissioner.*

Winton House Pencaitland Map DE 66. *Built 1620. Carved twisted stone chimneys unique in Scotland. Fine plaster ceilings in honour of visit by Charles I. Paintings, furniture, lovely grounds.* Sir David Ogilvy, Bt. *Open by arrangement with owner* Tel. Pencaitland 222. *Parties of 12–30 preferred.*

Books for further reading

History

W. T. BARR *For a Web Begun: the Story of Dunfermline* 1947
J. WILKIE *Bygone Fife from Culross to St Andrews* 1931

Travel and topography

M. BRANDER *Over the Lowlands* 1965
G. CHRISTIE *Harbours of the Forth* 1955
IAN FINLAY *The Lothians* 1960; *The Lowlands* 1967
W. GRANT *The Call of the Pentlands* 1951
THEO LANG *Edinburgh and the Lothians* 1952; *Kingdom of Fife and Kinross* 1951 (both in The Queen's Scotland series)
M. LINDSAY *The Lowlands of Scotland: Edinburgh and the South* 1956; *Glasgow and the North* (inc. Clackmannan, Kinross and Fife) 1953

GEORGE SCOTT-MONCRIEFF *The Lowlands of Scotland* 1939
MUIRHEAD'S 'BLUE GUIDES' *Scotland* 4th edn 1959
T. G. SNODDY *Afoot in Fife* 1950; *'Tween Forth and Tay* 1966
WARD LOCK'S 'RED GUIDES'

Edinburgh

J. BARCLAY *Edinburgh* 1965
R. CHAMBERS *Traditions of Edinburgh* 1967
CHIANG YEE *Silent Traveller in Edinburgh* 1948
ERIC LINKLATER *Edinburgh* (Cities of Enchantment series) 1960
MORAY MACLAREN *The Capital of Scotland* 1950
GEORGE SCOTT-MONCRIEFF *Edinburgh* 1947

Gazetteer

THE EDINBURGH LOWLANDS

Fife, Kinross, Clackmannan,
The Lothians

Craigmillar Castle   *Scottish Tourist Board*

Aberdour *Fife* (DB 68). Resort on the Firth of Forth, with ruined castle and old dovecote of 14th–17th cent. (AM). At near-by Dalgetty is the ruined Church of St Bridget (AM); while on Inchcolm Island, 1½ m. out to sea, is an Abbey, with some of the most complete monastic remains in the country.

Alloa *Clack.* (CJ 69) EC Tues (13,900). The largest town in the smallest of Scottish counties, to S of Ochil Hills (Ben Cleuch, 2,363 ft.), noted for worsted yarns. Note ancient Tower in modern Alloa House, and sundial on the 1695 house in Kirkgate.

Anstruther *Fife* (DF 70) EC Wed (3,300). With adjacent Cellardyke and Kilrenny, an important herring-fishing port and resort. The Manse, the oldest inhabited one in Scotland, bears the date 1590. Some 6 m. out to sea, the Isle of May is now a Nature Reserve.

Bo'ness (Borrowstounness) *W. Loth.* (CK 68) (10,280). Industrial town and port, where James Watt experimented with his steam engine in 1764. In Kinneil House (AM) note 16th-cent. wall paintings, possibly French or Flemish.

Borthwick Castle (*see* **Pathhead**).

Cakemuir Castle (*see* **Pathhead**).

Clackmannan (CK 69) EC Tues (2,350). Outside the old Tolbooth, note the Town Cross with its steps; also the ancient Clach (or stone) of Manau, from which the town derives its name. On a hill to the W the fine 15th-cent. Clackmannan Tower (AM), traditionally built by the Bruce.

Craigmillar Castle* *Midlothian.* 2 m. SE of Edinburgh (DC 67), this impressive ruined Castle (AM) was a favourite home of Mary Queen of Scots. From the massive 14th-cent. tower the view is especially fine.

Crail *Fife* (DG 70). Golf, and the number of old crow-stepped houses near the harbour, make this fishing village a popular resort. There is a good Tolbooth, and an interesting 13th-cent. Collegiate Church. Two m. SW are the Caiplie Caves, one of which is 40 ft. in length.

Crichton *Midlothian* (DD 66). The small 15th-cent. Collegiate Church, standing on the steep bank above Tyne Water, is remarkable for its squat tower and barrel vaulting. To the S the splendid Castle (AM), originally a single tower, developed into its present form with the addition of its unique Italianate N wing in the 16th cent.

Culross* *Fife* (CK 68). This loveliest of the Royal Burghs of Fife is now

681

cared for by the NT for Scot., which has done much to preserve its wealth of 17th-cent. buildings. Note particularly the Palace* (AM), with its painted and panelled rooms and terraced gardens; the Tolbooth; and the 'Study'. The present Church consists of the choir and central tower of the Abbey (AM), founded in 1217.

Dalkeith *Midlothian* (DD 66) EC Tues (8,860). Market town between the N and S Esk Rivers. The Palace was rebuilt by Vanbrugh *c*. 1700 for the Duchess of Buccleuch, widow of the Duke of Monmouth (executed in 1685). To SW is Newbattle Abbey, in fine parkland, the crypt and basement of which survive beneath an 18th-cent. mansion, now a college.

Dalmeny* *W. Lothian* (DB 67). Undoubtedly one of the finest small Norman churches in Scotland, with exceptionally rich carvings. Near by, overlooking the Firth of Forth, is the restored Barnbougle Castle.

Dirleton *E. Lothian* (DF 68). Midway between the famous golf courses of N Berwick and Gullane, this attractive village has the beautiful remains of a massive 13th-cent. Castle* (AM), with its three-storey Renaissance additions still standing, and an old bowling green.

Dollar *Clack.* (CK 69) EC Thurs (1,950). On the R. Devon, at the foot of the Ochils, the town is famous for its Academy, built by Playfair in 1819. One m. N, in a romantic setting between the Burn of Sorrow and the Burn of Care, stand the ruins of Castle Campbell (AM and NT); while, behind, King's Seat rises to 2,111 ft.

Dunbar *E. Lothian* (DG 67) EC Wed (4,000). Fishing port and resort, at the foot of the Lammermuirs. The Town House has an interesting six-sided tower; and in the Parish Church, with its 108-ft. tower, is the notable tomb of the 1st Earl of Dunbar, 1610. On a rock above the harbour are the scanty remains of the Castle, and near by is the battlefield where Cromwell defeated the Covenanters under Leslie in 1650.

Dunfermline *Fife* (DA 68) EC Wed (47,160). The magnificent Abbey Church* (AM), in which Robert the Bruce was buried, though much restored, still possesses the finest Norman nave in Scotland (1150), and its square battlemented tower. Andrew Carnegie, who founded the first of his Free Libraries here in 1881, was a native of the town, to which he bequeathed Pittencrieff Glen, with its fine flower gardens and 17th-cent. mansion, now a museum.

East Linton* *E. Lothian* (DF 67). Picturesque village on the Tyne, which flows through a small gorge, crossed by a 16th-cent. bridge. There is a monument to the great bridge-builder, John Rennie, who was born in the near-by mansion of Phantassie in 1761. Two m. SW is Hailes Castle, with original 13th-cent. watergate and dungeons; behind which rises Traprain Law (724 ft.), where in 1919 a hoard of 4th-cent. silver Roman coins was excavated.

Edinburgh** *Midlothian* (DC 67) EC Tues/Wed/Sat (468,375). Finely situated and famous for its University and Schools, as well as being the focus of the historical, political and cultural life of Scotland for centuries; any selection of the City's interesting features is bound to be invidious. The heart of the Old Town is the 'Royal Mile', the succession of streets amidst many-storeyed old houses and quaint Wynds, that follows the ridge E from the Castle to Holyroodhouse. The Castle★ (AM—*see p. s.55*) is the centre of a group of notable buildings: the restored Chapel of St Margaret dates from 1093; the Old Palace contains the Crown Room, with the Scottish regalia, the Royal Apartments and the Old Parliament Hall; while on the N side is the impressive National War Memorial (1927). In High St. is the fine Church of St Giles★, once the 'High Kirk', with its 'Crown' steeple, and Parliament House; and, within a stone's throw, the University, designed by Robert Adam in 1789 and completed by Playfair in 1827. Continuing down the Royal Mile, note John Knox's House, the splendid Canongate Tolbooth (1591), and White Horse Close and Inn (1791). In Holyroodhouse★, dating from 1500, are interesting relics and portraits of the Kings and Queens of Scotland, but of the Royal Chapel, once part of the adjoining Abbey, only part of the nave and W front are still standing. Very different in character is the 18th-

Edinburgh : John Knox's House   *J. Allan Cash*

cent. New Town, extending northwards from the famous thoroughfare Princes St. Its handsome streets and stately squares contain some of the most characteristic work of the great Robert Adam. Particularly outstanding are Drummond Place and Charlotte Square, while amongst individual buildings, the design of Register House containing the Scottish Archives, is of great beauty. Today, the annual Edinburgh Festival is a fitting tribute to the splendour of the Athens of the North.

Falkland★ *Fife* (DC 70). Ancient Royal Burgh, with old houses and cobbled streets, standing at the foot of the Lomond Hills. Of special interest is the Renaissance Palace★ (NT for Scot.), a favourite residence of James V, and his daughter Mary Queen of Scots. The fine S wing

Edinburgh: the Church of St Giles

J. Allan Cash

contains the Chapel, once a banqueting hall, with a good screen and tapestries; and the 1539 Tennis Court can still be seen.

Forth Bridge (*see* **Queensferry**).

Gifford *E. Lothian* (DF 66). A charming village, on the Gifford Water, from which to explore the Lammermuirs (4 m. S is Lammer Law, 1,733 ft.). A lime avenue leads to Yester House, a fine Adam mansion. Beyond are the remains of Yester Castle, with the curious underground chamber, 'Goblin Ha', referred to in Scott's *Marmion*.

Haddington* *E. Lothian* (DF 67) EC Thurs (5,500). On the R. Tyne, spanned by two fine 16th-cent. bridges, this fine little town has been carefully cleansed and preserved by the Town Council. The restored Church (AM), known as the 'Lamp of Lothian', retains the fine original 15th-cent. central tower, nave and W front. The Town House was designed by Wm. Adam; and there are three notable 17th-cent. buildings, Haddington House, Bothwell Castle and Moat House. Two m. N stands ruined Barnes Castle.

Kinross (DB 70) EC Thurs (2,360). To the W of **L. Leven** (*see below*), this resort is well known for its fishing, golf, skating and curling. Kinross House, with its beautiful gardens, is a fine achievement by the 17th-cent. architect, Sir Wm. Bruce. Note the old jougs (an iron collar for wrong-doers) attached to the Town Cross, and the Tolbooth, with Robert Adam's decoration.

Kirkcaldy *Fife* (DC 69) EC Wed (52,370). Coal port and manufacturing town, especially linoleum. At the old Burgh School, now closed, Adam Smith and Robert Adam, both natives

of the town, were pupils; and later Thomas Carlyle spent two years as a master there. Sailor's Walk (NT), near the harbour, contains several fine 17th-cent. houses. Behind the town, Beveridge Park, well-known for motor racing, leads to Raith House; and 2 m. W are the ruins of Balwearie Tower.

Kirkliston *W. Lothian* (DB 67). Notable for its partly 12th-cent. Church, with fine W tower and saddleback roof. Across the R. Almond is Turnhouse, the airport for Edinburgh. Two m. W is Niddry Castle, to which Mary Queen of Scots escaped from **L. Leven** (*see below*); and 2 m. SW is a fine Adam house, Newliston.

Lasswade *Midlothian* (DD 66). In the valley of the Esk River, this village is notable for its literary associations. Sir Walter Scott lived here 1798–1804, during which time he was visited by Wordsworth. Outside the ruined Norman Church is the grave of Wm. Drummond, the poet, who was born at Hawthorndown House, 2½ m. SW, in the grounds of which stands a tree commemorating Ben Jonson's visit to him in 1618–19. And near by is Mavisbush, the cottage where De Quincey lived from 1840–59.

Leuchars* *Fife* (DE 72). Notable for its very fine Norman Church, with its interesting bell turret above the apse, added in the 17th cent. To the E the ancient and picturesque house, Earlshall, has been admirably restored.

Linlithgow* *W. Lothian* (CK 67) EC Wed (4,330). In the precincts, on the edge of the small Loch, are the famous Palace* (AM), where Mary Queen of Scots was born, and St Michael's Church. The chapel and hall of the former are 15th-cent. work, and in the courtyard formed by the

Royal Apartments of the W wing is a notable 16th-cent. fountain. St Michael's is one of the finest 15th-cent. churches in Scotland. Note especially the nave and choir, and the flamboyant window tracery in the Katherine's aisle. There are a number of 16th-cent. houses in the town for which the NT for Scot. is responsible and the curious Cross Well, with its 13 water jets, is a careful reproduction of an earlier structure.

Loch Leven★ *Kinross* (D B 70). This very attractive Loch (*see also* **Kinross** and **Milnathort**), famous amongst fishermen for its pink-fleshed trout, is of great historical interest. From the Castle (AM) on the smaller of its two islands, William Douglas helped Mary Queen of Scots to escape after she had been imprisoned there for

Leuchars: the Norman church

almost a year. On the other island are the remains of St Serf's Priory.

Milnathort *Kinross* (D B 70). Besides being one of the two towns from which **L. Leven** is easily accessible, this little wool town is near the ruined Burleigh Castle (AM), once a Balfour fortress; a short distance S E are the interesting standing stones of Orwell.

Musselburgh *Midlothian* (DD 67) EC Wed Thur (17,600). The second largest burgh in Midlothian, with many historical associations (going back to Roman times), industrial interests and sporting facilities (horse-racing, golf, archery, etc.). The mussels which gave the town its name, though still to be found, are now contaminated and unfit for human consumption. Loretto School, now in Pinkie House (famous for its painted ceiling), until recently occupied a building on the former site of a chapel of Our Lady of Loretto whose stones were used in the construction of the present Tolbooth in the late 16th cent.

Newburgh *Fife* (D C 71) (2,460). Outside this harbour on the Firth of Tay is the Island of Mugdrum; the Mugdrum Cross in the town is more than 1,000 years old. To the E are the remains of Lindores Abbey; and beyond, 3 m. N E, ruined Ballanbreich Castle overlooks the Firth.

North Berwick *E. Lothian* (D F 68) E C Thurs (4,160). Well-known resort famous for its golf course. Three m. N E the Bass Rock, notable for its gannetry, rises 350 ft. out of the sea, with a powerful lighthouse. Three m. E beyond Canty Bay, moated Tantallon Castle★ (AM) is magnificently situated on a rocky headland.

Pathhead *Midlothian* (DD 66). On the steep banks of Tyne Water, at the foot of the Moorfoot Hills. N across the river is Oxenfoord Castle in its

Reece Winstone

fine park, while close to the village are two attractive old houses, Preston Hall and Ford House. The B636 to S, after passing through **Crichton** (*see above*), reaches a height of 900 ft., but about 1 m. before the summit the tiny village of Tynehead stands midway between the romantic Borthwick and Cakemuir Castles★. From the former massive stronghold, where Mary Queen of Scots lived after her marriage to Bothwell in 1566, she later escaped across the hills to Cakemuir, disguised as a page.

Pencaitland★ *E. Lothian* (DE 66). Picturesque village astride the Tyne Water. In the much earlier Church are a good W doorway and tower of the 17th-cent., with three sundials and a laird's loft. Across the river to N is the fine 1620 mansion, Winton House, with impressive entrance lodge, fine chimneys and decorated plaster ceilings. One and a half m. SW is Penkaet, a beautiful house of the same period, with two dovecotes and contemporary woodwork.

Pittenweem *Fife* (DF 70). Old houses surround this picturesque harbour, near to which is the cave-shrine of St Fillan. The Church has an impressive square tower dated 1592. Two m. NW Balcaskie House with its terraced gardens was designed by Sir Wm. Bruce; and 1 m. further on is the turreted, 16th-cent. Kellie Castle, with its notable interior and pictures.

Prestonpans *E. Lothian* (DD 67) EC Thurs (3,100). Here salt-panning was introduced by the monks in the 12th cent., and Prince Charles Edward won his one major battle over the English in the 1745 Rising. An exceptionally fine 17th-cent. Mercat Cross (AM), stands opposite Northfield House, of the same period. One m E, Hamilton House, restored by the NT for Scotland, is seen by prior arrangement only (Prestonpans 306).

Queensferry, South★ *W. Lothian* (DB 67) EC Wed (2,930). The inn at Hawes Ferry has been described in both Scott's *The Antiquary* and

R. L. Stevenson's *Kidnapped*. St Mary's, founded in 1330, and still possessing its 16th-cent. tower and barrel vaulting, is the only Carmelite Chapel still functioning as such in Britain. Overshadowing the town are the two great bridges*: the famous 19th-cent. engineering feat, the Forth Railway Bridge, 2,765 yds. long and 361 ft. above the water, and the magnificent new suspension bridge for road traffic, with its central span of 3,330 ft. One and a half m. S is the modernised 15th-cent. Dundas Castle. Three m. E, Hopetoun House, begun in 1699 by Sir Wm. Bruce and completed by Robert Adam, is a splendid mansion, now containing a most interesting museum.

Roslin* *Midlothian* (D C 66). Small mining village, famous for its Chapel and its Castle. In the former, note the elaborate carving, especially the Prentice Pillar, and the crypt. The latter, picturesquely situated on a cliff overlooking the Esk, dates from the 15th cent. and has been well restored.

Rumblingbridge* *Kinross* (D A 69). A famous beauty spot, where two adjacent bridges span the R. Devon into Perthshire. Devil's Mill and Caldron Linn are the finest falls, to N E and S W respectively; while 3 m. S E restored Aldie Castle looks out to the Cleish Hills.

Roslin Chapel: the Prentice Pillar
Scottish Tourist Board

St Andrews** *Fife* (D F 71) E C Thurs (9,890). This fascinating city and resort, standing on a promontory above long stretches of sand, has many claims to fame besides being the headquarters of golf (four courses, including the Royal and Ancient Club, founded in 1754). Its Cathedral (A M), though now largely ruined, was once the largest in the country, and still includes extensive monastic remains; while close by the choir and high tower of 12th-cent. St Rule's (A M) are still standing. Its University, since 1897 incorporating that of Dundee, is the oldest in Scotland, having been founded in 1412, and today has nearly 3,000 students. The College Chapel, once the Church of St Salvator, contains John Knox's pulpit, brought here from the Town Church, where he preached his first sermons; and in the quadrangle of St Mary's College a thorn tree, planted by Mary Queen of

St Andrews: the Castle

Scottish Tourist Board

Scots, still flourishes. Interesting local relics are to be found in the Sessions House (including two repentance stools and a scold's bridle) and in the Town Hall (portraits and a headsman's axe). In the ancient ruined Castle (AM), standing on a rock above the sea, note the 'bottle dungeon' and underground passage; while 2 m. SE are the curious basalt pillars, the 'Rock and Spindle'.

St Monance *Fife* (DF 70). Old and delightful little fishing port, with ancient St David's Church standing on the foreshore. Its shipyard, which once built the 'Fifie' trawlers, now builds yachts. Three m. W along the coast road that passes the ruins of Ardross Castle, are the twin resorts of Elie and Earlsferry, standing at the extremities of a bay with good beaches and bathing.

Torphichen *W. Lothian* (CK 67). High on the edge of the Bathgate Hills (the 1,017-ft. Knock provides a good view-point) the village is famous for its Church* (AM) which once belonged to the Knights of St John of Jerusalem. In appearance more like a fortress than a church, the tower with its saddle-back roof was once part of the domestic buildings; and its original nave is incorporated in the 16th-cent. Parish Church. Two m. E, at Cairn-apple Hill, a fine Bronze Age burial mound (AM), has recently been excavated, revealing an earlier Neolithic site.

Looking down the Firth of Lorn from Oban *Aerofilms*

ARGYLL AND BUTE
including Arran

AN INTRODUCTION BY ANGUS MACVICAR

When God had finished making Britain, some fragments of earth and stone were left in his ample apron. With a smile he flicked them out, and they fell into the western sea to form Argyll and Bute.

So runs an old Gaelic legend.

A more modern legend has it that the coastlines of the two counties stretch for 3,000 miles, approximately the distance between Glasgow and New York. This sounds less surprising when you consider that the area includes about a hundred islands, ranging in extent from giants like Mull, Islay, Jura and Arran to tiny skerries like Glunemore, off Sanda, and Pladda with its lighthouse in

689

the Firth of Clyde. It comes even more into perspective when you discover that by air the journey from Glasgow to Campbeltown is one of only 60 miles, while by road – a magic road cavorting through mountains and around blue sea-lochs – it is double that distance: 134 miles, to be exact.

Legend and statistics, however, supply no more than the background to a picture of land and sea inextricably mingled – a picture encompassing bleak moorlands in North Lorn and lush green pastures in Kintyre; bare, sand-blown *machars* in western Islay and sheltered glens in Arran pink with rhododendrons; Bidean nam Bian in Glencoe (at 3,766 feet higher by 77 feet than Ben Cruachan) and limpid Loch Awe, south of Dalmally, fringed with woods of pastel green; sombre pagan stones at Dunadd in mid-Argyll and a host of bright and hospitable little towns – Dunoon, Campbeltown and Oban on the mainland, Rothesay in Bute, Brodick in Arran, Port Ellen in Islay, Tobermory in Mull.

But everywhere in this picture of a region extending to 2,000,000 acres, which supports only 75,000 people as against 900,000 sheep and cattle – everywhere you are aware of the sea, calmly dreaming in Loch Etive and Loch Long, turbulent where the seven tides meet off the Mull of Kintyre.

Geology

Such dramatic scenic contrasts are due in part to a complicated variety of rock formations; and, in general terms, the area can be divided geologically into three parts.

In Mull and North Argyll igneous basalt and lava beds predominate, with some intrusions of granite and felsite, notably on the Moor of Rannoch and at Crarae, south-west of Inveraray, where a busy quarry provides paving-stones for Glasgow and chips for Argyll's 1,450 miles of roads. The main road south runs through this quarry, and travellers held up by warning notices are sometimes rewarded by the sound and spectacle of a mighty blast.

A central strip running south-west to north-east, which takes in Islay, Jura, North Kintyre, mid-Argyll, Cowal, the Isle of Bute and North Arran, contains rocks that are mainly metamorphic, quartzite alternating with softer schists and limestone. Hereabouts the soil produces protein-laden grass; milk is rich and mutton plentiful and sweet.

In South Kintyre and South Arran there occur considerable areas of sedimentary Old Red Sandstone. Here, for the artist, the cliffs glow red during a summer sunset. The practical farmer finds the dry soil ideal for potatoes.

But this story of successive periods of eruption, submergence and erosion has four interesting sub-plots. First, the raised glacial beaches – one at 25 feet, another at 100 feet – traceable throughout the area but most clearly visible along the western and southern coasts of Kintyre. Second, the whinstone (dolerite) dikes converging on Mull from the Clyde coasts – black intrusions in the ancient lava, marking the volcanic pipes of more recent eruptions. Third, the old coal-mine at Machrihanish near Campbeltown, oddly situated in a region of rich farmland and gorgeous yellow beaches, which betrays the presence at considerable depth of a small patch of carboniferous sediment. And fourth, the bed of white sandstone, 18 feet thick, near Lochaline in Morvern, which supplies material for the manufacture of high-quality glass.

Mountain and forest to the south-west of Loch Leven

Aerofilms

Flora and fauna

The weather in Argyll and Bute is mild and temperate, owing, it has been said, to the near presence of the Gulf Stream. Snow rarely falls before January; and though rain often drifts across the mountainous interior, the common impression that the whole area is perpetually damp and depressing can, without difficulty, be proved false. Statistically, the average annual hours of sunshine compare favourably with those in any other part of Britain.

As a result of this clement weather, all the common Scottish wild-flowers grow in profusion, while rare species like Norwegian sandwort and thyme broom-rape are native in the area. Colourful palms and fuchsias are cultivated in gardens open to the public; and strawberries from Bute have been sold in the Glasgow shops at Easter. Should you happen to be in Dunoon, try to visit the 'lucky' white heather farm up on the hill, near Toward.

State forests of pine, fir and larch blanket the lower slopes of the mountains. In older woodlands, alder and ash rub branches with beech and birch; elm and hazel grow alongside poplar, sycamore and yew. If you can, acquire a few pots of the local rowan and crab-apple jelly. It gives a royal flavour to soda scones.

Every second person in Argyll and Bute is an enthusiastic bird-watcher, which may be due to the fact that Kintyre and Arran provide a flight-line for comparatively rare south-bound migrants in autumn. But the golden eagle, the ptarmigan, the red grouse and the divers are all indigenous, while the only choughs now nesting in Scotland are to be found in the islands. Famed for its woodcock shooting, Islay also winters large flocks of barnacle geese.

Besides the native red and roe deer, the fallow deer and Japanese Sika deer – lately introduced – are fairly numerous. Hares have become a pest since the rabbit population was reduced by myxomatosis. Though less common than the otters, foxes, stoats and weasels, badgers and wild-cats still roam the lonelier parts of Argyll. When walking on the high moors, be wary of adders: they are quick and poisonous.

My own favourite local animals are the grey Atlantic seals. At sunrise on a cold, calm winter's morning they come up on the sea-rocks, sprawling and puffing. The professional salmon-fisher hates the sight of them, because 80 per cent of their food consists of salmon. But they are friendly in a way that is almost human. When there is talk of killing, a picture comes to my mind – one that any visitor may see in late autumn or early winter – the picture of a white-furred calf playing alone in a sea-pool, curiously turning over stones and shells.

For the amateur fisherman, Argyll and Bute are paradise. The number of lochs and streams is beyond reckoning, and salmon, sea-trout and brown trout are abundant. Loch Eck nurtures not only the salmonid powan – elsewhere found only in Loch Lomond and sometimes mistakenly called 'the freshwater herring' – but also its own distinct sub-species of charr.

Archaeology and history

After the last Ice Age, the first human beings to see the torn and tortured land of Scotland probably settled in Argyll and Bute about 6000 B.C. – Mesolithic men from Ireland, with flint arrows and flint tools stuck in their reindeer belts. They were followed by men of the Neolithic, Bronze and Iron Ages, whose arrow-heads, drinking utensils and primitive tools have all been found in the area. Some you can see in the Campbeltown Museum.

ARGYLL AND BUTE

The first Scots kingdom of Dalriada, founded in the third century A.D., had its headquarters at Dunadd, near Lochgilphead, where the tall stones of a Druid temple still commemorate a pagan power. Two centuries later, sacrificial knives were made redundant by the Cross.

There is a legend in Kintyre – which cannot be proved or disproved – that before going to Iona, St Columba and his disciples first landed on the shore at Kiel, six miles west of the Mull of Kintyre. There, on a grassy knoll above the kirkyard, you will find a flat stone bearing the prints of two right feet. More than likely they were carved out originally to mark a place where pre-Christian chiefs took their tribal vows; but they are called locally 'St Columba's footprints'. It is significant that only a hundred yards away stands a Druid altar. Columba, 'strong in stature, voice and spirit', built his new faith on the foundation of the old.

Iona itself – which you must surely visit (by steamer from Oban), to mingle with the pilgrims from every corner of the world and to see the Abbey, magnificently restored in the past few years by devoted hands – Iona itself provides proof of this. Before Columba made it the base for his Christian mission in Scotland, it had been a stronghold of Druidism.

Thereafter the history of Argyll and Bute merges with that of Scotland. Four centuries of Norse occupation were followed by the reign of the MacDonalds – the Lords of the Isles – whose ruined castles are strewn across the countryside. The breaking of their independent power by the royalist Campbells coincided with the Union of the Crowns in 1603. In the post-Jacobite period there began the slow decline of the old Gaelic civilisation. This continues.

Iona Abbey   *Reece Winstone*

Local industries

Farming is – and always has been – the paramount industry of the area. In view of the high proportion of rough grazings (94 per cent), the agricultural economy is based on livestock rather than on crop production. Sheep, mainly blackface, outnumber beef cattle and milking Ayrshires in the proportion of twelve to one. The chief dairying region is South Kintyre, where a creamery manufactures butter, condensed milk and lactic casein.

For centuries fishing was second in importance only to agriculture, which can be deduced from Inveraray's burghal motto: *Semper tibi pendeat halec* ('May you always have a catch of herring'). It continues to play an important part in the economy, but in fact more local people are now employed in forestry. To some extent this is due to the inexplicable disappearance of the fat Loch Fyne herring. But you can still buy wonderful kippers in Tarbert, Campbeltown and Oban, and the white fishing remains brisk. Now that trawl-nets are legal in the Clyde, the catching of prawns for *scampi* has become a lucrative business.

If you'd like a skiff built – or a yacht – try the up-to-date little yards at Sandbank, Port Bannatyne, Tarbert or Tighnabruaich. Other industrial activities range from a tweed mill in Oban, a modern sawmill in Strachur and a ropeworks and clothing factory in Campbeltown to a gurgle of distilleries in Islay. If someone offers you a dram of the comparatively rare Islay Mist, accept it with gratitude – but please do not ruin its gentle bouquet with ginger ale!

Roads to the Isles

After farming, today's main industry concerns yourself – the care and comfort of visitors.

By road from Glasgow you come into Argyll past Arrochar and Loch Long. Then you drive over the long steep hill appropriately called Rest-and-be-Thankful down through the woods to Inveraray. This is the ancient capital, a little town of white houses elbowing each other around a pier. Its turretted castle is owned by the Duke of Argyll – *MacCailein Mor* – whose family name is Campbell. One day soon, from beneath the sand and silt of Tobermory Bay, the present Duke hopes to salvage the treasure of the lost Armada galleon, *Florencia*.

If you have a moment to spare, visit the old Inveraray courthouse where James Stewart of the Glen was condemned to death in 1752 for the murder in Appin of Colin Campbell of Glenure ('the red fox'). James Stewart was almost certainly innocent, but the presiding judge and eleven of the fifteen jurors were Campbells. It was a notable trial, providing Robert Louis Stevenson with the inspiration for *Kidnapped*. Inveraray-born Neil Munro also wrote a story about it, but his best-known works are the Clyde-based *Para Handy* tales and historical romances like *John Splendid* and *Doom Castle*, which, their English style thirled to the Gaelic idiom, faithfully capture the spirit of Argyll and its islands.

From Inveraray you can double back to sail boats, catch fish or play golf in Cowal and Dunoon; you can strike west to climb mountains in Glencoe – the scene of the infamous massacre – or to experience the thrill of Oban's water-ski-ing and island sunsets; you can drive south to the administrative capital of Lochgilphead – pausing perhaps to visit the Druid temple at Dunadd – then on to Campbeltown with its astonishing cave picture of the crucified Christ. West of Campbeltown you can play golf on the championship links at Machrihanish

Inveraray: the waterfront

– birthplace of William MacTaggart, the artist – and in Southend study the whole history of Scottish civilisation in easily accessible prehistoric barrows, Columban remains and vitrified forts.

By air from Glasgow you may travel to Kintyre and Islay in a matter of minutes, while if steamers give you pleasure, whole fleets of them sail regularly to all the mainland and island ports of Argyll and Bute. In Rothesay, whose fairy lights make it the best illuminated town on the Clyde, you can again savour history in its mighty castle, built in 1098 as a MacDonald stronghold against the Norse invaders. In Arran you can rest on the shoulder of Goatfell and experience for yourself the scenes and emotions so brilliantly described by Robert Mc-Lellan in his *Sweet Largie Bay*.

People

How am I to convey to you in short the essential spirit of the two counties – the spirit of the people?

We are of mixed stock – Highland, Lowland and Irish. We are clannish, but sociable, and we like to sing and act and go to church. At the Mod – Gaelic equivalent of the Welsh Eisteddfod – the Campbeltown Gaelic Choir has won the premier trophy thirteen times. Our drama clubs are legion, and some have presented plays in Glasgow. Our kirks are legion, too, and generally well filled. But perhaps it is by joining us at one of our *ceilidhs* that you'll get to know us best. There you may find that under the influence of song and story – and 'a wee dram' – our gloss of modernity flakes off a little, revealing a Celtic heritage of humour and hospitality – and an independence that is as rugged as our history and sea-girt coasts.

Some houses and gardens open to the public

Achamore nr Ardminish, I. of Gigha *Map B G 64. Large gardens with roses and flowering shrubs.* Col. Sir James Horlick, Bt. *House not open.* (Ferry from Tayinloan, Kintyre, *Map* BH 64.) Tel. Gigha 217.

Benmore 7m N of Dunoon *Map* CB 67. *Famous woodland gardens in mountain scenery: rhododendrons, etc.* Ministry of Public Building and Works.

Brodick Castle I. of Arran *Map* CA 63. *Former home of the Dukes of Hamilton. Main structure dates from c. 1500. Silver, furnishings, china, pictures. Beautiful formal and woodland gardens.* NT for Scot.

Colonsay House Kiloran *Map* BD 69. *Subtropical gardens.* Lord and Lady Strathcona. *House not open.* (Steamer from Tarbert *Map* BJ 66.)

Crarae Lodge nr Minard on A83 road, *Map* BK 69. *Beautiful woodland garden by the shore of Loch Fyne. Best in early autumn.* Sir George Campbell of Succoth, Bt. *House not open.*

Inveraray Castle *Map* CA 70. *18th-cent. castle in magnificent setting near head of Loch Fyne. Headquarters of the Clan Campbell. Tapestries, furniture, china, early Scottish arms.* His Grace the Duke of Argyll.

Books for further reading

History

JOHN BUCHAN *The Massacre of Glencoe* 1933
IAN CARMICHAEL *Lismore in Alba* 1948
WM. MACARTHUR *The Appin Murder and the Trial of James Stewart* 1960
COLIN MACDONALD *History of Argyll up to the Beginning of the 16th Century* 1950
ANDREW MACKERRAL *Kintyre in the 17th Century* 1948
REV. A. J. MACVICAR *The Book of Blaan: A Personal History of Southend* 1966
LUCY MENZIES *St Columba of Iona* 1920
HUGH SHEDDEN *The Story of Lorn: Its Isles and Oban* 1938

Travel and topography

ARGYLL COUNTY COUNCIL *Argyll* (guide book) 1961
T. R. BARNETT *Land of Lorne and the Isles of Rest* 1933
G. BLAKE *Firth of Clyde* 1952
FORESTRY COMMISSION *National Forest Park Guides: Argyll* 1967
A. GARDNER *Sun, Cloud and Snow in the Western Highlands* 1933
T. HANNAN *The Beautiful Isle of Mull, with Iona and the Isle of Saints* 1926
JACK HOUSE *Down the Clyde* 1959
J. S. HUGHES *Harbours of the Clyde* 1954
M. LINDSAY *Clyde Waters* 1958

N. MUNRO *Clyde, River and Firth* 1907
W. A. POUCHER *Highland Holiday: Arran to Ben Cruachan* 1945
WARD LOCK'S 'RED GUIDES' *Glasgow and the Clyde* 1965; *Oban . . . and Western Scotland* 1965

Animal and bird life

S. GORDON *Land of the Hills and the Glens: Wild Life of Iona and the Inner Hebrides* 1920
H. D. GRAHAM *Birds of Iona and Mull* 1890
J. A. HARVIE-BROWN and T. E. BUCKLEY *Fauna of Argyll and the Inner Hebrides* 1892
J. M. MACWILLIAM *Birds of the Firth of Clyde* 1936

Bute, Arran and the Cumbraes

R. A. DOWNIE *Bute and the Cumbraes* 1934
V. A. FIRSOFF *Arran with Camera and Sketchbook* 1951
J. A. GIBSON *The Birds of the Island of Arran* 1955
T. S. HALL *Tramping in Arran* 3rd edn 1947
REV. J. K. HEWISON *The Isle of Bute in the Olden Time: Celtic Saints and Heroes* 1893-5
J. M. MACWILLIAM *The Birds of the Island of Bute* 1927
R. MEEK *Hill Walking in Arran* 1963

Gazetteer

ARGYLL AND BUTE

Acharacle *Argyll* (BG 76). Excellent angling headquarters at foot of freshwater Loch Shiel with steamer service to Glenfinnan. A road follows the stream from Shiel Bridge to the sea at Dorlin near romantically situated 14th-cent. Castle Tioram*. Bonnie Prince Charlie stayed at Kinlochmoidart to the N during the rally of the clans held at Glenfinnan before the 1745 rising.

Ardchattan Priory *Argyll* (BK 73). *See* **Connel Ferry.**

Ardgoil *Argyll* (CC 69). Loch Goil and Loch Long are on either side of this peninsula, known humorously as Argyll's Bowling Green because of its rugged nature. With the neighbouring estate of Ardgartan it forms part of Argyll National Forest Park, owned by the City of Glasgow.

Ardrishaig *Argyll* (BJ 68). Village at E end of the Crinan Canal, which is now mainly used by small craft. The canal has 15 locks in 5 m., but superb scenery compensates for the effort involved.

Ardtornish Castle *Argyll* (BG 74). *See* **Lochaline.**

Arran* *Bute* (BK 63). Owing to the policy of the Hamilton family, the chief owners, this mountainous island has 'escaped' development. It now has the fastest-shrinking population of any Scottish island. Car ferries from Ardrossan or Fairlie, in Ayrshire, call at Brodick, and other steamers (summer only) at Lochranza. Brodick Castle, famous for Old Masters and its gardens, was once the ducal seat, but is now owned by the NT for Scot. Those making the ascent of Goatfell (2,866 ft.) are sometimes rewarded by magnificent views of the Clyde, Inner Hebrides and Irish coast. A good road encircles the island. King's Cross village and King's Cave (Blackwaterfoot) are named for The Bruce. Holy Island, containing the cave of St Molios and runic inscriptions, lies off Lamlash. The Tormore standing stones, remains of six prehistoric stone circles and other features, are 1 m. from Machrie on the W. coast. The Carn Ban, a stone-built chamber tomb, is at the head of Kilmory Water in the S, and a Celtic monastery site at Kilpatrick in the SW.

Ballachulish *Argyll* (CA 75). Loch Leven flows towards Loch Linnhe at great speed, but this famous car ferry makes the passage in safety. To the NE the Corran Ferry takes cars across to Ardgour on the opposite side of Loch Linnhe.

Bridge of Orchy *Argyll* (CC 73). After passing the watershed between the North Sea and the Atlantic, the road from Glasgow to Fort William keeps the railway on the right and drops to Glen Orchy, haunt of fishermen.

Brodick *Bute* (CA 63). *See* **Arran.**

Bute (CA 66). Less spectacular than Arran, this island has a wide range of scenery and apart from the Royal Burgh of Rothesay, is little frequented. Car and passenger ferries from Wemyss Bay, and car ferry from Colintraive (CA 67). Fine rough country at N and S, with good sandy beaches at Ettrick Bay, Scalpsie Bay and Kilchattan Bay. Depends on agriculture, tourism and boatbuilding (at Ardmaleish and Port Bannatyne). The chapel of St Blain, and remains of a Celtic monastery, are in the S W, as is Dunagoil vitrified fort.

Campbeltown *Argyll* (BH 62) EC Wed (6,520). Royal burgh near S end of Kintyre, dependent on agriculture, rope-making and fishing. The Old Quay Head is notable for an elaborately carved 15th-cent. cross. Davaar Island at the mouth of the harbour has a cave in which Archibald Mackinnon, a local artist, painted the Crucifixion in 1887.

Carradale *Argyll* (BJ 63). Fishing village in sheltered bay, with lovely sands and good boating facilities.

Carrick Castle *Argyll* (CB 69). Romantic ruin of a stronghold of the Argyll clan on the shores of Loch Goil, burnt down by men of Atholl in the 17th cent.

Colintraive *Argyll* (CA 67). Car ferry to the Isle of Bute across the scenic Kyles of Bute, at a place where drovers years ago swam their cattle from the island.

Coll *Argyll* (BB 75). Island of small crofts reached by steamer from Oban. A ruined castle, lovely bays, good bathing and fishing. *See also* **Tiree**.

Colonsay *Argyll* (BD 69). Island connected with Oronsay at low tide. Reached by steamer from **Tarbert** (*see below*). The gardens of Lord and Lady Strathcona at Kiloran are on view during the summer, with azaleas and rhododendrons.

Connell Ferry *Argyll* (BK 73). A bridge now carries road travellers over the rapids made famous by Ossian as 'The Falls of Lora'. At very low tides the roar is deafening and daunting. Five m. to the N the twin-peaked hill of Benderloch may have been a Pictish capital, but a raised way between the peaks suggests Early Christian construction. Whichever it is, the summit gives a fine view. E of North Connel is 13th-cent. Ardchattan Priory, where Bruce's Parliament was one of the last to conduct business in Gaelic.

The Cumbraes *Bute* (CB 65). Two small islands off the Ayrshire coast. A Marine Biological Station combining Aquarium and Museum is on Great Cumbrae, near Keppel Pier. At Millport, on a beautiful sandy bay, stands the 'Cathedral of the Isles'. Car and passenger ferries from Wemyss Bay and passengers only from Largs or Fairlie on the mainland opposite.

Connel Ferry, at the entrance to Loch Etive *Aerofilms*

Glencoe: at the head of the Pass

Dalmally *Argyll* (CB 72). Situated on R. Orchy in delightful touring country. To the W the waters of Loch Awe rush headlong to Loch Etive and the sea. Ben Cruachan (3,689 ft.) looms above the Pass of Brander, where the MacDougals of Lorn were almost destroyed by Robert the Bruce.

Dunoon *Argyll* (CB 67) EC Wed (9,210). Deservedly popular resort, lively centre for road and steamer trips. Car ferry from Gourock. Holy Loch, famous submarine base, lies to the N opposite Sandbank. The botanic gardens of Benmore House, the Forestry Training School, (7 m. N) are open to the public (*see p.* S.72).

Dunstaffnage Castle★ *Argyll* (BJ 73). Magnificently placed on a sheer rock guarding the entrance to Loch Etive. The three round towers and 10-ft.-

thick walls of this rectangular stronghold are of the 15th cent., but tradition ascribes greater age to the ruins. A brass cannon salvaged from the Armada galleon sunk in Tobermory Bay is mounted on the ramparts. Robert the Bruce stormed the castle and Flora Macdonald was imprisoned here for a short time.

Gigha *Argyll* (BG 65). Small island off the W coast of Kintyre. A passenger ferry from Tayinloan on the mainland opposite calls at Ardminish and there are steamers from Tarbert. The gardens of Achamore House are worth seeing for their roses and flowering shrubs; they are on view during summer.

Glencoe★ *Argyll* (CB 75). Something of the dark events of 1692 seems to linger in this historic glen and yet contribute to its magnificence. Notices

699

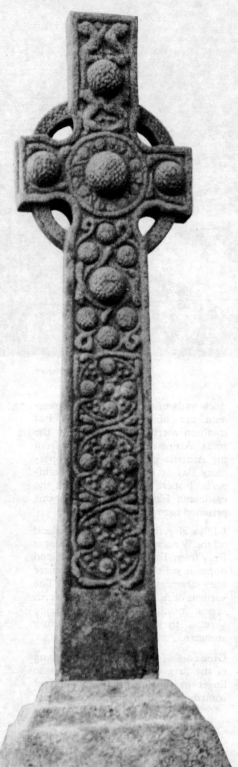

mark the site of the destroyed Macdonald homesteads. To the N a wall of rock, to the S 'naked crests fight to achieve the skies', and waters drop in cascades from the heights. The old winding route through the glen has been replaced by a good new road, which climbs beyond the watershed and over Rannoch Moor.

Holy Island (CA 62). *See* **Arran.**

Inveraray* *Argyll* (CA 70). Small but historic royal burgh situated on Loch Fyne and surrounded by beautiful woodlands. The massive castle greatly admired by Sir Walter Scott, and partly decorated by two of the Adam brothers, is built on the site of an earlier stronghold, and contains family portraits of the Argylls by Old Masters, historic relics, plate and tapestry. A 17th-cent. dovecote at Carlunan, 1 m. walk through the Castle grounds, is attractive, and so are the Falls of Aray (3¼ m.). Sir Walter Scott, R. L. Stevenson and the local novelist, Neil Munro, are amongst the writers who have used Inveraray as background for stirring tales. (*See also p. 694*).

Iona* *Argyll* (BC 72). This tiny isle off the SW corner of Mull (passenger ferry from Fionnphort and steamers from Oban in summer) was sacred to the Druids long before the missionary landing of St Columba in A.D. 563. Even Dr Johnson, never notably a lover of Scotland, remarked that 'the man is little to be envied . . . whose piety would not grow warmer among the ruins of Iona'. Norsemen continually pillaged the monastery, but it was later restored by the Scottish Queen Margaret, and early in the 13th cent. the Lord of the Isles founded

Iona: St Martin's Cross   Reece Winstone

a Benedictine abbey. This building was restored by the Church of Scotland in c.1905. The Chapel of St Oran on the supposed site of St Columba's cell has also been restored, and the nunnery Priory is well preserved. Since 1938 the Iona Community, a religious brotherhood for the training of students, has excavated and restored sites and buildings. Reilig Odhrain (the burial place of Kings) is believed to contain the remains of over sixty monarchs, including MacBeth and his victim, but their monuments were thrown into the sea at the time of the Reformation. Of 360 fine crosses known to have stood here, three remain: St John's Cross (9th cent.), St Martin's Cross (10th cent.) and Maclean's Cross (15th cent.).

Islay* *Argyll* (BD 65). The most southerly island of the Hebrides, reached by air (from Renfrew airport, Glasgow), steamer (from Tarbert, BJ 66) and car ferry from Kennacraig (West Loch Tarbert). From Port Ellen a good road system serves the island. A deep indentation almost divides the Rhinns district from Oa Peninsula, named after a legendary Danish princess, and shelters Bowmore (BD 65), a fascinating fishing village with a curious round church (18th cent.) at the head of the main street. U.S. troops lost from the *Tuscania* and the *Otranto* in 1918 are commemorated at Port Charlotte and Machir Bay.

Jura *Argyll* (BF 68). An island of great scenic beauty but poor in roads and tourist accommodation. Passenger ferry from Islay; steamers from Tarbert call at Craighouse (BF 66). The conspicuous breast-like Paps are each over 2,000 ft. high. To the N, though not easily accessible, the thunderous Corryvreckan whirlpool is a notorious menace to ships.

Kilchurn Castle *Argyll* (BK 70).

Strikingly situated 15th-cent. fortress reached from Loch Awe village. One tower was blown down by the 'Tay Bridge' gale of 1879.

Kilmartin *Argyll* (BJ 69). Picturesque village with a badly mutilated Celtic Cross and medieval sculptured stones in the churchyard. The ruins of 16th-cent. Carnassarie Castle lie 1½ m. to the N. The Hill of Dunadd (c. 500–850), 4 m. S, was the capital of an ancient kingdom, designated by carvings of a boar and a footprint at the summit. Fine view of Jura across the Sound.

Kyles of Bute* (BK 67). The narrow straits between Argyll and Bute, with some of the most enchanting scenery of the Firth of Clyde. *See also* **Colintraive** and **Tighnabruaich**.

Lamlash *Bute* (CA 63). *See* **Arran**.

Lismore *Argyll* (BJ 74). A long, flat island in the centre of Loch Linnhe, reached by passenger ferry from Port

Lismore lighthouse *J. Allan Cash*

Appin or steamer from Oban. The 18th-cent. Parish Church incorporates part of an early cathedral. Excavations have exposed the nave and site of its W tower. The ruins of the episcopal castle of Auchindown perch on the rocky W coast.

Lochaline *Argyll* (BG 74). On the Morven coast, facing Mull. Ardtornish Castle*, ancient home of the Lords of the Isles, overhangs the sea and is backed by cliffs and waterfalls which captured Sir Walter Scott's imagination. Silica sands for the making of optical glass have brought local employment.

Lochgilphead *Argyll* (BJ 68). The administrative capital of Argyll. Situated at the head of Loch Gilp near Dunadd, the crowning place of the kings of Dalriada.

Loch Leven *Argyll* (CB 76). Should not be confused with the Loch Leven of Mary Queen of Scots' flight from captivity (which is in Kinross-shire). Beautiful mountain scenery from lakeside road. At the head of the loch stands Kinlochleven's aluminium works.

Loch Leven, Argyllshire

Aerofilms

Oban

J. Allan Cash

Machrihanish *Argyll* (BG 62). Famous golf course on sand dunes facing open Atlantic. Airport on Campbeltown road.

Mull* *Argyll* (BG 73). Island of sea lochs and scenery rising to Ben More (3,169 ft.). Reached by steamer (cars carried) from Oban. Beloved of many, though Dr Johnson considered it 'worse than Skye'! Stevenson chose it for the escape of David Balfour in *Kidnapped*. One hundred miles of (rather poor) roads maintain touch with a fascinatingly indented coast culminating in the S with the granite cliffs of the Ross of Mull. Access by boat to **Iona** (*see above*). *See also* **Tobermory** *below*.

Oban* *Argyll* (BJ 73). EC Thurs (6,860). Centre of a network of steamer services linking the islands with the mainland, so that the comings and goings of islanders with provisions

crops and livestock create fascinating movement in this busy fishing port. Headquarters of the Royal Highland Yacht Club. Other sports well catered for. The ivy-clad keep of ruined Dunollie Castle stands above Loch Linnhe; the key is obtainable at Dunollie House, which proudly cherishes the Brooch of Lorne wrested from Bruce in a fight, and later returned to the MacDougalls. The cathedral (1932) was designed by Sir Giles Scott.

Oronsay *Argyll* (BD 68). A small island at the S of Colonsay, separated from it except at low tide. Remains of Augustinian priory of obscure origin, with cloisters similar to those in Saxon foundations in England. Finely executed 16th-cent. Cross with relief of Crucifixion. Recently restored Prior's House contains a collection of interesting tomb slabs.

Port Appin *Argyll* (BK 74). Delightful village on Loch Linnhe. Passenger ferry to Lismore. The Appin district was the scene of a famous murder of a Campbell in 1752, for which James Stewart of the Glens was hanged.

Rest and Be Thankful *Argyll* (CC 70). Highest point (860 ft.) on the old road from Loch Long which climbs through Glen Croe's wild scenery overlooked by 'The Cobbler' or Ben Arthur (2,891 ft.). The modern road has ironed out the worst of the bends and gradients.

Rothesay* *Bute* (CA 66). EC Wed (6,700). Capital of Bute and popular Clyde summer resort. The moated Castle*, conquered by Norsemen in the 13th cent., was originally circular in plan, with four towers. Worth seeing are Bute Museum, the 17th-cent. Mansion House and the ancient church of St Mary containing two 14th-cent. canopied tombs. Within easy access are the fine sandy beaches of Ettrick Bay and Kilchattan Bay.

Saddell *Argyll* (BH 63). Early 16th-cent. castle, and remains of a Cistercian monastery founded before 1207.

Seil *Argyll* (BH 71). Small island separated from the mainland by a narrow sound the width of a small river, and connected with it by the hump-backed Clachan Bridge 'over the Atlantic' (2½ m. NE of Balvicar).

Skipness *Argyll* (BJ 65). Panoramic views of Arran, Bute and Kilbrannan Sound. Remains of ruined church of St Columba and castle.

Southend *Argyll* (BG 60). Traditional landing-place of St Columba, within sight of Ireland. The golf course is near ruined Dunaverty Castle, where in 1647 Macdonald forces were overcome by shortage of water and butchered by Campbells.

Staffa* *Argyll* (BD 73). Uninhabited island with perpendicular cliffs S and W. Can be visited by steamer from Oban; landings may be made in calm weather to explore the basalt rocks which match those of Antrim's Giant's Causeway. Fingal's Cave, the most imposing of many, is 227 ft. long and correspondingly high, with grotesque formations which inspired Mendelssohn's music.

Tarbert *Argyll* (BJ 66). The E and W Lochs are separated by a mile of isthmus across which King Magnus (11th cent.) dragged his galley. The headquarters of Loch Fyne fishing. East Loch Tarbert is overlooked by a ruined castle once inhabited by James II of Scotland. Centre for steamer services to Islay, Jura, Gigha and Colonsay.

Tighnabruaich *Argyll* (BK 67). Small, delightful holiday resort and yachting centre on the **Kyles of Bute.**

Tiree *Argyll* (AK 74). The ancients said this was a kingdom whose 'summits were lower than the waves'. Windswept but fertile, specialising in bulb-growing. Quarries of unusual marble, pink spotted with green. Golf course and airport. Access by air from Renfrew airport, Glasgow, or by steamer from Oban. *See also* **Coll.** Ten m. W is the isolated Skerryvore lighthouse.

Tobermory *Argyll* (BF 75). Sheltered quayside resort and chief centre for the Isle of Mull. Many attempts have been made to recover the supposed treasure from the hold of the Spanish galleon sunk in the bay by a Scottish hostage in 1588. Golf course. *See also* **Mull.**

Opposite: Detail from the original painting by Maurice Wilson.
Wild life is found here in abundant habitation of land and water: salmon in the turbulent streams; red deer and wild-cats the soaring buzzard and the wandering gannet. The Scots pine is native, but forests of foreign spruce are widely planted, and rhododendrons flourish.

Loch Tay and Ben Lawers
Scottish Tourist Board

THE
SOUTH HIGHLANDS

Perth and Angus

AN INTRODUCTION BY WILFRED TAYLOR

The Highlands are defined as that part of Scotland (except for Caithness and the Buchan peninsula in Aberdeenshire) lying north of a line drawn from Helensburgh on the Clyde to Stonehaven on the North Sea, a few miles south of Aberdeen. This Highland line runs south-west to north-east, and almost three-quarters of it is in either Perthshire or Angus, the greater part of each county lying north of it, where the Grampian Mountains sweep up to heights of 3,500 feet or more. The main road north from Perth through the Grampians, the A9, follows the Tay and then the tumbling River Garry, to cross into Inverness-shire by the Drumochter Pass at 1,506 feet.

The Highland line is followed through all of Angus and much of Perthshire by the low-lying valley of Strathmore, which in the latter swells south-eastward to the Ochil Hills on the county boundary and in the former to the Sidlaw Hills. These (which extend some way into Perthshire also) are separated from the

Opposite: Detail from the original painting by Thomas Swimmer.

The foreground of this composite Tayside landscape represents some of the traditional exports of Perth and Dundee: cattle, marmalade, jute (used in the making of canvas, cordage, and sacking). The corner of MacGregor tartan recalls the free-booter Rob Roy, whose grave is in Balquhidder. The area is rich in historic buildings, such as Glamis Castle, the most romantic inhabited castle in Scotland.

Firth of Tay by another low-lying fertile strip, the Carse of Gowrie. Except for the clay in the vales and in the coastal strip of Angus, much of the soil in both counties is poor and suitable only for such growth as heather, bracken, silver birch and conifers – though often enough the scenery is magnificent, especially by loch or river side. In the Grampians, metamorphic and volcanic rocks rise to more than fifty peaks of over 3,000 feet. The Ochils, also volcanic, exceed 2,000 feet and are crossed through Glen Devon at 730 feet by the A823 to Gleneagles and Crieff. In contrast, the Sidlaw Hills, reaching 1,400 feet, are of Old Red Sandstone, a rock which gives fine coastal scenery north of Arbroath.

Perthshire

Perthshire, one of the largest of the Scottish counties, is roughly circular in shape and it offers an astonishing variety of scenery, from the bleak mountains in the north to the gentle and sweetly flowing Allan Water in the south. It is an entirely inland county, its margins at no point touching the open sea, a county of lofty mountains, rushing rivers, woodlands and romantic lochs. With, in its heartland, the incomparable Loch Tay, Loch Lubnaig, Loch Earn and Loch Tummel, it offers the nearest thing in Scotland to a Lake District. And through it flows the longest, most handsome and most majestic of Scottish rivers, the Tay, which as it approaches its estuary under craggy ramparts to the east of Perth has reminded many a visitor of the Rhine. With its high mountains, lonely glens and impressive ravines, Perthshire is essentially a dramatic county. But it has little of the wild drama of northern counties like Ross-shire: there is a gentle and settled atmosphere about it – a gentleness in stark contrast with savage battles once fought on its moors and by its rivers.

Undoubtedly the district most famous for beauty in Perthshire, if not in the whole of Scotland, is the Trossachs, in the extreme south-west of the county. This is a richly wooded gorge extending from Loch Achray to Loch Katrine, with Ben Venue, 2,393 feet, to the south and Ben A'an, 1,750 feet, to the north. It can be approached by car only from Callander to the east or from Aberfoyle to the south, since the road along Loch Katrine may be used by pedestrians only. The whole district is incredibly lovely – and its loveliness has been nowhere better described than in Sir Walter Scott's *Lady of the Lake* and *Rob Roy*.

Perth, the county town and the setting of Scott's *Fair Maid of Perth*, has all the appearance of a miniature capital. Lying mostly to the west of the Tay, which rolls under a number of graceful bridges, the town is fortunate in the possession of two vast green meadows, the North and the South Inch. It was on the North Inch that the last clan battle took place in Scotland. Here the Clan Kay and the Clan Chattan engaged in bitter and annihilating conflict, from which it is said only one man of Clan Kay escaped, by swimming the river, and less than a dozen of Clan Chattan—which was therefore awarded the victory. Nowadays the only strife of any consequence witnessed on the North Inch is when Perthshire county cricket club plays its rivals on one of the most pleasing cricket greens in the whole of Scotland.

Although its church spires and Georgian houses remind one of the antiquity of Perth, it has also recently built a modern and harmonious town centre. As the centre of an agricultural county Perth is an important centre for farmers, and its winter bull sales, which attract buyers from far overseas, add to the social life of the town, as do the Perth Hunt races run in the autumn. In addition to bleaching, dyeing and textile industries, it also boasts one of the largest

J. Allan Cash **On Loch Katrine in the Tross**

distilleries in Scotland. Nor does it neglect the arts: it has its own repertory theatre in which have played some of the liveliest companies in Scotland, and its art gallery houses an interesting collection.

Apart from Perth itself, there are a number of interesting little towns like Aberfeldy, Crieff, Callander and Dunblane. Of these the best known is Pitlochry, about 27 miles north of Perth on the A9 to Inverness. Lying in the richly wooded valley of the River Tummel, with the shapely peak of Ben Vrackie (2,757 feet) towering behind it, Pitlochry is an excellent touring-centre for such sights as the Queen's View (Victoria, it was), the Falls of Tummel or the Black Spout waterfall, the Pass of Killiecrankie and, indeed, for much of the best part of Perthshire. Its own attractions have been increased in recent years by two local developments. As part of a hydro-electric scheme, the waters of the Tummel have been harnessed by the construction of a dam on the outskirts of the town, creating the new Loch Faskally, which stretches up into the wooded hills. A big salmon-ladder has also been built, with a glass-sided observation-chamber underneath one of its steps, from which visitors can watch the salmon pausing on their climb up to the spawning-beds. And secondly, the 'Theatre in the Hills', founded shortly after the war by the late Mr John Stewart, who spent his entire fortune on it, now attracts thousands of visitors to Pitlochry every summer with its repertory of plays.

One of the charms of the county is its little, quiet villages, like Caputh or Inchture, with their whitewashed timbered houses and old-fashioned gardens. For lovers of trees, flowers, and of wild life in general, Perthshire offers endless possibilities. Rare plants are not unknown, and the higher slopes of Ben Lawers, in particular, are a favourite resort for botanists. Just outside the little church in Fortingall, right in the heart of Perthshire, there stands an ancient yew tree. It is popularly described as the most ancient example of vegetation in Europe, its age put at roughly 3,000 years. Fortingall, a pretty, trim hamlet lying at the foot of one of Scotland's longest glens, Glenlyon, also claims to be the northernmost point reached by the Roman legionaries. Legend has it that Pontius Pilate was born in Fortingall, while his father was there with an embassy. It is said that when a Fortingall man was asked if this was true he replied laconically, 'Aye, his mither was a Balquhidder wumman'. Balquhidder is another lovely village in central Perthshire, closely associated with the celebrated Scottish hero or rogue, Rob Roy.

The county abounds in historic buildings, and whether it is Blair Castle or the unexpected little public library on a loop of the River Earn at Innerpeffray, there is always something to fascinate the student of antiquity. Ecclesiastical architecture is to be found in great variety, from the cathedral churches at Dunkeld and Dunblane to the simple little churches at Kenmore or Struan.

With its abundance of lochs, rivers and burns, Perthshire is a favourite county for fishermen, who can take the choice of slipping up to some lonely little lochan in the hills or of renting one of the most expensive beats on the Tay near Stanley. In recent years sailing and water-skiing have become popular, especially on Loch Earn, where the Scottish water-skiing championships are held. In winter and spring, crowds of sportsmen flock to Ben Lawers at the week-end to ski. In all, it is a county of extraordinary richness and contrast – a county that wears its beauty serenely and enchantingly. Perhaps one can best respond to its spell by going to Loch Faskally on a bright, golden autumn day when the leaves in all their glory offer a breath-taking kaleidoscope of colour.

Trossachs: above Loch Achray   *J. Allan Cash*

Angus

Angus, a square and lumpish county, is contiguous with Perthshire on its western frontiers, but is totally different in atmosphere. Although it penetrates deeply into the southern Grampians, Angus is a maritime county. After its secluded passage through Perthshire, the River Tay, before it finally contracts between Dundee and Newport, to burst into the North Sea, puffs out its chest and in its tidal pride claims a breadth of about four miles to the opposite shore of Fife.

Angus is one of the most beautiful counties in Scotland; but no one could claim that Dundee, its metropolis, Scotland's third city in terms of population, resembles Florence. Though it is the portal to some of the finest scenery in Scotland, it does little to lure the tourist. However, recently the town centre has been cleared and a new shopping centre, incorporating the Angus Hotel, has been built. This reconstruction has considerably improved the town. In some ways it is a commercial and financial centre of the utmost importance. In the past, astute Dundee financiers did a great deal to open up the cattle lands of the American south-west.

Largely dependent on jute, the city was badly hit during the early thirties. After the last war it lifted itself out of the rut largely by strenuous local effort, and American industry was attracted to the industrial estates on the Kingsway. The young jute men sponsored great modernization projects; and now the new Queen's College, with its miniature skyscraper tower, dominates the intellectual life of Dundee in a brisk and ambitious way. For the rest, textiles, confectionery, engineering and linoleum comprise most of its industries.

But Dundee is not Angus. Angus is a county of little towns like Forfar, Kirriemuir, Brechin, Arbroath and Edzell, a county of pretty little villages like Cortachy and rock-bound Auchmithie. It is a rich and fertile farming county, traversed by the broad vale of Strathmore, with its fat farms and enchanting vistas of the Grampian rim. In its fields you will see the black, hornless Aberdeen-Angus cattle, which give, in the opinion of many good judges, the best beef in the world. It is, too, a county of romantic castles. Best known of these is Glamis, where Princess Margaret was born. Angus people are forthright and straightforward in their speech. They are men who love the soil and brook no nonsense. And Angus has its poets, writing in the rich vernacular, like Violet Jacob, Marion Angus and Sir Alexander Gray; and its authors, like Lewis Grassic Gibbon, whose prose runs to the lilt of the spoken Scots. Over Angus there is a lurid glow of theological memories, and near Invergowrie there is a rock in the shallows of the Tay which all decent Dundee children firmly believe was thrown, somewhat inaccurately, by the Devil in a tantrum at the parish kirk in Invergowrie. Sir James Barrie, probably the most famous Angus writer, (you can see his birthplace at Kirriemuir, the original 'Thrums') well knew the power of the kirk in the old days in Angus. The power of the minister to expose and humiliate transgressors was formidable.

Angus abounds in golden beaches and links – its golf courses are legendary, from the inland courses at Brechin, Kirriemuir and Forfar, to the seaside Carnoustie course, where the Open Championship has frequently taken place. But, best of all, Angus is the county of lonely lovely glens. Their names make music – Glenisla, Glen Prosen, Glen Clova, Glen Doll, Glenogil, Glenesk. These glens wind deeply into the hills (the famous Braes of Angus), and with their little farmhouses, their kirks, their inns, and their charming mansion houses and

Glamis Castle *Aerofilms*

castles they are an invitation to peace of mind. To those who want to feel sun-
burned with contentment there is nothing like those green, pastoral, mountain-
walled valleys. Go up Glenesk, for instance, as this writer did, and stop at the
little schoolhouse at Tarfside to watch the children, in their soft voices, rehears-
ing a poetic play written for them by the Angus poet, Helen Cruickshank, about
the animals they know, and you will not long for the West End. Or, if you are a
geologist, the rocks and glacial valleys of Angus will keep you busy. An antiquarian? Visit the little local folk museums and see how Angus folk in the past
lived, worked and amused themselves. A lover of landscape? Drive up Glen
Clova on a summer evening, up one side of the river and back by the other, and
you will experience a wonderful uplift of the spirits.

Angus is not a very sophisticated county. Essentially it is a county for those
who love the open air. You can play your golf on some of the finest courses in
the world; you can fish in wonderful rivers and lochs; you can swim in the pools

at Arbroath or from almost deserted beaches; you can climb up rock faces, or you can ski in appropriately named Glen Shee. You will be well catered for – mostly in unpretentious hotels specialising in homely food. But if you like a bracing wind in your face, and if you like the purple heather in lonely glens, if you like to stand on bridges and watch a brown burn purling over strewn boulders, if you thrill to the sight of deer silhouetted on a mountain ridge, if you like to listen to authentic Scottish voices, Angus is a peerless county.

Some houses and gardens open to the public

Blair Castle Blair Atholl *Map* CJ 76. *Imposing baronial mansion in superb scenery. See also p. 713.* The Duke of Atholl.

Doune Castle *Map* CH 70. *One of the best-preserved medieval castles in Scotland. See also p. 714.* The Earl of Moray.

Edzell Castle 6m N of Brechin *Map* D F 76. *16th-cent. castle with Renaissance garden. See also p. 716.* Ministry of Public Building and Works.

Glamis Castle *Map* D D 74. *Ancient and historic castle. See p. 717.* The Earl of Strathmore and Kinghorne.

Guthrie Castle *Map* D F 75. *15th-cent. castle on site of earlier stronghold. Unique 15th-cent. mural paintings. Renowned gardens (wild garden best late May and early June). Beautiful Walled Garden best from July onwards.* Col. Guthrie of Guthrie.

Books for further reading

Topography

I. F. ANDERSON *Loch Lomond and the Trossachs* 1934
G. CHRISTIE *Crieff Hydro 1869–1968* 1967
J. CORMACK *Forfarshire* 1912
V. A. FIRSOFF *In the Hills of Breadalbane* 1954
A. R. B. HALDANE *New Ways through the Glens* 1962
M. S. JOHNSTON *The County of Angus* 1939
H. MILES *Fair Perthshire* 1930
C. NAIRNE *The Trossachs and the Rob Roy Country* 1961
J. STIRTON *Glamis Castle* 1938
N. TRANTER *The Fortified House in Scotland*, Vol. II 1963

Scenery, geology and natural history

W. GARDINER *The Flora of Forfarshire* 1848
J. D. T. GRAY *Wild Nature in Strathearn* 1902
J. A. HARVIE-BROWN *A Fauna of the Tay Basin and Strathmore* 1906
D. G. HUNTER *Birds from Angus and the Far North* 1934
P. MCNAIR *Geology and Scenery of the Grampians* 1908

NT FOR SCOTLAND *Ben Lawers and its Alpine Flowers*
K. A. PYEFINCH *Trout in Scotland* 1960
F. WALKER *Tayside Geology* 1961
F. B. W. WHITE *The Flora of Perthshire* 1898

The 'feel' of the South Highlands

C. GIBSON *Folklore of Tayside* 1960
A. R. B. HALDANE *The Path by the Water* 1944
W. PATON *Hame Links* 1930
SIR J. WILSON *Lowland Scotch* 1915
J. M. YOUNG *A Dog at my Heels* 1951

History

P. R. DRUMMOND *Perthshire in Byegone Days* 1879
R. S. FITTIS *Chronicles of Perthshire* 1877
W. A. GILLIES *In Famed Breadalbane* 1938
J. HUNTER and others *Chronicles of Strathearn* 1896
T. HUNTER *Woods, Forests and Estates of Perthshire* 1883
W. MARSHALL *Historic Scenes in Forfarshire* 1875, *Historic Scenes in Perthshire* 1881
L. MELVILLE *The Fair Land of Gowrie* 1939

Gazetteer

THE SOUTH HIGHLANDS

Perth and Angus

Blair Castle　　　　　*J. Allan Cash*

Aberfeldy* *Perth* (CJ 74). A most attractive town on the Urlar Burn near its junction with the Tay. A delightful walk upstream along the Burn brings you to the three Falls of Moness. A cairn near General Wade's fine bridge over the Tay marks the place of enrolment in 1739 of the *Frecadan Dubh*, or Black Watch, whose duty it was to watch the Highlanders. An excellent nature trail (botany, trees and wild life) has been laid out at The Birks.

Aberfoyle *Perth* (CF 70). Small resort on the edge of **The Trossachs** *(see below)*. Popular with visitors from Glasgow and Scott enthusiasts who cherish associations with *Rob Roy*.

Abernethy *Perth* (DB 71). One of the three Round Towers of Scotland (similar in shape to those in Ireland) survives from a history which goes far back to Pictish and monastic community life.

Alyth *Perth* (DC 74). Busy small town at the foot of the Braes of Angus, with a burn running down the centre of the main street. Iron Age camp on Barry Hill (2 m. E). Airlie Castle (4 m. NE) incorporates remains of the 'Bonnie House o' Airlie' burnt by Argyll in 1640 and avenged by Montrose.

Arbroath *Angus* (DG 73) EC Wed (19,530). Industrial town and seaside resort convenient to Dundee. In the ruins of the fine old 12th–13th-cent. red-sandstone Abbey* see the unusual window named the 'O' of Arbroath, in which a beacon could be lit for the guidance of ships at sea. The Abbot's House has a fine kitchen and hall (restored), which functions as a Museum. St Vigean's Church (1½ m. N), of the 11th cent. but unrecognisably over-restored, contains early sculptured stones and the celebrated Drosten Stone which combines the Pictish language with Roman lettering.

Ardoch *Perth* (CJ 70). Extensive Roman encampment capable of accommodating over 30,000 men, the most perfect and clear example of Roman earthworks in Britain.

Balquhidder *Perth* (CF 72). Undoubted burial place of Robert MacGregor (Rob Roy), though the gravestones ascribed to him and his family appear to be of an earlier date.

Blair Atholl *Perth* (CJ 76). Imposing and dazzlingly white Blair Castle*, of various dates since the 13th cent., is the seat of the Duke of Atholl, who has the unique privilege of being permitted to retain a private army—the Atholl Highlanders. The Castle, with

713

its fine collection of historical relics and pictures, and its parkland, is open to the public.

Blairgowrie *Perth* (DB 74) EC Thurs (5,150). Though on the edge of the Highlands, this sheltered district is famous for soft fruit—raspberries in particular. Painting by Caravaggio in the Episcopal Church.

Brechin *Angus* (DF 76) EC Wed (7,110). Restoration work of 1901 has done much to atone for the barbarous demolition of the transepts of the Cathedral nearly a hundred years earlier. An 'Irish' Round Tower attached to the masonry of the cathedral tapers to a conical roof added in the 14th cent. Two prehistoric forts, the Brown and White Caterthuns (5½ m. NW), give a splendid view of the Grampians.

Broughty Ferry *Angus* (DE 73) EC Wed (12,520). Residential seaside suburb of Dundee much patronised by travellers from that city, and popular with holidaymakers. Permanent exhibition of Scottish Art in Orchar Gallery. Affleck Castle (6 m. NE) is a 15th-cent. tower-house with rooms still in good condition (open weekdays).

Cairnwell Pass *Perth* (DB 77). The highest point on any main road in Britain (2,199 ft.) lies between mountains a thousand feet higher. The Devil's Elbow to the S has severe gradients and sharp hairpin turns.

Callander *Perth* (CG 70). In proportion to its size has more good hotels than any other Scottish village. Centre for **The Trossachs** and the wonderful country of Sir Walter Scott's *Lady of the Lake.*

Carnoustie *Angus* (DF 73) EC Tues (5,500). Famous golf links and seaside resort. The sandbanks at Buddon Ness, at the mouth of the Tay, are a haunt of wildfowl. Ever since the flight of the Earl to France in 1715 the gates of Panmure House (1½ m.) have remained closed.

Comrie *Perth* (CH 72). Stands at the junction of two glens over the geological fault between the Highlands and the Lowlands, from which the rumble of harmless earthquakes is frequently heard. The beautiful castellated steeple of the Old Parish Church remains unaffected by these subterranean disturbances.

Coupar Angus *Perth* (DC 73). Named thus to distinguish it from Cupar in Fife, though it actually lies inside Perthshire. Traces of Cistercian abbey in churchyard. Very interesting earth-house at Pitcur (2 m. S) – key at Hallyburton House.

Crianlarich *Perth* (CD 72). Rail and road junction near mountainous border with Argyllshire. St Fillan's Pool (3 m. NW) provided old-time kill-or-cure treatment for the mentally deranged. The A82 south to Loch Lomond (7 m.) leads through the beautiful Glen Falloch.

Crieff *Perth* (CJ 72) EC Wed (5,592). Pleasant town with good hotel accommodation, at junction of two scenic roads. Antiquities include a fine Mercat Cross† with Runic carving, and cup and ring stones on the golf course. Drummond Castle (3 m. S) has formal terraced gardens open to the public, and a contemporary (1630) multiple sundial.

Doune Castle *Perth* (CH 70). Almost impregnable 15th-cent. stronghold* protected by two rivers and a moat. Entrance to courtyard through the

---

† Market cross or proclamation place.

great tower. Splendid example of Scottish medieval architecture. Doune itself was once the centre of a flourishing pistol-making industry.

Dunblane *Perth* (CH 70) EC Wed (3,500). The Cathedral (12th–15th cent.) is on the site of the Celtic church of St Blane, after which the town takes its name. Note especially the Celtic stone (c. AD 900) in the north aisle, the effigies of the 5th Earl of Strathearn and his Countess (1271) and the W window (to be seen only from outside) which was greatly praised by John Ruskin, and six carved stalls in the nave. The Cathedral Museum in the Dean's House, and Bishop Leighton's Library, which contains original 17th-cent. fittings and contemporary books, are both of great interest.

Dundee *Angus* (DD 73) EC Wed (183,000). Progressive city and port on the Firth of Tay, exporting more than the traditional 'jute, jam and journalists'. Prosperity is reflected in fine civic buildings, notably Caird Hall, which covers 2 acres. The 156-ft. Old Steeple, near the single roof of the three City Churches, is the one antiquity of importance. Rapidly expanding Queen's College has now become the independent University of Dundee. For a good view of

Doune Castle

Aerofilms

Dunkeld Cathedral

the city, docks and estuary of the Tay, go to the War Memorial on Dundee Law (571 ft.). Car ferry across the Tay to Newport (pending the construction of the new Tay road bridge). Five m. W, off the A85, is the 15th-cent. Castle Huntly. *See also* **Tay Bridge.**

Dunkeld *Perth* (DA 74). Very old and beautiful cathedral★ set on lawns beside the Tay. The 14th-cent. choir has been restored for use as the Parish Church. Roads follow both banks of the Tay and the Tummel to Pitlochry. An excellent nature trail (mainly trees) has been laid out at The Hermitage.

Dunsinane *Perth* (DC 73). Ancient fort at 1,012 ft. in Sidlaw Hills,

traditional site of Macbeth's castle to which 'Birnam Wood came'.

Edzell Castle★ *Angus* (DF 76). The Bower in the square Stirling Tower was frequented by Mary Queen of Scots. The Renaissance formal garden below the keep has walls showing allegorical subjects in low relief, and a turreted garden house in one corner.

Forfar★ *Angus* (DE 75) EC Thurs (10,250). Capital of the county, and a centre of the jute industry. An octagonal turret marks the site of the castle in which the Parliament of 1057 conferred surnames on Scottish noblemen. The Town Hall exhibits a specimen of the 'Forfar bridle', a gag for the witches who were so prevalent (and persecuted) in this region. Restenneth Priory (1½ m. E) is notable for having an 18th-cent. spire built over a 12th-cent. upper storey, itself in turn built over the remains of a 9th-cent. tower.

Fortingall *Perth* (CH 74). The upper part of Glen Lyon, the longest glen in Scotland (30 m.), has been greatly changed by the Breadalbane hydro-electric scheme, and some of the landmarks of historic clan warfare have disappeared. The yew tree in Fortingall churchyard is credited with 3,000 years; a trunk circumference of 56 ft. was recorded in 1772. (*See also p.* s.85).

Glamis Castle★★ *Angus* (DD 74). Probably the most attractive and evocative inhabited castle in Scotland, mainly 17th-cent. baronial style, but going back a thousand years in history. The seat of the Earls of Strathmore, forbears of the Queen Mother, and birthplace of Princess Margaret. Sir Walter Scott is chiefly responsible for perpetuating the story of a secret room known only to each heir. Armour, portraits, tapestries and fine furniture, as well as picturesque gardens. The view from the battlements is superb. The Angus Folk Museum in the village has an interesting collection of domestic and agricultural implements.

Gleneagles★ *Perth* (CK 71). Internationally renowned for its hotel and its fine golf course. There is no village. St Mungo's Chapel, higher up the glen, contains monuments of the Haldanes, whose family seat was built in 1624 from the stones of their ancestral castle.

Huntingtower Castle *Perth* (DA 72). Named Ruthven until all mention of that family was proscribed as a result of the Gowrie Conspiracy in 1600. The two 15th-cent. towers are joined by a later building which includes a great hall notable for wall and ceiling painting. The gap between the towers is the 'Maiden's Leap' of legend.

Innerpeffray *Perth* (CJ 71). Scotland's first public library, founded 1691.

Kenmore *Perth* (CH 74). Pretty village at lower end of Loch Tay, convenient for fishing, boating, touring and winter sports. Burns immortalised the view from the bridge by writing his appreciation over a fireplace in the inn. Taymouth Castle, previously a hospital for Polish officers, was the family seat of the Earls of Breadalbane, one of whom earned the gratitude of sportsmen by reintroducing the capercailzie (species of wood-grouse) to Scotland after it had become extinct in Britain.

Killiecrankie★ *Perth* (CK 76). A footpath from the car park leads down through the wooded gorge to the Soldier's Leap and the Bridge of Garry, every inch of which was fought over in the Highlanders' bloody victory over General Mackay's forces in 1691.

Killin *Perth* (CF 73). Village near the head of Loch Tay, not far from the junction of the Dochart and the Lochay. Sailing, and winter sports. Stronachlachan (1,708 ft.) rewards walkers with a magnificent view, but Ben Lawers (nearly 4,000 ft.) presents a greater challenge. Much of this country is NT property; the rare alpine plants should not be uprooted.

Kinloch Rannoch *Perth* (CG 75). Fishing centre at E end of Loch Rannoch, a natural loch which serves as a reservoir for part of the giant hydro-electric scheme that has altered the face of the country without detracting from the beauty of the mountains.

Kirriemuir★ *Angus* (DD 75) EC Thurs (3,480). Probably more people have heard of Sir James Barrie's

Thrums than of Kirriemuir, though it is decidedly a place in its own right and in the jute-manufacturing world. Number 9 Brechin Road, where Barrie was born, his grave, and many corners of the town made famous by him, are places of interest to lovers of his works.

Meigle *Perth* (DC 74). A small local museum contains 21 interesting carved Celtic stones found in or near the old churchyard.

Meikleour *Perth* (DB 73). The famous 580-yard beech hedge bordering the A93, planted 1746, is now nearly 90 ft. high.

Menteith, Lake of★ *Perth* (CF 69). The only 'lake' in Scotland. Mary Queen of Scots spent part of her childhood on Inchmahome, the largest of the three islands in the lake. The ruins

of 13th-cent. Inchmahome Priory are still to be seen.

Montrose *Angus* (DH 75) EC Wed (10,700). Ancient royal burgh from which Sir James Douglas embarked for the Holy Land carrying the heart of Bruce; where John Erskine of Dun established the first school in Scotland for the teaching of Greek (1534); where the great Marquess, James Graham, was born in 1612; and whence the Old Pretender fled by sea in 1716 at the collapse of the rebellion of the Earl of Mar. Now very popular as golfing and seaside resort.

Perth★ (DB 72) EC Wed (41,200). 'The Fair City', once the Scottish capital, and the scene of numerous historic events, is now prosperously occupied in dyeing, distilling and the marketing of cattle. It is built on the Tay between two green spaces, the

Hydro-electric scheme dam, near Pitlochry *Scottish Tourist Board*

The Trossachs: Loch Lubnaig near Callander

North and South Inches, one famous for the contest described in Scott's *Fair Maid*, and the other for those two great medieval sports: archery and witch-burning. John Knox preached his famous inflammatory sermon in the Church of St John in 1559, with the result that many of the churches of Scotland were 'purged of idolatry' – and of works of art beyond reclaim. Visitors will wish to see the Fair Maid's House in Curfew Row, now a crafts shop, with its quaint upstairs rooms. The Art Gallery and Museum in North St. contains paintings and antiques, as well as geological, zoological and botanical collections of special interest to travellers around the county. An excellent nature trail has been laid out at Kinnoull Hill.

Pitcairngreen *Perth* (DA 72). Delightful village on the Almond, which has been inspired to border its green with tall hedges clipped in the form of festoons.

Pitlochry* *Perth* (CK 75) EC Thurs (2,500). Claims to be the geographical centre of Scotland. Very lively resort, with Highland Games, sheep dog trials, golf, tennis, water sports and the go-ahead Festival Theatre (April–Oct.). Hydro-electric works have produced a new lake, Loch Faskally, with an underwater observation chamber* opening on to the Fish Ladder which thousands of salmon negotiate every year.

Sma' Glen *Perth* (CJ 72). Stony gorge 2 m. long on the road N from Crieff. An enormous flat stone (8 × 5 ft.) near the head of the glen is taken to mark the burial-place of Ossian, the legendary Gaelic bard.

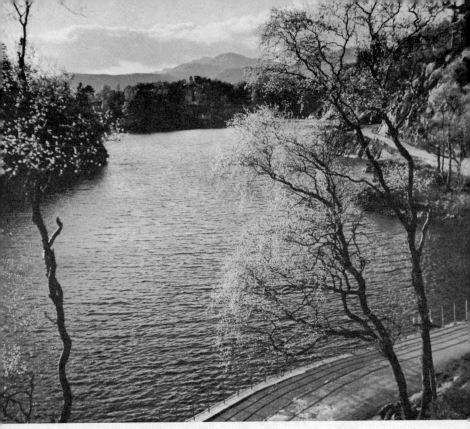

The Trossachs: Loch Katrine

J. Allan Cash

Tay Bridge (DD 72). Carries the main railway line from the south across the River Tay into Dundee. One of the longest railway bridges in the world – 2 m. long with 73 pairs of piers – it was built to replace the bridge blown down, along with a passenger-carrying train, in the 1879 disaster. The ferries have been discontinued, and the Tay Road Bridge is now in use – car tolls 2/6d.

The Trossachs ** *Perth* (CE 70). A wild, beautiful and tangled region, as shown by translation of its name: 'the bristly country'. The gorge leads from Loch Achray to beautiful Loch Katrine.

Tullibardine *Perth* (CK 71). Gives courtesy title of Marquis to the eldest sons of the Dukes of Atholl, who were Earls of Tullibardine before the dukedom was created. The chapel of the vanished castle has an interesting open roof, and has been used as a mausoleum.

Weem *Perth* (CJ 74). Castle Menzies, a good example of the Scottish baronial mansion, is not open to the public. The village inn is associated with General Wade, the great soldier-cum-engineer of the 18th cent. who was responsible for much of Scotland's road system and many beautiful bridges, with vast strategic, political and economic consequences.

The River Dee above Braemar

Allan Cash

NORTH-EAST SCOTLAND

Aberdeen, Kincardine, Banff, Moray, Nairn

AN INTRODUCTION BY JOHN R. ALLAN

The counties of Nairn, Moray, Banff, Aberdeen and Kincardine (the Mearns) have many local differences but a common character: they lie between the sea and the mountains. There is a continuous strip of ploughland, from a few to more than thirty miles wide, of the lowland sort which rises and thins away into sheep grazings and grouse moors. Then there is a steep ascent into the Grampians and the Cairngorms where the high tops are over 4,000 feet. So the roads through the cornland have blue water on one side and the near-blue mountains on the other, all the way from Nairn to the border of Angus at the North Esk. Lying far into the moors and lower slopes of the mountains there are the glens carved out by the rivers – the Nairn, the Findhorn, the Lossie, the noble Spey and its tributary the Avon, the Deveron, the Don, the Dee and the North Esk – glens that become narrower and emptier of people till they end in what fairly may be called highland country. Along the coast, just south of Peterhead and just south of Aberdeen, the farmland runs away into tremendous cliffs. So there is a great variety in this countryside, from the savage to the highly civilised. It is very much a land where men have imposed their will upon wild nature in a good sort of way, wherever they could.

The geology is complicated. For simplicity, the main divisions are: the Caledonian Granites, mostly in Aberdeenshire; Dalradian schists in Aberdeenshire and Banff; and Old Red Sandstone in the Howe of the Mearns, in some patches of Aberdeenshire and Banff, and in the coastal plain (The Laigh) of Moray and Nairn. In Aberdeenshire the overlying soils are very mixed owing to several periods of glacial action – several kinds of soil can be found on the same farm and even in the same field. The granite has been extensively quarried for building round Aberdeen, and sandstone near Elgin. The granite is a very hard clean stone, as may be seen in the town of Aberdeen.

Flora and fauna

In the high Cairngorms and Upper Glen Dee and Glen Derry there is a Nature Conservancy of about sixty square miles, rich in plants and wild life. In autumn the miles of heather spread a purple flush over the uplands which at other times may seem a little bare. Bracken has invaded too much hill pasture – a useless plant, but it dies to russet. The rosebay willow herb infests cut-over woodland, pretty enough and sending out clouds of seeds like drifting snow. The forests have suffered greatly in two wars; but the Forestry Commission have planted thousands of acres, mostly pines. There are still some noble hardwoods around the great houses, however. The silver birch, a very graceful creature, is a great volunteer in the cut-over, and the rowan (mountain ash) livens the glens with its clusters of red berries. At Culbin near Forres the Commission have established a forest on a vast area of drifting sand that smothered the farmland. Anyone interested in forestry and reclamation should go to see the work done there.

Red deer live on the hills and come to the low ground in winter – but even in summer they can be seen along the banks of the Dee between Balmoral Castle and Braemar. Foxes keep to the higher lands and are shot when they show themselves. There are plenty of hares and too many rabbits. The birds of the high ground are ptarmigan, golden eagles, black game, capercailzie, grouse, crossbill, siskin and the great spotted woodpecker. Oyster-catchers are becoming more common on the low ground. Wood-pigeons are a burden on the farms and the rooks are worse. At Hatton, near Turriff in Aberdeenshire, the rookery has about 6,000 nests and is the largest in Britain and perhaps anywhere. There are vast numbers of seabirds on the cliffs, that come inland and follow the plough. At Newburgh there is a delightful small bird sanctuary, and across the water on the Forvie Sands there are colonies of terns, besides shelduck and eider duck. Wild geese come in autumn to the estuaries, and there are often big flocks of whooper swans along the lower Don.

The coastline south of Stonehaven   *Aerofilms*

The climate

The natives are not enthusiastic about the climate – but then we are seldom enthusiastic about anything. In fact the climate is surprisingly good. It is rather a windy corner and the east winds are cold. But, for all that, Aberdeen is a very popular holiday place. Moray and Nairn are favoured places, always a little milder than the rest. Over the whole area the rainfall is low, about 32 inches a year. The great delight is the clarity of the air, in which all the world seems to have been swept clean, and the sunsets along the Moray Firth are magnificent as the sun goes down beyond the Ross-shire hills. It is a measure of the goodness of the climate that the grain and fruits ripen to the highest quality and that people survive it to a long age.

Industries

The chief industry is farming, which has been brought up to a high standard, in many places on land that seemed unpromising. The general pattern is that the largest arable farms are on the best land and the smallest on the poorest, which seems the wrong way round. You will find farms of 300 acres and more in the Howe of the Mearns, in central Aberdeenshire, in Banff and Moray. A common sort on poorer land is the family place of say 50 acres worked by the farmer and his family. There are many smaller ones which do not give a full-time job, so that the farmer works out. The larger ones are highly mechanised and nearly all the smaller ones have a tractor. The horse, the work-horse, has almost disappeared. The chief grain crops are oats, barley and wheat, and on the best lands the yields are high – over two tons an acre. The best of the barley goes to make the best of whisky. A lot of potatoes are grown, mostly for seed; and much more turnips, to feed stock. All those farmlands, on the low and the high ground, are famous for stock – the black Aberdeen-Angus, and the Shorthorn, and their crosses with other breeds. There are many thousands of sheep. Pigs are kept by the hundreds and hens by the thousands in conditions of excessive discomfort and restraint. The farms may look simple; but the operators in them can no longer afford to be so. However, you may find very primitive farming as well as the most sophisticated. It is as well not to go on first impressions.

Fishing is the second industry. All round the coast there are the fisher villages and towns, in coves with shelter and in some with none. Fishermen still live in the villages huddled against the wind by the open beaches, as at Inverallochy, or at the foot of the great cliffs, as at Pennan, which seems the end of the world; but they fish out from the big ports – Lossiemouth, Buckie, Peterhead, Fraserburgh and Aberdeen. The fortunes of those ports (except Aberdeen) were built on the herrings, which were silver from the sea. There are still many herrings caught; but there has been a change-over to the white fishing. The harbours at Peterhead and Fraserburgh are very busy and interesting when the herring drifters come in at morning. Aberdeen is a great white-fishing port, frequented by trawlers that go to the middle waters, and its fishmarket in the forenoon displays many strange wonders of the deep. Some of the fishing villages should be seen – but they may take some finding.

Industries live in these parts by skill, perseverance and high quality. There are famous textile mills at Grandholm near Aberdeen, at Huntly, Keith, Elgin and Peterhead, producing tweeds and knitwear famous in many parts of the world. Aberdeen has a great variety of industries, although it does not look like an industrial town. It has been famous for granite – especially from its Rubislaw Quarry, which is like a mountain in reverse, it is so deep. But the farming and the fishing give the north-east its distinctive character. Then there is the making of whisky. This is the art of making malt out of barley, using peat for firing; of brewing the malt in soft hill water, and then distilling the spirit. Each distillery produces its own distinctive spirit with its own flavour. Most of the spirit is blended to make the proprietary blends that are familiar on the market; but it is possible to get the matured whisky of one particular distillery, and that always carries the name of the distillery. The distilleries are not impressive buildings; but they produce millions of gallons of whisky and tens of millions of revenue. It can be seldom that so much is earned by so few.

History, castles and great houses

There has been a deal of busy and often bloody history here. On Bennachie and the Tap o' Noth in Aberdeenshire there are forts of the old people, and a village (perhaps Stone Age) on the Forvie Sands. There are many stone circles – we call them standing stones even when they are recumbent – of which a very good and accessible example is at Daviot in Aberdeenshire. The Romans came this way and left marching stations near Stonehaven, Peterculter, Kintore and

Scottish Tourist Board   **Tossing the caber at the Braemar Highland Gan**

Glenmailen near Ythanwells. They probably got to Fochabers, and even to the Moray Firth, but were likely unwelcome and did not stay long. Romans in these parts now sell ice-cream. The Danes and the Norsemen visited, killed some of the men and put some of the women with child, and so the stock is rather mixed – for there have been other wandering sailors since then. In later times (but still in the days of tell-tale) there was a Macbeth who may have been Thane of Cawdor near Nairn and met three witches on a blasted heath who told him he would be king thereafter. Out of that story Shakespeare made *Macbeth*. The blasted heath can still be seen near Forres – but not the witches.

The countryside is rich in castles and baronial houses. The great medieval castle of Kildrummy, chief house of the Earldom of Mar, is a magnificent ruin, arrested in decay; so is Dunnottar on the grim cliffs at Stonehaven. Huntly Castle and Tolquhon Castle, both in Aberdeenshire, are roofless but graciously preserved by the Ministry of Works. There are many others. Great castles still lived in are Cawdor (Nairn), Darnaway (Moray) and Fyvie (Aberdeenshire). Crathes Castle near Banchory is a very beautiful specimen of baronial, open to the public. So is Leith Hall near Huntly. Those castles and towers look peaceful enough now; but the people who lived in them were often a rowdy lot. They belonged to great families – Gordon Earls of Huntly, the Forbeses, the Frasers, the Farquharsons – who held gang warfare against each other in their own or the King's name. They were notorious disturbers of the peace. Also, the north-east being then a little out of the world, they were inclined to be Catholic when most of Scotland turned Episcopalian, or Episcopalian when the rest was Presbyterian. Some of the best Jacobites came from these parts, and some of them were noble men.

In settled times men built more comely houses – Gordonstoun near Elgin, now a famous public school with royal pupils, Cullen House, Duff House near Banff, Haddo House in Aberdeenshire and Park House near Aberdeen. There are many old houses – too many to name.

Out of all those treasures I would select two: Muchalls Castle on the Stonehaven road and the Ha' House at the Raemoir Hotel near Banchory (which may be seen on request): they are small, perfect examples of their kind. To complete all, I would have the great garden at Pitmedden, fifteen miles north of Aberdeen, which has been restored to its 17th-century style by the National Trust.

In medieval times there were two Roman Catholic sees in these parts – Moray and Aberdeen – and the good of their works remains in some shape. The Cathedral of Elgin is a ruin, but a noble one, in the bend of the River Lossie. Elgin, a county town and long prosperous, has an air of grace in its fine sandstone houses and quiet side streets, a grace that is perhaps supported by the whisky trade of which Elgin is the centre. Pluscarden Abbey, a few miles away in the glen of the Lossie, long time a ruin, is now being restored by a band of working monks, and there a traveller is taken into the Middle Ages whether or not he wishes to go that far back. The Cathedral in Aberdeen has been better cared for. Only the nave remains, as a parish church, but a sombre and stately one. And there in Old Aberdeen we have one of the treasures of Scotland. Besides the Cathedral the Chanonry remains, where the canons lived. Most of the old houses have been replaced; but the atmosphere is of age under old trees, and the rooks that defile the hats of gentlemen are probably descendants of those that did so a thousand years ago. King's College, founded in 1495, is of all ages from then till today. The chapel is a very fine medieval building with rare carvings in wood. Altogether Old Aberdeen is an experience of long life, always renewed by the students of the University that go to it for their little while.

Recreation and sport

Though an industrial town, Aberdeen is also a holiday place, with sandy beaches, public golf courses and pleasure parks. You may explore the country-side from it. There is plenty of good sport. The golf courses are excellent, especially the seaside ones. Visitors are welcome at most, and the fees are remarkably low – but the scores can be remarkably high, for the rough is rough. In summer the cattle-shows bring out all the country people. So do the Games, where young men and women compete in throwing hammers, putting weights, running, jumping, dancing and bagpipe music. At all those you can study the people of the north-east; and hear them. The biggest Games are at Aboyne and Braemar in early September. Those at Braemar are attended by the Queen and draw enormous crowds. There is much tartan, bagpipe music and Society.

The fishing is good – in the sea with the line or in the rivers with the rod for salmon, sea trout and brown trout. River fishing can be had by the day, often at hotels which have a stretch of water. Grouse are shot from August 12th, and partridges, pheasants and deer later on. Hill walking and mountain climbing are free to all, and in recent years skiing has become very popular. There are ski-lifts in the Cairngorms, and there is nearly always snow somewhere. It is as well to find out just where the snow and the facilities are.

Food and drink

It is fair to say that the people are good plain cooks. It is unwise to expect anything fancy to turn out well, though it often does. But the cooks understand the native foods – the salmon, the trout, the game, the poultry and the prime beef. The sea-fish, fresh out of the sea, can be a revelation to those accustomed to fish that tastes of mortality. The finnan, the smoked haddock, is a delicacy, either grilled or cooked in milk. Oatcakes, thin oatcakes, are another delicacy, with plenty of fresh butter. Porridge is usually taken with salt, but those who wish may have sugar instead. The home baking is often very good. Salads are not well understood, two leaves of lettuce being thought the limit of safety; but large salads can be had on persuasion. The coffee is weak, but the tea is virile. And in all these parts one can study the whisky. It is possible to get the single (un-blended) whiskies of the local distilleries and balance a Glenlivet against a Glendronach, with a Macallan on the side for reference. That can become quite a hobby and even a life-work.

Most of the people in the north-east do not think of themselves as highlanders and may be a little insulted if referred to as such. This is a difficult matter and too complicated to explain here. But you have been warned. Let them declare themselves. One last thing – never hesitate to ask a native for information. Either he will say, 'Och, I daena ken', or else he will tell you perhaps more than you wish to know, which is one of the better risks of travel.

Some houses and gardens open to the public

Balmoral Castle *Map* D C 79. *See p. 730* Her Majesty The Queen. *Gardens only. Not open when any member of the Royal Family is in residence.*

Braemar Castle *Map* D B 79. *'Fairy-tale' 17th-cent. castle of great historic interest. See p. 730.* Capt. A. A. C. Farquharson of Invercauld.

Crathes Castle *Map* D H 79. *Fine example of 16th-cent. Scots baronial architecture, with remarkable painted ceilings. Gardens renowned for yew hedges and rare shrubs.* N T for Scot.

Cullen House *Map* D F 86. *Imposing mansion in picturesque situation above Cullen Burn. Dates from 13th cent., with underground Monk's Passage, salon with painted ceiling, Grinling Gibbons carvings, etc.* The Countess of Seafield.

Dunnottar Castle 2m s of Stonehaven *Map* D J 78. *Impressive ruined fortress on rocky cliff 160 ft. above the sea. See also under Stonehaven, p. 736.* The Viscount Cowdray.

Haddo House Methlick *Map* D J 83. *Georgian house built 1732 by William Adam. Home of the Gordons of Haddo for over 500 years. Beautiful interiors, paintings, private chapel.* The Haddo House Choral Society.

Leith Hall nr Kennethmont *Map* D F 82. *Large picturesque mansion house dating from 17th cent. Family and Jacobite relics. Attractively situated rock garden.* N T for Scot.

Muchalls Castle *Map* D K 79. *17th-cent. fortified mansion with fine plasterwork ceilings.* Maurice A. Simpson, Esq.

Pitcaple Castle 4½m N W of Inverurie *Map* D H 82. *Family residence with many historical associations and relics. 15th cent. with 19th-cent. addition.*

Pitmedden nr Udny *Map* D J 82. *Renowned for its 'great garden' laid out by the first Baronet of Pitmedden in late 17th cent. Floral design, pavilions, fountain, sundials.* N T for Scot. *House not open.*

Provost Ross's House Shiprow, Aberdeen *Map* D K 80. *The oldest house in Aberdeen, built 1593.* N T for Scot.

Provost Skene's House Guestrow, Aberdeen *Map* D K 80. *A 16th–17th-cent. house furnished in period style, with painted and decorative plaster ceilings.* Aberdeen City Corporation.

Books for further reading

General

JOHN R. ALLAN *The North-East Lowlands of Scotland* (County Books series) 1952
PETER F. ANSON *Fishing Boats and Fisher Folk on the East Coast of Scotland* 1930
BRENDA MACROW *Speyside to Deeside* 1956
CHARLES MURRAY *Hamewith and other poems* reprinted 1960
JOHN ORD ed. *Bothy Songs and Ballads of Aberdeen, Banff and Moray, Angus and the Mearns* 1930
WARD LOCK'S 'RED GUIDES'

The Moray Firth

PETER F. ANSON *A Monastery in Moray: the story of Pluscarden Priory* 1959
RONALD G. CANT *Old Elgin* 1946; *Old Moray* 1948

JAMES ALAN RENNIE *Romantic Strathspey* 1952
JAMES B. RITCHIE *The Pageant of Morayland* 1953

Aberdeen and Kincardine

ABERDEEN CITY COUNCIL *The City of Aberdeen* 1961
IVOR BROWN *Balmoral: the history of a Home* 1955
A. D. FARR *The Royal Deeside Line* 1968
W. DOUGLAS SIMPSON *The Province of Mar* 1943; *The Earldom of Mar* 1949; *Dunnottar Castle* 1924
J. C. WATT *The Mearns of Old* 1914
FENTON WYNESS *Royal Valley: The Story of the Aberdeenshire Dee* 1968; *The Royal Deeside Line* 1968

Gazetteer

NORTH-EAST SCOTLAND

Aberdeen, Kincardine, Banff,
Moray, Nairn

St Machar's Cathedral *Radio Times Hulton P. L.*

Aberdeen** (DK 80) EC Wed/Sat
(182,117). Thriving University and
Cathedral city, important fishing port,
exporter of cattle and granite. The
city is built of locally-quarried granite
and set between two salmon rivers, the
Dee and the Don. The 7-arched
Bridge of Dee was imaginatively
widened over a hundred years ago
without losing its medieval face. The
14th-cent. gothic arched Brig o'
Balgownie over the Don is the oldest
important bridge in Scotland still in
use. In Castle St. the splendid 17th-
cent. City Cross depicts a unicorn presiding over the medallions of Scottish
sovereigns. The former Town House
to the N incorporates parts of the 14th-
cent. Tolbooth and houses an interesting collection of charters and records.
St Mary's Chapel, the crypt below the
E Church of St Nicholas in Union St.,
contains relics and was at one time
a prison for witches. Among many art
treasures, the Art Gallery shows the
Macdonald Collection of portraits of
famous painters *by* famous painters.
The University is represented in
Broad St. by Marischal College, with
frontage in imposing Perpendicular-
Gothic, and Mitchell Tower (233 ft.)
which provides a fine view of the City.
Old Aberdeen is the academic quarter
centred on King's College* (founded
1495). The lovely lantern tower of the
chapel was rebuilt in the 17th cent.;
note the carving of the stalls and
pulpit, the University War Memorial

behind the former rood screen, and
seven fine windows. The Cathedral of
St Machar* is chiefly 15th cent.; the
flat oak ceiling, painted splendidly
with emblems of spiritual and temporal
monarchs, was added in 1530. The
Harbour and Fish Market at the
mouth of the Dee are full of busy
activity; to the N are fine sandy
bathing beaches and golf links.

Aboyne *Aberdeen* (DF 79). Deeside
fishing, golf and touring centre built
around an attractive village green. The
Highland Gathering in early September is one of the principal events of the
Highland season.

Alford *Aberdeen* (DF 81). Stands in
hill-ringed farming land. Balfluig
Castle (16th cent.) was originally inhabited by the Lords Forbes, who
have now removed to 19th-cent.
Castle Forbes (4 m. NE).

Ballater *Aberdeen* (DD 79). Popular
holiday town on Deeside, surrounded
by beautiful woods and moorlands,
though some mountain walks may be
restricted during the shooting season.
Close to Abergeldie skiing slopes.

Ballindalloch *Banff* (DB 83). Fine
castle keep near the junction of Avon

729

Balmoral Castle

and Spey in a district world-famous for the waters which produce the whisky and the fish.

Balmoral Castle★ *Aberdeen* (DC 79). The Sovereign's Highland residence, built in Scottish baronial style and modified by direction of the Prince Consort. The grounds, including Queen Victoria's cottage and Queen Mary's sunken garden, are open to the public from May to July when the Royal Family is not in residence. Unassuming Crathie Church (1 m. E) contains the royal pew and memorials. *See also* **Braemar** *below*.

Banchory *Kinc*. (DG 79). Attractive village where the Feugh joins the Dee. Two miles NE, 16th-cent. Crathes Castle (NT for Scot. – *see p.* s.104) has treasures which include an oak-panelled ceiling unique in Scotland, allegorical paintings, and a jewelled ivory horn presented to a Burnett by Robert Bruce, as well as a beautifully laid-out 18th-cent. garden.

Banff (DG 86) EC Wed (3,330). Royal burgh and seaport at mouth of

R. Deveron, with a few remaining 17th-cent. houses on High Shore, vestiges of a royal castle and many interesting remains. Duff House by Wm. Adam was modelled on the Villa Borghese for a Duke of Fife, and later presented to the town.

Braemar★ *Aberdeen* (DB 79). Famous Highland resort in magnificent scenery, 1,100 ft. above sea-level, about 9 m. W of **Balmoral Castle** (*see above*). The Earl of Mar raised his standard here in the 1715 rebellion. Most popular nowadays during the famous Braemar Gathering in September, usually attended by a royal party, but it is also a good centre for winter sports. For Braemar Castle is by the R. Dee. *See also* **Cairngorm Mountains** *below*.

Burghead *Moray* (DB 86). Fishing village built on a headland fortified by Picts and Danes. The 'Roman' Well inside an Iron Age fort may be an early Christian baptistry.

Cairngorm Mountains★ (CK 80). Except for Ben Nevis, some of the highest and grandest mountain scenery

Crathes Castle, near Banch

in Scotland. Recognised ascents from Aviemore (CJ 81) in Inverness-shire and **Braemar** (DB 79) avoid conflict with shooting interests and give splendid views of mountain lochs and peat streams, with golden eagles, the quartz known as 'cairngorms', and even reindeer moss at times. Pony-trekking and winter sports in season.

Craigievar Castle (DF 80). *See* **Lumphanan.**

Cruden Bay *Aberdeen* (EA 83). Pleasant, quiet holiday resort with good golf course and sandy beach. The situation of Slains Castle, now ruined, was according to Dr Johnson the 'noblest he had ever seen'. He was equally impressed by the Bullers of Buchan, a deep, wide 'pot' with narrow opening to the sea, or, as he put it, 'a rock perpendicularly tubulated' – an awesome sight in rough weather.

Culbin Sands *Moray* (CK 86). Fertile cornland until engulfed by a sandstorm in 1694. The drifts (100 ft. high) have been known to shift and reveal traces of buildings. Afforestation is now reclaiming the land. Nearby Hardmuir, now under cultivation, is supposed to be the blasted heath of Macbeth's witches.

Cullen *Banff* (DF 86). Royal burgh, fishing port and holiday town. The older town was demolished in 1822 to make room for improvements to Cullen House, but the original Mercat Cross† still stands in the town square. The church founded by Bruce is notable for the interesting tomb of Alexander Ogilvy of Findlater, a tabernacle in the N wall of the chancel, and the carved Seafield pew.

Dufftown *Banff* (DD 83). A whisky-distilling centre. Mortlach Church (12th cent.) has ancient tombstones. Balvenie Castle, in turn owned by Comyns, Douglases and Atholls, has the Atholl family motto carved on the 15th–16th-cent. front.

Duffus *Moray* (DB 86). Gordonstoun School occupies the mansion built by Sir Robert Gordon (1647–1704), later known as the 'warlock of Gordonstoun'. Moated Duffus Castle, where David I of Scotland stayed, is in ruins.

Elgin* *Moray* (DC 86) EC Wed (15,720). County town where Charles James Stewart lodged before the Battle of Culloden. The ruined 13th-cent. cathedral* was known as the 'Lanthorn of the North', and in spite of a history of calamity and destruction the buildings retain a luminous beauty in the northern light. The W front and the Chapter House are magnificent. The town boasts good modern architecture of the early part of the present century, as well as beautiful Market Crosses and a High Street in which a few arcaded houses survive. Spynie Palace (2¾ m. N), the castle of the Bishops of Moray, has a tower originally 6 storeys high, and extensive fortifications.

Fettercairn *Kinc.* (DG 77). The old Town Cross of Kincardine has been erected in this pretty village. It shows the standard measurement of the Scottish ell. The ruins of Kincardine Castle (3 m. NE) are the sole remains of a historic town and royal residence.

Findhorn *Moray* (DA 86). A former village was overwhelmed by drifting sand, its successor by flood. The present village is the third of the name. Good sailing in Findhorn Bay. Remains of 12th-cent. Cistercian foundation, Kinloss Abbey (2 m. SE).

Fochabers *Moray* (DD 85). The old Market Cross near the site of Gordon Castle, now substantially

---

† Market cross or proclamation place.

demolished, is sole survivor of the wholesale removal of the village in the 18th cent. to its present position S of the park.

Forres *Moray* (DA 85) EC Wed (4,566). Ancient little royal burgh proud of a mention in *Macbeth*. Angling and touring centre. Sweno's Stone, in sandstone 23 ft. high with elaborate carvings in the Celtic tradition, may commemorate an early 11th-cent. Norse victory. A granite stone marks the spot where the witches of Forres were burnt.

Fraserburgh *Aberdeen* (DK 86) EC Wed (10,739). Herring-fishing port, with a good harbour founded in the 16th cent. by Sir Alexander Fraser, who built a square watchtower, now surmounted by a lighthouse, on Kinnaird's Head. Below is the Sealch's Hole, a 100 ft. cave. Note the fine 18th-cent. Mercat Cross at the top of the High Street.

Fyvie Castle *Aberdeen* (DH 83). Beautifully preserved fortified mansion. The gardens show traces of entrenchments thrown up by Montrose when pursued by Argyll in 1644. (No admission.)

Garmouth *Moray* (DD 86). Charles II landed here at the mouth of the Spey in 1650. Near-by Kingston is a shipbuilding village named by Yorkshiremen after their native Kingston-upon-Hull.

Grantown-on-Spey *Moray* (DA 82). On the county border with Inverness-shire. The village, with tree-lined main street and woodland surroundings, makes an excellent centre for exploration of the mountainous countryside. Salmon fishing in the R. Spey.

Huntly *Aberdeen* (DF 83) EC Thurs (3,812). The town has acquired several miles of fishing on the rivers Deveron and Bogie. Huntly Castle, once the home of the Gordons, is well worth visiting.

Insch *Aberdeen* (DG 82). Important village in agricultural district. Dunnideer, a conical hill, is surmounted by an early vitrified fort and remains of a 16th-cent. castle.

Fraserburgh Harbour

Radio Times Hulton Picture Library

Inverbervie *Kinc.* (DJ 77). Sometimes known as Bervie. Arbuthnott Church (13th cent.), 2½ m. W, has 2-storeyed 16th-cent. chapel. Arbuthnott House, continuously in the hands of one family since at least 1206, has attractive plaster ceilings which may be viewed on written application. Allardyce Castle, small 'fairy castle' of the early 17th cent., lies 1 m. to the NW.

Inverey *Aberdeen* (DA 78). The end of the road up Deeside into the heart of the Cairngorm Mountains. Walks in the glens and on the moors with wonderful views, including a strenuous one to Aviemore (CJ 81) in Inverness-shire, through the Larig Ghru. (Take local advice before setting out.)

Inverurie *Aberdeen* (DH 82) EC Wed (5,194). Prosperous burgh in agricultural district abounding in archaeological remains. The Bass, a mound S of the town, was the site of a Norman mote-and-bailey castle. The great battle fought at Harlaw (3 m. NW) in 1411 determined the whole course of Scottish history; this check to the Highland forces is described by Scott in a ballad in *The Antiquary*. Bennachie, a prominent hill 8 m. W, has an extensive Iron Age hill fort on the summit.

Keith *Banff* (DE 85) EC Wed (4,092). Well planned agricultural town. The Roman Catholic Church has giant statues of SS Peter and Paul incorporated in its façade, and an altarpiece presented by Charles X of France.

Kildrummy Castle★ *Aberdeen* (DE 81). Most imposing of the many historic remains of the Don Valley, and so ancient that it had to be *rebuilt* in 1303 for Edward I of England.

Kintore *Aberdeen* (DH 81). A royal burgh, though with a small population, having a delightful 18th-cent. Town House, and a church with 'sacrament house'. A stone in the churchyard combines pagan and Christian emblems.

Laurencekirk *Kinc.* (DH 77). Centre of the fertile Howe of the Mearns, with linen mills. The snuff-boxes made here have become collectors' pieces.

Lochindorb *Moray* (CK 83). Grim, off-the-beaten-track island-fortress once occupied by Edward I of England and later the stronghold of the Wolf of Badenoch.

Lossiemouth *Moray* (DC 87). EC Thurs (5,850). Fishing town serving as the port of Elgin, and catering for visitors. Birthplace of Ramsay Macdonald (1866–1937), first Labour Prime Minister.

Lumphanan *Aberdeen* (DF 80). Village close to traditional site of Macbeth's death. Neighbouring villages are Torphins, a pleasant summer resort, and Kincardine O'Neil, with its ancient ruined church and hospital. Craigievar Castle★ (4 m. N) has 7-storeyed keep of the early 17th cent., complete with turrets and high roofs. Unique Renaissance ceiling and fireplace exhortation 'Doe not vaiken sleiping dogs'.

Macduff *Banff* (DH 86) EC Wed (3,470). Large herring-fishing harbour and town, known as Down until the Earl of Macduff gave it his family name. Splendid view from the 70-ft. War Memorial Tower on Hill of Down.

Midmar Castle★ (DG 80). Fine turreted early-17th-cent. castle below the Hill of Fare, to the S of the A974 road.

Muchalls *Kinc.* (DK 79). One of several picturesque villages on the

Midmar Castle

coast S of Aberdeen. Red-sandstone cliffs. The 17th-cent. castle mansion* owned by the Burnetts of Leys is open to the public in summer.

Nairn (CJ 85) EC Wed (4,900). Three golf courses, bathing, fishing, and a share of the Gulf Stream. The attractive fishermen's quarter, Fishertown, has streets or 'mains' leading to the harbour. Moated Cawdor Castle (5¾ m. S), adopted by Shakespeare as the scene of Duncan's murder, includes among its treasures a pre-Elizabethan carving of monkeys smoking pipes. (Not open to the public.)

Newburgh *Aberdeen* (EA 82). Opposite a village overwhelmed by sand-drift at the mouth of the Ythan, whose freshwater mussels yield pearls – one of which is set in the Scottish Crown. Ellon (5 m. NW) has a Norman mote hill where in medieval times justice was administered.

Old Deer *Aberdeen* (DK 84). Village notable for the ruins of a 13th-cent. Cistercian abbey with 14th-cent. refectory and abbot's lodge. From an earlier (7th-cent.) monastery here came the famous Book of Deer, now in Cambridge University Library; it includes a 9th-cent. Latin fragment of the New Testament with 11th- and 12th-cent. marginal notes on contemporary happenings, the earliest Scottish Gaelic writing in existence.

Oldmeldrum *Aberdeen* (DJ 82). Robert Bruce fought a battle on the site of the prehistoric fort on Barra Hill. Four m. W is the Loanhead of Daviot prehistoric stone circle.

Peterhead *Aberdeen* (EB 84) EC Wed (12,500). Grey seaport near Scotland's furthest easterly point. Shipbuilding yards and busy harbour, a much-needed refuge on this rocky coast. The famous pink Peterhead granite is quarried at Boddam.

Pitmedden House *Aberdeen* (DJ 82). Old-world gardens* with pavilions, sundials and fountains reconstructed by the NT for Scot. The ruined Tolquhon Castle (1 m. NW) was built in the 16th cent. except for the earlier Preston's Tower; the splendid hall has original paving in good state of preservation.

Pluscarden Abbey* *Moray* (DB 85). The 13th-cent. monastic buildings, standing in the neck of a fertile valley, were partially restored by the Marquess

735

Pluscarden Abbey

Radio Times Hulton Picture Library

of Bute and presented to the Benedictine Order, who are completing the work. Admittance at reasonable hours.

Portsoy *Banff* (DF 86). Attractive holiday resort and fishing port, with double harbour. Notable for the distinctive rock formation, known as 'Portsoy marble'.

Stonehaven *Kinc.* (DJ 78). EC Wed (4,341). County town, busy harbour and holiday resort with fine cliff walks. The early 17th-cent. Tolbooth was formerly a storehouse. Dunnottar Castle★ (1½ m. S) stands in grim and isolated splendour on its rocky perch above the sea (*see p.* S.104). It was besieged unsuccessfully by Montrose, who ravaged the country and burned Stonehaven. In 1652 the Scottish regalia were smuggled out through the besieging Commonwealth lines by the

wife of the minister of Kinneff (6½ m. S) and hidden behind her husband's pulpit, as the monument to her testifies.

Tolquhon Castle (DJ 82). *See* **Pitmedden House**.

Tomintoul *Banff* (DB 81). The highest village of the Highlands (1,160 ft.). Summer and winter sporting resort surrounded by sparsely populated moors.

Turriff *Aberdeen* (DH 84) EC Wed (2,779). Country town above the Idoch Water. The first engagement of the Civil War, in which Forbes was routed by the royalist Gordons, was known as the 'Trot of Turriff'. Delgatie Castle, the tower-house belonging to the Hays of Errol, has beautiful painted ceilings.

Opposite: Detail from the original painting by Edgar Ainsworth.
Much of the east coast here is rugged cliffs. On its promontory, 160 feet above the North Sea, Dunnottar Castle near Stonehaven must surely be one of the most grimly situated fortress ruins in the world. Its most ancient portion, the L-shaped tower, is not far short of 600 years old. During the struggle against Cromwell, the crown and sceptre of Scotland were hidden in this building.

The Cuillins, Skye

THE
WEST HIGHLANDS

Inverness, Ross & Cromarty, The Western Isles

AN INTRODUCTION BY J. S. GRANT

Ross-shire and Inverness-shire are so large in area and so widely scattered that many of the inhabitants cannot visit their county town without an overnight sea-crossing or a journey by air. Both counties sprawl across Scotland from the North Sea far into the Atlantic, beyond the Outer Hebrides, to St Kilda which is an outlier of Inverness-shire, and to Rona and Sulisgeir, outliers of Ross-shire some forty miles north-west of Cape Wrath.

The Outer Hebrides, Skye, and the Western Seaboard have little in common with the Burgh of Inverness and the rich farmlands of the east, except the scenic magnificence of the whole area. East and west formed part of the old *Gaidhealtachd*, the Gaelic-speaking region of Scotland; but they have evolved – or failed to evolve – in different ways.

Opposite: Detail from the original painting by Leonard Rosoman.
In this composite landscape, the Cairngorms rise above an aboriginal forest of Scots pines. Here one might travel for many miles without seeing any sign of habitation. Six national nature reserves in the area include one for studying red deer. The birds are capercailzie (on the left) and black grouse; the plants are Scotch thistle, crowberry, and blaeberry (or whortleberry).

THE WEST HIGHLANDS AND THE WESTERN ISLES

In the east there is some of the richest, and best farmed, arable land in Scotland, and among the farmers are breeders of international repute. But at Iochdar, in Uist, the crofters still cultivate the *machair* in runrig – long narrow strips which are balloted for annually, and dispersed over several open fields, so that every shareholder gets some of the good and some of the bad at the price of cultivating a multiplicity of awkwardly shaped strips hundreds of yards apart.

In the Burgh of Inverness they recall with pride Defoe's comment in 1723: 'They speak as good English here as in London.' In the Outer Hebrides they also speak good English, because it is still an acquired language there as it was in Inverness in Defoe's time; but they take pride in their knowledge of Gaelic. Paradoxically, you may expect to find the kilt worn in Inverness, and every evening in the summer a tartan-clad pipe-band plays for the visitors; but you will see little sign of tartan in the Celtic west.

Although Inverness is a comparatively small town – the population is around 30,000 – it is much the largest in the two counties, and has been a place of importance since the days of St Columba. It was created a Royal Burgh by Alexander I, and it had a well-established foreign trade in the Middle Ages.

Dingwall, the county town of Ross-shire, has been a Royal Burgh since 1226, and, as its name implies, was a centre of government in Viking times. Tain and Fortrose are also ancient Royal Burghs, and Cromarty is an interesting little town with a number of 17th- and 18th-century buildings. The only towns in the west are Fort William, which lies in the shadow of Ben Nevis, and Stornoway in the Island of Lewis, which, after Inverness, is the largest in our area.

The two counties are poor in material resources but immeasurably rich in natural beauty: not the static beauty of a painted canvas, but a living beauty like the human face.

In full sunlight the mountains are richly draped in browns and greens, the colours of the vegetation and the rocks; but the light is always changing – and at times they are black as charcoal, as blue almost as the sea, or purple like grapes. When the mist comes down they melt into ghostly greys receding into the distance, ridge behind ridge.

Almost everywhere there is the sound of moving water: the slow rhythms of the sea, or the lighter music of an inland loch, or an impetuous mountain stream hurrying along as brown as beer or as black as stout, except where it leaps from rock to rock in glistening white.

The lochs are sometimes silver, sometimes sky-blue; but often they are variegated with all the colours of the birch and pine woods, the fields and the mountains, which they mirror.

Rock and soil

The beauty of this tumbled landscape of mountain, and loch, and sea, is in the geological bone which lies beneath the surface and is little changed by the hand of man.

Along the fertile east coast the underlying rock is Old Red Sandstone and Devonian; westward into the Hebrides it is hard, grey, unyielding Archaean Gneiss; Ben Nevis and the Cairngorms are massive intrusions of granite through the older rock; Skye is volcanic; and in Torridon Red Sandstone is crowned at the mountain tops with gleaming white Quartzite.

A geological fault reaching across Inverness-shire from coast to coast has

The Cairngorms, seen from Loch Morlich *J. Allan Cash*

created Glen More, the great glen of Scotland, with its chain of lovely lochs, of which Loch Ness, reputedly inhabited by a monster, is the largest and best known.

The Gneiss of the Outer Hebrides – known to geologists as Lewisian after the largest of the Islands – is one of the oldest rocks exposed on the surface of the earth, and the hills are smoothed by aeons of weathering, although still deeply scored by the ice. In Skye we have the youngest, and most dramatic, rocks in Scotland. The fantastic castle-like towers known as the Quirang and the Old Man of Storr are the remains of an eroded terrace of lava, and Dr Fraser Darling claims that the glacier-scored Cuillins provide some of the most spectacular scenery, not only in Britain but in the whole world. Similar claims are made for Glen Torridon, with its loch and the mountains on either side. Morar and Glen Affric, too, might claim the palm.

It is impossible to write of the geology of Inverness-shire and Ross-shire without using superlatives. In Inverness-shire alone there are more than fifty peaks over 3,000 feet high. On the north-east face of Ben Nevis we have the highest mountain cliff in Britain – 1,500 feet of granite wall; on the main Island of St Kilda we have the highest sea cliffs, just under 1,400 feet; and on the Shiant Islands the finest example of columnar basalt. The Falls of Glomach, although the amount of water is not great, are the highest in Britain and among the finest.

These dramatic natural features contrast not only with the rounded hills and rich fields of the Black Isle in the east of Ross-shire (which incidentally is neither black nor an island) but with the *machairs* of the west: the flat sandy plains and tidal reaches where the beauty is in the interplay of light and shade on the water, and in the rich colours of the wild flowers patterning the grass. It probably requires a more sophisticated taste to appreciate the *machairs*; but on a clear day after rain there is surely no lovelier place in Britain than the Uist *machairs*, unless it is the incredibly barren east coast of Harris with the backdrop of Skye twelve miles away across the Minch.

Fauna and flora

Six of the twenty National Nature Reserves in Scotland lie wholly within Ross and Inverness, and two others partly. On the Island of Rhum the Conservancy is studying principally the habits of the red deer, but Rhum also has its own breed of ponies, said to be descended from horses which swam ashore from the Spanish Armada. Loch Druidibeg in South Uist is the principal breeding-place of grey-lag geese in Britain. St Kilda has the largest gannetry in the world, the unique St Kilda wren and its own Soay sheep, the most primitive variety in Europe. North Rona is the largest breeding station in the world for the grey Atlantic seal, and, like the neighbouring Island of Sulisgeir, is a breeding-place of Leach's fork-tailed petrel, which comes ashore only at night. In the Cairngorms, on the fringe of Inverness-shire, the osprey has been re-established in Britain as a breeding bird within the past few years. On the Shiant Islands there is the largest puffinry in Britain, and in many of the wilder parts of the two counties the golden eagle, the peregrine falcon and the wild-cat are found.

The flora of the area is equally varied, ranging from the *machairs* of the Islands rich in wild, lime-loving flowers, through the acid heather moors, to the summits of the mountains, which Dr Fraser Darling has described as an immense archipelago of biological islands holding relic communities of the last glacial epoch. In contrast with the Alpine plants of the mountain-tops are the subtropical shrubs in the famous gardens at Inverewe. These remind us that while the Moray Firth is warmer and drier than the west (over a long period of years Fortrose has been one of the sunniest and driest places in Scotland), the North Atlantic drift keeps the western seaboard mild in winter – so that the mean temperature at Stornoway from November to March is exactly the same as at Kew. The Atlantic coast of the Hebrides is the windiest region of Britain except perhaps Shetland; but in May and early June it is also one of the sunniest, not excepting the south-east of England.

Sport and recreation

There are many famous salmon rivers within the two counties. Most of them are very closely preserved, like the Grimersta in Lewis, ranked by some as one of the finest in Europe. There are, however, many good hotels with fishing rights on trout and salmon waters. There are many extensive deer forests, and some snipe bogs and grouse moors; but these are even more closely preserved than the salmon fishings. Sea fishing for sport is now being developed at a number of centres, including Ullapool on Lochbroom, which is also a favourite

J. Allan Cash **Eilean Donan Castle, Loch Alsh and the Cui**

anchorage for the yachts which frequent the west coast and the islands. There is pony-trekking, especially round Aviemore, and ski-ing in the Cairngorms. There is probably the best walking and certainly the best climbing in Britain. There are some good golf-courses in the east and some smaller ones in the west. Football, as elsewhere in Scotland, is the principal team game; but shinty is still played, except, oddly enough, in some of the Western Isles. Highland Games are held regularly, and the Northern Meeting in Inverness is regarded as one of Scotland's premier piping contests. Skye Week brings visitors to the island in early summer, when the weather is at its best, and there are several Provincial Mods at which Gaelic singing can be heard.

Architecture

There are no great cathedrals; but St Duthus Chapel in Tain, ruined and restored, was a place of pilgrimage for Scottish kings, and there are the remains of ecclesiastical buildings worth seeing at Fearn and Rodel, while even in remote islands like the Flannans and North Rona there are the remains of humble dry-stone chapels built by the intrepid missionaries of the Old Celtic Church.

But the architectural glory of the two counties must be held to lie in its castles, often most picturesquely situated. Eilean Donan Castle, an ancient seat of the Mackenzies, must have one of the most magnificent sites of any castle in Britain, on a little island approached by a causeway and commanding the Sound of Sleat; Dunvegan Castle, with its 'Fairy Flag' and other priceless relics, still lived in by the chiefs of one branch of Clan MacLeod – but the list is a long one.

Outstanding monuments from prehistory are the Clava Stones near Culloden, one of the most extensive Bronze Age remains in Britain, and the Stone Circle at Callanish in Lewis, which is unique in design, and was obviously an important centre of some ancient cult, for there are numerous smaller circles in the neighbourhood – although some folk have suggested a little cynically that the smaller circles are really an early manifestation of the highlander's still strongly marked tendency towards religious schism.

There are the remains of various vitrified forts and Pictish towers or brochs, good examples being at Glenelg and Dun Carloway, and there is a very fine sculptured stone at Shandwick.

History

There is a sense in which Ross-shire and Inverness-shire are still possessed by the Jacobites: Prince Charlie first set foot on Scottish soil on the still Catholic Island of Eriskay; at Glenfinnan a monument, which looks like a lighthouse incongruously come ashore, commemorates the raising of his standard; Culloden Moor, scene of the final defeat, is a property of the National Trust and a place of pilgrimage for thousands. Flora Macdonald's birthplace can be seen at Milton in South Uist, and her grave at Kilmuir in Skye. In the West Highland Museum at Fort William there are several Jacobite relics, and almost every glen has some association with the early hopeful days of the rising, or with the massacre which followed Culloden. Am Fasgadh, the Folk Museum at Kingussie, reminds us that the ordinary people of the Highlands and Islands had a life apart from the clan and dynastic feuds in which they were so often and so bloodily embroiled; and, just as Dr Grant has rescued for posterity some of the implements, clothes and architecture of the peasantry, so Kenneth Macleod,

THE WEST HIGHLANDS AND THE WESTERN ISLES

Mr and Mrs J. L. Campbell of Canna and Marjorie Kennedy Fraser, among others (and, more recently, the School of Scottish Studies), have preserved some of the music and stories in which the Highlands and Islands were incredibly rich.

Local products

The main industries today are agriculture, fishing, distilling, and the manufacture of textiles. The best known of the textiles is Harris Tweed, handwoven in the Outer Hebrides; but excellent tweeds are also made in Skye and Inverness. The two counties produce an abundance of salmon, trout, venison, game-birds, prime beef and mutton; while the surrounding seas – the Minch and the Moray Firth – provide excellent white fish, lobster, scampi, and scallops. Barra cockles are famous; and those who know will rank a *matje* (or maiden) herring from the Minch in the month of June above any other fish from salt water or fresh.

In addition to producing whisky for the popular blends, Ross and Inverness produce several malt whiskies for the connoisseur. Talisker, Glen Morangie, and Dalmore are worthy to rank with the great wines of France, if you have the palate for them.

Preference in food and scenery alike depends on personal taste; but he is indeed hard to please who does not find in Ross-shire and Inverness-shire much to delight the eye, and the stomach, and to refresh the mind.

Harris: weaving tweed on a power-loom   *Radio Times Hulton Picture Library*

Some houses and gardens open to the public

Dunvegan Castle *Map* BC 84. *Medieval castle which has been the continuous residence of the chiefs of Clan MacLeod since 1200. Romantic situation on a rock partly surrounded by water. Bottleneck dungeon, the Fairy Flag, famous drinking-horn and other relics.* Dame Flora MacLeod of MacLeod, DBE.

Eilean Donan Castle *Map* BJ 82. *13th-cent. castle in situation of exceptional beauty and grandeur at meeting-point of three sea lochs.* J. D. H. MacRae, Esq.

Inverewe Gardens Poolewe *Map* BJ 87. *Famous sub-tropical gardens created by the late Osgood Mackenzie.* NT for Scot.

Kisimul Castle Castlebay, I. of Barra *Map* AG 79. *Probably the oldest existing stone castle in Scotland (begun 1030). Stands on island 200 yards off village. Stronghold of the chiefs of Clan Macneil from 1030 to 1838, and again from 1937 onwards. Greatly restored, and now summer residence of present chief.* The Macneil of Barra (XLV).

Books for further reading

Topography – general

ELIZABETH ORR BOYD *Cross Country Walks in the West Highlands*
F. REID CORSON *Beyond the Great Glen*
SETON GORDON *Days and Nights in the Highlands; Highways and Byways in the West Highlands*
A. R. B. HALDANE *The Drove Roads of Scotland*
DONALD B. MACCULLOCH *Romantic Lochaber*
J. HERRIES MCCULLOCH *The Charm of Scotland*
CALUM I. MACLEAN *The Highlands*
BRENDA G. MACROW *The Torridon Highlands*
GAVIN MAXWELL *Ring of Bright Water*
D. C. POCHIN MOULD *The Road from the Isles*

The Western Isles

I. F. GRANT *The Lordship of the Isles*
ANGUS MACLELLAN *Stories from South Uist*
MARTIN MARTIN *The Western Isles*
GEORGE SCOTT-MONCRIEFF *The Scottish Islands*
D. C. POCHIN MOULD *West Over Sea*
NIGEL NICHOLSON *Lord of the Isles*
ROLAND SVENNSON *Lonely Islands*
MRS O. F. SWIRE *Skye: the Island and its Legends*

History and tradition

KENNEDY FRASER *Songs of the Hebrides*
I. F. GRANT *The MacLeods: the Making of a Clan*
OSGOOD MACKENZIE *A Hundred Years in the Highlands*
ALEXANDER NICHOLSON *History of Skye*
MARGARET FAY SHAW *Folk Songs and Folk Lore of South Uist*

Flora and fauna

PHILIP BROWN and GEORGE WATERSTON *The Return of the Osprey*
F. FRASER DARLING *A Naturalist on Rona; Natural History in the Highlands and Islands*
A. E. HOLDEN *Plant Life in the Scottish Highlands*

Climbing

SCOTTISH MOUNTAINEERING CLUB *Climbing Guide to the Cuillin of Skye; The Cairngorm*

Fiction

NEIL M. GUNN *The Silver Darlings*
FIONA MACCOLLA *And the Cock Crew*
COMPTON MACKENZIE *Keep the Home Guard Turning; Whisky Galore*
ALASTAIR MACLEAN *The Islander*

744

Gazetteer

THE WEST HIGHLANDS & THE WESTERN ISLES

Inverness, Ross & Cromarty

Note—New car ferries are in operation, improving the links between the mainland and the islands. Motorists are advised to obtain the latest information from the RAC or the AA or local shipping companies.

Climbing in Glen Nevis
Scottish Tourist Board

Achnasheen *Ross & Cr.* (CB 85). Fine views of mountains, glens and lochs which have been deepened and lengthened by hydro-electric schemes without impairing their beauty.

Alness *Ross & Cr.* (CG 86). Village on N side of Cromarty Firth. Alness Bay was a wartime naval base. The Black Rock of Novar, an extraordinary deep ravine, 2 m. long, cut by the Allt Graat, 'the ugly burn', can be reached from Evanton.

Applecross *Ross & Cr.* (BH 84). Remote sea village reached with a sense of achievement and a storehouse of panoramic memories after negotiating the steep Bealachnam-Bo Pass (2,054 ft.). An ancient carved stone stands near the ruined church founded by Maelrubba, the Irish monk, in the 7th cent.

Ardgay *Ross & Cr.* (CG 89). Near the junction of beautiful, wild Strath Carron and Dornoch Firth, where Bonar Bridge leads into Sutherland. Carbisdale Castle (3½ m. NW), now a youth hostel, stands high above the River Oykell, where Montrose made his last stand against the Parliamentarians in 1650.

Arisaig *Inverness* (BG 78). The romantic Road to the Isles from Fort William reaches the sea at a bay studded with islets frequented by seals, with Rum and Eigg in the distance.

Aviemore* *Inverness* (CJ 81). Excellent touring, fishing and winter sports centre on the Spey between the Cairngorms and the Monadhliath Mountains. Unlimited range of expeditions: from echoing Loch-an-Eilean (3 m.) to the strenuous walk over the mountaintops to Braemar via Larig Ghru or Larig Laiogh. Imported reindeer flourish at Glenmore National Park (12,500 acres) and may be seen by arrangement.

Beauly *Inverness* (CF 84). This *beau lieu* of our ancestors was named in praise of the setting of the now-ruined Priory built by French monks in the 13th cent., of which the triangular windows and the W doorway are the most notable features. This is Lovat country.

Boat of Garten *Inverness* (CK 81). The ferry which earned this village its name has been superseded by a bridge

745

across the Spey. Strathspey is as famous for dance tunes (in slower tempo than the reel) as for whisky and fishing. The osprey has recently returned to Loch Garten as a breeding species; delightful to watch, especially during the nesting season.

Braemore* *Ross & Cr.* (CB 87). Finely wooded country at head of Strath More. The deep canyon of Corrie Halloch and the 150-ft. Falls of Measach are spectacular sights from the near-by suspension bridge.

Caledonian Canal *Inverness*. The 'longest short-cut' in Britain, running in a straight diagonal for over 60 miles from Corpach (CA 77) to the Moray Firth (CH 85), passing through 29 locks and Lochs Lochy, Oich and Ness. Increasingly used by pleasure craft, whose passengers revel in the lake and mountain scenery.

Canna *Inverness* (BC 80). Island of the Inner Hebrides NW of Rum. The rich iron deposits in Compass Hill affect the magnetic compasses of passing ships.

Carrbridge *Inverness* (CK 82). Village which caters for winter sports. The arch of the 18th-cent. bridge over the Dulnan survives alongside its successor, but for practical pictur-esqueness see General Wade's Slug-gan Bridge (2¼ m.).

Corrieyairick Pass* (2,507 ft.) *Inverness* (CE 79). Superb vantage-point reached by foot on 25-m. mountain track from Laggan to Fort Augustus. The suspension bridge above Glen Tarff was built by Edinburgh University students in 1932.

Cromarty *Ross & Cr.* (CH 86). At NE point of so-called Black Isle at the mouth of Cromarty Firth. Once famous for herring fisheries. Birth-place of Hugh Miller, the mason-geologist (1802–56), whose thatched cottage is kept as a museum. Passenger ferry across the Firth to Nigg, and launch to Invergordon.

Culloden *Inverness* (CH 84). The battle which spelt doom to the '45 rebellion is commemorated by a cairn and stones marking the graves of the fallen clansmen. 'Butcher' Cumber-land is said to have directed the fight from a near-by boulder. Near the River Nairn the Stones of Clava* con-sist of three Bronze-Age cairns ringed by standing stones and containing mysterious inner chambers.

Dingwall* *Ross & Cr.* (CF 85) EC Thurs (3,750). A royal burgh since 1226, county town of Ross, and har-bour at head of Cromarty Firth. Interesting Town House in the main street. Near the church is an obelisk to the first Earl of Cromartie, who chose his resting-place in order to frustrate his wife's avowed intention of dancing on his grave. Tenure of Foulis Castle (5 m. NE) is subject to an annual rent of a snowball at mid-summer – a condition difficult to fulfil in olden days.

Dornie *Ross & Cr.* (BJ 82). Village at junction of Loch Long, Loch Duich and Loch Alsh. The stronghold of the Earls of Seaforth on little Eilean Donan* was shelled by English war-ships in the 18th cent., but has recently been well restored. The romantic Falls of Glomach*, reached via the northern shore of Loch Long, have a 370-ft. drop over the spectacular black cliffs.

Drumnadrochit *Inverness* (CF 82). Vantage-point for monster-spotters on NW shore of Loch Ness. Castle Urquhart stands above the loch, well

The Caledonian Canal: Loch Lochy

Aerofilms

equipped for the repulse of rival clansmen. South of Divach Falls stands the monument to John Cobb, killed in 1952 when attempting the world's water speed record.

Eigg *Inverness* (BE 78). Small island reached from Mallaig, but with no hotels. Vengeful MacLeods from Skye suffocated 200 Macdonalds in a cave on the SE coast not far from the weird volcanic mass of the Sgurr of Eigg (1,289 ft.).

Eilean Donan Castle★. *See* **Dornie.**

Fearn *Ross & Cr.* (CJ 87). Centre of fertile Easter Ross. The roof of the Premonstratensian Abbey collapsed during a Sunday service in 1742, and has been tastelessly restored. Peter Fraser, Prime Minister of New Zealand 1940–9, was born and educated at Hill of Fearn ($\frac{1}{2}$ m.).

Fort Augustus★ *Inverness* (CD 80). Perfect centre for touring and fishing at S end of Loch Ness. The fort was built as a result of the 1715 rising, but was taken by the Highlanders in 1745, only to be lost after Culloden. In the late 19th cent. the site was presented by Lord Lovat to the Benedictine Order, who built their Abbey with a cloister and tower by Pugin.

Fortrose *Ross & Cr.* (CH 85). Formed in the 16th cent. by the amal-

Ben Nevis from the air

gamation of the towns of Chanonry and Rosemarkie, which still preserves its own name. Once an important port, but now visited mainly for golf and bathing. The 15th-cent. bell in the clock tower of the ruined Abbey is still rung for curfew.

Fort William* *Inverness* (CB 77). EC Wed (2,700). The advent of the railway brought rapid development to this town at the S end of the Caledonian Canal and on the steamer route to Oban, so that the fortifications built to restrain the Highlanders became obsolete and were superseded. The West Highland Museum in Cameron Square preserves relics of Scottish traditions, and historical mementoes of Bonnie Prince Charlie and Flora Macdonald. The 'easy' route to the summit of Ben Nevis*, 4,406 ft., highest mountain in the British Isles, begins through Glen Nevis, NE of the town. (4 hrs. up, 3 down – no guide necessary, but good weather essential.) Opposite the large aluminium works to the N are the ruins of 15th-cent. Inverlochy Castle, with massive round corner towers. The stretch of railway between Fort William and Mallaig is said to be one of the loveliest in Britain and the journey is often made by tourists for its scenery alone.

Gairloch *Ross & Cr.* (BJ 87). Village on sea loch near mouth of attractively named Flowerdale. Splendid views of Skye and the mountains.

Glenelg *Inverness* (BJ 81). Car ferry to Skye across Kyle Rhea in summer.

Glenfinnan *Inverness* (BK 78). Angling resort at head of Loch Shiel. A monument marks the historic spot where Prince Charles Edward raised his standard at the gathering of the Clans in 1745.

Glen Affric *Inverness* (CB 82). Now made more accessible by the work of the hydro-electric authority, which has taken great pains to preserve the natural beauty of this untameable glen.

Gruinard Bay *Ross & Cr.* (BK 89). Memorable both for its sands and for the first dramatic view as the road from the S tops a rise and prepares for a 1-in-4 descent to the shore.

Harris* *Inverness* (BB 89). Joined at the north to Lewis, the two together forming one island famous for hand-woven tweed and cloth. Wild, rocky and mountainous. South Harris has interesting funeral cairns, a church at Rodel with curious sculpture and Leverburgh, where Lord Lever-hulme's philanthropic fishery schemes met with failure. The Hebridean Car Ferry Service, sailing from Uig, Skye, is a pleasant and economical way of taking your car to this delight-ful island.

Invergarry *Inverness* (CD 80). A road to Skye swings west through the mountains from Loch Oich. Bonnie Prince Charlie and the clansmen marched S from here in August 1745.

Invergordon *Ross & Cr.* (CH 86). Ancient town on N side of landlocked Cromarty Firth. Its fine harbour was once an important naval base, and in 1931 was the scene of a mutiny against reductions in service pay.

Inverness** (CG 84) EC Wed (29,770). The 'capital' of the High-lands, full of life independent of the tourist season. Known for the sweet-ness of the air, the purity of the English language spoken by the inhabitants, and for a beautiful situation astride the River Ness, with mountains to E and W, two great firths to the N, and Loch Ness and the Caledonian Canal to the SW. The cream of the world's pipers meet in competition at the Northern Meeting which is followed by the Northern Meeting Balls, some-times graced by royalty.

Castles have come and gone since before the days of Macbeth. The ter-race of the most modern (which houses the county offices and law courts) has a statue of Flora Macdonald. 19th-cent. St Andrew's Cathedral is well-designed and impressive, with an interesting chapter house and a copy of the famous angel font in Copen-hagen. Note the many town houses of the 18th-cent. gentry, and the collec-tion of Jacobite relics in the Museum.

Kingussie *Inverness* (CH 80). Healthy resort on the Spey 745 ft. above sea-level, surrounded by high mountains. Fishing, golf and wonderful walks when these do not conflict with shoot-ing and stalking interests. *Am Fas-gadh** is a fascinating Highland Folk Museum founded by Miss Grant of Iona, and now administered by the Scottish universities.

Kinlochewe *Ross & Cr.* (CA 86). Near the head of Loch Maree and surrounded by mountains, the most spectacular being Beinn Eighe, formed of red sandstone powdered with white quartzite. Its western slopes are a nature reserve, haunts of the golden eagle and the wild cat.

Kyle of Lochalsh* *Ross & Cr.* (BH 82). Road and rail terminus for Skye, giving a taste of magnificent sea loch scenery. The royal wife of a Mac-donald living across the Kyle earned the name of 'Saucy Mary' for stretch-ing a chain across the channel in the hope of extorting toll money from passing ships. Car ferry to Kyleakin in Skye.

Lewis* *Ross & Cr.* (BC 93). Joined to Harris, which is in Inverness-shire. Cars can be shipped from Mallaig and Kyle of Lochalsh or by car ferry from Uig, then motor to Stornoway. Lord

Callanish Standing Stones, Lewis *Allan Cash*

Leverhulme presented his 19th-cent. mansion, Lewis Castle, to Stornoway, the chief town and fishing harbour. The land is peaty and acid, but is now being regenerated on a large scale. Callanish Standing Stones*, near the head of Loch Roag, are remarkable.

Mallaig *Inverness* (BG 79). Fishing port and centre for ships to the Western Isles (cars carried). Car ferry to Armadale in Skye (see also reference to car ferries under **Skye**).

Mallaig Harbour *Radio Times Hulton Picture Library*

Morar *Inverness* (BG 79). The deepest of all lochs empties into the sea through a well-disguised hydro-electric station. H.Q. of the Highland Home Industries overlooking famous white sands.

Muir of Ord *Ross & Cr.* (CF 84). Centre of fertile farmland. Students are admitted to library and museum of Tarradale House, near the Beauly Firth.

Poolewe *Ross & Cr.* (BJ 88). At head of Loch Ewe at the 'pool' famous for fishing where the waters from Loch Maree enter the sea. The gardens of Inverewe* are famous for a superb collection of subtropical plants and shrubs.

Roybridge *Inverness* (CC 78). Village at foot of Glen Roy, which has strange 'parallel roads' or terraces formed by lakes of the Ice Age.

Rhum *Inverness* (BD 80). Island nature reserve, where casual landing is discouraged. The group of peaks topped by Askival (2,659 ft.) is an impressive sight from Skye and the mainland.

Skye** *Inverness* (BE 83). Reached by car ferry from 'over the sea' via Mallaig, Glenelg or Kyle of Lochalsh; new car ferry in operation from the spring of 1964 linking Uig (BD 86) with the Outer Hebrides. The coast is broken by a maze of sea lochs, so that no inland point is more than 5 m. from the sea, and some of the wildest spots are best reached by boat. The rugged Cuillins, of which Sgurr Alasdair (3,309 ft.) is the highest, and many lesser mountains provide holiday pursuits for climbers and walkers. Loch Scavaig may have a forbidding grandeur, and Dunvegan Head with the basalt stacks called MacLeod's Maidens may be daunting, but alongside the magnificence there are peaceful beaches for fishing and bathing. Dunvegan Castle* (BC 84), the home of the MacLeods since time immemorial, was originally built without any possible approach from the land. The 15th-cent. tower and dungeons and the gracious 18th-cent. reception rooms are of great interest, together with a proud collection of historical and literary relics.

Portree, the chief town, sits on a platform of rock above its harbour, and is always busy with comings and goings, whilst most of the villages and many of the outlying crofts take in summer visitors.

Spean Bridge *Inverness* (CC 78). The memorial to the Commandos surveys the rugged terrain which was their wartime training ground.

Stornoway *Ross & Cr.* (BE 93) EC Wed (5,220). *See* **Lewis** *above.*

Stromeferry *Ross & Cr.* (BJ 83). A car ferry crosses Loch Carron, and roads lead N across unfrequented wild country to Applecross or Shieldaig.

Strathpeffer *Ross & Cr.* (CE 85). The one-time spa town has remained popular for golf, fishing and expeditions in a sheltered and wooded valley which contrasts strangely with neighbouring mountain wildness. Ben Wyvis (3,429 ft.), 10 m. distant, can be climbed by the inexperienced if adequate time is allowed.

Tain *Ross & Cr.* (CH 88). A royal burgh which derives its name from the Norse 'Thing', meaning an assembly. Sandy beach on Dornoch Firth, golf and water sports. The Tolbooth with its conical spire is near the 14th-cent. Church of St Duthus. The earlier chapel of the same saint was a place of pilgrimage and penance for two Scottish kings.

On the summit of Sgurr nan Gillean in the Cuillins   J. Allan Cash

Kisimul Castle off Castlebay, Barra

Tomdoun *Inverness* (CB 80). Hydro-electric works have deepened and lengthened Lochs Garry and Quoich, but care has been taken to preserve fishing amenities.

Uist (North & South)★, Benbecula★ and Barra★ *Inverness*. Southernmost islands of the Outer Hebrides, reached by air or steamship. North Uist is a pattern of inland waters, with Lochmaddy (AK 86) as capital. Benbecula (AH 85) lies sandwiched between North and South Uist, connected by two bridges. Benbecula and South Uist both boast historical connections with Bonnie Prince Charlie and Flora Macdonald; South Uist (AH 83) has a rocket range on its wild western shore. Barra (AG 80) is linked to South Uist by ferry. An ancestor of the Macneil of Barra is said to have refused to accompany Noah in the ark because he already had a boat of his own; the spirit of sturdy independence still survives on the island. Kisimul Castle is notable. In calm weather the smaller islands to the S, famous for rock formations, flowers and seabirds, are ideal for boating expeditions. Cars can be shipped to Uist by the Hebridean Car Ferry Service from Uig to Lochmaddy, but if one wishes to take a car to Barra, it is necessary to travel to Oban and ship the car by Messrs. Macbrayne's MV 'Claymore'. As there are only 14 m. of road on the island, few people trouble to do this but hire on the island.

Ullapool★ *Ross & Cr.* (CB 89). Most attractive lime-washed town with excellent harbour and sea-bathing in Loch Broom. Good centre for exploring the wild island-studded coast to the NW. The Summer Isles are to be recommended.

The Fish Market, Lerwick

THE

NORTH HIGHLANDS

Orkney and Shetland

AN INTRODUCTION BY ROBERT KEMP

Is any quality held in common by the two northernmost counties of Scotland, Caithness and Sutherland, and the two northern groups of islands, Orkney and Shetland? Sutherland, built up from ancient rocks that still seem to record some tortured spasm of the earth's crust, presents a wild and grandly mountainous aspect, whereas Caithness, with fields and moors resting on the Old Red Sandstone, is mainly flat, and seems to be swept still flatter by every wind. So too with the islands. The Orkneys, separated from Caithness by the Pentland Firth, share the geological basis of their mainland neighbour and astonish by the unexpected richness of their agriculture, while Shetland, much farther north, partakes to some extent in the geological formations of Sutherland

and in appearance is altogether fiercer and more spectacular than the gentle Orkneys.

Yet these four units might be said to compose 'Viking Scotland'. True, in days long past, the long ships with their raven-helmed crews thrust far down the west coast and imposed Norse rule on the Hebrides; but it is in our chosen territory that their influence most strongly persists. Sutherland, occupying the north-west corner of the Scottish mainland, is so called because it was 'southern land' to the Norsemen. The 'ness' in Caithness, the north-eastern county, is simply the Norse word for a headland. And in Orkney and Shetland the signature may be read even more clearly. The Cathedral of St Magnus in Kirkwall, the capital of the Orkneys, commemorates a claimant to the Old Norse earldom. In Shetland men often think of themselves as more Norse than Scots – and why not, for many things, from family names to dialect words and boat-design, remind us that Bergen is no farther away than Aberdeen? Indeed, both Orkney and Shetland were added to the Scottish Crown in a somewhat casual way – in 1468 they were pledged by the King of Denmark in payment of the dowry of his daughter on her marriage to the King of Scots. But the pledge was never redeemed.

Sutherland

Sutherland has one other distinction: it is the only part of the region which one thinks of as truly 'Highland'. For one thing, it contains many splendid mountains. Ben More in Assynt (3,273 feet) is the highest; but such summits as those of Ben Loyal, Ben Hope, Foinaven, Quinag and Suilven are very noble – in fact, many who should know maintain that the county encloses the best mountain scenery in Scotland. It also contains delectable glens and a multitude of lochs of all shapes and sizes, of which the largest is the attenuated Loch Shin. And this is 'clan country' – the Mackays, Sutherlands, Roses, as well as some Mackenzies and Macleods regard it as their cradle, and you may find a memorial to Rob Donn, the famous Mackay bard, in the churchyard at Durness. Rob spoke, and made his songs, in the Gaelic tongue, which is still the language of the western part of the county, in contrast to Caithness and the Islands.

Those who have driven through Sutherland, even once, observing not only the mountain masses but the expanses of bare moorland through which the shelves of rock project, are not surprised to learn that the proportion of arable land is the lowest in Scotland. Much of the territory is given over to sheep-runs and deer-forest – though here the word 'forest' is something of a misnomer, since such tracts are invariably bare of trees. Most of the inhabitants are 'crofters' and follow the way of life that is still general in the Highlands and Islands. A croft is a tiny farm, sometimes as small as five acres in extent (though in Sutherland at the last count the average size was thirteen acres, smaller than anywhere except Shetland). This tiny plot affords its owner and his family a bare basic living; but no crofter thinks of it as his sole support: he must always find additional work, such as fishing, working on the roads or weaving. He is generally intelligent and independent – and, if his sustenance seems meagre, remember that Sutherland had the reputation of rearing the tallest men in the British Isles.

The Norse were dominant here from 1034, when the Jarl Thorfinn colonized 'Sudrland', until the early 13th century, when they were driven out by the Scottish king. They have left traces in the place-names but no other visible remains. Their prehistoric predecessors, on the other hand, are remembered

Edwin Smith **Kirkwall, Orkney: the Cathedral of St. Mag**

by 'brochs' (or round towers), 'Picts' houses', mounds, cairns and hut-circles, the best being Dun Dornadilla, in the parish of Durness. Historically, the strongest as well as the most tragic memory is of the notorious 'Clearances' in the 19th century, when the crofters were driven from their holdings in such parts as Strathnaver. For this act the first Duke of Sutherland is never likely to receive forgiveness in popular memory, however his apologists may attempt to defend his policy.

The county can boast of no town of any size – even the county town of Dornoch had at the last census a population of under the thousand. So buildings of any size are lacking. Perhaps the most notable is the severely functional Cape Wrath Lighthouse. Difficult to reach except on foot across a wild peninsula called the Parph, it stands on a huge cliff, at the very north-west extremity of our island. But if Sutherland has no considerable towns, there are many hospitable fishing-inns, such as those at Tongue and Durness. And if many of the roads are narrow, they can lead the motorist through some of the grandest and lovelist scenery in Britain – especially the coast roads. If you like to get away from people, and find primeval landscape, Sutherland is your county.

Caithness

Caithness is the smallish triangular county in the extreme north-east of Scotland. Its boundaries are Sutherland on the west, the Pentland Firth on the north and the Moray Firth on the east. Alongside its western neighbour one thinks of it as flat and undramatic. But this is to forget that its southern corner is filled by a remarkable plateau at a level of 1,000 feet, and that three of the hills rising from this, Morven, Scaraben and Maiden's Pap, are conspicuous landmarks from afar. From these the county reaches to the north in a low-lying plain. There are two small towns – Wick, a royal burgh, and Thurso, both giving their name to rivers not large in volume but excellent in the eyes of fishermen, as are the inland lochs. Prehistoric man has left his signs here, in the brochs, cairns, forts and standing-stones. There are many traces of early Christian chapels, and the delightful kirks at Dunnet, Canisbay and Reay all have histories going back beyond the Reformation. Medieval times have bequeathed on us a number of stout castles, built by the independent and often lawless barons for their own survival, and one of these, the Castle of Mey, has achieved fresh fame in the present day by having been bought by the Queen Mother as her own Scottish residence. It is strange and surprising to find at Caithness, so far from what most regard as the centre of things, one of the most up-to-date buildings in the world – the atomic reactor, a great ball-shaped structure, at Dounreay near Thurso. Yet most of us may doubt whether Dounreay will ever be as famous a name as John o' Groats – so called from John de Groot, a Dutchman who settled here with his two brothers at the beginning of the 15th century. Soon there were eight families of de Groots, and to avoid disputes over precedence the peace-loving John built an octagonal room and table, so that each might boast of being at the head of the table.

Despite wide tracts of moorland suitable only for game or for grazing, Caithness offers more promise to the farmer than does Sutherland, which was given over to sheep and deer after the Clearances. On fertile ground next to the sea, cattle are bred for milk or for the stock market. Fishing is the second industry, and there is some distilling.

Between Caithness and Orkney is the Pentland Firth, one of the most perilous stretches of water round the shores of Britain. Through it races the tide from the

Ben Hope from Loch Hope, Sutherland *G. Douglas Bolton*

Atlantic to the North Sea and back again, at rates of from six to twelve knots. Many ships have met their end on the dangerous Skerries or reefs, and the local fishermen know they must avoid a number of boiling whirlpools with such picturesque names as the Swelkie, the Boars of Duncansby, the Merry Men o' Mey and the Wells of Swona. Many a ship has been wrecked on the Pentland Skerries or the cliffs of Hoy, and it is then that the world hears of the courage and seamanship of the crew of the Longhope lifeboat, which has its station in the south of Hoy.

Orkney

Across the Firth, only a little more than six miles broad at its narrowest point, the south isles of Orkney seem to beckon us. Orkney may be reached by air from Aberdeen or Wilk or by steamer from Leith, Aberdeen or Scrabster. And here we are truly in the old Norse earldom, although the history of the Orkneys is so ancient that sometimes even this can seem to be no more than a brief episode. These were the Orcades of the ancients and gave their name to the stirring *Orkneyinga Saga*. But in far earlier times their unknown inhabitants built at Stenness a stone circle which is worthy of comparison with Stonehenge. The tomb at Maeshowe and the underground village of Skara Brae, both on the largest island (which is usually called the Mainland), suggest to us strange, remote and primitive ways of life, when man seemed to be struggling for admittance on the very threshold of civilization. Orkney abounds with evidence of very old settlement by man, as far back as the Stone and Bronze Ages. At Birsay there are also the remains of a Celtic monastery of the Columban period and rule – an arrangement not of highly organized conventual buildings but of separate cells. One may find, too, such a curiosity as the Dwarfie Stone in Hoy, an enormous block of sandstone with chambers and a stone bunk hollowed out of it.

But it was the Norsemen, coming in the 9th century, who contributed the chief glory of these islands: the Cathedral of St Magnus in Kirkwall, once under the archdiocese of Trondheim, and now a parish church under the Presbyterian rule of the Scottish Kirk. This little masterpiece in the Norman style was begun in the 12th century and has been proudly preserved – unlike its neighbour, the ruined Bishop's Palace, still a reminder of the grandeur of the Norse period.

There are more than seventy islands in the Orkney group, but fewer and fewer are populated today – the number is under twenty. The largest islands, and those of the greatest importance, are grouped round an anchorage that bears a name known to naval men everywhere – Scapa Flow. Here the Grand Fleet established its northern base at the beginning of the First World War; and here the surrendered German Fleet was brought after the Armistice. Many still recall the day when the German sailors opened the sea-cocks of their vessels and scuttled the fleet – incidentally, the foundation of a salvage industry which Orkney found so much to its advantage between the wars. During the Second World War, as part of the Navy's defences against submarines, a barrier, now known as the Churchill Causeway, was built to link all the islands between the Mainland and South Ronaldsay. The Italian prisoners of war who did the work left behind them also a little chapel made from an army hut and decorated with loving care. Kirkwall and Stromness are both towns of character, huddled together about their narrow streets, with schools, newspapers and many other marks of lively communities.

Both the Orkneys and Shetland are virtually without trees: but in Orkney the soil is fertile and intensively farmed by a race of ingenious and up-to-date farmers, famous chiefly for their beef-cattle and eggs. Whisky is distilled near Kirkwall and supplied as the basis for some of the most widely advertised blends. The straw-backed Orkney chairs are much sought after and Orkney cheese, mild and with a tang of its own, is now made and exported by factories. Among the most faithful visitors to Orkney are the fishermen, who come for the sake of the excellent sport on such lochs as Stenness and Harray.

Shetland

Sailing or flying from Orkney across the stormy Atlantic waters to Shetland, the visitor passes half-way the Fair Isle, a solitary and sparsely inhabited rock. Its traditionally-patterned knitwear was popularized by the Duke of Windsor, when Prince of Wales, and its ornithological station is known to all bird-watchers.

Then, still farther north, he reaches Sumburgh Head, the southern tip of Shetland, a group of islands so rich in their appeal that it is hard to know how to begin. When he first sees them, the newcomer is probably struck by such features as the towering cliffs of Bressay and of Fitful Head or, in the north Mainland, of Ronas Hill. If he is somewhat appalled by the stern, naked moors, he will be delighted with the capital, Lerwick, where the narrow principal street is all paved, and from it steep lanes lead up the hill from the harbour. If his interests are archaeological, he will want to spend days at Sumburgh. Here, at Jarlshof, the evidence of several layers of civilization may be studied. There is, for example, a very fine 'broch' (another may be seen on Mousa) as well as the traces of Viking dwellings and underground houses. If he is interested in animals, he may watch the Shetland ponies running wild on the northernmost island of Unst. There are also a small breed of cattle, a small breed of dog (the Shetland collie) and the Shetland sheep, with wool so soft that it must be 'roo'd' or plucked, not sheared. It comes in various colours – black and 'moorit' (a brownish red), as well as white. This fine wool is, of course, the reason why Shetland garments are so soft and warm, and the visitor will certainly want to take back some of these, beautifully knitted in the home. As well as jerseys and cardigans, the Shetland women still knit baby-shawls of such fine texture that they could be drawn through a wedding-ring. If he comes at midsummer, he will realize that he is truly in a 'land of the midnight sun' and may watch the blazing orb descend to the horizon, rest there for a moment, as it seems, then begin to ascend the heavens again for another day. If he is an ornithologist, he will be out to study, in particular, the sea-birds which abound in such a sanctuary as Noss. If a fisherman, and at the right time of year, he may find himself fishing for sea-trout in the 'voes' or narrow arms of the sea. And perhaps he will revisit the islands in late January to participate in the festival of Up-Helly-Aa, during which a complete Norse galley is hauled through the streets of Lerwick and finally consumed in a bonfire made by the torches of its hundreds of attendants. Truly, there is no end to the attraction of Shetland and its vivid life.

The Shetlanders, unlike the Orcadians, are as much seamen as crofters. Fishing plays an important, if often unreliable, part in their economy, and that simple old man to whom you talk will very likely have sailed half a dozen times round the world. In his conversation he will use many words of Norse origin. He

Ardvreck Castle on Loch Assynt, Sutherland *G. Douglas Bolton*

may bear a name that is sturdy Norse and if he goes fishing he will sail a boat of the shapeliest Norse lines. He may talk of such things as 'scattald' – the common grazing on the hill – and 'udal' law, the Norse system so different from the feudal in many respects. We have passed through a region where the Vikings left many writings, but in Shetland one often feels that they have never left.

Some houses and gardens open to the public

Bishop's Palace Orkney At Kirkwall *Map* DE 101. *14th cent., in ruins; round tower built by Bishop Reid, with 17th-cent. additions by the Earl of Orkney.*

Bishop's Palace At Thurso *Map* DB 96. *Ruins of medieval palace, once home of the Bishops of Caithness; near the shores of Thurso Bay W of town.*

Castle of Mey 4m NE of Dunnet, 6m W of John O'Groats off A836 *Map* DC 97. *17th cent.; home of Her Majesty Queen Elizabeth the Queen Mother. Excellent views across the Pentland Firth towards the Orkneys. Gardens only; may be opened several days of the year.*

Earl Patrick's Palace At Kirkwall *Map* DE 101. *Renaissance-style, built by Patrick Stewart, Earl of Orkney; roofless; oriel windows.*

Jarlshof Prehistoric Site Sumburgh 27m S of Lerwick on A970. *Map* EE 110. *Bronze Age, Iron Age and Viking settlements with 13th-cent. medieval farmstead. 17th-cent. Laird's House is the 'Jarlshof' of Scott's novel* The Pirate.

Mousa Broch Sandwick 14m S of Lerwick *Map* EE 112. *Broch, 40-ft. high, exceptionally well preserved; reached by boat from Leebitton on Mousa Sound.*

Scalloway Castle 6½m W of Lerwick on A970 *Map* ED 113. *17th cent.; built by Patrick Stewart, Earl of Orkney; designed on the 'two-stepped' plan. Open on application to custodian.*

Skara Brae 7m N of Stromness off B9056 *Map* DC 101. *Collection of Stone Age dwellings engulfed in drift sand, well preserved; stone furniture and fireplaces.*

Rovie Lodge Rogart 9m NW of Golspie off A839 *Map* CH 90. *Gardens with herbaceous and heath borders; lawns, shrubs and water plants; near the Torbreck Burn.*

Books for further reading

The 'feel' of the North

G. M. BROWN *A Calendar of Love* 1968
IAN GRIMBLE *Chief of Mackay* 1965
NEIL M. GUNN *Highland River*
JOHN PREBBLE *The Highland Clearances* 1963
D. C. THOMSON and I. GRIMBLE (eds.) *The Future of the Highlands* 1968

Natural history

JAMES COUTTS *Game Fishing: A Guide to the Shetlands* 1967
MAURICE C. COX *The Shetland Pony* 1965
J. SAXON *Fossil Fishes of Caithness and Orkney* 1967
L. S. and U. M. VENABLES *Birds and Mammals of Shetland* 1955

KENNETH WILLIAMSON *Fair Isle and its Birds* 1965

Topography

JOHN R. ALLAN *North-East Lowlands of Scotland* 1952
ANDREW T. CLUNESS (ed.) *The Shetland Book* 1967
D. GRANT *Old Thurso* 1968
ERIC LINKLATER *Orkney and Shetland* 1965
JOHN SHEARER, et al. *The New Orkney Book* 1966
DOUGLAS SUTHERLAND *Against the Wind: An Orkney Idyll* 1966
F. T. WAINWRIGHT (ed.) *The Northern Isles* 1962

Gazetteer

THE NORTH HIGHLANDS, ORKNEY AND SHETLAND

Dornoch Cathedral, Sutherland
G. Douglas Bolton

Altnaharra *Suth.* (CF 93). Fishing centre at W end of Loch Naver with good hill-walking country all around. Brochs and hut-circles for archaeologists.

Armadale *Suth.* (CH 96). Farming and fishing village at the head of a pretty bay. Noted for its sheep. At Kirktomy Point, 2 m. NW, is curious tunnel-like cave through which boats can pass.

Berriedale *Caith.* (DB 92). The Langwell Water and Berriedale river enter the sea under the eye of the ruined 14th-cent. castle. Stags' antlers decorating houses remind one that the hills inland provide good stalking.

Bettyhill *Suth.* (CH 96) EC Wed. Coastal village with fine sands at point where the R. Naver flows into sea. Rocky scenery; mountains well seen from Strath Naver.

Brora* *Suth.* (CK 90). EC Wed. (1,074). Angling and holiday centre with fine sands, at the mouth of Strath Brora. On W side of Loch Brora, the Carrol Rock is 650 ft. high. There are several brochs in the neighbourhood, and a small coal-mine, which is owned by the miners themselves.

Cape Wrath *Suth.* (CC 97). Britain's NW corner, where the Atlantic hurls boulders at the 500-ft. cliffs. Ferry across the Kyle of Durness, and then a 10-mile walk over the moors. Tough walkers can follow a more varied route up the shore from Sheigra, past Sandwood Bay.

Dornoch *Suth.* (CH 88) EC Thurs (930). Attractive little town with a much-restored 13th-cent. cathedral, and the tower of an ancient castle, once the Bishop's palace. Excellent bathing, fishing and golf links. Skibo Castle, 5 m. W, was once owned by Andrew Carnegie.

Dounreay *Caith.* (CK 96). The experimental fast reactor of the U.K. Atomic Energy Authority was erected here to test the feasibility of deriving power from uranium instead of from coal (1 ton uranium = 3 million tons of coal). Step back a few years to contemplate the little old church at Reay, with external staircase.

Dunbeath *Caith.* (DB 92) EC Thurs (490). Fishing village with a notable broch and a 15th-cent. castle. Picts' houses beside the Dunbeath Water stand some 3 m. NW.

761

Dunnet *Caith.* (DC 97) EC Thurs (640). The Head is the most northerly point on the Scottish mainland, with views of Orkney (the Old Man of Hoy is conspicuous) across the swirling waters of Pentland Firth. There is a sandy beach and an ancient church with saddleback tower. 5 m. E is the 16th-cent. but restored Castle of Mey, formerly Barrogill Castle, the Scottish residence of Queen Elizabeth the Queen Mother.

Durness *Suth.* (CE 96) EC Wed (410). A village some 10 m. from Cape Wrath. Fine sands on Balnakill Bay. In another bay in the cliffs, 2 m. E, are the three Caves of Smoo, of which the outer one can be entered at low tide.

Golspie *Suth.* (CJ 89) EC Wed (1,330). Seaside village with excellent golf and sands. The church has notable Sutherland loft or gallery (1738) and pulpit. 1 m. E is Dunrobin Castle (Countess of Sutherland) embodying a 13th-cent. keep. Open to visitors (noteworthy pictures).

Halkirk *Caith.* (DB 95) EC Wed (1,530). Angling centre on Thurso river, with Loch Calder to W. Brawl Castle (14th cent.) has walls 10 ft. thick (*see* **Watten,** *below*).

Helmsdale *Suth.* (DA 91) EC Wed. Fishing village with harbour. Bathing, golf, sea and river fishing. Remains of 15th-cent. castle. Some 7 m. S is a fine broch; others lie N of the village towards the Ord of Caithness, a

Near John O'Groats: the church at Canisbay   *G. Douglas Bolton*

Lochinver, Sutherland

J. Allan Cash

Scourie, Sutherland: the manse and church   *J. Allan Cash*
Opposite: **Orkney: the stones of Stenness**   *J. Allan Cash*

headland that makes a wonderful viewpoint.

Hoy* *Ork.* (DC 99). Second largest of the Orkney islands and the hilliest of them. Ward Hill (botanists' hunting-ground) is 1,565 ft. high. Some of Britain's finest cliff scenery lies along the W coast. The Old Man of Hoy, a detached pillar, rises 450 ft. above the sea. At Rackwick on SW coast is the Dwarfie Stone, a Neolithic burial-chamber hollowed out of the rock. Fine gardens can be seen at Melsetter in the S of Hoy.

Inchnadamph *Suth.* (CC 92). Hotel and scattered crofts at SE end of Loch Assynt, beside which are the ruins of Ardvreck Castle (15th cent.) and of Edderchalder House (17th cent.). Quinag (2,399 ft.) is well seen to the NW. To the E is colourful Ben More Assynt (3,273 ft.).

Iverkirkaig *Suth.* (CA 91). Scattered crofting village at head of the bay where the Kirkaig river rushes out. There is a riverside path to the Falls of Kirkaig (2 m. away), from which the river drops into a chasm. To the S, a narrow winding road runs among lochs and hills to Ullapool.

John o' Groats *Caith.* (DD 97) EC Wed. The name is romantic, but the scene is not typically Scottish Highland. John's house was demolished years ago; his grave is at Canisbay Church. The northernmost point on the mainland is really Dunnet Head (*see above*). Duncansby Head, 1½ m. E, with its detached rocks, has a finer viewpoint.

Kirkwall *Ork.* (DE 101) EC Wed (4,492). Stone-paved streets and narrow alleys characterize the capital of Mainland (and indeed of the Orkneys as a whole). St Magnus Cathedral (mainly 12th cent.) has a notable nave and memorials of many periods. There are ruined palaces of

765

bishops (16th cent.) and earls (17th cent.). S of the town, the sandy bay opens out into Scapa Flow, the naval anchorage.

Kylesku *Suth.* (CC 93). The ferry (free) is beautifully placed where lochs Glendu and Glencoil join Loch Cairnbawn. Near the head of Loch Glencoil is Eas Coul Aulin, the highest waterfall in Britain (some 600 ft.).

Lairg *Suth.* (CF 90) EC Wed (960). Village where miscellaneous supplies brought up by rail are transferred to road vehicles for further transport to crofts and villages all over Sutherland. Instructive to town dwellers. Very good centre, with boating, bathing and fishing. Loch Shin, 15 m. long and nowhere more than 2 m. wide, is now used by the North of Scotland Hydro-Electricity Board.

Latheron *Caith.* (DB 93). Sights include a whalebone arch, an ancient standing stone and an old tower in which the church bells used to hang. 2 m. N is Forse, with its ruined castle and primitive stone dwellings.

Laxford Bridge *Suth.* (CC 93). Where the Laxford river (noted for salmon) enters Loch Laxford amid a glorious tangle of rocks and lochs.

Lochinver *Suth.* (CA 92). Amphibious parish containing nearly 300 named lochs and many without names. It is strung out beside the final half mile or so of the R. Inver. Small pier, excellent fishing, both sea and freshwater. SE, Suilven (2,399 ft.) rises as a rounded height, seemingly inaccessible.

Orkney Islands. 28 of the 67 islands are inhabited. The largest, Mainland, has over 180 m. of motor roads. *See* **Kirkwall, Hoy, Stromness,** etc.

Rhiconich *Suth.* (CC 95). Here a narrow road goes NW by Kinloch-

bervie (a fishing village) to Sheigra, the northernmost village on the W coast. Primitive scenery. A rough 4-m. walk leads N to Sandwood Bay and strong walkers can continue to Cape Wrath.

Scourie *Suth.* (CB 94) EC Wed (340). Village on a small bay in the rocky coast. Offshore 2 m. N is Handa Island, with great cliffs and flights of raucous sea-birds.

Shetland Isles. Fewer than 20 of the 100 are inhabited. The largest is Mainland, whose capital is Lerwick (5,932), a fishing port on the W side of Bressay Sound. To the W is Scalloway, with its ruined castle (1600); to the S, Sandwick, whence boats cross to Mousa island (fine broch). 25 m. S of Lerwick is Sumburgh, with fine beaches and the remains of Jarlshof, a late Bronze Age settlement with fascinating evidence of occupation. From Sumburgh Head the view includes Fair Isle.

Stoer *Suth.* (CA 92). Crofting village on rocky indented coast extending to the Point of Stoer, where cliffs are 300 ft. high. The views are remarkable. Clachtoll, 1 m. S, has white sands and rugged rocks. 2 m. S is Achmelvich, a township on a fine sandy bay.

Stromness *Ork.* (DC 100). EC Thurs (1,578). Hillside town with harbour. 5 m. E are the Standing Stones of Stennis and Maeshowe, a great chambered burial mound, 300 ft. in circumference and 25 ft. high, with Runic inscriptions in the central chamber. 7 m. N of Stromness is Skara Brae, a wonderfully preserved Neolithic settlement. 15 m. N is Birsay with its ruined 16th-cent. Earl's palace and the remains of an 11th-cent. church: this was Orkney's first cathedral.

harbour, Stromness, Orkney *J. Allan Cash*

Thurso *Caith.* (DB 96) EC Thurs (9,012). Town and port at the head of the bay sheltered by Dunnet Head (*see above*). For long it was the centre of the Caithness paving-stone industry and the stones are still much in evidence. The museum contains the collection of the geologist Robert Dick (1811–66). On the W side of the bay, beyond the ruins of the Bishop's palace (13th cent.) is Scrabster, whence boats cross to and from Orkney. E of the town stands ruined Thurso Castle. Nearby, Harold's Tower marks where the Earl of Caithness was killed in 1136.

Tongue *Suth.* (CF 95) EC Sat (830). Picturesque village on the Kyle of Tongue, with bathing, fishing, boating and some circular routes through wonderful mountain and loch scenery. Nobody knows the age of Castle Varrick, now in ruins. To the S are stately Ben Loyal (2,504 ft.) and Ben Hope (3,040 ft.).

Watten *Caith.* (DC 95). Village headquarters for those who fish for trout in the neighbouring loch.

Wick★ *Caith.* (DD 94) EC Wed (7,418). Ancient town, the centre for herring fishery, with a harbour in a rocky coast sprinkled with castles. To the S are the ruined castle of Old Wick and a rock arch known as Brig o' Tram. Northwards, precariously placed on a cliff edge, stand the ruins of Girnigoe and Sinclair castles and Ackergill tower. N of Keiss is Bucholie Castle, with brochs nearby.

Wick, Caithness   *G. Douglas Bolton*

Opposite: Detail from the original painting by Richard Eurich.
The most northerly point of Britain – and of Caithness – is not John O'Groats but Dunnet Head. The picture shows the bones and beakers, and a passage-grave, left by invaders 4,000 years ago. Wild life is represented by the Arctic tern and the Scottish primrose. A contrastingly modern touch is given by the *John O'Groats Journal*, which presents a photograph of the atomic station at Dounreay.

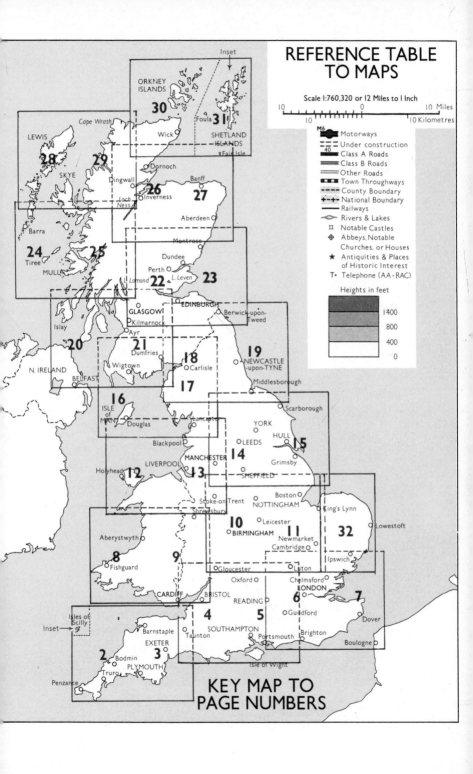

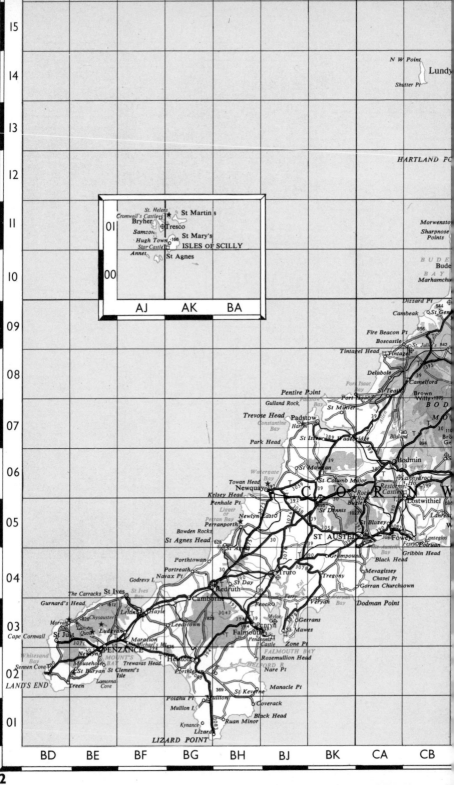

15

14
N W Point   Lundy
Shutter Pt

13

12
HARTLAND PO

11
St. Helens ★ St Martin's
Cromwell's Castle
Bryher ⌐Tresco
Samson   St Mary's
Hugh Town ₁₆₆ ISLES OF SCILLY
Star Castle
Annet   St Agnes
Morwenstow
Sharpnose
Points

01

00

AJ   AK   BA

B U D E
Bude
BAY
Marhamchu

10

09
Dizzard Pt   844
Cambeak   St Gen
Fire Beacon Pt   856
Boscastle St Julio's 842
Tintagel Head   Tintagel
Delabole   Camelford
Brown
Willy ₁₃₇₅
Pentire Point   B O D
Gulland Rock   Port Isaac   M O
Trevose Head   St Teath
Constantine   Port Isaac   30 11
Bay   Bay   Bra
Padstow   Blisland   Ge
Harlyn   894
Park Head   St Issey ₃₈₉ Wadebridge

08

07

06
Watergate   Bodmin
Bay   St Mawgan   Lanhydrock
Towan Head   St Columb Major   Ho
Newquay   Roch   Restormel
Kelsey Head   Roc   Castle
Penhale Pt   Bugle   Lostwithiel
Ligger   St Dennis
Newlyn East   St Blazey   Lanhea
Petranporth   St Austell   Fowey Lanteglos
Bawden Rocks   Gribbin Head
St Agnes Head   ST AUSTELL   Black Head
Porthtowan   Grampound   Mevagissey
Portreath   Truro   Chapel Pt
Godrevy I.   St Day   Tregony   Gorran Churchtown
Navax Pt   Redruth   Veryan   Dodman Point
The Carracks St Ives   Camborne   Probus   Bay
Gurnard's Head   St Ives   Gerrans
Bay   Penryn   St Mawes
Morvah   Leedstown   Mylor
Chysauster   Falmouth   Zone Pt
Lanyon   Ludgvan   Pendennis   FALMOUTH BAY
Quoit   Marazion   Castle   Rosemullion Head
Cape Cornwall   St Just   Michael's Mt   Nare Pt
PENZANCE   Helston
Newlyn   MOUNT'S   Manacle Pt
Whitesand   Mousehole BAY Trewavas Head
Bay   St Buryan St Clement's   Porthleven
Sennen Cove   Isle   Poldhu Pt   St Keverne
LAND'S END   Treen   Lamorna   Mullion   Coverack
Cove   Mullion I.   Black Head
Kynance   Ruan Minor
Lizard
LIZARD POINT

05

04

03

02

01

BD   BE   BF   BG   BH   BJ   BK   CA   CB

2

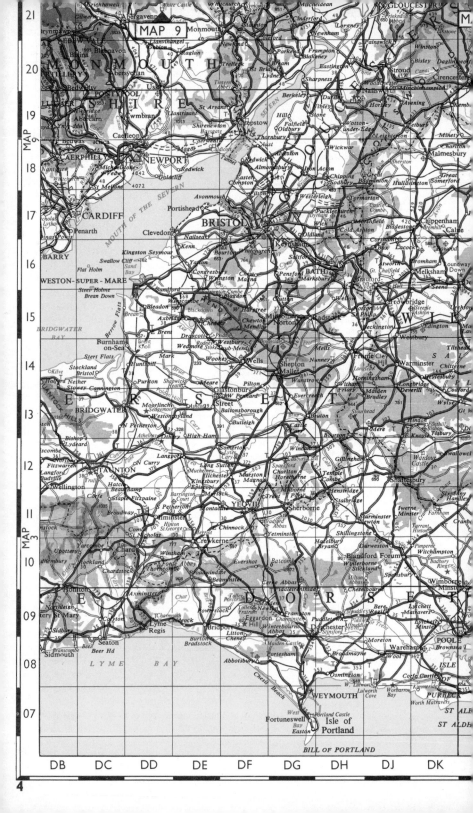

MAP II

MAP 6

EB   EC   ED   EE   EF   EG   EH   EJ   EK   FA

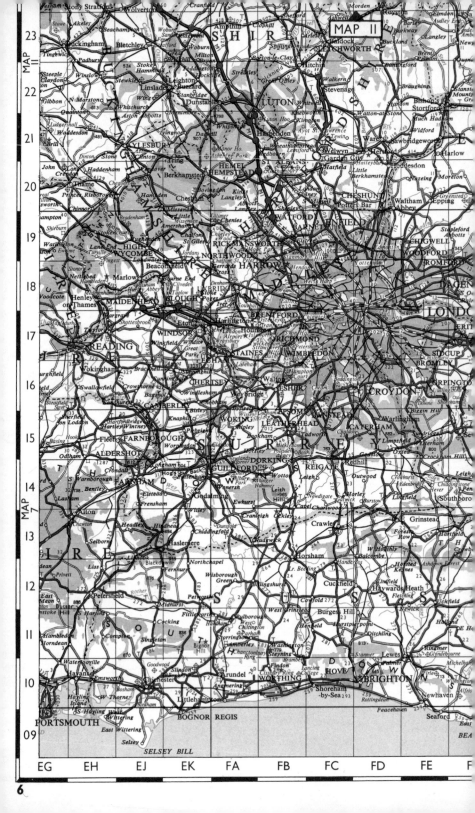

MAP II

MAP 32

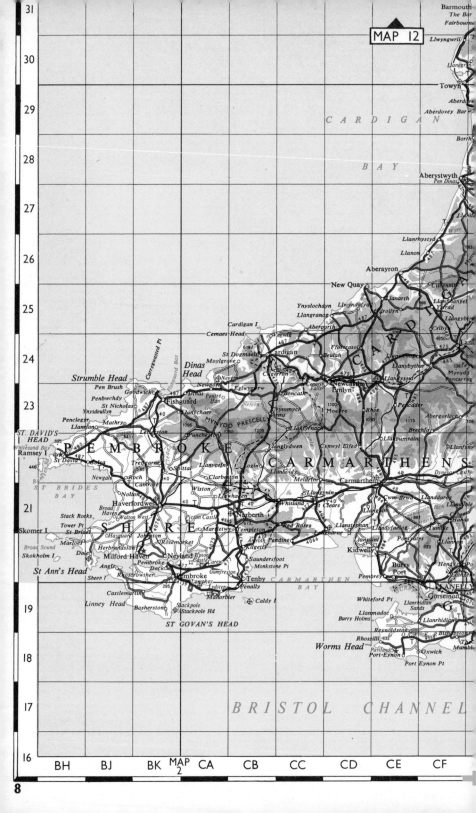

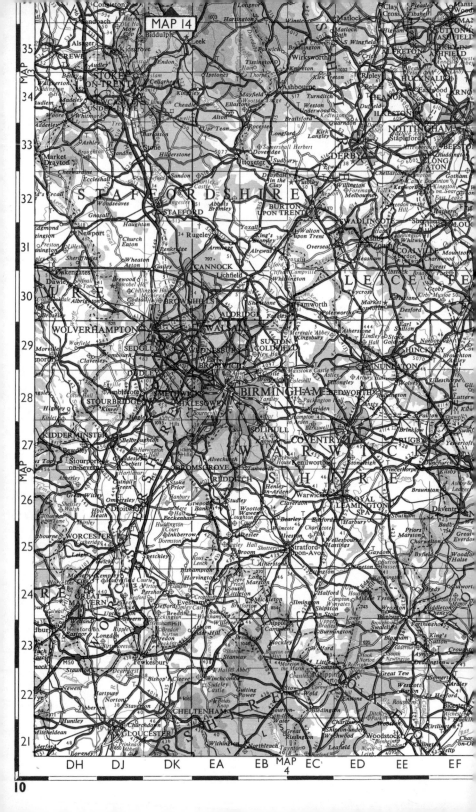

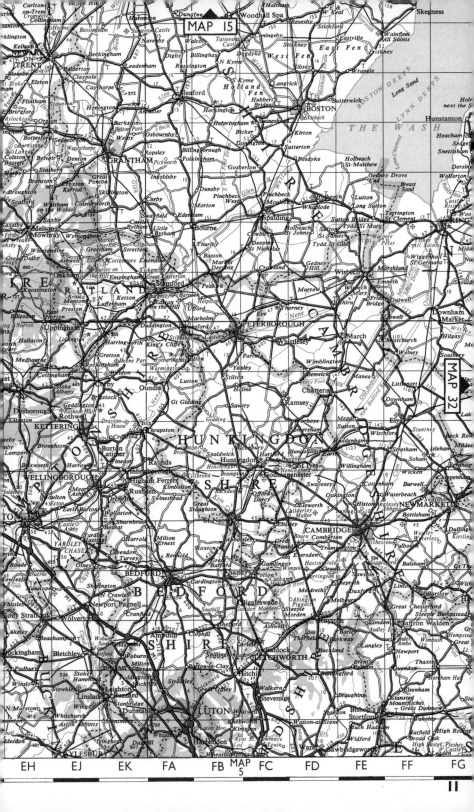

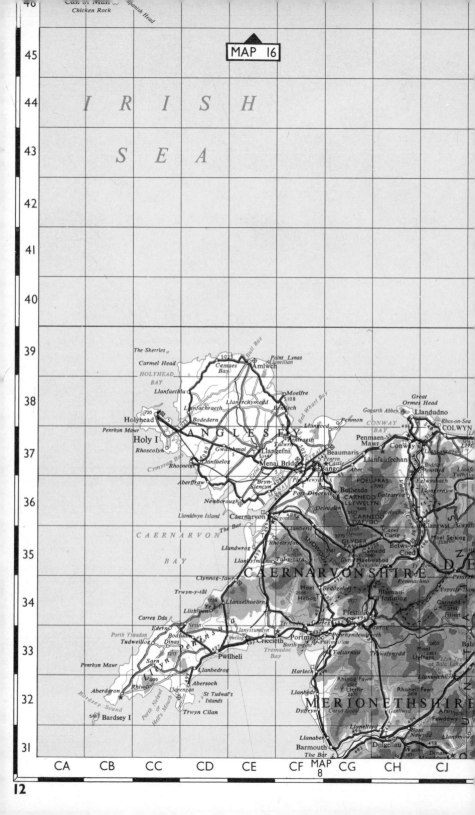

MAP 16

IRISH

SEA

The Skerries
Chicken Rock
Carmel Head
Bull Bay
S028
Cemaes
Bay
Amlwch
Paint Lynas
Llaneilian
HOLYHEAD
BAY
Llanfaethlu
Moelfre
S108
Great
Ormes Head
Llandudno
Llanerchymedd
Gogarth Abbey
Rhos-on-Sea
Llanfachraeth
Benllech
Red Wharf Bay
CONWAY
COLWYN
720
Holyhead
Bodedern
Penmon
BAY
49
Penrhyn Mawr
ANGLESEY
Llangoed
Conwy
Holy I
Penmaen-
Mawr
Llanrwst
Rhoscolyn
Gwalchmai
Llangefni
Talwrn
Beaumaris
Llanfairfechan
Cymyran Bay
Llanfaelog
Menai Bridge
Penrhyn
Castle
Bangor
Aber
POELFRAS
Moel Seisiog
S384
Rhosneigr
Bodrial
Penrhyn
Talhaia
Aberffraw
Bryn-
Siencyn
Port Dinorwic
Bethesda
3992
Eglwysbach
Llansernyw
Newborough
Deiniolen
CARNEDD
LLYWELYN
3485
Capel
Curig
Llanddwyn Island
Caernarvon
CARNEDD
DAFYDD
Bettws-y-
Coed
CAERNARVON
The Bar
Llanberis
GLYDER
FAWR
Dysb
Owen
D
Llandwrog
Rhostryfan
Z
BAY
Llanllyfni
Tal-y-llyn
SNOWDON
Carnedd
3561
Moel-siabod
CAERNARVONSHIRE
Clynnog-Fawr
Moel
2506
Hebog
Beddgelert
Penmachno
Yspyty-Ifan
Trwyn-y-tâl
Llanaelhaearn
Blaenau-
Ffestiniog
Carnedd-y-
2194
Filiast
Carres Ddu
Yr Eifl
1849
Tremadoc
Ffestiniog
Nevin
Llanystumdwy
Carreg
2800
Edern
Bodfuan
Dinas
Criccieth
Portmadoc
Penrhyndeudraeth
Talsarnau
Trawsfynydd
Bala Lake
Porth Ysgaden
Tudweiliog
1217
Borth-y-gest
Portmeirion
Llanuwchllyn
Penrhyn Mawr
Sarn
Pwllheli
Tremadoc
Bay
Harlech
Rhinog Fawr
2362
Rhobell Fawr
2408
Llanbedrog
Y Llechr
Rhives
Abersoch
Llanbedr
MERIONETHSHIRE
Aberdaron
Llanengan
St Tudwal's
Islands
Dyffryn
Gamlwyd
Aran
Fawddwy
548
Bardsey I
Porth Neigal
or Hell's Mouth
Trwyn Cilan
Llanelltyd
Bont
Newydd
Llanaber
Barmouth
Dolgellau
The Bar
Waun
Dinas
CA   CB   CC   CD   CE   CF   MAP   CG   CH   CJ
8

12

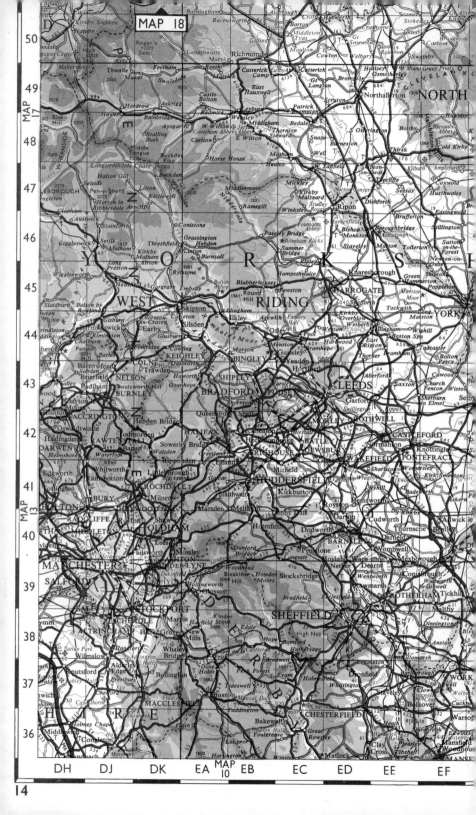

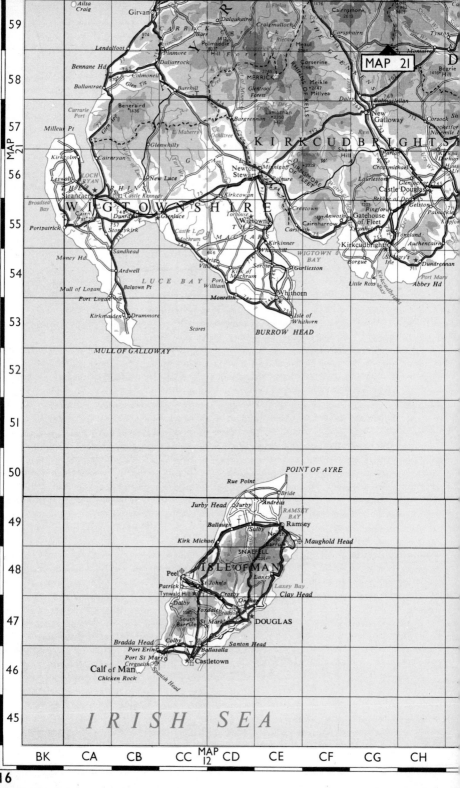

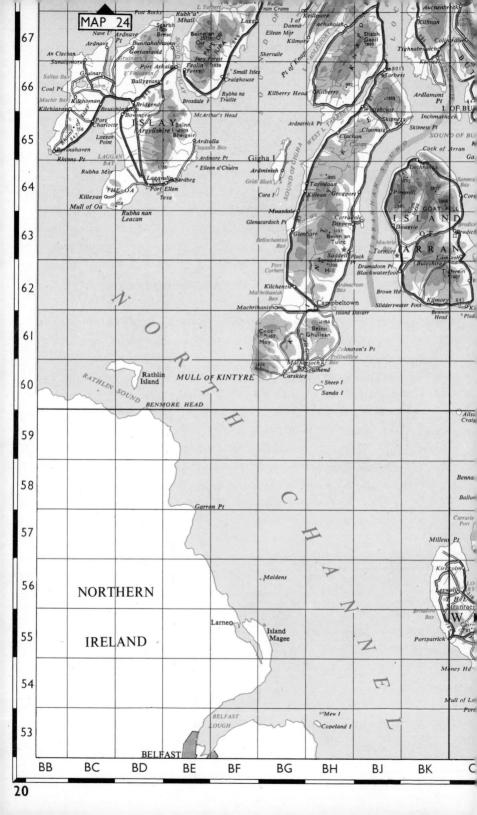

MAP 24

67

66

65

64

63

62

61

60

59

58

57

56

55

54

53

NORTH

Post Rocks
Rubh'a'
Mhail
L. Tarbert
Rubha
nan Crann
Auchenbreck
Keillmore
Achahoish
Kilfinan
Scarbh
Breac
I. of
Danna
Ellean Mòr
Kilmore
Shiab
Gaoil
1840
Tighnabruaich
Colintraive
Beinn an
2571
Kilmory
Skerville
Pt of Knap
8015
Kames

An Clachan
Ardnave
Pt
Gortanlaoid
Bunnahabhainn
PASS OF JURA
Jura Forest
Feolin
Ferry
1839
Port Askaig
Small Isles
Craighouse
Tarbert
992
1363
Ardlamont
Pt
I. OF BU
Inchmarnock

Salligo Bay
Coul Pt
Machir Bay
Kilchiaran
Gruinart
L. Finlaggan
Ballygrant
Bridgend
Brosdale I.
Rubha na
Traille
Kilberry Head
Kilberry
Whitehouse
SOUND OF BU

Bowmore
ISLAY
Argyllshire
Beinn
1609
Bheigeir
McArthur's Head
Ardpatrick Pt
WEST L. TARBERT
Skipness
Skipness Pt
Cock of Arran
Ga

Port
Charlotte
Kilchoman
Bruichladdich
Ardtalla
Claggan Bay
Clachan
L. Ciaran
Claonaig
Luchrubia
1570
Sannox
Bay

Rhinns
758
847
Laggan
Point
1136
Gigha I.
Ardminish
Grob Bagh
Tayinloan
935
Grogport
Pirnmill
2345
2817
GOAT FELL
2866

Port
Ellen
Lagavulin
Ardbeg
Texa
Eilean a'Chuirn
Cara I.
Killean
Carradale
Dippen
1091
ISLAND
Douerie
Brodic
Brodic

THE OA
Killeyan
Mull of Oa
Rubha nan
Leacan
658
Muasdale
Glenacardoch Pt
Glenbarr
Beinn an
Tuirc
Saddell
1298
Torrmore
Pluck
ARRAN
Buteshire
Tighvein
1497

Bellochantuy
Bay
Port
Corbert
Spreadan
Hill
Drumadoon Pt
Blackwaterfoot
Lamlash

Kilchenzie
Machrihanish
Bay
Machrihanish
Ardnacross
Bay
Brown Hd.
Slidderywater Foot
Kilmory
841

Campbeltown
Island Davarr
Bennan
Head
Plade

NORTH
Cnoc
1462
Moy
1154
Beinn
Ghuilean
Johnston's Pt
Polliwilline
Bay

CHANNEL
RATHLIN SOUND
Rathlin
Island
MULL OF KINTYRE
1204
Macharioch
Carskiey
Southend
Sheep I.
Sanda I.
Ailsa
Crai

BENMORE HEAD

Garron Pt
Benna
Balla

Currarie
Port
Milleu Pt

NORTHERN
Maidens
Kirkcolm
Lesswalt
W
Stranraer

IRELAND
Larneo
Island
Magee
Broadsea
Bay
Portpatrick
Par

Money Hd
Mull of Lo
Por

BELFAST
LOUGH
Mew I.
Copeland I.

BELFAST

BB   BC   BD   BE   BF   BG   BH   BJ   BK   C

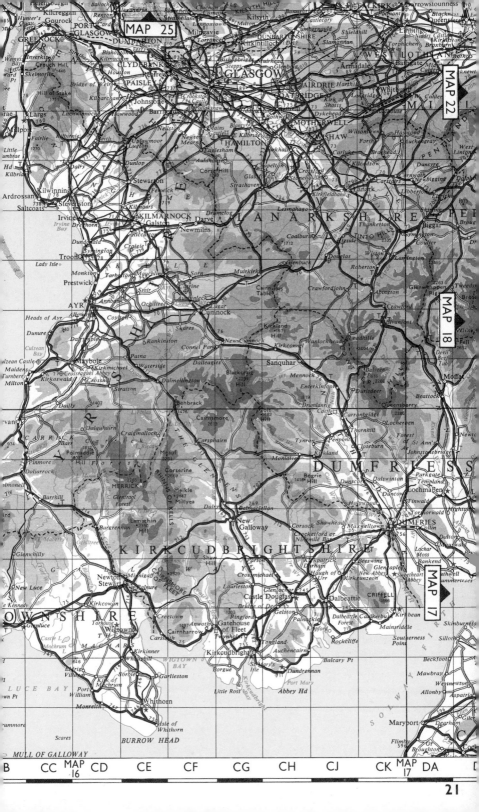

MAP 26

HOWE OF THE MEARNS
White Hill
2544
Fettercairn
Roadside
Kinneff
Allardice
Castle
Arbuthnott
Inverbervie
LAURENCEKIRK
Gourdon
Luthermuir
Bridgend
Garvock
Kirkton of
Menmuir
Inchbare
Marykirk
Johnshaven
Milton Ness
St Cyrus
Fern
Brechin
Hillside
Careston
Tannadice
Aberlemno
Farnell
Bridge
of Dun
Montrose
Scurdie Ness
Ferryden
Kirriemuir
Ketcobie
Guthrie
Friockheim
Inverkeilor
Lunan Bay
Forfar
Letham
Vigeans
Glamis
Inverarity
Carmyllie
Affleck
Castle
Monikie
Arbirlot
Arbroath
Newbigging
Barry
Muirdrum
East Haven
Carnoustie
Monifieth
Buddon Ness
Broughty Ferry
Tayport
Newport-on-Tay
Inchcape or
Bell Rock
Kilmany
Leuchars
919
ST ANDREWS
BAY
St Andrews
Strathkinness
Boarhills
Pitscottie
Kingsbarns
Ceres
Peat Inn
Dunino
Carr Briggs
Largo
Wood
Carnbee
FIFE NESS
Kellie
Castle
Crail
Largo
Kilconquhar
Kilrenny
Leven
Elie
Anstruther
Pittenweem
Methil
St Monance
Buckhaven
Earlsferry
Isle of May
OF
FORTH
Fidra
Craigleith
Bass Rock
North Berwick
Craigenon
Dirleton
Gullane
Tantallon Castle
Whitekirk
Cockenzie
Aberlady
Dirleton
Dunbar
Drem
Linton
W Barnes
Preston
Longniddry
Athelstaneford
Halles Castle
Barns Ness
Tranent
Haddington
Spott
GREAT
EAST
LOTHIAN
Stenton
Innerwick
Cockburnspath
Fast Castle
Gifford
Oldhamstocks
ST ABB'S HEAD
Pencaitland
Garvald
Clints
Dod
Meikle
Black Law
St Abb's
Coldingham
E & Saltoun
1307
1283
Hoart
Law
1107
Buss Craig
Eyemouth
Pathhead
Humble
Crichness
Grantshouse
Reston
Burnmouth
Fala
LAMMERMUIR
Abbey
St Bathans
Ayton
Cakemuir
Castle
Meikle Law
HILLS
Preston
Chirnside
Foulden
Heriot
Coxton
Longformacus
Cranshaws
Duns
Berwick-upon-Tweed
Thirlestane
Castle
Edgarhope
Forest
Dirrington
Great Law
Hutton
Paxton
Tweedmouth
intonhall
Lauder
Westruther
Potwarthin
Whitsome
Cheswick
Edgarhope
Swinton
Ladykirk
Goswick
Legerwood
Greenlaw
MERSE
Norham
Grindon
Ancroft
Holy Island
Langshaw
Gordon
Eccles
Leitholm
Duddo
Bowsden
Beal
Burrows Hole
Mellerstain Ho
Stichill
Coldstream
Cornhill
Etal
Lowick
Farne Islands
Clovenfords
Galashiels
Newstead
Earlston
Birgham
Carham
Crookham
Ford
Ross
Bamburgh
Abbotsford
Smailholm
Sprouston
Branxton
Lucker
Seahouses
Melrose
Dryburgh Abbey
Kelso
Floddon
Milfield
Belford
Sunderland
Eildon Hills
Boswell
Kilham
Doddington
Beadnell
Selkirk
Maxton
Roxburgh
Kirknewton
926
Akeld
Chatton
Newham
Chathill
Lilliesleaf
Midlem
Nisbet
Linton
Town
Yetholm
Newton Tors
1762
Yoolie
Chillingham
Newton-by-the-Sea

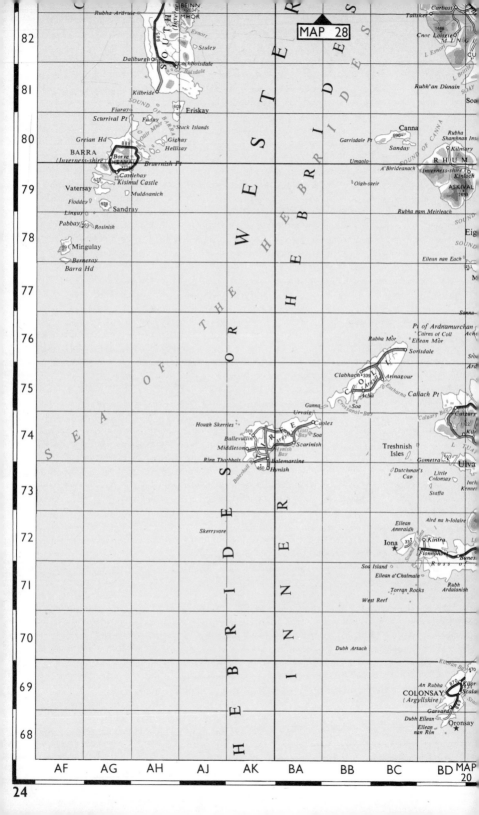

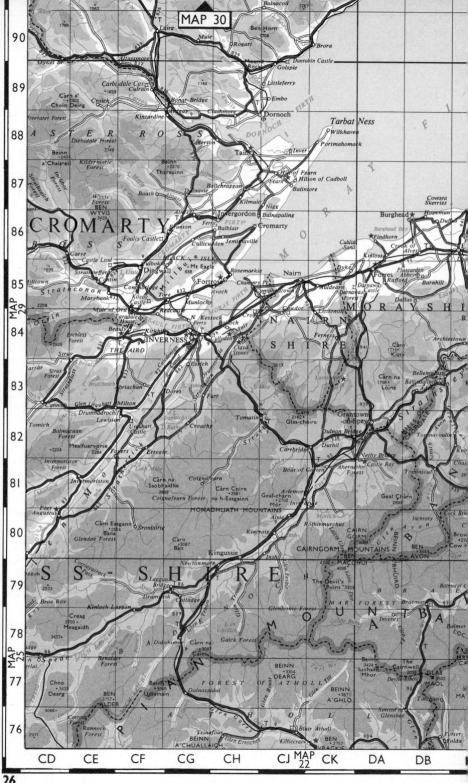

MAP 30

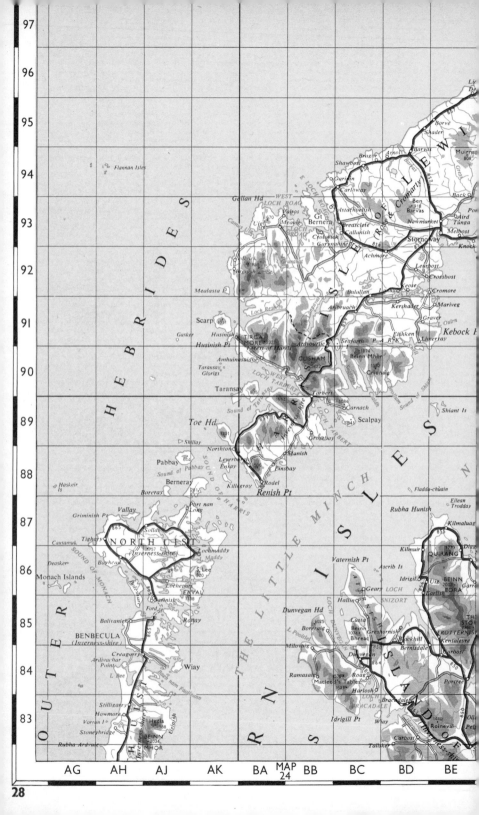

CAPE WRATH

Faraid Head

Whiten Hd

EWIS

Durness

Melness

Balnakill
Achmore
Kyle of Durness
976
1498
Keoldale
Fashven
1592

Meall
Meddhonach
Eilde
Beinn
Spionnaidh *2537*
Eriboll

Am Balg

Sheigra
Oldshore
L. Eriboll

Kinlochbervie
L. Inchard

Cranstackie *2630*
2980

Eilean an Roin Mòr

BEN
HOPE

BEN
LOYAL

FOINAVEN
2554

Handa
Island

Laxford
Bridge
ARKLE *2580*

Saval Beg
Ben Hee
2010

Scourie
2544
2393

Badcall
Ben Stack *2364*
2364

Kylestrome
Ferry
Kylesku
Glendhu

EDDRACHILLIS
BAY
Meall Mòr
Oldany I.

Altnaharra

Point of Stoer
530
Drumbeg

S U T H E R
SUTHER

Culkein
Clashnessie
2658
2010

QUINAG *2653*
Ben Hee

Stoer
2541
2410

Loch Inver
Ardvreck Castle
Inchnadamph
BEN MORE

Lochinver
ASSYNT *3273*
Shinness

Inverkirkaig
Glencanisp Forest
CANISP
2779

Rubha Còigach
2399
SUILVEN *2545*
1562

ENARD
BAY
Brae of
Achnahaird

Cam Loch

Reiff

Stingascaig
Cul Mòr
Elphin

Polbain
2786

Summer Isles
2523

Urigill
1765

Tanera Mòr
CROMALT
HILLS

Priest I.
Isle
Martin
Strathkanaird

CÒIGACH
Meall an
Fhuarain

Ben More
Coigach
2438

Oykel Br.
Rosehall

Greenstone Pt
Cailleach
Head

Rhidorroch
Forest
1298

Carbisdale Castle
Culrain
1659
Croick

Mellon Udrigle
Gruinard I.
Ullapool
Loch Achall

Rubha Rèidh
Badluchrach

Carn a'
Choin Deirg

Kincardine

Mellon
Charles
Laide
Aultbea

Leckmelm
SEANA
BHRAIGH *3040*
Freevater Forest

Diebidale Forest

Caves
L. of
Ewe

Ardessie
Ardcharnich

BEINN
DEARG *3547*

EASTER R

Melvaig
AN
TEALLACH *3483*

Beinn
a'Chaisteil

Kildermorie
Forest

N. Erradale

Naust
Fisherfield
Forest
2814
3974
Braemore

BEN
WYVIS

Longa I.
Poolewe

Sgurr Ban *3194*

MAP 26

LOCH
GAIRLOCH
Gairloch
Letterewe
Forest

Sgurr Mòr
3637
3276
2178
Fannich Forest
Kinlochluichart
Forest

Opinan
Badachro
637

Foulis Castle

Red Point
SLOCH

Fannich Forest

ROSS and CROMARTY
ROSS
CROMARTY

Rubha
na Fearn
Talladale

Diabaig
Shieldaig
Forest
3232

Kinlochewe Forest
Kinlochewe
3059
Achanalt
Garve
Castle Leod
Strathpeffer
Contin

Rona
404

Inver
Alligin

L. a'Chroisg
Achnasheen

Sgurr a'
Mhuilinn
Milltown

Strathconon
Forest
Marybank

Cononbridge

Torridon
Coulin
Forest
Carn
Breac
Scardroy
2298

Mains of Ord
Tarradale
House
Beauly

Shieldaig
Ben-damph
Forest
3060
3425
3220

Kilcoy
Castle

Arnish
Maol
Chean-dearg

Loch
Achnashellach
Forest

Strathconon
Forest

Erchless
Forest
INV

Applecross
Forest
2936
286
Balnacra

Sgurr
a'Chaorachain
3452
3294

Glen Orrin
3554
Struy

THE AIRD

RAASAY
Achintee
Lochcarron
Monar Forest
Glen Strathfarrar
Strathglass
Forest

Kirkhill
Beauly

Toscaig
Ardarroch

SGURR NA
LAPAICH *3773*
2676

Crowlin
Is

Stromemore
Plockton
Stromeferry
Sguman

Glen Cannich
Glencannich
Forest
Cannich
Drumnadrochit
Milton
Lewiston

1298
Duirinish
Balmacara
Kirkton
Killian
Coinntich
Glen Cannich

Longay

Kyle of
Lochalsh
L. Long

Calnay

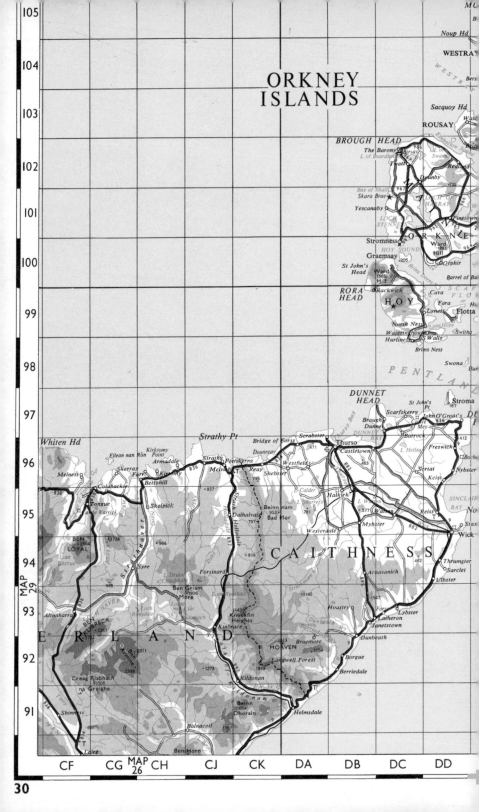

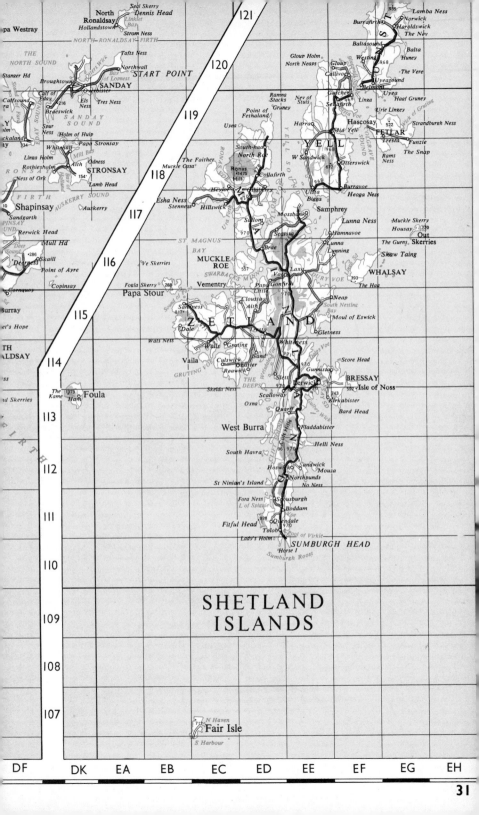

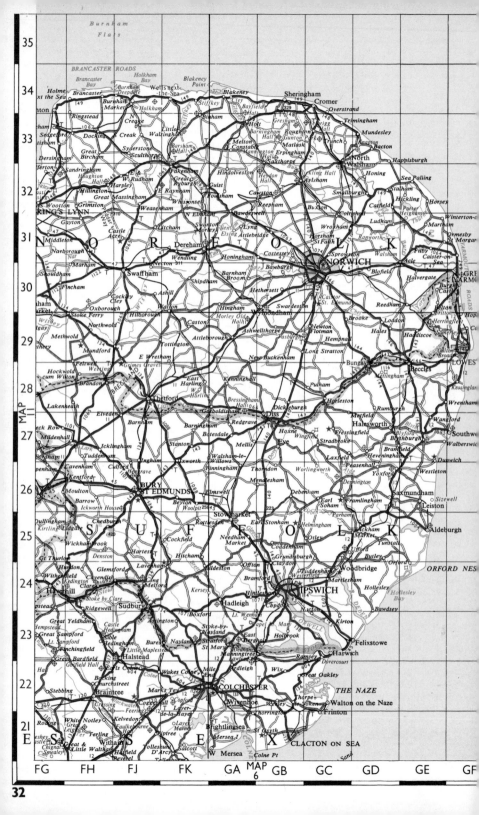

INDEX

The following is a list of place names which appear in the Gazetteer of each chapter. The Gazetteer page number appears first, followed by the corresponding map number and reference.